HBJ
LANGUAGE
Medallion Edition

6

Dorothy S. Strickland
Richard F. Abrahamson
Roger C. Farr
Nancy R. McGee

6

Karen S. Kutiper
Patricia Smith

HBJ
LANGUAGE
Medallion Edition

HARCOURT BRACE & COMPANY
Orlando   Atlanta   Austin   Boston   San Francisco   Chicago   Dallas   New York
Toronto   London

Requests for permission to make copies of any part of the work should be mailed to: Permissions Department, Harcourt Brace Jovanovich, Publishers, 8th Floor, Orlando, Florida 32887

Material from earlier edition: copyright © 1990 by Harcourt Brace Jovanovich, Inc. All rights reserved.

Printed in the United States of America

ISBN 0-15-301056-8

5 6 7 8 9 10   069   96 95 94

Acknowledgments

For permission to reprint copyrighted material, grateful acknowledgment is made to the following sources:

Kathleen Benally, on behalf of Alethea Benally: "Autumn" by Alethea Benally from *The Charging Nest,* edited by Gail Newman and Kristina McGrath. © 1988 by Alethea Benally.

Stephanie Brown, on behalf of Pablo Siguenza: "The Sky Is as Vast as the World" by Pablo Siguenza from *A Red Sky of Lilacs,* edited by Gail Newman. © 1984 by Pablo Siguenza.

Childrens Press: From p. 4, 16, and 18 in *Olympic National Park* by Ruth Radlauer. Copyright © 1978 by Regensteiner Publishing Enterprises, Inc.

Philip Corsi: From *In the Shadow of Liberty: The Chronicle of Ellis Island* by Edward Corsi. © 1935 by The Macmillan Company.

Victor Hernández Cruz: From "The Latest Latin Dance Craze" in *Tropicalization* by Victor Hernández Cruz. © 1976 by Victor Hernández Cruz. Published by I. Reed Books.

E. P. Dutton, a division of Penguin Books USA Inc.: Adapted from *Immigrant Kids* (Retitled: "Coming Over") by Russell Freedman. Copyright © 1980 by Russell Freedman.

Dilys Evans: Illustrations by Les Morrill from "The Cub" by Walter Dean Myers in *Cricket* Magazine, July 1987.

Ronald Everson: From "The Loaves" in *The Wind Has Wings: Poems from Canada,* edited by Mary Alice Downie and Barbara Robertson.

Tia Greenfield, on behalf of Lars Smith, and Marcy Castillo, on behalf of Marc Almond: "Spirit of the Grizzly Bear" by Lars Smith and Marc Almond from *Paper of Life,* edited by Gail Newman. © 1985 by Lars Smith and Marc Almond.

Harcourt Brace Jovanovich, Inc.: Short pronunciation key and entries from *HBJ School Dictionary.* Copyright © 1985 by Harcourt Brace Jovanovich, Inc. "Study Steps to Learn a Word" from *HBJ Spelling,* Signature Edition, Level 6 (Brown) by Thorsten Carlson and Richard Madden. Copyright © 1988, 1983 by Harcourt Brace Jovanovich, Inc.

HarperCollins Publishers: Text from pp. 13, 14, and 16 and illustration from p. 15 in *The Land I Lost* (Retitled: "Catching a Python") by Huynh Quang Nhuong, illustrated by Vo-Dinh Mai. Text copyright © 1982 by Huynh Quang Nhuong; illustrations copyright © 1982 by Vo-Dinh Mai.

Alfred A. Knopf, Inc.: "African Dance" from *Selected Poems of Langston Hughes* by Langston Hughes. Copyright 1926 by Alfred A. Knopf, Inc., renewed 1954 by Langston Hughes.

Little, Brown and Company: From p. 9 in *Blue Highways: A Journey into America* by William Least Heat Moon. Copyright © 1982 by William Least Heat Moon.

Lothrop, Lee and Shepard Books, a division of William Morrow and Company, Inc.: From "Two to Nothing" in *The Break Dance Kids* by Lillian Morrison. Text copyright © 1985 by Lillian Morrison.

Modern Curriculum Press, Inc.: From "A Modern Dragon" in *Songs from Around a Toadstool Table* by Rowena Bastin Bennett. Copyright © 1967 by Rowena Bastin Bennett.

Walter Dean Myers: "The Cub" by Walter Dean Myers from *Cricket* Magazine, July 1987. © 1987 by Walter Dean Myers.

The New York Times Company: "Terror by Radio" from *The New York Times,* November 1, 1938. Copyright © 1938 by The New York Times Company.

Ruth Ramirez, on behalf of Emma Moreno: "Looking Out My Window" by Emma Moreno from *Sassy as Ice,* edited by Gail Newman. © 1987 by Emma Moreno.

Random House, Inc.: "Sand-Jar Ant Ranch" from *The Incredible Year-Round Playbook* by Elin McCoy. Copyright © 1979 by Elin McCoy.

Marian Reiner, on behalf of Lilian Moore: "Winter Dark" from *I Thought I Heard the City* by Lilian Moore. Copyright © 1969 by Lilian Moore.

San Francisco Chronicle: "The Right Place for News Is in Newspapers" from *San Francisco Chronicle,* November 1, 1938. © 1938 by San Francisco Chronicle.

Sandra M. Simons, on behalf of Ashley Simons: From "The Mystery of the Missing Coin" by Ashley Simons.

William Jay Smith: From "The Owl" in *LAUGHING TIME: Nonsense Poems* by William Jay Smith. Copyright © 1955, 1957, 1980 by William Jay Smith. Published by Delacorte Press, 1980.

Viking Penguin Inc.: From "Lone Dog" in *Songs to Save a Soul* by Irene Rutherford McLeod. All rights reserved.

Lloyd Washington, on behalf of De-Shun Washington: "There is Danger" by De-Shun Washington from *My Skills Are for Survival,* edited by Gail Newman. © 1986 by De-Shun Washington.

The H. W. Wilson Company: Entries from "HISTORIC HOUSES, SITES, ETC." in *Readers' Guide to Periodical Literature,* August 1988. Copyright © 1988 by The H. W. Wilson Company.

continued at the end of the book

Contents

Giving Instructions

Comparing and Contrasting 152

Reading ⟷ Writing Connection

Composition Focus: Paragraphs of Comparison and Contrast

Language Focus: Verbs

Communicating Your Opinions

Reading ⬌ Writing Connection

Composition Focus: Persuasive Paragraph in a Business Letter

Language Focus: Pronouns

Creating Images 252

7 Persuading Others

Reading ←→ Writing Connection

Composition Focus: Persuasive Essay

Language Focus: Adverbs

8 Reporting Information

Reading ⟷ Writing Connection

Composition Focus: Research Report

Language Focus: Prepositions, Conjunctions, Interjections, Phrases, and Clauses

9 Inventing Stories

Reading ⟷ Writing Connection

Composition Focus: Suspense Story

Language Focus: Mechanics Wrap-up

Study Skills 455

Extra Practice 1

Dear Student,

English plays a key role in your everyday life. You use language when you listen to a weather forecast, answer the phone, read a newspaper, or write a letter.

It makes sense to learn more about something that is such a big part of your life. In HBJ Language, Medallion Edition, you will read examples of how other people — students as well as adults — have used English. You will learn how to communicate more effectively when you write and speak.

We hope that HBJ Language, Medallion Edition, will help you discover the joy of being able to say exactly what you mean when you speak or write and to understand what others are saying when you read and listen.

Sincerely,

The Authors

Understanding the Writing Process

Writing a story, a poem, or an article is like sailing a boat from one harbor to another. A sailor plans such a trip carefully to ensure that the boat arrives safely. Similarly, a good writer follows a plan to produce a carefully crafted message that travels smoothly to the reader. The writer's plan is called the **writing process**. This process includes five stages:

1. Prewriting
2. Drafting
3. Responding and Revising
4. Proofreading
5. Publishing

The five stages of the writing process are not separate steps. Often writers move back and forth between the stages as they shape their ideas, just as a sailor may have to adjust his or her plans because of changes in the weather. The diagram shows how a writer might make the journey through the writing process.

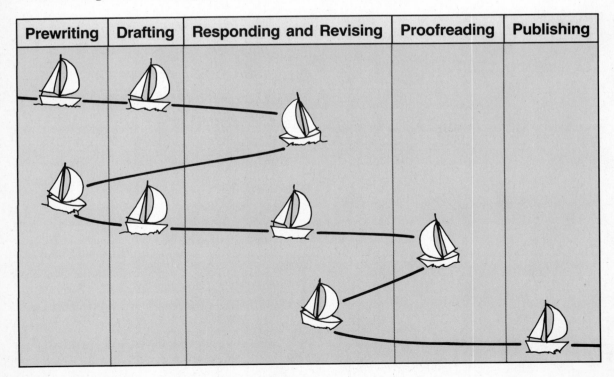

Prewriting	Drafting	Responding and Revising	Proofreading	Publishing

1 Prewriting

weekend at the beach
field trip to the art museum
Uncle Jake's visit
summer vacation in the mountains
the baseball game on Saturday
the sixth-grade science fair

Beginning to write is sometimes difficult. That is why prewriting is such an important stage of the writing process. During the prewriting stage, you

- identify your audience, the person or persons for whom you are writing.
- define your purpose, or reason for writing, and decide on a form for your writing.
- brainstorm a list of possible topics for writing.
- select one topic that is appropriate for your audience and your purpose.
- gather and organize information about your topic.

The chart shows examples of various writing forms, audiences, and purposes.

Writing Form	Audience	Purpose
friendly letter	grandparents	**to inform** about a trip
poem	self	**to express** feelings about a problem
story	friend	**to entertain** by telling exciting events
letter to the editor	community	**to persuade** readers to support an issue

Graphic Organizers

Graphic organizers will help you in the prewriting stage of the writing process. Use graphic organizers to generate ideas and to organize and focus information.

Cluster Use a cluster to help you generate ideas and details about your topic. This graphic organizer can be very useful when you are planning to write a description.

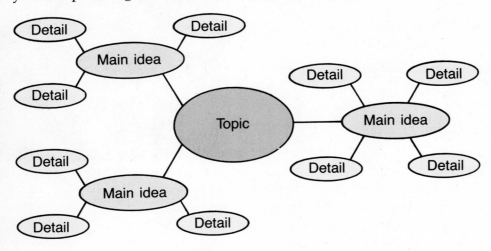

Chart Use a chart to help you organize ideas that involve several categories of details and a process or actions that must be carried out in sequence. This graphic organizer is helpful when you are planning to write a how-to paragraph.

	Category A	Category B	Category C
Step 1	Detail 1A	Detail 1B	Detail 1C
Step 2	Detail 2A	Detail 2B	Detail 2C
Step 3	Detail 3A	Detail 3B	Detail 3C

Time Line Use a time line to help you organize information in the order in which events occur in time. This graphic organizer is very effective when you are planning to write a story.

First event ・ Second event ・ Third event ・ Fourth event

Beginning |——————————————————————————————————| End
    Time 1   Time 2   Time 3   Time 4

Inverted Triangle   Use an inverted triangle to help you narrow your topic. This graphic organizer can help you limit your topic when you are planning to write a persuasive paragraph, a research report, or a short story.

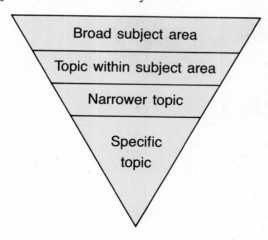

Venn Diagram   Use a Venn diagram to help you identify the similarities and differences between two items. This graphic organizer is very helpful when you are planning to write a paragraph of comparison and contrast.

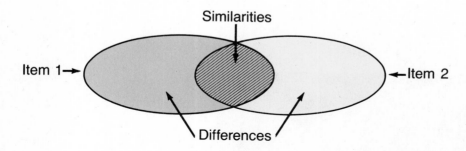

Outline   Use an outline to help you organize almost any topic. It is best suited for a broad topic with many main ideas and details, such as the topic of a research paper.

Topic
I. Main idea
   A. Detail
   B. Detail
   C. Detail
II. Main idea
   A. Detail
   B. Detail
III. Main idea
   A. Detail
   B. Detail
   C. Detail

2 Drafting

    In the drafting stage, you use the ideas developed in prewriting to write a first, rough version of your composition. Write freely, without worrying about errors. As you write, you may find that you need more information about your topic or that some of your ideas are not appropriate for your audience and your purpose. If so, you can return to the prewriting stage and rethink your earlier decisions.

3 Responding and Revising

    Responding and revising is the next stage in the writing process. By yourself or with a partner, respond to your writing by checking the organization, the information, and the language in your draft. Be sure each is suited to your audience and your purpose. Then revise your writing, making appropriate changes and improvements.

4　Proofreading

In the proofreading stage, you polish your writing, correcting errors in grammar, spelling, capitalization, and punctuation.

5　Publishing

Publishing means "making public." During this final stage of the writing process, you share your writing with your audience in some written or oral form. Thinking again about your purpose and your audience will help you decide the best way in which to publish your work.

UNIT

Relating Your Experiences

◆ **COMPOSITION FOCUS:** **Personal Narrative**
◆ **LANGUAGE FOCUS:** **Sentences**

Taking part in a conversation is one way to tell others about your life. Another way is to write a personal narrative. A personal narrative tells a story about something that happened to you.

Writer Huynh Quang Nhuong wrote a personal narrative about his childhood in Vietnam. He called it *The Land I Lost: Adventures of a Boy in Vietnam.* By reading his recollections of the funny, sad, and exciting experiences he had, you will learn about him and about a way of life in a faraway place. Then you, too, will write a personal narrative.

◆  *WARMING UP* ◆

 IN YOUR JOURNAL
Write about your favorite vacation. Tell about some of the things you saw and did. Tell why it was your favorite.

 CREATIVE DRAMATICS
Imagine that you have just made a telephone call to someone you admire but have never met. Act out what happened when you made that call.

Huynh Quang Nhuong wrote *The Land I Lost to inform* and *to entertain* readers. His personal narrative won the American Library Association Notable Books for Children Award.

Reading with a Writer's Eye
Personal Narrative

A python is a powerful snake that can grow to 20 feet in length. Its bite is not poisonous, but it can squeeze small animals to death. Huynh Quang Nhuong wanted a python for a pet. As you read what happened to him, imagine how you might have felt in his place.

Catching a Python
by Huynh Quang Nhuong

One day my cousin told me that a man from a tribe nearby had taught him the technique of catching a live python and taming it. Pythons, like wild elephants, can be tamed and become faithful friends to people. My cousin said that when a python attacked you, you should raise both hands high to keep them free while the python coiled around you. Then, with one hand, you should grab its tail, and with the other hand, you should hold its head away from you, to avoid getting bitten. As the python started squeezing, you should lightly bite its tail. For some reason that would keep the python at bay. Afterward you could call for help if the python was too big, or better yet, walk home with the python wrapped around you. But, my cousin added, you should never make the mistake of biting the python's tail too hard. If you did that, the python would get very angry and squeeze you to death.

A few months later we heard one of our roosters cry very loudly. We rushed out of our house and saw a python squeezing the rooster. My cousin used the technique he had learned and caught the python easily.

I was very much impressed by my cousin's python and wished I had a smaller one that I could bring with me to the lowlands, where I went to school. It would certainly impress my friends at the boarding house, especially the young daughter of my landlady!

The next time I was home from school, my mother asked my cousin and me to go to the edge of the jungle to gather some firewood. At the jungle's edge we saw birds hopping on the ground and singing in the bushes, a sign that there were no dangerous beasts around. So we went a little farther into the jungle and looked for a type of mushroom my parents were very fond of. But secretly, I hoped we might find a small python.

We did not find any mushrooms or pythons, and since we had gathered enough firewood, we started the journey home. A little later we stopped and rested on a fallen tree trunk half buried in dead leaves. My cousin whistled a song and I beat the time to it on the dead tree with my sharp woodcutting knife. Suddenly the tree moved. We looked at each other. Each of us thought the other had moved the tree. Then we realized that it was not a tree we were sitting on but a very angry python!

We threw everything into the air and ran as fast as we could. When we were far enough away, we looked back and saw the python raising its head about two meters above the ground and opening its huge mouth in our direction. This python certainly wasn't the one I wanted for a pet! And after that, whenever we went into the jungle, my cousin and I looked very carefully at any tree we wanted to sit on.

Respond

1. How do you think you would have felt in Huynh Quang Nhuong's place? What details in the story make you think so?

Discuss

2. What main event does Huynh Quang Nhuong tell about in this personal narrative? What information does he give to lead up to the main event? How does this information help make the story interesting?

3. How does the writer himself feel about the events he describes in this personal narrative? How does he show these feelings by the details he includes and the words he uses?

Thinking As a Writer
Analyzing a Personal Narrative

A personal narrative gives the story of a true event in the writer's own life from the writer's **point of view.** The narrative has a **beginning,** a **middle,** and an **ending.** In personal narratives, writers usually describe their feelings about their subjects.

Reread parts of Huynh Quang Nhuong's narrative.

Writer's Guide

A personal narrative
- is written in the first-person point of view.
- has a beginning, a middle, and an ending.
- usually reveals the writer's feelings.

Catching a Python

One day my cousin told me that a man from a tribe nearby had taught him the technique of catching a live python and taming it.

The **title** captures the reader's attention.

The **beginning** gives the background for the story.

. . . My cousin whistled a song and I beat the time to it on the dead tree with my sharp woodcutting knife. Suddenly the tree moved. We looked at each other. Each of us thought the other had moved the tree. Then we realized that it was not a tree we were sitting on but a very angry python!

The **point of view** is **first person,** which means it is the writer's point of view. The pronouns *we, my,* and *I* are used.

The **middle** tells the main events of the story.

Time order is the order in which details are usually given in a personal narrative. Words like *suddenly* or *then* provide time-order clues.

. . . This python certainly wasn't the one I wanted for a pet! And after that, whenever we went into the jungle, my cousin and I looked very carefully at any tree we wanted to sit on.

The **ending** provides the readers with a sense that the story is "over."

Discuss

1. Read the first paragraph aloud in the third person, replacing every pronoun that refers to the writer and his cousin with the third-person pronouns *he* or *they*. Then reread it in the first person. Which do you prefer? Explain your preference.

2. In addition to the words *suddenly* and *then,* how do you know these events are described in the order in which they occurred?

Try Your Hand

A. Identify the Point of View Read the following journal entry. Identify what point of view is used in this narrative, and explain the narrative in a way that a fourth-grader could understand.

> I did it! I entered the pie-eating contest at the fair on Saturday! Five of us entered the contest, and we had to go up on the stage. We sat at a long table. A lady put a pie in front of each of us and then gave all of us bibs. Suddenly, a buzzer sounded. We had to gobble down our pies as fast as we could. As we finished, the judge wrote down each person's speed. Eating the pie was easier said than done because we had to keep our hands behind our backs while we ate! That was the first round. Then we did the whole thing again—five more pies were set on the table. I didn't win. In fact, I really lost. I lost my taste for cherry pie!

B. Identify the Order of Events
Look back at the journal entry. List the main events in the order in which they happened.

C. Label Parts of a Personal Narrative
Use brackets to label the beginning, the middle, and the ending of the list you made in **B.**

D. Analyze the Writer's Feelings
Reread the journal entry. Briefly describe how you think the writer felt about the contest; give details to support your opinion.

E. Read Personal Narratives Choose a personal narrative. Read it to a partner; then analyze these elements: point of view, beginning, middle, ending, and the writer's feelings about the subject.

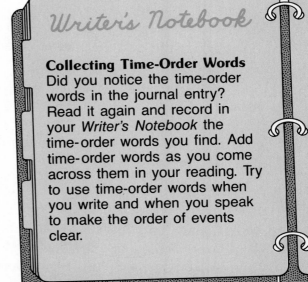

Writer's Notebook

Collecting Time-Order Words
Did you notice the time-order words in the journal entry? Read it again and record in your *Writer's Notebook* the time-order words you find. Add time-order words as you come across them in your reading. Try to use time-order words when you write and when you speak to make the order of events clear.

Thinking As a Writer
Connecting Cause and Effect

Writer's Guide

To write a personal narrative, good writers

- look for cause-and-effect connections among events.
- build stories around cause-and-effect chains.

People have reasons for what they do, and their actions have definite effects. Good personal narratives are built around such connections between events or feelings and the events or the feelings to which they lead. One cause can have several effects, and one effect can have several causes.

Good writers use **transition words,** such as *because, due to, whenever,* and *as a result,* to signal a cause-and-effect relationship. Notice the transition words in the following captions.

1.

Because she had practiced, she won.

2.

As a result, she got a prize.

3.

Whenever she receives a prize, she feels happy.

When planning a personal narrative, look for cause-and-effect connections among events. Be especially on the lookout for cause-and-effect chains that can make interesting stories.

Discuss

1. Look back at the personal narrative on pages 10–11. What are the causes for the narrator's being in the woods?
2. In the same personal narrative, what is the effect on the narrator when his cousin captures a python?
3. Look again at the personal narrative on pages 10–11. Find a chain of events that is set off by the narrator and his cousin's sitting on the "tree trunk."

Try Your Hand

Connect Causes and Effects   With a partner, make a list of cause-and-effect connections about a recent event at school, such as a sports competition. First, choose an event. Next, list several causes. Then, list several effects. Draw a chain of events if you find one.

Developing the Writer's Craft
Using Examples

Because writers want their writing to interest their readers, they use examples to help bring their writing to life. Although several examples might come to a writer's mind, good writers decide which example is the most effective. Good writers also consider which examples the reader will enjoy and how many examples would be best for the reader.

In "Catching a Python," the writer gives one effective example of why he wanted a python—to impress his landlady's daughter. The example works well because readers understand just what the writer means. Readers might laugh with the writer at his trying to show off. They might enjoy his honest admission that he is trying to impress someone. One measure of a well-chosen example is whether the reader remembers it after finishing the story.

When you write your personal narrative, try to choose examples that your readers will remember.

Discuss

1. Look at "Catching a Python" on pages 10–11. Find specific examples of how the writer responds when he is afraid. Does he use enough examples? Explain your answer.
2. Look again at "Catching a Python." You are told in the fourth paragraph that birds are hopping and singing. What is the writer trying to show you with this example? Is it an effective example? Explain your answer.

Try Your Hand

Use Examples List three causes and three effects that might be part of a personal narrative about the event in the picture. Give specific examples of causes or effects that you might use if it were your personal narrative.

1 Prewriting
Personal Narrative

Judith wanted to write a personal narrative for her friend Carmen. She used the checklist in the **Writer's Guide** to help her plan her narrative. Look at what she did.

◆ Brainstorming and Selecting a Topic

First, Judith looked for topics for her narrative by searching her memory and by browsing in her journal. The journal was a notebook she kept just for herself. In it she wrote down her thoughts and feelings every day. She also wrote brief notes about events of the day. Here are parts of three journal entries that caught Judith's eye.

As Judith browsed through her journal, she looked for stories she especially wanted to share with Carmen. She knew that the mix-up with Joey's lunch would make Carmen laugh. Since humor was a big part of her friendship with Carmen, she circled the topic. She wanted to be sure to include that story in her narrative.

Oct. 11—Took Joey's lunch to school by mistake. Yuk! Papaya and peanut butter sandwich? Green milk? Never again!

Oct. 15—I should have paid more attention on the hike, because I got poison ivy on my ankle. Mom says Calamine lotion might help.

Oct. 16—Finally! I beat Dad at checkers. I wonder if he just let me win. I hope not.

Discuss

1. Would the events of October 15 and 16 make good stories? Why or why not? Should Judith include those events in her personal narrative? Explain your answer.
2. Suppose that Judith were writing her personal narrative for a pen pal in another country, a girl whom she had never met. Which topic might interest her pen pal the most? Why?

◆ Gathering and Organizing Information

After Judith had chosen a story she wanted to tell Carmen, she listed the events of the story. She decided to list the events in the order in which they happened. She tried to include every detail that might have helped cause the mix-up with Joey's lunch.

After finishing her list, she went back and added information about her feelings. When she checked her list, she found a detail that was out of time order. She used an arrow to show where the detail belonged.

oatmeal for breakfast
woke up late
dressed and ate in a hurry
Joey shouted "Zot Vodilla!" (felt flustered)
grabbed lunch
ran for bus
lunchtime opened bag (I was really hungry.)
found a papaya and peanut butter sandwich
    and a thermos filled with green milk
traded the sandwich for an apple and a roll
no one wanted the milk

Judith also noticed that some of her information told about causes and effects. To make sure she would correctly explain the cause-and-effect relationships, she made a chart. Here is part of Judith's chart.

Cause	Effect
woke up late	dressed and ate in a hurry
	felt flustered
ran for the bus	grabbed the wrong lunch

Discuss

1. Look at the events that Judith listed. Do all the details seem important? If not, which ones would you leave out?
2. What additional events or information might Judith put on her list?

Try Your Hand

Now plan a personal narrative of your own.

A. Brainstorm and Select a Topic   Brainstorm interesting experiences you have had recently. If you keep a journal, look through it for ideas. Write a list of possible topics to cover in your personal narrative. Then look at each topic and think about your audience.

◆ Cross out topics that will not interest your audience.
◆ Cross out topics that you do not want to share.
◆ Cross out topics that will not be fun to write about.
◆ Circle the topic left on your list that involves the most interesting cause-and-effect chain of events. This will be the topic of your personal narrative.

B. Gather and Organize Information   When you are satisfied with your topic, plan how you can gather and organize information about it. If you lose interest in your topic as you are planning your personal narrative, brainstorm more topics and select a new topic.

◆ Think about the story you want to tell. If you keep a journal, check it to refresh your memory.
◆ List the events that make up the story. Include all the details that led up to and helped cause the main event.
◆ Look over your notes. Add any important details you left out. Add any information about your feelings that you want to include in your personal narrative.
◆ Decide the order in which you want to give the details of your story. Then arrange the details in this order. Circle any item that you want to move, and use an arrow to show where it belongs. Make a clean copy of your list if it becomes hard to read.

 Save your notes and your final list in your *Writer's Notebook*. You will use them when you draft your personal narrative.

WRITING PROCESS

2 Drafting
Personal Narrative

Writer's Guide

Drafting Checklist
- ☑ Use your notes for ideas.
- ☑ Write a beginning that gets your readers ready for your story.
- ☑ Write about your experience and how you feel about it.
- ☑ Write about the effects the experience had on you.

Judith followed the **Writer's Guide** to draft her personal narrative. Look at what she did.

Discuss

1. Look at Judith's first sentence. Why did she begin her paragraph this way?
2. What background has Judith given so far for the main event in her story?

What a Day!

I love my little brother Joey, but he sure does drive me crazy sometimes. His weird taste in food, for example, caused me a real headache last week. Looking back, I have to laugh, but at the time it was not very funny.

Try Your Hand

Now draft a personal narrative.

A. Review Your Information Think about the information you gathered and organized in the last lesson. Decide whether you need more information. If so, gather it.

B. Think About Your TAP Remember that your task is to write a personal narrative to share with a classmate. Your purpose is to tell an interesting story about an event in your life.

C. Write Your First Draft Follow the steps in the **Drafting Checklist** to write your personal narrative.
  When you write your draft, put all your ideas on paper. Do not worry about spelling, grammar, or punctuation. You can correct the draft later.

Task: What?
Audience: Who?
Purpose: Why?

Save the first draft in your *Writer's Notebook*. You will use it when you revise your personal narrative.

3 Responding and Revising
Personal Narrative

Judith used the checklist in the **Writer's Guide** to revise her personal narrative. Look at what she did.

◆ Checking Information

Judith decided to add a detail that would show by example why she felt as she did about the main event of her story. She then cut some information to add a more effective example. She used this mark ∧ to show her addition. She used this mark ℐ to show what she was cutting.

◆ Checking Organization

Judith moved some sentences to put events in time order. She used this mark ◌ to show what she was moving.

◆ Checking Language

Judith replaced one word with another word that she found in a thesaurus, because it expressed more exactly how she felt. She used this mark ∧ to show the replacement. She also added a phrase to emphasize the cause-and-effect connection between two events.

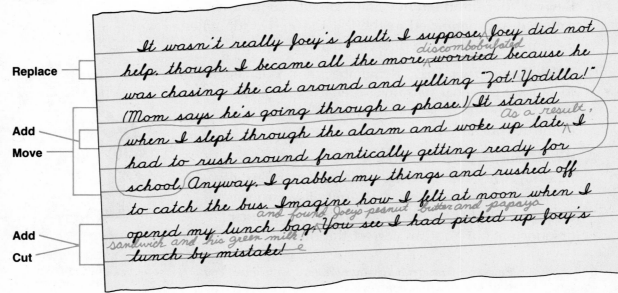

Replace — It wasn't really Joey's fault. I suppose. Joey did not help. though. I became all the more ~~worried~~ discombobulated because he was chasing the cat around and yelling "Zot! Yodilla!" (Mom says he's going through a phase.) It started

Add / Move — when I slept through the alarm and woke up late. As a result, I had to rush around frantically getting ready for school. Anyway. I grabbed my things and rushed off to catch the bus. Imagine how I felt at noon when I

Add / Cut — opened my lunch bag and found Joey's peanut butter and papaya ~~sandwich and his green milk!~~ You see I had picked up Joey's lunch by mistake!

Discuss

1. Do you agree that adding details about Joey's lunch helps explain Judith's feelings? Why or why not?
2. Look back at the sentences that Judith moved. In what way does this change improve her personal narrative? Explain your answer.
3. Would you make any other changes in Judith's narrative? Why?

Try Your Hand

Now revise your first draft.

A. Read Your First Draft   As you read your personal narrative, think about your audience and your purpose. Read your narrative silently or to a partner to see if it is complete and well organized. Ask yourself or your partner the questions in the box.

Responding and Revising Strategies

✔ **Respond**
Ask yourself or a partner:

◆ Does my personal narrative make clear what happened and why it happened?

◆ Is my personal narrative easy to follow?

◆ Does my narrative show how I felt and why I felt that way?

◆ Do my words express exactly the meaning and the feeling I intend?

✔ **Revise**
Try these solutions:

◆ **Add** any missing events. **Move** information and add transition words to make cause-and-effect connections clearer.

◆ **Move** information to give events in the order in which they happened.

◆ **Add** concrete examples. **Cut** dull details or **replace** them with more vivid ones.

◆ **Replace** words that do not express what you intend. See the **Revising Workshop** on page 22 and the **Writer's Thesaurus** in this book.

B. Make Your Changes   If the answer to any question in the box is *no,* try the solution. Use the **Editor's Marks** to show your changes.

C. Review Your Personal Narrative Again   Decide whether there is anything else you want to revise. Keep revising your narrative until you feel it is well organized and complete.

EDITOR'S MARKS

∧ Add something.
✗ Cut something.
◯ Move something.
∧ Replace something.

 Save your revised narrative in your *Writer's Notebook.* **You will use it when you proofread your personal narrative.**

Revising Workshop
Using a Thesaurus

Good writers pay attention to the words they use in their writing. One way in which writers find the exact words they need is by looking in a thesaurus. A **thesaurus** is a book that lists **synonyms,** or words with similar meanings, and **antonyms,** or words with opposite meanings. In a thesaurus, entry words are listed alphabetically, as in a dictionary.

Here is a sentence from a sixth-grader's personal narrative.

He became <u>sad</u>.

The writer wanted to show a special kind of sadness, so he looked up *sad* in a thesaurus and found this entry.

---

sad *adj.* Unhappy or depressed, sorrowful. The little boy was
  sad when his pet rabbit escaped from its cage.
joyless Lacking in joy; dreary. Cleaning my bedroom is a
  joyless task.
melancholy Having low spirits; gloomy or dejected. He was
  melancholy after being cut from the basketball team.

The writer was puzzled by the word *melancholy* because it was a new word for him. He read the entry carefully and thought that the meaning of *melancholy* was just what he wanted.

However, the writer decided *not* to use *melancholy* because he didn't want his readers to be puzzled, as he had been. Instead, he chose *joyless,* an unusual word but a clear one. It fit this writer's purpose because it expressed both the meaning and the feeling he intended, and because his audience would understand it.

Practice

Rewrite each sentence to be more exact. Use a thesaurus or the **Writer's Thesaurus** at the back of the book to replace the underlined word.

1. She <u>walked</u> slowly up to the door.
2. She <u>looked</u> inside the dark house but could see nothing.
3. The house seemed to be <u>empty</u>.
4. When she stepped inside, she noticed the <u>shiny</u> decorations.
5. The house looked <u>pretty</u> with all the birthday decorations.

Listening and Speaking
Tips on How to Listen and Speak in a Response Group

Responding to Another Student's Writing

1. Listen carefully while the piece is being read. Pay attention to your own thoughts and feelings as you listen.
2. After the reading, wait for your turn to speak. Then explain what you thought and felt about the work. Be sure to cover what you liked as well as what you did not like. Tell which parts held your interest, which parts did not, and which parts, if any, confused you. Identify specific words and details that stood out for you. Tell why they stood out.
3. Respond to the writing, not to the comments of others.

Receiving Other Students' Responses to Your Writing

1. Read your work aloud clearly and smoothly.
2. Listen quietly to the responses. Let each person speak without interruption. Do not argue with what anyone says. Try not to get angry or upset with any criticism you hear.
3. As you listen, try to see how your writing affected your audience and which parts affected them most. Notice what message they received and which parts of your writing expressed this message. Do not think about how to change your writing at this point. You can do that later.
4. If you want specific information about your writing, wait until everyone has responded. Then, if no one has given you the information you want, ask specific questions.

4 Proofreading
Personal Narrative

After revising her personal narrative, Judith used the **Writer's Guide** and the **Editor's Marks** to proofread it. Look at what she did.

Writer's Guide

Proofreading Checklist

- ☑ Check for errors in capitalization.
- ☑ Check for errors in punctuation.
- ☑ Check to see that all your paragraphs are indented.
- ☑ Check your grammar.
- ☑ Circle any words that you think may be misspelled. Find out how to spell them. Use a dictionary to check your spellings.
- ⇒ For proofreading help, use the **Writer's Handbook.**

¶ Luckily a student named Ron must be
going through the same phase as Joey. He
~~traided~~ *traded* me an apple and a roll for the
~~sandwhich~~ *sandwich* I could not get anybody
interested in the milk. though—and i'm
surprised not ~~surprized~~ !

EDITOR'S MARKS

- ≡ Capitalize.
- ⊙ Add a period.
- ∧ Add something.
- ⩓ Add a comma.
- ⱽⱽ Add quotation marks.
- ⌀ Cut something.
- ⋀ Replace something.
- ~ Transpose.
- ○ Spell correctly.
- ⊬ Indent paragraph.
- / Make a lowercase letter.

Discuss

1. Look at Judith's proofread narrative. What kinds of corrections did she make?
2. Why did Judith make the spelling errors that she made?

Try Your Hand

Proofread Your Personal Narrative Now use the **Writer's Guide** and the **Editor's Marks** to proofread your personal narrative.

Save your corrected narrative in your *Writer's Notebook*. You will use it when you publish your narrative.

WRITING PROCESS

5 Publishing
Personal Narrative

Judith made a clean copy of her personal narrative. Then she and her classmates published their personal narratives by posting them on a bulletin board. You can find Judith's narrative on page 41 of the **Writer's Handbook** at the back of this book.

Here is how Judith and her classmates made a bulletin board display of personal narratives.

Writer's Guide

Publishing Checklist

☑ Make a clean copy of your personal narrative.

☑ Be sure that nothing has been left out.

☑ Be sure that there are no mistakes.

☑ Share your narrative in a special way.

1. First, they typed each personal narrative, leaving space for the writer's photograph. Then, they mounted each narrative on a sheet of construction paper.

2. Next, they covered a bulletin board with colored paper and cut out paper letters of another color to spell out the title *Stories of Ourselves.* Finally, they pinned the title and the narratives on the board.

Discuss

1. Why are the colors you choose for your bulletin board important?
2. How might you decide on the order in which to pin the personal narratives on your bulletin board?

Try Your Hand

Publish Your Personal Narrative Follow the checklist in the **Writer's Guide.** If possible, make a class bulletin board of personal narratives, or try one of these ideas for sharing your narrative.

◆ Write your personal narrative in the form of a friendly letter, and mail it to a friend.
◆ Call a friend on the telephone, and tell that friend about the event in your personal narrative.

Writing in the Content Areas

Use what you learned to write the story of some true, interesting event from the first-person point of view. Use one of these ideas or an idea of your own.

Writer's Guide

When you write, remember the stages of the Writing Process.
- Prewriting
- Drafting
- Responding and Revising
- Proofreading
- Publishing

History

Select a famous figure in history, and imagine that you are that person. Write a friendly letter to someone you know. In the letter, tell about an important event in "your" life. Look in a history book or an encyclopedia for information. Write about the event as the person might have experienced it and told about it.

Literature

Fictional characters are often faced with realistic problems. Imagine that you are one of your favorite characters from fiction. Tell a classmate the story of how you solved some problem. What caused the problem? What actions did you take to solve the problem? What happened as a result of your actions?

Science

Scientists study the world in order to explain natural events. Read about some great scientists and their discoveries. Then write a journal entry that one of the scientists might have written, telling about his or her greatest discovery.

Social Studies

Imagine a day in the life of the President of the United States, a senator, or another government leader. Find out what people like this do and what sorts of events usually fill their days. You can get ideas by reading newspapers and news magazines as well as books on government and social studies.

Writers tell interesting stories about themselves when they write personal narratives. Often they use a friendly, conversational tone to tell these stories. What gives this personal narrative its conversational tone?

Listen to this crazy story. You know the noises we've been hearing in our attic? Boy, I thought we had ghosts up there! Well, I was totally wrong. Yesterday I was on the lawn by our house, and a mothball hit me. I looked up and let out a gasp. Shaking its fist at me from the attic window was a raccoon. It had collected mothballs from all our trunks and was flinging them at people passing by on the street below. My family and I had a good laugh over the whole episode.

MOTH BALLS

◆ **Sentences in a Personal Narrative** Study the variety of sentences used in the personal narrative. Notice that the first sentence gives a command, the second one asks a question, the third expresses a strong feeling, and the fourth makes a statement. The writer used other kinds of sentences, too. Such variety makes the personal narrative interesting to read.

◆ **Language Focus: Sentences** The following lessons will help you form and use many kinds of sentences correctly in your writing.

1 Sentences

A **sentence** is a group of words that expresses a complete thought.

Compare these two groups of words.

1. the author
2. The author wrote a book.

Notice that the first group of words seems incomplete. It leaves us wanting to know something about *the author*. The second group of words is a sentence because it expresses a complete thought. We know whom the words are about (*the author*) and what the person did (*wrote a book*). A sentence always begins with a capital letter and ends with a punctuation mark.

3. The book described his childhood.

Guided Practice

A. Tell whether each group of words is a *sentence* or is *not a sentence.*

1. Wilson Rawls wrote a story.
2. Writers sometimes tell about their own lives.
3. Back to his childhood.
4. Was called *Where the Red Fern Grows.*
5. The author grew up in the Ozark Mountains.
6. The Ozark Mountains extend across four states.
7. From southern Illinois to Oklahoma.
8. The Ozark region is covered with timber.
9. He set the story in the same area.
10. The woods in the Ozark Mountains.
11. About a poor family during the Great Depression.
12. Scarcely enough money for food.
13. They live in Arkansas.
14. The finest hunting country in the world.

> **THINK AND REMEMBER**
> ◆ Remember that a **sentence** expresses a complete thought.

Independent Practice

B. Identifying Sentences For each group of words, write *sentence* or *not a sentence*.

15. The story's young hero.
MODEL> not a sentence

16. The hero is named Billy.
17. Billy wants two dogs.
18. Cost too much money.
19. The boy works to earn the money.
20. Sells worms to a fisherman.
21. His grandfather buys his berries.
22. Fills a bank with nickels and dimes.

C. Proofreading: Correcting Sentences Find the errors in capitalization or punctuation in each sentence. Write the sentence correctly.

23. the boy liked to read
MODEL> The boy liked to read.

24. he read a book about farming
25. He found a sunny part of the yard
26. He followed the instructions in the book
27. the pumpkins won a prize at the state fair
28. The boy smiled proudly
29. today he is famous for his books on gardening

D. Completing Sentences Add words to complete the sentences. Write each sentence.

30. _____ visited the shop.
MODEL> The girl visited the shop.

31. A little dog _____.
32. _____ enjoyed stories about animals.
33. Snakes and lizards _____.
34. _____ held a pet show.
35. The whole class _____.

36. The frightened bird _____.
37. _____ visited the zoo.
38. _____ rode a bus.
39. All of us _____.
40. _____ gave us a tour of the training area.

Application — Writing

Journal Entry Imagine that you are the man in the picture. You are thinking back to a good time you had when you were younger. Write a journal entry about that time. Tell what you did and what made the event special. Use complete sentences.

2 Four Kinds of Sentences

◆ FOCUS   The four kinds of sentences are declarative, interrogative, imperative, and exclamatory.

There are four kinds of sentences to express different feelings and purposes. A **declarative** sentence makes a statement. An **interrogative** sentence asks a question. An **imperative** sentence gives an order or makes a request. An **exclamatory** sentence expresses strong feeling.

1. Ads give information.   declarative
2. Have you heard this ad?   interrogative
3. Please listen to it.   imperative
4. This cereal is great!   exclamatory

Notice that declarative and imperative sentences end with periods. An interrogative sentence ends with a question mark. An exclamatory sentence ends with an exclamation point.

> **Link to Speaking and Writing**
> Varying the kinds of sentences you use can help make your speech and writing lively.

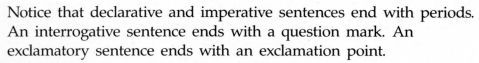

We went to the store. Would you believe it? The place was packed! Go see for yourself.

Guided Practice

A. Tell whether each sentence is *declarative, interrogative, imperative,* or *exclamatory.*

1. The ad just started.
2. What is it selling?
3. Look at those shoes.
4. Those are nice shoes!
5. Please turn up the sound.
6. I want to buy those shoes.

> **THINK AND REMEMBER**
> ◆ Use a **declarative** sentence to make a statement.
> ◆ Use an **interrogative** sentence to ask a question.
> ◆ Use an **imperative** sentence to give an order or to make a request.
> ◆ Use an **exclamatory** sentence to express strong feeling.

Independent Practice

B. Identifying Kinds of Sentences For each sentence, write *declarative, interrogative, imperative,* or *exclamatory.*

7. Look at the ad on that billboard.
> MODEL > imperative

8. A car is moving down a dusty road.
9. A coyote watches the car.
10. What is the ad trying to sell?
11. The ad is for a new kind of car.
12. Have you ever seen a car like that?
13. The coyote is certainly handsome!
14. Why is the coyote watching the car?
15. How sleek and shiny the car is!
16. That car must move fast!
17. How much does that car cost?
18. Go find out.
19. I would love to own a car like that!
20. Wait until you grow up.

C. Revising: Rewriting Sentences Rewrite each group of sentences to make it more lively. Change at least two sentences in each group into different kinds of sentences.

21. Brazil is a lovely country. The weather is wonderful. It is a pleasant place to visit.
> MODEL > What a lovely country Brazil is! Isn't the weather wonderful? Please visit this pleasant place.

22. You should look at a map of Brazil. Brazil is big. It fills half the continent of South America. That is a big country.
23. You may wonder where the world's biggest river is. It is in Brazil. It is called the Amazon River. The Amazon runs through the world's largest jungle.
24. A tour company offers cruises on the Amazon River. I wonder if the cruises are exciting. Can we take a cruise on our next vacation?

Application — Writing and Speaking

Advertisement Write a television advertisement for cereal or for another product. Tell the audience what your product is and why they should buy it. Be sure to use all four kinds of sentences. Present your advertisement aloud to some of your classmates, and try to convince them to buy your product.

3 Subjects and Predicates

◆ **FOCUS** Each sentence is made up of two parts: the subject and the predicate.

In order to express a complete thought, a sentence must have a subject and a predicate. The **subject** tells whom or what the sentence is about. It can be one word or more than one word. The subject in each of these sentences is in color.

1. Young Alicia Frank wrote a postcard.
2. She put it in the mailbox.

The **predicate** expresses something about the subject. It can tell what the subject does, has, feels, or is. The predicate, too, can be one word or more than one word. The predicate in each of these sentences is in color.

3. Her grandfather in Ohio smiled .
4. The postcard was a pleasant surprise .

All the words in a sentence are either part of the subject or part of the predicate.

Guided Practice

A. Identify the subject in each sentence.

1. The postal service is important in everyday life.
2. Mail carriers deliver letters to your home.
3. Letters travel by truck and by plane.
4. Many letters arrive overnight.
5. Workers at the post office weigh letters and packages.
6. Machines sort 50,000 letters per hour.

B. 7.–12. Identify the predicate in each sentence in **A.**

THINK AND REMEMBER
- ◆ Include a subject and a predicate in every sentence.
- ◆ In the **subject,** tell whom or what the sentence is about.
- ◆ In the **predicate,** tell something about the subject.

Independent Practice

C. Identifying Subjects Write the subject of each sentence.

13. Innkeepers handed out letters in colonial times.

MODEL > Innkeepers

14. The United States printed its first stamps in 1847.

15. A picture of George Washington was on the 10-cent stamp.

16. New York and Boston had the first collection boxes.

17. The pony express operated from 1860 to 1861.

18. Riders on horses carried mail.

19. Western settlers waited eagerly for letters.

20. People picked up mail at the post office until 1863.

21. Mail carriers began delivering mail in 1863.

D. 22.–30. Identifying Predicates Write the predicate of each sentence in C.

22. Innkeepers handed out letters in colonial times.

MODEL > handed out letters in colonial times

E. Completing Sentences Add a subject or a predicate to complete each sentence. Write the sentence. Then write *subject* or *predicate* to show what you added. Remember to begin each sentence with a capital letter and to end it with a punctuation mark that shows what kind of sentence it is.

31. the workers

MODEL > The workers are busy.   predicate

32. arrived from a good friend

33. an Italian postage stamp

34. my friend Sally

35. the letter

36. told me about the trip

37. Rome, the capital of Italy,

38. is a pleasant place

39. enjoy getting those letters

40. the train from Milan to Florence

41. according to my friend Sally, the weather in Italy

Application — Writing

Postcard Imagine that you are on vacation in a faraway place. Write a postcard to a classmate about your vacation. Tell your classmate where you are and what you are doing. Be sure that every sentence has a subject and a predicate.

4 Complete and Simple Subjects

◆ The **complete subject** is all the words that make up the subject of a sentence.
◆ The **simple subject** is the main word or words in the complete subject.

Read the sentence below. Notice the words that make up the complete subject. The word in color is the simple subject.

┌─ complete subject ─┐
1. The sixth-grade `class` attended a play.

Sometimes the simple subject is more than one word.

2. The talented `Ann Young` played Deborah Sampson.

Sometimes the complete subject is only one word. The complete subject and the simple subject are then the same.

3. `She` smiled at the audience.

Guided Practice

A. Identify the complete subject of each sentence.

1. The dark red curtains opened.
2. Every eye in the audience watched the stage.
3. The title of the play was *Daring Deborah*.
4. Deborah Sampson was a hero of the American Revolution.
5. A gifted actress played the leading role.
6. She spoke her lines with great force.
7. Her performance captivated the audience.
8. The audience responded with a standing ovation.
9. The entire cast took a bow.

B. 10. – 18. Identify the simple subject of each sentence in **A.**

THINK AND REMEMBER
◆ Remember that the **complete subject** is all the words in the subject.
◆ Remember that the **simple subject** is the main word or words in the subject.

Independent Practice

C. Identifying Complete Subjects   Write the complete subject of each sentence.

19. Many people have written books about Molly Pitcher.

MODEL > Many people

20. Molly Pitcher lived during the American Revolution.
21. The stories about her may be just legends.
22. Molly's real name was Mary Ludwig.
23. Molly's husband joined the army.
24. Molly Ludwig came along to help.
25. A very important battle began on June 28, 1778.
26. The terrible heat made Molly's husband faint.
27. Brave Molly took her husband's place.

D. 28.–36. Identifying Simple Subjects   Write the simple subject of each sentence in **C.**

28. Many people have written books about Molly Pitcher.

MODEL > people

E. Adding Subjects to Sentences   Add a complete subject to each sentence. Write the sentence. Underline the simple subject.

37. _____ wrote a play.

MODEL > My best friend in school wrote a play.

38. _____ is about the Civil War.
39. _____ is the hero's name.
40. _____ meets some enemy soldiers.
41. _____ try to capture him.
42. _____ talks to the soldiers.
43. _____ end up respecting the hero.
44. _____ helped our class produce the play.
45. _____ built the sets for the scenery.
46. _____ turned the auditorium into a theater.
47. _____ enjoyed the play a great deal.

Application — Writing and Speaking

Speech   Imagine that you are writing a play about a real or fictional hero of the American Revolution for your class to perform. Write a speech for one character in your play. Be sure that all of your sentences have subjects. Then read the speech for your class. If you need help writing a speech for a play, see page 45 of the **Writer's Handbook** at the back of this book.

5 Complete and Simple Predicates

FOCUS

◆ The **complete predicate** is all the words that make up the predicate of a sentence.
◆ The **simple predicate** is the main word or words in the complete predicate.

Remember that all the words in the subject make up the complete subject. Look at the words that make up the complete predicate in the sentence below. The word in color is the simple predicate.

```
        ┌─── complete predicate ───┐
```
1. Sam explained the game to Tommy.

The simple predicate is always one or more verbs. A **verb** is a word that expresses an action or links the subject to a word in the predicate. The words in color below are verbs.

2. Four Quarters is fun.
3. Two to four people can play .

Notice that the complete predicate in sentence 3 contains only verbs. In this sentence the complete predicate is also the simple predicate.

Link to Speaking and Writing
Using precise verbs in the simple predicate can sharpen a whole sentence.

The person with the most points does the best. wins

Guided Practice

A. Identify the complete predicate in each sentence.

1. Four Quarters is an enjoyable game.
2. I will explain the rules to you.
3. Each player in Four Quarters has an area.
4. Players stay in their areas.
5. One person throws the ball up.
6. You bat the ball away from your area.

B. 7.–12. Name the simple predicate in each sentence in **A.**

> **THINK AND REMEMBER**
> ◆ Remember that the **complete predicate** is all the words in the predicate.
> ◆ Remember that the **simple predicate** is the main word or words in the predicate.

Independent Practice

C. Identifying Complete Predicates Write the complete predicate of each sentence.

13. Lacrosse is the national sport of Canada.

MODEL ▷ is the national sport of Canada

14. It may be the oldest game in North America.
15. Indians of the Iroquois nation played the game.
16. The Indians called it *baggataway*.
17. The game has changed greatly.
18. A modern lacrosse team has ten members.
19. The Indian version of lacrosse was different.
20. A thousand Indians might have played in some games.

D. 21.–28. Identifying Simple Predicates Write the simple predicate of each sentence in **C.**

21. Lacrosse is the national sport of Canada.

MODEL ▷ is

E. Revising: Sharpening Sentences Sharpen each sentence by changing the complete predicate. Write the new sentence. Use the **Writer's Thesaurus** to help you find precise verbs.

29. Mighty Casey missed the baseball with his bat.

MODEL ▷ Mighty Casey struck out.

30. Mudville baseball fans made sad sounds for weeks.
31. They began to have no memory of Casey's mighty deeds.
32. The fans used the name "Strike-out Casey" for him.
33. One day Casey was face to face against the same pitcher.
34. This time his bat came together with the ball.
35. Mighty Casey had succeeded in the game!

Application — Writing

Rules for a Game Think of a game you enjoy. Write rules to explain the game. Tell how many people can play and what each player should do. Use precise, active verbs as simple predicates.

6 Word Order in Sentences

◆ **FOCUS** Words in a sentence can be in natural or inverted word order.

Remember that every sentence has a subject and a predicate. If the subject comes before the predicate, the sentence is in **natural word order.** Most sentences are in natural word order.

1. The blue whales swam in the ocean.

If the predicate comes before the subject, the sentence is in **inverted word order.**

2. In the ocean swam the blue whales.

Link to Speaking and Writing
Inverted word order sometimes makes a sentence stand out and show more emphasis. Which sentence shows more emphasis?

Its tail moved up and down.
Up and down moved its tail.

Guided Practice

A. Tell whether the word order in each is *natural* or *inverted.*

1. The blue whales spent the summer in the Arctic.
2. Huge glaciers surrounded them.
3. Colder and colder grew the northern waters.
4. Around them formed great blocks of ice.
5. To the south headed all the whales.
6. By March they were off the coast of Mexico.

THINK AND REMEMBER
◆ To write a sentence with natural word order, put the subject before the predicate.
◆ To write a sentence with inverted word order, put the predicate before the subject.
◆ Use inverted word order to make a sentence show more emphasis.

Independent Practice

B. Identifying Word Order in Sentences   Write *natural word order* or *inverted word order* for each sentence.

7. Many types of animals have died out.

MODEL ▷ natural word order

8. Gone are the mastodons and the passenger pigeons.

9. On the island of Mauritius lived a bird called the dodo.

10. Sailors hunted the dodo for its meat.

11. The last dodo died more than 100 years ago.

12. In danger today is the California condor.

C. Changing Word Order in Sentences   Rewrite each sentence in different word order. Then label the new sentence *natural* or *inverted*.

13. The baby lions romped in the grass.

MODEL ▷ In the grass romped the baby lions.   inverted

14. A man crouched behind the lions.

15. A shiny black movie camera was in his hands.

16. Two feet long was the little cub.

17. Off a little ridge leaped the mother lion.

18. Her great body shot through the air.

19. The lioness roared angrily.

D. Completing Sentences in Natural and Inverted Order   Write a sentence using each group of words given. Write the sentence in the word order named in parentheses.

20. in the water (inverted)

MODEL ▷ In the water swam a seal.

21. steadily coasted (inverted)

22. one little seal (inverted)

23. rocked gently (natural)

24. a curious girl (inverted)

25. played and splashed (natural)

26. a small bird (natural)

27. on a tree limb (inverted)

28. into the sky (inverted)

29. a flock of birds (natural)

30. three boys (natural)

Application — Writing and Speaking

Eyewitness Account   Suppose you are a reporter for a radio station. You are on the scene where the whales in the picture have been sighted. Describe the whales for your radio audience, and tell what they are doing. First, write your sentences; then, read them to your classmates. Use inverted word order to add emphasis to some sentences.

7 Finding Subjects of Sentences

◆ **FOCUS** The subject is not always found at the beginning of the sentence.

Remember that in most sentences, the simple subject comes before the predicate. In an interrogative sentence, however, it usually comes after the simple predicate or between two parts of the simple predicate. To determine the subject of an interrogative sentence, make the sentence declarative. Then ask yourself whom or what the sentence is about.

1. Did you hear about the party?
   (You did hear about the party.)

In imperative sentences, the subject is rarely stated. It is understood, however, to be *you*. Notice that an imperative sentence with *you* (understood) follows natural word order.

2. (*you*) Go to Sally's slumber party.

In declarative sentences that begin with *here* or *there*, the simple subject follows the simple predicate. The simple subjects are in color.

3. Here are the presents .
4. There will be food at the party.

Guided Practice

A. Identify the simple subject of each sentence.

1. Is Amy going to Sally's party?
2. Here is the invitation.
3. Look at the pretty drawing on the front.
4. Does the invitation tell the time of the party?
5. Please tell me about Sally's house.
6. There is an elm tree in her yard.
7. How old will Sally be?
8. There will be a slumber party later.
9. When will Amy have a slumber party?
10. Where does she live?
11. Here is a map to her house.
12. Follow the streets I marked in red.
13. There will be ten people at the party.
14. Would you like to ride with me?
15. What time should we leave?
16. Don't be late.

Independent Practice

B. Identifying Simple Subjects Write the simple subject of each sentence.

17. Do you know a good game?

MODEL> you

18. Here is a great game.
19. Is it a scavenger hunt?
20. Look at all those presents.
21. Here is a hat from Elaine.
22. Will you open that box next?
23. Now, cut the cake.

C. Identifying Subjects in Different Kinds of Sentences

Write the simple subject for each sentence. Then write *declarative, interrogative,* or *imperative.*

24. Tell me about the history of birthday celebrations.

MODEL> (You)—imperative

25. Did the Egyptians start the custom?
26. There were birthday parties for the Pharaohs.
27. Did the Greeks celebrate their birthdays?
28. Here is a way to find out.
29. Look in this book about the subject.
30. There were birthday parties only for kings and nobles.
31. Did ordinary Greeks have birthday parties?
32. There is no information on that subject.

Application — Writing

Friendly Letter Imagine that you have just attended a friend's birthday party. Write a letter to another classmate, describing the party. Use interrogative and imperative sentences and sentences beginning with *here* and *there* in your letter. If you need help writing a friendly letter, see page 52 of the **Writer's Handbook.**

8 Compound Subjects

◆ **FOCUS** A **compound subject** is two or more subjects that have the same predicate.

Remember that a simple subject is the key word or words in the complete subject. A compound subject has two or more simple subjects. The parts of a compound subject are usually joined by the connecting word *and* or *or*. In these examples, the compound subjects are in color.

1. Rome and Athens were two ancient cities.

2. Kings or emperors ruled ancient cities.

When a compound subject has three or more subjects, a comma comes after all but the last.

3. Nobles, workers, and merchants lived there.

Link to Speaking and Writing
To use fewer words, combine sentences with similar predicates into one sentence with a compound subject.

and
Uxmal ~~was an ancient city in Mexico.~~ Tulum *were* ~~was~~ also an ancient *cities* city in Mexico.

Guided Practice

A. Name the simple subjects in each sentence. Tell what connecting word joins the simple subjects.

1. An old pot or statue can give clues about ancient life.

2. Ancient cities and towns were surrounded by high walls.

3. Ancient Athens, Beijing, and Rome had large populations.

4. Rulers and high priests were part of the upper class.

THINK AND REMEMBER
◆ Remember that two or more simple subjects with the same predicate are called a **compound subject.**
◆ To save words, combine sentences with similar predicates into one sentence with a compound subject.

Independent Practice

B. Identifying Simple Subjects   Write the simple subjects and the connecting word from each sentence. Underline the connecting word.

5. My parents and I went to Rome last year.

MODEL > parents <u>and</u> I

6. Rome and my city are very different from each other.
7. New buildings and old buildings seem jumbled together in Rome.
8. Time and nature have left their mark on Rome.
9. Invading armies and harsh weather have damaged some of the buildings.
10. Even now, however, a statue or a beautiful column greets your eye wherever you look.

C. Identifying Compound Subjects and Their Parts   Write the complete subject of each sentence. Then underline each simple subject once, and underline the connecting word twice.

11. My aunt and uncle are archaeologists.

MODEL > My <u>aunt</u> <u>and</u> <u>uncle</u>

12. Historians and archaeologists study the past.
13. Old books and documents are what historians examine.
14. Most archaeologists and their helpers dig in the ground.
15. The tools people used, the food they ate, and the things they made interest archaeologists.

D. Writing Sentences with Compound Subjects   Use each set of words in a sentence with a compound subject.

16. Dallas, Miami

MODEL > Dallas and Miami are modern cities.

17. airports, train stations
18. subways, buses
19. offices, museums, theaters
20. factories, warehouses
21. parks, playgrounds
22. students, parents, teachers
23. brothers, sisters
24. bicycles, skateboards
25. sidewalks, parking lots
26. friends, neighbors

Application — Writing

Social Studies Report   Imagine that you are an archaeologist digging in the ruins of an ancient city. Write a brief report for other archaeologists about one object you found and how you found it. Use at least two sentences that have compound subjects.

9 Compound Predicates

◆ **FOCUS** A **compound predicate** is two or more predicates that have the same subject.

Remember that a simple predicate is the key word or words in the complete predicate. A compound predicate has two or more simple predicates. The parts of a compound predicate are usually joined by the connecting word *and, but,* or *or.* The words in color below are compound predicates.

1. Newscasters observe and report the weather.
2. The wind blows hard but feels quite warm.

If a compound predicate contains three or more simple predicates, a comma comes after all but the last simple predicate.

3. Leaves dance , drift , and float in the air.

Link to Speaking and Writing

A compound predicate can help you tell more about the subject.

We go indoors , sit by the fire, and talk

Guided Practice

A. Identify the compound predicate in each sentence. Then tell the connecting word that joins the simple predicates.

1. Fall leaves rustle and crackle underfoot.
2. A fierce wind whistles and sighs in the chimney.
3. Bare trees bend but do not break in the wind.
4. The days cool down and grow shorter.

THINK AND REMEMBER
- ◆ Remember that two or more predicates with the same subject are called a **compound predicate.**
- ◆ Use a compound predicate to say more about a subject.

Independent Practice

B. Identifying Compound Predicates Write the compound predicate from each sentence.

5. The air was cold but felt refreshing.

MODEL was, felt

6. Ice crystals shimmered, glistened, and sparkled on the grass and the trees.

7. A snowflake floated down and landed on my hand.

8. I looked at my brother and laughed.

9. He knew what I was thinking or read my thoughts.

10. We hurried to the garage and dragged out the red sled.

11. Albert had a sled and knew we wanted to race him.

12. He would race us today or would face disgrace.

C. Identifying the Parts of Compound Predicates Write the complete predicate from each sentence. Underline each simple predicate once. Underline the connecting word twice.

13. Rain taps and patters on the earth.

MODEL taps and patters on the earth

14. The sun comes out and warms the ground.

15. Water turns into steam and rises.

16. The moist air expands, cools, and finally condenses into clouds.

17. Some clouds look white and bring no rain.

18. Other clouds look dark and cover the sky.

D. Revising: Expanding Sentences Expand each sentence by forming a compound predicate. Write the new sentence.

19. The sun shines.

MODEL The sun shines and sparkles on the sea.

20. A dog runs across the sand.

21. People come to the beach.

22. Children splash in the water.

23. The sky is blue.

Application — Writing and Speaking

Weather Report Write a weather report for a television news program. Describe the day shown in the picture. Discuss temperature, wind, and general conditions. Use at least two sentences with compound predicates. Read your weather report to your classmates as if you are on television.

10 Compound Sentences

◆ **FOCUS** A **compound sentence** is two or more simple sentences joined by *and, or, but,* or a semicolon.

If a sentence expresses only one complete thought, it is a **simple sentence.** Two or more simple sentences can be joined to make a compound sentence.

1. I read the novel. I liked it.   simple sentences
2. I read the novel, and I liked it.
   compound sentence

A compound sentence contains two or more simple sentences, each with its own subject and predicate. The simple sentences are often connected by *and, but,* or *or.* A comma comes after each simple sentence, except for the last one, and before the connecting word. Each connecting word is in color in the compound sentences below.

3. I started it yesterday , and I finished it today .
4. The book has sad parts , but it ends happily .
5. You can read it here , or you can take it home .

If the ideas in two or more simple sentences are closely related, you can use a semicolon to join them instead of a comma and a connecting word.

6. There are many copies available ; this library has three.

Do not confuse a simple sentence that has a compound subject or a compound predicate with a compound sentence.

7. The hero survives and saves his town.   compound predicate
8. The hero survives, and he saves his town.   compound sentence

Guided Practice

A. Tell whether each sentence is a *compound sentence* or a *simple sentence.*

1. Marguerite de Angeli wrote *The Door in the Wall.*
2. The story is set in the Middle Ages, and it is exciting.
3. Robin's father has gone away and cannot help him.
4. Robin and some servants stay behind in London.
5. An illness strikes Robin, and he cannot walk.
6. Robin calls for help; no one hears him.

Independent Practice

B. Identifying Compound and Simple Sentences Write *simple* or *compound* for each sentence.

7. Brother Luke takes Robin to a hospital.

MODEL ▷ simple

8. Robin likes the hospital, but he misses his parents.
9. Robin cannot walk, but he learns to use crutches.
10. His hopes and dreams of knighthood vanish.
11. A nearby town is attacked; the people flee to the castle.
12. Robin must get help, or the castle will be captured.

C. Recognizing Compound Subjects, Compound Predicates, and Compound Sentences For each sentence, write *compound subject, compound predicate,* or *compound sentence.*

13. The Roman Empire collapsed, and Europe changed forever.

MODEL ▷ compound sentence

14. Small kingdoms arose, and they replaced the empire.
15. Roads and bridges crumbled away.
16. Vikings came from the north and attacked the towns.
17. Kings ruled nobles, nobles ruled vassals, and vassals ruled serfs.
18. Nobles lived in castles and protected their vassals.

D. Writing Sentences Use each pair of words in a compound sentence. Use semicolons in at least two of the sentences.

19. fought, won

MODEL ▷ They fought well, and they won.

20. king, knights
21. smiled, laughed
22. sang, listened
23. rider, horse

Application — Writing and Speaking

Description Write a description of medieval times based on the picture and on any other information you wish to gather. Use at least two compound sentences in your report. Read your report aloud to some of your classmates.

11 Avoiding Sentence Fragments and Run-on Sentences

◆ FOCUS   Two common sentence errors are sentence fragments and run-on sentences.

Remember that a sentence expresses a complete thought. A group of words that does not express a complete thought is called a **sentence fragment.** You can correct a sentence fragment by adding words to give it a complete subject and a complete predicate.

1. made videos in Hawaii   sentence fragment
2. My family made videos in Hawaii.   sentence

A **run-on sentence** strings together two or more thoughts without separating them clearly. To correct a run-on sentence, you can use capitalization and punctuation to separate the thoughts.

3. Many tourists go to Hawaii they visit the volcanoes.
   run-on sentence
4. Many tourists go to Hawaii. They visit the volcanoes.
   correct sentences

Sometimes when you break up a run-on sentence, your writing sounds choppy. To avoid this, change the run-on sentence into a compound sentence or into a sentence with a compound subject or a compound predicate.

5. Many tourists go to Hawaii and visit the volcanoes.
   compound predicate

Guided Practice

A. Identify each group of words as a *sentence,* a *sentence fragment,* or a *run-on sentence.*

1. A fault is a crack in the earth's surface.
2. Millions of years ago a long fault.
3. The fault opened in the ocean bottom it was 2,000 miles long.

THINK AND REMEMBER

◆ Avoid using a **sentence fragment,** which does not express a complete thought.
◆ Avoid using a **run-on sentence,** which strings together two or more sentences without clearly separating them.

Independent Practice

B. Identifying Sentences and Sentence Errors Write *sentence,* *sentence fragment,* or *run-on sentence* for each group of words.

4. Riding on a long board called a surfboard.

MODEL▷ sentence fragment

5. We filmed surfers riding the waves.
6. Captain Cook discovered Hawaii in 1778 he saw Hawaiians surfing.
7. Early Hawaiians had long surfboards made of heavy wood.
8. The balsa-wood or plastic surfboards of today.
9. Julie had a hard time standing up we enjoyed taking pictures of her earnest attempts.

C. Revising: Correcting Sentence Fragments Rewrite each sentence fragment as a complete sentence.

10. The weather on the island.

MODEL▷ The weather on the island is mild.

11. Has deep-blue seas.
12. Softly at night.
13. Filmed acres of bananas.
14. Photographs of some islands.
15. Grow sugar cane.
16. Crash against the shore.

D. Proofreading: Correcting Run-on Sentences Rewrite each run-on sentence. Use the correct punctuation and capitalization.

17. Some volcanoes are active they may erupt.

MODEL▷ Some volcanoes are active. They may erupt.

18. The Hawaiian Islands are mountaintops the bottoms of the mountains are on the ocean floor.
19. Mauna Loa is on the island of Hawaii it is the world's most active volcano.
20. Hawaii has many active volcanoes tourists can see them.
21. Tourists watch the volcanoes they stay a safe distance away in special buildings.

Application — Writing and Speaking

Eyewitness Account Imagine that you are a reporter for your hometown radio station. You are visiting Hawaii and have just seen a volcano erupt. Write a report telling what you saw, where you saw it, who was there, and when the event happened. Avoid using sentence fragments or run-on sentences. Read your report as a radio broadcast to your classmates.

Building Vocabulary
Context Clues: Words in Sentences

Are you the cooper?   Of course, I make barrels. Can't you tell?

The situation shown in the picture helps you recognize that a cooper makes barrels. The whole situation surrounding an event or an item is called the **context.** Good writing creates a strong context for words a reader may not know so that the reader does not have to stop to look up each word. Instead, the written context, or the words around the new word, gives clues to the word's meaning.

Sometimes when you write, you may use words that your readers do not know. There are several ways to help your readers understand these words. You can give a definition. In example **1** the underlined words provide a definition for the highlighted word.

1. The cooper turned staves into barrels and pails. Staves are narrow strips of wood.

You can give a word with a similar meaning.

2. Traveling workers dispersed , or spread, news through the colonies.

You can give a word with an opposite meaning.

3. Colonists waited for them, not with disinterest but with anticipation .

You can give other information that suggests the meaning of the word. In example **4** the underlined information provides a clue that *itinerant* means "moving from place to place."

4. In colonial times many workers were itinerant because there was not enough work for them to stay in one place very long.

Reading Practice

Read each sentence. Write the meaning of the underlined word in each sentence. Then write *definition, information,* or *similar meaning* for the kind of context clue that helped you know the word's meaning.

 1. Many colonists lived in <u>hamlets,</u> settlements so small they could not even be called villages.
 2. Hamlets were in <u>isolated</u> areas, so strangers were rarely seen in them.
 3. Tradespeople <u>congregated,</u> or gathered, in larger settlements.
 4. In most colonial towns, the <u>cobbler,</u> or shoemaker, was often the harness maker, too.
 5. The <u>tanner</u> was an important member of the community. A tanner turns the skins of animals into leather.
 6. <u>Tinkers</u> usually traveled from place to place, fixing metal household objects.
 7. Some workers used the <u>windlass</u> for hauling and lifting heavy objects.
 8. Colonial farmers used many different <u>implements,</u> or tools, to harvest their crops.
 9. The <u>scythe,</u> with its long curved blade and long handle, made cutting hay a relatively easy job.
10. Hard stones were used to <u>hone,</u> or sharpen, the blades.

Writing Practice

Find the meaning of each word below in a dictionary. Then write a sentence containing a context clue for each word.

11. sickle	13. wreak	15. covertly	17. stylus
12. guile	14. anvil	16. impromptu	18. terse

Project

With a group of classmates, look in the library for a book on a topic that interests all of you. Have each person in the group read the same chapter and list ten or more difficult words. Compare your lists and, as a group, choose ten words that no one knows. Find the meanings of the words in a dictionary. Then each person should write sentences containing context clues for each word. Compare your sentences to see which context clues make the meanings of the words clearest.

Language Enrichment
Sentences

Use what you know about sentences to do these activities.

 ### What's So Funny?

Clip a comic strip from the Sunday newspaper. Cover the word balloons with blank balloons that you have cut from a sheet of white paper. Fill in the balloons with your own dialogue. Use the four different kinds of sentences, including some in inverted order.

I've got an idea. Do you want to play kick ball?

That sounds great! Ask Tommy if he wants to play.

 ### Silly Sentences

For this activity, you will need 25 index cards. Number five cards with a *1*, five with a *2*, five with a *3*, five with a *4*, and five with a *5*. On the first set of cards, write either *A* or *The*. On cards of the second set, write words that describe people, places, or things. On each card of the third set, write the name of an object, an animal, or a person. On cards of the fourth set, write a word that ends in *s* and tells about an action taking place now. On each card of the last set, write a word that ends in *ly* and describes how an action takes place. Put a period after each word in the last set.

Shuffle the cards in each stack and lay the stacks in order on a desk. Put cards together in number order to form sentences. Share these silly sentences with the class.

 ### Compound Circles

With a group of classmates, form a circle. Go around the circle and form longer and longer sentences by adding subjects, predicates, or complete thoughts to make compound subjects, compound predicates, or compound sentences.

For example, the first player might say, "My sister went to the beach." The next player might add, "My sister and her dog went to the beach." The third player might say, "My sister and her dog went to the beach and saw an elephant." Continue in this way until a player cannot remember all the parts of the sentence.

CONNECTING
LANGUAGE ⟷ WRITING

In this unit you learned that sentences express complete thoughts. They can tell, ask, give commands, or express feelings. They are made of subjects and predicates that may come in natural or inverted order. You learned to recognize and form compound subjects, compound predicates, and compound sentences.

◆ **Using Sentences in Your Writing**   Sentences are the building blocks of paragraphs and longer works. Using different kinds of sentences gives you the ability to communicate effectively. Pay special attention to your sentences as you do these activities.

> **Boy:** *I am Diego.*
> **Girl:** *Who are you?*

What's the Question?

With a classmate, play an answer-question game. Write declarative, exclamatory, and imperative sentences. Include some sentences in inverted order, some compound sentences, some sentences with compound subjects, and some with compound predicates. Have your partner write questions that the sentences answer.

Context Contests

You learned about context clues on the **Building Vocabulary** pages. See how well you can guess words from a context created by a partner.

Write a paragraph that is part of a mystery story or another kind of story. Then go back through your work and pick the four most difficult words. Make sure the contexts for the words are clear. Paste strips of blank paper over the words, and have your partner guess what they are.

1 Unit Checkup

Think Back	Think Ahead
◆ What did you learn about personal narratives in this unit? What did you do to write one?	◆ How will what you learned about personal narratives help you analyze the stories you read?
	◆ How will you use examples to make your writing clearer?
◆ Look at the writing you did in this unit. How did varying your sentences improve your writing?	◆ How can you use what you learned about run-on sentences and fragments to improve your writing?

Personal Narratives   *pages 12–13*

Read the journal entry. Then follow the directions.

> Saturday was the best day I've had in a long time. My Uncle Jordan came to visit. After we picked him up at the airport, he took us to lunch at Luigi's, my favorite restaurant. We spent the afternoon at the Aquarium. Then we had a relaxing dinner at home. Finally, we fell asleep watching an old movie on TV.

1. List the main events in the order in which they happened.
2. Label the *beginning, middle,* and *ending* of the list in 1.
3. Identify the entry's point of view. Give clue words.

Connecting Cause and Effect   *page 14*

Write each sentence. Underline the cause once and the effect twice.

4. Andy and I cooked dinner because the restaurant was closed.
5. Since Andy is a good cook, our dinner was good.
6. The meat defrosted after I took it from the freezer.
7. Our salad was fresh; we picked the lettuce from our garden.

Using Examples   *page 15*

Write an effective example to express each description.

8. an unusual house   9. an exciting game   10. an attractive landscape

The Writing Process   *pages 16–25*
Write the letter of the correct response to each question.

11. When planning a personal narrative, what should you do last?
    a. Organize facts for your story.
    b. Gather information.
    c. Brainstorm interesting events.

12. Imagine that you are writing a personal narrative about a fishing trip for your class. You find out that your class knows nothing about fishing. What would you do?
    a. Change your topic.
    b. Add background information about fishing.
    c. Cut some information.

13. Which is not a good way to publish a personal narrative?
    a. in a letter
    b. in a book of stories
    c. as directions on how to make something

Sentences   *pages 28–29*
For each group of words, write *sentence* or *not a sentence*.

14. Many people who cannot hear use sign language.
15. Means "Help me" in sign language.
16. Finger spelling is a different system.
17. Each letter is represented by a motion of the fingers.
18. Stand for entire words rather than for single letters.

Four Kinds of Sentences   *pages 30–31*
For each sentence, write *declarative, interrogative, imperative,* or *exclamatory.*

19. Have you ever written a secret message in invisible ink?
20. One kind of invisible ink is made from lemon juice.
21. Write with a toothpick dipped in the lemon juice.
22. When heated, the dried lemon juice will turn brown.
23. What a surprise the receiver of the letter will have!

Subjects and Predicates   *pages 32–33*
Write the subject and the predicate of each sentence.

24. In the 1930's and 1940's, people listened to their favorite programs on the radio.
25. Families gathered around the radio in the evening.
26. Listeners of all ages laughed at "Fibber McGee and Molly."
27. "The Shadow" frightened both children and adults.
28. Of course, the radio gave listeners news as well as entertainment.

Complete and Simple Subjects   *pages 34–35*
Add a complete subject to each sentence. Write the sentence.
Underline the simple subject.

29. _____ brought their taste in food to the New World.

30. _____ was huge.   **32.** _____ was grown by the Incas.

31. _____ is corn.   **33.** _____ helped the explorers.

Complete and Simple Predicates   *pages 36–37*
Write the complete predicate from each sentence. Underline the simple predicate.

34. Astro explorer Kincaid closed the door to her Planetcoach.

35. UV642 greeted Kincaid at the Venus spaceport.

36. The host mumbled strange sounds into a small box.

37. Kincaid heard the box's automatic translation.

38. The translation box had changed interplanetary travel.

Word Order in Sentences   *pages 38–39*
Rewrite each sentence in different word order. Then label the
new sentence *natural* or *inverted*.

39. From the audience came a chorus of cheers.

40. Loud clapping thundered in the dancers' ears.

41. Through the air flew bouquets of flowers.

42. Lower and lower curtsied the dancers.

Finding Subjects of Sentences   *pages 40–41*
Write the simple subject for each sentence. Then write *declarative,*
interrogative, imperative, or *exclamatory.*

43. There are many different kinds of telephones.

44. Bring me that portable telephone.

45. How do portable telephones work?

46. Cellular car phones are so expensive!

Compound Subjects   *pages 42–43*
Write the complete subject of each sentence. Then underline each
simple subject once. Underline the connecting word twice.

47. Typing and shorthand are important office skills.

48. Speedwriting and Gregg Shorthand are two methods.

49. A letter or letter groups represent words in Speedwriting.

50. Letters and special symbols make up the Gregg system.

51. Letters and memos are frequently taken down in shorthand.

Compound Predicates   *pages 44–45*

Write the complete predicate from each sentence. Underline each simple predicate once. Underline the connecting word twice.

52. Music expresses feelings and entertains the listener.
53. The words to songs can tell a story or describe a thought.
54. The strings of an orchestra can sing sweetly or thunder darkly.
55. Some music soothes and calms frazzled nerves.
56. Other music stirs the blood and inspires people.

Compound Sentences   *pages 46–47*

Write each sentence and label it *compound subject, compound predicate,* or *compound sentence.*

57. Johann Gutenberg was born in Germany and lived in the fifteenth century.
58. This printer and inventor created movable type.
59. Movable type made the printing of books possible and helped spread ideas throughout the world.
60. Before Gutenberg, monks copied books by hand, but this task was slow and difficult.
61. Some of Gutenberg's books still exist, and they are valuable.

Avoiding Sentence Fragments and Run-on Sentences   *pages 48–49*

Write *sentence, sentence fragment,* or *run-on sentence* for each group of words.

62. Frederic Remington was a great American painter.
63. He was educated at Yale he went west in 1880.
64. Remington as a war correspondent.
65. Was responsible for over 2,700 paintings and drawings.
66. He worked in oils he worked in bronze as well.

Context Clues   *pages 50–51*

Read each sentence. Write the meaning of the underlined word in each sentence. Then write *information, similar meaning,* or *opposite meaning* for the kind of context clue that is given.

67. Newspaper writers must <u>verify</u> all the facts they write to make sure they are true.
68. Workers called fact checkers <u>ascertain</u>, or make sure, that the writers' facts are correct.
69. <u>Unsubstantiated</u> rumors cannot be reported as facts.
70. <u>Unscrupulous</u> writers, those with no principles, will not last long on the staff of any good newspaper.

UNIT

2

Painting Pictures with Words

◆ **COMPOSITION FOCUS:** **Descriptive Paragraph**
◆ **LANGUAGE FOCUS:** **Nouns**

Close your eyes and think of a beautiful place you have visited or have seen in a picture. Think of that place's colors, shapes, smells, and sounds. All these details help you form a vivid mental picture.

Writer Ruth Radlauer writes descriptions of America's national parks, which she has loved since she was a child in Wyoming. She writes so that other people will appreciate the parks as she does.

In this unit you, too, will use your senses and your memories to write descriptions of a place that is special to you.

◆══ *WARMING UP* ══◆

IN YOUR JOURNAL

Imagine that you are a master chef. You are creating your finest meal. Write notes about the flavors, smells, textures, and appearance of the meal so that customers will want to order it.

ORAL LANGUAGE

WORK IN A GROUP

Think of a familiar place, but don't identify it. Then describe it by how it looks, feels, smells, and sounds. Have your group guess where it is.

Ruth Radlauer has written books *to inform* readers about the beauty and splendor of national parks.

Reading with a Writer's Eye
Description

At Olympic National Park, you can visit the mountains, the seashore, and a rain forest all in the same day. Try to picture these places as you read Ruth Radlauer's descriptions. Notice the details she gives about what you would see, hear, and feel if you were in the park.

What Is Olympic National Park?
by Ruth Radlauer

Olympic National Park is three parks in one: high mountains, rain forests, and a seacoast.

At the seacoast, this park is the rushing of ocean waves on the sand. It's the lonely call of gulls looking for food in the water. Mysterious rocks, the sea stacks, stand among driftwood thrown on the beach by the waves. Here you can see starfish on the rocks of a tide pool.

A cool, green rain forest grows thick in the valleys. You can walk through this forest and gaze at huge trees and tiny mosses. You'll see small trees growing on a nurselog, the old trunk of a fallen tree. Many ferns, mosses, and lichens grow in this wet, green world.

Your family can drive to the high mountains on Hurricane Ridge Road. At the end of the road, an easy trail takes you up Hurricane Hill. As you get above the tree line, mountain meadows may be white with avalanche lilies or blue with lupine. Watch for a furry ball of life the size of a small dog. When you hear the Olympic marmot's whistle, you'll know you've arrived at Olympic National Park.

Trees—Lowland Forest

At Kalaloch (klāy′lŏk) Beach Campground, you can meet with a ranger for a walk through the lowland forest. On the walk you learn that forests usually have levels or stories. Close to the ground is the first story, where low plants and seedling shrubs grow. Higher off the ground, young trees and shrubs grow on the second level. The third story has bigger trees, and the biggest trees make the fourth story. This story forms a covering, or canopy, over the others.

In this wet, lowland forest, the canopy lets very little sunlight reach the ground. Only shade-loving trees do well here. They are the western red cedar, western hemlock, and Sitka spruce.

A busy animal kingdom works in the lowland forest. Insects like termites, wood beetles, and carpenter ants clean up the forest by eating dead leaves and wood.

If you see something that looks like a pile of sawdust, it's the chickaree's trash pile. The chickaree, or Douglas squirrel, cuts down Sitka spruce cones and eats the seeds. It leaves the scales and cores of the cones in a pile under the tree.

The Lowest and Slowest

In forests below 500 meters elevation, you may come upon a very strange greenish yellow creature with spots. Bigger than most garden slugs, it's the banana slug.

You can pick up this animal carefully and take a good look. The slug has two pairs of antennae. The long upper antennae are used to sense light. The lower antennae, at each side of the mouth, sense smells. Can you think why such an animal needs to be able to smell?

On the slug's right side is a small hole. When the slug gets used to you, you may see the hole open and close as the animal breathes. Looking at

the underside, you'll see a rippling muscle that makes the banana slug move along. When you put it down, the slug breaks no speed limits as it slowly oozes away, leaving a trail of thick slippery liquid, or mucus. (Try not to get the mucus on your fingers, unless you want to glue them together.)

Along with the black slug, this one eats decaying things like dead leaves and bark, or debris. As the debris passes through the slug's body, it turns into good soil. You see, even the lowest and slowest creature in the forest is important.

Respond

1. Would you enjoy visiting Olympic National Park? What information does the writer include to make you think as you do?

Discuss

2. What details does the writer give to let you know what you would see, hear, and feel in Olympic National Park?
3. Does the writer choose words and arrange details that create vivid pictures of the park in your mind? Give examples.

Thinking As a Writer
Analyzing a Descriptive Paragraph

Writer's Guide

A descriptive paragraph
- creates a picture with words.
- presents sensory details in a clear order.
- has a topic sentence and detail sentences.

A descriptive paragraph uses words to create a picture. It presents sensory details about someone or something in an order that is easy to follow. It has a topic sentence and detail sentences.

Reread one of Ruth Radlauer's descriptions. These descriptive paragraphs are from "What Is Olympic National Park?"

Olympic National Park is three parks in one: high mountains, rain forests, and a seacoast.

At the seacoast, this park is the rushing of ocean waves on the sand. It's the lonely call of gulls looking for food in the water. Mysterious rocks, the sea stacks, stand among driftwood thrown on the beach by the waves. Here you can see starfish on the rocks of a tide pool.

A cool, green rain forest grows thick in the valleys. You can walk through this forest and gaze at huge trees and tiny mosses. You'll see small trees growing on a nurselog, the old trunk of a fallen tree. Many ferns, mosses, and lichens grow in this wet, green world.

Your family can drive to the high mountains on Hurricane Ridge Road. At the end of the road, an easy trail takes you up Hurricane Hill. As you get above the tree line, mountain meadows may be white with avalanche lilies or blue with lupine. Watch for a furry ball of life the size of a small dog. When you hear the Olympic marmot's whistle, you'll know you've arrived at Olympic National Park.

The **topic sentence** tells what will be described in the paragraph.

Detail sentences tell what can be observed with the senses.

Sensory words appeal specifically to sight, hearing, smell, touch, or taste.

Comparisons help make the picture clear. Here the writer compares the Olympic marmot to a furry ball and then provides a mental picture of the marmot's size by comparing it to a small dog.

No matter what kind of paragraph you write, you must put your sentences in some kind of order, or **sequence**. The sequence you use depends on the kind of paragraph you are writing. For example, if you are writing about an event, you could sequence your sentences in **time order**. That is, you could describe events in the order in which they take place, from the earliest event to the latest one. If you are giving advice, you might want to present your sentences in **order of importance**. When you write a descriptive paragraph, the best order to use is usually **space order**. For example, you could describe items from left to right, from near to far, or from top to bottom. In this paragraph from "What Is Olympic National Park?" the writer organizes her details in space order from low to high.

> At Kalaloch Beach Campground, you can meet with a ranger for a walk through the lowland forest. On the walk you learn that forests usually have levels or stories. Close to the ground is the first story, where low plants and seedling shrubs grow. Higher off the ground, young trees and shrubs grow on the second level. The third story has bigger trees, and the biggest trees make the fourth story. This story forms a covering, or canopy, over the others.

Discuss

1. In the paragraph above, what words does the author use that indicate that the paragraph is written in space order? How would the paragraph be different if the writer did not use these words? Explain your answer.
2. Which details in the paragraphs about Olympic National Park tell what can be seen? Which tell what can be heard? Which tell what can be felt? Why are there no details about what the writer tasted? Would such details improve the paragraphs? Why or why not?
3. Find another paragraph with space order on pages 60–61. What kind of space order does the writer use?

Try Your Hand

A. Identify the Subject of Descriptions Read each paragraph. Write the topic sentence.

1. Beamly Park has an old merry-go-round. The horses have been repainted in bright colors. How smooth they are! What a charming, bell-like music is heard as they go around!

2. Half Moon Lane has 10 old houses that face each other. Most of them are blue, with yellow shutters. You can smell the smoke from the fireplaces on a cold day.

B. Identify Sensory Details Make five columns labeled *see, hear, smell, taste,* and *feel.* Write each detail from the paragraphs in **A** in one of the columns.

C. Identify Space Order For each set of sentences, write *top to bottom, near to far,* or *side to side* to show how the details are sequenced. Then write one comparison from each set of sentences.

3. Birds of all colors sat on the top branches. Monkeys chattering like babies swung on the limbs just below.

4. The building had a sloping red roof. The eaves stuck out one foot beyond the walls. The windows were as tall as full-grown men.

5. Sheila woke up in a field of tall grass. Low, scrubby bushes surrounded the saucer-shaped field. Cows were grazing on the hill beyond the bushes.

D. Read Descriptive Paragraphs Find a descriptive paragraph in a magazine. With a partner, identify the details and discuss how each one helps to create a word picture.

Writer's Notebook

Collecting Words That Appeal to the Senses Look at the word *rushing* in the second paragraph of the selection on page 60. How does the sound of the word help create a picture in your mind? As you read, be on the lookout for other words that appeal sharply to your senses. In your *Writer's Notebook*, write each word, its meaning, and a sample sentence using the word. Use the words when you write your own descriptions.

Thinking As a Writer
Observing Details

To write good descriptions, a writer must learn to observe details clearly and thoroughly. Here is the most important rule to remember about observing details: Use all your senses. Notice not only what you see but also what you hear, feel, taste, and smell. Using a graphic organizer can help you.

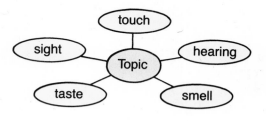

Use your senses to fill in the ovals with details about your topic.

Categorizing the details you observe may also help strengthen your powers of observation. Put the details you observe into categories. Group words according to whether they describe size, color, action, or sound.

When you write a descriptive paragraph, be sure to include specific details that appeal to the reader's senses. Also, remember to arrange the details in a logical order.

Discuss

1. Read the passage under the heading "The Lowest and Slowest" on page 61. What details does the writer give about the slug?
2. Suppose that you wanted to make a chart of details about the banana slug. What categories would you use as column headings in your chart? Would the same categories be useful for observing the sea stacks? Why or why not?

Try Your Hand

Observe Objects and People   Choose an object or a person in your classroom to observe for one full minute. Then look away and write down all the details you can remember. Have a partner observe the same object or person and write down the details he or she observes. Trade papers with your partner, and compare the details you observed.

Developing the Writer's Craft
Using Precise Words

To describe objects and events clearly, good writers use words with precise and specific meanings.

Look at the underlined words in these sentences.

1. Several plants stood behind the thing.
2. Six cactuses stood behind the boulder.

Several, in sentence 1, is a vague word. How many are several? The word *six,* in sentence 2, gives an exact number. The word *plant* in sentence 1 is also vague because it has a very general meaning. A plant could be a flower, a bush, a cornstalk, or even an herb. The word *cactus* is specific. It tells us exactly what kind of plant the writer has in mind. Notice, too, how vague the word *thing* is in sentence 1. The word *boulder* in the second sentence leaves no doubt about what the writer means.

When you write your descriptive paragraph, help your readers feel as if they themselves are experiencing what you are describing. Use precise words to show exactly what you have observed.

Discuss

1. Look again at the description on page 60. What words does the writer use to name the objects found by the seashore in Olympic National Park? What picture do you have of the seacoast after reading the second paragraph?
2. In the third paragraph of the description on page 60, the writer uses the words *nurselog, ferns, mosses,* and *lichens.* Are these words precise? Explain your answer. If you wanted to add to the paragraph, what are some precise words you might use?

Try Your Hand

Use Precise Words   Look at the picture of the man on the beach. Write sentences using precise words to describe what you see in the picture. If you need help, use the **Writer's Thesaurus** at the back of the book.

1 Prewriting
Descriptive Paragraph

Writer's Guide

Prewriting Checklist

☑ Brainstorm topics.

☑ Select a topic.

☑ Think about your audience and your purpose.

☑ Gather specific details.

☑ Organize the details.

Hannah wanted to describe a local landmark for people who might want to visit her area. She used the checklist in the **Writer's Guide** to help her plan her description. Look at what she did.

◆ Brainstorming and Selecting a Topic

First, Hannah brainstormed local places and landmarks that she might want to describe. Look at Hannah's list.

Next, Hannah crossed off topics that were too broad and places that would not be interesting to see. She also crossed off sights that were likely to resemble others her audience had seen.

Finally, Hannah decided to write about the highest point in the city. She remembered how the view had thrilled her the first time she saw it. She wanted to share that feeling with others. She knew she could collect information for her description by visiting the spot again.

statue of soldier

30-story building

natural history museum

the courthouse

old post office

highest point in city

St. Paul's cathedral

the zoo

famous writer's home

Discuss

1. Look at each topic Hannah crossed off her list. Why do you think she crossed it off?
2. How might Hannah have narrowed down the topics that were too broad?

◆ Gathering Information

After Hannah selected her topic, she gathered information for her description. She went to the highest point in the city with a notebook. She stood on a big rock and observed the scene, paying attention to all five of her senses. She jotted down the details. Look at Hannah's chart of details.

Saw	Heard	Smelled	Felt
trees. grass 5 pigeons path. rocks playground	squeaking wheels people talking birds. traffic kids yelling	wet ground burning rubber	rain sticky rock sharp glass wind

Discuss

1. Why do you think Hannah did not record a column of details about things she tasted?
2. Was Hannah wise to list her details under different headings? Why or why not?

◆ Organizing Information

When Hannah got home, she visualized, or pictured in her mind, the scene she had just visited. She decided to describe the place as it looked from the big rock, using space order from near to far. She mapped what she saw on a diagram that showed the position of each item. Look at Hannah's diagram.

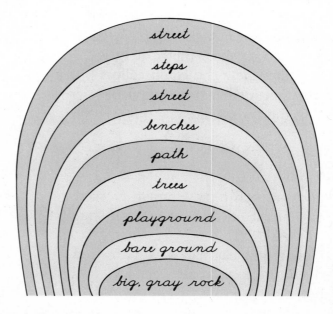

street
steps
street
benches
path
trees
playground
bare ground
big. gray rock

WRITING PROCESS

Discuss

1. Why did Hannah decide to describe the highest place in the city from one particular spot? Why did she choose space order from near to far to organize her description? Explain your answers.
2. What other kinds of space order might Hannah have used in her description? Did she choose the best order? Explain your answer.
3. How will Hannah's diagram help her keep details in space order when she writes?

Try Your Hand

Now plan a descriptive paragraph of your own.

A. Brainstorm and Select a Topic Brainstorm a list of possible topics. Include all the local landmarks you can think of. Then think about each topic and your audience.

- ◆ Cross out topics that are too broad, too dull, or too much like other sights your audience may have seen.
- ◆ Mark the topics you can visit or can picture vividly.
- ◆ Decide which of these topics interests you the most. This will be the topic of your description.

B. Gather Information When you are satisfied with your topic, plan how to gather information about the place you have chosen. If you lose interest in the topic as you go along, brainstorm more topics and select a new one.

- ◆ Visit your place, or picture it in your mind.
- ◆ Make observations about the place with all five of your senses.
- ◆ Jot down the details you notice and any descriptive words that occur to you.

C. Organize Information Decide how you will organize your descriptive paragraph. Choose the kind of space order that is the most effective for your topic. Then make a map or a diagram that shows where all the details you will describe are located.

 Save your chart and your diagram in your *Writer's Notebook*. You will use them when you draft your descriptive paragraph.

2 Drafting
Descriptive Paragraph

Writer's Guide
Drafting Checklist
- ☑ Use your charts and diagram for ideas.
- ☑ Write a topic sentence for your paragraph.
- ☑ Write details in the space order you have chosen.
- ☑ Include details you have observed with all five senses, if possible.

Hannah followed the **Writer's Guide** to draft her descriptive paragraph. Look at what she did.

A View Worth Seeing

The highest natural point in the city is at the top of a rock in Bennett Park. It is a lovely, quiet place in late fall. The rock is long and gray, with a fat, round end. You can smell damp soil when you stand on it, and you can feel water on your face.

Discuss

1. Look at Hannah's topic sentence. Does it prepare the audience for the description that is to come? Explain your answer.
2. What details has Hannah given so far? Is she following the order she planned when she organized her information? Explain your answer.

Try Your Hand

Now draft a descriptive paragraph.

A. **Review Your Details**   Think about the information you gathered. Decide whether you need more information. If so, gather it.

B. **Think About Your TAP**   Remember that your task is to write a description for anyone who might visit your area. Your purpose is to give your audience a vivid picture of the place you are describing.

C. **Write Your First Draft**   Follow the steps in the **Drafting Checklist** to write your descriptive paragraph.
   When you write your draft, just put all your ideas on paper. You can correct the draft later.

Task: What?
Audience: Who?
Purpose: Why?

Save your first draft in your *Writer's Notebook*. You will use it when you revise your descriptive paragraph.

3 Responding and Revising
Descriptive Paragraph

Hannah used the checklist in the **Writer's Guide** to revise her description. Look at what she did.

◆ **Checking Information**

Hannah cut a piece of information that did not help create a picture of her topic. She used this mark ✄ to show the cut. She also added a detail to make her description more concrete. She used this mark ∧ to show the addition.

◆ **Checking Organization**

Hannah moved a sentence to keep her description in clear space order. To show what she wanted to move, she used this mark ◌ .

◆ **Checking Language**

Hannah added a comparison to make her description more lively. She also replaced a vague, general word with a more precise one. She used this mark ⌐ to show what she was replacing.

Writer's Guide

Revising Checklist
- ☑ Read your description to yourself or to a partner.
- ☑ Think about your audience and your purpose. Add or cut information.
- ☑ Check to see that your description is organized in clear space order.
- ☑ Check to see that your language is concrete and specific.

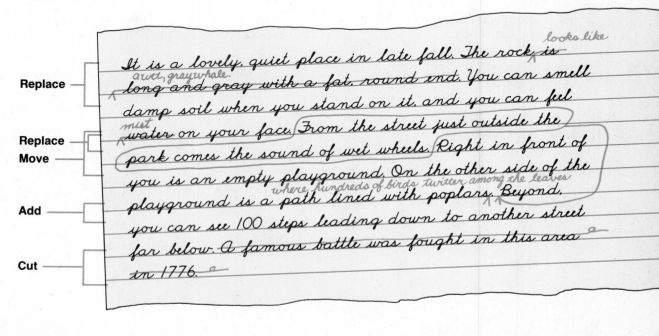

Replace — It is a lovely, quiet place in late fall. The rock ~~is~~ looks like ~~long and gray~~ a wet, gray whale. with a fat, round end. You can smell damp soil when you stand on it, and you can feel ~~water~~ mist on your face. From the street just outside the park comes the sound of wet wheels. Right in front of you is an empty playground. On the other side of the playground is a path lined with poplars where hundreds of birds twitter among the leaves. Beyond, you can see 100 steps leading down to another street far below. A famous battle was fought in this area in 1776.

Replace / Move / Add / Cut

Discuss

1. Did Hannah improve her paragraph by comparing the rock to a whale? Explain your answer.
2. Do you agree with Hannah that the word *mist* is more precise than the word *water*? Explain your answer.

Try Your Hand

Now revise your first draft.

A. **Read Your First Draft** As you read your description, think about your audience and your purpose. Read your description silently or to a partner to see if it is complete and well organized. Ask yourself or your partner the questions in the box.

Responding and Revising Strategies

✔ **Respond** Ask yourself or a partner:	✔ **Revise** Try these solutions:
◆ Is my topic clear to the reader?	◆ **Add** a topic sentence.
◆ Are my details given in an order that is easy to follow?	◆ **Move** sentences as needed to give details in space order.
◆ Does every detail help make my description vivid?	◆ **Cut** details that do not give sensory observations.
◆ Will the reader know exactly how the things I am describing look, sound, smell, feel, and taste?	◆ **Replace** vague language with precise details. See the **Revising Workshop** on page 73 and the **Writer's Thesaurus** in this book.
◆ Is my description interesting?	◆ **Add** fresh or surprising comparisons.

B. **Make Your Changes** If the answer to any question in the box is *no*, try the solution. Use the **Editor's Marks** to show your changes.

C. **Review Your Descriptive Paragraph Again**
   Decide whether there is anything else you want to revise. Keep revising your paragraph until you feel it is well organized and complete.

> **EDITOR'S MARKS**
> ∧ Add something.
> ✗ Cut something.
> ◠ Move something.
> ∧ Replace something.

 Save your revised description in your *Writer's Notebook.* You will use it when you proofread your description.

WRITING PROCESS

Revising Workshop
Expanding Sentences

A good description paints a complete picture for the reader. Skillful writers add to this picture with every sentence. To make a sentence richly descriptive, they expand it with details. There are many ways to expand sentences with details. Notice the underlined portions of these sentences.

1. The car rattled through the entrance.
2. The <u>rusty old</u> car rattled through the entrance.
3. The rusty old car rattled through the <u>tree-lined</u> entrance.
4. The rusty old car <u>and the rickety trailer</u> rattled through the tree-lined entrance.
5. The rusty old car and the rickety trailer rattled <u>and bumped</u> through the tree-lined entrance.

Sentence 1 offers very little detail. In sentence 2, the writer has added descriptive details about the subject. In sentence 3, the writer has added a descriptive detail about an item in the predicate. In sentence 4, the writer has added a descriptive detail by adding a second subject. In sentence 5, the writer has added a detail by adding a second predicate. Notice that sentence 5 is much more detailed and descriptive than sentence 1.

Practice

Expand each sentence with descriptive details. Follow the instructions in parentheses ( ) to rewrite the sentences.

1. The boy walked along the seashore. (Add descriptive details about the subject.)
2. The huge flock of birds flew over the lake. (Add another predicate.)
3. Joan set up the tent. (Add another subject.)
4. A deer stood near the campsite. (Add a descriptive word about an item in the complete predicate.)
5. The boys fished for hours. (Add descriptive words about the subject, and add a second predicate.)
6. Terry swam in the stream. (Add a second subject, a second predicate, and a descriptive word about an item in the complete predicate.)

4 Proofreading
Descriptive Paragraph

Writer's Guide

Proofreading Checklist

☑ Check for errors in capitalization.

☑ Check for errors in punctuation. Be sure that every sentence ends correctly.

☑ Check to see that paragraphs are indented.

☑ Check your grammar.

☑ Circle any words you think are misspelled. Find out how to spell them correctly.

⇨ For proofreading help, use the **Writer's Handbook.**

After Hannah revised her description, she used the **Writer's Guide** and the **Editor's Marks** to proofread it. Look at what she did to fix part of her descriptive paragraph.

> In the playground, tire swings *climb* hang from beams. you can (clime) up inside a small red rocket and slide out of it You can (kwench) *quench* your thirst at the silver drinking fountain. this is a good place for children and adults.

EDITOR'S MARKS

≡ Capitalize.

⊙ Add a period.

∧ Add something.

⋏ Add a comma.

ᵛᵛ Add quotation marks.

✄ Cut something.

⋏ Replace something.

~ Transpose.

◯ Spell correctly.

⌗ Indent paragraph.

／ Make a lowercase letter.

Discuss

1. What kinds of corrections did Hannah make?
2. Why did Hannah use this mark ⊙ ?

Try Your Hand

Proofread Your Description   Use the **Writer's Guide** and the **Editor's Marks** to proofread your description.

Save your corrected descriptive paragraph in your *Writer's Notebook.* You will use it when you publish your description.

WRITING PROCESS

5 Publishing
Descriptive Paragraph

Hannah made a clean copy of her descriptive paragraph and checked it to be sure that she had not left out anything. Then she and her classmates published their paragraphs in a sightseeing guidebook. You can find Hannah's paragraph on page 38 of the **Writer's Handbook.**

Here's how Hannah and her classmates published a sightseeing guidebook.

You can find Hannah's paragraph on page 38 of the **Writer's Handbook.**

> ### Writer's Guide
> **Publishing Checklist**
> - ☑ Make a clean copy of your paragraph.
> - ☑ Check to see that nothing has been left out.
> - ☑ Check that there are no mistakes.
> - ☑ Share your descriptive paragraph in a special way.

1. First, they chose a title and designed a cover for the guidebook. Then, they planned what would appear on each page and where it would be placed.

2. Next, they pasted the descriptions in place, added illustrations where they were needed, and numbered each page.

3. Then, they made copies of each page and stapled the pages for each guidebook together.

WRITING PROCESS

4. Finally, they distributed copies of the guidebook to another class. They saved several copies for out-of-town visitors too.

Discuss

1. How might you decide on the order in which to place the descriptions in a guidebook?
2. Would a map be useful in a guidebook? Why?
3. What other people and groups might find your guidebook interesting?

Try Your Hand

Publish Your Descriptive Paragraph   Follow the checklist in the **Writer's Guide** on page 75. If possible, create a class guidebook, or try one of these ideas for sharing your descriptive paragraph.

◆ Form groups of five. Put your paragraphs in a box. Have each student draw a paragraph from the box and read it to the others. Before you begin, read **Tips on How to Read Aloud** on page 77.
◆ Make a poster-size map of your area on butcher paper, and tape each description on the map where the place it describes is located.
◆ Send your description in the mail to someone you know who is planning to visit your community.

WRITING PROCESS

Listening and Speaking
Tips on How to Read Aloud

1. Practice reading the piece to yourself or to a classmate before you read it to an audience. As you practice, think about what the words mean and how you want them to make the audience feel. Then try out different ways of saying the words to find out which way best expresses the meaning and feeling you think the writer intended. You can vary the way you read words in several ways.

   ◆ Vary your **pitch,** the rise and fall of your voice.
   ◆ Vary what you **stress,** or emphasize, with your voice.
   ◆ Vary the **volume** of your voice—how loudly you speak.
   ◆ Adjust the **rate,** or speed, of your reading to the content. Do not speak too fast or too slowly. Avoid long, unnecessary pauses. You can, however, pause on purpose before or after an important passage, to emphasize the words.

2. Use gestures to emphasize and dramatize what you are reading.

3. Do not keep your eyes glued to the page that you are reading. Look up and make eye contact with your audience.

4. When you read to the audience, pronounce your words clearly, and speak loudly enough for everyone to hear you.

Writing in the Content Areas

Use what you learned to write a description for your classmates about something you have seen or done during a trip. Use one of these ideas or an idea of your own.

Social Studies

Have you taken a trip to a historical site? Describe what you saw as you wandered through the place. Did you get the feeling you were visiting the past when you were there? Tell what objects gave you that feeling. Remember to include relevant details using all five senses, if possible.

Fine Arts

Have you visited an art museum lately? Describe a painting that particularly appealed to you. Describe the painting itself and the colors, shapes, and style used by the artist.

Science

The time of day and the way light shines on objects affect the look of those objects. Recall a scene you saw during a trip, and describe how it looked at two different times. Tell how the light changed the colors and shadows.

Literature

The setting of a story is the place where the action happens. A good writer can describe a setting so vividly that you feel as if you are there. Describe the setting from one of your favorite books. Tell what a person would see, hear, feel, and smell in that setting. Name the book and its author in your description.

CONNECTING

WRITING ⟷ LANGUAGE

A writer can describe something in a way that makes the reader "see" it with one or more of the senses. What do you see when you read this description?

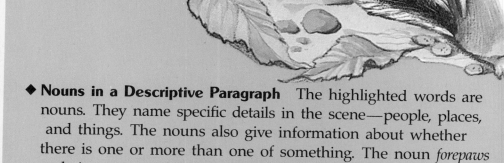

The small chipmunk darts out of its burrow. Nearby, a woodcutter has chopped down an elm. Under the trunk, the chipmunk finds a few buttercup seeds. It picks one up, turns it over in its forepaws, cracks the hull with its teeth, and eagerly eats the kernel.

The chipmunk nips the points off the remaining seeds and puts them in the pouches of its cheeks. Then it scurries back into its hole.

◆ **Nouns in a Descriptive Paragraph** The highlighted words are nouns. They name specific details in the scene—people, places, and things. The nouns also give information about whether there is one or more than one of something. The noun *forepaws* ends in *s*, so you know that it names more than one thing. Writers use nouns in their descriptions to give clear pictures of people, places, and things.

◆ **Language Focus: Nouns** In the following lessons you will learn more about different kinds of nouns you can use in your writing.

1 Nouns

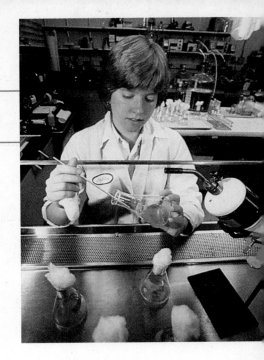

◆ **FOCUS** A **noun** names a person, a place, a thing, or an idea.

The simple subject of a sentence tells whom or what the sentence is about. Often, the simple subject is a noun. Here are some examples of nouns.

Persons man, scientist, Galileo, Marie Curie
Places city, Europe, fields, Gulf of Mexico
Things map, lamp, spark plug
Ideas imagination, kindness, century, answer

Notice that some nouns are more than one word.

Link to Speaking and Writing
A precise noun gives a clear message without wasting words. How was a noun used to edit this sentence?

Galileo looked through a long, ^telescope^ *round, hollow thing.*

Guided Practice

A. Identify the nouns in the sentences.

1. The Renaissance was an exciting time in Europe.
2. Many great thinkers lived in Italy.
3. Galileo Galilei had both curiosity and imagination.
4. This man gained great fame for his ideas.
5. Scientists of the time wondered about the stars.
6. Galileo invented the telescope.

B. **7. – 12.** Tell whether each noun in **A** names a *person*, a *place*, a *thing*, or an *idea*.

THINK AND REMEMBER
◆ Remember that a **noun** names a person, a place, a thing, or an idea.
◆ Use precise nouns to express clear messages.

Independent Practice

C. Identifying Nouns List the nouns from the sentences.

13. How does blood move through the body?

MODEL > blood, body

14. A scientist in London studied this question.

15. William Harvey was doctor to the king of England.

16. Dr. Harvey looked closely at the heart throughout his career.

17. The heart is a pump, Harvey decided after much thought.

18. This pump makes blood move through arteries and veins.

19. This man worked without a microscope.

20. Harvey published a book in Frankfurt about his work.

21. Many people around the world read about his ideas.

D. 22.–30. Classifying Nouns Write each noun you listed in C. Label it *person, place, thing,* or *idea.*

22. How does blood move through the body?

MODEL > blood—thing   body—thing

E. Revising: Using Precise Nouns Rewrite each sentence, using exact nouns to express a clear message.

31. The boy entered his place.

MODEL > Joe entered his workshop.

32. The boy got out his science equipment.

33. He used it to look at some liquid.

34. He saw some life forms in the liquid.

35. A small, furry animal that lived with him climbed on some furniture.

36. It knocked over a tall glass container.

37. Some smelly stuff spilled into some dustlike stuff.

38. The boy saw a sudden change in the dusty powder.

39. The room in which he conducted experiments was filled with scientific odds and ends.

40. He looked at the dusty stuff through a magnifying device.

Application — Writing

Profile Imagine that you are a reporter for your community newspaper. You have just visited the scientist in the photograph. Write a profile of the scientist for your newspaper. Describe who she is, where she works, and what she has done. Use precise nouns.

2 Common and Proper Nouns

FOCUS

◆ A **common noun** names any person, place, thing, or idea.
◆ A **proper noun** names a particular person, place, or thing.

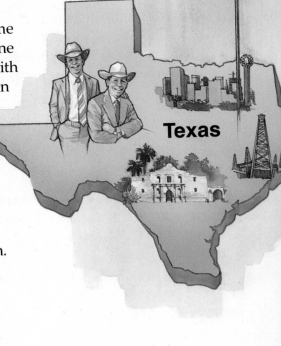

Texas

Compare the words in color in this sentence.

1. Frank Dobie , the writer , has studied cowboys.

The word *writer* is a common noun because it refers to any person of a certain category. The name *Frank Dobie* is a proper noun because it refers to one particular person. A proper noun always begins with a capital letter. Here are more examples of common nouns and proper nouns.

Common Nouns	Proper Nouns
mayor	Kathryn Whitmire
city	Houston
river	San Jacinto River

The same word may be a proper noun in one sentence and a common noun in another. Capitalizing proper nouns helps prevent confusion.

2. The Tigers won the World Series in 1984.
3. We saw the tigers in the zoo.

Guided Practice

A. Identify the nouns. Tell whether each one is *common* or *proper.*

1. Texas is a very large state.
2. Only Alaska is larger.
3. Corpus Christi touches the Gulf of Mexico.
4. Ports and beaches line the shore.
5. Alonso Alvarez de Piñeda of Spain mapped the coast of Texas.

THINK AND REMEMBER

◆ Use a **common noun** to name any person, place, thing, or idea.
◆ Use a **proper noun** to name a particular person, place, or thing.
◆ Capitalize all proper nouns.

Independent Practice

B. Identifying Common and Proper Nouns Write the nouns in each sentence, and label each one *common* or *proper*.

6. New York is one of the oldest cities in America.

MODEL⟩ New York—proper cities—common
America—proper

7. Henry Hudson claimed the region for the Netherlands.
8. Explorers from England later took over the area.
9. The first governor of the colony was George Clinton.
10. New York State has beautiful valleys and lakes.
11. Niagara Falls attracts many tourists.
12. Lake Placid is a popular town for vacations.
13. The Olympic Games once took place there.
14. The professional basketball team from New York City is called the Knicks.
15. That name is short for the Knickerbockers.
16. The capital of the state is Albany.

C. Proofreading: Capitalizing Proper Nouns Write the sentence in each pair that has the proper noun. Use capital letters where they are needed.

17. Jim drives a mustang.
    The mustang is grazing in the meadow.

MODEL⟩ Jim drives a Mustang.

18. The boat raced through the waters of bass lake.
    We caught a bluegill and some bass in the lake.
19. The vacation was a treat for cliff.
    The boys peered over the cliff.
20. Up ahead was a big bend in the road.
    The family passed through big bend on their vacation.
21. My aunt grew up in that small white house.
    American presidents live in the white house.
22. We can cross the lake in our boat, the *sea trout*.
    During our trip, I caught a sea trout.

Application — Writing

Description Imagine that you are a travel writer. Write a description of an important building, bridge, or sight in your area. Tell travelers where it is located and how it is used. Give some details about its history. Use common and proper nouns.

3 Capitalization of Proper Nouns

◆ **FOCUS**   Each important word in a proper noun begins with a capital letter.

Remember that a proper noun begins with a capital letter. If a proper noun has more than one word, capitalize the first word and all other important words. Do not capitalize a word such as *of, and, in,* or *the* unless it is the first word in the title of a book or other work.

Alice   *The Living Sea*   Bay of Biscayne

The chart shows some kinds of nouns that must be capitalized.

Types of Nouns	Examples
Names of people and pets	Martin Luther King, Amy Hill, Americans, Spot
Names of days, months, and holidays	Saturday, May, Columbus Day, Fourth of July, Cinco de Mayo
Names of particular places	Texas, Lake Erie, Gulf of Mexico, Astrodome
Names of particular things and events	Pulitzer Prize, *Houston Gazette*, *Titanic*, the Civil War, the Alamo
Names of clubs, businesses, and organizations	Sierra Club, Mi Casa, Lakeville Dance Corps

Guided Practice

A. Identify the proper nouns. Tell which letters should be capitalized.

1. The friends of the sea is a club in my town.

2. The club meets in the pacific building every tuesday.

3. On june 15, mario pinza spoke to the group.

4. He is dean of anza college.

5. He talked about fish life in the mediterranean sea.

6. On memorial day the club made a trip to monterey bay.

7. We visited gus's shell and fish shop on drew lane.

Independent Practice

B. Proofreading: Capitalizing Proper Nouns   Write the sentences. Capitalize the proper nouns correctly.

8. Jacques cousteau was born on june 11, 1910, in france.

MODEL ▷ Jacques Cousteau was born on June 11, 1910, in France.

9. During world war II he served on the warship *dupleix*.

10. Later he received a medal from the legion of honor.

11. In 1945 cousteau set up the undersea research group.

12. The group explored sunken ships built by the ancient greeks and romans.

13. His movie world without sun won an academy award.

14. His television series "the undersea world of jacques cousteau" showed his undersea adventures.

C. Completing a Registration Form   Make up information to complete the following form. Write the appropriate information next to each numeral.

MODEL ▷

REGISTRATION FOR SCUBA DIVING CLASS
Name **15.** Tim McCready
Address **16.**
City **17.**   State **18.**
Date of Birth **19.**
School **20.**
Person to Call in an Emergency **21.**

Application — Writing

Poster   Write a paragraph for a poster advertising a trip being organized by the Friends of the Sea. Tell where the group will go, when it will go, and how people can get information about the trip. Remember to capitalize all proper nouns.

4 Abbreviations

◆ **FOCUS**   An **abbreviation** is a shortened form of a word.

When you write lists and addresses or fill out forms, you can abbreviate, or shorten, certain words. Abbreviations usually begin with a capital letter and end with a period. Most titles for people are abbreviated.

Mister: Mr.   Doctor: Dr.   Reverend: Rev.
Senator: Sen.   Junior: Jr.   Senior: Sr.
Honorable: Hon.   Professor: Prof.

An **initial** is the first letter of a name and is used in place of the complete name. It is capitalized and followed by a period.

Leslie Marie Fane: L. M. Fane   James Jay Troy: J. J. Troy

Common Abbreviations	
Days	Sun. Mon. Tues. Wed. Thurs. Fri. Sat.
Months	Jan. Feb. Mar. Apr. Aug. Sept. Oct. Nov. Dec. (May, June, and July are never abbreviated.)
Businesses	Company: Co. Incorporated: Inc. Corporation: Corp. Department: Dept.
Kinds of streets	Street: St. Avenue: Ave. Road: Rd. Route: Rt./Rte. Boulevard: Blvd. Drive: Dr. Lane: Ln.
Times	"before noon": A.M. "after noon": P.M.

The United States Postal Service has a special set of abbreviations for the states. You will find the state postal abbreviations on page 56 of the **Writer's Handbook.**

Guided Practice

A. Give the abbreviations or initials for these groups of words. Give initials only for first and middle names.

1. John Foster Dulles Street
2. Sunday
3. Senator Jay Long
4. October 10
5. Mister John Louis Best
6. 8:00 in the morning

Independent Practice

B. Writing Abbreviations and Initials   Write each group of words, using abbreviations or initials.

   7. Alan Drive

   MODEL ▷ Alan Dr.

   8. Mister Evan Carr
   9. Monday, April 10
   10. Reverend Dale Kay
   11. Kelly Road
   12. 9:00 in the evening
   13. Poe Avenue

C. Using Abbreviations and Initials in Sentences   Write the sentences, using abbreviations for any words that can be abbreviated. Use initials only in place of middle names.

   14. James Peter Hanes built a robot.

   MODEL ▷ James P. Hanes built a robot.

   15. Leah Joyce Hunley invented a folding bicycle.
   16. Doctor Joseph Luce helped her.
   17. He works at the corner of Robin Avenue and Black Boulevard.
   18. A science fair will take place on Tuesday, November 13.
   19. The fair will last from 9:00 in the morning until 5:00 in the afternoon.
   20. Mister Leonard Collins thinks that Professor Albertine Corona's soil tester will win first prize.

Application — Writing

Catalogue Entry   Write a poster announcement for an imaginary invention. Tell what your invention looks like, what it does, and when it will be available. Space will be limited, so use initials and abbreviations wherever you can.

5 Singular and Plural Nouns

◆ A **singular noun** names one person, place, thing, or idea.

◆ A **plural noun** names more than one person, place, thing, or idea.

Remember that nouns name people, places, things, and ideas. All nouns and pronouns have number: they are either singular or plural.

| Singular | painter | ship | sail |
| Plural | painters | ships | sails |

You can turn most singular nouns into plural nouns by adding *s* or *es*. Sometimes the spelling of the noun changes. The rule for forming a plural noun depends on how the singular form ends.

Forming Plural Nouns		
Singular Ending	**Rule**	**Examples**
s, ss, ch, sh, x, and *z*	Add *es.*	gas—gases grass—grasses lunch—lunches wish—wishes fox—foxes waltz—waltzes
consonant + *y*	Change *y* to *i* and add *es.*	guppy—guppies baby—babies
vowel + *y*	Add *s.*	turkey—turkeys boy—boys

Guided Practice

A. Tell whether the underlined nouns are *singular* or *plural.*

1. Joe and his friends went to England.
2. Buses and trains carried them from city to city.
3. The boys visited many museums.
4. They saw many pictures and sculptures.
5. Their favorite paintings were in the Tate Gallery.

◆ End most plural nouns with *s* or *es*.
◆ Follow the rules in the chart to form most plural nouns.

Independent Practice

B. Identifying Nouns as Singular or Plural Write each underlined noun and label it *singular* or *plural*.

6. J.M.W. Turner was a great painter.

MODEL ▷ J.M.W. Turner—singular   painter—singular

7. He created many paintings of the canals in Venice.
8. Houses, boats, and workers appear in the mist.
9. Turner also did a great many drawings of rivers in France and England.
10. Some of the pictures show castles and churches.
11. Some have puppies and other animals in them.
12. Sometimes, girls are seen strolling in patches of sunlight.

C. Proofreading: Spelling Plural Nouns Correctly Find the spelling error in each sentence. Write the misspelled word correctly.

13. Sue has many hobbys.

MODEL ▷ hobbies

14. Painting landscapes is among her favorite activitys.
15. Beachs can be wonderful places to paint pictures.
16. You need brushs, a sketch pad, and some paints.
17. Look for shells, sea creatures, and butterflys.
18. Are there gulls in the sky or boates in the water?
19. A bush with berrys makes a good subject.
20. Painting by the sea has problems as well as joyes.
21. Colores change, and waves never stand still.
22. Sue could spend dayes wrestling with such problems.

Application — Writing and Speaking

Description Discuss the painting with a classmate and compare it with other pictures you have seen. Then write a paragraph describing the painting for someone who has never seen it. Use at least five plural nouns.

6 More Plural Nouns

◆ FOCUS The plural forms of some nouns follow special rules.

Remember that the spellings of most plural nouns depend on how the singular forms end. The chart shows how to form some plural nouns that follow special rules.

Forming Plural Nouns		
Singular Ending	**Rule**	**Examples**
most words that end in *f* or *fe*	Add *s*.	chief—chiefs reef—reefs
some words that end in *f* or *fe*	Change *f* to *v* and add *s* or *es*.	calf—calves knife—knives
consonant + *o*	Add *s* or *es*.	auto—autos potato—potatoes
vowel + *o*	Add *s*.	radio—radios

Not all plural nouns end in *s* or *es*. Some words, such as *deer* and *trout,* are spelled the same way in the singular and the plural. Other nouns change spelling completely when they are made plural.

Singular	man	woman	child	tooth	mouse
Plural	men	women	children	teeth	mice

Guided Practice

A. Spell the plural form of each noun.

1. woman
2. solo
3. hoof
4. tooth
5. piano
6. hero
7. half
8. shelf
9. stereo
10. life

THINK AND REMEMBER
- ◆ Follow the rules in the chart to form some plural nouns.
- ◆ Memorize the spellings of nouns that change completely when the plural is formed.

Independent Practice

B. Forming Plural Nouns Write the plural form of each noun. Use a dictionary for help if you wish.

11. pant

> MODEL pants

12. muff
13. scarf
14. goose

15. tomato
16. man
17. rodeo

18. foot
19. ox
20. studio

21. child
22. moose
23. scissors

C. Proofreading: Spelling Plural Nouns Correctly Find the misspelled word in each sentence and write it correctly.

24. Winter has come to the land where the deers live.

> MODEL deer

25. The leafs have fallen from the trees.
26. Wolfs hunt in the cold for rabbits.
27. Mouses scurry through the snow, looking for crumbs.
28. We saw two video showing winter on the plains.
29. The people's tooth are chattering in the cold.
30. One of the womens spots a bear on a distant ridge.
31. They have not seen a bear that large in all of their lifes.
32. The bear was over eight foots tall.
33. The men sharpen their knifes before the hunt.
34. One knife broke into two halfs.
35. Four of the mans went to hunt for the bear.
36. A flock of gooses flew over their heads.
37. Everyone wore scarfs to help them stay warm.
38. All of the childs stayed at home.

D. Using Plural Nouns in Sentences Write a sentence using the plural form of each noun below. Use a dictionary for help in spelling the plural forms.

39. roof

> MODEL I saw the sun glinting off the roofs.

40. elf
41. soprano

42. echo
43. safe

44. hero
45. sheep

46. gulf
47. goose

Application — Writing

Science Report Write a report for your class about how several wild animals, such as wolves and deer, spend the winter. Find information in an encyclopedia or in a library book. Tell how the animals find food, where they live, and what they do. Use at least five plural nouns.

7 Possessive Nouns

◆ **FOCUS**   A **possessive noun** shows ownership or possession.

In the sentences below, the words in color are possessive nouns.

1. Andy's backpack is filled with supplies.
2. The pack's straps are very sturdy.

In the first sentence, the possessive noun shows that the backpack belongs to Andy. In the second sentence, the possessive noun shows that the straps are part of the pack.

Forming Possessive Nouns	
Rule	**Examples**
To form the possessive of most singular nouns, add an apostrophe and the letter *s*, even if the noun already ends in *s*.	a frog's legs a boat's oars Mr. Harris's glasses
To form the possessive of plural nouns that end in *s*, add only an apostrophe.	the owls' hoots the Ameses' house
To form the possessive of plural nouns that do not end in *s*, add *'s*.	the children's toys the sheep's tails

Link to Speaking and Writing

Use possessive nouns to make your sentences more direct. How do the changes improve this sentence?

Jim's
~~The campground belonging to Jim~~ is pleasant.

Guided Practice

A. Identify each possessive noun. Tell whether it is *singular* or *plural*.

1. Andy's family is going camping.
2. Mrs. Jones packed the family members' tents.
3. Tess's tent is green.
4. The next six days' weather should be dry.

Independent Practice

B. Identifying Possessive Nouns   Write the possessive noun from each sentence. Label it *singular* or *plural*.

    5. The boys saw an animal's footprints.

> MODEL   animal's—singular

    6. They followed the tracks to the river's edge.
    7. John pointed Andy's flashlight into a cave.
    8. A little bear cub's eyes shone in the light.
    9. Suddenly a roar caught the boys' attention.
    10. Andy and John ran back to the Browns' campsite.

C. Forming Possessive Nouns   Write the possessive form of each noun. Label the possessive nouns *singular* or *plural*. Some nouns may be singular or plural.

    11. eagles

> MODEL   eagles'—plural

    12. field   **14.** foxes   **16.** grass   **18.** oxen   **20.** Alice
    13. sheep   **15.** parents **17.** men   **19.** fish   **21.** girls

D. Revising: Using Possessive Nouns in Sentences   Use a possessive noun to make each sentence more direct. Write the new sentence.

    22. Yellowstone is the largest park in Wyoming.

> MODEL   Yellowstone is Wyoming's largest park.

    23. The parks of America are a national treasure.
    24. Some of the most beautiful scenery of the country is in Yellowstone National Park.
    25. Visitors come to see the many geysers of the park.
    26. Early explorers described the beauty of the region.

Application — Writing

Travel Brochure   Write a travel brochure about Jim's Campground for people planning a vacation in the area. Describe the campground in a way that will make them want to stay there. Use at least four possessive nouns.

8 Appositives

◆ **FOCUS** An **appositive** identifies or renames the word or words that precede it.

An appositive can be a single word, or it can be a phrase. The words in color in these sentences are appositives.

1. The sun, a medium-sized star , gives us light and heat.
2. The second planet from the sun, Venus , is very hot.
3. We, the students of Oakview Middle School , like astronomy.

Notice the comma before and after the appositive in each sentence. Do not use commas, however, if the appositive is needed to complete the meaning of the word or words it follows.

4. The planet Earth is the third planet in our solar system.

If an appositive comes at the end of a sentence, replace the second comma with end punctuation.

5. In the sky we saw Mars , the "red planet ."

Guided Practice

A. Identify the appositive in each sentence and the word or words that it renames.

1. Earth, our home, has just one moon.
2. A red moon, the harvest moon, is often seen in autumn.
3. Moon craters, a puzzle to scientists, may be dead volcanoes.
4. You, a student of astronomy, will find this interesting.
5. One crater, Copernicus, is larger than Rhode Island.

THINK AND REMEMBER

◆ Use an appositive after a word or words to identify or rename them.

Independent Practice

B. Identifying Appositives Write each sentence. Underline the appositive. Underline twice the word or words it renames.

    6. Astronomy, the study of stars, is an old science.

    MODEL▷ Astronomy, the study of stars, is an old science.

    7. Ptolemy, an ancient astronomer, studied the night sky.

    8. This man, an important thinker, wrote some famous books.

    9. He said the sun moved around the Earth, our own planet.

    10. Copernicus, a Polish scientist, had a different idea.

    11. He, a bold thinker, believed Earth and the other planets moved around the sun.

C. Proofreading: Using Commas with Appositives Write each sentence correctly. Use commas where they are needed.

    12. Yesterday Monday was Manuel's birthday.

    MODEL▷ Yesterday, Monday, was Manuel's birthday.

    13. Mr. Marquez Manuel's father brought home a box.

    14. In the box was a telescope Manuel's birthday present.

    15. Manuel an amateur astronomer was excited.

    16. He set up the telescope a shiny white tube.

    17. He looked for Saturn a planet with rings.

    18. The rings several flat disks were too dim to see.

D. Revising: Adding Details to Sentences Rewrite the sentences, using appositives to add information.

    19. Their ship was fast.

    MODEL▷ Their ship, the *Flash*, was fast.

    20. The three scientists were flying to a planet.

    21. A meteor hurled toward their spaceship.

    22. Dr. Winkle stared through the window.

    23. He could see the stars.

    24. How could the ship survive the meteor?

Application — Writing and Speaking

Science Fantasy Imagine that you are a scientist traveling to one of the planets. Describe your trip for a radio audience back on Earth. Tell what you see, hear, and feel. Present your report to the class as a radio broadcast. Use appositives to add interesting details.

Building Vocabulary
Compound Words: Word Teams

Many nouns as well as other kinds of words are formed by joining two or more smaller words. These words are called **compound words.**

One kind of compound word is written as one word. This is called a **closed compound.**

    bullfrog   groundhog
    rosebud   evergreen

A second kind of compound is written as two words. The words, however, are used together as one word. This kind of compound is called an **open compound.**

boa constrictor home run blue whale

In a third kind of compound, the smaller words are connected by hyphens. This kind of compound word is called a **hyphenated compound.**

blue-green   thirty-six   jack-in-the-box

New compound words enter the language all the time. As a writer, you can create compound words to express new ideas. For example, you can combine nouns, color words, or words that appeal to the senses to name or describe things as you see them. Notice the new compounds used in these sentences.

1. The swallow queen chirped her song.
2. The bird spread its gray-gold wings.
3. The butterfly landed on the dew-damp grass.

Reading Practice

Read each sentence. Write the compound word. Then write *closed, open,* or *hyphenated* to tell what kind of compound word it is.

1. My bookcase is full of books about insects.
2. Insects live everywhere.
3. They are found at seashores and in mountains and forests.
4. Insects are six-legged creatures.
5. Farmers wage a never-ending battle against some insects.
6. Pest-eating insects are helpful to people.
7. The dragonfly eats many mosquitoes.
8. The praying mantis gets rid of harmful insects.
9. Insects visit plants and become pollen carriers.
10. The firefly is a kind of beetle.
11. It is often called a lightning bug.
12. People use honey and wax made by honeybees.
13. These bees are excellent housekeepers.
14. Silk comes from cocoons made by silkworms.
15. Some scientists use fruit flies in their studies.

Writing Practice

Use the words below to make your own compound words. Then use each compound word in a sentence.

16. eating
17. moon
18. eye
19. news
20. talk
21. house
22. pink
23. dog
24. writer
25. weed
26. plane
27. flower

Project

Look through a newspaper or a book for compound words. List the words you find in three columns, titled *closed compounds, open compounds,* and *hyphenated compounds.* Time yourself as you write your list. Keep reading until you have listed a total of 50 words. You may be surprised by how quickly you complete your list.

Language Enrichment
Nouns

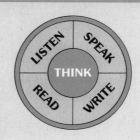

Use what you know about nouns to do these activities.

Name Mobiles

Write the name of a state or a country in 9-by-12-inch letters. Cut out the letters and write a topic, such as famous people, cities, mountains, products, or songs, on each letter. Then write nouns to fit under each topic. Punch holes at the top and the bottom of each letter, and tie the letters together with yarn or string. Hang your mobile in the classroom.

Rhyme Time

Have you ever seen a bug's mugs or a sheep's jeeps? Write down between 5 and 10 rhyming possessives and illustrate them. Share your drawings with some of your classmates, and see if they can guess what the rhyming possessives are.

What's It All About?

Think of a topic you would like to write about. List at least 10 nouns that you would use in your writing. Exchange papers with a classmate. See how quickly the classmate can guess the topic.

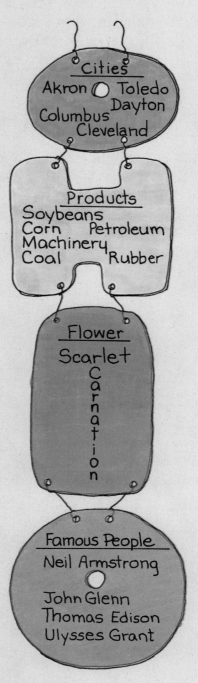

CONNECTING
LANGUAGE ↔ WRITING

In this unit you learned that nouns do more than name people, places, things, or ideas. They can show whether something is a particular thing or a general thing. They can tell whether something is singular or plural. Nouns can show who or what owns something. They can also be used next to other nouns to add information.

◆ **Using Nouns in Your Writing** Using clear nouns can make your writing crisp and easy to understand. Nouns help your reader focus on the main ideas, characters, or settings you are describing. Pay close attention to the nouns you use as you do these activities.

 Danger at Sea

Study the picture. Then describe it, using as much detail as you can. Name each item in the picture with a clear, precise noun. Name feelings you think characters in the picture might have.

Tall-Tale Towns

You learned about compound words on the **Building Vocabulary** pages. Many town names are compound words. Have you ever been to Baconrind Creek, Montana, or Fiddletown, California?

Look on a United States map or on a state map for interesting names that are compound words. Choose one name and write your own tall tale explaining how the town got the name. Use your imagination!

2 Unit Checkup

Think Back	Think Ahead
◆ What things did you learn about a descriptive paragraph in this unit? What did you do to write one?	◆ How will what you learned about a descriptive paragraph help you observe with your senses? ◆ How will observing details carefully help you write a descriptive paragraph?
◆ Look at the writing you did in this unit. How did nouns help you express your ideas?	◆ What is one way you can use nouns to improve your writing?

Descriptive Paragraphs   *pages 62–64*

Read the descriptive paragraph. Then follow the directions.

Savannah is an old city built near the river. Warehouses line the riverbank. Behind them are steep flights of cool stone steps worn smooth by the flooding river. These lead to the street shops. Further back are gracious squares of private homes. In the center of each square is a green, grassy park like an emerald set within a ring.

1. Write the topic sentence.
2. Write one sensory detail.
3. Write one comparison.
4. Write whether the description is in *time order, space order,* or *order of importance.*

Observing Details   *page 65*

Write whether each detail appeals to the sense of *sight, hearing, touch, taste,* or *smell.*

5. In the forest the evergreens seem to reach to the clouds.
6. The spongy moss is a soft cushion for our feet.
7. In every tree busy birds chirp and tweet like a thousand flute players.
8. The buttery scent of fish cooking brings us back to reality.
9. As we bite into each salty morsel, we talk about the day's events.

Using Precise Words   *page 66*

Write each sentence, replacing the underlined word with one or more precise words.

10. Jenny and Doug <u>ran</u> onto the beach.
11. They laid their <u>things</u> down on the sand.
12. "This sand is <u>hot!</u>" shouted Doug, jumping up and down.
13. The two children dove into the icy <u>water</u>.
14. They <u>played</u> in the water for nearly an hour.

The Writing Process   *pages 67–76*

Write the letter of the correct response to each question.

15. To gather information for a description of a place, what is the best thing for a writer to do?
    a. Ask people about the place.
    b. Read about the place.
    c. Visit the place.
16. When writing a topic sentence, what should you do?
    a. Include several details.
    b. Include one important detail.
    c. Prepare the audience for the description.
17. Your descriptive paragraph of a place could be published in a
    a. guidebook.
    b. catalogue.
    c. textbook.

Nouns   *pages 80–81*

List the nouns from the sentences.

18. When people think of deserts, they probably think of miles and miles of the same thing.
19. The landscape of the desert is, however, always changing.
20. Sand piles up on itself to form enormous dunes.
21. In the spring the desert comes to life as flowers bloom everywhere.
22. Cactuses form fantastic shapes, and some of them even produce colorful blossoms.

Common and Proper Nouns   *pages 82–83*

Write the nouns, and label each one *common* or *proper.*

23. In 1988 there was a terrible fire in Yellowstone National Park.
24. Firefighters from all over the United States came together to fight the blaze.
25. An area almost as large as the state of Massachusetts burned in just a few weeks.
26. The flames from this huge fire threatened many homes.
27. The geyser Old Faithful continued to shoot water into the air.

Capitalization of Proper Nouns *pages 84–85*
Write the sentences. Capitalize the proper nouns correctly.

28. On thursday night we are going to seaside park to see the meteor showers.
29. There are meteor showers all year, but the perseid meteor showers come during the second week of august every year.
30. The name *perseid* comes from the latin name *perseus*.
31. My friend betsy read about the meteor showers in the *sunday tribune*.
32. I called the hayden planetarium in new york, new york, to get more information about meteors.

Abbreviations *pages 86–87*
Write the sentences, using abbreviation when appropriate. Use initials only in place of middle names.

33. Doctor Ostroff is going to a conference. He wrote himself a note that read "Friday, at 2:30 in the afternoon," so he wouldn't forget.
34. He is a member of the Susan Ann Smith Institute for Marine Biologists.
35. The Institute has gotten the support of Senator Schwartz and Reverend Akdag and is trying to convince Mister Louis Greenwald to support it too.
36. Helaine Kathryn Blanchord posted a sign in the lobby that read "Breakfast will be served at 7:30 in the morning on Saturday, February 10 for all members of the institute."
37. Members of the institute send their yearly dues to this address: Susan Ann Smith Institute, 1414 Bay Avenue, New York, New York, 10025.

Singular and Plural Nouns *pages 88–89*
Write each underlined noun and label it *singular* or *plural*.

38. <u>Nature</u> provides us with many different <u>colors</u> and <u>shades</u>.
39. The azure <u>sky</u> is decorated by fleecy white <u>clouds</u> and the golden <u>disk</u> of the <u>sun</u>.
40. Sandy <u>beaches</u> lapped by the glassy green <u>ocean</u> are trimmed in frothy white <u>foam</u>.
41. <u>Deserts</u> at <u>sunset</u> seem to be painted with gold, rose, and blue colors.
42. <u>Trees</u> and <u>grass</u> are tender green against the gray and brown <u>rocks</u> on the <u>hill</u>.

More Plural Nouns   *pages 90–91*

Find the misspelled word in each sentence and write it correctly.

43. Danny packed two loafs of whole wheat bread and a thermos of juice in his knapsack.
44. The hiking trail had plenty of bushs loaded with edible berries.
45. Danny and his friend Burt had two-way radioes in case they needed to speak to one another on the trail.
46. The trail would take the two boys through two countys.
47. After their nature hike Danny and Burt wrote reportes for their botany teacher.

Possessive Nouns   *pages 92–93*

Write the possessive form of each noun. Label the possessive nouns *singular* or *plural*. Some nouns may be singular or plural.

48. planets
49. garden
50. women
51. dish
52. mesa
53. cranberries
54. Alexis
55. chief
56. deer

Appositives   *pages 94–95*

Write each sentence. Underline the appositive once. Underline twice the word or words it renames.

57. Robert Hutchings Goddard, the father of modern rocket science, lived in Worcester, Massachusetts.
58. Goddard, a physicist, was born in 1882 and lived until 1945.
59. He was the first to launch a liquid-fuel rocket, the predecessor of rockets still in use today.
60. Solid rocket fuel, a later development, powers most modern rockets.
61. Today at Cape Canaveral, which used to be called Cape Kennedy, rocket launchings are a common event.
62. Space travel, a dream in Goddard's time, has become a reality.

Compound Words: Word Teams   *pages 96–97*

Read each sentence. Write the compound word. Then write *closed, open,* or *hyphenated* to tell what kind of compound word it is.

63. At sunrise we left for our fishing trip.
64. A school bus took us to the lake.
65. We put our ice chests over by the tents.
66. Donny and I used an entire bottle of insect-repellent lotion.
67. Clarissa won a prize for catching sixteen walleyed pike.

1-2 Cumulative Review

Four Kinds of Sentences   *pages 30-31*

For each sentence, write *declarative, interrogative, imperative,* or *exclamatory.*

1. The mid-1960's brought the launch of the communications satellite Telstar.
2. What wonders Telstar and similar satellites have brought to the eyes of viewers!
3. Have you ever seen a television program broadcast "live via satellite"?
4. Look for those words at the beginning of news broadcasts from faraway countries.
5. The 1988 Summer Olympic Games came to us live from halfway around the world by satellite.
6. Are today's communications satellites more advanced than Telstar?
7. Hundreds of communication satellites are in orbit around our planet.
8. NASA is responsible for launching most of the satellites for companies in the United States.
9. Please change the station and turn up the volume on the radio.
10. Did the news broadcaster say anything about next week's launch?

Subjects and Predicates   *pages 32-33*

Write each sentence. Draw a vertical line between the complete subject and the complete predicate. Underline the simple subject once. Then underline the simple predicate twice.

11. The sixth-grade students from our middle school visited the television studio.
12. The manager of the television station spoke to our group about careers in television.
13. A few volunteers helped to run a television camera during a rehearsal of a news broadcast.
14. Others sat at the news anchor desk.
15. We watched them on the television monitor.
16. The television studio was a great place to visit!

Compound Subjects   *pages 42–43*

Write the complete subject of each sentence. Underline each simple subject once, and underline the connecting word twice.

17. Painters and sculptors express their thoughts through their art.
18. Oil paints and watercolors are two choices artists have.
19. Blues or greens can give pictures a cool, peaceful feeling.
20. Clay and stone work equally well for large heads or figures.
21. Both potters and sculptors use a special kind of clay.
22. Beginners and experienced artists alike get pleasure from creating art out of raw materials.
23. Museums and art galleries display artists' work.

Compound Predicates   *pages 44–45*

Write the compound predicate from each sentence. Underline the connecting word.

24. People have come together and lived in groups for many centuries.
25. Southwest American Indians built and lived in apartment houses in the faces of cliffs.
26. The ruins of one of these apartment buildings amaze and impress modern visitors to Mesa Verde in Colorado.
27. Pueblo Bonito in Chaco Canyon, New Mexico, is huge and could hold almost 300 families.
28. The residents of Pueblo Bonito raised cotton, grew corn, and mined turquoise for jewelry.

Compound Sentences   *pages 46–47*

Write *simple* or *compound* for each sentence.

29. Amateur radio operators send and receive messages; they are called "hams."
30. Ham radio operators often get messages through to people in disaster areas.
31. The hams send messages from relatives, or they help lost people find one another.
32. Storms and earthquakes frequently knock down telephone wires, but hams don't need wires.
33. Hams can talk to other hams in many other countries all around the world.
34. Many ham radio operators make friends with other hams in countries hundreds of miles away.

Avoiding Sentence Fragments and Run-on Sentences
pages 48–49

Rewrite each sentence fragment as a complete sentence. Rewrite each run-on sentence as one or more sentences. Use the correct punctuation and capitalization.

35. When you write a friendly letter.
36. You should always write a return address on the envelope you never know when the letter itself might get lost.
37. A business letter should be typed if at all possible a friendly letter need not be typed.
38. When you think about it, in fact, a typed letter.
39. Use a comma after a greeting capitalize the first letter of the word "Dear."
40. I'm waiting for a letter from Aunt June has the mail come yet?
41. The last word in the closing.
42. A business letter should always be written on white or ivory paper other colors are all right for personal letters.
43. I wrote a letter to a company asking for a refund the refund arrived today.
44. Six weeks to receive a response.
45. Most companies are very busy it takes that long for them to process a request.

Common and Proper Nouns   *pages 82–83*

Write the nouns. Use capital letters where they are needed.

46. Except for the dead sea, all seas and oceans contain about the same amount of salt.
47. The worldwide cruise of the ship HMS *challenger* provided that information.
48. The atlantic ocean is just about as salty as the pacific ocean and the indian ocean.
49. Among the saltiest bodies of water is the great salt lake in northern utah.
50. The dead sea is a smaller salty lake located between israel and jordan in the middle east.
51. The mediterranean sea is bordered by three continents: africa, europe, and asia.
52. Ships can enter through the strait of gibraltar and exit through the suez canal.

Possessive Nouns *pages 92–93*

Write the possessive form of each noun. Label the possessive
nouns *singular* or *plural*.

53. Mr. Mendez
54. sun
55. peaches
56. plates
57. children
58. knife
59. program
60. sky
61. captains
62. corral

63. grade
64. sock
65. trucks
66. star
67. leaf
68. Annette
69. necklaces
70. lunch
71. soil
72. mountains

Appositives *pages 94–95*

Write each sentence. Underline the appositive phrase once.
Underline twice the word or words it renames.

73. The Old Man of the Mountains, a natural rock formation, is
    an amazing sight to see.
74. It is the perfect profile of a man's face formed in stone on a
    mountainside in the White Mountains, a New Hampshire
    mountain range.
75. The 40-foot-high head, a series of five separate ledges, rises
    1,200 feet above Profile Lake.
76. This lake, a clear and deep oval, was once known as "The
    Old Man's Wash Bowl."
77. Near the Old Man of the Mountains is a large recreation area,
    Franconia North State Park.
78. The Flume, a series of spectacular waterfalls, is only a few
    miles from the Old Man of the Mountains.
79. The park ranger, Jack Bartwick, said he would take us on an
    exciting tour.
80. The expedition, a hike through the mountains, will last about
    four hours.
81. We will have to pack some supplies, food, water, and other
    necessities.

UNIT

3

Giving Instructions

◆ **COMPOSITION FOCUS:** How-to Paragraph
◆ **LANGUAGE FOCUS:** Verbs

What is something special that you can do well? Are you good at playing checkers, perhaps? Can you balance a stick on the end of your nose? Do you have a knack for guessing tomorrow's weather? Whatever your special skill, you can be sure of one thing—many other people in the world would like to learn to do what you can do.

Elin McCoy knows how to have fun. She has ideas for interesting things to do indoors or outdoors, in every kind of weather. To share her many ideas for games, hobbies, and activities, she wrote a "how-to" book called *The Incredible Year-Round Playbook*. She has divided her book into four parts, one for each of the seasons. In each part she gives step-by-step instructions for dozens of pastimes. Young people can use her book the way a cook uses a cookbook. They can browse through it to look up "recipes for fun." In this unit you will read instructions written by Elin McCoy. Then you will learn how to write instructions so that you, too, can share your recipes for fun.

◆ ══ *WARMING UP* ══ ◆

IN YOUR JOURNAL
Write about a time you followed directions either to get to someone's house or to put something together. Explain what made those directions easy or difficult to follow.

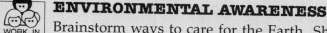

ENVIRONMENTAL AWARENESS
WORK IN A GROUP
Brainstorm ways to care for the Earth. Share your ideas.

Reading with a Writer's Eye
Instructions

Ants can be fascinating to watch as they scurry through the tunnels and rooms of their underground cities. Find out by reading Elin McCoy's instructions how to make an ant city that you can watch. Notice what materials you need and what steps you need to follow.

Sand-Jar Ant Ranch
by Elin McCoy

Catch some ants yourself so you can watch them build tunnels in sand. You'll need:

- cheesecloth (You can buy this at a dime store.)
- 2 large glass jars with screw-on lids
- a paper-towel (or toilet-paper) tube
- a sheet of paper with a dab of honey on it
- dry sand with a little dirt mixed in
- a brown paper bag
- a hammer
- a big nail
- scissors

Cut the paper-towel tube so that it's 1 inch (2.5 centimeters) shorter than one jar. Put it in the middle of the jar and fill the space around it with sand. (The cardboard tube will keep your ants from making their tunnels in the center of the jar, where you couldn't see them.) The sand should come nearly to the top of the tube. Your jar should look like this:

Punch a lot of small holes in the lid of the jar with the hammer and nail. Cut two squares of cheesecloth bigger than the lid. Leave the lid and the cheesecloth next to the jar while you go to find some ants.

Take the honey paper and the other jar and lid on your ant hunt. Look for anthills or look under flat stones in your yard or in empty lots. When you find one spot with plenty of ants, put out the honey paper for bait. As the ants walk onto the paper, brush them off into the jar. Collect a few dozen—all from the same spot.

Then take the ants home and dump them into the sand jar. Quickly put the squares of cheesecloth over the top of the jar and screw on the lid. Put the paper bag over the jar (ants like to work in the dark). When you take the bag off in a day or two, you'll see the ants tunneling away! Keep the bag over the jar when you're not looking at them.

P.S. When you're tired of running an ant ranch, let the ants go—in the yard!

Ant food: bits of honey, scraps of lettuce, a couple of bread crumbs, and a few drops of water. Feed your ants once a week.

Respond

1. Could you build a sand-jar ant ranch using these instructions? What does the writer do to make the instructions easy to follow? Do you like her way of presenting information? Why or why not?

Discuss

2. What information does the writer give about materials you will need?
3. Some of the information in the instructions is not directly related to building an ant ranch. What is this information? Why do you think the writer included it?

Thinking As a Writer
Analyzing a How-to Paragraph

Writer's Guide

A how-to paragraph
- tells how to do something.
- has a topic sentence and detail sentences.
- tells what materials to use and what steps to follow.

A how-to paragraph gives instructions for doing some project or activity, such as building an ant ranch or making a terrarium. A good how-to paragraph has a **topic sentence** that tells what will be explained. **Detail sentences** list the materials that will be needed and the steps that should be followed. Time-order words, such as *first, then,* and *finally,* help the reader understand the order in which the steps should be completed.

If you like models and miniatures, try making a terrarium, or bottled landscape. You will need a big jar, some potting soil, a rubber band, a sheet of plastic, and a trowel. First, begin by washing and drying the jar. Put an inch or two of potting soil in it. Then, go out to a forest, a meadow, or your backyard. Add enough soil to your jar to make hilly shapes. Dig up moss, grass, weeds, and small shrubs. Try not to damage the roots as you dig them up. Next, arrange your plants and shrubs on the soil to create a landscape. Add stone "cliffs" and twig "logs" if you like. Finally, put plastic over the jar and seal it with a rubber band. You do not have to water your terrarium. It will create its own weather!

The **topic sentence** states the activity or project to be explained.

A **materials list** identifies in one or more detail sentences the tools and supplies you will need.

The **detail sentences** tell what you should do step-by-step, in time order. Any special information or advice the reader may need is given where it will be most useful.

Discuss

1. What project or activity do these instructions explain?
2. What kind of information is given in the first sentence? What kind of information is given in the second sentence? What kind of information is given in the rest of the paragraph?
3. Would a how-to paragraph be easy to follow if the writer gave the steps first and the materials second? Why or why not?

Try Your Hand

A. Analyze Instructions Read the instructions. Then write the information from the paragraph under the headings *Purpose, Materials Needed,* and *Steps to Follow.*

1.
> Beautiful pictures can be created with seeds. You will need seeds of different colors, such as pea, bean, and grain seeds. You will also need a piece of cardboard, a pencil, some glue, two eyehooks, and some string. First, draw a design on the board. Next, spread the glue for one kind of seed. Glue those seeds down. Then, do the same for each other type of seed you have. When the picture is dry, attach the eyehooks to the back. Tie the string to each eyehook and hang the picture up.

B. Arrange Sentences in Time Order Rewrite the sentences so that the steps are in the order in which they should be followed.

2. Now put your white mice in their new home.
   Get a medium-sized cardboard box.
   Place an exercise wheel at the other end of the box.
   Put a food dish in the box at one end.
   Put an inch of sawdust in the box.

C. Read Instructions Find and read a set of instructions such as the one on pages 110–111. Find the sentences that tell the purpose of the instructions. Find the list of materials. Find the sentences that tell what steps to follow. Discuss with a partner whether the instructions are well written and why you do or do not think so.

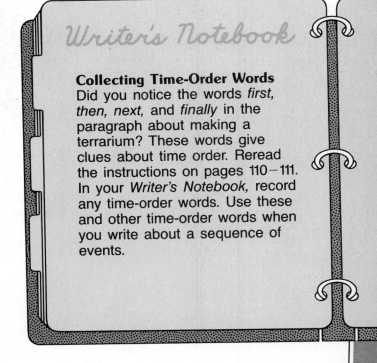

Writer's Notebook

Collecting Time-Order Words
Did you notice the words *first, then, next,* and *finally* in the paragraph about making a terrarium? These words give clues about time order. Reread the instructions on pages 110–111. In your *Writer's Notebook,* record any time-order words. Use these and other time-order words when you write about a sequence of events.

Thinking As a Writer
Visualizing Steps in a Process

To write a good how-to paragraph, writers often visualize the activity. **Visualizing** means "making a movie in your mind." You picture someone going through the steps and "watch" what he or she does. Writers can visualize with their eyes open or closed.

As writers visualize an activity, they make notes about each step. Writers make their notes in the order in which they "see" the steps. A column is often the most convenient form for these notes. Writers leave space between the steps so that they can add any forgotten steps or information later on.

Materials:		
Steps:		
1.		
2.		
3.		

When you plan a how-to paragraph, be sure to visualize the steps in the activity. Take notes as you "watch" someone doing the activity.

Discuss

1. Look back at the instructions on pages 110—111 for making an ant ranch. Do you think Elin McCoy visualized someone doing the activity? Why do you think as you do?
2. In brief phrases, list the main steps in making an ant ranch. Could someone who had never seen the instructions decide whether they were useful by looking at your list? Why or why not?

Try Your Hand

Visualize an Activity With a partner, visualize the steps for making a peanut butter and jelly sandwich, and make notes for a how-to paragraph telling someone how to make one. As one partner visualizes the steps, the other partner should record them.

Developing the Writer's Craft
Adjusting for Audience and Purpose

Writers make adjustments for audience and purpose. They ask, "For whom am I writing this? What does my audience know about this subject? How can I interest my audience?" They use these questions to help them adjust their language and choose their details.

Read these sentences from "Sand-Jar Ant Ranch."

◆ Punch a lot of small holes in the lid of the jar with the hammer and nail.

◆ P.S. When you're tired of running an ant ranch, let the ants go— in the yard!

The writer, Elin McCoy, adjusted her instructions for an audience of sixth-graders. She chose a topic that was likely to interest this audience. She used informal language to make her instructions inviting. She knew that her audience was old enough to use tools, so she left out unnecessary advice about how to hammer nails.

Had Elin McCoy been writing for first-graders, she would have explained how to use the tools. Her language would have been simpler and her instructions easier to follow. Had she been writing for adults, her language would have been more formal.

When you write your how-to paragraph, adjust your language and details to fit not only the people you are trying to reach but also what you are trying to explain to them.

Discuss

1. Look at "Sand-Jar Ant Ranch" on pages 110–111. Find another sentence that shows that the writer was thinking of her audience and her purpose. Explain your choice.
2. Find a sentence in "Sand-Jar Ant Ranch," and adjust it for a first-grader. What changes did you make? Why?

Try Your Hand

Adjust for Audience and Purpose   Find a set of instructions. With a partner, identify the intended audience for the instructions. Then choose a different audience and take turns rewriting the steps for the new audience.

1 Prewriting
How-to Paragraph

Writer's Guide
Prewriting Checklist
☑ Brainstorm project ideas.
☑ Select a project.
☑ Think about your audience and your purpose.
☑ Gather information and determine what materials are needed.
☑ Organize the information into logical steps.

Ken wanted to write a how-to paragraph for his classmates. He used the checklist in the **Writer's Guide** to help him plan his instructions. Look at what he did.

◆ Brainstorming and Selecting a Topic

First, Ken brainstormed interesting hobbies, projects, and activities he had done. Look at Ken's list.

Next, Ken scanned his list. He crossed out projects if the materials seemed hard to find. He crossed out projects that seemed hard to explain or very hard to do. Ken also crossed out projects that he thought would not interest his audience.

Finally, Ken decided to write about kite making. He remembered the hours of enjoyment he had gotten from a kite he had made the previous summer. Ken thought that few of his classmates knew how to make a kite, and he believed he could explain the process to them clearly.

building a model car
building a tree house
starting a fossil collection
taking photographs
making a kite
raising tropical fish
collecting fingerprints

Discuss

1. Look at each item Ken crossed off his list. Why do you think he did not choose these topics?
2. Suppose that Ken wanted to tell adults about a hobby they could do both in the city and in the country. Which idea might he have chosen? Explain your answer.

◆ Gathering and Organizing Information

Ken gathered information for his how-to paragraph by picturing each step he had followed to make a kite. As he visualized this process, he took notes on a three-column chart. First, he listed the steps in the middle column. Then, he filled in the other two columns, using his notes in the middle column to help him visualize each step again.

Tools, materials	Steps	Tips, extra information
two sticks, knife, ruler	1. cut sticks	24 inches, 30 inches
file	2. file notches	both ends, each stick
marker, ruler	3. mark sticks	at 12 inches, at 8 inches
string	4. tie sticks	cross-like shape
string	5. make string frame	tie from notch to notch
marker, newsprint paper	6. trace outline	lay frame on paper
scissors	7. cut kite shape	leave one-inch flap over string
glue	8. fold and glue	

After Ken finished his chart, he numbered the steps to make sure they were in time order, the order in which the steps should be followed. He crossed out some words in the left-hand column so that each tool or material was mentioned only once.

Discuss

1. Ken began by listing the steps of kite making. Was this wise? Why or why not?
2. Look at the information in the middle and right-hand columns of Ken's chart. Where will this information appear when he writes his instructions?
3. Did the order in which Ken listed the steps of kite making matter? Why or why not?

Try Your Hand

Now plan a how-to paragraph of your own.

A. Brainstorm and Select a Topic   Brainstorm a list of possible projects and activities. Write down every interesting activity that occurs to you. Then look at each topic and think about your audience.

- ◆ Cross out projects that may not interest your audience.
- ◆ Cross out projects for which your audience may not be able to get materials.
- ◆ Cross out projects that you may not be able to explain.
- ◆ Circle the most interesting project left on your list. This will be the project for which you will write your how-to paragraph.

B. Gather Information   When you are satisfied with your topic, plan how to gather the information you will need to write your paragraph.

- ◆ Make a three-column chart with plenty of space to list materials, steps, and useful tips your audience may need to know.
- ◆ Visualize the activity or project you want to explain. Picture each step in order. Think about what you do, what you use, and what a person would need to know to complete each step.
- ◆ Fill in your chart as you picture the activity. Leave room between lines so you can add words later.

C. Organize Information   After you complete your chart, look it over.

- ◆ Review the steps you have listed. Be sure you have included all the necessary steps.
- ◆ Make sure the steps you have listed are in the correct time order.
- ◆ Cross out tools or materials that are listed twice. Cross out information your audience may not need to know.
- ◆ Add any special advice or information that may help your audience understand and follow your instructions.

 Save your chart and any other notes you have made in your *Writer's Notebook*. You will use them when you draft your how-to paragraph.

2 Drafting
How-to Paragraph

Writer's Guide
Drafting Checklist
☑ Use your notes and chart for ideas.

☑ Write a topic sentence that tells the purpose of the instructions.

☑ Write detail sentences that tell the tools and materials needed and the steps to be followed.

☑ Use time-order words.

Ken followed the **Writer's Guide** to draft his how-to paragraph. Look at the beginning of his first draft.

> Kite making is easy and lots of fun. You need two long, thin sticks, lots of string, some newsprint paper, and glue. Also collect some scissors, a knife, a ruler, a file, and a marker. First of all, cut the sticks to size. Be careful because a knife is sharp.

Discuss

1. Does Ken's topic sentence make the purpose of his instructions clear? How?
2. Which words signal that Ken has finished listing materials and is beginning step 1?

Try Your Hand

Now draft a how-to paragraph.

A. **Review Your Information**   Think about the information you gathered and organized in the last lesson. Decide whether you need more information. If so, gather it.

B. **Think About Your TAP**   Remember that your task is to write a set of instructions. Your purpose is to explain to your classmates how to do the project or activity.

Task: What?
Audience: Who?
Purpose: Why?

C. **Write Your First Draft**   Follow the steps in the **Drafting Checklist** to write your how-to paragraph.
When you write your draft, just put all your ideas on paper. Do not worry about spelling, punctuation, or grammar. You can correct the draft later.

Save your first draft in your *Writer's Notebook*. You will use it when you revise your how-to paragraph.

3 Responding and Revising
How-to Paragraph

Ken used the checklist in the **Writer's Guide** to revise his how-to paragraph. Look at what he did.

◆ Checking Information

When Ken read over his draft, he decided to cut some advice his audience would not need and to add a useful tip. Ken also added a time-order word. He used this mark ✄ to show what he was cutting. He used this mark ∧ to show what he was adding.

◆ Checking Organization

Looking at his instructions again, Ken noticed a step out of time order. To show that the sentence should be moved, he used this mark ↺ .

◆ Checking Language

Ken also found that he had used more words than he needed in one sentence, so he replaced a long phrase with one word. He used this mark ⌒ to show what he replaced.

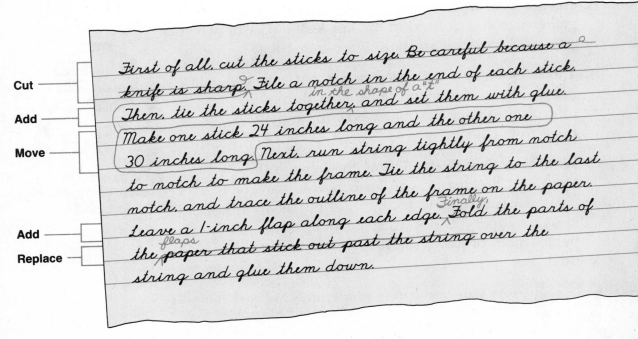

Cut · Add · Move · Add · Replace

First of all, cut the sticks to size. Be careful because a knife is sharp. File a notch in the end of each stick. in the shape of a "t" Then, tie the sticks together, and set them with glue. Make one stick 24 inches long and the other one 30 inches long. Next, run string tightly from notch to notch to make the frame. Tie the string to the last notch, and trace the outline of the frame on the paper. Finally, leave a 1-inch flap along each edge. Fold the parts of flaps the paper that stick out past the string over the string and glue them down.

Discuss

1. Was the detail Ken added useful? Why or why not?
2. Look at the sentence Ken cut. Do you agree that this advice was unnecessary? Why or why not? For what audience might the advice have been useful?
3. Why did Ken add a time-order word?

Try Your Hand

Now revise your first draft.

A. Read Your First Draft As you read your how-to paragraph, think about your audience and your purpose. Read your paragraph silently or to a partner to see if it is complete and well organized. Ask yourself or your partner the questions in the box.

Responding and Revising Strategies

✔ Respond **Ask yourself or a partner:**	✔ Revise **Try these solutions:**
◆ Do readers know from the start what the how-to paragraph is about?	◆ **Add** a topic sentence that states the purpose of your paragraph.
◆ Have I listed all the materials needed before I tell what steps to follow?	◆ **Add** information that is needed, or **move** it from another part of the paragraph.
◆ Are the steps clear and easy to follow?	◆ **Move** sentences that are out of time order. **Add** time-order words.
◆ Does each sentence express its message in the fewest words needed?	◆ **Cut** or **replace** words to make your language more concise. See the **Revising Workshop** on page 122.

B. Make Your Changes If the answer to any question in the box is *no,* try the solution. Use the **Editor's Marks** to show your changes.

C. Review Your Instructions Again Decide whether there is anything else you want to revise. Keep revising your how-to paragraph until you feel it is well organized and complete.

EDITOR'S MARKS

- ∧ Add something.
- Cut something.
- Move something.
- Replace something.

Save your revised how-to paragraph in your *Writer's Notebook.* You will use it when you proofread your paragraph.

Revising Workshop
Avoiding Wordy Language

Good writers make every word count by avoiding wordy language. Look at these two sentences. Notice the underlined words in each sentence.

1. In June of every year, in the city of Hartford, boys and girls are welcome to have a frog take part in a frog jumping contest.
2. Every June in Hartford, children can enter a frog in a frog jumping contest.

Both sentences express the same message, but in the second sentence the writer uses concise language. Concise language expresses a message in the fewest words needed. For example, *every June* is a concise way of saying *in June of every year*. The phrase *enter a frog* is a concise way of saying *have a frog take part*. Notice, too, that in the second sentence the writer dropped the phrase *the city of* because it adds no necessary information. In your own writing, look for words and phrases that add no necessary information. Drop or replace them to make your writing concise.

Practice

Rewrite each sentence. Drop or replace the words in parentheses ( ) to make the sentence concise.

1. (The best of times to catch a frog) is (to do so at night).
2. Go to the edge of (a pond of water) with a (flashlight that has a strong beam of light).
3. Point the light (at different places near the edge of the water toward the shore).
4. (Then, at the moment that) you see a frog, shine the light into (the frog's two eyes).
5. Gently reach behind (where the frog's body is located), and (grab it successfully from the) back.
6. (You could) then bring your frog (with you) to the (place where the frog jumping contest is going to happen).
7. Each frog will (have a chance to) take three jumps (one right after another), and the frog who goes farthest wins.

4 Proofreading
How-to Paragraph

Ken wrote another paragraph about how to fly a kite. He used the **Writer's Guide** and the **Editor's Marks** to proofread it. Look at what he did.

> *easy*
> Flying a kite is ~~eazy~~. Here is what you
> *space*
> do. First, find a big open ~~spase~~, face away
> from the wind and hold the string. Next,
> have a friend hold the kite, and wait for
> a strong gust. when a strong wind comes,
> tell your friend to let go, and the wind
> will carry your kite up into the air.

EDITOR'S MARKS

≡ Capitalize.

⊙ Add a period.

∧ Add something.

⅄ Add a comma.

ᵛᵛ Add quotation marks.

✂ Cut something.

⋀ Replace something.

〰 Transpose.

◯ Spell correctly.

⌇ Indent paragraph.

╱ Make a lowercase letter.

Discuss

1. Look at Ken's proofread paragraph. What kinds of corrections did he make?
2. Why did Ken add commas? Why did he remove a comma?

Try Your Hand

Proofread Your How-to Paragraph   Now use the **Writer's Guide** and the **Editor's Marks** to proofread your how-to paragraph.

Save your corrected how-to paragraph in your *Writer's Notebook.* **You will use it when you publish your paragraph.**

5 Publishing
How-to Paragraph

Ken made a clean copy of his how-to paragraphs and checked to be sure he had not left anything out. Then he and his classmates published their paragraphs in a class book called *31 Fun Projects*. You can find Ken's paragraphs on page 32 of the **Writer's Handbook.**

Here's how Ken and his classmates published a book of projects and activities.

1. First, they typed each set of instructions and pasted them onto book-sized pages. Then, they pasted in the illustrations that went with the instructions. Next, they numbered each page.

2. Ken typed the table of contents. Then, they gave the book a title, and made a cover. Ken made several copies of each page and stapled the pages together to make books.

Discuss

If you were making a book of activities, how would you group the projects? Why?

Try Your Hand

Publish Your Instructions Follow the checklist in the **Writer's Guide.** If possible, create a class hobby-starter book, or try this idea for sharing your how-to paragraph.

◆ Paste the how-to paragraphs on stiff cards. File everyone's paragraphs in a box labeled *Hobby Starters*. Browse through the box when you are looking for something to do.

Listening and Speaking
Tips on How to Give and Follow Instructions

Giving Instructions

1. Speak clearly.
2. Use language that is right for your audience. For example, when giving instructions to young children, keep your language simple enough for them to understand.
3. Give your audience all the information it needs, but give no extra or unnecessary information.
4. Give the steps in time order. Use time-order words such as *first, next, after that, then,* and *finally.*
5. Watch the audience for signs that they are confused or are not keeping up. If necessary, stop to invite questions.

Listening to Instructions

1. Watch the speaker.
2. Concentrate on what the speaker is saying.
3. Think about each step and try to picture it as you hear it.
4. If you do not hear or understand something, ask questions.
5. When the speaker is finished, go over the steps in your mind. If the instructions are not clear or if you think you missed a step, ask the speaker for help.

Writing in the Content Areas

Use what you learned to write instructions for students your own age about how to do or make something. You could write a paragraph or a booklet. Use one of these ideas or an idea of your own.

Health/Physical Education

What steps can you take to make sure you become and stay healthy? Talk to the physical education teacher about good exercises for people your age. Talk to the school dietitian, or read about creating balanced meals.

Mathematics

Is there a secret to success on mathematics tests? Find out what steps experts recommend that people take to prepare for mathematics tests and other tests. Interview friends to discover what preparation techniques work best for them. Talk to teachers to learn what steps they think are most helpful.

Literature

How do people become authors and illustrators? Find out what kind of training is recommended for people interested in these careers and what steps they must take to enter these fields after they have been trained. Read biographies of writers and artists, or interview people in these fields.

Science

Scientists perform the same experiments over and over to make sure their findings are correct. What experiments have you performed at school or at home? How well can you explain the steps that you followed? Will the results be the same when someone else follows your directions?

CONNECTING

WRITING ↔ LANGUAGE

Doing anything the first time can be difficult. Clear instructions make the job easier. What makes these instructions easy to follow?

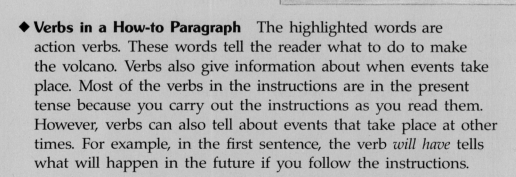

How to Make Your Own Volcano

Follow these directions step-by-step, and you will have your own active—but perfectly safe—volcano. First, fill a large pan with sand. Wet the sand with water, and shape it into a mountain around a large, empty orange-juice can. Next, mix together one cup of water, ¾ cup of vinegar, ½ cup of liquid dish soap, and 10 drops of red food coloring. Pour the mixture into the center of your mountain, and watch your volcano erupt.

◆ **Verbs in a How-to Paragraph** The highlighted words are action verbs. These words tell the reader what to do to make the volcano. Verbs also give information about when events take place. Most of the verbs in the instructions are in the present tense because you carry out the instructions as you read them. However, verbs can also tell about events that take place at other times. For example, in the first sentence, the verb *will have* tells what will happen in the future if you follow the instructions.

◆ **Language Focus: Verbs** In the following lessons you will learn more ways to use verbs to make your writing clear and exciting.

1 Action Verbs

◆ **FOCUS** An **action verb** tells what the subject does or did.

Remember that the simple predicate of a sentence is made up of one or more verbs. The simple predicate is often an action verb. In this sentence the word in color is an action verb.

1. Tammy relaxes in her chair.

Some action verbs tell about action that cannot be seen.

2. Tammy dreams about a horse show.

Link to Speaking and Writing

Strong action verbs help make a sentence vivid. How does replacing the verb change this sentence?

The horse went over the hurdle.
soared

Guided Practice

A. Identify the verb in each sentence.

1. Tammy wants a horse.
2. Her parents buy a horse.
3. The horse struts proudly.
4. She names him Rex.
5. Tammy practices with Rex.
6. She works with him every day.
7. They jump a high fence.
8. Tammy enters a horse show.
9. She wins a blue ribbon.
10. Her parents smile happily.

B. 11.–20. Tell whether each verb in **A** expresses an action that *can be seen* or that *cannot be seen*.

THINK AND REMEMBER

◆ Use an **action verb** to tell what a subject does or did.
◆ Use strong action verbs to help make your sentences more vivid.

Independent Practice

C. Identifying Verbs   Write the verb from each sentence.

21. Leonardo da Vinci lived in the fifteenth century.

MODEL > lived

22. He had many interesting daydreams.
23. Daydreams helped Leonardo's creativity.
24. Leonardo saw pictures of airplanes in his daydreams.
25. He drew pictures of those airplanes.
26. The first real airplane flew in 1903.
27. Most of us probably have daydreams.
28. People's hopes and goals shape their daydreams.
29. A boy plays for a Little League team.
30. In his daydreams the boy pitches for a famous team.
31. He pitches a perfect game in the World Series.
32. A girl wants a new bicycle.
33. She needs the money for it.
34. In a daydream she wins a ten-speed bicycle.

D. Revising: Using Strong Action Verbs   Rewrite each sentence. Use a strong action verb to make the sentence more vivid.

35. Josie went home.

MODEL > Josie dashed home.

36. She looked at the table.
37. Her eyes grew wide.
38. She wanted this!
39. She showed delight.
40. She moved to the box.
41. The puppy made noise.

E. Writing Sentences with Strong Action Verbs   Use each simple subject in a sentence with a strong action verb.

42. lightning

MODEL > Lightning ripped across the sky.

43. stallions	46. airplane	49. rain
44. runner	47. car	50. stars
45. waves	48. hawk	51. dishes

Application — Writing

News Story   Imagine that you are a reporter writing about a horse show or another kind of show for a community newspaper. Tell about one event in the show. Use vivid sentences with strong action verbs.

2 Linking Verbs

◆ **FOCUS** A **linking verb** connects the subject to a word or words in the predicate.

Remember that action verbs tell what the subject does or did. Linking verbs do not express action. They connect the subject to a word or words in the predicate. In these sentences the words in color are linking verbs.

1. My father is a good cook.
2. His meals taste delicious.

Common Linking Verbs	
Forms of *Be* am, is, are, was, were, been	**Other Linking Verbs** taste, look, smell, feel, appear, seem, become

Link to Speaking and Writing
You can add variety to your sentences by varying your linking verbs. Do the changes make the paragraph more interesting? Why?

Dinner is ready. The salad is ~~is~~ *tastes*
crisp. The bread ~~is~~ *feels* warm. The
chicken ~~is~~ *smells* delicious.

Guided Practice

A. Identify the linking verb in each sentence.

1. Fishing was once Dad's hobby.
2. Now, cooking is his hobby.
3. It became his hobby recently.
4. Dad's kitchen smells good!
5. His sherbet tastes creamy.
6. We are Dad's biggest fans.

THINK AND REMEMBER
◆ Remember that a **linking verb** joins the subject of a sentence with a word or words in the predicate.
◆ Vary your linking verbs to add interest and variety to your sentences.

Independent Practice

B. Identifying Linking Verbs   Read the sentences. Write the linking verbs.

    7. Mr. and Mrs. Drew are farmers.

> MODEL   are

    8. They appear proud of their vegetables.
    9. Their tomatoes taste fresh and juicy.
  10. Their carrots become bigger every year.
  11. Their fields are in the hot sun.
  12. A hat with a wide brim is important out there.

C. Recognizing Linking and Action Verbs   Write the verb from each sentence. Label it *action* or *linking*.

  13. Mrs. Ames works hard.

> MODEL   works—action

  14. Mrs. Ames is a construction worker.
  15. A construction company employs her.
  16. The company builds apartment houses.
  17. Construction sites are dangerous places.
  18. Cranes lift heavy loads.
  19. Sometimes a brick falls from above.
  20. A hard hat seems necessary there.
  21. Mrs. Ames likes her job.
  22. She is surely one of the best workers in the company.

D. Revising: Varying Linking Verbs   Rewrite the sentences, using a different linking verb in each one.

  23. The air is fresh.

> MODEL   The air smells fresh.

  24. The weather is warmer in early summer.
  25. How clean the air is today!
  26. The sky is clear and blue.
  27. The breeze is soft against my cheek.
  28. This is a perfect day for the beach.

Application — Writing, Speaking, Listening

Menu   Talk with classmates about a meal you would like to plan. Then write a menu for the meal. List the foods, and describe each one. Tell how the foods look, taste, and smell. Describe the textures of the foods, too. Use a variety of linking verbs.

3 Main Verbs and Helping Verbs

FOCUS
◆ The **main verb** is the most important verb in a verb phrase.
◆ A **helping verb** works with the main verb to express action or being.

A **verb phrase** is two or more verbs that work together. The main verb is always the last word in a verb phrase. It expresses action or being. All the other words in the phrase are called helping verbs because they help the main verb express its meaning. In these sentences, the words in color are verb phrases.

1. The boys are building a clubhouse.
2. They have been given some tools.

Some helping verbs can also be main verbs.

   helping verb   main verb

3. John has drawn some plans; he has a lot of talent.

The most common helping verbs are forms of *be, have,* and *do.* Other helping verbs include *could, can, must, would, will, should, may,* and *might.* One or more words may come between the helping verbs and the main verb.

4. I have never seen such a project.

Forms of *Be*	Forms of *Have*	Forms of *Do*
is, am, was, were, been	has, had	does, did

Guided Practice

A. Identify the verb phrase in each sentence. Tell whether each part is a *main verb* or a *helping verb.*

1. The boys had been dreaming about a clubhouse.
2. They were holding their meetings in the park.
3. Now they have finished their clubhouse.
4. Did you see their faces?
5. Never have I seen such happy boys!

Independent Practice

B. Identifying Verb Phrases, Main Verbs, and Helping Verbs
Write the verb phrase from each sentence. Underline each helping verb once. Underline the main verb twice.

6. The house has needed a new roof for a long time.

MODEL▷ <u>has</u> <u>needed</u>

7. The roofers have measured the roof carefully.
8. A big truck is bringing the shingles.
9. Were you watching the roofers?
10. The sky had been getting cloudy.
11. The workers did not notice the clouds.
12. Suddenly rain was pouring down.
13. Now the roofers are sitting on the porch.

C. Identifying Verbs and Verb Phrases   Write the complete verb from each sentence. Label it *verb* or *verb phrase*. Underline the helping verb once, and underline the main verb twice.

14. They were always laughing.

MODEL▷ <u>were</u> <u>laughing</u>—verb phrase

15. The girls in the class have formed a club.
16. The club has a funny name.
17. The girls have called it "The Slogwatch Circle."
18. The club has rules for all members.
19. The girls do many activities in their clubhouse.
20. The group is probably meeting right now.
21. The president of the club is Amy Lewis.
22. Does Amy enjoy being president?

Application — Writing

Journal Entry   Imagine that you have watched some classmates build a clubhouse. Write an entry for your journal describing what you saw. Tell what your classmates were doing and how the clubhouse looked. Use at least four verb phrases. If you need help writing a journal entry, see page 40 of the **Writer's Handbook.**

4 Principal Parts of Verbs

◆ FOCUS The **principal parts** of a verb are the present, the present participle, the past, and the past participle.

Every verb has four basic forms called principal parts. These are used to express many different **tenses,** or times. The principal parts are the present, the present participle, the past, and the past participle. **Participles** are the forms used with helping verbs such as *is, am, was, were, has,* and *have.*

Present	Present Participle	Past	Past Participle
ask	(is, are) asking	asked	(have, has, had) asked
earn	(is, are) earning	earned	(have, has, had) earned
have	(is, are) having	had	(have, has, had) had

The past and the past participle of regular verbs, such as *ask* and *earn,* are formed by adding *ed* to the present. The past and past participle of irregular verbs, such as *have* and *do,* are formed in other ways. Notice that the present participle of both kinds of verbs is formed by adding *ing* to the present.

Remember these spelling rules for regular verbs.

◆ If the verb ends in *e,* drop the *e* before you add *ed* or *ing.*
◆ If the verb ends with a consonant plus *y,* change *y* to *i* before you add *ed.*
◆ If a one-syllable verb ends in a single vowel plus a consonant, double the consonant before you add *ed* or *ing.*

change	—changed
	—changing
hurry	—hurried
	—hurrying
slam	—slammed
	—slamming

Guided Practice

A. Tell the other three principal parts of each verb.

1. wait
2. seem
3. grin
4. supply
5. close
6. clap
7. cry
8. tame

THINK AND REMEMBER
◆ Remember that the **principal parts** of verbs are the present, the present participle, the past, and the past participle.

Independent Practice

B. Writing the Principal Parts of Verbs Write the other three principal parts of each verb.

9. worry

MODEL (is, are) worrying, worried,
(have, has, had) worried

10. play	12. tap	14. apply	16. dust
11. sail	13. graze	15. talk	17. amaze

C. Identifying the Principal Parts of Verbs Write the main verb from each sentence. Label it *present, present participle, past,* or *past participle.*

18. George Washington Carver loved plants.

MODEL loved—past

19. People have called Carver a genius and a pioneer.
20. Carver studied agriculture in the 1890's.
21. He experimented with plants and soil.
22. Carver spoke to many farmers.
23. He had discovered new uses for crops such as peanuts.
24. Farmers have changed their techniques because of Carver.
25. They grow a variety of plants on their farms.
26. This practice is helping the soil.
27. Farmers are raising many of the plants Carver studied.
28. For example, they have produced peanuts for years.

D. Proofreading: Checking for Spelling Errors Find the misspelled word in each sentence and write it correctly.

29. Alice plantted peanuts.

MODEL planted

Peanut

30. She has applyed her skills in gardening.
31. The plants have thrivd in the rich soil.
32. The plants have supplyed plenty of peanuts.
33. Alice roastted the peanuts.
34. She was worryed that the peanuts would taste burnt.
35. She placd some oil in a blender.
36. Then, she droped in plenty of peanuts.
37. She turnned the peanuts into peanut butter.

Application — Writing

Description Write eight sentences to share with classmates about a plant that you have grown or that you have seen growing. Use the present forms of verbs in two sentences, the present participle forms in two sentences, the past forms in two sentences, and the past participle forms in two sentences.

5 Present, Past, and Future Tenses

◆ **FOCUS** The **simple tenses** are the present, the past, and the future.

The **tense** of a verb expresses the time when the action or state of being takes place. The **present tense** tells about what is happening now.

1. Juana works on her painting.

The **past tense** tells what happened before now. It is usually formed by adding *ed* to the present.

2. Joe admired the painting.

The **future tense** tells what will happen later. The helping verb *will* is used with the present to express the future tense.

3. Juana will be famous someday.

Link to Speaking and Writing
Using the same tense throughout a description helps make the description clearer.

> The painting shows a forest. A deer
> ~~stood~~ *stands* by a tree. A stream ~~will flow~~ *flows*
> quietly nearby.

Guided Practice

A. Identify whether the tense of each underlined verb is *present, past,* or *future.*

1. Juana <u>painted</u> a picture for her mother.
2. The picture <u>hangs</u> in her mother's room.
3. Last week she <u>entered</u> the picture in a contest.
4. I <u>will go</u> to the gallery one of these days.
5. Perhaps Juana <u>will win</u> a prize.

THINK AND REMEMBER
◆ Use the **simple tenses** to express what is happening now, what happened before, and what will happen later.
◆ Remember that the **simple tenses** are the present, the past, and the future.

Independent Practice

B. Identifying Verb Tenses Write the verb from each sentence, and label it *present, past,* or *future.*

 6. Juana attended an art show.

MODEL▷ attended—past

 7. She asked the artists questions.
 8. She looked closely at their art.
 9. Now she has an idea for a picture of her own.
10. She writes the idea in her journal.
11. Juana will paint a desert landscape.
12. She will experiment with different colors.
13. She learned many things at the art gallery.
14. She will try some new techniques in her landscape.
15. She will mix her paints with sand and powdered leaves.
16. She never mixed colors that way before.

C. Using Verb Tenses Write a sentence with each verb, using the tense given in parentheses.

17. play (past)

MODEL▷ She played the guitar.

18. jump (future)   20. call (present)   22. rinse (past)
19. laugh (past)   21. dance (past)   23. pick (future)

D. Using Consistent Verb Tenses Use each set of verbs to write three sentences that all express the same verb tense. Use each of the simple tenses in at least one set of sentences.

24. work, sketch, add

MODEL▷ The artist worked quickly. He sketched the house.
         Then he added details.

25. look, paint, fix   31. write, revise, proofread
26. knock, reply, enter   32. walk, attend, return
27. finish, show, admire   33. shop, buy, wrap
28. start, help, complete   34. call, listen, reply
29. regret, search, locate   35. enter, display, win
30. cherish, keep, love   36. throw, swing, hit

Application — Writing

Business Letter Write a letter to a gallery where you would like to display your paintings. Describe a beautiful place you saw, the painting you did of the scene, and the next painting you plan to do. Remember to use verb tenses consistently. If you need help writing a business letter, see page 53 of the **Writer's Handbook.**

6 Perfect Tenses

◆FOCUS   The **perfect tenses** are the present perfect, the past perfect, and the future perfect.

Remember that the present tense expresses what is happening now. The **present perfect tense** expresses action that took place at some indefinite time before the present and may still be going on. Use *has* or *have* with the past participle to express the present perfect.

1. Tim has run every day for more than two months.
2. We have noticed him running on the school track.

The **past perfect tense** expresses action that was completed before some moment or action in the past. Use *had* with the past participle to express the past perfect.

3. By last Tuesday, Tim had beaten the team record.

The **future perfect tense** expresses action that will be completed before some moment or action in the future. Use *will have* with the past participle to express the future perfect.

4. By next year, Tim will have broken the city record.

Guided Practice

A. Identify whether the tense of each underlined verb is *present perfect, past perfect,* or *future perfect*.

1. Tim <u>had worked</u> hard to make the school track team.
2. The time <u>had arrived</u> for the tryouts.
3. He made the school track team and <u>has practiced</u> every day since then.
4. Tim's hopes <u>have focused</u> on today's race.
5. By dinnertime, Tim <u>will have finished</u> the big race in the district track meet.
6. Tim and his teammates <u>have decided</u> to practice on the weekends.

Independent Practice

B. Identifying Verbs in the Perfect Tenses   Write the verb from each sentence, and label it *present perfect*, *past perfect*, or *future perfect*.

7. Park School never had experienced a winning season.

MODEL ▷ had experienced—past perfect

8. They had lost most of their games each year.
9. This season, however, the team has defeated its rivals.
10. The players have earned our support.
11. In fact, the team has reached the championship game.
12. The other team has played well this season, too.
13. By next week, one team will have earned the championship trophy.
14. No one had expected such a good season from our team.
15. By next year, many of the best players on our team will have graduated.

C. Using the Perfect Tenses   Write each sentence, using the correct perfect tense of the verb in parentheses.

16. Meg _____ for the past five years now. (bowl)

MODEL ▷ Meg has bowled for the past five years now.

17. Before I met Meg, she _____ never _____ a league. (join)
18. Now she _____ in my league for two years. (play)
19. Meg _____ six tournaments in the past year. (enter)
20. She _____ the trophy in every tournament. (capture)
21. By next month, she _____ a plaque. (receive)
22. I say she _____ it. (earn)

Application — Writing and Speaking

Sportscast   Imagine that you are a sportscaster. Write a sportscast for a radio station in your community. Tell who won a big track meet, what led to his or her success, and what this athlete's prospects are for the future. Use all three perfect tenses. Read your sportscast to your class.

7 Subject-Verb Agreement

◆ **FOCUS**   A subject and its verb should agree in number.

Verbs, like nouns, express number. That is, they can be singular or plural. Singular verbs must be used with singular subjects. Plural verbs must be used with plural subjects.

1. Kitty O'Neil is a stuntwoman.   singular
2. Dangerous tricks are her specialty.   plural

Most verbs have two present-tense forms. One form ends in *s* or *es*. This form is used with *he, she, it*, and all singular nouns. The other form does not end in *s* or *es*. This form is used with *I, you, we, they*, and all plural nouns. Compare the verbs in color in sentences 3 and 4.

3. Kitty jumps off buildings and leaps through windows.
4. Stuntpeople often jump off buildings and leap through windows.

In a verb phrase, the helping verb agrees with the subject.

5. Few people have faced such dangers.

Guided Practice

A. Identify the verb in parentheses that correctly completes each sentence.

1. Kitty O'Neil (has, have) been brave all her life.
2. During a stunt, she (concentrate, concentrates) hard.
3. Kitty (learns, learn) each stunt step by step.
4. Stuntpeople (does, do) dangerous work.
5. Caution (is, are) very important during a stunt.
6. (Is, Are) you interested in this type of job?

THINK AND REMEMBER
◆ Use the singular form of a verb with a singular subject.
◆ Use the plural form of a verb with a plural subject.

Independent Practice

B. Using Verb Forms Correctly   Write the verb in parentheses that correctly completes each sentence.

7. All movie actors (wear, wears) makeup.

MODEL ▷ wear

8. Makeup artists sometimes (turn, turns) actors into monsters.
9. They (has, have) made actors look older or younger.
10. Many monster faces (are, is) really masks.
11. A makeup artist (has, have) spent seven hours on one job.
12. Afterwards, the actor (look, looks) very different.
13. (Isn't, Aren't) movie makeup amazing?
14. Sometimes, I (dreams, dream) of becoming a makeup artist.
15. I can make it if I (works, work) hard enough.
16. On the other hand, luck (play, plays) a part, too.
17. I just (hope, hopes) my luck will be good.

C. Proofreading: Checking for Subject-Verb Agreement   Rewrite each sentence to correct the error in subject-verb agreement.

18. Movies has changed.

MODEL ▷ Movies have changed.

19. They says movies are not what they used to be.
20. I certainly believes that!
21. Nowadays, most movies is in color.
22. There is also many other differences.
23. Modern sound systems provides realistic sound.
24. Today's directors often uses computers.
25. They creates action scenes with special effects.
26. You sees a huge rocket fly across the screen.
27. A whole city burn down dramatically.
28. Scenes like these often seems almost too real.
29. Yes, movies have changed, but is they better?
30. Some old movies looks great to me.
31. I is trying to find videotapes of some of my favorite old movies.

Application — Writing

Movie Scene   Imagine that you want to make an action movie. Write a description of one action scene from the movie to present to a movie producer. Tell what happens in the scene step by step. Be sure that all your verbs agree with their subjects.

8 Agreement of Verbs with Compound Subjects

◆ **FOCUS** Some compound subjects and verbs follow special rules of agreement.

Remember that a verb must agree with its subject in number. If the subject is a compound and the parts are joined by *and*, the verb must be plural.

1. Violet and blue look good together.
2. Reds and oranges look good together.

In some compound subjects the parts are joined by *or, either/or,* or *neither/nor.* If both parts are plural, use a plural verb. If both parts are singular, use a singular verb.

3. Either reds or blues go well with violet.
4. Either red or blue goes well with violet.

If one part is plural and the other is singular, make the verb agree with the subject closest to it.

5. These reds or that blue goes well with violet.
6. This blue or those reds go well with violet.

Guided Practice

A. Identify the verb in parentheses that agrees with the subject.

1. Jon and his family (moves, move) into a new house.
2. The dining room and the kitchen (is, are) painted yellow.
3. Neither Jon nor the twins (likes, like) this color.
4. They or their parents (has, have) to paint these rooms.
5. Some rugs or a carpet (is, are) needed in the living room.
6. "The chairs or the couch (goes, go) here," say the twins.
7. Neither the couch nor the chairs (fits, fit) there.
8. Jon and his family (makes, make) their new house beautiful.

THINK AND REMEMBER
◆ When the parts of a compound subject are joined by *and*, use a plural verb.
◆ When the parts of a compound subject are joined by *or* or *nor*, use the verb form that agrees with the subject closest to it.

Independent Practice

B. Identifying Verbs That Agree with Compound Subjects Write the verb in parentheses that correctly completes each sentence.

9. Joe, Tom, and May (has, have) started a business.

MODEL▷ have

10. They and their parents (hopes, hope) it will grow.
11. Friends or relatives often (hires, hire) them.
12. A house or an apartment (needs, need) painting.
13. May and the boys (does, do) the job.
14. Either the clients or Joe (chooses, choose) the colors.
15. Then, either May or the boys (buys, buy) the paint.
16. Today, neither the paint store nor the three hardware stores (is, are) open.
17. Tom, Joe, and May (takes, take) the day off.
18. May and her brothers (wonders, wonder) what to do.
19. A swim or some outdoor games (sounds, sound) good to May.

C. Proofreading: Correcting Errors in Subject-Verb Agreement Rewrite each sentence, correcting the error in subject-verb agreement.

20. The house and the neighborhood appeals to me.

MODEL▷ The house and the neighborhood appeal to me.

21. My family and I wants to move here.
22. Perhaps some new paint or wallpaper are needed.
23. The kitchen and the dining room is rather small.
24. The banister or the stairs creaks when you walk in.
25. Neither the creaks nor the small size bother me.
26. The yard and the view makes up for the problems.
27. A mooing cow or even barking dogs relaxes me.
28. Loud sirens or a clattering jackhammer, on the other hand, make me tense.

Application — Writing

Friendly Letter Imagine that you have recently moved to a new town. Write a letter to a classmate. Describe your new home and how you have improved it since you moved in. Use at least three compound subjects. Make sure all your verbs agree with their subjects. If you need help writing a friendly letter, see page 52 of the **Writer's Handbook.**

Building Vocabulary
Prefixes: Parts for the Word Builder

A large vocabulary can help you express ideas and information clearly. You can expand your vocabulary by building new words out of words you already know. For example, you can add one or more letters to the beginning of some words to form new words. The letter or letters you add to the beginning of a word are called a **prefix**. In the following sentence, the prefix *dis* added to the verb *like* makes a new verb that means the opposite of *like*.

I dis like complicated instructions.

Study this chart of prefixes.

Prefix	Meaning	Examples
un	not, opposite of	untie, unfair
im	not, opposite of	imperfect, impossible
in	not, opposite of	incomplete, incorrect
re	back, again	retrace, retell
dis	away, off, not	dislike, displease
mis	badly, wrongly, not	misjudge, misunderstand
pre	before	preheat, preteen
post	later, after	postgame, postscript
over	too much, above	overcook, overshoot

Reading Practice

Read each sentence. Write each word formed with a prefix. Then underline the prefix.

1. Sally is an unusual girl.
2. She has a preschool gymnastics practice every day.
3. Sometimes, she gets overtired.
4. I will be unable to go to her show.
5. I am very disappointed.
6. Sally rearranges her day to put on a show just for me.
7. We meet in the gym during a postlunch break.
8. She disappears into the locker room.
9. She reappears a moment later wearing her costume.
10. Sally gives me a preview of the whole show.
11. Some of her moves seem impossible.
12. Her jumps and handstands are incredible.
13. I don't see any missteps.
14. Suddenly she overshoots the mark in a jump.
15. She is unsure about what went wrong.
16. I think she misjudged the distance.
17. She retraces her steps and does the jump correctly.

Writing Practice

Form a new word by adding a prefix to each word below. Then use each new word in a sentence.

18. print
19. lock
20. polite
21. agree
22. do
23. proper
24. heat
25. clear
26. understand
27. aware
28. obey
29. please

Project

Look through library books and magazine articles for more examples of words with prefixes. With classmates, list the words on long strips of paper according to the prefix they contain. Use each prefix as a list title. Post the word lists, and keep adding to them as you come across more words.

re
replay
readjust
react
remake
recover
reapply
reunite

Language Enrichment
Verbs

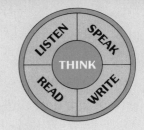

Use what you know about verbs to do these activities.

Then What Happened?

Write an ending to the story. Use past-tense verbs to tell what happened.

Last summer I took a walk in Founders Forest. The day was beautiful, and I wandered off the path. Suddenly I found myself in a meadow filled with yellow flowers.

Share your story ending with the class. Practice reading it dramatically in front of a mirror before presenting it to the class.

Name That Sport

List at least 10 action verbs that describe movements in a particular sport. For example, for baseball your list might include *swing* and *pitch*. Then act out the movements for the class. See how quickly your classmates can name the sport.

Eyes on the Future

Write sentences describing 10 dramatic events from the past. Use the past tense. For example, one sentence might say "The *Titanic* sank in 1912." Then make a prediction related to each event. Use the future tense. For example, a sentence about the *Titanic* might say "Divers will find long-lost treasures inside the sunken *Titanic*." Share your predictions with the class. See how many classmates agree with you.

CONNECTING
LANGUAGE ↔ WRITING

In this unit you learned that some verbs show action. Others link the subject to words in the predicate. Some verbs work together to express meaning. Verbs have four main forms, or principal parts, to express different tenses. Verbs also have different forms to agree with singular and plural subjects.

◆ **Using Verbs in Your Writing** Verbs can help you tell about actions clearly and vividly. They can help you communicate precisely how people and objects behave, move, and feel. Pay special attention to the verbs you use as you do these activities.

 ## On the Move

Imagine one of the races pictured. Describe the race as if it is going on as you write. Use present-tense verbs. Tell how the people, animals, or vehicles in the race move, how the spectators react, and what happens at the end of the race.

 ## Verbs Times Two

You learned about prefixes on the **Building Vocabulary** pages. Make a list of verbs relating to cooking, sports, or schoolwork. See how many of the verbs can be changed with the addition of a prefix. Write at least five sets of sentences using the verbs with and without their prefixes.

Example: skiing—wax, rewax

1. I waxed my skis before getting on the lift.
2. I rewaxed them the next morning.

Unit Checkup

Think Back	Think Ahead
◆ What did you learn about how-to paragraphs in this unit? What did you do to write one?	◆ How will what you learned about writing a how-to paragraph help you explain things clearer? ◆ How will visualizing help you plan steps in a how-to paragraph?
◆ Look at the writing you did in this unit. How did subject-verb agreement help you express your ideas?	◆ What is one way action verbs help improve your writing?

How-to Paragraphs   *pages 112–113*

Read the how-to paragraph. Then follow the directions.

> You can print designs with a potato! First, gather your materials: a potato, a sharp knife, thick paper, and some watercolor paints (temperas). Wash the potato, and cut it in half. On the cut side of the potato, carve a design. When cutting, make sure that the shape to be printed stands out at least ¼ inch. Dip the design in paint, and press on the paper. Let the paint dry.

1. Write the topic sentence.
2. List the materials needed.
3. Write the first step.
4. In what order are all the steps listed?
5. Write the last step.

Visualizing Steps in a Process   *page 114*

Visualize potting a plant. Rewrite these steps in the correct order.

6. Water the plant.
7. Put the plant in the soil, covering the roots.
8. Put soil in the pot about halfway to the top.
9. Add more soil to fill the pot.
10. Place small stones in the bottom of a pot.

Adjusting for Audience and Purpose *page 115*

Read the short paragraph about making a tuna sandwich. Write how you would change the paragraph for each of the following audiences.

> Chop tuna finely, and add diced celery. Add mayonnaise to moisten. Mix ingredients well. Spread them on bread.

11. someone from another country where tuna in cans is not common

12. a preschool child

13. restaurant cooks

The Writing Process *pages 116–124*

Write the letter of the correct response to each question.

14. In preparing a how-to paragraph, a chart helps you to
    a. select a topic.
    b. organize your information.
    c. brainstorm ideas.

15. When writing the topic sentence of a how-to paragraph, be sure to
    a. state the activity or project to be explained.
    b. give the first step.
    c. tell what materials will be needed.

16. In revising, you notice a step is out of time order. What editing mark would you use to show that the sentence needs to be moved?
    a. ⟳   b. ∿   c. ﻭ

17. If how-to paragraphs were placed in a class book, what should be in the front of the book?
    a. a sample project
    b. a table of contents
    c. an index

Action Verbs *pages 128–129*

Write the verb from each sentence.

18. All his life, Simon dreamed of a career as an astronaut.
19. He joined the Air Force after college.
20. Alas, Simon was not qualified for the astronaut program.
21. Simon became an even better and more determined student because of this disappointment.
22. Today, Simon works behind a huge control panel at the NASA Space Center in Houston, Texas.

Linking Verbs *pages 130–131*

Write the verb from each sentence. Label it *action* or *linking.*

23. The sixth grade at the Sagamore School raised money for a local shelter.
24. Their money provided nutritious meals for homeless people.
25. The students held car washes, bake sales, rummage sales, and a walkathon.
26. Mr. Romero, the pet shop owner, was a big contributor.
27. The students felt proud of their good deeds.

Main Verbs and Helping Verbs *pages 132–133*

Write the verb phrase from each sentence. Underline each helping verb once. Underline the main verb twice.

28. Have you heard of the great architect Frank Lloyd Wright?
29. A house's relationship to its environment did matter a great deal to Wright.
30. Many homes of his time did not fit well into their environment.
31. Frank Lloyd Wright would always include the landscape— trees, rocks, even a waterfall—in his overall design.
32. Wright will long be remembered as a true creative genius.

Principal Parts of Verbs *pages 134–135*

Write the main verb from each sentence. Label it *present, present participle, past,* or *past participle.*

33. Allie has studied dancing for seven years now.
34. She is currently taking dance classes four afternoons a week after school and on Saturday mornings.
35. Allie loved dancing and music even as a very young child.
36. Allie and her friend Melissa are creating a dance routine of their own for the spring show.
37. Mr. and Mrs. Tanzer are very proud of Allie's hard work and accomplishments.

Present, Past, and Future Tenses *pages 136–137*

Write a sentence with each verb, using the tense in parentheses.

38. arrange (future)
39. smell (present)
40. cook (present)
41. clean (past)
42. list (past)

43. enter (future)
44. skip (present)
45. capitalize (present)
46. plan (future)
47. laugh (past)

Perfect Tenses   *pages 138–139*

Write each sentence, using the correct perfect tense of the verb in parentheses.

48. David was very disappointed. He _____ to improve his math grade this term, but he received only a C. (hope)
49. The teacher is pleased, however, because David's English and social studies grades _____. (improve)
50. She said, "You _____ very hard this term. I'm proud of you!" (work)
51. "I know," she continued, "that by next report card, you _____ 10 points to your math grade." (add)
52. When David got home that day, his father told him not to feel so glum. He _____ even _____ math once when he was a boy, and now he worked with numbers in the bank every day. (fail)

Subject-Verb Agreement   *pages 140–141*

Rewrite each sentence to correct the error in subject-verb agreement.

53. The Martons has lived in the United States since 1956.
54. Mrs. Marton teach French and Italian at Cliffside College.
55. Both Ferenc and Eva speaks several languages.
56. The Marton children is American citizens because they were born in this country.

Agreement of Verbs with Compound Subjects

pages 142–143

Rewrite each sentence, correcting the error in subject-verb agreement.
57. Bottles, cans, and papers litters the beaches of our town.
58. Jodi and Ed thinks we should select a clean-up committee.
59. Either Tucker's Hardware or Beach Bluff Supermarket provide the trash bags.
60. Lian's Coffee Shop and Dembrowski's Restaurant donates refreshments for the workers.

Prefixes: Parts for the Word Builder   *pages 144–145*

Read each sentence. Write each word formed with a prefix. Then underline the prefix.

61. Lurene talked about her performance in a postgame interview.
62. She wished that the game could be replayed.
63. "We are going to discontinue our schedule of weekly practices," the coach said.
64. "The number of practices is unimportant. It's what we do at those practices that counts," said Mr. Enriquez.

UNIT

4

THIRD ANNUAL COMEDY COMPETITION

Comparing and Contrasting

◆ **COMPOSITION FOCUS:** **Paragraphs of Comparison and Contrast**

◆ **LANGUAGE FOCUS:** **Verbs**

What is your favorite sport? Who is your favorite singer? To decide, you first think about how two or more sports, or singers, are alike and different. In other words, you compare and contrast.

Writers often entertain their readers by comparing and contrasting characters, places, or events. Omar S. Castañeda enjoys writing about characters from different cultures. In this unit you, too, will write paragraphs that compare and contrast.

◆ === *WARMING UP* === ◆

IN YOUR JOURNAL

Compare and contrast ways that you now spend your free time with ways that you used to spend it.

WORD GAME

WORK IN A GROUP

"*Hot* is to *cold* as *summer* is to *winter*" is an example of an analogy. An analogy can tell how words with different meanings are alike in at least one way. Complete the following analogies. Create others to share with classmates.

1. *Up* is to *down* as *high* is to _____ .
2. *Gulp* is to *swallow* as *screech* is to _____ .

Omar S. Castañeda writes stories *to entertain* readers.

Reading with a Writer's Eye
Comparison and Contrast

How can two boys be best friends when they seem to be completely different? How can they agree on a way to do a school project? You'll find out when you read this funny story by Omar S. Castañeda. As you read, notice how the writer describes the ways in which the main characters are alike and different.

The Most-Least Pizza to Go
by Omar S. Castañeda

Steve and Orlando lived in the same building in New York City, but that's right where their similarities ended. "It's beyond me how you two can be best friends," Mrs. Zhang said to them on the day of their assignment on cooperation. "And I sure don't know how you two are going to manage."

"Don't you worry," Steve said. "We're going to show the class that we can make something really big."

Orlando shook his head. "When we're done you're going to see the smallest project ever, but it'll also be the best."

Mrs. Zhang laughed. "If I see you two agree on anything, I'll see the most surprising project, I know that!"

After school, Orlando took the elevator from the first floor to Steve's apartment on the top floor. They were going to brainstorm as they watched boats work their way up and down the Hudson River. Steve's father had left them a box of cereal and apple juice so they would have energy to think.

Steve took a gulp from a big tumbler of apple juice. "We have to come up with something really good. Ours is the last project."

Orlando nodded. He drank his apple juice through a straw. "Some of the other kids have already said we won't be able to do it. They think we can't agree on anything."

Both of the boys remembered how the Urdang twins had done a project on similarities. They both wore the same clothes, wore their hair the same, and danced so that they looked like two sides of a mirror.

"We'll show them."

"You bet!" Orlando agreed.

And the two boys began to brainstorm. They thought a trip would be a good project. Steve wanted them to be class guides to the World Trade Center. Orlando thought it would be more fun to be guides on the ferry around Manhattan. Next, Steve wanted to do a project with a telescope, but Orlando wanted to do a project with a microscope. Orlando said they should write something on the head of a pin.

"Yeah!" Steve said. "We can make a gigantic pin and write the Gettysburg Address on it and put it on top of the school."

Orlando shook his head. "Are you crazy? Everyone will think the school is a pincushion."

"This is hopeless," Steve said. "Maybe everyone is right: we'll never agree on anything."

"I know," Orlando sighed. "There's only one thing we both like, and that's pizza—and we can't . . ."

"Hey! Let's make a pizza!"

"Great idea!" Orlando answered. "We'll make a cheese pizza."

"No, let's make a pizza with everything on it."

"Here we go again," Orlando said.

And the two boys slumped down in their chairs overlooking the Hudson River and thought and thought. Maybe it was their stomachs growling or the fact that neither could get the pizza out of his head, but both of them suddenly shot up together from the chairs and shouted, "I got it!" Since they were best friends, they knew they both had the same idea.

The next day, rumors started to fly around school that Orlando and Steve had agreed on a project. But the biggest surprise was that they were going to make a Most-Least Pizza to Go. What that meant, no one knew, but everyone had fun trying to guess.

The other students thought the boys would make pizzas different in size, number, and kind. Some thought Steve would make the biggest pizza and Orlando would make the littlest. Some thought Orlando would make one pizza and Steve would make more pizzas than they could count. Some thought that the boys would make two very different kinds of pizzas.

The only thing everyone knew for sure was that Steve and Orlando weren't going to let their secret out. They would all have to wait until the great pizza day.

Then, after days of whispers and days of friends trying to spy on their plans, the day came when both boys walked into the classroom with a huge box completely wrapped in plain brown paper. It smelled wonderful. Everyone was quiet. They studied social studies and literature and they went to gym class, but no one could get the delicious smell of that pizza out of his or her head. Finally, it came time for the two boys to reveal their project to the class.

Steve stood on one side and Orlando stood on the other. With one big pull, the paper fell away to reveal their fabulous Most-Least Pizza to Go. The students were flabbergasted to see two pizzas, one above the other, separated by tall pepperoni sticks. The top pizza had cheese, sausage, onions, and all the other things normal pizzas have, but it also had peanut butter, pitted dates, pineapple, cereal, sunflower seeds, and other things too weird to mention. The bottom pizza was a crispy thin crust with just the faintest white of cheese and the faintest red of tomato sauce and nothing else. No one moved a muscle as they looked at the Most-Least Pizza to Go.

"Try mine," Steve said, pointing to the top pizza.

"Try mine," Orlando said, showing off the bottom pizza.

Then, as the class sat there wondering who was going to be the first to try the strange thing, the top pizza started to bend down. It sagged under the weight of all that stuff until suddenly the pizza just split apart. Half of the things on top plopped down on the bottom.

The two boys shouted, "Oh, no!" But it was too late: their pizzas were mixed. "Oh, no," they said again. "Now it's not the Most-Least Pizza to Go anymore."

Someone shouted, "Actually it's now both most *and* least!"

"Does that mean it is just right?" Mrs. Zhang said. She spoke the words as if she were reading "Goldilocks and the Three Bears."

The whole class laughed. "Just right" was probably the one phrase that least described the pizza. Steve and Orlando looked at each other and then at their strange pizza. Steve thought that maybe they could fix it by adding just one item. Orlando thought that maybe they should remove just one item. Mrs. Zhang called for volunteers to try the most-least pizza. For once, however, the whole class was silent.

Respond

1. Which way of doing things do you like better, Steve's or Orlando's? What information about the boys' differences helped you decide on your answer?

Discuss

2. What details does the writer give to show how Steve and Orlando are alike? What details does he give to show how they are different?

3. Which do you think are more important to the story—the boys' similarities or their differences? Why?

Thinking As a Writer
Analyzing Paragraphs of Comparison and Contrast

Writer's Guide

A paragraph of comparison or contrast

◆ tells about the similarities or differences of two or more items.

◆ answers the same questions about each item.

A **paragraph of comparison** tells how two or more people or things are similar. A **paragraph of contrast** tells how two or more people or things are different. Often a topic sentence tells what will be compared or contrasted. Detail sentences describe the similarities or the differences.

> Steve and Orlando were alike in a few ways. They both lived in the same building in New York City, and they were both in Mrs. Zhang's class. They both liked apple juice and pizza. They liked each other, too.

The **topic sentence** in a paragraph of comparison tells what will be compared.

Detail sentences describe features the items have in common.

> What most people noticed about Steve and Orlando, though, was the ways they were different. Orlando, for example, was quieter than Steve. Orlando used a straw to sip his drinks. Steve preferred to drink out of a glass. The difference that really mattered, however, was that Steve liked everything big. Orlando, in contrast, liked things that were small. It should have been no surprise that Steve's part of their "Most-Least Pizza" had everything on it and Orlando's part had just a little tomato sauce and cheese. Only such unusual friends could have made such an unusual pizza!

The **topic sentence** in a paragraph of contrast tells what will be contrasted.

Detail sentences describe differences.

Transition words such as *both* show the writer is making a comparison. Other signal words such as *in contrast* and *however* show the writer is making a contrast.

Discuss

1. What do the two paragraphs compare and contrast? Which sentences give this information?
2. How is information in the first paragraph organized differently from the information in the second paragraph?

Try Your Hand

A. Analyze Topic Sentences Read each topic sentence. Write what items will be compared and contrasted in the paragraph.

1. The Rose Brothers' Circus and Big Top both put on good circus shows.
2. We used to like camping at Chenago State Park, but we don't like it anymore.
3. Both Jan and Tyson work at Bayview Aquarium.
4. Starr Flyte and her sister, Wing, have very different circus acts.

B. Identify Comparison and Contrast Write each item. Label it *comparison* or *contrast*. Then underline the key words that tell the similarity or difference.

5. The Rose Brothers' Circus is a one-ring circus, just like Big Top.
6. In the old days we never saw bears at Chenago State Park, but now there are lots of bears.
7. Jan tells people about the fish, while Tyson feeds the fish.
8. Starr is a trapeze artist and so is Wing.

C. Identify Categories of Information Read each pair of sentences. Write what question they both answer.

9. The Rose Brothers' Circus has a two-hour show. The Big Top show lasts only an hour.
10. Food used to be safe in camp in Chenago, but now the bears eat everybody's lunch.
11. Jan works on Mondays and Wednesdays, and Tyson works on Thursdays and Saturdays.
12. Starr wears a leotard. Wing, by contrast, wears a black suit, a bow tie, and a top hat.

D. Read Stories That Compare and Contrast Find a short story that compares and contrasts two characters. Read the story aloud to a partner, identifying the characters and discussing their similarities and differences.

Writer's Notebook

Collecting Transition Words
Look at the word *both* and the phrase *in contrast* in the paragraphs about the two boys. Notice how these words keep the writer's ideas organized. Look for other such signal words and phrases as you read. Record them in your *Writer's Notebook*, along with a sentence showing how each one is used. Use the words you collect to keep ideas and information organized when you write paragraphs of comparison and contrast.

Thinking As a Writer
Evaluating to Compare and Contrast

Writer's Guide

To write paragraphs of comparison or contrast, good writers

◆ observe similarities and differences between two items.

◆ choose categories of information that reveal characteristics of both items.

◆ compare and contrast the items based on the categories of information.

Before a writer is ready to compare or contrast two items, he or she observes them carefully. The writer chooses several categories of information that reveal characteristics of both items. The categories may be size, color, purpose, or other important qualities. Then the writer discusses the same categories of information in the same part of a paragraph.

Writers often use a Venn diagram to plan paragraphs of comparison and contrast. Study this Venn diagram that shows the differences and similarities between Steve and Orlando.

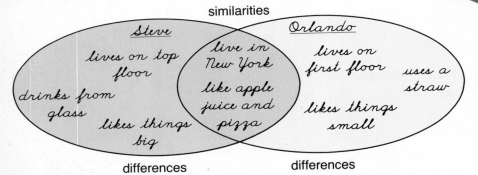

similarities

Steve
lives on top floor
drinks from glass
likes things big

live in New York
like apple juice and pizza

Orlando
lives on first floor
uses a straw
likes things small

differences   differences

Before you write paragraphs of comparison and contrast, choose several characteristics of each item. Then categorize the information, and compare or contrast the same kind of information in the same part of the paragraph.

Discuss

1. Reread the paragraphs on page 155. Are these good examples of comparison and contrast? Why or why not?
2. Read this sentence: *Orlando was tall and quiet, but Steve's brown hair seemed to stick straight up when he was thinking hard.*
   Why is this sentence a poor example of comparison and contrast?

Try Your Hand

Chart Similarities and Differences Make a Venn diagram showing the similarities and differences between two classmates. Then compare diagrams with a classmate, and discuss any differences.

Developing the Writer's Craft
Using Enough Details

When good writers compare or contrast two items, they discuss a range of different features. In this way they make sure that readers really understand the similarities and differences between the items. For example, Omar S. Castañeda shows three projects Steve and Orlando consider before they make their pizza. Each example shows a specific difference of opinion between the boys. The three examples together, however, reveal the general difference of personality between the boys.

Good writers also make sure that the features they discuss are important ones. The most important difference between Steve and Orlando, for example, is that Steve likes everything big and Orlando likes everything little. Omar S. Castañeda gives many examples that show this important difference. We would not understand this difference if the writer had focused only on the boys' hair color.

When you write your paragraphs of comparison and contrast, focus on important features. Include enough details to reveal the main similarities and differences between your subjects.

Discuss

1. Look at the paragraph on page 156 that describes the most-least pizza. Does the writer give enough important details to show the difference between the two parts? Explain your answer.
2. In another story the appearance of the boys might be important. What details might you give to compare and contrast their appearance?

Try Your Hand

Use Enough Details   Think of two foods you like. Think of several important ways in which those foods are alike and several in which they are different. Write three or four sentences telling how the foods are alike and different, but do not name the foods in your sentences. Trade papers with a partner, and see if your partner can guess what your foods are.

1 Prewriting
Paragraphs of Comparison and Contrast

Writer's Guide

Prewriting Checklist

☑ Brainstorm characters to write about.

☑ Select two characters.

☑ Think about your audience and your purpose.

☑ Gather details to compare and contrast.

☑ Organize the facts.

Hector, a student at Wedderburn School, wanted to write some paragraphs of comparison and contrast to amuse and inform his classmates. He used the checklist in the **Writer's Guide** to help him plan his paragraphs. Look at what he did.

◆ Brainstorming and Selecting a Topic

First, Hector brainstormed a list of possible characters to write about in his paragraphs. Look at Hector's list. He included as many pairs of characters as he could think of.

Next, Hector read over his list and crossed out characters his audience might not know. Because he wanted to amuse his readers, he also crossed off characters who would have to be taken seriously.

Finally, Hector decided to write about two candidates for "Dog Days" mascot. Every year his school had a "Dog Days of Summer" party to celebrate the end of the school year, and the students chose a dog to serve as the mascot for this party. Hector was sure his audience would find a report on the two leading candidates for "Dog Days" mascot both interesting and amusing.

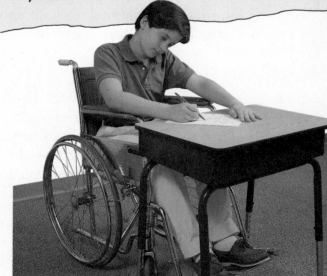

my two best friends

two candidates for state senate

two candidates for "Dog Days" mascot

two best teachers in the school

two comic book characters

two candidates for student body president

Discuss

1. Look at each pair of characters Hector crossed off his list. Why do you think he decided not to write about these topics?
2. If Hector were writing a serious story for his student newspaper, which might he have chosen? Why?

◆ Gathering Information

When he was ready to gather information, Hector wrote the questions he wanted to answer about each character. Look at some of Hector's questions.

> What do the dogs look like?
> What kinds of dogs are they?
> How do they get along with people?
> How do they spend their time?
> What trouble, if any, do they cause?

Next, Hector went to look at the two dogs, Couch Potato Pete and Moxie Maxie. Then, he interviewed the owners of the dogs. He also interviewed neighbors and classmates who knew the dogs. He recorded information about each dog under a separate heading. Look at some of his notes.

Couch Potato Pete	Moxie Maxie
setter (English)	red coat
watches TV all day	Irish setter
doesn't bark much	good dog
black and white	doesn't bark
won obedience contest	runs and plays a lot
16 ways to play dead	hides her toys
eats too much	very friendly
loves people	

Discuss

1. Was Hector wise to prepare questions before he started gathering information? Why or why not?
2. Which source of information might Hector have found most useful? Which was probably least useful? Why?
3. What are some other questions Hector might ask?

◆ Organizing the Facts

After Hector had gathered all the information he needed, he scanned his notes. He decided which of the facts he had gathered showed similarities between the two dogs and which ones showed differences. Then he organized his facts by copying the most important ones onto a Venn diagram that showed the similarities and differences between the two dogs.

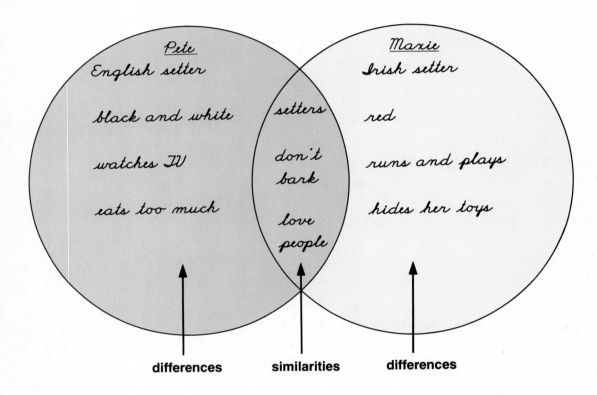

Pete
English setter

black and white

watches TV

eats too much

setters

don't bark

love people

Maxie
Irish setter

red

runs and plays

hides her toys

differences   **similarities**   **differences**

Discuss

1. Hector drew a Venn diagram—two overlapping circles. What does each circle stand for? What kind of information did he write in the area where the circles overlapped? Is this a good way to diagram similarities and differences? Why or why not?
2. Look at the list of features that the dogs do not share. Will Hector's chart help him to keep his paragraph of contrast organized so that he discusses the same categories of information about each dog? Explain your answer.
3. What else can Hector do to organize his information before he starts writing?

WRITING PROCESS

Try Your Hand

Now plan paragraphs of comparison and contrast of your own.

A. Brainstorm and Select a Topic Think of several categories of characters, such as people you know, people in the news, and characters from books. Choose one category that interests you and will interest and amuse your audience. List as many pairs of characters as you can in this category. Think about your topic and your audience.

◆ Cross out characters who may not want you to write about them.

◆ Cross out characters about whom you will not be able to gather information.

◆ Cross out characters who will not interest and amuse your audience.

◆ Of the characters left on your list, circle the pair with the most interesting similarities and differences. They will be the topic of your paragraphs of comparison and contrast.

B. Gather Information When you are satisfied with your topic, prepare a list of questions you will want to answer about your two characters. Then gather information to answer the questions, using any of the following techniques that fit your topic.

◆ Talk to or observe the characters.

◆ Read about the characters, or watch them on TV or in movies.

◆ Interview people who know the characters or know about them. Take notes during the interview. If you need help, follow the suggestions in **Tips on How to Conduct an Interview** on page 166.

C. Organize the Facts Review your notes. Then group the facts that show similarities and, separately, those that show differences. You may want to copy the facts you want to use onto a diagram like the one Hector made.

◆ Draw a Venn diagram—two overlapping circles.

◆ List differences between the characters where the circles are separate.

◆ List similarities between the characters where the circles overlap.

 Save your notes and your diagram in your *Writer's Notebook.* **You will use them when you draft your paragraphs of comparison and contrast.**

Listening and Speaking
Tips on How to Conduct an Interview

1. Prepare your questions before the interview. Base your questions on the kind of information you want to gather.
2. At the interview, introduce yourself if necessary, and tell why you want to conduct the interview.
3. Ask questions clearly. Use polite language.
4. After you ask a question, pay close attention to the answer. Listen for details that relate to the main idea of your question. If you do not understand the answer, ask the person to explain further.
5. Take notes. Write only a few key words about each detail. Learn to keep listening while you write your notes. You may also want to use a tape recorder, if the person you are interviewing does not mind.
6. If any additional questions occur to you during the interview, ask them.
7. Be sure you know how to spell the name of the person you are interviewing. Check the spelling of any other names that come up during the interview. Make sure you know how to get back in touch with the person you have interviewed in case you have further questions.
8. When you are finished, thank the person for the interview.
9. After the interview, look over your notes as soon as you can to make sure you can read them and to make sure that you have enough information. Add any information you still remember that you may not have written down.

2 Drafting
Paragraphs of Comparison and Contrast

Writer's Guide
Drafting Checklist
- ☑ Use your notes and your diagram for ideas.
- ☑ Write how the characters are alike.
- ☑ Write how the characters are different.
- ☑ Answer the same questions about each character.

Hector followed the checklist in the **Writer's Guide** to draft his paragraphs. Look at what he did.

> Who will be our "Dog Days Dog" this year — Couch Potato Pete or Moxie Maxie? Before you decide, consider the facts. Both dogs are setters, so either one could set the mood for "Dog Days." People who know them say that both dogs love people and neither one barks much. Couch Potato Pete once won an obedience contest by showing 16 ways to play dead.

Discuss

1. Look at Hector's topic sentence. What information does he use to connect Couch Potato Pete and Moxie Maxie?
2. What kind of information will Hector probably give in the next paragraph? What are some details he may mention?

Try Your Hand

Now draft your paragraphs of comparison and contrast.

A. Review Your Information Think about your information. Gather more information if you need to.

B. Think About Your TAP Remember that your task is to write paragraphs comparing and contrasting two characters. Your audience is your classmates. Your purpose is to amuse your audience and to give information about the two characters.

Task: What?
Audience: Who?
Purpose: Why?

C. Write Your First Draft Follow the steps in the **Drafting Checklist** to write your paragraphs.

When you write your draft, just put all your ideas on paper. Do not worry about spelling, punctuation, or grammar. You can correct the draft later.

Save your first draft in your *Writer's Notebook*. You will use it when you revise your paragraphs.

3 Responding and Revising
Paragraphs of Comparison and Contrast

Hector used the checklist in the **Writer's Guide** to revise his paragraphs. Look at what he did.

◆ Checking Information

Hector cut one detail and replaced another in order to keep his paragraphs focused on similarities and differences between the characters. He used this mark ✗ to show what he was cutting. He used this mark ∧ to show what he was replacing.

◆ Checking Organization

Hector moved one sentence so that his ideas would flow more logically. He used this mark ↺ to show the move.

◆ Checking Language

Hector also added some transition words to make his language flow more smoothly. He used this mark ∧ to show where he wanted to add words.

Cut

Replace

Add

Move

> Who will be our "Dog Days Dog" this year — Couch Potato Pete or Moxie Maxie? Before you decide, consider the facts. Both dogs are setters, so either one could set the mood for "Dog Days." People who know them say that both dogs love people and neither one of them barks much. Couch Potato Pete once won an obedience contest by showing 16 ways to play dead.
>
> The dogs look different, however. Couch Potato Pete is a black-and-white dog, but Maxie ~~is an~~ *has a red coat* Irish Setter. Couch Potato Pete's favorite activity is sitting around watching TV. Maxie loves to *in contrast,* run and play. "She wears us all out, but she's such fun that we don't care," Betty Hernandez says. The dogs behave differently, too.

Discuss

1. Hector cut one detail and replaced another. How did these changes improve his paragraphs?
2. Hector moved one sentence to make his ideas flow more logically. Do you agree with Hector? Why or why not?
3. Are there other changes Hector should have made? Explain your answer.

Try Your Hand

Now revise your first draft.

A. Read Your First Draft As you read your paragraphs, think about your audience and your purpose. Read your paragraphs silently or to a partner to see whether they are complete and well organized. Ask yourself or your partner the questions in the box.

Responding and Revising Strategies

✔ **Respond**
Ask yourself or a partner:

- Do I make clear what characters I am comparing and contrasting?

- Do I tell completely how the characters are similar and different?

- Does each paragraph flow in a way that makes sense?

- Does my language flow smoothly?

✔ **Revise**
Try these solutions:

- **Add** a topic sentence to each paragraph.

- **Add** details to answer the same questions about both characters.

- **Move** information so that your ideas follow in logical order.

- **Add** transition words. See the **Revising Workshop** on page 170.

B. Make Your Changes If the answer to any question in the box is *no,* try the solution. Use the **Editor's Marks** to show your changes.

C. Review Your Paragraphs Again Decide whether there is anything else you want to revise. Keep revising your paragraphs until you feel they are well organized and complete.

EDITOR'S MARKS

∧ Add something.

⌿ Cut something.

◡ Move something.

⋀ Replace something.

 Save your revised paragraphs in your *Writer's Notebook.* You will use them when you proofread your paragraphs.

Revising Workshop
Using Effective Transitions

Good writers use language that flows smoothly. They arrange their ideas so that each sentence follows from the one before. They also use transition words to show how sentences are related. Compare these two groups of sentences.

1. The more Mavis cooked, the fatter Avis got. Mavis solved their problem by learning to cook low-calorie foods. Mavis was a wonderful cook. She ate very little. Her sister, Avis, hated to cook but loved to eat.

2. Mavis was a wonderful cook. However, she ate very little. Her sister, Avis, in contrast, hated to cook but loved to eat. The more Mavis cooked, the fatter Avis got. Finally, Mavis solved their problem by learning to cook low-calorie foods.

Notice that in the second group of sentences, the writer has put the ideas in logical order. The writer has also added the underlined transition words, which help carry the reader smoothly from one sentence to the next. Writers may use transition words to link and to group ideas. Notice that the transition words are separated from the rest of the sentence with commas.

Practice

Write each group of sentences in a smooth, logical order. Add any transition words that are needed. Use transition words from the box.

1. Rob told wonderful stories. His handwriting and spelling were terrible. Rob asked his friend Ahmed to record his stories for him. Ahmed always won spelling bees in school, and his handwriting was beautiful. The two boys learned to use their strengths to help each other.

2. Petra was not as good as she seemed. Fuzzball, the big gray cat, was always in trouble. Petra, the orange one, seemed like a little angel. When Fuzzball did something wrong, everybody knew it. Petra made sure that all her mischief was blamed on Fuzzball.

| in contrast |
| however |
| although |
| on the one hand |
| on the other hand |
| then |
| finally |
| therefore |
| in fact |
| indeed |

4 Proofreading
Paragraphs of Comparison and Contrast

Writer's Guide

Proofreading Checklist

- ☑ Check for errors in capitalization.
- ☑ Check for errors in punctuation.
- ☑ Check to see that all your paragraphs are indented.
- ☑ Check for errors in grammar. Be sure that your subjects and verbs agree.
- ☑ Circle any words you think are misspelled. Find out how to spell them correctly.
- ⇨ For proofreading help, use the **Writer's Handbook.**

After revising his paragraphs, Hector used the **Writer's Guide** and the **Editor's Marks** to proofread them. Look at what he did.

> ⁀Is⁀ Are Couch Potato Pete or Moxie Maxie the best "Dog days Dog?" i couldn't say. However, when you're voting, you might think about how you want to spend your "Dog Days." Will you spend summer lying around like Couch Potato Pete or playing outside like Moxie Maxie. After all, our mascot represent us—so let's pick one that show what we want to be.

Discuss

1. Look at Hector's proofread paragraph above. What kinds of corrections did he make?
2. Why did Hector change *Are* to *Is* in the first sentence? Why do you think he may have made this mistake?

Try Your Hand

Proofread Your Paragraphs   Now use the **Writer's Guide** and the **Editor's Marks** to proofread your paragraphs.

 Save your corrected paragraphs in your *Writer's Notebook.* You will use them when you publish your paragraphs.

EDITOR'S MARKS

- ≡ Capitalize.
- ⊙ Add a period.
- ∧ Add something.
- ⋏ Add a comma.
- ⱽⱽ Add quotation marks.
- ⸲ Cut something.
- ⌒ Replace something.
- ⁀ Transpose.
- ◯ Spell correctly.
- ⊓ Indent paragraph.
- / Make a lowercase letter.

5 Publishing
Paragraphs of Comparison and Contrast

Hector made a clean copy of his paragraphs and checked them to be sure he had not left anything out. Then he and his classmates published their paragraphs in a book called *Portrait Gallery: Wedderburn School Characters.* You can find Hector's paragraphs on pages 33–34 of the **Writer's Handbook.**

Here's how Hector and his classmates published their book of portraits.

1. Hector and his classmates made and decorated a title page for their book. They decided on the order in which their paragraphs would appear in the book. They allowed two facing pages for each set of paragraphs.

2. A student typed each set of paragraphs so that they fit on two facing pages.

3. They pasted the paragraphs onto the pages and added a drawing or a photograph of one of the characters described in the paragraphs. They numbered the pages.

4. They made a table of contents for their book of portraits. Then they duplicated and stapled the pages and the cover of the book.

5. The class put copies of the book of portraits in the school library for other students to see.

Discuss

1. Why would photographs or drawings of the characters be useful to include in a book of comparisons and contrasts?
2. Why is a table of contents important to have in a book that gives character sketches and comparisons of many different people or animals?

Try Your Hand

Publish Your Paragraphs of Comparison and Contrast Follow the checklist in the **Writer's Guide.** If possible, create a book of portraits, or try one of these ideas for sharing your paragraphs.

◆ Write the words *Portrait Gallery* on construction paper, and use the words as a title for a bulletin board display. Place your paragraphs on the bulletin board along with photographs or drawings of the characters being described.
◆ Read your paragraphs aloud to the class, but leave out the names of the characters. See whether your classmates can guess the two characters being described in the paragraphs.

Writing in the Content Areas

Use what you learned to write paragraphs that compare two people, animals, or things. Write a report or paragraphs for friends who share your interests. Use one of these ideas or an idea of your own.

Writer's Guide

When you write, remember the stages of the Writing Process.
- Prewriting
- Drafting
- Responding and Revising
- Proofreading
- Publishing

Science

Animals such as the lynx and the bobcat or the frog and the toad are similar in some ways and different in others. Read about two similar animals. What do they look like? Where do they live? What do they eat? How do they move?

Social Studies

What was life like before the invention of the computer, the telephone, or the automobile? Read about life before the development of some important invention. In what ways did the invention improve life? Are there ways in which life was better before the invention?

Literature

Who is your favorite fiction writer? What makes this author's books more interesting to you than those of another writer? Compare the characters, settings, and styles of two authors. Explain why one author's work appeals to you more than another's.

Mathematics

What would make a career in mathematics more or less interesting to you than a career in another field? Find out about one career in mathematics and one career in another area. What tasks does each job involve? Would you be working with people more in one job than in the other? Would traveling be part of either job?

A good comparison helps the reader look at things more closely to see how they are alike and how they are different. Which sister would you be more interested in meeting after reading these paragraphs of comparison and contrast?

Ramona and Beezus are two characters created by writer Beverly Cleary. They live in the same house. They have the same parents. They are, in fact, sisters.

However, these two sisters are very different. Ramona, the younger sister, is a little firecracker. She means well, yet she fights a great deal with her classmates and—sometimes—with the whole world. Once, she tore up an owl that one of her classmates had drawn because the girl had copied Ramona's work. Beezus, in stark contrast, is calm and practical. She is the kind of girl who follows rules and speaks only when spoken to.

◆ **Verbs in Paragraphs of Comparison and Contrast** The highlighted words are forms of irregular verbs. Notice the important role these highlighted words play in showing the similarities and differences between Ramona and Beezus.

◆ **Language Focus: Verbs** In the following lessons you will learn more about using irregular verbs correctly in your writing.

1 Irregular Verbs

REGULAR

◆ **FOCUS** An irregular verb does not end with *ed* to form the past and the past participle.

Remember that the past and the past participle of regular verbs are formed by adding *ed*. The past and the past participle of irregular verbs are not formed by adding *ed*.

Regular Verb bloom bloomed bloomed
Irregular Verb do did done

IRREGULAR

Three of the most important irregular verbs are *be, have,* and *do.* These are important helping verbs. Each one is also a main verb. The verb *be* is the most important linking verb. It has many forms, as shown in this chart.

The Verb *Be*				
	Present	**Present Participle**	**Past**	**Past Participle**
I	am	being	was	been
he, she, it, and singular nouns	is	being	was	been
we, you, they, and plural nouns	are	being	were	been

The verb *have* is used as a helping verb to form the perfect tenses. The helping verb *do* is often used in questions. The following charts show the forms of *have* and *do* used with various subjects.

The Verb *Have*				
	Present	**Present Participle**	**Past**	**Past Participle**
I, we, you, they, and plural nouns	have	having	had	had
he, she, it, and singular nouns	has	having	had	had

The Verb *Do*				
	Present	**Present Participle**	**Past**	**Past Participle**
I, we, you, they, and plural nouns	do	doing	did	done
he, she, it, and singular nouns	does	doing	did	done

Guided Practice

A. Identify the verb form in parentheses that correctly completes each sentence.

1. Roses (is, are) beautiful flowers.
2. (Does, Do) they bloom in your yard?
3. No, weeds (has, have) overtaken our garden.
4. I (has, have) pulled up all of the flowers and left the weeds.
5. I never said I (was, were) a gardener.
6. (Is, Are) you planning to plant a flower garden in your backyard?
7. I don't (has, have) any flowers to plant, but I may plant vegetables.
8. My grandmother (has, have) a large vegetable garden in her backyard.
9. She (does, do) all the work herself.
10. When (do, does) you think she will harvest the potatoes, corn, and green beans?
11. I'm not sure, but the vegetables will (has, have) to be harvested soon.
12. (Do, Does) you get to eat any of the vegetables?
13. Oh, yes! My grandmother's vegetables (is, are) the most delicious vegetables I (has, have) ever eaten.

THINK AND REMEMBER
- Form the past and past participle of **regular verbs** by adding *ed* to the present.
- Form the past and past participle of **irregular verbs,** such as *be, have,* and *do,* in other ways.

Independent Practice

B. Using the Correct Forms of *Be*, *Have*, and *Do*   Write the correct form of the verb in parentheses.

14. My mom (has, have) always liked daffodils.

MODEL > has

15. She (is, are) glad to see the first daffodils of spring.
16. However, I (does, do) not know a daffodil from a rose.
17. (Does, Do) you like flowers?
18. I (does, do) like to look at them, but I can't grow any.
19. Like you, I (am, is) not a gardener.
20. I (has, have) planted seeds before.
21. Weeds (was, were) all I grew.

C. Using *Be*, *Have*, and *Do* in Sentences   Use the correct present form of *be*, *have*, or *do* to complete each sentence.

22. We _____ roses and lilacs in our garden.

MODEL > We have roses and lilacs in our garden.

23. Lilacs _____ such a lovely smell!
24. A lilac bloom _____ actually a cluster of tiny flowers.
25. Each flower _____ four small petals.
26. _____ lilacs grow easily?
27. I _____ sure I can kill a lilac as easily as any other plant.

D. Proofreading: Checking for Correct Verb Usage   Find the error in each sentence. Write the sentence correctly.

28. Some flowers being tropical.

MODEL > Some flowers are tropical.

29. They is grown in warm climates.
30. One example are the orchid.
31. Orchids be not grown outdoors in New England.
32. Orchids does grow outdoors in Florida, however.
33. Do an orchid plant need a long growing season?
34. Weeds does not need any special season at all.
35. I is good at growing weeds.

Application — Writing, Speaking, Listening

Comic Dialogue   With a partner, brainstorm an argument that two flowers in a garden might have. Think of funny things the flowers might say. Write down the dialogue, and read it to the class. Use *be, have, do,* and other irregular verbs correctly. If you need help writing a dialogue, see page 39 of the **Writer's Handbook.**

2 More Irregular Verbs

◆ **FOCUS** Some irregular verbs follow a pattern when they change form.

The principal parts of irregular verbs are not formed according to a single rule. However, most do follow a certain pattern in their principal parts. In one group of irregular verbs the past participle is formed by adding *n* or *en* to the present form.

Present	Present Participle	Past	Past Participle
take	taking	took	taken
grow	growing	grew	grown
know	knowing	knew	known
eat	eating	ate	eaten
see	seeing	saw	seen
draw	drawing	drew	drawn
give	giving	gave	given

In another group of verbs, the past participle is formed by adding *n* or *en* to the past form.

Present	Present Participle	Past	Past Participle
speak	speaking	spoke	spoken
break	breaking	broke	broken
freeze	freezing	froze	frozen
choose	choosing	chose	chosen

In a third group of irregular verbs, the form of the past participle is the same as the present form.

Present	Present Participle	Past	Past Participle
become	becoming	became	become
come	coming	came	come
run	running	ran	run

In a fourth group of irregular verbs, the form of the past participle is the same as the past form.

Present	Present Participle	Past	Past Participle
say	saying	said	said
make	making	made	made
sell	selling	sold	sold
tell	telling	told	told
hold	holding	held	held
meet	meeting	met	met
spend	spending	spent	spent
mean	meaning	meant	meant
bend	bending	bent	bent
lend	lending	lent	lent
catch	catching	caught	caught
fight	fighting	fought	fought
think	thinking	thought	thought
buy	buying	bought	bought
stand	standing	stood	stood

Guided Practice

A. Identify the past and the past participle of each verb.

1. run   3. spend   5. freeze   7. give   9. eat
2. come   4. think   6. speak   8. meet   10. buy

THINK AND REMEMBER

- Remember that some irregular verbs can be grouped according to the way their past participles are formed.
- In one group of irregular verbs, add *n* or *en* to the present form.
- In another group of irregular verbs, add *n* or *en* to the past form.
- In a third group of irregular verbs, write the past participle in the same way as the present form.
- In a fourth group of irregular verbs, write the past participle in the same way as the past form.

Independent Practice

B. Writing Principal Parts of Irregular Verbs Write the past and the past participle of each verb.

11. rise

MODEL> rose, risen

12. grow	**15.** see	**18.** make	**21.** tell
13. know	**16.** choose	**19.** sell	**22.** mean
14. take	**17.** draw	**20.** fight	**23.** become

C. Using Irregular Verbs Correctly Write the past or the past participle form of the verb in parentheses that correctly completes each sentence.

24. I _____ the book *Don Quixote.* (buy)

MODEL> bought

25. The book has _____ a classic. (become)
26. The author has _____ a portrait of a peculiar man. (draw)
27. The hero, Don Quixote, _____ he was a knight. (think)
28. One day he _____ across some giants. (run)
29. Don Quixote _____ a battle with the giants. (fight)
30. Soon, he _____ his lance. (break)
31. The giants he had _____ were really windmills. (meet)
32. One evening Don Quixote _____ to an inn. (come)
33. He _____ everyone the inn was a castle. (tell)

D. Proofreading: Checking for Errors in Verb Usage Find the error in each sentence. Write the sentence correctly.

34. Cervantes telled stories.

MODEL> Cervantes told stories.

35. He had a life as exciting as any story he maded up.
36. Pirates selled him into slavery.
37. He spended five years as a slave.
38. He seen many things during his travels.
39. In 1605 Cervantes choosed to publish *Don Quixote.*
40. Soon, many people had buyed the book.

Application — Writing

Character Sketch Write a character sketch to share with your classmates. Describe the knight in the picture or another humorous character from a book you have read. Use irregular verbs correctly. If you need help writing a character sketch, see page 47 of the **Writer's Handbook.**

3 Direct Objects

◆ FOCUS   A **direct object** receives the action of the verb.

In the following sentence, *clown* is a direct object because it receives the action expressed by the verb *splashed*.

1. The water splashed the clown .

A direct object follows the verb. Some sentences are not complete without a direct object.

2. The clown wore makeup .   incomplete without *makeup*

A verb can have two or more direct objects.

3. One clown juggled dishes , bottles , and torches .

One or more words may come between a verb and its direct object. To find a direct object, say the verb, and then ask yourself "What?" or "Whom?"

4. Jugglers did many tricks .   did what?

5. We saw many talented and nimble acrobats .   saw whom?

Guided Practice

A. Identify the direct object in each sentence.

1. Peggy Willis joined the circus.
2. She chose *JoJo* as her clown name.
3. Older clowns helped Peggy.
4. The crowds liked Peggy's costume.
5. She greeted children and parents.
6. She performed cartwheels and other tricks.
7. Girls and boys clapped their hands.

THINK AND REMEMBER
◆ Remember that a **direct object** follows an action verb and shows who or what receives the action.
◆ To find the direct object, say the verb and ask yourself "What?" or "Whom?"

Independent Practice

B. Identifying Direct Objects Write the direct object in each sentence.

8. The Ringling brothers had a circus.
MODEL > circus
9. Charles and Alf Ringling played musical instruments.
10. John Ringling sang funny songs.
11. The brothers made tent poles and wooden stakes.
12. They bought some canvas and some wagons.
13. The young men opened a circus.
14. They advertised their show.
15. By 1889, the brothers had bought many circus animals.
16. They had 110 horses and three elephants.
17. People enjoyed the Ringling Brothers Circus.
18. By 1902, their circus filled sixty railroad cars.

C. Proofreading: Checking for Complete Sentences Add a direct object to each incomplete sentence. Write *complete* for each sentence that already expresses a complete thought.

19. Vendors sold.
MODEL > Vendors sold popcorn.
20. Sally and her family went to the circus.
21. Sally's father had gotten.
22. In the middle ring, the clowns were throwing buckets of water at one another.
23. The tightrope walkers wore.
24. Oh, look at the jugglers!
25. Sally's mother smiled at the children.
26. Sally's father bought.
27. The ringmaster announced.
28. During the parade, each elephant carried.
29. The horse pranced around the ring.
30. Under her seat Sally found.
31. Sally went to sleep smiling that night.

Application — Writing

Announcement Imagine that you are the circus ringmaster. Write an announcement introducing a circus act to your audience of children and adults. Give the names of the performers, and tell what they will be doing. Be sure to include a direct object in every sentence that needs one.

4 Indirect Objects

◆ **FOCUS**   An **indirect object** tells to whom or for whom the action of the verb is done.

Remember that an action verb may have a direct object. Sometimes a noun or a pronoun comes between the verb and its direct object. This word is an indirect object. It tells to whom or for whom the action of the verb is done.

indirect object   direct object

1. Tina gave Jeffrey a large book of jokes.

Notice that without the direct object, sentence 1 makes no sense. A sentence cannot have an indirect object unless it also has a direct object.

Indirect objects often follow the verbs *give, tell, show, promise, send, buy, sell, bring,* and *lend.* An indirect object can replace a phrase that begins with the words *to* or *for* without changing the meaning of the sentence. In these sentences, the words in color are indirect objects.

2. Jo told the joke to Bob.
3. Jo told Bob the joke.
4. Steve bought a book of jokes for Sally.
5. Steve bought Sally a book of jokes.

Guided Practice

A. Identify the direct object and the indirect object in each sentence.
1. Amy Foster showed her father the joke book.
2. Her father told his friends the funniest joke.
3. One friend lent Mr. Foster an even funnier book.
4. The librarian gave Sarah the same book.
5. I showed Jim the page with the funniest joke.
6. I wrote my pen pal the shortest joke.
7. I told Kate the title of the book.
8. Did Kate buy her aunt the book?

Independent Practice

B. Identifying Direct and Indirect Objects   Write the direct and the indirect object from each sentence. Label each word or words *DO* for *direct object* or *IO* for *indirect object.*

  9. Jack gives his family funny presents.

MODEL> family—IO   presents—DO

  10. Jack mailed Uncle Mike a huge package.
  11. He showed Mrs. Lucas the contents of the package.
  12. Jack had sent his uncle piles of tissue paper.
  13. Jack's uncle bought Jack a present.
  14. He gave the boy quite a fine present.
  15. Mike gave his nephew a jar of water.
  16. Jack mailed his uncle a thank-you note.
  17. He promised Uncle Mike something special for Christmas.

C. Revising: Writing Sentences with Indirect Objects
Rewrite each sentence using an indirect object.

  18. Mr. Souza bought some tickets for the Kelly twins.

MODEL> Mr. Souza bought the Kelly twins some tickets.

  19. The twins gave their tickets to a ticket collector.
  20. A young woman offered help to people in finding their seats.
  21. A vendor sold some popcorn to the children.
  22. The comedian told jokes to the crowd.
  23. He showed magic tricks to the audience.
  24. At the end of the show, he gave a special wink to the twins.

Application — Writing and Speaking

Joke   Write a joke to share with your classmates. Make up a new joke or recall one you already know. Practice telling the joke. Then tell it to your classmates. Use at least two indirect objects in your joke. Remember, a sentence cannot have an indirect object unless it also has a direct object.

5 Predicate Nominatives

◆ FOCUS A **predicate nominative** is a noun or a pronoun that follows a linking verb.

Remember that a linking verb connects the subject of a sentence with a word or words in the predicate. If the word is a noun or a pronoun, it is called a predicate nominative. A **pronoun** is a word such as *he, she,* or *it* that takes the place of a noun. A predicate nominative renames the subject or tells who or what the subject is.

predicate nominative

1. The parade was a special event .

predicate nominative

2. The person who organized the event was she .

A predicate nominative also may appear in an interrogative sentence that begins with a linking verb.

predicate nominative

3. Is she the person standing on that float?

Guided Practice

A. Identify the predicate nominative in each sentence.

1. Mrs. Ames was the planner of the parade.
2. She was also its coordinator.
3. One parade float was a seaweed cave.
4. The giant octopus inside was Rick.
5. Angelo was the giant clam.
6. My favorite person is he.
7. He is my best friend.
8. Was he the one in the strange costume?

THINK AND REMEMBER

- ◆ Remember that a noun or a pronoun that follows a linking verb is called a **predicate nominative.**
- ◆ Remember that a predicate nominative renames or tells who or what the subject is.

Independent Practice

B. Identifying Predicate Nominatives Write the predicate nominative from each sentence.

9. Mrs. Ellis is a sculptor.

MODEL > sculptor

10. She was the assembler of the reef float.
11. The ticket collector was Wilma's father.
12. He was also the printer of the tickets.
13. Tony was the first person to arrive.
14. The most excited boys were Angelo and Jim.
15. Jim's grandmother was the float's Loch Ness Monster.
16. Was his dad a character on the float, too?
17. Yes, he was a giant squid.
18. George was a sea creature.
19. Was he that weird, squiggly thing?
20. The woman who prepared and served the refreshments was Mrs. Page.
21. *Sea Sludge* was the name of the drink.
22. The only ice-cream flavor was "bluelagoony."

C. Completing Sentences Complete each sentence with a predicate nominative that fits the description given in parentheses.

23. The maker of the seaweed was _____. (a man)

MODEL > The maker of the seaweed was Mr. Walker.

24. The costume designers were _____. (two women)
25. The mechanics were _____. (two parents)
26. The funniest marchers in the parade were _____. (a boy and a girl)
27. The winning float was _____. (a sea-related name)
28. The two hardest workers on this year's parade committee were _____. (two students)

Application — Writing

Invitation Imagine that you and some classmates and parents are putting on a parade for the community. Write an invitation asking members of the community to attend. Tell when and where the parade will be, who and what will be in it, how people will be dressed, and who will organize it. Use at least three predicate nominatives in your work. If you need help writing an invitation, see page 54 of the **Writer's Handbook.**

6 Transitive and Intransitive Verbs

FOCUS
◆ A transitive verb has a direct object.
◆ An intransitive verb does not have a direct object.

An action verb followed by a direct object is called a **transitive verb.** An **intransitive verb** has no direct object. Action verbs can be transitive or intransitive. Linking verbs are always intransitive.

         subject   verb

1. The strange device awoke the sleeping
direct object
    student. **transitive**

       subject verb

2. The device was an original Rube
(no direct object)
    Goldberg invention. **intransitive**

The following sentences show how a single verb can be either transitive or intransitive.

3. Goldberg drew his contraptions. **transitive**

4. He drew carefully. **intransitive**

Your ear can sometimes tell you whether an action verb is transitive or intransitive. Read a sentence to yourself, and then repeat the verb, followed by the question "What?" or "Whom?" If the question has an answer, the verb is transitive.

5. We grinned at the silly contraption.

Notice that the questions "Grinned what?" and "Grinned whom?" make no sense. Therefore, *grinned* is an intransitive verb.

Guided Practice

A. Identify each underlined verb as *transitive* or *intransitive.*

  1. Rube Goldberg <u>drew</u> cartoons for a newspaper.
  2. One day his cartoon <u>showed</u> a complicated machine.
  3. People <u>laughed</u> heartily.
  4. They <u>wanted</u> more crazy machines.
  5. Soon Goldberg <u>was</u> famous.
  6. His machines <u>became</u> very popular.

Independent Practice

B. Identifying Transitive and Intransitive Verbs Write the verb from each sentence. Label it *transitive* or *intransitive.*

7. One Goldberg invention was a page turner.

MODEL › was—intransitive

8. The page turner has many parts.
9. The first part is a pump.
10. The pump pushes air into a whistle.
11. The whistle blows.
12. A goldfish mistakes the sound for a dinner bell.
13. The goldfish eats a worm.
14. A shelf drops.
15. A boxing glove punches a balloon.
16. The balloon breaks.
17. Air blows against a sail.
18. The sail turns in the breeze.
19. The sailor turns the page.

C. Proofreading: Checking for Complete Sentences Check each sentence. If it is complete, write *complete*. If it is incomplete, rewrite it with a direct object.

20. I like.

MODEL › I like funny inventions.

21. The children laughed.
22. The man found.
23. Amy described.
24. The newspaper arrived.
25. The boys departed.
26. Pablo wanted.
27. Yoshiko smiled.
28. The truck moved.

Application — Writing

Cartoon Caption Draw a silly invention for a humor magazine that might be read by sixth-graders. It should be a complicated or unusual machine to solve a simple problem. Describe your invention. Tell what it does and how it works. Use transitive and intransitive verbs.

7 Easily Confused Verb Pairs

◆ **FOCUS**   Sometimes a verb is confused with another verb.

Some verbs have very similar spellings or meanings. These verbs are sometimes confused with each other. Study these verb pairs carefully.

Verb	Meaning	Example
teach	give knowledge	Mr. Ito *teaches* science.
learn	receive knowledge	I *learned* about comets.
lend	give something that must be given back	The library *lends* books.
borrow	take something that must be given back	Max *borrowed* my pen.
let	permit or allow	*Let* your father sleep.
leave	go away from	The plane *leaves* shortly.
rise	get up or move higher	People *rise* for a judge.
raise	lift something up	I *raise* my hand.
set	place something somewhere	*Set* the book there.
sit	rest, as in a chair	*Sit* here by me.
lie	rest or recline	I *lie* in bed.
lay	put or place something	*Lay* the pillow here.

Guided Practice

A. Identify the verb in parentheses that correctly completes each sentence.
1. (Let, Leave) us watch the rest of the show.
2. (Borrow, Lend) me your pillow, too.
3. I'll (lay, lie) here and watch it.
4. This program can (teach, learn) us something.
5. The TV mime (sat, set) in a chair.
6. Then she pretended to (rise, raise).

THINK AND REMEMBER
◆ Avoid confusing pairs of verbs that look or sound similar.

Independent Practice

B. Using Verbs Correctly   Write the verb that correctly completes each sentence.

  7. The TV mime (borrows, lends) a hat from a passerby.

  MODEL ⟩ borrows

  8. She (raises, rises) the hat over her head.
  9. Then, she (sits, sets) the hat on a bench.
  10. The mime (sits, sets) down on the hat!
  11. Next, the mime (lies, lays) down on the floor.
  12. She pretends to (lie, lay) her head on a pillow.
  13. A loud noise makes her (rise, raise) suddenly.
  14. Now, she (sits, sets) a book on her lap.
  15. She wants someone to (lend, borrow) her money.
  16. Some of the audience begin to (let, leave).
  17. She pretends that she won't (let, leave) them go.
  18. She (teaches, learns) the audience about bees.
  19. I (teach, learn) about acting by watching the mime.

C. Proofreading: Checking for Correct Verb Usage   Find the error in each sentence. Rewrite the sentence correctly.

  20. Leave me stay up late.

  MODEL ⟩ Let me stay up late.

  21. This performer may learn me how to make people laugh.
  22. In one skit, someone pretends to let glue on the seat of a chair.
  23. The man sets down in the chair.
  24. He cannot raise out of the chair.
  25. The man asks a friend to borrow him a saw.
  26. The friend leaves him have the saw.
  27. The man lays on his stomach and pretends to saw himself off the chair.
  28. He sits the saw on the floor.
  29. Then he rises his head and smiles at the audience.
  30. Does the incident learn the man a lesson?

Application — Writing

Review   Write a review of a television show that you watch regularly. Tell about the main characters, and explain why you like or dislike the show. Give examples to support your opinion. Use each of the verbs in this lesson in your review. Be sure to use the verbs correctly.

8 Contractions

◆ FOCUS   A **contraction** is a shortened form of two words.

When you speak, you may run words together. When you write with an informal tone, you may include these words by using contractions. A contraction is two words put together with one or more letters left out. An apostrophe shows where letters are missing.

He is looking at the oars.   He's looking at the oars.

Many contractions are formed by combining the words *I, you, he, she, it, we,* and *they* with helping verbs such as *is, are, am, has, have, had, would,* and *will.* Many other contractions are formed by combining a verb with the word *not.*

Some Common Contractions		
I'm (I am)	they've (they have)	isn't (is not)
I'll (I will)	they'll (they will)	aren't (are not)
I've (I have)	they're (they are)	wasn't (was not)
he'd (he had)	they'd (they would)	wouldn't (would not)
he'd (he would)	they'd (they had)	don't (do not)
it's (it is)	you're (you are)	doesn't (does not)
it's (it has)	we'd (we would)	shouldn't (should not)
she's (she is)	we'll (we will)	mustn't (must not)
she's (she has)	we've (we have)	won't (will not)

Guided Practice

A. Identify the contractions and the words from which they are formed.
1. All these rowers won't fit in the boat.
2. It's not big enough for them.
3. They'll have to leave some rowers behind.
4. Who'll the team choose to stay in the boat?
5. Well, they didn't choose me.

THINK AND REMEMBER
◆ Form contractions by putting certain pairs of words together and replacing one or more letters with an apostrophe.
◆ Use contractions only when you mean to give your writing an informal tone.

Independent Practice

B. Identifying Contractions in Sentences   Write the contraction from each sentence and the words from which it is formed.

6. The rower who wasn't chosen met a friend on his way home.

MODEL ▷ wasn't—was not

7. "Your shoes don't match," said the friend.

8. "Why, it's true!" said the rower.

9. "I'm wearing a brown shoe and a blue shoe."

10. "I'd better change my shoes," he thought.

11. His other shoes weren't any better.

12. "That's not possible!" cried the rower.

13. "I've got another pair just like these in my closet!"

C. Proofreading: Checking for Errors in Contractions   Identify the error in each sentence. Rewrite the sentence correctly.

14. The rower was annoyed; "I'l stay on land," he decided.

MODEL ▷ The rower was annoyed; "I'll stay on land," he decided.

15. He thought, "Im going to visit my farmer friend."

16. "Ive been worried about the moon," said his friend.

17. "Its getting lower and lower every night."

18. "It looks as though i'ts on fire," said the rower.

19. "Soon it'l burn the crops."

20. "Wed better frighten it away," said the farmer.

21. The two men threw rocks until the'yd used them all up.

22. Finally, the moon set, but theyl never know where it went.

D. Using Contractions   Write a sentence using the contraction for each word or pair of words.

23. are not

MODEL ▷ These jokes aren't funny.

24. I will	**28.** you have	**32.** they had	**36.** cannot
25. we are	**29.** I would	**33.** could not	**37.** you had
26. has not	**30.** must not	**34.** we shall	**38.** she has
27. he is	**31.** is not	**35.** were not	**39.** will not

Application — Writing, Speaking, Listening

Nonsense Story   Tell a round-robin nonsense story with a small group. Have group members take turns adding to the story. Create funny characters and nonsensical situations. Then, write your own version of the story. Use contractions in your version.

Building Vocabulary
Homographs and Homophones: Humor with Puns

> Well, yesterday I went out in the rain with my purse open. I was expecting some change in the weather. Ha, ha. I'm just kidding. Have you heard any good jokes lately? Send them next time you write.
>
> Your friend,
>
> *Yoko*
>
> Yoko

The writer of this letter is playing with words. She is using *change* as a pun. A **pun** is a joke that uses one word to suggest two different meanings.

Many puns are based on homographs. **Homographs** are words that are spelled alike but have different meanings and sometimes have different pronunciations as well.

The joke in the letter makes sense only when you know that *change* can mean "to become different" as well as "money you get back." The double meaning of the homograph *change* is what makes the joke funny.

When you read a homograph, you usually use context clues to decide the word's meaning. Look at the highlighted words below.

1. My watch ticks as it keeps time.
2. The vet treated my dog for ticks .

From the context you can tell that *ticks* in the first sentence means "makes a clicking sound." In the second sentence *ticks* refers to tiny animals.

Some puns are based not on homographs but on homophones. **Homophones** are words that sound alike but have different meanings and spellings. Read this joke:

3. How can you kill time in the winter? You can sleigh it.

To understand the humor in this joke, you need to know about the homophone pair *slay* and *sleigh*. The word *slay* means "to kill." A *sleigh*, on the other hand, is a kind of sled.

You can use homophones and homographs to create humor in your writing. Think of the different meanings a word has, or of interesting homophone pairs. Then use the homophones or homographs in ways that refer to two very different contexts.

Reading Practice

Read each joke. Write the word that is used as a pun. Tell whether the pun is based on a homophone or a homograph. For homographs write both meanings of the word. For homophones write the two words.

1. What insect would make the best outfielder?
   A spider because it always catches flies.
2. What is the principal part of a horse?
   The mane part.
3. Why isn't a dog's nose 12 inches long?
   Because then it would be a foot.
4. What do bees do to earn a living?
   They cell their honey.
5. Why did the silly girl Sally sleep on the lamp?
   She was a light sleeper.
6. Why is a game of baseball like a pancake?
   Because they both need batters.

Writing Practice

A. Write two definitions for each homograph. Then use each word in a sentence. Use the sentence context to make the word meaning clear. Use a dictionary if you need help.

7. pick   9. pit   11. rib   13. date
8. quiver   10. grate   12. rest   14. trip

B. Write a homophone for each word. Use a dictionary if you need help. Then pick two of these homophone pairs and write your own jokes.

15. foul   17. peace   19. tail   21. eight
16. deer   18. plane   20. pear   22. steal

Project

Look in your school or classroom library for collections of jokes. Write ten jokes on ten separate index cards. Write five jokes that are based on homophones and five that are based on homographs. On the reverse side of the homograph cards, write the two homograph meanings that relate to the joke. On the reverse side of the homophone cards, write the homophone pairs. Share the jokes with classmates. Help any classmates who don't understand the jokes by showing them the backs of the cards.

Language Enrichment
Verbs

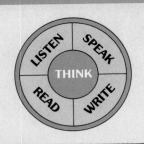

Use what you know about verbs to do these activities.

 Busy, Busy City

What happens on a busy city street? Write sentences describing things that you might see and hear at noon in the middle of a city. Use ideas from the picture. Add ideas from your own experience. Use both transitive and intransitive verbs in your sentences. Be sure that transitive verbs have direct objects.

 Word Wheel

Make a word wheel by cutting a small circle and a larger circle out of construction paper. With a pen, divide the large circle into eight sections. Then attach the small circle to the center of the large circle with a paper fastener. On the large circle, write eight direct objects. Use objects that can be found in a classroom. On the small circle, write a transitive verb commanding students to do something they could do in a classroom. Then draw a line from the center of the small circle to its edge. This will be the pointer. Spin the small circle to see what a player must do or pretend to do.

 Past Participle Search

Find eight past participles in this word search puzzle. Then create your own past participle puzzle. Use past participles from both regular and irregular verbs. Ask classmates to solve your puzzle.

B	E	C	O	M	E	P
X	M	R	X	F	J	Q
K	C	T	A	K	E	N
N	S	H	N	O	A	H
O	F	O	F	E	T	Y
W	R	U	L	G	E	R
N	B	G	W	D	N	D
C	J	H	I	Y	K	J
L	M	T	O	V	N	A
A	E	K	M	A	E	L
E	T	R	X	I	B	N

CONNECTING
LANGUAGE ↔ WRITING

In this unit you learned the patterns of many common irregular verbs. You learned that transitive verbs have direct objects but intransitive verbs do not. You looked closely at some verbs that are often confused with each other. You also practiced using contractions.

◆ **Using Verbs in Your Writing**   By using verbs and their objects correctly, you help others recognize what you are trying to communicate. Pay special attention to using verbs, their objects, and contractions correctly as you do these activities.

 What Was It? What Is It?

Look at the animals in the picture. Both of them once looked very different. Tell what each animal once was, how it looked, and what it did. Then describe each animal as it appears in the picture. Use past-tense and present-tense forms of the verbs *be, have,* and *do.*

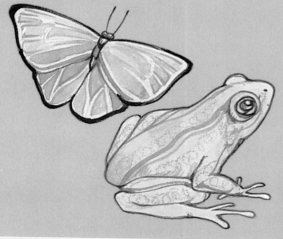

 Name Those Words

You have learned about homographs and homophones on the **Building Vocabulary** pages. Make a list of 5 pairs of words—a verb and a homophone or a homograph for the verb. Then play this game.

Using words from your list, write a total of 5 sentences. In each sentence, use a homophone or a homograph in two places. Read your sentences to the class, saying *homophone* or *homograph* instead of the words. See how quickly your classmates can guess the missing words.

Example: An airplane can (homograph) faster than a (homograph). (fly, fly)

Think Back	Think Ahead
◆ What did you learn about paragraphs of comparison and contrast in this unit? What did you do to write them?	◆ How will what you learned about making comparisons and contrasts help you make decisions? ◆ How will using details help you when writing a report?
◆ Look at the writing you did in this unit. How did using exact verbs help you write clearer and more accurately?	◆ What is one way verbs can show comparisons or contrasts?

Paragraphs of Comparison and Contrast *pages 158–159*
Read each sentence. Tell whether it shows *comparison* or *contrast*.

1. Eric rides his bike, while Michael prefers to skateboard.
2. Arthur and Spencer both had spiked haircuts.
3. Records are large and flat, while tapes are small and thick.
4. Michelle and Sarah love green clothes.

Evaluating to Compare and Contrast *page 160*
Rewrite each sentence that does not compare or contrast similar characteristics.

5. Dave is tall, but Adam is very quiet.
6. The blanket is dirty, but the sheet is clean.
7. Spaghetti is tasty, and salad is nutritious.
8. Ann loves to write poems, but Bill prefers to write stories.
9. Sailboats are quiet, and powerboats are large.

Using Enough Details *page 161*
Write two detail sentences that compare or contrast each of the following.

10. summer and winter
11. winter in Maine and winter in Florida
12. collies and dachshunds
13. deserts and beaches

The Writing Process *pages 162–173*

Write the letter of the correct response to each item.

14. When brainstorming a list of characters to write about, choose characters who are
    a. interesting to your audience.
    b. famous.
    c. fictional.

15. In revising, if the paragraph does not flow smoothly, then
    a. completely rewrite it.
    b. add important details.
    c. add transition words.

16. Which editor's mark would be used to correct the error in this sentence?
    Jerry told the jokes he had written for his his audience.
    a. cut something ℯ
    b. add something ∧
    c. move something ○

Irregular Verbs *pages 176–178*

Write the correct present-tense or past-tense form of *be, have,* or *do* to complete each sentence.

17. Many people say that Larry _____ a great sense of humor.
18. Larry _____ very funny in the show last week.
19. _____ you see his act?
20. Larry _____ the audience laughing so hard that they didn't hear the bell.
21. Nobody _____ imitations of famous people better than Larry!
22. Larry is _____ interviewed by the newspaper right now.

More Irregular Verbs *pages 179–181*

Write the past or the past participle form of the verb in parentheses that correctly completes each sentence.

23. Mark Twain has _____ to be one of our most-beloved humorists. (come)
24. Born Samuel L. Clemens in Hannibal, Missouri, Twain _____ stories about life on the Mississippi River. (tell)
25. This writer _____ many hours watching the riverboats. (spend)
26. Twain has _____ many fine portraits of people he met in the course of his travels around the world. (draw)
27. As an adult, Twain _____ many famous people. (meet)

Direct Objects *pages 182–183*
Write the direct object in each sentence.

28. Marceline Connell's family owned a well-known joke shop.
29. Connell's Joke Shop sold magic tricks as well as joke items.
30. Famous performers often visited the shop when they were in town.
31. Once a magician from Hollywood came in and purchased a thousand items.
32. Mr. Connell occasionally taught classes in magic at the community center.
33. Sometimes he performs magic tricks for his customers.

Indirect Objects *pages 184–185*
Rewrite each sentence, using an indirect object.

34. Celia promised a part in the new musical comedy show to Lynn.
35. The actors would sing some funny songs for the audience.
36. Mariann will sell tickets to the Hadley School students.
37. Compass Trucking Company bought new costumes for the entire cast.
38. Can you send an invitation to my sister Donna?

Predicate Nominatives *pages 186–187*
Write the predicate nominative from each sentence.

39. Those drawings over there are really cartoons.
40. Bob is a very witty man.
41. It was he who drew that funny comic strip.
42. Art was always Bob's best subject in school.
43. He was the president of the Art Club.
44. Now Bob is a professional cartoonist.

Transitive and Intransitive Verbs *pages 188–189*
Write the verb from each sentence. Label it *transitive* or *intransitive*.

45. A man slips on a banana peel.
46. People roar with laughter.
47. A clown wears baggy pants.
48. One clown rides a unicycle.
49. Another clown squirts seltzer in his face.
50. The audience giggles again.
51. All the world loves a clown!

Easily Confused Verb Pairs *pages 190–191*

Find the error in each sentence. Rewrite the sentence correctly.

52. Watching old movies on television can learn you a lot about comedy.
53. Tomorrow I will go to the library to see if they will borrow me a book on the great comedians.
54. Just set down in that chair, and I'll tell you all about Charlie Chaplin.
55. If you are having trouble with your back, you might want to lay down.
56. Here, leave me help you get comfortable.
57. You will never be able to raise from that position on the floor.
58. Lie those books down on the table, and I'll help you get up.

Contractions *pages 192–193*

Write the contraction from each sentence and the words from which it is formed.

59. We mustn't let Felicia find out about her birthday surprise.
60. Richie and Marlene aren't finished with the song they have written for Felicia.
61. She'll laugh when she hears the funny words they wrote to the tune of "Twist and Shout."
62. I think they're doing a very good job.
63. I'm surprised because I never realized that Richie and Marlene were so talented!
64. We'll all have to learn the words before the party so that we can sing it.

Homographs and Homophones: Humor with Puns
pages 194–195

Write whether the key word in the answer to each riddle is a *homophone* or *homograph*. If it is a homophone, write both spellings. If it is a homograph, write its two meanings.

65. Why does a piece of wood fall asleep all the time?
    It's a little board.
66. How do you know when the sun is angry?
    It glares at you.
67. How do you know fish are smart?
    They swim in a school.
68. Why is flat land not pretty? It is plain.
69. Why does Mr. Sloan complain so much? He is a groan man.

1-4 Cumulative Review

Compound Subjects *pages 42–43*
Write the compound subject in each sentence. Underline the connecting word.

1. Latin and Greek use different alphabets.
2. The letter *j* and the letter *k* are not in the Latin language.
3. Modern English and Old English also differ.
4. Spanish, French, and Italian are related languages.
5. German and Latin are two languages that influenced English.

Compound Predicates *pages 44–45*
Write the compound predicate from each sentence. Underline the connecting word.

6. One factory rarely prints and binds the same books.
7. A printer prints and cuts huge sheets of paper.
8. A bindery sews or glues together the pages of a book.
9. Some fine editions of books are covered with leather and stamped in gold.
10. After the books are bound, workers count the books, put them in boxes, and ship them to big warehouses.
11. Bookstores across the country advertise the books and sell them to their customers.

Plural Nouns *pages 88–91*
Find the misspelled word in each sentence, and write it correctly.

12. Almost all puppys cry and bark a lot to get their owner's attention.
13. Cates often rub against their owner's legs when they want to be fed.
14. A family of bunnys lives and plays in our woods.
15. A few deers become tame, but most won't even go near a human being.
16. Some monkies love to play with people and chatter away merrily to them.
17. I think the finchs are prettier than any of the other birds.
18. Some animals dug up the tomatos that my parents had planted in the garden.
19. We'll give gardening a few more trys.

Possessive Nouns   *pages 92–93*

Write the possessive noun from each sentence. Label it *singular* or *plural.*

20. This telescope's lens isn't very strong.
21. You can see Mars's red color and its canals if you look carefully.
22. The amateur astronomers' meeting will be held next Thursday in town.
23. Give me a list of the women's names.
24. I'm sure they will be interested in many of the program's speakers.
25. The professors' topics will range from the "The History of Astronomy" to "Recently Discovered Stars."

Action Verbs   *pages 128–129*

Write the action verb or verbs from each sentence.

26. The entire family climbed into the car.
27. Mrs. Halliburton drove through the busy city streets.
28. Before long, they reached the pleasant scenery of the country.
29. Now, the roads rose and fell between the hills.
30. The roads twisted around trees, lakes, and woods.
31. The hungry Halliburtons ate their delicious picnic lunch quickly.
32. The children hurried over to a beautiful little waterfall in the woods.
33. All afternoon the children played by the swift, clean river.
34. At night, Mom and the children sat around the campfire and told stories.

Linking Verbs   *pages 130–131*

Read the sentences. Write the linking verbs.

35. Charlie looks more confident every time I see him.
36. He is quick and agile during tennis practice.
37. Charlie appears controlled and serious.
38. Things are wonderful for Charlie at a time like this.
39. The world seems a brighter and a more pleasant place than ever before.
40. Even his food tastes better every day at breakfast, lunch, and dinner.
41. The air smells fresher to him.
42. Charlie is on top of the world!

Main Verbs and Helping Verbs *pages 132–133*

Write the verb phrase from each sentence. Underline each helping verb once. Underline each main verb twice.

43. Hank has been working on his new recipes.
44. He is studying for a test at the Good Cook's Cooking School.
45. Do Hank's parents own a restaurant?
46. His mother, Janet, had once run a restaurant in Tucson.
47. Janet sold the restaurant to Bill Osserman.
48. Janet and Bill bought another restaurant together much later.
49. They were married in 1972.
50. Hank was born to the Ossermans in 1976.

Past and Future Tense *pages 136–137*

Write each verb, using the tense in parentheses ( ).

51. write (future)
52. wash (past)
53. cough (past)
54. try (future)
55. wiggle (past)
56. compete (future)
57. complete (future)
58. stir (past)
59. grip (future)
60. own (past)
61. cry (past)
62. twist (past)
63. put (future)
64. spray (past)
65. grant (future)
66. shine (future)
67. aspire (past)
68. address (future)

Perfect Tenses *pages 138–139*

Write the perfect-tense verb from each sentence. Label it *present perfect, past perfect,* or *future perfect.*

69. Wendy and Kevin have planted a garden this year.
70. They had planned to have a garden last year, but Kevin broke his wrist.
71. Of course, that turn of events had disappointed Kevin at the time, but he eventually got over it.
72. Wendy has decided to plant tomatoes, corn, beans, lettuce, and squash.
73. By the end of the summer, they will have pulled enough weeds to fill a large wagon!
74. Kevin has rented a truck to take their produce to a farmer's market.
75. They hope that by the closing of the farmer's market, they will have earned enough money to buy new skis.

Subject-Verb Agreement   *pages 140–143*

Rewrite each sentence to correct the error in subject-verb agreement. Keep the verb in the present tense.

76. Jaclyn practice very hard at the music studio and at home.
77. She hope to be a concert pianist someday and to play all around the world.
78. Jaclyn's parents understands how badly she wants to reach her goal.
79. This determined young woman enter piano competitions every year.
80. Ms. Ingemi and Ms. Miller-Phillips is Jaclyn's favorite piano instructors.
81. The school concert and the spring competition comes one week apart.

Direct and Indirect Objects   *pages 182–185*

Write each sentence. Underline the direct object once. Underline the indirect object twice.

82. I bought my parents tickets to the Hal Grinspoon Show.
83. Mrs. Taylor showed us a clip of Grinspoon's new video.
84. In it, he told a friend hilarious stories about moving from one school to another.
85. He showed his audience the costume he had worn to a Halloween party when he was a boy.
86. Hal once sent his mom a telegram telling her that her son had been chosen for the Olympic Diving Team.
87. He later brought his mother a fake Olympic gold medal.
88. She gave him a standing ovation!
89. His mother must have given Hal his sense of humor.

Easily Confused Verb Pairs   *pages 190–191*

Find the error in each sentence. Rewrite the sentence correctly.

90. Can you learn me how to have a sense of humor?
91. Maybe you can borrow me a book on the subject.
92. I'm going to set down in my chair and practice being funny.
93. Perhaps while I lay on the beach, I can think of some new jokes to tell you.
94. When I raise from my chair, I'll be funnier than before.
95. Leave me tell you, I'm just joking, of course.

Communicating Your Opinions

◆ **COMPOSITION FOCUS:** **Persuasive Paragraph in a Business Letter**
◆ **LANGUAGE FOCUS:** **Pronouns**

A baby boy cries and bangs a spoon on the floor. A four-year-old girl eating her dinner exclaims, "Mmm! This is yummy!" A presidential candidate gives a speech on television.

All these people are expressing opinions. The baby, however, is not stating his opinion clearly. The four-year-old is making her opinion clear but is not giving convincing reasons for it. However, the presidential candidate on television may be doing both. If the candidate can persuade enough people to accept his or her views, that person may be elected President.

People hear and express a great many opinions in the course of daily life. Almost every newspaper, for example, has a page devoted to **editorials,** essays that give the writer's opinions about various issues. In this unit you will learn how to state your own opinions clearly in a business letter and how to present convincing reasons for your views.

◆ **WARMING UP** ◆

IN YOUR JOURNAL
Should sixth-grade students be allowed to choose the subjects they study? Write your opinion, and list some reasons.

CURRENT EVENTS
Find a newspaper editorial that interests you. Discuss what you think the writer is trying to get you to think or do.

Reading with a Writer's Eye
Editorials

In 1938 a director named Orson Welles produced a radio play called *The War of the Worlds*. The play was about an invasion of Earth by creatures from Mars. Orson Welles presented it in the form of a news broadcast. Many people mistook the play for real news and panicked. Read these editorials to find out what people thought about this event. Notice the opinions the writers state and the reasons they give. Decide how well you think the writers support their opinions.

This editorial is from the *New York Times*, November 2, 1938.

Terror by Radio

Radio ought to act promptly to prevent a repetition of the wave of panic in which it inundated the nation Sunday night by its "realistic" attempt to transfer to the air H. G. Wells's horror story of a mythical invasion by creatures from Mars. The inability of so many tuning in late to comprehend that they were listening to the account of an imaginary catastrophe has its ridiculous, even its pathetic, aspects. But the sobering fact remains that thousands from one end of the country to the other were frightened out of their senses, starting an incipient flight of hysterical refugees from the designated area, taxing the police and hospitals, confusing traffic, and choking the usual means of communication. What began as an "entertainment" might readily have ended in disaster.

Common sense might have warned the projectors of this broadcast that our people are just recovering from a psychosis brought on by fear of war. But the trouble goes much deeper than that. It is inherent in the method of radio broadcasting as maintained at present in this country. It can only be cured by a deeply searching self-regulation in which every element of the radio industry should join.

Radio is new but it has adult responsibilities. It has not mastered itself or the material it uses. It does many things which the newspapers learned long ago not to do, such as mixing its news and its advertising. Newspapers know the two must be rigidly separated and plainly marked. In the broadcast of the "The War of the Worlds" blood-curdling fiction was offered in exactly the manner that real news would have been given and interwoven with convincing actualities, such as an ordinary dance program, a definite locale, and the titles of real officials.

Radio officials should have thought twice before mingling this news technique with fiction so terrifying. Horror for the sake of the thrill has been legitimately exploited on the air. But to disguise it as news, with the deplorable results achieved from coast to coast, underlies the need of careful self-searching in American broadcasting.

This editorial is from the *San Francisco Chronicle*, November 1938.

The Right Place for News Is in Newspapers

The radio broadcast that caused panic in many parts of the United States by dramatizing an imaginary invasion shows how dangerous the ill-judged use of the air can be. More, it is warning of what might be the consequence of the deliberately conceived hoax for some sinister purpose.

This broadcast was not a hoax. It was innocently intended. The persons responsible did try to create a spectacular illusion and give their listeners the horrors, but there is no doubt that they thought it would be understood by all listeners as a piece of fiction.

Doubtless the broadcasters would have been right if radio listeners had the habit of keeping an ear glued to the program of a single station. Instead, there is much shifting of dials. It is extremely alarming to tune into the sudden declaration of a state of emergency and advice to seek safety, in a voice strangely like that of the President, a voice familiar to many listeners.

This is a danger not present in other methods of public information. The whole script of the broadcast as given probably could be published in print without misleading any reader. Even if it were intended as a hoax, which the broadcast was not intended to be, the mischief would be minimized.

The suddenness of the announcement over the air, the element of surprise, had the effect of creating panic in persons who, this incident further indicates, are in a panicky state of mind.

In this present state of the public mind, it is essential to avoid unbalancing influences. Certainly it is not a state in which to encourage experiments with agencies whose psychological effects are not as yet fully determined. The public mind is jittery enough without such things.

Respond

1. In what ways are the opinions expressed in the two editorials the same? In what ways are they different? Which do you find more persuasive? Explain your answer.

Discuss

2. Look at the editorial from the *New York Times*. Who does the writer mainly blame for the panic? For what reasons?
3. After reading these editorials, do you think some people might have admired and approved of the program *The War of the Worlds*? Explain your answer.

Thinking As a Writer
Analyzing a Persuasive Paragraph in a Business Letter

A letter to the editor is a **business letter,** a formal letter written for a specific purpose. A business letter has six parts: a **heading,** an **inside address,** a **greeting,** a **body,** a **closing,** and a **signature.**

Writer's Guide

A business letter

◆ is a formal letter written for a specific purpose.

◆ has a heading, an inside address, a greeting, a body, a closing, and a signature.

421 West End Avenue
New York, NY 10025
October 31, 1993

Editor
New York Times
229 West 43rd Street
New York, NY 10036

Dear Editor:

Radio and television should never again present plays disguised as real news broadcasts. In 1938 the Orson Welles program The War of the Worlds caused panic all across the country. A similar program today could still frighten children. It could also frighten adults who had not read the program guides. Worst of all, such programs could make people distrust and disbelieve real news shows. Allowing programs like The War of the Worlds on the air is not only foolish but could someday cost lives as well.

Sincerely yours,

Esther Conroy

Esther Conroy

The **heading** gives the writer's address and the date. Notice how the heading is punctuated.

The **inside address** gives the address of the person, the company, or the group that will receive the letter.

The **greeting** gives the title of the person being addressed. It includes the person's name if it is known. The greeting ends with a colon.

The **body** contains the main message of the letter.

The **closing** is formal in a business letter. Other possible closings are *Yours truly, Best regards,* or *Sincerely.*

The **signature** is the writer's name, signed in handwriting. It may be typed as well.

A letter to the editor is written to state an opinion convincingly. Therefore, the body usually contains one or more persuasive paragraphs. A **persuasive paragraph** has a topic sentence that states the issue and gives the writer's opinion. It also has detail sentences that give the writer's reasons for holding the opinion. Often it has a final "clincher" sentence that repeats and emphasizes the main idea of the paragraph.

Writer's Guide

A persuasive paragraph
- states an opinion and gives supporting reasons.
- has a topic sentence and detail sentences.
- often has a "clincher" sentence.

Radio and television should never again present plays disguised as real news broadcasts. In 1938 the Orson Welles program The War of the Worlds caused panic all across the country. A similar program today could still frighten children. It could also frighten adults who had not read the program guides. Worst of all, such programs could make people distrust and disbelieve real news shows. Allowing programs like The War of the Worlds on the air is not only foolish but could someday cost lives as well.

The topic sentence identifies the issue and gives the writer's opinion.

Detail sentences give reasons that support the writer's opinion. Often these reasons are arranged in order of importance. The most important reason is given last, where it is most likely to be noticed.

The clincher repeats the main idea in a way that leaves the reader with a strong impression.

Discuss

1. Why is each part of a business letter important?
2. How many reasons does Esther Conroy give in the body of her letter to support her opinion? Which is the most important reason? Why do you think so?
3. What warning does Esther Conroy give? In which part of her letter do we find this warning? Why did she place it there?
4. Reread the topic sentence. What is the issue that Esther will discuss in her letter? What is her opinion about this issue?
5. What other reasons might Esther have included in her letter?
6. Is the tone of Esther's letter formal or informal? Why did she choose this tone?

Try Your Hand

A. Identify Letter Parts Write each business letter. Add any missing words, punctuation marks, or letter parts. Then label each part of the letter.

1.
```
                    21 Samson Rd.
                    Riverside, IL
Dear Sir
    I spent $20 on a
fishing pole made by your
company. It broke in no
time. Please send my
money back.
                    Gary
```

2.
```
                    June 12, 1993
Amy Gault
Toad Press
534 5th Ave.
    Your book about the
gold rush was great! It
was very informative.
Thank you for publishing
it.
                    Sincerely,
```

B. Identify Parts of a Persuasive Paragraph Read these sentences from a persuasive paragraph. For each sentence, write *topic sentence, detail sentence,* or *clincher.*

3. For one thing, so many pets need good homes.
4. Everyone should have a pet.
5. Statistics show that people with pets live longer.
6. The next time you go past a pet shop and see a pair of brown eyes gazing at you, give in to your feelings—go inside and ask the clerk: "How much is that doggy in the window?"
7. Taking care of a pet helps people feel good about themselves.

C. Read and Analyze a Letter to the Editor Find a persuasive letter to the editor in a current newspaper. Read the letter aloud to a partner, pointing out the writer's opinion, the supporting reasons, and the clincher, if it has one. Discuss whether the letter is persuasive and why you do or do not think so.

Writer's Notebook

Collecting Powerful Words In the editorial on page 208, the writer has chosen some words for their powerful effect on the reader. The word *panic* gives a stronger impression than *fright.* The word *pathetic* is more forceful than *sad,* another word the writer might have chosen. Watch for powerful words like these when you read, and add them to your *Writer's Notebook.* Use these powerful words when you write or speak to persuade.

Thinking As a Writer
Evaluating Reasons to Support an Opinion

In a good persuasive paragraph, the writer supports an opinion with one or more good reasons. A good reason is **relevant,** which means it is "closely related to the opinion." It is **logical,** which means it "uses clear reasoning." Finally, a good reason is **distinct.** That is, it is different from any other reason you have given. Read this opinion and the reasons that follow it.

> **Writer's Guide**
>
> To write a persuasive paragraph, good writers
>
> ◆ support their opinions with reasons that are relevant, logical, and distinct.

Opinion: Summer vacation should be longer.

Reasons:
1. Summer vacation was longer in the past.
2. Children would learn more if they had longer vacations.
3. Children could spend more time with their parents.
4. Parents could enjoy more time relaxing with their children.

The first reason is not relevant. It has nothing to do with whether vacations *should* be longer. The second reason is not logical. Why would children learn more if vacations were longer? The writer does not explain. The third and fourth reasons are not distinct. They are really two different ways of stating the same reason.

When you write a persuasive paragraph, be sure that your reasons support your opinion. Look at each reason you have written and ask yourself: Is it relevant? Is it logical? Is it distinct?

Discuss

1. Look at the editorials on pages 208–209. Which reasons are good ones? Give two examples. Explain your answers.
2. Read these sentences. *Children should not attend weddings for these reasons: Children make too much noise. They are loud. They do not enjoy adult parties. They are short.* Do you think each reason is a good one? Explain why or why not.

Try Your Hand

Write Good Reasons Write three good reasons for one of these opinions.

◆ Summer vacation should be shorter. ◆ Summer vacation should be longer.

Developing the Writer's Craft
Using Formal and Informal Language

Good writers use a tone that fits their audience and their purpose. An informal tone, for example, may suit a friendly letter or certain stories. A business letter requires a more formal tone.

Pay attention to the language in these sentences.

1. In my opinion, far too many shows of low quality appear on television today.
2. Hey, if you ask me, most of the stuff on TV these days is junky.

Both of these sentences express the same message. The underlined words in the first sentence, however, give the sentence a formal tone. The underlined words in the second sentence give it an informal tone. For example, *in my opinion* is a formal way of introducing an idea, while *Hey, if you ask me* is an informal way of doing so. When you use formal language, do not use words such as *hey*, abbreviations such as *TV*, or informal adjectives such as *junky* to mean "of low quality."

Informal language has its place. When you write a business letter, however, use formal language to give your letter a serious tone and to help persuade your audience to accept your views or respond to your request.

Discuss

1. Look at the editorials on pages 208–209. Do these writers use formal or informal language? Give examples.
2. In the editorial on page 209, the editor writes, "This is a danger not present in other methods of public information." Which words give this sentence its formal tone? What words might the editor have used to create a more informal tone?

Try Your Hand

Use Formal and Informal Language   Write several sentences about a television or radio program, using formal language such as you might use in a business letter. Then rewrite the sentences, using informal language such as you might use in conversation or in a letter to a good friend.

1 Prewriting
Persuasive Paragraph in a Business Letter

Leo wanted to write a letter to the editor of his local newspaper. He used the checklist in the **Writer's Guide** to help him plan his letter. Look at what he did.

Writer's Guide

Prewriting Checklist
- ☑ Brainstorm topics.
- ☑ Select a topic.
- ☑ Think about your audience and your purpose.
- ☑ Brainstorm reasons that support your opinion.
- ☑ Organize your reasons in the order of their importance.

◆ Brainstorming and Selecting a Topic

First, Leo listed possible topics for his letter. He read his local newspaper to get ideas. He listened to people he knew. He brainstormed changes that he wanted to see or did not want to see in his world.

Next, he crossed off topics about which he had no strong opinion. He also crossed off topics if he could not support his opinions on those topics.

Finally, Leo decided to write about an idea he got one day after spending time with his grandfather. Leo thought someone should start a program that would bring together children who had no grandparents with older adults who had no grandchildren. He knew he could give good reasons for such a program.

> making summer vacation longer
> new hairstyles
> making work week shorter
> closing city parks to traffic
> laws for bike riders
> keeping dogs off buses
> (adopted grandparent program)
> bus stop signs in braille
> too much rudeness in world
> Is TV bad for kids?

Discuss

1. Look at the topics Leo crossed off. Why do you think he decided against each topic he crossed off?
2. If Leo were writing for an audience made up entirely of children, which topic might he cross off right away? Why?

◆ Gathering and Organizing Information

After Leo selected his topic, he brainstormed reasons to prove that his idea was a good one. He made a cluster diagram showing what groups of people would benefit from his idea and what the program would do for each group. He reviewed his diagram to make sure all his reasons were strong ones. Then he numbered his reasons in the order of their importance to his audience. Look at Leo's diagram. He numbered his least important reason with a 1 and his most important reason with a 3.

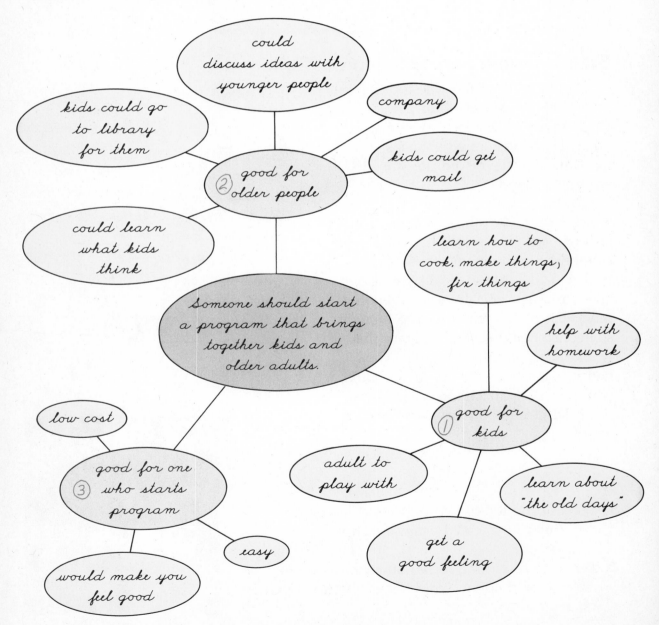

WRITING PROCESS

Discuss

1. Look back at Leo's cluster diagram. What three main reasons does he give to show that the program he has in mind is a good one? How will he persuade his audience to believe his reasons?
2. Who will be most convinced by each of Leo's reasons? Whom does Leo most need to convince? Why?
3. In what order should Leo present his three reasons? Explain your answer.
4. What are some other reasons that Leo might use to support his opinion?

Try Your Hand

Now plan your own persuasive paragraph in a business letter.

A. **Brainstorm and Select a Topic**   Decide who your audience will be. Then list possible topics for your letter. Brainstorm issues that have been on your mind. Browse in newspapers and magazines. Listen to people you know, and list the topics on their minds. Then look at each topic and think about your audience.

   ◆ Cross out topics that would not interest your audience.
   ◆ Cross out topics about which you have no strong opinions. Also cross out topics if you cannot support your opinions about them with convincing reasons.
   ◆ Circle the remaining topic about which you feel most strongly. This will be the topic of your letter.

B. **Gather and Organize Information**   When you are satisfied with your topic, plan what to say in your letter.

   ◆ Write the opinion you will present.
   ◆ Write down every reason you can think of that supports your opinion.
   ◆ Write examples and details that might make each of your reasons more convincing. A cluster diagram like Leo's may help you keep your reasons organized.
   ◆ Number your reasons in the order of their importance to your audience.

 Save your notes and your diagram in your *Writer's Notebook*. You will use them when you draft your persuasive paragraph in a business letter.

2 Drafting
Persuasive Paragraph in a Business Letter

Using his notes and his diagram, Leo followed the checklist in the **Writer's Guide** to draft his persuasive paragraph. Look at what he did.

> I think someone should start a program to get children and older adults together. Whoever makes this idea work is sure to feel good about it. The program would be good for kids.

Discuss

1. What opinion did Leo state in his first sentence?
2. What groups of readers has Leo appealed to so far? In what way?
3. What should Leo write in the rest of his paragraph to make his opinion convincing?

Try Your Hand

Now draft a persuasive paragraph in a business letter.

A. Review Your Information Think about the information you gathered and organized in the last lesson. Decide whether you need more information. If so, gather it.

B. Think About Your TAP Remember that your task is to write a persuasive paragraph in a business letter to a newspaper editor. Your purpose is to persuade the readers of the newspaper to agree with your opinion.

C. Write Your First Draft Follow the steps in the **Drafting Checklist** to write your business letter.

When you write your draft, just put all your ideas on paper. Do not worry about spelling, punctuation, or grammar. You can correct the draft later.

Task: What?
Audience: Who?
Purpose: Why?

Save your first draft in your *Writer's Notebook.* You will use it when you revise your persuasive paragraph in a business letter.

3 Responding and Revising
Persuasive Paragraph in a Business Letter

Leo used the checklist in the **Writer's Guide** to revise his business letter. Look at what he did.

◆ **Checking Information**

Leo cut a sentence that did not help support his opinion. He used this mark ✐ to show what he was cutting. He also added a point that he felt made his paragraph more persuasive. He used this mark ∧ to show the addition.

◆ **Checking Organization**

Leo decided to move one of his reasons to the end of his letter because he wanted it to stand out To show which words should be moved and where they should go, he used this mark ⟳ .

◆ **Checking Language**

Leo decided his tone was too informal for a business letter. He replaced one phrase with more formal language. To show this change, he used this mark ⌒ . He also corrected a sentence fragment. He used this mark ∧ to show the change.

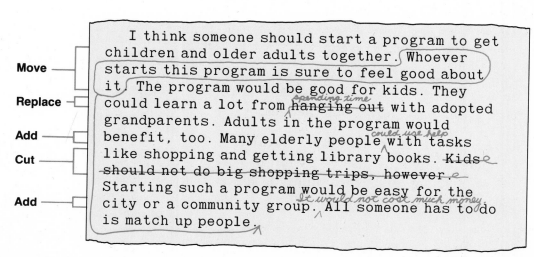

Move — Replace — Add — Cut — Add

I think someone should start a program to get children and older adults together. Whoever starts this program is sure to feel good about it. The program would be good for kids. They could learn a lot from *spending time* hanging out with adopted grandparents. Adults in the program would benefit, too. Many elderly people *could use help* with tasks like shopping and getting library books. Kids should not do big shopping trips, however. Starting such a program would be easy for the city or a community group. *It would not cost much money.* All someone has to do is match up people.

Discuss

1. Look at the changes Leo made. Do these changes make his paragraph more persuasive? Why or why not?
2. Study the sentence Leo moved. To whom is this sentence relevant? Why did Leo move the sentence to the end of his letter?

Try Your Hand

Now revise your first draft.

A. Read Your First Draft As you read your business letter, think about your audience and your purpose. Read your letter silently or to a partner to see whether it is complete and well organized. Ask yourself or your partner the questions in the box.

Responding and Revising Strategies

✔ **Respond**
Ask yourself or a partner:

◆ Do I make my opinion clear?

◆ Have I supported my opinion with persuasive reasons?

◆ Is my tone proper for a letter to the editor?

◆ Are all my sentences clear and complete?

◆ Have I included all six parts of a business letter?

✔ **Revise**
Try these solutions:

◆ **Add** a topic sentence that states your opinion, or **replace** your topic sentence with a clearer one.

◆ **Add** new reasons, and **replace** weak reasons with strong ones.

◆ **Replace** informal language with more formal words and phrases.

◆ **Correct** any sentence fragments and run-on sentences. See the **Revising Workshop** on page 221.

◆ **Add** any missing parts.

B. Make Your Changes If the answer to any question in the box is *no*, try the solution. Use the **Editor's Marks** to show your changes.

C. Review Your Business Letter Again Decide whether there is anything else you want to revise. Keep revising your letter until you feel it is well organized and complete.

EDITOR'S MARKS

∧ Add something.

⟋ Cut something.

◯ Move something.

⟋⟍ Replace something.

Save your revised business letter in your *Writer's Notebook.* You will use it when you proofread your letter.

Revising Workshop
Correcting Sentence Fragments and Run-on Sentences

In talking to a friend, you might run ideas together and use sentence fragments, yet make yourself understood. When you write a business letter, however, you must be more formal. Look at this excerpt from a business letter. It needs to be revised.

> Dear Mr. Tanzer:
>   I have a wonderful idea for your company I think you'll like it. A package that turns into a wastebasket. Every time people buy your product—boom: a free wastebasket.

This letter probably will not convince Mr. Tanzer of anything because he won't understand it. It begins with a run-on sentence. It continues with two groups of words that are sentence fragments. Neither group expresses a complete thought. Here is one way to correct the letter.

> Dear Mr. Tanzer:
>   I have a wonderful idea for your company. I think you'll like it. Sell your product in a package that turns into a wastebasket. This way, every time people buy your product, they would get a free wastebasket.

Learning how to correct sentence fragments and run-on sentences can help you write confidently and persuasively.

Practice

Rewrite these sentence fragments and run-on sentences as correct sentences.

1. Please let me be in charge I have a lot of experience.
2. My older sister last year.
3. She taught me how to organize a dinner she can help me.
4. This year, while I've had more practice.
5. I will work hard I will expect everyone else to work hard, too.
6. Won't regret it if you pick me.

4 Proofreading
Persuasive Paragraph in a Business Letter

Writer's Guide

Proofreading Checklist

- ☑ Check for errors in capitalization.
- ☑ Check for errors in punctuation. Be sure that you have used colons and commas correctly.
- ☑ Check to see that paragraphs are indented.
- ☑ Check your grammar.
- ☑ Circle any words you think are misspelled. Find out how to spell them correctly.
- ⇒ For proofreading help, use the **Writer's Handbook.**

After revising his business letter, Leo used the **Writer's Guide** and the **Editor's Marks** to proofread it. Look at what he did.

> 1129 Wabash Street
> Harbin, Arizona 92008
> March 10, 19--
>
> City pages
> 125 Main Street
> Harbin Arizona 92008
>
> Dear Editor,

> An idea like this was tried in fresh Springs, nebraska. It worked well there. Let's start a program that gets together the young and the elderly in our community, too.
>
> sincerely,
> *Leo Parks*
> Leo Parks

Discuss

1. What kinds of corrections did Leo make?
2. Why did Leo use a colon instead of a comma after his greeting?

Try Your Hand

Proofread Your Business Letter Now use the **Writer's Guide** and the **Editor's Marks** to proofread your business letter.

Save your corrected business letter in your *Writer's Notebook.* You will use it when you publish your letter.

EDITOR'S MARKS

- ☰ Capitalize.
- ⊙ Add a period.
- ∧ Add something.
- ∧ Add a comma.
- ᵛᵛ Add quotation marks.
- ✌ Cut something.
- ⌐ Replace something.
- ∼ Transpose.
- ◯ Spell correctly.
- ⊤ᐤ Indent paragraph.
- / Make a lowercase letter.

5 Publishing
Persuasive Paragraph in a Business Letter

Writer's Guide

Publishing Checklist

☑ Make a clean copy of your letter.

☑ Check to see that nothing has been left out.

☑ Check that there are no mistakes.

☑ Share your letter in a special way.

Leo made a clean copy of his letter and checked to see that he had not left anything out. Then he and his classmates published their letters by mailing them to the local newspaper. You can find Leo's paragraph on page 36 of the **Writer's Handbook.**

Here's how Leo published his persuasive letter.

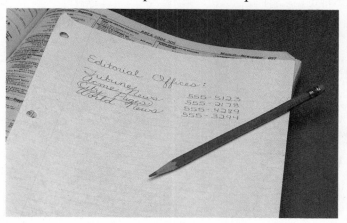

1. First, he decided which newspaper he wanted to send his letter to. He found the correct address for that newspaper.

2. Next, Leo addressed and stamped an envelope. He folded his letter as shown, put it in the envelope, and sealed the envelope. For information about envelopes, see page 56 of the **Writer's Handbook.**

3. Then, he mailed his letter by putting it in the nearest mailbox, and waited for a reply. Also, he checked the newspaper to see whether his letter got printed.

4. Finally, Leo shared the printed letter with his classmates.

Discuss

1. How can you get the correct address for a newspaper?
2. Why is it important for a letter to the editor to be written in a business-letter format?

Try Your Hand

Publish Your Letter to the Editor   Follow the checklist in the **Writer's Guide** on page 223. If possible, prepare your letter to the editor and mail it to a newspaper, or try one of these ideas for sharing your letter.

◆ With your classmates, post your letters on a bulletin board, under a title such as *Point of View.* Invite students from other classes to read and respond to the letters.

◆ Form a small group and read your letters aloud to one another. Discuss each letter after it is read. Discuss the writer's opinion, the reasons given for the opinion, whether members of the group agree with that writer, and why they do or do not agree. Read **Tips on How to Listen and Speak in a Group Discussion** on page 225 for helpful information.

Listening and Speaking
Tips on How to Listen and Speak in a Group Discussion

1. Make sure everyone understands the topic of the group discussion.
2. Decide the purpose of your discussion. Is it to make a decision, to reach an agreement, or just to find out what everybody in the group thinks?
3. Make sure that everyone gets an opportunity to speak. You could do this by simply having each person speak in turn or by electing one member of the group to lead the discussion. If you elect a leader, people should raise their hands when they want to speak. The leader would choose the next speaker.
4. Listen politely to others and do not interrupt. If you disagree with someone, explain your disagreement when it is your turn to speak.
5. Watch and pay attention to other people as they speak. Listen carefully for their opinions. Notice the reasons they give to support their opinions.
6. Take notes to help you remember what others have said and what you want to say in response. Jot down only key words. Remember to keep listening as you write.
7. If you do not understand what someone has said, ask questions after he or she has finished speaking.
8. Speak clearly when your turn comes. Remember your purpose in speaking: to present your opinion and to persuade others to agree with you. Therefore, state your opinion directly. Then present good reasons why the others should agree with your opinion.
9. Give your reasons in order of importance. State last the reason you want the group to remember most.
10. As you speak, make eye contact with different members of the group. Do not stare down at your desk or keep your eyes glued to your notes.
11. Be concise and keep to the topic. Otherwise, people will stop listening to you.
12. Avoid repeating the same points that other speakers have already made.

Writing in the Content Areas

Use what you learned to write about something you would like to see happen in your school or community. You could write a business letter or a persuasive paragraph. Use one of these ideas or an idea of your own.

Writer's Guide

When you write, remember the stages of the Writing Process.
◆ Prewriting
◆ Drafting
◆ Responding and Revising
◆ Proofreading
◆ Publishing

Social Studies/Science

Is traffic or pollution a cause for concern in your community? Tell your mayor, your state senator, or another public official how you feel. Think about how the problem affects you personally. Talk to others about how the problem affects them. Then draw your own conclusions about how the problem could be solved.

Social Studies

Does your community need a new pool, a park, or a gathering place for young people? Talk to classmates about additions to the community they might like to see. How would these additions benefit people? Where might they be located? How could you and your classmates help to build them?

Physical Education

Public figures sometimes visit schools. What sports figure would you like to invite to your school? Write the invitation, and include a set of reasons that will convince the person to accept.

Literature

Do people in your community make good use of the library? How might people benefit from going to the library more often? What useful services does the library provide? What other useful services should the library provide?

CONNECTING
WRITING ↔ LANGUAGE

Skillful persuasive writers get their message across directly, clearly, and in the fewest words possible. What message do you get from this persuasive paragraph?

Advertisements should not be allowed on television programs for very young children. Young children cannot tell when advertisers are telling the truth and when they aren't. One young boy we know saw a television advertisement for a candy bar. It led him to believe that candy was good for his health. A young girl from Oregon saw a dangerous toy advertised by a stuntperson. She thought she could try the same stunt at home—and she hurt herself. Some children who do not understand the value of money ask for products their families cannot afford. Others are frightened by ads. Shouldn't we protect young children from being fooled and frightened in these ways?

◆ **Pronouns in a Persuasive Paragraph** The highlighted words are pronouns. They make the paragraph read smoothly by replacing nouns. Notice that pronouns work as both subjects and objects in the sentences. Many of them refer to a specific person, place, or thing named earlier in the paragraph. Some, such as *others*, refer to indefinite people, places, or things. Pronouns help writers express themselves clearly without repeating the same words again and again.

◆ **Language Focus: Pronouns** In the following lessons you will learn more about using pronouns correctly in your writing.

1 Pronouns

◆ FOCUS   A **pronoun** takes the place of a noun or nouns.

Remember that a noun names a person, a place, a thing, or an idea. A pronoun is a word that takes the place of a noun or nouns.

1. The Oleniks celebrated Thanksgiving.   noun

   They celebrated Thanksgiving.   pronoun

Pronouns, like nouns, have number: they can be singular or plural. A singular pronoun replaces a singular noun. A plural pronoun replaces a plural noun. A plural pronoun may also replace two or more nouns.

2. Pauline invited Peter and Lynn .   Pauline invited them .

The most commonly used pronouns are the **personal pronouns.** The chart shows the singular and plural personal pronouns.

Singular Pronouns	I me my mine you your yours he she it him her his hers its
Plural Pronouns	we us our ours you your yours they them their theirs

Link to Speaking and Writing
Pronouns help you express yourself without using the same words again. How does the editing improve the sentence? Why do you think so?

Maria admitted that ~~Maria~~ she was tired after all ~~Maria's~~ her cooking.

Guided Practice

A. Identify the pronoun in each sentence.

1. Pauline Olenik's dinner wins her many compliments.
2. The turkey is done, and it smells delicious.
3. Pauline's parents say they like being with the family.
4. William smiles as he dishes up some mashed potatoes.
5. They all have warm feelings about the family dinner.

B. 6.–10. Name the nouns that the pronouns in **A** replace.

Independent Practice

C. Identifying Pronouns Write the pronoun from each sentence.

11. When William first came to America, he felt homesick.

MODEL ▷ he

12. One day William's mother gave him some money.
13. Mrs. Olenik said that she wanted to make stuffed cabbage.
14. William was glad to help her prepare the stuffed cabbage.
15. Mrs. Olenik and William shopped for what they needed.
16. The bag was so heavy that William could hardly lift it.
17. Mrs. Olenik hummed a tune as she cooked.

D. 18.–24. Identifying the Nouns Replaced by Pronouns
Write the noun or nouns that each pronoun in **C** replaces.

18. When William first came to America, he felt homesick.

MODEL ▷ William

E. Revising: Using Pronouns to Avoid Repetition Rewrite each sentence by replacing the underlined words with pronouns.

25. Pauline entered Pauline's room.

MODEL ▷ Pauline entered her room.

26. When Pauline reached the desk, Pauline saw a note.
27. Pauline picked up the note and read the note.
28. Pauline learned that Pauline's father was at the airport.
29. Since Mr. Olenik was in sales, Mr. Olenik often traveled.
30. Pauline and Ann had talked about how much Pauline and Ann missed Pauline's and Ann's father.
31. When Mr. Olenik returned from a trip, Mr. Olenik would be tired, and Mr. Olenik would be hungry.

Application — Writing and Speaking

Friendly Letter Suppose you were at a dinner party. Discuss with a classmate what might happen. Notice the pronouns you use. Then write about the party in a letter to a friend. Use pronouns to avoid repeating nouns again and again. If you need help writing a friendly letter, see page 52 of the **Writer's Handbook.**

2 Agreement of Pronouns with Antecedents

◆ **FOCUS** A pronoun should agree with its antecedent in number and gender.

When using a pronoun, you must make clear what noun it replaces. You can do this by providing a clear antecedent. The **antecedent** of a pronoun is the noun to which it refers. The antecedent may be in the same sentence or in another sentence.

1. Mother was quite surprised when she found the picture.

2. The photo was very old. It showed great-grandfather Chen.

Like nouns and verbs, pronouns have number. They can tell about one or more than one. Pronouns also have **gender.** They may refer either to a male, to a female, or to neither gender in particular. A pronoun should agree with its antecedent in number and gender. For example, the pronoun *she* in sentence 1 agrees with *Mother* because both words are singular and both name a female. A pronoun with more than one antecedent is always plural.

3. Mu Tan and Mu Lan liked the photo of their ancestor.

Guided Practice

A. Identify the antecedent of each underlined pronoun. The antecedent may be in another sentence.

1. Great-grandfather Chen came to America when <u>he</u> was ten.
2. Mother's parents had told <u>her</u> many stories about <u>him</u>.
3. One story involved Chen and <u>his</u> adventures in gold mining.
4. Chen and a friend once thought they had really found gold.
5. An expert, however, found <u>it</u> to be "fool's gold."

THINK AND REMEMBER
- ◆ When using a pronoun, make sure its **antecedent,** the noun to which it refers, is clear.
- ◆ Make sure pronouns agree with their antecedents in number and gender.

Independent Practice

B. Recognizing Pronoun Antecedents   Write each sentence. Draw an arrow from each underlined pronoun to its antecedent.

6. Hoy published an essay <u>he</u> wrote.

MODEL> Hoy published an essay he wrote.

7. Hoy's essay is about <u>his</u> grandmother, Ma Chan.

8. Ma Chan knows that Hoy is proud of <u>her</u>.

9. Ma Chan came to Copper Junction when <u>she</u> was a young woman.

10. The town was young then, too, and <u>it</u> had no library.

11. Ma Chan convinced the townspeople that <u>they</u> needed a library.

12. The library that Ma Chan started is named after <u>her</u>.

C. Recognizing Pronouns and Their Antecedents   Write each pronoun. Then write its antecedent. The antecedent may be in another sentence.

13. Li Hua is proud she is in the Hing family.

MODEL> she—Li Hua

14. Li Hua found a scrapbook when she cleaned the attic.
15. "What a great family record," she thought.
16. Shing saw her with it later.
17. "What are you looking at?" he asked Li Hua.
18. "A scrapbook," she said. "It's about our family."
19. "What a wonderful way to learn about our ancestors!" said he.
20. "Why don't we start a new family scrapbook," she said.

Application—Writing and Speaking

Family Scrapbook   Imagine that you have found a trunkful of souvenirs that belonged to a great-grandparent of yours. Discuss with a classmate what you might find in the trunk. Then write a paragraph for your family scrapbook about your great-grandparent. Be sure all your pronouns have clear antecedents; be sure they all agree with their antecedents in number and gender.

3 Subject and Object Pronouns

◆ **FOCUS**   Pronouns can be subjects or objects in sentences.

A pronoun that replaces the subject of a sentence is called a **subject pronoun.** The subject pronoun *I* is always capitalized. The words in color are subject pronouns.

   1. He is Wyatt Brooks.   **2.** I like his novels.

Pronouns that replace objects are called **object pronouns.** Object pronouns can be used as direct or indirect objects. They are also used after words such as *to, from, at,* and *by.* The words in color are object pronouns.

   3. Customers ask him for autographs.

   4. Angela gave him a book to sign.

   5. Mr. Brooks returned the novel to her .

Look at the chart of subject and object pronouns. Notice that *you* and *it* can be either subject pronouns or object pronouns.

Subject Pronouns	I	you	he	she	it	we	you	they
Object Pronouns	me	you	him	her	it	us	you	them

Use subject pronouns as predicate nominatives. Never use an object pronoun as a predicate nominative.

   6. The author who won the award is he .

Guided Practice

A. Identify each pronoun as a *subject pronoun* or an *object pronoun.*

   1. Mr. Brooks smiled at me.

   2. He wrote in the book.

   3. He gave me some advice.

   4. "You can write a novel, too."

   5. "Write it with joy."

   6. I liked the message.

> **THINK AND REMEMBER**
> ◆ Use subject pronouns as subjects and as predicate nominatives in sentences.
> ◆ Use object pronouns as direct or indirect objects in sentences.

Independent Practice

B. Identifying Subject and Object Pronouns Write the pronoun from each sentence. Label it *subject pronoun* or *object pronoun*.

7. A good novel can touch us deeply.

MODEL us—object pronoun

8. It can also supply food for thought.
9. We may treasure favorite books like old friends.
10. Do you ever read historical novels?
11. Many people enjoy them.
12. They like to learn about other times.
13. A historical novel can teach you about history.
14. I recommend a book called *Johnny Tremain.*
15. It is an adventure story, and Johnny is the hero.
16. He lives at the time of the American Revolution.
17. The colonists depend on him for help.

C. Choosing the Correct Pronoun Write the pronoun in parentheses that correctly completes each sentence.

18. (We, Us) like novels.

MODEL We

19. (I, me) liked *A Gathering of Days.*
20. The book is about a girl named Catherine. (Her, She) lives on a farm.
21. Her mother is dead, and Catherine misses (she, her).
22. Catherine's father is lonely, so (him, he) remarries.
23. Catherine and her stepmother do not agree. (They, Them) are not happy with the situation.
24. Catherine's stepbrother comes to live with (they, them).
25. Catherine makes friends with (he, him).

D. 26. – 33. Using Pronouns in Sentences List each pronoun you did not use in **C.** Use each pronoun in a sentence.

26. (We, Us) like novels.

MODEL Us Some of us like books about real people.

Application — Writing and Speaking

Book Report Discuss with a classmate a book you have read and liked. Then prepare a report about the book and present it orally to your class. Describe the characters, and tell what you liked about the book. If you need help writing a book report, see page 49 of the **Writer's Handbook.**

4 Possessive Pronouns

◆ **FOCUS** A **possessive pronoun** shows ownership or possession.

Remember that a possessive noun shows that a person, a place, a thing, or an idea owns or has something. A possessive pronoun takes the place of a possessive noun.

1. John states John's opinion.   **possessive noun**

   John states his opinion.   **possessive pronoun**

Some possessive pronouns are used in front of nouns. Other possessive pronouns stand alone.

in front of noun   stands alone

2. My debate team will beat yours.

Possessive Pronouns That Are Used in Front of Nouns	Possessive Pronouns That Stand Alone
my your our his her its their	mine yours ours his hers theirs

Do not confuse contractions with possessive pronouns. A possessive pronoun never has an apostrophe.

3. It's our turn to speak.   **contraction**
4. Your team had its turn.   **possessive pronoun**

Link to Speaking and Writing
Possessive pronouns can help simplify a cluttered sentence.

~~~~~~
                                      your
          Practice ^the speech that you will
make.
~~~~~~

Guided Practice

A. Identify each possessive pronoun. Tell whether it is a pronoun that is used *in front of* a noun or a pronoun that *stands alone*.

1. Our debate is on Thursday.
2. My team is the Titans.
3. Theirs is the Eagles.
4. Your team works hard.
5. Mine works even harder.
6. Their practice lasts an hour.
7. Ours lasts almost two hours.
8. Each team does its best.

Independent Practice

B. Identifying Possessive Pronouns Write and underline once each possessive pronoun that is used in front of a noun. Write and underline twice each possessive pronoun that stands alone.

9. Everyone has his or her opinion.

MODEL ▷ his, her

10. When we debate, we present our ideas to an audience.
11. You state your ideas and I state mine.
12. The audience may show its opinion by clapping.
13. Debate is part of our way of life in America.
14. My candidate for President may debate yours.
15. Their debate may help to shape this nation of ours.

C. Revising: Using Possessive Pronouns Rewrite each sentence. Use possessive pronouns to make each sentence less cluttered.

16. Athens was famous for the speakers of Athens.

MODEL ▷ Athens was famous for its speakers.

17. Perhaps the best-known speaker of Athens was Demosthenes.
18. As a boy, Demosthenes was troubled by Demosthenes' lisp.
19. Demosthenes improved the speech that he used.
20. He practiced speaking with pebbles in the mouth that he had.
21. He overcame the problems that he had as a speaker.

D. Using Possessive Pronouns and Contractions in Sentences Use each set of words correctly in one or two sentences.

22. your, ours

MODEL ▷ That is your tent. This one is ours.

23. it's, theirs	25. my, yours	27. their, theirs
24. his, hers	26. there's, its	28. your, mine

Application — Writing, Speaking, Listening

Opinion Choose an interesting topic for a class debate. Explore your opinion by discussing the topic with a classmate. Then write a paragraph stating your opinion and your reasons for it. Use possessive pronouns to make your message clear.

5 Reflexive Pronouns

FOCUS
◆ A **reflexive pronoun** refers to the subject.
◆ A reflexive pronoun ends in *self* or *selves.*

Remember that pronouns such as *my, your, him,* and *them* are called personal pronouns. The endings *self* or *selves* can be added to some personal pronouns to make reflexive pronouns. A reflexive pronoun usually refers to the subject of the sentence. The word in color is a reflexive pronoun.

1. We went by ourselves to the natural history museum.

A reflexive pronoun can be used as a direct or an indirect object, or after words such as *to, by,* and *from.* It may also be used as a predicate nominative. It should agree with the subject in number and gender.

2. Almost immediately Al found himself in the fossil room.

3. Jeena was left by herself in the museum lobby.

4. "I'm not quite myself today," she mused.

Reflexive Pronouns				
Singular	myself	yourself	himself	herself	itself
Plural	ourselves	yourselves	themselves		

Guided Practice

A. Identify the pronouns in each sentence. For each reflexive pronoun, name the subject to which it refers.

1. Jeena introduced herself to one of the museum guides.
2. "I'd like to see the crystal displays for myself," she said.
3. "Follow these directions, and you will find yourself in the right room," advised the guide.
4. She soon saw that she had the crystal room to herself.
5. "I'm so glad I convinced myself to come here," she thought.

Independent Practice

B. Identifying Reflexive Pronouns Write each pronoun, and label it *personal* or *reflexive*. After each reflexive pronoun, write the subject to which it refers.

   6. The director prides herself on the natural history museum.
   MODEL ▷ herself—reflexive—The director
   7. "You can really educate yourself here," she claims.
   8. The Ellises taught themselves about native plants.
   9. Later, they bought themselves souvenirs.
   10. Jimmy found himself a museum calendar for next year.
   11. Jenny bought a book about plants for herself.

C. Completing Sentences with Reflexive Pronouns Complete each sentence with a reflexive pronoun that agrees with the subject of the sentence.

   12. Jenny bought _____ a book.
   MODEL ▷ Jenny bought herself a book.
   13. Jimmy bought _____ some amber, a hard, clear plant resin.
   14. "I can see _____ in the amber's smooth surface," he said.
   15. Dad found a beautiful amber necklace for Mom but nothing for _____.
   16. "Maybe we should set up a display for _____," Jenny suggested.
   17. "I can make a wooden display case by _____," answered Jimmy.
   18. We can see _____ in the display case he made.
   19. Jenny feels proud that she chose the specimens by _____.

Application — Writing

Description Imagine that you are an exhibit at the natural history museum. Write a paragraph for your fellow fossils and minerals describing the people who come to see you and telling how you feel about being an exhibit. Use reflexive pronouns in several sentences.

6 Indefinite Pronouns

◆ **FOCUS** An indefinite pronoun does not refer to a particular person, place, thing, or idea.

Remember that personal pronouns refer to specific people, places, things, or ideas. An **indefinite pronoun** is a pronoun that has no definite antecedent. It does not refer to a specific person, place, or thing. The words in color below are indefinite pronouns.

1. Nearly everyone in my class likes animals.
2. Somebody volunteers at the animal shelter each week.

Indefinite pronouns can be singular or plural. When an indefinite pronoun is used as a subject, the verb must agree with it in number.

3. Anybody is welcome to come to the shelter.
4. Several of my classmates spend many hours there on weekends.

Guided Practice

A. Identify the indefinite pronoun(s) in each sentence.
1. All of my classmates believe in treating animals humanely.
2. A few work hard convincing others to agree with them.
3. Many write letters to elected officials.
4. Most of my friends focus on humane treatment for pets.
5. Some work toward helping farm animals.

Indefinite Pronouns	
Singular	
anybody	everything
anyone	nobody
anything	nothing
each	somebody
everybody	someone
everyone	something
Plural	
all	most
both	others
few	several
many	some

THINK AND REMEMBER
◆ Remember that an **indefinite pronoun** is a pronoun that does not refer to a specific person, place, or thing.
◆ Remember that indefinite pronouns can be singular or plural.
◆ Follow the rules for subject-verb agreement when using indefinite pronouns as subjects.

Independent Practice

B. Identifying Indefinite Pronouns Write the indefinite pronoun or pronouns from each sentence. Identify each one as *singular* or *plural.*

6. Some of the adults think we won't accomplish anything.

MODEL ⟩ some—plural; anything—singular

7. In fact, several think we're wasting time.
8. Most of our parents, however, are proud of us.
9. They believe that everything helps.
10. Several of my friends also volunteer at a hospital.
11. Some like working with little children.
12. A few prefer to visit the elderly in convalescent homes.
13. Does anyone know what is involved in this work?
14. Almost anybody can do small errands for the elderly.
15. Someone may like to work with handicapped children.

C. Choosing Verbs That Agree with Indefinite Pronouns Write the verb form in parentheses that correctly completes each sentence.

16. Nobody in Grade 5 (has, have) ever done volunteer work.

MODEL ⟩ has

17. Most (realizes, realize) that volunteering is worthwhile.
18. Now, someone (wants, want) to help at the animal shelter.
19. Others (goes, go) along with her.
20. (Has, Have) anybody in Grade 5 volunteered at a hospital?
21. Yes, a few (has, have) just started at Mercy Center.

D. Proofreading: Checking for Errors in Pronoun-Verb Agreement Find the error in each sentence. Then write the sentence correctly.

22. Most of my friends concentrates on helping animals.

MODEL ⟩ Most of my friends concentrate on helping animals.

23. Many refuses to ignore an animal in need.
24. Some has persuaded their friends to adopt stray dogs.
25. A few of these animals needs medical attention.

Application — Writing, Speaking, Listening

Survey Results Take a survey in your class. Ask at least ten of your classmates to tell how they feel about helping animals. Prepare and present for your classmates a report about the results. Use at least four indefinite pronouns in the report. Be sure all the subject pronouns agree with their verbs.

7 Subject or Object Pronoun?

◆ FOCUS   Subject and object pronouns should be used correctly.

Subject pronouns are used as subjects and as predicate nominatives. Object pronouns are used as direct or indirect objects, or after such words as *by*, *for*, and *with*. Remember these rules especially when using pronouns as part of compound subjects and compound objects.

1. **Sally and I** took a computer class.
   compound subject

2. The best students were **she and I** .
   compound predicate nominative

3. Mr. Lee praised **Sally and me** .
   compound direct object

4. He gave **her and me** books.
   compound indirect object

The pronouns *we* and *us* are sometimes used with nouns for emphasis. Use *we* only with subjects and with predicate nominatives. Use *us* with direct and indirect objects, and with nouns that follow such words as *by*, *for*, and *with*.

5. The computer fans are **we** students.   **predicate nominative**
6. Computers can really help **us** students.   **direct object**

Your ear may help you decide which pronoun to use in a compound or with a noun. Leave out the rest of the compound or the noun with which the pronoun is used. Then notice how the pronoun sounds by itself in the sentence.

7. **We** (students) depend on information.
8. The computers are for (the teachers and) **us** .

Guided Practice

A. Identify the pronoun that correctly completes each sentence. Identify it as a *subject pronoun* or an *object pronoun*.
   1. (We, Us) students have a new computer.
   2. It is for the seventh-graders and (we, us).
   3. Mr. Lee is teaching (they and we, them and us) to use it.
   4. He showed Sally and (I, me) the keyboard.
   5. A future computer expert am (I, me)!

Independent Practice

B. Using Pronouns Correctly   Complete each sentence by using the correct pronoun. Write the sentence. Then write whether the pronoun is a *subject pronoun* or an *object pronoun*.

6. (We, Us) engineers build computers.

MODEL▷ We engineers build computers. subject pronoun

7. Tom and (I, me) studied computers in college.
8. Professor Chu taught Tom and (I, me) about programming.
9. A very fine teacher was (she, her).
10. (He, Him) and Ann became computer programmers.
11. The best programmers here are Ann and (he, him).
12. Ann and (he, him) write programs for computer games.
13. Sometimes Professor Chu gives Ann and (he, him) ideas.
14. People ask (we, us) engineers to make faster computers.

C. Proofreading: Checking for Correct Pronoun Usage   Find the error in each sentence. Write the sentence correctly.

15. I and Judy listened.

MODEL▷ Judy and I listened.

16. Mr. Terada told we students about Charles Babbage.
17. A man with brilliant ideas was him.
18. Judy and me found his life fascinating.
19. It was him who invented a computer in the 1820's.
20. Him and his machines met with much disapproval.
21. A young countess and him worked together.
22. One of the first computer programmers was her.
23. Mr. Terada showed me and Judy pictures of Babbage.
24. Us girls would like to have met him.

Application

Business Report   Imagine that you are a businessperson taking a class about some special equipment. Write a report for your boss about how your company might use this new equipment. Be sure to use subject and object pronouns correctly.

8 *Who, Whom, Whose*

◆ **FOCUS** The pronouns *who, whom,* and *whose* should be used correctly.

The pronouns *who, whom,* and *whose* are often used in questions. *Who* is a subject pronoun. It is used as the subject of an interrogative sentence. *Whom* is an object pronoun. It is used as a direct object, as an indirect object, or after words such as *to, by, for,* and *with.*

1. Who sorted these clothes? **subject pronoun**

2. Whom did you see? **object pronoun**

3. You gave whom the coats? **object pronoun**

4. To whom should I send all these children's clothes? **object pronoun**

Whose is a possessive pronoun. It is often used in questions about ownership. Do not confuse *whose* with *who's,* the contraction of *who is.* Remember that a possessive pronoun never has an apostrophe.

5. Whose shirt is this? **shows ownership**

6. Who's going to wear it? **replaces *who is***

Turning a question into a statement can sometimes help you decide whether to use *who* or *whom.* If you cannot easily turn the question into a statement, you should generally use *who.*

7. *Whom* did you choose? **You did choose *whom.***
8. *Who* said so? **cannot easily be turned into a statement**

Guided Practice

A. Tell whether *who, whom, whose,* or *who's* correctly completes each sentence.

1. _____ feels good about this work?
2. _____ did she bring to help us?
3. _____ group is Mark working with?
4. _____ going to keep track of all these boxes?
5. To _____ should I give this list?
6. _____ idea was this, anyway?

Independent Practice

B. Using *Who* and *Whom* Correctly   Decide whether *who* or *whom* correctly completes each sentence. Write the correct word.

7. _____ wants to help me here?

MODEL > Who

8. _____ can we call for extra assistance?
9. _____ feels like changing jobs with me?
10. With _____ would you like to work?
11. _____ will you ask to the benefit concert after the game?
12. For _____ is the concert being given?
13. _____ heard that it will benefit the earthquake victims?
14. _____ will the performers be?
15. If I go, _____ will go with me?

C. Using *Whose* and *Who's* Correctly   Decide whether *whose* or *who's* correctly completes each sentence. Write the correct word.

16. _____ idea was it to have the concert?

MODEL > Whose

17. _____ going to travel there to aid the victims?
18. _____ planning to help them rebuild their country?
19. Do you know _____ embassy I should call to volunteer?
20. You want to help, but _____ permission will you get?
21. _____ going to let a sixth-grader give that kind of help?
22. Can't you find someone _____ working for them here?
23. _____ going to let you start working for a different group when you have to finish this job first?

Application — Writing, Speaking, Listening

Interview Questions   Imagine that you are a reporter interviewing the victims of a disaster such as an earthquake or a flood. Make a list of questions to ask the people. Use *who, whom,* and *whose* in at least seven questions. Then have a partner play the part of one of the victims, and use your questions to interview him or her.

Building Vocabulary
Denotations and Connotations: Word Overtones

Dear Mayor Finn:
   I am writing to you about those quaint cabins by the lake. The owners are working with great persistence to preserve them.

Dear Mayor Finn:
   I am writing to you about those outmoded shacks by the lake. The owners are working with great stubbornness to preserve them.

As you read the letters above, you can probably tell that one writer wants to save the buildings and the other does not. Yet the letters are almost the same. Only the words in color are different. Even these words have the same **denotation,** or surface meaning. For example, both *cabin* and *shack* refer to a small, one-story building.

The letters communicate different messages because the words in color have different connotations. The **connotation** of a word is an extra layer of meaning made up of the feelings and the associations that the word suggests. The word *cabin*, for example, sounds cozy and appealing. It has a

positive connotation. A *shack*, on the other hand, sounds like a cold and miserable place. This word has a negative connotation. The connotations of the words in color give the two letters to Mayor Finn their overall positive or negative feelings.

Not all words have connotations. For most people, words such as *chair, go,* and *beside* suggest no particular emotion. As you speak and write, however, watch for words that do have connotations. Make sure that your words not only mean what you intend but also carry the connotation you want to express.

Reading Practice

Read each sentence. Write the word in parentheses that has the more positive connotation.

1. Sally's family spends the summer at a (quiet, boring) beach.
2. Usually Sally wears very (stylish, flashy) clothes.
3. Often, she buys (cheap, inexpensive) clothes.
4. During vacation she dresses in a more (sloppy, casual) way.
5. Sally has always been (skinny, slender).
6. Emily is Sally's (curious, snoopy) sister.
7. Emily likes to (entertain, aggravate) Sally.
8. She (pesters, asks) Sally to take her everywhere.
9. Sally has a (group, gang) of friends at school.
10. She tells her (playful, bothersome) sister to leave her alone.
11. Emily just (smiles, smirks) at her.
12. The family likes swimming in the (brisk, frigid) water.
13. The waves (beat, slam) against the shore.
14. Sally loves the salty (smell, stench) of the water.
15. Children (shout, shriek) as they run in the waves.

Writing Practice

Write the word in each pair that has a more positive connotation. Then use the word in a sentence.

16. plump, fat
17. clever, sly
18. soggy, wet
19. eat, gobble
20. tell, betray
21. thrifty, stingy
22. awkward, bungling
23. observe, spy on
24. laugh, snicker
25. chat, gossip
26. ambitious, pushy
27. take, steal

Project

Read the editorials and the letters on the editorial page of your local newspaper to find more examples of words with positive or negative connotations. Make a list of the words on a long strip of paper. Beside each word, write a word with a similar meaning but with a different connotation. Post the list on a bulletin board, and continue adding to it.

Language Enrichment
Pronouns

Use what you know about pronouns to do these activities.

 A Room for Two

Study the picture of the room. Imagine that you and a brother or a sister share this bedroom. Describe the room. Use possessive pronouns as you describe what belongs to you and what belongs to your brother or sister. Use subject and object pronouns as you tell how you use things in the bedroom. Imagine additional objects that might be on a shelf or inside a closet.

 Singing Telegram

Imagine that you write singing telegrams "to order" for special events. Fill this order: "We need a singing telegram to be delivered at a little girl's birthday party. The girl will be six years old. She loves kangaroos, spaghetti, and gymnastics." Use subject, object, and indefinite pronouns in your telegram.

 Interviewer

Imagine you are a reporter on a program that interviews famous historical figures. Pick two or three people from the past whom you would like to meet. List questions you would ask them. Begin at least half of your questions with *who, whom,* or *whose.* Have a different classmate pretend to be each person. Use your questions during several interviews.

Somebody loves you...

CONNECTING

In this unit you learned that pronouns can take the place of nouns. They can be subjects or objects and can show possession. They can reflect action back to the subject as well as tell about people, places, things, and ideas. Pronouns such as *who, whose,* and *whom* can be used to ask questions. You learned how to choose which pronouns to use, and how to make their antecedents clear.

◆ **Using Pronouns in Your Writing** When used correctly, pronouns can help you express yourself clearly without repeating yourself or using unnecessary words. Pay close attention to how you use pronouns as you do these activities.

Take a Guess

You have learned about connotation on the **Building Vocabulary** pages. Now use connotations to play this game. Write five or six sentences giving information about a person. Do not mention any names or express your feelings directly. Instead, choose words with connotations that reveal your feelings. Read your sentences to your classmates. See how quickly they can guess whom you are describing and how you feel about the person.

Example: He was born in a log cabin.
He rose to greatness.
He was an eloquent speaker.
He believed in justice.
His Presidency was a
turning point in U.S. history.

Who Are They?

Study the person and the animal in the picture. Tell who and what they are and what they normally do. Then imagine a story that would involve the girl and the parrot. Write a short summary of the story. Use pronouns to make your writing smooth. Make sure all your pronouns have clear antecedents.

5 Unit Checkup

Think Back	Think Ahead
◆ What did you learn about persuasive letters in this unit? What did you do to write one?	◆ How will what you learned about persuasive letters help you persuade someone? ◆ How will thinking about your audience help you evaluate reasons to support an opinion?
◆ Look at the writing you did in this unit. How did pronouns help you express your ideas?	◆ What is a way to check whether using pronouns helps to make your writing smoother?

Persuasive Paragraphs in Business Letters   *pages 210–212*
Read the persuasive paragraph. Then follow the directions.

> Students from other schools should be allowed to attend our school dances. Many students have friends who go to other schools. Our school would earn more in ticket sales. To promote friendship and goodwill among the different schools, let's open our dances to these students, and let the good times roll!

1. Write the topic sentence.
2. What opinion does the writer have?
3. How many reasons are given to support this opinion?
4. Where is the most important reason written? Why?
5. Write the clincher. Do you think it is effective? Why or why not?

Evaluating Reasons to Support an Opinion   *page 213*
Several reasons are given to support the following position. For each reason, write whether it is *good, not relevant, not logical,* or *not distinct.*

Students should be given homework every night.

6. It helps them practice what they learned that day.
7. It is an aid in reviewing material covered in class.
8. Doing homework helps build discipline.
9. Doing homework is boring.
10. We have plenty of time to work in school.

Using Formal and Informal Language   *page 214*
Write whether each sentence uses *formal* or *informal* language.

11. Let's face it. This story is excellent!
12. Your information seems to be incorrect.
13. The attire is not appropriate for the occasion.
14. Give me a break! Your rules are too bad to believe.

The Writing Process   *pages 215–224*
Write the letter of the correct response to each question.

15. When drafting a persuasive letter to a newspaper, your letter should be
    a. amusing.   **b.** angry.   **c.** businesslike.
16. Which sentence should be rewritten to make it more suitable for a letter to a newspaper?
    a. Our schools need more volunteers.
    b. I have a super idea for our schools!
    c. Perhaps people will think about this problem.
17. Which mark would show that the underlined word and comma in the sentence must be deleted?
    Our big, enormous budget must be trimmed.
    a. ⋀̲   **b.** ᵖ   **c.** ≡
18. When typing a persuasive letter to send to a newspaper, you should not
    a. write it on clean, white paper.
    b. use decorated stationery.
    c. send it to the editor of a newspaper.

Pronouns   *pages 228–229*
Write the pronoun or pronouns from each sentence.

19. A trembling Ryan couldn't believe that he was actually going to the haunted mansion.
20. The mansion was so dilapidated that it was almost falling down.
21. Ellie said bravely that she wanted to go to the mansion before the new owners arrived.
22. Ellie told Ryan that they should go to the mansion on Thursday afternoon.
23. When Ellie and Ryan arrived in front of the mansion, there was a surprise for them.
24. "Do you believe it?" said Ryan to Ellie, a bit relieved.
25. "The mansion! It's gone!" Ellie exclaimed.

Agreement of Pronouns with Antecedents   pages 230–231

Write each sentence. Draw an arrow from each underlined pronoun to its antecedent.

26. Lupe was disappointed that <u>her</u> team, the Diggers, had lost.

27. Mr. Parker told the team that <u>they</u> had tried hard.

28. Miranda was right when <u>she</u> said that the team played well.

29. "When the Diggers play the Rockets again, <u>we</u> will show <u>them</u>!" said Lupe.

Subject and Object Pronouns   pages 232–233

Write the pronoun in parentheses that correctly completes each sentence.

30. Kara and Cindy are best friends, and (they, them) do a lot of things together.
31. If Cindy is feeling sad, (she, her) calls Kara to have a little chat.
32. Kara often asks Cindy for advice because she trusts (she, her).
33. "(We, Us) will never be separated!" the girls claim.

Possessive Pronouns   pages 234–235

Rewrite each sentence. Use possessive pronouns to make the sentence less cluttered.

34. Albert Einstein spent much of Albert Einstein's life at Princeton University.
35. Einstein and many other scholars chose to leave Europe when the Nazis gained power in the land in which they lived.
36. Did you know that the grandparents I have once met Einstein?
37. It seems that every family has the family's own stories of meeting famous people.
38. The favorite story in the family that belongs to us will always be that of our grandparents meeting the great scientist.

Reflexive Pronouns   pages 236–237

Write the pronouns in each sentence, and label each pronoun *personal* or *reflexive*. After each reflexive pronoun, write the subject to which it refers.

39. I am teaching myself to speak Spanish.
40. Why don't you two teach yourselves?
41. Do you see that table standing over in the corner all by itself?
42. Why don't we sit ourselves down at the table, and I will give you a short Spanish lesson!
43. Max taught himself French, and he feels proud of it.

Indefinite Pronouns *pages 238−239*

Write the verb form in parentheses that correctly completes each sentence.

44. Somebody (is, are) buying our house.
45. It seems that nobody (like, likes) moving to a new school.
46. It is hard for newcomers when everyone else (has, have) friends.
47. Most others (goes, go) along and don't realize that the new person might be lonely.
48. A few, however, (do, does), and they introduce themselves.

Subject or Object Pronoun? *pages 240−241*

Complete each sentence by using the correct pronoun. Then write whether the pronoun is a *subject pronoun* or an *object pronoun*.

49. (We, Us) students were very angry.
50. Bobby said that (he, him) had been treated unfairly.
51. We called the president and the vice president of the club and told (they, them) how we felt.
52. In fact, the president apologized to Bobby and (I, me).
53. A very happy young man was (he, him)!

Who, Whom, Whose *pages 242−243*

Decide whether *who* or *whom* correctly completes each sentence. Write the correct word.

54. To _____ should we send the invitations for the walkathon?
55. _____ will actually be doing the walking?
56. To _____ did you give permission?

Decide whether *whose* or *who's* correctly completes each sentence. Write the correct word.

57. _____ idea was the walkathon?
58. _____ in charge of refreshments?
59. Do you know _____ walking shoes these are?

Denotations and Connotations: Word Overtones *pages 244−245*

Read each sentence. Write the word in parentheses that has the more positive connotation.

60. Our theater club will have to be very (careful, stingy) with its money for the rest of the year.
61. Does that mean we can't repaint those (dark, gloomy) walls?
62. I have a (plan, scheme) for raising the money we need.
63. Janet is so (quiet, aloof) that I didn't realize she could sing.
64. The audience was (noisy, enthusiastic).

UNIT

6

Creating Images

◆ **COMPOSITION FOCUS:**   Lyric Poem
◆ **LANGUAGE FOCUS:**   Adjectives

The poet Robert Frost once wrote, "Poetry begins as a lump in the throat." Frost was saying that poetry often expresses strong feelings. Poetry that expresses a writer's feelings is called lyric poetry. In lyric poetry the writer describes people, places, and things instead of telling a story about them.

Gail Newman teaches a poetry workshop at a middle school in California. Her students are among those who have participated. Their lyric poetry appears on the next few pages. In this unit you will use observation and imagination to create your own poetry.

◆ === *WARMING UP* === ◆

 IN YOUR JOURNAL
Describe images of early morning in the outdoors.

 CHORAL READING
WORK IN A GROUP
Study the picture on page 252, and discuss how it makes you feel. Then look in poetry books for a poem that expresses your feelings. Rehearse the poem before reading it to the class.

These students in Gail Newman's class create poetry *to express* their feelings, observations, and ideas.

Alethea Benally

De-Shun Washington

Lars Smith

Pablo Siguenza

Emma Moreno

Reading with a Writer's Eye
Lyric Poems

Almost anything can be the subject of a poem. Read these poems by student poets from the San Francisco Community School. Notice what they wrote about, what pictures they present, and what feelings they express.

Autumn
by Alethea Benally

Walking down the street is like
    walking into an enchanted forest.
        Brown and green leaves
            falling at the slightest
wind.
    So quiet all I can
        hear is the crunching
            of the leaves as
I step down.
        Autumn is like
            millions of ants
                crawling around.

The Sky Is as Vast as the World
by Pablo Siguenza

The sky is as vast as
the world.
    Clouds like
puffs of smoke
flames streak by
fast as light
    dark clouds
        come rolling in
like bowling balls.
Birds fly by.
    The night creeps
up like a robber as
the day sinks down west.

Looking Out My Window
by Emma Moreno

Looking out my window
the children playing tag in the street
the sun hitting my face
the smell of the pine trees
Mrs. Baker and Mrs. Simon
gossiping
a yellow bird sitting on a
telephone pole

Spirit of the Grizzly Bear
by Lars Smith and
Marc Almond

Night its nose,
He follows me
Stars its eyes,
He follows me,
Wind its breath,
He follows me
Thunder its growl,
He follows me,
Lightning its claws,
He follows me,
Thorns its teeth,
He's caught me,
A cave its stomach,
He's swallowed me.

There Is Danger
by De-Shun Washington

Jack-o'-lanterns falling from the sky vanish
in vapor, rain drops softly kiss the ground like
foxes and rabbits dancing in the shower
you better be careful because . . .

They sing the harmony of the forbidden
song. It summons their names
screaming out like lightning
you better be careful because . . .

They sway back and forth in a
winter breeze. A bee follows a bright
butterfly. You better not follow because

There is danger up ahead
snow flakes dance in the
wind.

Respond

1. Which poem do you like best? What do you like about the
   poem? What words and details create the quality you enjoy?

Discuss

2. Which poem creates the most vivid pictures in your mind?
   What words does the writer use to create these pictures?
3. What is the main subject of each poem? What mood does it
   express? How does the poet use details to express the mood?
   How does the writer's choice of words add to the mood?

Thinking As a Writer
Analyzing a Lyric Poem

A **lyric poem** expresses the poet's feelings. Often it does so by describing a person, an object, or a scene in nature. In a lyric poem, the language creates vivid **images,** or pictures, in your mind. The poem may or may not rhyme.

Writer's Guide

A lyric poem
- expresses feelings, often through description.
- presents vivid images.
- may or may not rhyme.

Winter Dark
by Lilian Moore

Winter dark comes early
mixing afternoon
and night.
Soon
there's a comma of a moon,

and each street light
along the
way
puts its period
to the end of day.

Now
a neon sign
punctuates the dark
with a bright
blinking
breathless
exclamation mark!

The **title** sets the tone for the poem. It may also give an idea of what the poem is about.

A **stanza** is a group of lines. An extra space separates one stanza from the next. Each stanza may have the same number or a different number of lines.

Rhyming words end with the same sound. In the second stanza, the words *way* and *day* rhyme. A lyric poem may or may not have lines that rhyme.

An **analogy** describes a surprising similarity between two very different items. A **simile** uses the word *as* or the word *like* to compare the items. A **metaphor** compares the items by saying or implying that one of the items *is* the other item. In the third stanza, the poet makes an analogy between a neon sign and an exclamation mark.

Discuss

1. What is the poet describing in the poem "Winter Dark"?
2. Which lines in the poem create images? What pictures do they create in your mind?
3. What analogies does the poet make in the poem? Are these analogies similes or are they metaphors? In what way is the whole poem an analogy?

Try Your Hand

A. Explain Poems   Read each set of lines from a lyric poem. Write what the poet is describing. Then in your own words, describe the image it makes you see.

1.
> Amid the mist in the
> dark, solemn forest, a
> cathedral of trees
> towered above the
> unwelcomed intruders.

3.
> Pots and dishes
> crowded in a sink
> stare at me
> like grumpy trolls.

2.
> Graceful as a cheetah,
> in three bounding
> soundless strides,
> the runner goes by.

4.
> During the storm, the
> waves pounded the
> beach . . . A battle of land
> and sea.

B. Analyze Analogies   Choose two sets of lines from **A**. Find one analogy in each set. Write the analogy, and label it *simile* or *metaphor*. Name the two items compared in the analogy, and describe how the items are similar.

C. Write Titles for Poems   Decide what mood each set of lines in **A** expresses. Write a title for each poem to help express its mood.

D. Read Lyric Poems   With a partner, choose some lyric poems that you like. Take turns reading the poems to each other. Discuss what the poems describe, what feelings they express, and how they use language to express these feelings. Look for images and comparisons in the poems.

Writer's Notebook

Collecting Double-Duty Words
Look at the word *punctuates* in the poem "Winter Dark." Usually, the word tells what you do to a sentence. The poet uses the word to express that same action, but in a surprising new context. In doing so, she adds rich layers of meaning and feeling to her description of lights on a winter night. When you come across a word used in an unusual context, record in your *Writer's Notebook* the word and its use. Look for opportunities to use these words in these new ways when you write poetry.

Thinking As a Writer
Visualizing Comparisons

Writer's Guide

To write an analogy, good poets
◆ visualize one item.
◆ select one characteristic of the item.
◆ visualize other items with the same characteristic.

When poets use analogies to compare items, they are mainly interested in one of those items. They use the analogy to help describe that item. To write a good analogy, therefore, poets begin by thinking about the item they wish to describe.

Suppose that you are writing a poem about a hot day and you want to describe the sun. You could begin by visualizing the sun and noticing its characteristics.

Sun—round, yellow, hot

For your purpose, the most important of these qualities would be heat. Therefore, you would visualize items that give off heat.

Sun = heat: flames,
stove, sparks
red-hot horseshoe being pounded by a blacksmith

Comparing the sun to a blacksmith may strike you as interesting. You could express the analogy as a simile or as a metaphor.

1. The sun hammered the world like a blacksmith.
2. The sun was a blacksmith, hammering the world.

When you write poetry, include interesting comparisons to create vivid images for your audience.

Discuss

1. The poem by Pablo Siguenza on page 254 contains this analogy: "Dark clouds come rolling in like bowling balls." Did the poet begin by visualizing clouds or bowling balls?
2. Choose another analogy from the same poem. Explain the process the poet may have gone through to think of this comparison.

Try Your Hand

Use Metaphors and Similes   Picture a place where you spent a happy time. Write an analogy that shows what was special about the place. Choose one important item in the place, and use visualization to write an effective metaphor or simile.

Developing the Writer's Craft
Avoiding Overused Words and Clichés

Good poets use fresh language because they want to make the world seem new to readers. They avoid overused words and clichés. **Clichés** are expressions that have been used so often that they have become dull and lifeless. Contrast the poem on the left with the livelier one on the right.

1. The sun rose bright as a button. It would be a nice day!

2. The sun rose like the space shuttle. This day would glow!

Does "bright as a button" really make you picture the brightness of the day? It probably doesn't. The phrase has been used so often that it has lost its power to bring images to mind. The phrase "like the space shuttle," by contrast, may still invite most readers to picture images because it is unusual and new.

Also compare the third line of the poems. People talk about "nice" days so much that *nice* no longer says much about a particular day. The word *glows,* however, remains fresh in this context. After all, how often have you heard someone say, "Have a day that glows"?

Learn to recognize overused words and expressions in your writing. Replacing these clichés with original language will make your writing more powerful.

Discuss

1. On page 254, Pablo Siguenza writes that "night creeps up like a robber." Is this a cliché? Why or why not?
2. Look at the poem by Lilian Moore on page 256. Explain what makes her language fresh.

Try Your Hand

Replace Clichés Read each cliché. Then write a phrase or sentence expressing the same idea in fresh language.

1. busy as a bee
2. hard as a rock
3. a stream of traffic
4. straight as an arrow
5. a flood of requests
6. like a ton of bricks

1 Prewriting
Lyric Poem

Mindy wanted to write a lyric poem for her aunt's birthday. She used the checklist in the **Writer's Guide** to help her plan her poem. Look at what she did.

Writer's Guide

Prewriting Checklist

☑ Brainstorm topics.

☑ Select a topic.

☑ Think about your audience and your purpose.

☑ Gather fresh images and ideas.

☑ Plan your poem.

◆ Brainstorming and Selecting a Topic

First, Mindy listed possible topics for her lyric poem. She looked around her room, her house, and her neighborhood for ideas. She thought about things she had seen and done recently in other places. She brainstormed all sorts of items about which she had special feelings.

my friend Patty
my school
hamburgers
✓ cantaloupe in summer
my favorite mystery novel
✓ summer camp
✓ the street I live on

Next, Mindy looked at her list. She circled the topics about which she had the strongest feelings. She crossed off the circled topics that would not bring vivid images to mind. Then, she thought about the feelings that each remaining topic gave her. Mindy put checks by the topics that brought to mind the strongest images. She decided to write about cantaloupes because they reminded her of summer. Mindy's aunt often came to visit her during the summer.

Discuss

1. Look at the topics Mindy listed but did not choose. Why do you think she did not choose these topics?
2. What topic might you have chosen from Mindy's list? Why?

◆ Gathering Images and Details

After Mindy selected her topic, she gathered images and details for her poem. She studied a cantaloupe closely, using all five of her senses. She also brainstormed everything the cantaloupe reminded her of, no matter how farfetched or odd the comparisons seemed. Mindy recorded her images and details in a cluster diagram.

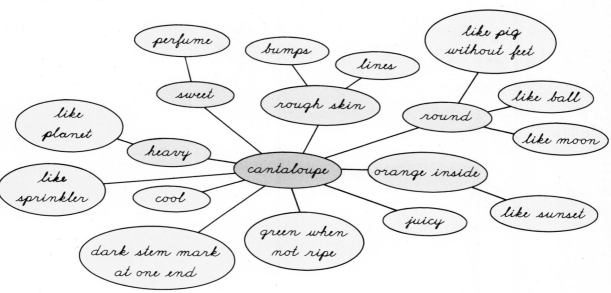

Mindy remembered that she wanted her poem to remind her audience of summer. Therefore, she brainstormed another cluster of words and details about summer. Look at Mindy's second cluster.

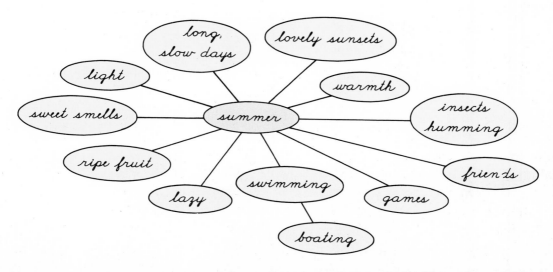

Discuss

1. Look back at the sensory details Mindy recorded in her cluster about the cantaloupe. Did she have to study an actual cantaloupe to record these details? How might Mindy have listed sensory details without having the object in front of her?
2. Look at the comparisons Mindy listed in her first cluster. Why did she think of each one? Which ones might work best in her poem? Why do you think so?
3. How might Mindy's cluster of details about summer help her compose her poem?

◆ Organizing the Images and Details

When Mindy was ready to plan her poem, she looked at her two clusters of details. The phrase "long, slow days" caught her eye. That was the feeling that she wanted to express. She decided to write about eating a cantaloupe—slowly, taking time to enjoy it. She made a time-order list of actions to help her organize her details.

Describe,
holding cantaloupe
feeling it
lifting it
smelling it
cutting it
tasting it

Discuss

1. Mindy decided to organize her poem around the eating of a cantaloupe. Why do you think she chose this plan? What are some other ways she could have organized her details?
2. How will Mindy's time-order list help her keep her details organized?
3. What other steps might Mindy add to her list?

Try Your Hand

Now plan a lyric poem of your own.

A. Brainstorm and Select a Topic Brainstorm a list of possible topics for your poem. Search your memory for ideas. Also, look at the world around you. Include any people, places, things, times, and events about which you have strong or special feelings. Then think about each topic and your audience.

◆ Notice the images that come to your mind as you think about each topic. Mark the topics that evoke the most vivid images.

◆ Decide which of the topics you have marked have special meaning for your audience. Of these topics, circle the one about which you have the strongest feelings. This will be the topic for your poem.

B. Gather Images and Ideas When you are satisfied with your topic, gather information for your poem. If you lose interest in your topic as you go along, brainstorm more topics and select a new one.

◆ Observe your topic, or picture it in your mind.

◆ Brainstorm details, sensory words, images, similes, and metaphors related to your topic. You may want to brainstorm more than one cluster of words and ideas, as Mindy did. To think of comparisons, visualize the topic, select one main characteristic, and then think of other items that have that same characteristic.

C. Organize Your Images and Ideas Plan a way to tie your images and ideas together.

◆ Look over the notes you have made. If you have made two or more sets of details, look for connections among them.

◆ Decide what central image or idea you want to express in your poem. Think about how the images and details in your notes help express this idea.

◆ Think of a pattern or a plan for your poem. You may want to make a time-order list, as Mindy did, or another kind of diagram. You may want to decide only where to begin and let the poem take its own course from there.

 Save your notes and your diagrams in your *Writer's Notebook*. You will use them when you draft your lyric poem.

Listening and Speaking
Tips on How to Listen to Poetry

Good poetry often pleases the ear because of the way it sounds. Here are some sound patterns often found in poetry.

Rhyme

A **rhyme** is a similar end sound in two or more words. *Spruce* and *goose,* for example, are rhyming words. Poets often place rhyming words at the ends of lines. Read aloud these lines from the poem "The Loaves" by Ronald Everson, and listen for the rhymes.

> Half a dozen white loaves lie
> in the oven of the sky,
> round above and flat below.
> Who is baking? I don't know.

Notice that in these lines, the first line rhymes with the second, and the third line rhymes with the fourth. A pattern of rhymes is called a **rhyme scheme.** In another rhyme scheme, for example, every other line may rhyme.

Rhythm

A **rhythm** is a regular pattern of stressed, or accented, syllables that give a poem a beat. The rhythm of a well-written poem goes with, and sharpens, what the poem is saying. Notice the rhythm in these lines from Irene R. McCleod's poem "Lone Dog."

> I'm a lean dog, a keen dog, a wild dog, and lone;
> I'm a rough dog, a tough dog, hunting on my own;

Listen now to the gentle rhythm in these lines from "The Owl and the Pussycat" by Edward Lear. Notice how this rhythm goes with the meaning of the lines.

> The owl and the pussycat went to sea
> In a beautiful pea-green boat.

Alliteration

Alliteration is what you hear when several nearby words begin with the same sound. Read these lines from the poem "Fly Away, Fly Away" by Christina Rossetti. Notice the words that begin with the /s/ sound.

> Fly away, fly away over the sea,
> Sun-loving swallow, for summer is done.

Assonance

Assonance means that several nearby words contain the same vowel sound. Read these lines from William Jay Smith's poem "The Owl." Listen for the repetition of the long /ō/ sound.

> The Owl that lives in the old oak tree
> Opens his eyes and cannot see

Consonance

Consonance means that several nearby words contain the same consonant sound. The sound is not necessarily at the beginning of each word. Listen for the repeated /r/ sound in these lines from "A Modern Dragon" by Rowena Bastin Bennett.

> A train is a dragon that roars through the dark.
> He wriggles his tail as he sends up a spark.

Onomatopoeia

Onomatopoeia is what you hear when the sound of a word imitates the meaning of the word. *Clang, buzz,* and *hiss* are onomatopoetic words. Notice the onomatopoeia in these lines from Alfred Lord Tennyson's poem "The Princess."

> The moan of doves in immemorial elms,
> And murmuring of innumerable bees.

2 Drafting
Lyric Poem

Writer's Guide

Drafting Checklist

☑ Use your notes and diagrams for ideas.

☑ Begin writing lines of poetry.

☑ Read aloud your poem as you write, and listen for appealing sounds.

☑ If sounds make you think of other lines, write those lines down.

☑ Try to establish a rhyming pattern or a rhythm in your poem.

☑ Include interesting comparisons and examples of alliteration, assonance, consonance, or onomatopoeia.

Mindy followed the **Writer's Guide** to draft her poem. Look at what she did.

> Cantaloupe
>
> Cradle a cantaloupe in both hands.
> cool as a cucumber.
> Lift the fragrant fruit
> to your face.
> It's ripe for eating
> if it smells sweet.

Discuss

1. Does Mindy's first line make you want to read on? Why or why not?
2. Why do you think Mindy decided to begin each new line where she did?

Try Your Hand

Now you are ready to write a lyric poem.

A. Review Your Information Think about the ideas and details you gathered and organized in the last lesson. Decide whether you need more ideas. If so, gather them.

B. Think About Your TAP Remember that your task is to write a lyric poem. Your purpose is to create vivid images that express your feelings to your audience.

C. Write Your First Draft Follow the steps in the **Drafting Checklist** to write your lyric poem.

When you write your draft, just put all your ideas on paper. Do not worry about spelling, punctuation, or grammar. You can correct the draft later.

Task: What?
Audience: Who?
Purpose: Why?

 Save your first draft in your *Writer's Notebook*. You will use it when you revise your lyric poem.

3 Responding and Revising
Lyric Poem

Writer's Guide

Mindy used the checklist in the **Writer's Guide** to revise her poem. Look at what she did.

◆ Checking Information

Mindy added an analogy that occurred to her as she was reading her first draft. She thought it deepened the feeling in her poem. She used this mark ∧ to add the words. She also cut one line that did not fit in with the rest of the poem. She used this mark ✄ to show what she was cutting.

◆ Checking Organization

Mindy moved one line to improve the rhythm and flow of her poem. She used this mark ◯ to show this change.

◆ Checking Language

Mindy realized that one analogy in her poem was a cliché. She replaced it with a comparison that expressed her own feelings about cantaloupes. She used this mark ∧ to show this change.

Writer's Guide

Revising Checklist

☑ Read your poem to yourself or to a partner.

☑ Think about your audience and your purpose. Add or cut details.

☑ Be sure that your poem has a sense of rhythm.

☑ Check for dull or overused words. Replace these words with fresh language that brings vivid images to mind.

☑ Check the unity of your poem. Be sure you have kept to the topic.

Replace

Add

Move

Cut

Cantaloupe
Cradle a cantaloupe in both hands.
cool as a ~~cucumber~~. (mossy stone)
Lift the fragrant fruit,
(heavy as a small planet,)
to your face.
It's ripe for eating
if it smells sweet
Slice apart
two sunsets.
Save one. Taste the other.
~~You always had such good taste!~~
Savor summer on your tongue.

Discuss

1. Look at the analogy Mindy added and the one that she changed. What feeling does each one express?
2. Do you think that moving the sixth line improves Mindy's poem? Explain your answer.

Try Your Hand

Now revise your first draft.

A. Read Your First Draft As you read your poem, think about your audience and your purpose. Read your poem aloud to yourself or to a partner to see if it expresses your feelings. Ask yourself or your partner the questions in the box.

<table>
<tr><td colspan="2" align="center">Responding and Revising Strategies</td></tr>
<tr><td>✔ Respond
Ask yourself or a partner:</td><td>✔ Revise
Try these solutions:</td></tr>
<tr><td>◆ Does my poem express what I want it to say?</td><td>◆ Cut words that are not related to your topic. Add ones that are. See the Revising Workshop on page 269.</td></tr>
<tr><td>◆ Does my poem sound pleasing when I read it aloud?</td><td>◆ Move words or lines to improve the poem's rhythm and flow and to add pleasing sound patterns.</td></tr>
<tr><td>◆ Is my language fresh?</td><td>◆ Replace clichés and overused words with fresh, vivid language. Use the Writer's Thesaurus.</td></tr>
<tr><td>◆ Will my poem create new images in the reader's mind?</td><td>◆ Add imaginative similes or metaphors.</td></tr>
</table>

B. Make Your Changes If the answer to any question in the box is *no*, try the solution. Use the **Editor's Marks** to show your changes.

C. Review Your Lyric Poem Again Decide whether there is anything else you want to revise. Keep revising your poem until you feel it expresses what you want it to express.

EDITOR'S MARKS

∧ Add something.
‿ Cut something.
◡ Move something.
∧ Replace something.

Save your revised poem in your *Writer's Notebook.* You will use it when you proofread your poem.

WRITING PROCESS

Revising Workshop
Keeping to the Topic

Good writers stick to their topic. In prose, they make sure that every sentence relates to the main idea. In poetry, writers face a special challenge. Good poems often touch on several topics in order to make interesting comparisons or draw surprising connections. Even so, however, a poem must be unified by one central image or idea. Good poets use every line of a poem to build the same mood, feeling, and idea. They avoid switching metaphors in the middle of a description. Compare these poems.

1. Roaring like jungle animals,
   waves of people washed across the plaza.
   Hey, it was a happy time. What more can I say?
2. Roaring like ocean waves,
   people washed across the plaza.
   The tide of merriment was rising.

In the first poem, the writer switches metaphors between the first line and the second. Are the people like jungle animals, or are they like waves? They cannot be both. The third line is jarring because it expresses a different mood. Notice that these problems are corrected in the second version.

Practice

Replace the words in parentheses ( ) to make each set of lines more unified.

1. Wind shrieked orders right and left.
   The trees bowed low.
   (Man, they looked scared or something.)
   The sun began to sink.
2. Setting foot upon the fairground
   like Columbus and his crew,
   we faced this bright new world.
   (Would there be something to eat here?)
3. Trucks rumbled
   like rogue elephants.
   Sports cars bounded past them
   (like shiny metal sharks.)

4 Proofreading
Lyric Poem

After revising her poem, Mindy used the **Writer's Guide** and the **Editor's Marks** to proofread it. Look at what she did to the last stanza.

Writer's Guide

Proofreading Checklist

☑ Check for errors in capitalization.

☑ Check for errors in punctuation.

☑ Check your grammar.

☑ Circle any words you think are misspelled, and find out how to spell them correctly. Be sure you have followed spelling rules for verbs.

⇨ For proofreading help, use the **Writer's Handbook.**

> as you savor it, remember
> other summers we have (spended) *spent*
> (tasteing) cantaloupes *tasting*
> when whole days (hurryed) past *hurried*
> like jets, and yet the hours
> *seemed* (seemmed) to last and last and last⊙

EDITOR'S MARKS

≡ Capitalize.

⊙ Add a period.

∧ Add something.

⋏ Add a comma.

ⱽ ⱽ Add quotation marks.

✄ Cut something.

⋏ Replace something.

↔ Transpose.

◯ Spell correctly.

⁋ Indent paragraph.

╱ Make a lowercase letter.

Discuss

1. Look at Mindy's proofread poem. What kinds of corrections did she make?
2. What spelling rules did Mindy use to correct the misspelled words in her poem?

Try Your Hand

Proofread Your Lyric Poem Now use the **Writer's Guide** and the **Editor's Marks** to proofread your poem.

Save your corrected poem in your *Writer's Notebook.* You will use it when you publish your poem.

WRITING PROCESS

5 Publishing
Lyric Poem

Writer's Guide

Publishing Checklist

☑ Make a clean copy of your poem.

☑ Check to be sure that nothing has been left out.

☑ Check that there are no mistakes.

☑ Share your poem in a special way.

Mindy made a clean copy of her lyric poem and checked it to be sure she had not left out anything. Then she and her classmates published their poems by giving a class poetry reading. You can find Mindy's poem on page 46 of the **Writer's Handbook.**

Here is how Mindy and her classmates gave a poetry reading.

1. First, each student read his or her poem silently and pictured images as he or she read. Each student identified the feeling he or she wanted to express.
2. The students practiced their poems until they nearly knew them by heart. Each student worked with a partner. The listener gave suggestions for improvement to the reader.
3. When everybody in the class was ready, they invited guests in to enjoy their class poetry reading.

Discuss

1. How can students use their voices to help express the feeling in their poems?
2. How might preparing for a class poetry reading be different if each student read someone else's poem?

Try Your Hand

Publish Your Lyric Poem Follow the checklist in the **Writer's Guide.** If possible, prepare for a class poetry reading, or try one of these ideas for sharing your lyric poem.

◆ Mount your poems on sheets of colored construction paper that have been folded in half. Make a cover, a title page, and a table of contents. Sew or staple the pages together to make a book. Share the book with another class.
◆ With a group of classmates, read your poems to one another and discuss the feelings they express.

Writing in the Content Areas

Use what you learned to write a poem about the world around you. Your poem can tell a story, paint a picture, or express feelings. Use one of these ideas or an idea of your own.

Writer's Guide

When you write, remember the stages of the Writing Process.

◆ Prewriting
◆ Drafting
◆ Responding and Revising
◆ Proofreading
◆ Publishing

Physical Education

A well-trained athlete can be poetry in motion. Describe a runner, a baseball player, a diver, or another athlete. How does the athlete move? What is beautiful about the athlete's movements? You may want to bring out the drama of competition in a poetic way.

Fine Arts

How does a piece of popular or classical music make you feel? How do you move to the music? What do the words, and the rhythms, melodies, or harmonies "say" to you? You may want to re-create the rhythms of a piece of music in your poem.

Health

How can you use rhyme and rhythm to urge people to eat healthier foods? Write a poem about the importance of balanced meals. Describe the benefits of eating good foods and the problems caused by having too many sugary or fatty foods in the diet.

Science

Look for poetry in the world of nature. Read a poem about an animal. How does it move? Where does it live? What sound does it make? What does it eat? Write a short poem describing the animal. You may want to make a sketch based on the images you see.

CONNECTING
WRITING ↔ LANGUAGE

Poets describe feelings and paint pictures with expressive language. What pictures do you see as you read this poem? What feelings do you get?

Glenwood Springs, Colorado

High on the bulky flank
of mountainside we see
one stubborn structure:
worn planks
pinned together by
red rust—an old shack,
as frail as a swallow's breath,
perched
up there,
where all day the hammering wind
pries at it and punches it.
Old-timers say the shack has been there
for a hundred years.

◆ **Adjectives in a Lyric Poem** The highlighted words are adjectives. Each one tells you more about a noun. Notice that some of the adjectives tell about number or amount. Others tell what kind of item the noun names. Imagine how bare this poem would be without the adjectives.

◆ **Language Focus: Adjectives** In the following lessons you will learn more about using adjectives correctly in your writing.

1 Adjectives

◆ **FOCUS** An **adjective** modifies a noun or a pronoun.

One word can change or add to the meaning of another word. Changing or adding to meaning is called **modifying.** Adjectives are words that modify nouns or pronouns. Many adjectives answer the questions *What kind? How many?* or *How much?*

what kind?   how many?   how much?

1. From her rich imagination come many drawings of great interest.

Most adjectives are placed just before the nouns they modify. Sometimes, however, adjectives can follow nouns. When they do, they are usually set off by commas.

2. The artist , eager and skillful, adds color to the pages.

The words *a, an,* and *the* are special adjectives called **articles.** *The* tells about one or more particular items. *A* or *an* tells about any item. Use *a* before words that begin with consonant sounds. Use *an* before words that begin with vowel sounds.

3. The artist will draw a picture of an elf.

Link to Speaking and Writing
Adjectives can change the mood, or tone, of a sentence. How does the editing change the tone of this sentence?

Graceful
Somber trees surround the ~~lonely~~ shining lake.
Graceful trees hide the shining lake from view.

Guided Practice

A. Identify each adjective. Tell whether it is an *article* or an *adjective that describes.*

1. The Grimms, two brothers, collected old tales.
2. The stories, rich and colorful, had been told for years.
3. Wise kings, courageous princes, and odd creatures appeared in the popular tales.
4. Small children have enjoyed the stories for many generations.
5. Most adults enjoy reading the entertaining tales, too.

Independent Practice

B. Identifying Adjectives Write each adjective. Label it *article* or *adjective that describes.*

6. The story is about a beautiful princess.

MODEL▷ The—article   a—article   beautiful—adjective that describes

7. The artist drew a handsome prince standing in the great hall, asking the evil king if he could marry the lovely princess.
8. The king demanded some impossible tasks of the brave hero.
9. The tasks led the prince into a deep forest.

C. Using Articles Correctly Use each pair of words in a sentence with the article *a* or *an.*

10. old story

MODEL▷ The artist illustrated an old story.

11. ancient wish   13. clever idea   15. elegant gown
12. wicked queen   14. brave deed   16. strange land

D. Revising: Changing Sentence Tone Change the tone of each sentence by replacing the adjectives. Write each new sentence.

17. A warm, glowing sun rose over the shining trees.

MODEL▷ A pale, wintry sun rose over the icy trees.

18. The frail princess, shy and trembling, woke up.
19. A strange meadow of shimmering flowers surrounded her.
20. The artist drew unusual blossoms and vines in bright colors.
21. She gave each bud and flower several green leaves.
22. She drew the princess with a pale face and long, shining, golden hair.

Application — Writing

Modern Fantasy Tale Rewrite part of an old tale or legend using modern words and modern surroundings and customs. Then imagine that you are the artist who will illustrate the tale. Write a description of the characters as you imagine them to be. Use clear, precise adjectives that will paint pictures in your readers' minds.

2 Proper Adjectives

◆ **FOCUS**   A proper adjective is formed from a proper noun.

Remember that a **proper noun** names a particular person, place, or thing. An adjective formed from a proper noun is a **proper adjective.** A proper adjective is always capitalized.

```
          proper noun          proper adjective
           ┌──────┐             ┌──────┐
The creature from  Venus  is selling  Venusian  plants.
```

Proper adjectives are often formed by adding a **suffix,** or ending, to a noun. When this happens, the spelling of the noun may change.

Suffix	Proper Nouns	Proper Adjectives
n, an, or *ian*	Africa, Asia, Europe, Egypt	African, Asian, European, Egyptian
ish	Poland, Ireland, England, Sweden	Polish, Irish, English, Swedish
ese	Burma, Nepal, Malta	Burmese, Nepalese, Maltese

Guided Practice

A. Identify the proper adjectives.

1. The Martian fellow demonstrated some toys.
2. The Italian booth was filled with shoes.
3. Sally bought some Venusian plants.
4. The space visitors admired the Colombian jewelry.
5. The Brazilian handbags sold quickly.

B. **6. – 10.** Name the proper noun from which each proper adjective in **A** was formed.

THINK AND REMEMBER
◆ Remember that a **proper adjective** is formed from a proper noun.
◆ Capitalize proper adjectives.

Independent Practice

C. Identifying Proper Adjectives Write the proper adjective in each sentence.

11. The space visitors tasted Asian foods at a banquet.
MODEL> Asian
12. Irish craftspeople had made the napkins.
13. The tables had been decorated by Nigerian carvers.
14. The chairs had been covered with Moroccan leather.
15. Chefs had made Polish sausages from old recipes.

D. 16.–20. Identifying Roots of Proper Adjectives
Write the proper noun from which each proper adjective in **C** was formed.

E. Forming and Using Proper Adjectives Write a sentence using a proper adjective formed from each proper noun. Use a dictionary if you wish.

21. Algeria
MODEL> Algerian traders brought salt and dates from the desert.

22. America	24. Canada	26. India	28. China
23. Russia	25. Vietnam	27. Mexico	29. Alaska

F. Proofreading: Checking for Errors in Capitalization Find the error in each sentence. Write the sentence correctly.

30. A merchant sold me a chilean dress.
MODEL> A merchant sold me a Chilean dress.
31. The venusian visitors enjoyed the dance.
32. The band played turkish melodies.
33. A group performed some guatemalan folk songs.
34. A woman performed a spanish dance.
35. The hawaiian hula was very popular.
36. Everyone sampled the swedish meatballs.
37. The space visitor enjoyed driving my german sports car.

Application — Writing

List Imagine that an intergalactic fair will be held in your community. Make a list of items to be sold at the fair. The list will be displayed in local shop windows for passersby to read. Name and briefly describe the items that will be brought by people from Earth as well as by imaginary beings from space. Use at least six proper adjectives.

3 *This, That, These, Those*

◆ **FOCUS** A **demonstrative adjective** points out a noun.

The words *this, that, these,* and *those* are called demonstrative adjectives. They answer the question *Which one?* The word in color is a demonstrative adjective.

1. The author of this book works hard to complete the story.

This and *these* point out nearby nouns. *That* and *those* point out more distant nouns. *This* and *that* are used with singular nouns. *These* and *those* are used with plural nouns.

2. He used these notes for the book he is writing now. **nearby**

3. He has discarded those pages. **distant**

If a noun does not directly follow *this, that, these,* or *those,* the word is considered a pronoun.

4. Those are confusing. **pronoun**
5. Those notes are confusing. **adjective**

Guided Practice

A. Identify the demonstrative adjective or adjectives in each sentence.

1. This book tells about the adventures of a little girl.
2. The hardworking writer invented all these characters.
3. The writer uses these adjectives to describe this girl.
4. Only time will tell whether that story will be good.
5. All those long writing sessions will result in success.

B. **6.–10.** Identify each demonstrative adjective in **A** as singular or plural.

THINK AND REMEMBER
◆ Remember that the **demonstrative adjectives** *this, that, these,* and *those* answer the question *Which one?*

Independent Practice

C. Identifying Demonstrative Adjectives Write the demonstrative adjective from each sentence.

11. This copy of *The Wind in the Willows* is very old.

MODEL This

12. That edition on the table is new.
13. Kenneth Grahame wrote this book.
14. These pictures are by Ernest Shepard.
15. Those illustrations were drawn by Sir John Tenniel.
16. These books are both children's stories.
17. Many adults enjoy this one.
18. Several movies have been made of that story.

D. 19.–26. Identifying Singular and Plural Demonstrative Adjectives Label each demonstrative adjective in **C** as *singular* or *plural*.

19. This copy of *The Wind in the Willows* is very old.

MODEL This—singular

E. Identifying Demonstrative Adjectives and Pronouns Label each underlined word as an *adjective* or a *pronoun*.

27. I really like these.

MODEL pronoun

28. This character is Toad.
29. That is his.
30. Badger found this.
31. This cap is Mole's.
32. These oars belong to Rat.
33. That table is Toad's.
34. They shared those.
35. This is the wrong way.

Application — Writing

Character Sketch Write a character sketch that describes an animal in an imaginary story for young children. Imagine an animal that lives and behaves like a person. Give the animal amusing, interesting, or annoying traits. Begin by describing the animal. Then tell what the animal does. Use *this, that, these,* and *those* at least once. If you need help writing a character sketch, see page 47 of the **Writer's Handbook**.

4 Predicate Adjectives

◆ **FOCUS** A **predicate adjective** is an adjective that follows a linking verb.

Remember that a linking verb connects the subject of a sentence to a word in the predicate. If the word in the predicate is a noun or a pronoun, the word is a predicate nominative. If the word in the predicate is an adjective, it is a predicate adjective.

1. The scientist was an inventor .
   predicate nominative
2. His invention was shiny . **predicate adjective**

In a sentence with inverted word order, the predicate adjective comes before the linking verb.

3. Fearful were the time travelers.
   inverted word order

> **Link to Speaking and Writing**
> Using a predicate adjective in an inverted sentence can add variety to your writing. Would you use this kind of sentence often? Why or why not?

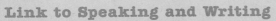
Loud was the roar of the engine.

Guided Practice

A. Identify each predicate adjective and the noun it modifies.

1. The machine was ready.
2. Inside, the leather seats felt comfortable.
3. The volunteers seemed nervous.
4. The scientist was proud indeed.
5. Impressive was the work he had done.

> **THINK AND REMEMBER**
> ◆ Remember that a **predicate adjective** is used with a linking verb to describe the subject of a sentence.

Independent Practice

B. Identifying Predicate Adjectives Write the predicate adjective from each sentence. Then, write the noun it modifies.

6. Stories about space travel are popular.
MODEL> popular—stories
7. Distant are the planets.
8. Voyages to the stars are difficult.
9. The tall rocket ships look rugged.
10. Brave indeed are the travelers who fly these ships.
11. Sometimes the travelers become ill with strange fevers.
12. Often, the planets they visit appear barren.
13. The travelers may feel homesick on a long journey.
14. After months in space, the food may no longer taste fresh.
15. At times, success may seem impossible.

C. Recognizing Predicate Adjectives and Predicate Nominatives Write *PA* for each sentence that has a predicate adjective. Write *PN* for each sentence that has a predicate nominative.

16. Time travel is simple.
MODEL> PA
17. This is a time machine.
18. This is the door.
19. The START button is red.
20. The pilot is he.
21. Your trip will be great.
22. You'll be surprised.

D. Completing Sentences Complete each sentence with a predicate adjective. Write the sentence.

23. The captain felt _____.
MODEL> The captain felt nervous.
24. The stars are _____.
25. The astronaut _____.
26. The rocket looked _____.
27. _____ was the crater.
28. The creature looked _____.
29. The moon rock felt _____.

E. Writing Sentences Use each word as a predicate adjective in a sentence with inverted word order.

30. sturdy
MODEL> Sturdy seemed the moon buggy.
31. icy   32. calm   33. reckless   34. flimsy   35. peaceful

Application — Writing

Fantasy Imagine that you are a scientist who has used the machine in the picture to travel into outer space or through time. Describe for other scientists where you have landed. Tell how things look and feel. Use at least five predicate adjectives.

5 Comparison with Adjectives: *er, est*

◆ **FOCUS** Adjectives can be used to compare nouns.

Adjectives have three forms, two of which are used in comparisons. The **positive form** is used when no comparison is made. The **comparative form** is used to compare two items. The **superlative form** is used to compare three or more items.

1. Maria is small . **positive**
2. Maria is smaller than the giant. **comparative**
3. The elf is the smallest of the three. **superlative**

Add *er* to the positive form of most one-syllable adjectives and some two-syllable adjectives to form the comparative. Add *est* to form the superlative. Sometimes you have to change the spelling of the positive form of an adjective before adding *er* or *est*.

Spelling Changes in Comparative and Superlative Forms			
In words that end in *e*, drop the final *e*.	fine close	finer closer	finest closest
In words that end in a consonant followed by *y*, change *y* to *i*.	dry hardy	drier hardier	driest hardiest
In most words that end in one vowel and one consonant, double the final consonant.	wet big	wetter bigger	wettest biggest

Guided Practice

A. Name the comparative and the superlative forms of each adjective. Tell which of these spelling changes is needed.

> no change   drop final *e*
> change *y* to *i*   . double final consonant

1. thin   **2.** dark   **3.** strong   **4.** large   **5.** shiny

---

THINK AND REMEMBER

◆ Use a **comparative adjective** (*er*) to compare two items.
◆ Use a **superlative adjective** (*est*) to compare three or more.

Independent Practice

B. Writing Comparative and Superlative Adjectives   Write the comparative and the superlative forms of each adjective.

6. bright

MODEL ▷ brighter, brightest

7. rosy	**11.** ripe	**15.** sad	**19.** safe
8. high	**12.** hot	**16.** fresh	**20.** sunny
9. dry	**13.** fierce	**17.** bold	**21.** wet
10. soggy	**14.** healthy	**18.** sweet	**22.** red

C. Completing Sentences with Adjectives   Write the form of the adjective in parentheses that correctly completes the sentence. The answer may be the positive, comparative, or superlative form.

23. The shepherd was (smart) than the giant.

MODEL ▷ smarter

24. Maria read the stories of Denmark's (great) writer, Hans Christian Andersen.
25. One of his (sad) stories was "The Little Mermaid."
26. "The Snow Queen" is also a sad story, but it has a (happy) ending.
27. Thumbelina was the (tiny) girl in the world.
28. Her walnut-shell bed was (tiny) than your thumb.
29. The (small) boy in fiction is Tom Thumb.
30. Tom Thumb was (small) than your hand.
31. Tom's size helped him in his (wild) adventures.
32. It is not (hard) to bring you the stories you like.

D. 33.–38. Writing Sentences with Adjectives   Choose five adjectives from **B.** Use the comparative and the superlative forms of each adjective in sentences.

33. bright

MODEL ▷ The sun seems brighter today than it was yesterday. This is the brightest day we've seen all summer.

Application — Writing, Speaking, Listening

Summary of a Conversation   Choose two partners, and imagine that all three of you are story critics. Each of you should read the same three short fairy tales or folk tales. In discussing the three tales, use the adjectives *happy, scary, bright, sad, long, dull,* and *lively*. Write a summary of your conversation to share with the class. Use comparative and superlative adjectives in your sentences.

6 Other Comparisons

◆ **FOCUS** Some adjectives that compare have special forms.

Remember that you add *er* and *est* to the positive form of most adjectives to form the comparative and the superlative forms. If an adjective has two or more syllables, however, the word *more* or *less* is usually used to form the comparative. *Most* or *least* is used to form the superlative.

good

better

Comparisons
Formed
While-U-Wait

1. Some machines are   more useful   than others.
   comparative
2. The inventor has made the   most wonderful
   machine in the room.   superlative

Never use *more* and *er* or *most* and *est* with the same adjective.

3. This machine does the   fastest   job of all.
4. This is the   most rapid   machine I have ever seen.

Some adjectives are irregular. Their spellings change completely in the comparative and the superlative forms.

Positive	Comparative	Superlative
much	more	most
good	better	best
bad	worse	worst

Some adjectives, such as numbers, articles, and demonstrative adjectives, do not have comparative forms.

Guided Practice

A. Tell the comparative and the superlative forms of each adjective.

1. serious   **2.** painful   **3.** productive   **4.** much   **5.** good

> **THINK AND REMEMBER**
> ◆ Use *more* or *less* and *least* or *most* to form the comparative and the superlative of most adjectives with two or more syllables.
> ◆ Memorize adjectives that change spelling completely in the comparative and the superlative forms.

Independent Practice

B. Writing Comparative and Superlative Adjectives Write the comparative and the superlative forms of each adjective.

6. efficient

MODEL more/less efficient, most/least efficient

7. troublesome 9. curious 11. dangerous 13. bad
8. amazing 10. colorful 12. intelligent 14. courageous

C. Proofreading: Checking for Errors in Adjective Usage Find the error in each sentence. Write the sentence correctly.

15. The inventor made the most usefullest robot.

MODEL The inventor made the most useful robot.

16. I would give my robot the carefullest instructions.
17. I would have the more spotless room in the neighborhood.
18. My difficultest chores would be done in a flash.
19. I would have mucher time for baseball than I do now.
20. My homework would be gooder than anyone else's.

D. Making Comparisons with Adjectives Write the form of the adjective in parentheses that correctly completes each sentence.

21. What is the world's (useful) machine?

MODEL most useful

22. The wheel may be the (good) invention of all time.
23. The computer is very (complicated).
24. The wheel, however, may be the (remarkable) tool we have.
25. Life would be far (bad) without the wheel.
26. Edward is the (dedicated) inventor I know.

E. 27.–32. Writing Sentences with Adjectives Choose four adjectives from **B.** Use the comparative and the superlative forms of each adjective in sentences.

27. efficient

MODEL A car is more efficient than a horse.
A car is the most efficient way to travel.

Application — Writing

Advertisement Write an advertisement telling students about an invention they might like to build. Describe what makes this invention better than other products of its type. Use at least four comparative and four superlative adjectives formed with *more* and *most*. Also, use at least two adjectives with irregular comparisons.

Building Vocabulary
Synonyms and Antonyms: A Wealth of Words

Sometimes, you may think of two or more words to express a feeling or to describe a scene. Two or more words that have the same or similar meanings are called **synonyms.** The highlighted words are synonyms.

1. The waves slapped noisily against the dock.
2. The waves slapped loudly against the dock.

You can add variety to your speaking and your writing by using a synonym instead of repeating a word.

3. The motor boat raced away from the dock and then raced back.
4. The motor boat raced away from the dock and then sped back.

Although synonyms have similar meanings, no two words have exactly the same meaning. Think about the words *stone, boulder,* and *pebble.* All are synonyms for *rock,* but they have different shades of meaning. A pebble, for example, refers to a small rock. A boulder refers to a large one. *Stone* is the word you use to focus on the material itself. Thus, you might say you found a cup made of stone, but you would never say you found a cup made of boulder or pebble. When you speak or write, therefore, be sure to choose the synonym that expresses the exact shade of meaning you intend.

Antonyms are words that have opposite meanings. Antonyms are useful when you want to discuss differences. Choose antonyms carefully to provide clear contrasts.

5. Jan caught a huge fish.
6. The fish Julie caught was tiny.

Reading Practice

Read each sentence. Find a word in each sentence that is a synonym or an antonym for the word in parentheses. Write the word from the sentence, and label it *synonym* or *antonym*.

1. The fish swam through the sparkling water. (gleaming)
2. Overhead the sun was hot. (blazing)
3. A burning wind moved through the trees. (icy)
4. Boats wandered through the bay. (roamed)
5. By evening the weather had changed. (morning)
6. Heavy clouds filled the sky. (light)
7. The wind grew chilly. (bitter)
8. People closed their windows tightly. (loosely)
9. The air felt cold and damp. (moist)
10. When it was dark, rain pattered on rooftops. (bright)
11. The rain made driving difficult. (hard)
12. Children played indoors. (worked)

Writing Practice

Complete each sentence with a synonym or an antonym for the underlined word. Add the kind of word named in parentheses ( ). If you need help, use a dictionary or a thesaurus.

13. Ira chose a <u>beautiful</u> picnic spot near a _____ lake. (synonym)
14. He spread a <u>bright</u> blanket on the _____ ground. (antonym)
15. He <u>remembered</u> the apples, but he _____ the grapes. (antonym)
16. I <u>loved</u> Ira's sandwiches, but I _____ the salad. (antonym)
17. Ira said that swimming would be <u>risky</u>, and wading would be _____, too. (synonym)
18. We <u>walked</u> across a field and then _____ to the lake. (synonym)
19. We had a <u>quiet</u> nap near the _____ water. (synonym)

Project

Make a series of synonym and antonym trees. Draw trees with branches and roots. On each trunk, write a word that you often use in speaking and in writing. You might use such words as *happy, run,* and *cold.* On the branches, write as many synonyms as you can. On the roots, write as many antonyms as you can. Put the trees on a bulletin board, and refer to them when you are writing.

Language Enrichment
Adjectives

Use what you know about adjectives to do these activities.

Leave It Out

Copy one or more paragraphs from a favorite book. Cross out all the adjectives. Then read the passage to classmates. Ask them to supply an unusual adjective for each blank. Write the adjectives as they are given. Then read the passage again with the suggested adjectives. You may find the results strange and interesting.

Weather Forecast

Play the part of a weather forecaster. Look carefully at the sky and the clouds. Then predict the next day's weather. Use adjectives to describe the skies, the clouds, the wind, the temperature, and the rainfall. The following day, read your prediction to the class, and check it against the actual weather.

I'll See You on the Telephone

In the future, when you use a telephone, you may be able to see the person with whom you are talking. Write an advertisement for such a telephone. Tell what it looks like and what special features it offers. Explain why it is better than today's phones. Use positive, comparative, and superlative adjectives.

CONNECTING
LANGUAGE ⟷ WRITING

In this unit you learned that adjectives give important details by telling *how many, how much, what kind,* or *which one.* They can be used in comparisons to show differences between things. Adjectives can be placed before or after nouns or pronouns, or after linking verbs.

◆ **Using Adjectives in Your Writing** Adjectives give you the power to describe people, places, and things vividly. Pay special attention to adjectives you use as you do these activities.

 How's the Food?

Imagine that you have traveled to another planet. Write a review of a restaurant there. Describe the food and the service, and tell how it was decorated. Tell whether you would recommend the restaurant to people from Earth. Use adjectives that compare. Also use adjectives before and after nouns or pronouns, and after linking verbs.

 Adjective Switch

You learned about synonyms and antonyms on the **Building Vocabulary** pages. Use synonyms and antonyms to change a familiar poem. Find a poem that many of your classmates know well. Then rewrite the poem, using either synonyms or antonyms for as many of the adjectives as you can. Read your poem to some classmates. See how many of them can guess what the original poem was. Discuss what your changes show about the poet's own choice of words.

6

Unit Checkup

Think Back	Think Ahead
◆ What did you learn about lyric poems in this unit? What did you do to write one?	◆ How will having written a lyric poem help you read other poems? ◆ How will avoiding clichés help you when you write poetry?
◆ Look at the writing you did in this unit. How did using adjectives help you express more colorful ideas?	◆ What is one way you can use adjectives to help avoid clichés?

Lyric Poems   *pages 256–257*

Read the lyric poem. Then answer the questions.

Anticipation

The sky is a sagging ceiling;
Great cotton clouds turn dirty.
We wait.

The air turns sharp and dampens;
The ceiling sky moves lower.
It snows.

1. How does the title give an idea of what the poem is about?
2. How many stanzas does the poem have?
3. What type of analogy is used for the sky?
4. What does the poem compare the sky to?
5. Does this poem have rhyming words? If so, what are they?

Visualizing Comparisons   *page 258*

Visualize and write an analogy comparing the following topics.

6. sunshine—music notes
7. hair—ocean waves
8. trees—giants

9. green lawns—soft fabric
10. whispers—gentle breeze

Avoiding Overused Words and Clichés   *page 259*

Replace each underlined cliché with words expressing the same idea in fresh language. Write the sentences.

11. Marla's tired fingers were <u>as stiff as a board</u>.
12. The students were <u>as busy as beavers</u>.
13. Your idea isn't <u>worth a dime</u>.
14. The baby's skin felt <u>as smooth as silk</u>.
15. Candy <u>sings like a bird</u>.

The Writing Process   *pages 260–271*

Write the letter of the correct response to each question.

16. After gathering images and details for a lyric poem, what should you do?
    a. Read them to a friend.
    b. Write the poem in the order in which you thought of them.
    c. Decide what central image or idea you want to express.
17. Which line needs to be revised because it contains a cliché?
    a. The sky looked like soft, blue velvet.
    b. The sky was as dark as night.
    c. The gray clouds swallowed up the blue sky.
18. When reading your poem aloud, you should
    a. read from your paper, not looking at the audience.
    b. ask someone else to read it.
    c. use your voice to express tone.

Adjectives   *pages 274–275*

Write each adjective. Label it *article* or *adjective that describes*.

19. Beth, the helpful flight attendant, brought the bored children two coloring books.
20. Soon the children were asking for cold drinks and small packages of nuts.
21. Beth did not get much rest on the long, crowded flight to California.
22. Pleasant thoughts, however, were always on her tired mind.
23. In two weeks Beth would be taking a vacation in beautiful, peaceful Tahiti!
24. Beth had a good job, and for very little money she got to fly anywhere her airline went.

Proper Adjectives   *pages 276—277*

Write the proper adjective in each sentence.

25. Maybe I'll take my vacation in a European city this summer.
26. Since Italian food is my favorite, maybe I will travel to Rome.
27. The Spanish people are justly proud of their greatest museum, the Prado in Madrid.
28. Of course, who wouldn't want to see a Parisian sunset behind the Eiffel Tower?
29. The Danish countryside is supposed to be gorgeous.
30. Maybe I should stay home and visit an American city.
31. Some Mexican chili would taste very good to me right now.

This, That, These, Those   *pages 278—279*

Write the demonstrative adjective from each sentence.

32. That room has been reserved for the Career Day program and exhibits.
33. Could you please put these registration forms by the door?
34. This speaker is Mrs. Moltz, who will tell the students about careers in publishing.
35. Each person will set up a booth over by those pillars at the end of the hallway.
36. Is that woman from the Environmental Protection Agency?
37. These speakers represent many different kinds of companies.
38. Are any of those people employed in health services occupations?
39. Is this Career Day the first our school has ever held, or was one held last year?

Predicate Adjectives   *pages 280—281*

Write the predicate adjective from each sentence. Then write the noun it modifies.

40. Chess is interesting.
41. Checkers seems quite easy.
42. The old tried-and-true games are really the best.
43. Some games, however, seem never-ending.
44. Pocket games are convenient.
45. "Geography," that old travel game, becomes challenging after the easy place names are used up.
46. Kendra's knowledge of geography is excellent for such a young child.

Comparison with Adjectives: *er, est* *pages 282–283*

Write the form of the adjective in parentheses that correctly completes each sentence.

47. Claudia wanted to go to an amusement park, but Inez felt like doing something (quiet).
48. Claudia made a (strong) argument than Inez did, however, so the girls spent their day at Fiesta World.
49. Did you know that Fiesta World has the (tall) Ferris wheel in this part of the United States?
50. Inez said she was feeling (tired) until she got to the park.
51. Once she got there, however, Inez said she felt (happy) than before.

Other Comparisons *pages 284–285*

Find the error in each sentence. Write the sentence correctly.

52. What do you think is the most challengingest job in the medical field?
53. I think being a nurse would be gooder than being a laboratory technician.
54. Because Syrie loves helping people, she thinks being a nurse would be the most pleasantest job of all.
55. Syrie did the beautifullest job of setting up trays for all the patients yesterday.
56. Jonathan says that just sitting behind a desk waiting for things to happen would be the worstest kind of job he could imagine.

Synonyms and Antonyms: A Wealth of Words
pages 286–287

Complete each sentence with a synonym or an antonym for the underlined word or words. Add the kind of word named in parentheses. If you need help, use a dictionary or thesaurus.

57. On our vacation we <u>viewed</u> the White House and _____ the Capitol. (synonym)
58. Our guide <u>spoke</u> about some of the Presidents who had lived there and _____ several funny stories. (synonym)
59. The weather was <u>sunny</u> when we left our hotel, but it turned _____ as soon as we got to the park. (antonym)
60. We ended up eating a <u>fancy</u> lunch at a restaurant instead of the _____ one we had planned for the park. (antonym)
61. I want to <u>go back</u> to Washington next year, and I hope to _____ to the Air and Space Museum while I'm there. (synonym)

UNIT

7

Persuading Others

◆ **COMPOSITION FOCUS:** Persuasive Essay
◆ **LANGUAGE FOCUS:** Adverbs

Save the whales! Vote for Kay Jimenez! Buy a steel bike lock! Persuasion is a part of our everyday lives. Our friends, our leaders, and our family members often tell us their opinions and try to persuade us to feel the same way. Television, radio, and newspapers are filled with advertisements and other forms of persuasion.

Many professional writers publish articles to persuade people to take certain actions. Toni Volk writes about the environment, hoping to convince people to take better care of our natural resources. In this unit you will also write a persuasive essay.

◆ === *WARMING UP* === ◆

IN YOUR JOURNAL

Write about a time someone persuaded you to try something new. What did that person say or do to convince you?

LIBRARY

WORK IN A GROUP Identify the people who said the following famous lines in a speech. Then use the library to find out what they were trying to persuade people to do. Share and discuss your answers.

1. "Ask not what your country can do for you. Ask what you can do for your country."
2. "I have a dream today."

Toni Volk writes *to persuade* people to care about the environment.

Reading with a Writer's Eye
Persuasive Essay

You may have heard the slogan "Give a hoot. Don't pollute." In the following essay, Toni Volk goes beyond slogans. She takes a close look at some of the threats facing our environment. As you read her article, think about the dangers she describes. Notice the evidence she gives to prove her points.

Earth Is Our Home
by Toni Volk

Would you ever think of gathering garbage and poisonous chemicals from your kitchen, dumping them in your bedroom, and then settling down to eat and sleep and live in the mess? Of course not. Yet we, the people of the earth, are behaving this way on a grand scale by polluting the air, soil, water, and other resources we need for our survival. We must take action, starting now, to rescue and restore the earth.

Action begins with understanding. We have to understand, for example, the importance to our lives of ozone, a type of gas found in the upper atmosphere. A layer of this gas surrounds the earth, keeping out dangerous parts of sunlight known as ultraviolet rays. Some of the chemicals we produce, however, have been floating up and turning ozone into oxygen. Oxygen does not keep out ultraviolet rays. Once these rays reach the earth they may cause skin cancers. They can damage crops and change the climate.

In fact, as more and more ozone turns into oxygen, the whole earth may begin to heat up, a process that scientists call the "greenhouse effect." Rising temperatures can lead to storms and droughts. The ice in the polar regions may melt as well, which could result in floods around the world. Scientists are now studying a large hole in the ozone shield above Antarctica. Sunbathing under that hole, according to one science writer, would be "a death-defying act." What will happen if that hole grows larger—or if the entire ozone layer is destroyed?

Toxic wastes are another serious problem. Certain factories and chemical plants produce these poisonous materials as a by-product. Toxic wastes are "leftovers" just like the garbage that we produce at home in the course of daily life. Rotten fruit, stale bread, and paper cartons, however, can be buried in a landfill, where they soon break down and become part of the soil. Toxic wastes are another matter. Some of these chemicals do not break down for thousands of years. If burned, they pollute the air. If buried, they can poison the soil and then turn up in the plants that people, livestock, and wild animals eat. They can mix with the water in the soil and eventually leak into rivers, lakes, streams, and the ocean.

Consider what can happen when toxic wastes get into a stream. The chemicals enter tiny plants, animals, and insects that live on or near the stream. Fish become poisoned as they eat these plants, animals, and insects. Deer and livestock absorb the poison too as they drink from the stream or eat poisoned plants. Eventually all these animals may end up on our dinner tables. As we eat the tainted fish or meat, the toxic wastes enter our bodies. Worst of all, the poison becomes more concentrated as it moves up the chain, from water into plants, from plants into animals, and from animals into people's bodies.

A third serious problem facing the earth is deforestation—the cutting down of forests. Deforestation is under way all over the world, yet human survival depends on these great stretches of trees, bushes, and vegetation. Forests provide the earth with oxygen. Forests hold moisture, thus making rain possible. Rain is important, of course, because it returns water to the earth. Forests provide shade for plants that hold the topsoil. Without these plants, rain or melting snow either evaporates or runs along the top of the ground, picking up silt as it eats away the earth. This silt ends up in rivers and lakes or blows around the world as dust storms that cause droughts. For all these reasons, trees are called "the skin of the earth."

Scientists say this is the most critical period in the history of the earth. They say the whole globe must cooperate to solve the problems we face. Is the situation hopeless? Not at all. Many times in human history, a few people have launched movements to bring about enormous changes. Many of these changes directly affect your life today. For example, in the early 1900's, young children worked in factories for as many as sixteen hours a day. They worked for extremely low wages under dirty and dangerous conditions. Then a few people took action, more people joined in, and eventually a great movement succeeded in passing laws to protect children from such abuses in the future.

You, too, can take action to affect the future. Here are just a few of the ways in which you can help.

◆ Avoid products that deplete the ozone. These products include aerosols and solvents. Remember that products containing harmful chemicals create waste problems even as they are made.

◆ Many communities have collection points where people can bring dangerous household wastes for safe storage and disposal. If your community has such a service, offer to help your parents find and collect empty containers around your home that have held dangerous materials. Dangerous household wastes include paint and paint thinners, furniture strippers, used motor oil, drain openers, bleach, disinfectants, and fertilizers.

◆ Recycle aluminum cans, bottles, and newspapers. Do you know people who do not recycle these materials? Offer to pick up their recyclables on a regular schedule. You can earn money and help the environment at the same time.

◆ Plant just one tree and commit yourself to nourishing it. See that the tree gets water. Be grateful to the tree for the oxygen it is adding to the earth.

Today more than ever the earth needs our concern and care. Your help is needed. Begin by writing just one letter. You could write to the president, a senator, the governor of your state, or a newspaper, for example. Express your concerns for the environment and ask the person to help. By taking action yourself, you encourage everyone else to take action too. Earth—our home—is worth the trouble.

Respond

1. Which part of Toni Volk's article interests you the most? What information does it contain that makes you care about environmental pollution?

Discuss

2. Toni Volk says our environment is in trouble. That is one opinion she holds. What other main opinion does she state in this essay?

3. Do you agree with the opinions Toni Volk presents? What evidence does she present that leads you to agree with her?

Thinking As a Writer
Analyzing a Persuasive Essay

A persuasive essay presents facts and reasons to support an opinion and a course of action. A persuasive essay has an **introductory paragraph,** **supporting paragraphs,** and a **conclusion.**

Reread parts of Toni Volk's persuasive essay.

Earth Is Our Home

Would you ever think of gathering garbage and poisonous chemicals from your kitchen, dumping them in your bedroom, and then settling down to eat and sleep and live in the mess? Of course not. Yet we, the people of the earth, are behaving this way on a grand scale by polluting the air, soil, water, and other resources we need for our survival. We must take action, starting now, to rescue and restore the earth.

The **title** gives an idea of what the essay is about.

The **introductory paragraph** often begins with a strong statement to catch the reader's interest. It includes a **position statement** that gives the writer's main opinion.

You, too, can take action to affect the future. Here are just a few of the ways in which you can help.

◆ Avoid products that deplete the ozone. These products include aerosols and solvents. Remember that products containing harmful chemicals create waste problems even as they are made.

The **supporting paragraphs** give reasons or facts that support the writer's opinion. Here the writer is stating actions the reader can take to help save the environment.

Today more than ever the earth needs our concern and care. Your help is needed. Begin by writing just one letter. You could write to the president, a senator, the governor of your state, or a newspaper, for example. Express your concerns for the environment and ask the person to help. By taking action yourself, you encourage everyone else to take action too. Earth—our home—is worth the trouble.

The **conclusion** sums up the writer's main idea in a way that leaves a strong impression. It often contains a **call to action,** encouraging readers to do something about the issue discussed in the essay.

Good writers use strong reasons and persuasive language. They do not, however, try to mislead their readers with **propaganda techniques.** These are techniques for influencing beliefs without presenting correct facts or logical reasons. Here are examples of some common propaganda techniques.

Over 100,000 people drive a Guzzla luxury sedan. Don't miss out! Join the parade!

The bandwagon technique tries to persuade an audience to believe or do something because many others supposedly believe it or are doing it.

Use Air-O-Blast deodorant spray. Glenda Powers, the famous actress, does!

A testimonial tries to make a belief or an action seem right by claiming that some well-known person recommends it.

Get RID of UGLY, DISGUSTING oil stains. Use Grimex degreaser!

Emotional words are words with powerful connotations, used to affect the emotions of the audience and distract them from the facts.

Nine out of ten dentists surveyed recommended Sparkly. Buy the toothpaste most dentists recommend.

A faulty generalization bases a conclusion on too few examples. How many dentists were asked about toothpaste? This ad does not say.

Everyone agrees that using Lilac Air Freshener is fun. So, get your Lilac today and start having fun.

Begging the question is taking for granted the matter or item in question.

Discuss

1. Look at the introductory paragraph, the supporting paragraph, and the conclusion of Toni Volk's persuasive essay. How is the information in each part different?
2. What is wrong with each of the propaganda techniques described? Why are they sometimes convincing?
3. Does Toni Volk use any of these techniques in her essay? Explain your answer.

Try Your Hand

A. Identify Position Statements and Supporting Reasons Read each set of sentences. Then write the position statement. Below it, write only the sentences that support it.

1.
> Recycling used cans and bottles is a good idea. The labels on some bottles are really quite attractive. It also helps prevent a lot of junk from getting dumped into the environment. Food in metal cans stays fresh for a long time, too. Recycling is a good way to earn extra money. Recycling also helps to conserve our natural resources.

2.
> Do you ever share a ride to school or to work? I believe that sharing rides is good for almost everybody. Sharing rides means fewer cars on the road. That means less traffic and less pollution. Also, people who share rides save money on gas and car repairs. Sharing rides is more fun if everybody has a comfortable car.

B. Write and Analyze an Opening Sentence Choose one of the position statements you wrote in **A.** Write a sentence you could use to begin a persuasive essay on this topic. Then explain why the sentence would make a good opener.

C. Write and Analyze a Conclusion Write at least three sentences you could use in the conclusion of an essay about the topic you chose in **B.** Then write why the sentences would make a good conclusion.

D. Analyze an Editorial Find a magazine or newspaper editorial and cut it out. Underline the position statement and the supporting sentences.

Writer's Notebook

Collecting Science Words Did you notice the science words, such as *oxygen, ozone,* and *ultraviolet,* in the persuasive essay by Toni Volk? Reread the essay, and record in your *Writer's Notebook* as many science words as you can find. Look up the words in a dictionary, and write their definitions and a sample sentence as well. Try to use the words you collect when you write and speak.

Thinking As a Writer
Classifying Fact and Opinion

Writer's Guide

To write a persuasive essay, good writers

♦ back up opinions with facts.

♦ keep opinions and facts separated.

In a persuasive essay, a writer states one or more opinions and backs them up with facts. A **fact** is a statement that can be proved true or false. An **opinion** is a statement of a person's attitudes or feelings.

Facts	Opinions
1. Ozone is a gas. 2. It is located in the upper atmosphere. 3. It acts as a shield.	1. We need to understand the importance of ozone. 2. We should conduct more studies of the ozone layer.

Careful writers keep facts and opinions clearly separated. They avoid expressing an opinion as if it were a fact. Often they include signal words such as *I think* or *I believe* to let readers know that they are expressing an opinion. Good writers recognize that words such as *silly, hopeless, awful,* and *best* usually signal opinions because they express judgments. If a sentence includes such words, a good writer checks to see whether it is an opinion and adds supporting facts if needed.

Recognizing the difference between facts and opinions can help you write stronger persuasive essays. As you write, watch for sentences that express judgments and attitudes. Remember to back up with accurate facts any opinions that you express.

Discuss

1. Look at the second paragraph of "Earth Is Our Home" on page 296. What opinions are expressed in the paragraph? What facts are given to back up the opinions?
2. Read this statement: *Spending money to rescue whales is just plain silly.* Is this a fact or an opinion? Explain your answer.

Try Your Hand

Write Facts and Opinions   Write three facts and three opinions. Have a partner do the same. Read your sentences to each other in random order. Identify each sentence you hear as *fact* or *opinion.*

Developing the Writer's Craft
Using Vivid Words

Writer's Guide

Good writers
◆ use vivid words and phrases.

"It's not just what you say but how you say it." You have probably heard these or similar words before. They mean that the words you use to express your ideas are important.

1. Sunbathing under the hole in the ozone layer would be *very, very dangerous.*
2. Sunbathing under the hole in the ozone layer would be a *death-defying act.*

In sentence 1 the writer tries to increase the impression of danger by repeating the word *very.* The attempt fails because *very* and *dangerous* are both ordinary words. They do not create a vivid mental picture. In sentence 2 the writer has replaced these ordinary words with the vivid phrase *death-defying act.* Notice how much more forcefully these words work to express danger.

When you write a persuasive essay, use vivid words to make your writing come alive for the reader. Instead of common words like *rain, run,* and *red,* use words like *downpour, gallop,* and *scarlet.* The more vivid your language, the more persuasive you will be.

Discuss

1. Look at the first paragraph of "Earth Is Our Home" on page 296. What words does the writer use to create a vivid impression of the dangers threatening our environment?
2. Read these two sentences: "The whales were tired." "The giant mammals were exhausted." Which sentence makes you more sympathetic to the whales? Why?

Try Your Hand

Use Vivid Words Look at the picture of the whales and their rescuers. Write five sentences that describe their appearance and actions. Use vivid words.

1 Prewriting
Persuasive Essay

David wanted to write an essay for the members of his school's Cleaner World Club. He used the checklist in the **Writer's Guide** to help him plan his essay. Look at what he did.

Writer's Guide

Prewriting Checklist
- ☑ Brainstorm topics.
- ☑ Select a topic about which you have a strong opinion.
- ☑ Think about your audience and your purpose.
- ☑ Gather facts that support your opinion.
- ☑ Organize the information.

◆ Brainstorming and Selecting a Topic

First, David brainstormed a list of possible topics for his essay. Look at David's list. David included many environmental issues.

Next, David looked down his list and crossed out topics that he thought would not interest his audience. He also crossed off topics for which he would have trouble finding or understanding information.

Finally, David circled the third topic on his list. He felt that of all the problems remaining on his list, this was the one his club could do the most to help solve. He knew that since all the members of his club go to the school, they would be interested in having a clean place to play and to spend time with their friends. David also knew that he could find all the information he would need by reading and by speaking to other students and adults.

~~Saving the endangered gorillas in Africa~~
~~"Scrubbers" and how they clean factory waste~~
(Cleaning up the schoolyard)
The problem of acid rain
Pollution in Ancient Rome

Discuss

1. Look at each topic David crossed off his list. Why do you think he decided against each topic?
2. Suppose David were writing an essay for a wildlife club. Which topic do you think he might have chosen? Why?

◆ Gathering Information

After David selected his topic, he gathered information for his essay. To help develop his opinions, he read several articles and interviewed a number of people to get their ideas. He prepared to interview the people by thinking of questions that he could ask them. Look at David's questions.

How do you feel about a school clean-a-thon?
What can you do to help?
How can we get others involved?

David interviewed the principal, the school custodian, several students in each grade, and a salesperson for a professional cleaning company. The salesperson told David that the students could never clean up the mess themselves. The salesperson used emotionally charged words such as *back-breaking, deadly, horrendous, filthy,* and *unqualified.* Fortunately, David recognized this as a sales propaganda technique and did not become discouraged.

David took notes on the information he gathered.

Information from a written source
Magazine article. Schools where students help with chores have more school spirit.
Newspaper article. Stanley School held a successful cleanup day last year.

Main question asked in interviews
Should students clean schoolyard? Why?

Reasons to support position
Principal Drew. Self respect and pride
Sally and Tony. The yard is dirty.
People should try to solve problems. not just grumble about them.
We can do a good job right now.

Propaganda
Dirty Trick Cleaning Company says we'll need "professional" help.

Discuss

1. Look at David's notes. Which ones contain information he might use in his introduction? Which ones might he use to write his supporting paragraphs?
2. Who else might David have interviewed to gather information for his essay?

WRITING PROCESS

◆ Organizing the Information

After David had gathered enough information for his persuasive essay, he was ready to organize his notes. First, he had to make sure that he had one clear opinion to express and a reasonable action to recommend. He also wanted to get a clear sense of the facts and arguments he would present in support of his opinion.

Looking through his notes, David listed the items he wanted to use in his essay. Then he made a chart showing his main opinion and listing his supporting reasons in order from most important to least important. He ended his chart with the action he planned to recommend.

> *Opinion: We students should clean up our own schoolyard.*
> *Reasons:*
> *1. It will make us feel good about ourselves—pride and self-respect.*
> *2. It will build school spirit, which can help make other school events successful.*
> *3. We can get it done now, and not have to wait.*
> *Action: Clean-a-thon on November 5*

David had only one opinion to state: that students should clean up the schoolyard. He knew he had to state the opinion in a **position statement**. A **position statement** is a sentence that clearly gives the writer's opinion. This is the position statement David wrote.

> *We students can clean up our own schoolyard—and we should.*

Discuss

1. How is putting notes in chart form helpful?
2. Why do you think David left out any mention of the salesman from the Dirty Trick Cleaning Company when he made his chart?

Try Your Hand

Now plan a persuasive essay of your own.

A. Brainstorm and Select a Topic Brainstorm a list of possible topics for a persuasive essay. Begin by thinking of the audience you wish to reach. For example, your audience might be your classmates, your neighbors, or the members of some club or organization. List all the issues you think might interest this audience.

- Cross off the topics that your chosen audience would not find interesting.
- Cross off topics for which you would have trouble finding information.
- Cross off topics that might be so complicated that you would have trouble understanding the information you could find about them.
- Circle the topic left on your list that you and your audience could do the most about. This will be the topic of your persuasive essay.

B. Gather Information When you are satisfied with the topic you have chosen, plan how to gather information.

- Browse through reference books, newspapers, and other sources for information related to your topic.
- Interview people who know something about your topic and who can give you facts that support your position statement. Take notes as you listen to these people, but be aware of any motive or bias they have that might make their information unreliable. If you need help, read **Tips on How to Recognize Bias and Motive** on page 309.

C. Organize the Information Look over your notes, and circle the ones that may help you write your essay.

- Write a statement giving your opinion on the topic.
- Make sure your opinion involves something you can persuade others to do or think.
- List the facts and reasons that support your opinion.
- Arrange the facts from most important to least important. You may want to make a chart like David's.
- Write a position statement on your topic.

 Save your notes and your chart in your *Writer's Notebook*. You will use them when you draft your persuasive essay.

WRITING PROCESS

Listening and Speaking
Tips on How to Recognize Bias and Motive

Bias is an attitude about a subject based on feelings, not facts. **Motive** is a speaker's purpose for saying something. A statement is not false just because the speaker has a bias, nor do all speakers stretch the truth to suit their motives. Nonetheless, you can better judge any messages you hear if you know the speaker's bias and motive. Ask yourself these questions to help you recognize bias and motive.

1. **Does the speaker have a close friend or a relative involved in the issue?**

    If so, the speaker may be biased. Suppose, for example that Henry says, "The umpires at that baseball game were unfair." If Henry's brother was a player on the losing team, he may be biased. You may want to check his opinion by talking to someone who does not know any of the players.

2. **What is the speaker's point of view?**

    Sometimes people can see one side of an issue more clearly than another. A person's point of view may depend on his or her job, interests, experiences, or some other factor. A police officer, for example, may say that crime is the most important problem in America. Someone whose job involves fighting water pollution may say, "Water pollution is the most important problem today." These two speakers have different opinions because they have different points of view. To weigh what they say, you need to take their points of view into account.

3. **Does the speaker have something to gain from convincing you to share a particular opinion?**

    If so, the speaker's motive casts doubt on his or her statements. Suppose that a man on television claims that air pollution is harmless. "In fact," he says, "it is good for people." If he is the president of a company that causes air pollution, he has a motive for making his statement. He will not have to spend money on antipollution measures if he can convince people that he is right. Before you believe him, you may want to consult with someone who has nothing to gain from convincing you that air pollution is either good or bad.

2 Drafting
Persuasive Essay

David followed the **Writer's Guide** to draft his essay. Look at what he did.

Writer's Guide

Drafting Checklist
- ☑ Use your notes and chart for ideas.
- ☑ Write an introductory paragraph.
- ☑ Write supporting paragraphs.
- ☑ Write the conclusion.
- ☑ Write a title for your persuasive essay.

Time to Clean Up!

Recently, a student grumbled, "The schoolyard is a mess. Why don't they do something about it?" I think that is the wrong question. Instead, when we see a problem, we should ask, "What can I do?" We students, for example, can clean our own schoolyard — and we should.

Discuss

1. Where did David put his position statement? Why?
2. What additional information would you add to David's essay to support his statement? Where would you add it? Why?

Try Your Hand

Now draft a persuasive essay.

A. Review Your Information Think about the information you gathered and organized in the prewriting section. Decide whether you need more information. If you do, gather it.

B. Think About Your TAP Remember that your task is to write a persuasive essay. Your purpose is to persuade your audience to agree with your opinion.

C. Write Your First Draft Follow the steps in the **Drafting Checklist** to write your persuasive essay.

　　When you write your first draft, just put all your ideas on paper. Do not worry about spelling, punctuation, or grammar. You can correct the draft later.

Task: What?
Audience: Who?
Purpose: Why?

Save your first draft in your *Writer's Notebook.* You will use it when you revise your persuasive essay.

3 Responding and Revising
Persuasive Essay

David used the checklist in the **Writer's Guide** to revise his persuasive essay. Look at what he did.

Writer's Guide
Revising Checklist
- ☑ Read your essay to yourself or to a partner.
- ☑ Think about your audience and your purpose. Add or cut information.
- ☑ Be sure that your persuasive essay is well organized.
- ☑ Be sure that you have facts to support your opinion.
- ☑ Be sure that your language is vivid and your sentences are varied.

◆ Checking Information

David cut one sentence because it expressed an opinion without offering any facts. To show what he was cutting, David used this mark ✁ . He also added a point about the school spirit because he thought it would make his essay more persuasive. To show this addition, he used this mark ∧ .

◆ Checking Organization

David moved a paragraph closer to the end of his essay because he wanted this information to stand out for his readers. To show that the paragraph should be moved, he used this mark ◌ .

◆ Checking Language

David replaced a dull phrase with a vivid one to increase the impact of his essay. He also combined two sentences to vary his sentence length. He used this mark ⌒ to show the changes.

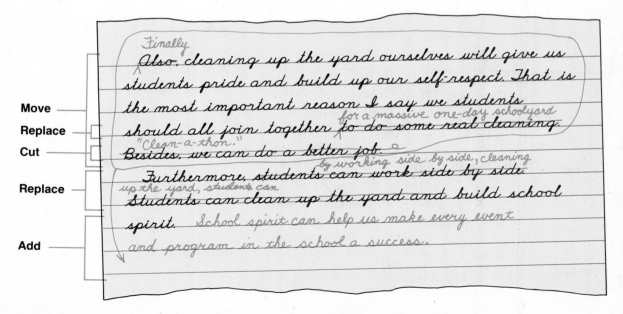

Move
Replace
Cut

Replace

Add

Finally
Also, cleaning up the yard ourselves will give us students pride and build up our self-respect. That is the most important reason I say we students should all join together to do some real cleaning. for a massive one-day schoolyard
"Clean-a-thon."
Besides, we can do a better job.
Furthermore, students can work side by side. by working side by side, cleaning up the yard, students can
Students can clean up the yard and build school spirit. School spirit can help us make every event and program in the school a success.

Discuss

Did adding the point about school spirit make David's essay more persuasive? Explain your answer.

Try Your Hand

Now revise your first draft.

A. Read Your First Draft As you read your persuasive essay, think about your audience and your purpose. Read your essay silently or to a partner to see if it is complete and well organized. Ask yourself or your partner the questions in the box.

Responding and Revising Strategies

✔ **Respond**
Ask yourself or a partner:

✔ **Revise**
Try these solutions:

◆ Have I made my opinion clear?	◆ **Add** a clear position statement.
◆ Have I made my opinion convincing?	◆ **Add** facts to back up each opinion. **Cut** opinions you cannot support.
◆ Does each word give the picture clearly so as to persuade the reader?	◆ **Replace** dull words with vivid ones. Use the **Writer's Thesaurus** at the back of the book.
◆ Do I vary my sentences?	◆ **Move** or **add** words and combine sentences to create sentence variety. See the **Revising Workshop** on page 313.
◆ Does my title give an idea of what I want to persuade people to do or think?	◆ **Replace** your title with one that is more closely related to your essay.

B. Make Your Changes If the answer to any question in the box is *no,* try the solution. Use the **Editor's Marks** to show your changes.

C. Review Your Essay Again Decide whether there is anything else you want to revise. Keep revising your persuasive essay until you feel it is well organized and complete.

> **EDITOR'S MARKS**
>
> ∧ Add something.
> ﹏ Cut something.
> ◌ Move something.
> ⋏ Replace something.

Save your revised essay in your *Writer's Notebook*. You will use it when you proofread your essay.

WRITING PROCESS

Revising Workshop
Varying Sentence Structure and Length

If you ate only one kind of food, your meals would soon begin to bore you. If you use only one kind of sentence, you will soon bore your readers. Notice how similar the sentences are in this paragraph.

> Composting is a valuable activity for people who have gardens. It is a process for making fertilizer. Composting uses kitchen garbage. A gardener can save money by composting. Composting is free. Commercial fertilizer costs money. Many people like the idea of composting. They like growing food with natural fertilizer.

To vary your sentences, you can combine some of them or add words and phrases to create longer sentences. You can also vary the structure of your sentences by varying the placement of words and phrases. Notice how these techniques were used to create sentence variety in the paragraph about composting.

> Composting, a process for making fertilizer out of kitchen garbage, is a valuable activity. By composting, a gardener can save money. Composting is free, after all, whereas commercial fertilizer costs money. Many people, however, simply like the idea of composting. They like growing food with natural fertilizer.

Practice

Rewrite the following paragraph. Create sentence variety by combining sentences, adding words, and shifting the placement of words.

I think Sandra Locke should run the school cleanup effort. Sandra has organized several group projects. She has been successful in doing so. She is a hard worker, too. Sandra has a great ability to work with people. She expresses herself calmly and clearly. She is a patient woman. She has excellent listening skills. These are all qualities of a leader. Sandra Locke is just the person we need to coordinate our school cleanup project.

4 Proofreading
Persuasive Essay

Writer's Guide

Proofreading Checklist

☑ Check for errors in capitalization. Be sure all your proper nouns and abbreviations are capitalized.

☑ Check for errors in punctuation.

☑ Check to see that all your paragraphs are indented.

☑ Check for errors in grammar.

☑ Circle any words you think are misspelled. Find out how to spell them correctly.

⇨ For proofreading help, use the **Writer's Handbook.**

David added a paragraph to his persuasive essay. Then he used the **Writer's Guide** and the **Editor's Marks** to proofread it. Look at what he did.

¶ Our principal, mr. Drew, said we can have the Clean-a-thon on Saturday, november 5. The town's department of sanitation will send a dumpster for us us to use. Everyone should meet at the Whitman Road entrance to the School at 9 o'clock. Please join us. You'll be glad you did.

Discuss

1. Look at David's proofread paragraph. What kinds of corrections did he make?
2. Why did David capitalize *department* and *sanitation* but not *of*?

Try Your Hand

Proofread Your Paragraph   Now use the **Writer's Guide** and the **Editor's Marks** to proofread your paragraph.

EDITOR'S MARKS

≡ Capitalize.

⊙ Add a period.

∧ Add something.

⋏ Add a comma.

ⱽⱽ Add quotation marks.

ℓ Cut something.

⟋⟍ Replace something.

∼ Transpose.

◯ Spell correctly.

⊬ Indent paragraph.

⁄ Make a lowercase letter.

Save your corrected persuasive essay in your *Writer's Notebook.* You will use it when you publish your essay.

5 Publishing
Persuasive Essay

David made a clean copy of his persuasive essay and checked to be sure he had not left out anything. Then he and his classmates published their persuasive essays as a display for the Cleaner World Club at a school activities fair. You can find David's persuasive essay on page 37 of the **Writer's Handbook.**

Here's how David and his classmates published their essays as a display.

First, David mounted his essay on a large dark-colored poster board and neatly pasted his photos and illustrations related to his topic around his essay. Then, he cut letters out of a contrasting color of construction paper to form his title. Finally, David pasted the title above his essay and displayed his poster.

Discuss

1. Why would it be important to display your essay in an attractive way for an activities fair?
2. Where else could you display your poster of your persuasive essay?

Try Your Hand

Publish Your Persuasive Essay   Follow the checklist in the **Writer's Guide.** If possible, create a display for your own persuasive essay, or try one of these ideas for sharing your essay.

◆ Make a book of your class's persuasive essays.
◆ Use your essay as the basis for a talk to an interested group.

Writing in the Content Areas

Use what you learned to write your opinion about an important issue in a way that will convince others. You can write an essay or a paragraph. Use one of these ideas or an idea of your own.

Writer's Guide

When you write, remember the stages of the Writing Process.
◆ Prewriting
◆ Drafting
◆ Responding and Revising
◆ Proofreading
◆ Publishing

Literature

Choose a book that you either liked or disliked very much. Explain your opinion of the book, and give your reasons. Try to convince others who have read the book to share your opinion. Try to convince those who have not read the book to read it or to avoid it, according to your position.

Social Studies

Imagine that you have been asked to recommend a destination for a tour. Choose the most interesting place you have been to or have heard about. Explain what makes this country, state, or geographic area an attractive place to visit. Give facts about the place to back up your opinions.

Health

Do you know of a habit that could improve a person's health? Describe the habit, and explain how it affects health. Give facts to prove that what you say about the habit is true. Try to persuade your readers to take up the habit and make it a part of their own lives.

Physical Education

Do you have a favorite sport? What do you like about it? Get an audience interested in your sport by describing it. Give facts to show what makes the sport challenging and fun. Try to convince your audience to try or to watch your sport.

CONNECTING
WRITING ⬌ LANGUAGE

In good persuasive essays, writers use precise language to express strong opinions and to move their readers to action. What points are made in this introductory paragraph from a persuasive essay?

Many years ago , people thought the earth was too big to damage. Certainly few people thought we had a responsibility to protect nature! Mere humans, after all, could never affect something so powerful as the weather! Today, unfortunately , we know that we do have this power. For example, we work in factories that produce polluting gases. We drive around in cars that add to this pollution. The wastes we produce may be heating up the earth and changing the climate. We must take action now . Otherwise , life here on earth may soon become difficult or even impossible.

◆ **Adverbs in a Persuasive Essay** The highlighted words are adverbs. In this paragraph, they give important information by telling when, how, and where actions took place. Some adverbs also help tell more about adjectives by showing to what extent and in what manner the adjectives apply to the nouns they describe.

◆ **Language Focus: Adverbs** In the following lessons you will learn more about using adverbs correctly in your writing.

1 Adverbs

◆ **FOCUS** An **adverb** modifies a verb, an adjective, or another adverb.

Remember that adjectives modify nouns or pronouns. An adverb is a word that modifies a verb, an adjective, or another adverb. Adverbs that modify verbs tell *how, when, where,* or *to what extent.* In these sentences, the words in color are adverbs.

1. The train moved swiftly .   how
2. Soon it reached the station.   when
3. Many passengers waited there .   where
4. People totally filled the platform.   to what extent

Adverbs that modify adjectives or other adverbs tell *how* or *to what extent.*

5. Quite suddenly the train began to move.   how
6. The night was completely silent.   to what extent

Most adverbs end in *ly.* However, many common adverbs, such as those in this chart, do not.

Common Adverbs That Do Not End in *ly*								
somewhat	then	always	rather	quite	well	often	away	late
yesterday	already	seldom	almost	very	also	today	here	still
everywhere	tomorrow	first	nearby	just	now	later	there	soon

Guided Practice

A. Identify the adverb in each sentence.

1. Today people enjoy trains.
2. Trains travel everywhere.
3. Usually they follow schedules.
4. People travel comfortably.
5. Trains move quietly.
6. Bridges are very strong.

B. 7.–12. Tell whether each adverb in **A** tells *how, when, where,* or *to what extent.*

> **THINK AND REMEMBER**
> ◆ Use an **adverb** to modify a verb, an adjective, or another adverb.

Independent Practice

C. Identifying Adverbs Write the adverb from each sentence. Write whether each adverb tells *how, when, where,* or *to what extent.*

13. Traveling in America was very hard before 1850.
> MODEL > very—to what extent
14. Railroads had already developed in the East.
15. In the West, however, people still used wagons and horses to make journeys.
16. Then Congress passed the Pacific Railroad Act.
17. This bill clearly called for a railroad track to be built across the continent.
18. Two companies began immediately to lay tracks.
19. One company slowly worked its way west from Omaha.
20. The other company had a much harder job.
21. It laid tracks across the Sierra Nevada Mountains, and there the work was difficult.
22. The two companies competed fiercely.
23. On May 10, 1869, the two tracks finally met in Utah.

D. Identifying Adverbs and the Words They Modify Write each adverb and the word it modifies. Label the modified word *verb, adjective,* or *adverb.*

24. Casey Jones worked very hard.
> MODEL > very—hard, adverb   hard—worked, verb
25. Seldom did he miss a day's work.
26. Children often hear about Casey Jones.
27. Casey really loved trains.
28. One day, Casey's train was quite late.
29. Water from a rainfall almost covered the tracks.
30. Suddenly, Casey saw another train on his track.
31. Casey's wet brakes failed completely.
32. This brave man firmly believed one thing.
33. An engineer always stays with his train.

Application — Writing

Journal Entry Imagine that you were a passenger on a train. Write an entry for your journal describing the weather and telling what you and the other passengers did. Use at least five different adverbs. If you need help writing a journal entry, see page 40 of the **Writer's Handbook**.

2 Placement of Adverbs in Sentences

◆ FOCUS   The placement of an adverb in a sentence can vary.

An adverb that modifies an adjective or another adverb usually comes just before the word it modifies. It cannot be moved without changing the meaning of the sentence. Notice the adverbs in color in these sentences.

1. The day was incredibly beautiful.
2. The climb was very enjoyable.

Most adverbs that describe verbs can come almost anywhere in a sentence. They can come before the verb, after the verb, or between the helping verb and the main verb. Often, they can be moved without changing the meaning of the sentence.

3. Swiftly the mountaineers climbed up the slope.
4. The mountaineers swiftly climbed up the slope.
5. The mountaineers climbed swiftly up the slope.

> **Link to Speaking and Writing**
> Varying the placement of your adverbs can add variety to your sentences.

Guided Practice

A. Identify the adverbs. Tell whether each one *can be moved* or *cannot be moved* without changing the meaning of the sentence.

1. Usually, expert mountain climbers are thoroughly trained.
2. Mountain climbers scale very steep cliffs carefully.
3. People can climb safely with special equipment.
4. At the very highest peaks, the air is extremely thin.
5. Sometimes, breathing is quite difficult.

> **THINK AND REMEMBER**
> ◆ Place most adverbs that modify adjectives or other adverbs just before the word they modify.
> ◆ Place most adverbs that modify verbs almost anywhere.

Independent Practice

B. Identifying Adverbs Write the adverbs from the sentences. Label each one *yes* if it can be moved or *no* if it cannot be moved.

6. Skillfully, two very brave women climbed the mountain.
   MODEL> Skillfully—yes   very—no
7. The peak loomed dangerously above.
8. Once, they saw a thundering avalanche.
9. Luckily, the avalanche missed them.
10. Sometimes, the extremely bright sun burned their skin.
11. These women climbed very well.
12. They really enjoyed mountain climbing.
13. Of course, it is rather hard work, but they consider it an adventure.
14. The Rocky Mountains are located nearby.
15. They can practice their sport often.

C. 16. – 25. Identifying Words Modified by Adverbs Write each adverb from **B**. Then write the word it modifies, and label the word *verb, adjective,* or *adverb.*

16. Skillfully, two very brave women climbed the mountain.
    MODEL> Skillfully—climb, verb   very—brave, adjective

D. Completing Sentences with Adverbs Add the adverb in parentheses to each sentence, and write the sentence. Vary the placement of the adverbs.

26. Mount Everest towers above its neighbors. (majestically)
    MODEL> Mount Everest towers majestically above its neighbors.
27. Sir Edmund Hillary climbed the mountain. (courageously)
28. His team worked together well. (extremely)
29. Tenzing Norgay led the way for the team. (skillfully)
30. Hillary smiled at the top. (joyfully)
31. People applauded the feat. (everywhere)
32. Mount Everest remains a great challenge. (still)
33. It will be a challenge. (always)

Application — Writing

Description Imagine that you were one of the climbers in the picture. Write a description of the climb for your classmates. Tell what the weather and snow conditions were like. Use at least five adverbs. Vary their placement to add variety to your sentences.

3 Comparison with Adverbs

◆ **FOCUS**   Adverbs can be used to make comparisons.

Adverbs, like adjectives, have three forms, two of which are used in comparisons. The **positive form** of an adverb is used when no comparison is made. The **comparative form** is used to compare two items. The **superlative form** is used to compare three or more items.

1. Mike ran fast in the race. positive
2. Alex ran faster than Mike. comparative
3. Robert ran fastest of all. superlative

Add *er* and *est* to form the comparative and the superlative of most one-syllable adverbs. Use *more* or *less* and *most* or *least* if the adverb ends in *ly* or has two or more syllables. Never use *more* and *er* or *most* and *est* with the same adverb.

4. In yesterday's track meet, Grace jumped more skillfully than her rival. comparative
5. She was the most amazingly agile athlete in the event. superlative

Some adverbs change spelling completely to form the comparative and the superlative. Other adverbs, such as *never, always,* and *here,* cannot be used to make comparisons.

Positive	Comparative	Superlative
well	better	best
badly	worse	worst
little	less	least
much	more	most
far	farther/further	farthest/furthest

Guided Practice

A. List the comparative and the superlative forms of each adverb.

1. lightly
2. near
3. hard
4. often
5. patiently
6. carelessly
7. shyly
8. deeply
9. well
10. much

> **THINK AND REMEMBER**
> ◆ To form the **comparative** or the **superlative** of most short adverbs, add *er* or *est*.
> ◆ Use *more* or *less* and *most* or *least* instead of *er* and *est* with adverbs that end in *ly* or have two or more syllables.

Independent Practice

B. Writing Comparative and Superlative Forms of Adverbs Write the comparative form and the superlative form of each adverb.

11. eagerly

MODEL ▷ more/less eagerly, most/least eagerly

12. quickly   **14.** little   **16.** bravely   **18.** patiently
13. far   **15.** softly   **17.** soon   **19.** expertly

C. Choosing Adverbs That Compare Write the adverb in parentheses that correctly completes each sentence.

20. No one trained (harder, hardest) than Jesse Owens.

MODEL ▷ harder

21. Jesse Owens ran (more swiftly, swiftlier) than any other athlete in the 1936 Olympics.
22. He won many races because he ran (fastest, most fast).
23. He did (weller, better) at most sports than other people.
24. Owens jumped (more skillfully, most skillfully) than the other long jumpers in the Olympics.
25. His record lasted (longer, longest) than any other record.

D. Writing Sentences with Adverbs That Compare Write two sentences for each adverb, one sentence using the comparative form and the other using the superlative form.

26. well

MODEL ▷ I play baseball better than I play basketball.
I play football the best of all.

27. badly   **28.** little   **29.** slowly   **30.** far   **31.** often

Application — Writing and Speaking

Sportscast Imagine that you are a sportscaster for your community radio station reporting on the race shown in the picture. Write a description of the event, comparing the performances of the athletes. Use at least five adverbs that compare. Read the completed sportscast to your class.

4 Negatives

◆ **FOCUS**   Two negative words should not be used together.

Negatives are words that mean "no." Some common negatives, such as *not*, *never*, and *nowhere*, are adverbs. Other common negatives include *no*, *nobody*, *nothing*, *none*, and *no one*. A negative can reverse the meaning of a sentence. The word in color is a negative.

1. People will forget the work of Father Hidalgo.
2. People will not forget the work of Father Hidalgo.

The use of two negatives in a sentence is called a **double negative.** Avoid using double negatives because they confuse the meaning of a sentence.

Incorrect: 3. He would not never stop working for freedom.
Correct: 4. He would never stop working for freedom.
Correct: 5. He would not ever stop working for freedom.

To correct a double negative, you can drop one negative, as in sentence 4. You can also replace one negative word with a positive word, as in sentence 5. Most negative words have one or more opposite words that are positive.

never—ever   nobody—anybody, somebody
none—some, any   nothing—something, anything
hardly—almost   neither/nor—either/or

Watch for the negative *not* hidden in some contractions. The word in color contains a negative.

6. Mexico wasn't independent until 1821.

Guided Practice

A. Identify the word in parentheses that makes each sentence negative.

1. In Mexico, the Creoles could hold (no, any) power.
2. The mestizos and Indians were (ever, never) given any education.
3. These groups (did, didn't) revolt until 1810.
4. They wanted (no, some) more Spanish rule.
5. (No one, Anyone) could stop the fight for independence.

Independent Practice

B. Identifying Negative Words Write the word in parentheses that makes each sentence negative.

6. (Someone, No one) worked harder than Father Hidalgo.

MODEL ▷ No one

7. (Everybody, Nobody) knows when he first dreamed of independence.

8. Hidalgo (did, didn't) just dream, however.

9. He let (nothing, anything) stand in his way.

10. Most of his soldiers had (no, some) formal training.

11. Hidalgo (never, ever) lived to see independence.

C. Revising: Reversing the Meaning of Sentences Change or add words to reverse the meaning of each statement.

12. After independence, Mexico had no problems.

MODEL ▷ After independence, Mexico still had problems.

13. Running the country was easy.

14. Some people had almost everything.

15. Others were not very wealthy.

16. Juarez wanted special privileges for the few.

17. Many Mexicans said they would accept his reforms.

D. Proofreading: Checking for Double Negatives Find the error in each sentence. Write the sentence correctly.

18. Today, Mexico is not a colony of no country.

MODEL ▷ Today, Mexico is not a colony of any country.

19. Mexican Independence Day isn't not just a one-day festival.

20. Mexicans don't never fail to celebrate their independence.

21. There aren't no limits to the country's future.

22. I didn't have no idea Mexico was so interesting.

Application — Writing and Speaking

Biography Write a short biography of a person in history who worked for freedom. Look in your history book for ideas and information. Write at least five sentences that contain negative words. Present the biography to your class.

5 Adverb or Adjective?

FOCUS
◆ An **adverb** modifies a verb, an adjective, or another adverb.
◆ An **adjective** modifies a noun or a pronoun.

Many adjectives and adverbs look similar. Whenever two such words confuse you, remember that words that end in *ly* are usually adverbs.

Adjectives	real	happy	easy	bad
Adverbs	really	happily	easily	badly

The words *bad* and *badly* are frequently misused. Use *bad* as a predicate adjective after a linking verb. Use *badly* with action verbs to tell how something was done.

1. The work went badly .   adverb
2. The nurse felt bad .   predicate adjective

Also, be careful not to misuse *good* and *well*. *Good* is always an adjective. *Well* is an adjective when it means "healthy," but it is an adverb when it tells how something is done.

She was a brave woman.
She worked bravely.

3. Clara Barton was a good nurse.   adjective
4. She helped soldiers who did not feel well .   adjective
5. She did her job well .   adverb

Guided Practice

A. Identify the word that correctly completes each sentence.

1. The soldiers needed help (bad, badly).
2. Clara Barton was a (careful, carefully) worker.
3. Supplies did not arrive (regular, regularly).
4. Her medicines did not always work (good, well).
5. Barton was a (real, really) brave woman.

THINK AND REMEMBER
◆ Remember that most words ending in *ly* are adverbs.
◆ Use *good* only as an adjective.
◆ Use *well* as an adjective to mean "healthy" and as an adverb to tell how something is done.

Independent Practice

B. Using Adjectives and Adverbs Correctly   Write the word in parentheses that completes each sentence correctly.

6. During World War II, soldiers needed blood (desperate, desperately).

MODEL ▷ desperately

7. Stored blood was (good, well) for only a few days.
8. Dr. Charles Drew saw the problem (clear, clearly).
9. Drew did (careful, carefully) research with plasma.
10. This work was (real, really) important.
11. People got (good, well) with transfusions of plasma.
12. Plasma, which is the liquid part of blood, could be stored (easy, easily).
13. Plasma could be given (safe, safely) to anybody.
14. Drew organized blood banks (quick, quickly).
15. Drew's (good, well) work saved millions of lives.
16. Now, anyone who needs blood can get it (swift, swiftly).

C. Proofreading: Checking Adjective and Adverb Usage   Find the error in each sentence. Write the word that would make the sentence correct.

17. Sir Alexander Fleming studied bacteria close.

MODEL ▷ closely

18. During World War I, infections killed people real often.
19. No medicines fought infection good enough.
20. Fleming treated people without real effective medicines.
21. He felt badly that he could not do more to help.
22. Later, Fleming was working careful in his lab.
23. Mold landed sudden on some bacteria.
24. The mold destroyed the bacteria quick.
25. Fleming had accidental discovered penicillin.
26. Penicillin fights bacteria good.
27. Fleming felt well about his discovery.
28. In 1945 he proud accepted a Nobel Prize.

Application — Writing

Story Scene   Write a scene from a story about a medical worker. Write the story for students your age. Your character can be a real person or someone you make up. Look in an encyclopedia for information if you wish. Use at least five adverbs and five adjectives. Use the words *bad, badly, good,* and *well* at least once.

Building Vocabulary
Suffixes: Word Changers

You have learned that many adverbs end with the letters *ly*. The letters *ly* are a **suffix**, a letter or letters added to the end of a base word. A suffix changes the meaning of a word. Usually it changes the way the word is used in a sentence as well. For example, a suffix can change a noun into an adjective and an adjective into an adverb.

noun	adjective	adverb
effect	effect ive	effective ly

A suffix can also change an adjective into a noun, or a noun into a verb.

shy	adjective	shy ness	noun
light	noun	light en	verb

Study the suffixes in this chart.

	Suffix	Meaning	Example
Noun-Forming Suffixes	er	one who	builder
	ist	one who	artist
	or	one who	sailor
	ness	act of, state of	kindness
	ment	as a result of being	enjoyment
	ance	act of	assistance
Adjective-Forming Suffixes	ful	full of, worthy of	powerful
	less	without	careless
	y	having	dirty
	ous	full of	dangerous
	able	having qualities of	comfortable
	ish	being like	childish
Verb-Forming Suffixes	en	make, add	thicken
	n	make, add	widen

Reading Practice

Read each sentence. Write the word formed with a suffix. Underline the suffix.

1. Aesop was a Greek fable teller.
2. People still find Aesop's fables enjoyable.
3. Each fable has a useful moral.
4. One humorous story tells about a dog.
5. The greedy dog is carrying a bone.
6. It sees its likeness in a river.
7. The dog's eyes widen.
8. The foolish dog thinks it sees another dog with another bone.
9. The other bone looks more flavorful than its own.
10. It opens its powerful jaws and drops its own bone.
11. It leaps into the chilly river to get the other dog's bone.
12. Of course, the selfish dog gets no bone at all!

Writing Practice

Complete each sentence. Use a word formed by adding a suffix to the word in parentheses ( ).

13. A (care) mouse runs over a lion's face.
14. The lion wakes with (annoy).
15. The (might) lion is about to kill the mouse.
16. The (help) mouse pleads for its life.
17. "Let me go, and someday I will repay your (kind)," it whimpers.
18. The lion chuckles in (amuse), but it lets the mouse go.
19. One day a (hunt) traps the lion in a net.
20. The mouse hears the lion's (sorrow) cries.
21. It gnaws a hole in the net and sets the (luck) lion free.
22. You cannot always judge others by their (appear).

Project

Reread a chapter from a favorite book. As you read, list all the words containing suffixes from the chart. Compare your list with lists made by your classmates. Then create a class bulletin board display of suffixes. List suffixes on strips of paper. Use individual suffixes as list titles. List words beneath the suffix they contain. Post the lists, and continue adding to them.

Language Enrichment
Adverbs

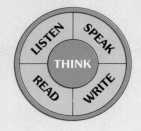

Use what you know about adverbs to do these activities.

 Sportswriter

Imagine that you are a sportswriter. Write a description of a race, a baseball game, a tennis match, or another sporting event. Tell how and where athletes move and when different plays occur. Use adverbs to tell more about verbs, adjectives, and other adverbs.

 Negative Positives

Imagine that it is New Year's Eve—time to make a list of resolutions. List at least 10 things that you plan not to do in the coming year. Use contractions with negatives, and use negative words such as *not, never,* and *nothing* in your resolutions.

 The Adverb Walk

Complete the command "Walk _____" with 10 different adverbs on 10 different index cards. Use common adverbs such as *fast* as well as unusual adverbs such as *jauntily.* Have classmates act out the different ways of walking.

 Noun-Verb-Adverb Shuffle

Write 10 nouns, 10 intransitive verbs, and 10 adverbs on separate cards. Shuffle the cards together, and then use the cards in a game for two players. The object of the game is to form as many sentences as possible.

Give each player three cards. Players take turns drawing cards until they can form sentences. They set the sentence-forming cards in a row face up and draw three new cards. The game ends when all the cards in the stack have been used up. The winner is the player who has formed the most sentences.

CONNECTING
LANGUAGE ↔ WRITING

In this unit you learned that adverbs tell about verbs, adjectives, and other adverbs. Adverbs can be used in comparisons. Some negative words are adverbs. You learned to avoid using double negatives and not to confuse adverbs with adjectives.

◆ **Using Adverbs in Your Writing** Adverbs can add important details in sentences. Often they can change the word pictures you create. Knowing how to use adverbs correctly gives you the power to express your ideas clearly and convincingly. Pay special attention to the adverbs you use as you do these activities.

 Pet Point of View

Imagine that you are a dog, a cat, a bird, or another pet. Write a paragraph telling how you think the world should be changed to suit your needs. Describe how you feel about your home, your owners, your neighborhood, the way you are treated, and the way other people and animals in your world live. Use adverbs to describe verbs, adjectives, and other adverbs.

 Career Corner

You learned about suffixes on the **Building Vocabulary** pages. Many career titles end with suffixes. Make a dictionary of careers.

Write the name of a career at the top of each of ten different sheets of paper. Then write one or two sentences defining the career and another sentence or two describing the kind of person who does that type of work well. Use adjectives, words with suffixes, and adverbs in the sentences. Combine your career sheets with those of classmates. Put them in alphabetical order. Make a table of contents for the career dictionary, and number the pages. Make a cover and put the career dictionary in a reading corner.

Example: *guitarist* A guitarist is a person who plays the guitar. A good guitarist plays very skillfully.

7 Unit Checkup

Think Back	Think Ahead
◆ What did you learn about persuasive essays in this unit? What did you do to write one?	◆ How will what you learned about writing persuasive essays help you in other classes? ◆ How will using vivid words add spice to your writing?
◆ Look at the writing you did in this unit. How did adverbs help make an essay persuasive?	◆ What is one way you can use adverbs to help make your writing more vivid?

Persuasive Essays   *pages 300–302*

Read each sentence. Write the propaganda technique used: *bandwagon, testimonial, emotional words, faulty generalization,* or *begging the question.*

1. Sally Somebody, famous actress, says, "I never go outside without my Sunblaster Sunglasses."
2. Greenscene gardening tools are preferred by 99 out of 100 gardeners.
3. Come on! Join your neighbors in voting for Sam Teel for mayor.
4. Are you repulsed by the vile, horrible smell of cooking odors? Use Odorex and you'll smile!
5. You'll love using Glisten shampoo because it's a pleasure to wash your hair with Glisten!

Classifying Fact and Opinion   *page 303*

Write *F* if the sentence is factual and *O* if it is an opinion.

6. Dogs and cats dream just like humans.
7. I feel that students should learn the facts.
8. Movies about space travel are always fun.
9. Satellites orbit the earth.

Using Vivid Words   *page 304*

Rewrite each sentence, replacing the underlined word with a more vivid word.

10. Space travel is <u>interesting</u>.
11. The moon is <u>small</u>.
12. Astronauts <u>came</u> back to Earth.
13. The spacecraft travels <u>fast</u>.

UNIT CHECKUP Unit 7

The Writing Process   *pages 305–315*

Write the letter of the correct response to each question.

14. In a persuasive essay, the position statement usually comes

    a. at the beginning.
    b. in the middle.
    c. at the end.

15. When revising, you should

    a. add or delete information as needed.
    b. forget about organization for the time being.
    c. not worry about the difference between fact and opinion.

16. Which editor's mark is used to correct the error in this sentence?

    Young children shoudln't travel alone.

    a. cut something
    b. add something
    c. transpose

17. In sharing your persuasive essay, you probably would not make it

    a. part of a display.
    b. an editorial in a newspaper.
    c. part of a novel.

Adverbs   *pages 318–319*

Write the adverb from each sentence. Write whether each adverb tells *how, when, where,* or *to what extent.*

18. Everyone knows that the future will be somewhat different from the present.

19. Of course, most changes will come gradually.

20. We can, however, imagine a completely different world.

21. Rockets will transport passengers speedily between planets and space stations.

22. Earth people may be able to communicate easily with people from other worlds.

23. Food may be grown in specially equipped space stations, leaving more room on Earth for people.

24. Modern science, combined with our imaginations, can give us some clues as to what the world will soon be like.

25. No matter what happens in the future, one thing will never change.

26. People will still wonder and dream about life in the future.

Placement of Adverbs in Sentences   *pages 320–321*

Write the adverbs from the sentences. Label each one *yes* if it can be moved or *no* if it cannot be moved.

27. Amazingly, Gene and Betsy created that fabulous stage set in a week.
28. The scenery was perfectly matched to the mood and the plot of the play.
29. Some rather unusual materials were used to build the stage set.
30. Very long strips of torn plastic wrap were suspended from hooks above the curtain.
31. These strips glowed eerily whenever the blue or purple stage lights were turned on them.
32. Occasionally, they seemed to take on a life of their own!
33. Aluminum foil was carefully glued to foam bases and placed around the stage.
34. Green and silver glitter, strewn generously over everything, gave the stage even more sparkle.
35. Mirrors covered almost every flat surface on the entire stage.
36. The viewer truly could believe that he or she was in an enchanted forest!
37. Betsy and Gene did an absolutely wonderful job, and they can be proud of their achievement.

Comparison with Adverbs   *pages 322–323*

Write the adverb in parentheses ( ) that correctly completes each sentence.

38. Can you think of an animal you'd (less, least) rather meet than a dragon?
39. The dragon may be the (most commonly, commonliest) feared beast in all of literature.
40. In stories of the imagination, the dragon roars (more fiercely, most fiercely) than a lion.
41. The dragon bites (viciouslier, more viciously) than the tiger.
42. In their quests, many storybook heroes meet a dragon (jealously, more jealously) guarding some treasure.
43. Some heroes suffer (worse, worser) fates than others in trying to slay these beasts.
44. Those heroes who fight (nobliest, most nobly) often win their battles.
45. The reader of tales of the imagination knows that (more soon, sooner) or later, he or she will encounter still another dragon.

Negatives *pages 324–325*

Find the error in each sentence. Write the sentence correctly.

46. Some people will tell you that they don't never dream.

47. Dreams aren't not unique to human beings.

48. Scientists know that animals dream, even if they can't never tell us about it.

49. Don't believe no one who tells you that he or she doesn't dream.

50. You may not have no dreams every night of your life.

51. I haven't got no idea of how much time the average person spends dreaming every night.

Adverb or Adjective? *pages 326–327*

Write the word in parentheses that completes each sentence correctly.

52. Dr. Martin Luther King, Jr. imagined a world where all people, regardless of race or religion, lived together (peaceful, peacefully).

53. He spoke very (clear, clearly) about this in his famous speech, "I Have a Dream."

54. Dr. King always spoke very (good, well), but he spoke with special fire on the day that he gave that speech.

55. This (real, really) important speech led many people to imagine the future as Dr. King described it.

56. A famous song by John Lennon, "Imagine," asks us to think (serious, seriously) about a world in which people celebrate their similarities rather than their differences.

Suffixes: Word Changers *pages 328–329*

Read each sentence. Write the word or words formed with a suffix. Underline each suffix.

57. A producer is in charge of arranging finances for a movie.

58. Most movies are very expensive.

59. A director tells the actors how to perform in every scene.

60. Films have become one of the most popular forms of entertainment.

61. Some film stars can create very believable characters.

62. Watching good movies can challenge and strengthen our minds.

63. Many meaningful ideas are communicated through movies.

Cumulative Review

Four Kinds of Sentences   *pages 30—31*

For each sentence, write *declarative, interrogative, imperative,* or *exclamatory.*

1. Justin wrote a letter to a video game company.
2. Why didn't Jamie write the letter herself?
3. It was Jamie who bought the video game that didn't work.
4. What a disappointment that was!
5. Justin, did Jamie ask you to write the letter for her?
6. Next time, Jamie, take care of your problem yourself.
7. Put the broken video game on the table in the den.

Avoiding Sentence Fragments and Run-on Sentences   *pages 48—49*

Rewrite each sentence fragment as a complete sentence. Rewrite each run-on sentence as one or more sentences. Use the correct punctuation and capitalization.

8. When Guglielmo Marconi invented the radio in 1876.
9. Marconi was an Italian citizen he worked in the United States.
10. Marconi Station, which stands on Cape Cod.
11. Alexander Graham Bell's great invention, the telephone, which was once seen as so revolutionary.
12. Today, people can send a message in a matter of seconds they can punch in a few numbers on a phone and talk to someone halfway around the world.

Singular and Plural Nouns   *pages 88—91*

Find the misspelled word in each sentence, and write it correctly.

13. Most of the planets in our solar system have satellites, or moones, revolving around them.
14. Some of these satellites have smooth surfaces while others are covered with volcaneos.
15. Although some are made of rock, others are composed of ice and different frozen gass.
16. We can never see both halfs of our moon because the same side always faces the Earth.
17. The craters and seas on this side look to some people's eyies like the face of a man.
18. It's fun to learn the identitys of these craters and seas from a moon map.

Subject-Verb Agreement *pages 140–143*

Rewrite each sentence to correct the error in subject-verb agreement.

19. I still insists that basketball is the hardest sport.
20. Basketball players runs for almost the entire game.
21. Some practices sprinting as part of their training.
22. Track coaches and trainers sometimes works with the teams.
23. Defense and passing is two other important skills.
24. Of course, everything still depend on shooting the ball into the basket.

Irregular Verbs *pages 176–178*

Write each sentence. Use a form of *be, have,* or *do* to complete the sentence.

25. The characters in the comic strip "Peanuts" _____ among the most popular ever created.
26. _____ you know that Charles Schultz created these characters over 25 years ago?
27. Lucy, Charlie Brown, Linus, and the other characters _____ many of the same problems most people share.
28. Linus _____ a security blanket that he carries around with him at all times.
29. His sister, Lucy, _____ a bossy know-it-all.
30. Lucy thinks that whatever she _____ is right.
31. Actually, Charlie Brown's pet beagle, Snoopy, seems to _____ the best outlook on life.
32. Snoopy _____ a vivid imagination that can take him away from his troubles.

Transitive and Intransitive Verbs *pages 188–189*

Write the verb from each sentence. Label it *transitive* or *intransitive.*

33. That joke is very old.
34. That joke has a beard!
35. Why did the chicken cross the road?
36. It crossed the road for some fowl reason!
37. Can you name a thing that crosses a filthy road twice?
38. You could call it "a dirty double-crosser."
39. Why do cows wear bells?
40. The cows' horns do not work!
41. Yuck! Find some newer jokes!

Agreement of Pronouns with Antecedents *pages 230–231*

Write each sentence. Draw an arrow from each underlined pronoun to its antecedent.

42. Khaleef was sad because <u>his</u> best friend, Anthony, was moving away.

43. Now his street would have no other children living on <u>it</u>.

44. Khaleef's mother said that the same thing had happened to her when <u>she</u> was a young girl.

45. As it turned out, twin boys Khaleef's age moved into Anthony's house, and <u>they</u> enjoyed many of the same activities as Khaleef.

46. Anthony's mother got a new job, and <u>she</u> decided to move her family back to the old neighborhood.

47. Now Khaleef has three good friends on <u>his</u> street instead of just one.

48. When Anthony, Richard, and Khaleef get together, <u>they</u> have a wonderful time.

Possessive Pronouns *pages 234–235*

Write and underline once each possessive pronoun that is used in front of a noun. Write and underline twice each possessive pronoun that stands alone.

49. Ladies and gentlemen, could you please give me your attention?

50. I would like to tell you a little about my plans if I'm elected class president.

51. I have some excellent ideas, and I'd like to hear yours, if you will share them with me.

52. Our class should get involved in some kind of community project.

53. So, when you write a name on your ballot next Tuesday, please let it be mine.

54. I need your vote to make a difference.

Subject or Object Pronoun? *pages 240–241*

Complete each sentence, using the correct pronoun.

55. Can you give (we, us) some ideas of what we can do for Grandma and Grandpa's anniversary?
56. Carolyn and (I, me) would like to make something special for them.
57. Why don't you make a collage of family photographs for (they, them)?
58. Dad has some pictures taken when (he, him) was a little boy.
59. I'm sure Aunt Beverly will make copies of the pictures for you if you ask (she, her).
60. (We, Us) think that's an excellent suggestion. Thank you very much.

Adjectives *pages 274–275*

Write each adjective. Label it *article* or *adjective that describes*.

61. The Hopi, for many centuries, produced a beautiful and unusual pottery.
62. The unique pottery had a yellowish color.
63. Nampeo, a young potter, found fragments of the pottery in the late 1800's.
64. The gifted Nampeo set out to reproduce the great lost craft.
65. She tried first one formula, then another.
66. Finally, Nampeo was successful.
67. She not only reproduced the ancient craft but turned it into a modern art.
68. Nampeo was soon hailed as an artist with a superior and original gift.
69. Many years later, other Hopi continue to preserve a centuries-old art.

Proper Adjectives *pages 276–277*

Write the proper adjectives formed from these proper nouns, and then use each proper adjective in a sentence. Use a dictionary if you wish.

70. Italy
71. China
72. Mexico
73. Asia
74. France
75. Switzerland
76. Alaska
77. America
78. California
79. Sweden

Predicate Adjectives   *pages 280−281*

Write the predicate adjective from each sentence. Then write the word or words it modifies.

80. Jerry was feeling very excited.
81. His band, the Tornadoes, had sounded very professional at practice today.
82. Alexandra, the lead singer, was actually quite talented.
83. The drummer seemed unstoppable.
84. Max, on keyboards, sounded really sharp.
85. Lucky was the person who had hired the Tornadoes for tonight!

Comparison with Adjectives   *pages 282−285*

Write the form of the adjective in parentheses that correctly completes each sentence.

86. Sandy was angry, and he became even (furious) as time went on.
87. "Of all the kits I've ever put together," he said, "this one is the (annoying)."
88. "Was that the (cheap) one they had?" his sister Henrietta asked.
89. "No," he replied, "but it certainly is the (bad) one, and I'm returning it!"
90. Then he laughed, "There must be an (easy) way to have fun than this."

Adverbs   *pages 318−319*

Write the adverb from each sentence.

91. A movie director often sees a whole movie in his or her head before it is made.
92. A talented person can actually transform words on paper into a finished film.
93. Unconnected parts of a plot come together to form a unified story.
94. A good director can draw inspiration or ideas from almost any source.
95. When one movie is finished being filmed, a good director may already have another one or two in mind!
96. Later, those movie ideas may appear in another film.

Comparison with Adverbs *pages 322−323*

Write the adverb in parentheses that correctly completes each sentence.

97. The human brain can process information even (more swiftly, most swiftly) than a sophisticated computer.
98. Our brains can usually be trained, through work and study, to work (more efficiently, efficientlier).
99. Most people do get (weller, better) at a particular skill if they practice.
100. The brain may be the (most fast, fastest) "computer" ever developed.
101. The brain, however, can act (more creatively, most creatively) than a computer, and that is a major difference.

Negatives *pages 324−325*

Write the word in parentheses that makes each sentence negative.

102. Training for an Olympic event is (ever, never) an easy task.
103. (Everybody, Nobody) really understands the time and dedication needed to become an Olympic athlete.
104. Most athletes have (no, some) life outside of training and attending meets.
105. However, (none, any) of the athletes would trade his or her opportunity to compete in the Olympic Games.
106. Even after the Olympics, most athletes (do, don't) want to stop participating in their sport.

Adverb or Adjective? *pages 326−327*

Write the word in parentheses that correctly completes each sentence.

107. All artists work (hard, hardly) to create their paintings and sculptures.
108. Those who work with huge canvases and large, bulky pieces of wood or metal find their work (physically, physical) difficult.
109. Heavy tools are needed to cut the wood or metal (proper, properly).
110. It is (real, really) important to prepare canvases in the right way, too.
111. (Incorrect, Incorrectly) stretched canvases will wrinkle and crease, spoiling the artist's work.

UNIT

8

Reporting Information

◆ **COMPOSITION FOCUS:** Research Report
◆ **LANGUAGE FOCUS:** Prepositions, Conjunctions, Interjections, Phrases, and Clauses

Imagine that you are a scientist who has been asked to present information that will affect the health of the entire nation. You must be sure your information is accurate. You carefully research your topic to get the information you need.

Writers also do research to report information accurately. Author Russell Freedman, whose research report appears on the next few pages, enjoys doing research. His research has been published in books and has won awards. In this unit you, too, will gather information to write a research report.

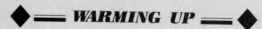 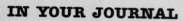 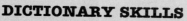

◆══ *WARMING UP* ══◆

IN YOUR JOURNAL

Look through magazines and newspapers to find a picture of someone or something you would like to know more about. Tell what you want to know and why.

DICTIONARY SKILLS

WORK IN A GROUP Find the meaning of the word *research*. Use a dictionary to find the exact meaning of this word and of the prefix *re-*. Discuss your findings.

Russell Freedman writes books *to inform* readers about interesting historical topics.

Award
Author
Winning

Reading with a Writer's Eye
Research Report

Ellis Island lies at the mouth of New York's Hudson River. Four out of every ten Americans have ancestors who had to pass through Ellis Island before they could be admitted to this country. In the nineteenth century, Ellis Island was the main point of entry for immigrants to the United States. Read Russell Freedman's report about Ellis Island and the immigrants who arrived there. Notice how he uses facts and quotations to give a sense of the people and the times in which they lived.

Coming Over
by Russell Freedman

Between 1880 and 1920, twenty-three million immigrants arrived in the United States. They came mainly from impoverished towns and villages in southern and eastern Europe. The one thing they had in common was a fervent belief that, in America, life would be better.

Most of these immigrants were poor, and many immigrant families arrived penniless. Often, the father came first, found work, and sent for his family later.

Immigrants usually crossed the Atlantic as steerage passengers. Reached by steep, slippery stairways, the steerage lay deep down in the hold of the ship. It was occupied by passengers paying the lowest fare.

Men, women, and children were packed into dark, foul-smelling compartments. They slept in narrow bunks stacked three high. They had no showers, no lounges, and no dining rooms. Food served from huge kettles was dished into dinner pails provided by the steamship company. Because steerage conditions were crowded and uncomfortable, passengers spent as much time as possible up on deck.

The great majority of immigrants landed in New York City, at America's busiest port. Edward Corsi, who later became United States Commissioner of Immigration, was a ten-year-old Italian immigrant when he sailed into New York harbor in 1907. He wrote, "My first impressions of the New World will always remain etched in my memory, particularly that hazy October morning when I first saw Ellis Island. The steamer *Florida,* fourteen days out of Naples, filled to capacity with sixteen hundred natives of Italy, had weathered one of the worst storms in our captain's memory; and glad we were, both children and grownups, to leave the open sea and come at last through the Narrows into the Bay.

"My mother, my stepfather, my brother Giuseppe, and my two sisters, Liberta and Helvetia, looked with wonder on this miraculous land of our dreams.

"Passengers all about us were crowding against the rail. Jabbered conversation, sharp cries, laughs, and cheers—a steadily rising din filled the air. Mothers and fathers lifted up babies so that they, too, could see, off to the left, the Statue of Liberty. . . ."

But the journey was not yet over. Before they could be admitted to the United States, immigrants had to pass through Ellis Island, which became the nation's chief immigrant processing center in 1892. There they would be questioned and examined. Those who could not pass all the exams would be detained; some would be sent back to Europe. And so their arrival in America was filled with great anxiety. Among the immigrants, Ellis Island was known as Heartbreak Island.

When their ship docked at a Hudson River pier, the immigrants had numbered identity tags pinned to their clothing. Then they were herded onto special ferryboats that carried them to Ellis Island. Officials hurried them along, shouting "Quick! Run! Hurry!" in half-a-dozen languages.

Filing into an enormous inspection hall, the immigrants formed long lines separated by iron railings that made the hall look like a great maze.

First the immigrants were examined by two doctors of the United States Health Service. One doctor looked for physical and mental abnormalities. When a case aroused suspicion, the immigrant received a chalk mark on the right shoulder for further inspection: *L* for lameness, *H* for heart, *X* for mental defects, and so on.

The second doctor watched for contagious and infectious diseases. He looked especially for infections of the scalp and at the eyelids for symptoms of *trachoma*, a blinding disease. Since trachoma caused more than half of all medical detentions, this doctor was greatly feared. He stood directly in the immigrant's path. With a swift movement, he would grab the immigrant's eyelid, pull it up, and peer beneath it. If all was well, the immigrant was passed on.

Those who failed to get past both doctors had to undergo a more thorough medical exam. The others moved on to the registration clerk, who questioned them with the aid of an interpreter: What is your name? Your nationality? Your occupation? Can you read and write? Have you ever been in prison? How much money do you have with you? Where are you going?

Some immigrants were so flustered that they could not answer. They were allowed to sit and rest and try again. About one immigrant out of every five or six was detained for additional examinations or questioning.

Most immigrants made it through Ellis Island in about one day. Carrying all their worldly possessions, they waited on the dock for the ferry that would take them to Manhattan, a mile away. Some of them still faced long journeys over land before they reached their final destinations. Others would head directly for the teeming immigrant neighborhoods of New York City. But no matter where they went, they all hoped to find the same thing: a better life for themselves and their children.

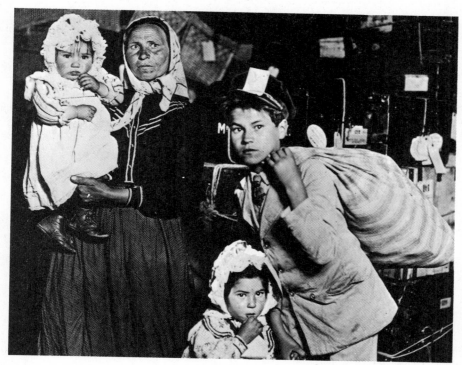

Respond

1. What information in the article do you find most interesting? Why does this information interest you?

Discuss

2. How do you think most immigrants felt on Ellis Island? What facts in the article show this to be so? How does the writer use quotations to support this impression?
3. What feeling do you have about Ellis Island after reading the article? How does the writer select and organize details to leave you with this feeling?

Thinking As a Writer
Analyzing a Research Report

A **research report** presents information drawn from various sources such as books, magazines, and interviews about a certain topic. A research report has an **introduction,** a **body,** and a **conclusion.**

Reread parts of Russell Freedman's report.

Coming Over

Between 1880 and 1920, twenty-three million immigrants arrived in the United States. They came mainly from impoverished towns and villages in southern and eastern Europe. The one thing they had in common was a fervent belief that, in America, life would be better.

The title gives a sense of what the report is about.

The introduction identifies the topic and arouses interest in the subject of the report. Notice how the first sentence offers a striking statistic to catch the reader's attention.

Immigrants usually crossed the Atlantic as steerage passengers. Reached by steep, slippery stairways, the steerage lay deep down in the hold of the ship. It was occupied by passengers paying the lowest fare.

The body gives specific information that the writer has gathered. Each paragraph in the body deals with a different main idea.

Most immigrants made it through Ellis Island in about one day. Carrying all their worldly possessions, they waited on the dock for the ferry that would take them to Manhattan, a mile away. Some of them still faced long journeys over land before they reached their final destinations. Others would head directly for the teeming immigrant neighborhoods of New York City. But no matter where they went, they all hoped to find the same thing: a better life for themselves and their children.

The conclusion signals the end of the report and gives a sense of completeness. It may sum up the information given and draw a conclusion about the subject. Often, it leaves the reader with a desire to find out more about the topic.

Discuss

Why does a research report need an introduction? Why does it need a body? Why does it need a conclusion?

Try Your Hand

A. **Identify Parts of a Research Report** All of the following paragraphs come from the same research report. For each paragraph, write whether it comes from the *introduction,* the *body,* or the *conclusion* of the report, and tell why you think so. Then write a phrase that identifies the subject of the whole report.

1.   As we have seen, Ellis Island has served many functions over the years. It has been a fort, a storage depot, and a processing center for immigrants. Now Ellis Island is on its way to becoming a museum of immigration. In this land of dreams and opportunities, however, who knows what part Ellis Island may play in the future of the United States?

2.   "Give me your tired, your poor, your huddled masses yearning to breathe free . . ." These words by Emma Lazarus are written on the base of the Statue of Liberty. They are fitting words with which to begin a study of immigration to the United States.

3.   Immigrants from northwestern Europe joined those from eastern and southern Europe. From 1890 to 1914, about 15 million newcomers from Europe and the Middle East arrived in the United States.

B. **Identify Details** Make a list of specific facts and details included in the paragraphs in **A.**

C. **Write a Title** Write a title for the research report that includes the paragraphs in **A.**

D. **Read a Research Report** With a partner, read aloud the research report on pages 344–347 or another research report about a topic that interests you. Identify the introduction, the body, and the conclusion of the report. Discuss whether each part is well written and why you do or do not think so.

Writer's Notebook

Collecting Social Studies Words Notice social studies words such as *immigration* and *commissioner* in "Coming Over." List the social studies words in the article that you do not know. Use a dictionary to find out what they mean. Record in your *Writer's Notebook* the words and their meanings. Watch for opportunities to use these new words when you speak or write about social studies topics.

Thinking As a Writer
Connecting Ideas in a Summary

The following postcard summarizes a vacation.

I just spent three weeks camping from Yellowstone to Yosemite. Old Faithful is still gushing, but I didn't see many bears. We camped in a lodge in the middle of Yosemite and hiked to the top of a waterfall. See you soon.

Summarizing is a useful tool when you are taking notes for a research report. It helps you write only the main idea and the most important details from your reading.

Study how the information in the original source has been summarized. Notice that the summary includes the most important information in the original source.

Original Source	Summary
Though forty percent of all Americans can trace their ancestry to a relative who came through Ellis Island, other ports of entry, located in Virginia and Texas, have also been important in American history.	Forty percent of Americans have an ancestor who passed through Ellis Island. However, Virginia and Texas have also been ports of entry.

When you take notes for a research report, summarize only the main ideas and important details from each original source.

Discuss

1. Look back at both the original source and the summary on this page. How else could the writer have summarized the information?
2. In the last paragraph of "Coming Over" on page 347, which sentence is used to summarize the immigrant dream?

Try Your Hand

Connect Ideas in a Summary Summarize the key steps in the immigration process described in "Coming Over." Compare your summary with a partner's. Discuss any differences between the two summaries.

Developing the Writer's Craft
Catching the Reader's Interest

Good writers know that to inform readers, they must keep them interested. Therefore, writers often begin a research report with a striking question or fact to catch the reader's attention. They also hold the reader's interest by giving concrete examples, instead of stating general ideas. In "Coming Over," Russell Freedman gives these facts to show that traveling as a steerage passenger was uncomfortable.

◆ Steerage passengers occupied dark compartments.
◆ They slept in narrow bunks.
◆ They ate out of dinner pails.

Details like these make information real for readers. Writers also convey information through quotations to make their writing more vivid. Russell Freedman used this quotation to show that immigrants approaching America were excited.

> "Passengers all about us were crowding against the rail. Jabbered conversation, sharp cries, laughs, and cheers—a steadily rising din filled the air. Mothers and fathers lifted up babies so that they, too, could see, off to the left, the Statue of Liberty. . . ."

When you write a research report, begin with a striking sentence. Use concrete details and direct quotations to catch and hold your reader's interest.

Discuss

1. Reread the opening paragraph of "Coming Over" on page 344. What makes the first sentence of this paragraph striking?
2. What other concrete details does Russell Freedman use in "Coming Over"? What does he convey with these details?

Try Your Hand

Catch a Reader's Interest Talk with someone you know about his or her family history. Then write a striking fact you learned from the talk, and give a direct quotation to illustrate the fact.

1 Prewriting
Research Report

Rosa wanted to write a research report about her heritage to share with her classmates. She followed the checklist in the **Writer's Guide** to help her plan her report. Look at what she did.

Writer's Guide

Prewriting Checklist
- ☑ Brainstorm topics.
- ☑ Select a topic.
- ☑ Narrow the topic.
- ☑ Think about your audience and your purpose.
- ☑ Gather information.
- ☑ Organize the facts.

◆ Brainstorming and Selecting a Topic

When Rosa thought about her heritage, she realized that the topic was too broad to cover in a short report. To narrow it down, she made an inverted triangle diagram. Under each topic, Rosa thought of a smaller, more specific topic. Finally, she had narrowed her topic down to the food of Mexico. She thought she could get information about this topic that would interest and surprise her classmates.

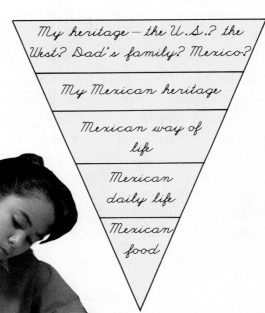

My heritage – the U.S.? the West? Dad's family? Mexico?

My Mexican heritage

Mexican way of life

Mexican daily life

Mexican food

Discuss

1. How did using the inverted triangle diagram help Rosa narrow her topic?
2. Should Rosa have narrowed her topic further? Why or why not?
3. Starting from her heritage, could Rosa have narrowed down to a different topic? Explain how and give examples.

WRITING PROCESS

◆ Gathering Information

After Rosa selected her topic, she gathered information. She began by interviewing her grandmother, Delia, who had grown up in Mexico. Rosa asked her grandmother some questions and took notes during the interview. During the interview, Rosa and her grandmother also looked in an **atlas,** a book of maps. They found Jalisco, the Mexican state where Rosa's grandmother was born. After the interview, Rosa reviewed her notes to make sure they were clear.

Rosa decided to look for more information about Mexican food in the library. In an encyclopedia, she found an entry for Mexico in the volume labeled *M—ME.* Rosa read the encyclopedia article and summarized in her notes the main idea and details. She also made sure she included information for her bibliography. A **bibliography** lists the sources of information that are used in writing a research report (see pages 436—437 for information on bibliographies).

Then Rosa looked in the card catalogue for books on her topic. She knew that the card catalogue is arranged by title, author, and subject. Since she did not have a particular book or author in mind, Rosa looked at subject cards under these topics: *Mexico, Mexican Foods, Foods of the World.* She recorded the call numbers of books that looked interesting. Rosa read a few of these books and took notes.

What is the food like there?
Spicy, lots of chili peppers
Is the food the same
everywhere in Mexico? No,
but tortillas are everywhere.

Mexican food
Food varies from place to place.
Turkey mole among best-
known dishes.
Turkey mole contains chili
peppers and chocolate.
Miller, Frank C. Mexico. The
People" Encyclopedia
Americana.
Vol. 18, pp. 828-829 Danbury,
C.T. Grolier Encyclopedia Inc.
1982

4-course lunch in Mexico City.
sopa (rice or pasta)—meat and vegetables—frijoles
(beans)—a sweet dessert
Montez, Maria. The Mexican Heritage Cookbook
San Antonio, TX, Sandpiper Press, 1985.

Finally, Rosa asked the librarian to help her find interesting magazine articles about Mexican food. By looking in a book called the *Readers' Guide to Periodical Literature,* the librarian found a listing for "Olé! The Festive Foods of Mexico," an article in *Parents* magazine. This article gave Rosa just the kind of information she was looking for. Again, Rosa took notes, including information for her bibliography.

Discuss

1. Why do you think Rosa interviewed her grandmother? Who else might Rosa have interviewed to get more information?
2. Of all the sources Rosa used, which do you think she found most useful? What other sources might she have used?
3. Why did Rosa include in her notes information for her report's bibliography?
4. Why is it important to include a bibliography in a research report?

◆ Organizing Information

Rosa gathered many pages of notes about the foods of Mexico. Now she was ready to plan her report. She read over her notes and circled each piece of information that seemed important. She scanned the circled notes to get a sense of the main ideas she wanted to cover in her report. Then she made an outline for her report. She gave the outline a title to identify the topic of her report. Look at Rosa's outline.

Each Roman numeral stands for the main idea of a paragraph. Each capital letter stands for a detail that supports the main idea. Each entry is brief and begins with a capital letter. All entries are parallel in structure, which means that they use similar wording. Notice that Rosa's entries are built around nouns.

Mexican Food

I. Variety
    A. Example from Jalisco
    B. Example from Yucatán
II. History
    A. Indian influence
    B. Spanish influence
III. Turkey Mole
    A. Ingredients
        1. Turkey
        2. Mole sauce
    B. Importance
IV. Other foods
    A. Some main dishes
    B. Some desserts
    C. Some drinks

Discuss

1. What main point will Rosa make in her first paragraph? How do you think she will support this point?
2. Using this outline, could Rosa include an explanation of how tortillas are made? Could she discuss what foods Mexico gave to the world? Explain your answers.
3. Has Rosa outlined her conclusion? Explain your answer.

Try Your Hand

Now plan a research report of your own.

A. Choose and Narrow a Topic Decide on a general subject for your research report. You may need to brainstorm a list of possible subjects. Then choose one that interests you, and narrow it down to a specific topic. You may want to use an inverted triangle diagram like the one Rosa made.

B. Gather Information Gather facts for your report from at least three sources. When you take notes from written sources, remember to include information for your bibliography. If you need help in writing a bibliography, see page 436.

- ◆ Interview people who can give you information about your subject. Include in your notes the name and address of the person you interviewed.
- ◆ Read reference books in the library. For information about reference sources, see page 465.
- ◆ Read books about your subject. Use subject cards in the card catalogue to find these books.
- ◆ Look for information in newspapers, magazines, and other periodicals. Use the *Readers' Guide to Periodical Literature* or ask the librarian to help you locate articles.
- ◆ Summarize in your notes the main ideas and details from each source.

C. Organize the Information Look over your notes. Decide what main ideas your notes suggest. Select the details you may want to use to support these main ideas. Sort your notes into groups of related facts. Then make an outline of your information like the one Rosa made.

 Save your notes and your outline in your *Writer's Notebook*. You will use them when you draft your research report.

2 Drafting
Research Report

Rosa followed the **Writer's Guide** to draft her research report. Look at what she did.

Writer's Guide

Drafting Checklist
- ☑ Use your notes and outline for ideas.
- ☑ Write the introduction first. Remember to use a striking sentence.
- ☑ Write the body next.
- ☑ Write the conclusion.
- ☑ Write a title.

> Land of Many Flavors
>
> When you think of Mexican food, do you always picture tacos? Actually, Mexican food includes a great variety of dishes. These dishes come from many different regions.
> In Jalisco, for example, you can enjoy pozole, a stew made with various contrasting ingredients.

Discuss

1. Look over Rosa's introduction. Is her first sentence striking enough to catch the reader's attention? Why or why not?
2. Has Rosa followed her outline so far? Explain your answer.

Try Your Hand

Now draft a research report.

A. **Review Your Information** Think about the information you gathered and organized in the last lesson. Decide whether you need more information. If so, gather it.

B. **Think About Your TAP** Remember that your task is to write a research report. Your purpose is to inform your audience about your topic.

Task: What?
Audience: Who?
Purpose: Why?

C. **Write Your First Draft** Follow the steps in the **Drafting Checklist** to write your research report.
   When you write your draft, just put all your ideas on paper. Do not worry about spelling, punctuation, or grammar. You can correct the draft later.

Save the first draft of your report in your *Writer's Notebook*. You will use it when you revise your research report.

3 Responding and Revising
Research Report

Rosa used the checklist in the **Writer's Guide** to revise her research report. Look at what she did.

Checking Information

Rosa decided she could make her report more interesting by replacing some general information with a concrete detail and adding a quotation. She used this mark ∧‾ to show the replacement. She used this mark ∧ to show her addition.

Checking Organization

Rosa decided to move a sentence so that her ideas would develop more logically. She used this mark ↺ .

Checking Language

Rosa cut some words to combine two sentences and create variety. She used this mark ⌿ to show what she cut.

Writer's Guide

Revising Checklist

- ☑ Read your report to yourself or to a partner.
- ☑ Think about your audience and your purpose. Add or cut information.
- ☑ Be sure that your introduction captures the reader's interest.
- ☑ Be sure that your report is complete and well organized.
- ☑ Check to see that your sentences are varied. Combine sentences to create variety.

Land of Many Flavors

When you think of Mexican food, do you always picture tacos? Actually, Mexican food includes a great variety of dishes~~. These dishes come~~ from many different regions. (Cut)

In Jalisco, for example, you can enjoy pozole, a stew made with ~~various contrasting ingredients~~ *chunks of pork, corn, and chilies*. In the Yucatán, you can dine on sac-kol de jambali— wild boar with peppermint sauce. (Replace)

Turkey mole combines two of the most important foods Mexico gave to the world—turkey and chocolate. Turkey with mole sauce is one of the most interesting dishes from Mexico. Mole sauce has 40 ingredients, including chocolate! *My grandmother says, "It's practically the national dish of Mexico."* (Move; Add)

Discuss

1. How did Rosa's change improve her first paragraph?
2. What else did Rosa do to make her report more interesting?

Try Your Hand

Now revise your first draft.

A. Read Your First Draft   As you read your report, think about your audience and your purpose. Read your report silently or to a partner to see whether it is complete and well organized. Ask yourself or your partner the questions in the box.

Responding and Revising Strategies

✔ **Respond**	✔ **Revise**
Ask yourself or a partner:	**Try these solutions:**
◆ Does my research report catch and hold the reader's interest?	◆ **Add** a striking first sentence. **Replace** general information with concrete details. **Add** interesting quotations.
◆ Is my information complete and correct?	◆ **Add** or **replace** information by checking your notes.
◆ Will readers understand how the information I provide is connected?	◆ **Move** information so that the order makes sense.
◆ Are my sentences varied and interesting?	◆ Vary your sentences by combining some of them. See the **Revising Workshop** on page 359.

B. Make Your Changes   If the answer to any question in the box is *no,* try the solution. Use the **Editor's Marks** to show your changes.

C. Review Your Research Report Again   Decide whether there is anything else you want to revise. Keep revising your report until you feel that it is well organized and complete.

D. Complete Your Bibliography   List your sources alphabetically by the authors' last names. If you need help writing a bibliography, see page 436.

> ### EDITOR'S MARKS
> ∧ Add something.
> ✗ Cut something.
> ⌒ Move something.
> ∧ Replace something.

Save your revised report in your *Writer's Notebook*. You will use it when you proofread your report.

WRITING PROCESS

Revising Workshop
Combining to Embed a Word or a Phrase

Writers vary their sentences by combining some of them. Often they place, or **embed,** only a word or a phrase from one sentence in the other. For example, writers can combine sentences by embedding an adjective, an adverb, an appositive, or a phrase that begins with a word such as *from, in, to,* or *by.*

Before Combining	After Combining
1. Many immigrants flocked to the United States. Many of them were ambitious and hardworking.	Many *ambitious, hardworking* immigrants flocked to the United States.
2. Edward Corsi struggled to get ahead. He struggled mightily.	Edward Corsi struggled *mightily* to get ahead.
3. This man was an immigrant. He became the Commissioner of Immigration.	This man, *an immigrant,* became the Commissioner of Immigration.
4. He came from Italy. He came in 1907.	He came from Italy *in 1907.*

Notice that in the first example, the writer embedded two adjectives. In the second example, the writer embedded an adverb. In the third example, the writer embedded an appositive. In the fourth example, the writer embedded the phrase *in 1907.*

Practice

Combine these sentences by embedding a word or a phrase.

1. Many Hispanic Americans fought in World War II. They fought courageously.
2. Manuel Gonzalez was a sergeant in World War II. He was heroic.
3. New immigrants from Puerto Rico came to the United States. They came after the war.
4. Herman Badillo arrived in the United States in 1947. He was an orphan.
5. He became a United States congressman. He became successful.

4 Proofreading
Research Report

After revising her research report, Rosa used the **Writer's Guide** and the **Editor's Marks** to proofread it. Look at what she did to her conclusion and the first entry of her bibliography.

Writer's Guide

Proofreading Checklist

☑ Check for errors in capitalization.

☑ Check for errors in punctuation. Make sure you have punctuated your bibliography correctly.

☑ Check to see that all your paragraphs are indented.

☑ Check your grammar.

☑ Circle any words you may have misspelled. Find out how to spell them correctly.

⇨ For proofreading help, use the **Writer's Handbook.**

¶From ensenada to the Yucatán, from
Veracruz to Mazatlán, Mexico is a land of
many flavors. The goodest *best* way to learn
about this real *really* delicious cuisine is to
visit Mexico. Bring your appetite.

Bibliography
H. Garrison, Olé! The Festive Foods
of Mexico. Parents April 1985,
pp. 103–106.

Discuss

1. What kinds of corrections did Rosa make?
2. What errors did Rosa make in punctuating her bibliography entry?

Try Your Hand

Proofread Your Research Report Now use the **Writer's Guide** and the **Editor's Marks** to proofread your report.

Save your corrected research report in your *Writer's Notebook.* You will use it when you publish your report.

EDITOR'S MARKS

≡ Capitalize.

⊙ Add a period.

∧ Add something.

⩘ Add a comma.

∨∨ Add quotation marks.

✄ Cut something.

⋀ Replace something.

∼ Transpose.

◯ Spell correctly.

⊬ Indent paragraph.

／ Make a lowercase letter.

WRITING PROCESS

5 Publishing
Research Report

Rosa made a clean copy of her research report and checked it to be sure she had not left out anything. Then she and her classmates published their reports in a class book. You can find Rosa's report on pages 50–51 of the **Writer's Handbook.**

Here is how Rosa and her classmates published a class social studies book.

1. First, Rosa met with her classmates and shared ideas about possible ways to publish their research reports.

2. Next, Rosa and her classmates decided in what order they wanted their reports to appear and what illustrations and maps they wanted to include.

3. Then, they mounted each report on construction paper and put illustrations and maps in place.

4. Next, they numbered each page and prepared a table of contents and a cover.

5. Last, they bound their class social studies book and displayed it in their classroom.

Discuss

1. Suggest some of the ways in which reports in a class social studies book might be arranged. Which do you prefer, and why?

2. Do you think every student should be free to make whatever illustration or map he or she chooses? Why or why not?

Try Your Hand

Publish Your Research Report   Follow the checklist in the **Writer's Guide.** If possible, create a class book, or try one of these ideas for sharing your research report.

◆ Present your research report to your classmates or to another group as an oral report. Before you begin, read **Tips on How to Give and Listen to an Oral Report** on page 363.

◆ Make an illustration or draw a map to accompany your report, and display it on the bulletin board under a large heading, such as *One World.*

WRITING PROCESS

Listening and Speaking
Tips on How to Give and Listen to an Oral Report

Giving an Oral Report

1. Choose a topic that will interest your audience.
2. Prepare for your talk by making notes on index cards. The notes are to remind you of points you want to make during your talk. Write only a few key words on each card so you can remember what you want to say at a glance. If you have already written a research report on your topic, use it to make your notes.
3. Think of a way to start your talk that will catch the listeners' attention. For example, you could open with a striking question, a brief story, a joke, or an interesting quote. Summarize this "opener" on your first note card.
4. Arrange the rest of your note cards in the order that you want to give your talk, and number the cards.
5. Practice your speech with a partner until you feel comfortable with it. Ask your partner for comments to help you improve your presentation. Learn to avoid nervous habits such as talking too fast or saying "Uh" too often.
6. When you are ready to begin speaking, take a deep breath and relax. You may want to pick out a friendly face in the audience and pretend that you are speaking only to that person.
7. During your talk, maintain eye contact with your audience. Glance at your notes only to refresh your memory. Do not read directly from your cards.
8. Speak clearly, vary your voice, and use appropriate gestures. Refer to your visual aids if you have any.
9. End by restating your most important point. Then thank your audience for their attention.

Listening to an Oral Report

1. Keep your eyes on the speaker and pay attention.
2. Listen for the main topic of the report. Then listen for important details, and notice how they are related to the topic.
3. Make notes about any questions you have. You may have a chance to ask your questions after the talk.

Writing in the Content Areas

Use what you learned to gather information about a topic of interest. Write a research report or a paragraph about your research findings. Use one of these ideas or an idea of your own.

Writer's Guide

When you write, remember the stages of the Writing Process.
- Prewriting
- Drafting
- Responding and Revising
- Proofreading
- Publishing

Mathematics

Devices and machines such as the abacus, the adding machine, the slide rule, the calculator, and the computer are used in making mathematical calculations. Find out the history and the uses of one of these items.

Physical Education

Has tennis, football, or soccer always been played in the same way? Research the history of a sport. Have the rules changed? Is the sport more or less popular than it once was? Do people wear the same kinds of clothes to play the sport?

Social Studies

How old is your town or city? Who were its earliest settlers? How has your town or city changed since its beginnings? Read about the history of your town or city. Ask the librarian at the local library to help you find information. Perhaps your parents or other adults may be able to give you information as well.

Science

What fruits and vegetables grow best in your area? When should they be planted, and what kind of care do they need? Talk to a local plant nursery owner, or find information in a planting guide. If you know people with gardens, ask them for information as well.

CONNECTING
WRITING ↔ LANGUAGE

Both writers and readers can gain information from a well-written research report. What can you learn from this section of a report about alligators?

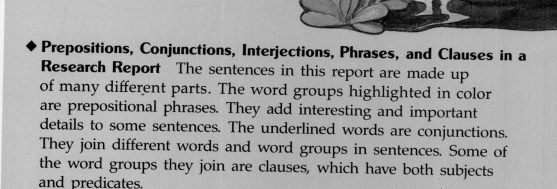

Alligators

Alligators live in the southeastern United States and in parts of China. A male alligator can measure up to 12 feet long, but a female seldom measures more than 9 feet. An alligator's eyes seem to stick up above its skull. Therefore, an alligator can see above the water while its body is beneath the surface. Alligators are the only reptiles with loud voices, and their bellows can be heard a mile away.

◆ **Prepositions, Conjunctions, Interjections, Phrases, and Clauses in a Research Report** The sentences in this report are made up of many different parts. The word groups highlighted in color are prepositional phrases. They add interesting and important details to some sentences. The underlined words are conjunctions. They join different words and word groups in sentences. Some of the word groups they join are clauses, which have both subjects and predicates.

◆ **Language Focus: Prepositions, Conjunctions, Interjections, Phrases, and Clauses** In the following lessons you will learn more about using prepositions, conjunctions, interjections, phrases, and clauses to help you write interesting and varied sentences.

1 Prepositions and Prepositional Phrases

FOCUS

◆ A **preposition** relates a noun or a pronoun to another word in the sentence.

◆ A **prepositional phrase** is made up of a preposition, the object of the preposition, and all the words in between.

Read this sentence. The word in color is a preposition. It shows the relationship between the verb *sailed* and the noun *world*.

1. Magellan sailed around the world.

The noun or pronoun that follows a preposition is the **object of the preposition**. The preposition, its object, and any words that modify the object make up a prepositional phrase. If the object of a preposition is a pronoun, it is an object pronoun. A preposition can have more than one object.

       preposition   object

2. The king of rich, powerful Spain helped him.

               object pronoun

3. The king provided ships for him and his crew.

If a sentence has a prepositional phrase, you may be able to combine it with another sentence. Notice how the two previous sentences are combined in this sentence.

4. The king of rich, powerful Spain provided ships for him and his crew.

Some Common Prepositions						
in	to	from	near	below	during	across
of	at	with	by	above	between	behind
on	for	over	into	under	through	against

Guided Practice

A. Identify each prepositional phrase. Tell which word is the *preposition* and which is the *object of the preposition*.

1. The fleet sailed across three oceans.
2. The voyage ended without Magellan.
3. Magellan died in the Philippines.
4. He was killed during a battle.
5. Few of the sailors survived the journey.

Independent Practice

B. Identifying Prepositions and Objects of Prepositions Write each prepositional phrase. Then underline the preposition once. Underline the object of the preposition twice.

6. Jim Beckwourth was a mountain man from St. Louis.

MODEL▷ from St. Louis

7. He took part in fur-trading expeditions.
8. He made many trips across the Rockies.
9. Beckwourth was also a scout for the army.
10. During one journey he discovered Beckwourth Pass.
11. This pass opened a route to California.
12. He built a ranch near this pass.
13. Beckwourth led a life of high adventure.

C. Revising: Combining Sentences Use a prepositional phrase to combine each pair of sentences. Write each new sentence.

14. There is a new frontier. It is under the waves.

MODEL▷ There is a new frontier under the waves.

15. People study undersea life. They use special equipment.
16. They take many photographs. They photograph sea plants.
17. Someday, people may live under the oceans. They may inhabit giant colonies.
18. The people must have oxygen. They need oxygen for survival.
19. Oxygen will be pumped into the colonies. Enormous tanks store the oxygen.
20. Each colony will have several tanks. The tanks will hold a three-month's supply of oxygen.

Application — Writing

Letter Imagine that you are on Magellan's expedition or on another journey in the past, the present, or the future. Write a letter to a friend telling about a day during the expedition. Describe what you see and do. Use at least five prepositional phrases.

2 Prepositional Phrases Used as Adjectives

◆ **FOCUS** A prepositional phrase that modifies a noun or a pronoun is an **adjective phrase.**

Remember that an adjective modifies a noun or a pronoun. A prepositional phrase can also modify a noun or a pronoun. When it does, it is called an adjective phrase. In this sentence the group of words in color is an adjective phrase.

1. The hotel near the ruins is new.

Most adjectives come before the words they describe. Adjective phrases usually follow the word they describe.

2. Many European tourists stay there.   adjective

3. Many tourists from Europe stay there.
   adjective phrase

> **Link to Speaking and Writing**
> You can use adjective phrases to add enriching details to sentences.

with long white hair
Llamas live in the ruins.

Guided Practice

A. Identify the adjective phrase in each sentence.

1. The Incas of Peru built Machu Picchu.
2. These ruins in the mountains are very old.
3. The population of the city was never large.
4. The main building was a temple on the hillside.
5. A building above the city was a lookout point.
6. The builders used rocks of incredible size.
7. Today, many tourists visit the city in the jungle.
8. People can climb the peaks near the ruins.
9. The views from the peaks are spectacular.

B. **10. – 18.** Identify the word modified by each adjective phrase in **A.**

Independent Practice

C. Identifying Adjective Phrases Write the adjective phrase in each sentence.

19. Houston, a city in southern Texas, is very modern.

MODEL ▷ in southern Texas

20. Skyscrapers line the streets of the downtown area.
21. Buildings with glass sides are common.
22. Texas Commerce Tower is a building with many floors.
23. People from many places visit Houston.
24. Residents of the city enjoy its shops.
25. Stores in underground malls are popular.
26. Universities in Houston educate many students.

D. 27. – 34. Identifying Words Described by Adjective Phrases
Write the word that each adjective phrase in C modifies.

27. Houston, a city in southern Texas, is very modern.

MODEL ▷ city

E. Revising: Expanding Sentences with Adjective Phrases
Rewrite each sentence. Use one or more adjective phrases to add enriching details.

35. The house is large.

MODEL ▷ The house with the yellow awning is large.

36. The woman is an architect.
37. The boy climbed the hill.
38. The street was busy.
39. Listen to the sound.
40. The hotel is empty.
41. Bob painted a picture.
42. I looked in the window.
43. He sat in the car.

Application — Writing

Description Imagine that you have hired a builder to build a hotel like the one in the picture. Write a description of the hotel for the builder so that he or she will have a clear idea of what you want. Tell where the hotel should be and how the buildings and the grounds should look. Use at least five adjective phrases.

3 Prepositional Phrases Used as Adverbs

◆ **FOCUS** A prepositional phrase that modifies a verb, an adjective, or an adverb is an **adverb phrase.**

An adverb phrase does the same job in a sentence that an adverb does. It tells *how, when, where,* or *to what extent* about a verb, an adjective, or another adverb. The groups of words in color are adverb phrases.

1. The museum opens at ten . **modifies verb**
2. Carla is curious about dinosaurs .
   modifies adjective
3. She arrives early in the morning .
   modifies adverb

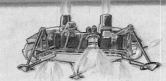

Link to Speaking and Writing
For sentence variety, place an adverb phrase at the beginning of an inverted sentence.

Through the leaves peered the dinosaur.

Guided Practice

A. Identify the adverb phrase in each sentence.

1. Carla studies dinosaurs with great interest.
2. Soon after her arrival she visited the dinosaur room.
3. Dinosaurs flourished for 150 million years.
4. The Stegosaurus was protected with bony plates.
5. Dinosaurs made life dangerous for other animals.

B. 6.–10. Identify each word modified by an adverb phrase in **A,** and tell whether it is a *verb,* an *adjective,* or an *adverb.*

THINK AND REMEMBER
◆ Remember that a prepositional phrase that modifies a verb, an adjective, or an adverb is an **adverb phrase.**

Independent Practice

C. Identifying Adverb Phrases Write the adverb phrase from each sentence.

11. Robert Goddard studied at Clark University.
MODEL> at Clark University

12. Goddard did research during the early twentieth century.
13. This scientist experimented with rockets.
14. The Goddard rocket lifted up into the air.
15. Goddard was happy with this success.
16. Goddard's experiments led to space exploration.
17. Late in his life, his work became well known.
18. Today, Goddard is famous for his work.

D. 19. – 26. Identifying Words Modified by Adverb Phrases
List the words modified by adverb phrases in **C.** Label each one *verb, adjective,* or *adverb.*

19. Robert Goddard studied at Clark University.
MODEL> studied—verb

E. Adding Adverb Phrases to Sentences Complete each sentence with an adverb phrase.

27. The shuttle rose _____.
MODEL> The shuttle rose into the sky.

28. Tongues of bright orange flame leaped _____.
29. The astronauts headed _____.
30. A vast crowd of spectators watched _____.
31. The ship sped _____.
32. The astronauts saw Earth spinning far away _____.

F. 33. – 38. Revising: Changing Word Order in Sentences
Rewrite the completed sentences from **E** in inverted word order. Begin each sentence with an adverb phrase.

33. The shuttle rose into the sky.
MODEL> Into the sky rose the shuttle.

Application — Writing and Speaking

Speech Imagine that you are a tour guide at a museum. Write a speech describing the museum for a group of elementary schoolchildren who will be visiting it. Tell the students how to find their way around the museum and what exhibits to look for. Use at least five adverb phrases. Present your speech to your class.

4 Choosing the Correct Preposition

◆ **FOCUS** Some prepositions are frequently misused.

The prepositions *in* and *into* have slightly different meanings. The preposition *in* means "already inside." The preposition *into* shows movement from the outside to the inside.

1. Sally is `in` her costume.
2. John is getting `into` his costume.

The preposition *between* refers to two persons or things. The preposition *among* refers to three or more.

3. Sally chose `between` the brown hat and the headband.
4. She stood `among` her four best friends.

The words *different from*—not *different than*—are used to tell about differences.

5. This compass is `different from` that one.

The preposition *of* and the helping verb *have* may sound similar when you say them quickly. Be sure not to write *of* when you mean *have.*

6. We `should have` practiced more.

getting INTO costume

IN costume

Guided Practice

A. Identify the word that correctly completes each sentence.

1. Sally is starring (in, into) a play about Sacajawea.
2. The play is (different from, different than) most others.
3. The students chose (between, among) three plays.
4. A tent is on the stage (between, among) five cardboard trees.
5. The play (could have, could of) been longer.

THINK AND REMEMBER

◆ Use *in* to mean "already inside." Use *into* to tell about movement from the outside to the inside.
◆ Use *between* for two and *among* for three or more.
◆ Use *different from* to tell about differences.
◆ Do not use *of* in place of *have* when you write.

Independent Practice

B. Using Prepositions Correctly   Write the preposition in parentheses that correctly completes each sentence.

6. My class went (in, into) the auditorium for the play.

MODEL ▷ into

7. My friend Kelly had been offered three roles, and she chose (between, among) them.
8. Kelly played Sandra Day O'Connor (in, into) the play.
9. O'Connor is one of the nine justices of the Supreme Court (in, into) Washington, D.C.
10. The play begins with O'Connor going (in, into) the Supreme Court Building.
11. Sandra Day O'Connor is (different from, different than) the other judges.
12. She is the only woman (between, among) the nine judges.
13. The play took place (between, among) nine o'clock and twelve o'clock.
14. Back (in, into) our classroom, we discussed the play.
15. I wish I (could have, could of) played Justice O'Connor.

C. Proofreading: Checking Preposition Usage   Find the error in each sentence. Write the sentence correctly.

16. Our play could of been about anything.

MODEL ▷ Our play could have been about anything.

17. Eugene and I went in the bookstore.
18. We looked between all the plays in the play corner.
19. We could of chosen a play about space.
20. In this play, some astronauts go in a black hole.
21. My favorite play was different than the space play.
22. It was set into ancient Greece.
23. We just couldn't choose among the two plays.
24. We might of flipped a coin, but we didn't.
25. A clerk put both plays in a bag for us.

Application — Writing

Journal Entry   Imagine that you were in a play about frontier life in early America. Write a journal entry that describes the experience. Tell what part you played, how you got ready backstage, and what happened during the performance. Use the prepositions *in, into, between,* and *among* correctly in your account. If you need help writing a journal entry, see page 40 of the **Writer's Handbook.**

5 Conjunctions

◆ **FOCUS** A **conjunction** connects words or groups of words in a sentence.

A conjunction joins two words or two groups of words. Use a comma and a conjunction to combine two simple sentences into one compound sentence. The words in color are conjunctions.

1. The car engine sputters and stops.

2. A farmer appears, and I ask him to help me.

Three of the most common conjunctions are *and, but,* and *or.* These conjunctions join words or word groups of equal importance. *And* is used to show additions or inclusions. *But* is used to show contrast. *Or* is used to show a choice.

3. The horse is hot and tired.

4. The car moves slowly but surely into town.

5. Would you rather have a horse or a car?

Link to Speaking and Writing
You can use conjunctions to connect words and combine sentences. How do the changes improve these sentences? Why was a verb changed?

The farmer ~~looks relaxed.~~ ^{and} His horse looks relaxed. ^{but} The driver seems nervous.

Guided Practice

A. Identify the conjunction in each sentence. Then name the words or groups of words that it joins.

1. Long ago, people used horses for work and transportation.

2. Horses pulled wagons and plows.

3. They pulled barges and uprooted tree stumps.

4. Some people traveled in horse-drawn coaches, but this kind of travel was expensive.

5. Most people traveled on horseback or on foot.

Independent Practice

B. Identifying Conjunctions Read each sentence. Write the conjunction and the words or groups of words it joins. Then underline the conjunction.

6. In the 1800's, ships and trains were powered by steam.

MODEL ▷ ships <u>and</u> trains

7. Many people were curious but uncertain about trains.
8. By 1900, trains had become common in Europe and North America.
9. A train ride from New York to San Francisco took only a week or a little more.
10. The same trip took weeks or even months by stagecoach.
11. Steam trains were fast, but people wanted to go faster.
12. Electric trains traveled more quickly and safely.
13. When gas engines were first invented, they were not used for cars and trucks.
14. Gas engines were built in Germany and used in bicycles.

C. Revising: Combining Sentences Write each pair of sentences as one sentence. Use the conjunction in parentheses to join words or groups of words.

15. Car travel is fast. It is convenient. (and)

MODEL ▷ Car travel is fast and convenient.

16. Most American cars are built in Detroit. Some are built elsewhere. (but)
17. Cars travel on streets. Cars travel on highways. (and)
18. Engineers design new cars. They test the cars. (and)
19. Some cars may look plain. They may move fast. (but)
20. Tomorrow's cars may be lighter. They may be safer. (and)
21. Future cars may run on sunlight. They may run on electricity. (or)

Application — Writing, Speaking, Listening

Announcement With a partner, brainstorm what the car of the future should be like. Together, write an announcement describing the car to a group of reporters. Use *and, but,* and *or* to join words and word groups.

6 Interjections

◆ **FOCUS** An **interjection** is a word or group of words that expresses feeling or emotion.

Interjections can express strong or mild feeling. An interjection that expresses strong feeling is usually followed by an exclamation point. It stands alone as if it were a sentence.

1. Wow ! Watch that man run!

An interjection that expresses mild feeling is followed by a comma. The first word after it is not capitalized unless it is a proper noun or the word *I*. This kind of interjection cannot stand alone.

2. Oh , he missed that catch.

Common Interjections						
phew	hey	well	ah	aha	alas	bravo
wow	eek	ugh	hurray	oh	oops	ouch

Link to Speaking and Writing
Interjections can help written dialogue sound like real speech.

Hey,
Did you see that?

Guided Practice

A. Identify the interjection in each sentence. Then tell what punctuation mark should follow it and whether the next word should be capitalized.

1. Bravo you won the game!
2. Ouch watch your step!
3. Well I guess it's over.
4. Oh I forgot my bag.
5. Aha here it is.
6. Ah I see Luis over there.

THINK AND REMEMBER
◆ Use **interjections** to express strong or mild feeling.

Independent Practice

B. Identifying Interjections Write the interjection in each sentence. Label each interjection *strong* or *mild*.

7. Wow! I love this parade!

> MODEL > Wow!—strong

8. Ah, the clowns are coming.
9. Oops, she dropped her baton.
10. Whew! It's getting hot!
11. Oh! That band was great!
12. Well, it's time to go.

C. Proofreading: Finding Errors in Punctuation and Capitalization Find the error in each sentence. Write the sentence correctly.

13. Eek this movie is scary.

> MODEL > Eek! This movie is scary!

14. Oh there's someone hiding in that closet.
15. Whew that girl just escaped.
16. Ugh that monster is ugly.
17. Psst let's leave now.
18. Hey hurry up.

D. Revising: Adding Interjections to Sentences Add an interjection to each sentence. Write the new sentence. Add punctuation marks where they are needed.

19. That speech was good.

> MODEL > Bravo! That speech was good!

20. This speech is exciting.
21. Please talk more softly.
22. I hope this candidate wins.
23. Please pass the program.
24. That's a great idea.

Application — Writing, Speaking, Listening

Conversation Choose a partner. Imagine that you are watching the same event as the people in the picture. Decide what the event is and what the spectators find so exciting. Then express your reactions to each other in a short conversation. Begin some sentences with interjections. Write down the parts of the conversation you like best.

7 Phrases and Clauses

◆ A **phrase** is a group of words that is used as a part of speech.
◆ A **clause** is a group of words that has a subject and a predicate.

A group of words can work as a unit in a sentence. If the group does not have a subject and a predicate, it is a phrase. For example, a group of words that works as an adjective is an adjective phrase. A group of words that works as an adverb is an adverb phrase. A group of words that works as a verb is a verb phrase. A phrase does not express a complete thought.

          verb phrase   adverb phrase

1. Tacos will be served at the fiesta .

A clause is a group of words that contains both a subject and a predicate. A clause may or may not express a complete thought.

2. They will dance. complete thought
3. as the moon is shining not a complete thought

A sentence can have one clause or more than one clause.

4. Mrs. Torres is tired. one clause
5. Mrs. Torres rests, and Pepe sets the table while the tamales cook. three clauses

---

Link to Speaking and Writing

Use phrases and clauses to produce a rich variety of sentences. What phrases and clauses does this sentence contain?

In the afternoon the people gather, and the mayor begins the fiesta with a funny speech.

Guided Practice

A. Tell whether each group of words is a *phrase* or a *clause.*

1. the fiesta begins
2. during the afternoon
3. have been singing
4. for the children
5. they break the piñata
6. with guitar music
7. when night comes
8. the stars twinkle

Independent Practice

B. Identifying Phrases and Clauses Write *phrase* or *clause* to describe each group of words.

9. Japanese cooking is delicious

MODEL > clause

10. on the table
11. sashimi is raw fish
12. into a large pot
13. when the food is hot

14. with unusual spices
15. on colorful china plates
16. before the meal ended
17. with wooden chopsticks

C. Completing Sentences Complete each sentence with the kind of word group named in parentheses.

18. I eat my hamburger _____. (phrase)

MODEL > I eat my hamburger with ketchup.

19. When _____, I take my dish to the sink. (clause)
20. I drink milk _____. (phrase)
21. After I eat my favorite dessert, _____. (clause)
22. Some people cook chicken _____. (phrase)
23. I like popcorn, and _____. (clause)

D. Revising: Expanding Sentences Add a phrase or a clause to each sentence. Write each new sentence, and label it *phrase* or *clause* to show what you added.

24. I ate turkey on my birthday.

MODEL > I ate turkey on my birthday since it was on Thanksgiving. clause

25. Last year we tried something different.
26. We had a whole salmon for Thanksgiving.
27. It didn't seem very much like Thanksgiving.
28. Thanksgiving was the day after my birthday.
29. I missed having turkey.

Application — Writing

Food Review Imagine that you are a food critic. Describe a delicious meal you have recently eaten. Tell what you ate, what you liked about it, and how it was served. Build an interesting variety of sentences with clauses and phrases.

8 Independent and Dependent Clauses

FOCUS
◆ An **independent clause** expresses a complete thought and can stand alone.
◆ A **dependent clause** does not express a complete thought and cannot stand alone.

Remember that a clause is a group of words with a subject and a predicate. An independent clause expresses a complete thought. It can stand alone as a sentence or be part of a larger sentence.

independent clause

1. Bill Robinson was a great tap dancer.

independent clause   independent clause

2. He moved gracefully, and audiences loved him.

A dependent clause cannot stand alone. It has a subject and a predicate, but it does not express a complete thought. In this sentence, the words in color are a dependent clause.

3. The dancers moved while the music played .

Dependent clauses often begin with such words as *while, before, after, when, where, who, that, if, which, until, though, because,* and *since.* Look for these words to help you locate dependent clauses in sentences.

Guided Practice

A. Tell whether each clause is *independent* or *dependent*.

1. Americans admired Bill Robinson
2. they called him "Bojangles"
3. though he appeared in movies
4. before he danced
5. he was greeted warmly

THINK AND REMEMBER

◆ Remember that an **independent clause** can stand alone as a sentence or can be used with other words as part of a sentence.
◆ Remember that a **dependent clause** cannot stand alone as a sentence.

Independent Practice

B. Identifying Independent and Dependent Clauses
Write *dependent* or *independent* to describe each clause.

6. the Cossack dancers perform spectacular leaps

MODEL > independent

7. though they land on their knees
8. they dance on the tips of their boots
9. because they turn so fast
10. when they toured the United States
11. this dancing takes enormous energy

C. Identifying Clauses Within Sentences
Write each sentence. Underline the independent clause once. Underline the dependent clause twice.

12. Flamenco dancers tap their feet loudly as they dance.

MODEL > Flamenco dancers tap their feet loudly as they dance.

13. The gypsies created flamenco, which many now perform.
14. Before the dance begins, a guitarist plays and sings.
15. Flamenco dancers are graceful when they move.
16. As the women twirl, their costumes are a mass of color.
17. Some dancers play the castanets when they dance.

D. 18.–23. Identifying Words That Begin Dependent Clauses
Write the word that begins each dependent clause in C.

18. Flamenco dancers tap their feet loudly as they dance.

MODEL > as

E. Revising: Expanding Sentences
Add a clause to each sentence. Write the new sentence. Label it *dependent* or *independent* to show what kind of clause you added.

24. I know a dance _____.

MODEL > I know a dance that you'll like. dependent

25. It's called "Rubberneck Chicken," and _____.
26. Before _____, let me show you how it's done.
27. Raise your right arm and _____.
28. Then, hop forward while _____.
29. After you finish, _____.

Application — Writing

Photo Captions Write a caption for each picture in this lesson. Describe the photographs for readers, and point out important details. Use at least four sentences with dependent clauses.

9 Complex Sentences

◆ **FOCUS** A **complex sentence** contains an independent clause and one or more dependent clauses.

Every sentence must have at least one independent clause. If it also contains any dependent clauses, it is a complex sentence. A comma comes after a dependent clause that begins a sentence. No comma separates the clauses if the independent clause comes first. The dependent clauses are in color in these complex sentences.

1. John Chapman lived when America was young .
2. Although the country was young , it was growing fast.

Do not confuse complex sentences with compound sentences. A compound sentence is made up of two or more independent clauses joined by such words as *and, but,* and *or.*

independent clause		independent clause

3. The wagons rolled west, and Chapman followed them.

Link to Speaking and Writing
A complex sentence can show how two ideas are related. Does combining these sentences make the message clearer? In what way?

As Chapman walked along. He planted apple seeds.

Guided Practice

A. Tell whether each sentence is *compound* or *complex.*

1. Wherever he went, John Chapman helped people build.
2. He gave people seeds, and they planted apple trees.
3. People called him Johnny Appleseed, and his fame spread.
4. When Johnny rested, children gathered around him.
5. They listened while he told about his adventures.
6. As the years passed, Johnny's trees grew bigger.
7. Johnny is gone now, but his trees still live.

Independent Practice

B. Identifying Complex and Compound Sentences Write whether each sentence is *compound* or *complex.*

8. When railroads first began, tunnels had to be blasted through mountains.

MODEL ▷ complex

9. John Henry hammered holes where explosives were placed.
10. He was strong, and he disliked machines.
11. When the steam drill was invented, he raced against it.
12. The machine roared as it started.
13. Though the machine was fast, John Henry was faster.
14. He beat the machine, but the contest killed him.
15. As he lay dead, his hammer was still in his hand.

C. Combining Sentences Combine each pair of sentences into one complex sentence, using the word in parentheses. If the dependent clause begins the sentence, put a comma after it.

16. Paul Bunyan traveled. Strange things happened. (wherever)

MODEL ▷ Wherever Paul Bunyan traveled, strange things happened.

17. Paul Bunyan came to America. There were no mountains, lakes, or rivers. (before)
18. He dug the Great Lakes. His men needed water. (because)
19. The lakes were dug. He hauled water from the Atlantic to fill them. (after)
20. Paul was walking to Louisiana. He got sand in his shoes. (while)
21. He poured out the sand. It formed the Kiamichi Mountains of Oklahoma. (when)

Application — Writing

Tall Tale Write your own version of a familiar tall tale, or write your own tall tale. Describe a character with amazing strength, intelligence, or goodness. Tell about one amazing feat the character performs. Use at least three complex sentences.

Building Vocabulary
Roots: Clues to Word History

You can learn something about the history of a word by looking at its root. The **root** is the core of a word, the part left over when you take away all the prefixes and suffixes.

Look, for example, at the word *martial*, which means "warlike." It contains the root *mart*. This root comes from the Latin word *Mars*. Latin was the language spoken by the Romans. The Romans believed in many gods, one of whom was Mars, the god of war. From *Mars* we also get the name *March*. The Romans named this month after Mars because it was the time of year when they usually went to war.

Many English words have Greek roots. The Greeks built a great civilization hundreds of years before the Romans. Words with Greek origins have been passed down through the centuries. The word *microscope*, for example, contains the Greek roots *micro*, which means "small," and *scope*, which means "see."

You may find the same root in many different words. Think of the words *visible, visit, vista, vision, invisible*, and *visual*. All of these words come from the Latin root *vis*, meaning "to see."

Study these roots from Greek and Latin.

	Root	Meaning	Example
from Latin	capt	take, hold	captive
	equ	same	equality
	loc	place	local
	spect	see	spectacles
	tract	pull	subtract
	vent	come	convention
from Greek	ology	study	biology
	hemi	half	hemisphere
	astro	star	astronomy
	graph	writing	paragraph
	phone	sound, voice	telephone
	thermo	heat	thermostat

Reading Practice

Read each sentence. Write the word that contains a root from the chart. Underline the root.

1. There are many interesting stories in mythology.
2. Atalanta was the daughter of a respected king of Greece.
3. No one could equal her swiftness in running.
4. She captured the hearts of many young men.
5. Atalanta's astrological sign was Capricorn.
6. Hippomenes was attracted to the lovely girl.
7. They agreed on a location for a race.
8. In the race, Hippomenes distracted Atalanta by dropping golden apples in her path.
9. Spectators cheered as Hippomenes raced past Atalanta.
10. She could not prevent him from winning the race.

Writing Practice

Complete each sentence with a word containing the root in parentheses. Use a dictionary if you need help.

11. The study of the earth is called _____. (ology)
12. We measure temperature with a _____. (thermo)
13. When you sign your name, you write your _____. (graph)
14. A storm can stop, or _____, a plane from landing. (vent)
15. Firefighters check, or _____, buildings. (spect)
16. Things that cannot be seen are _____. (vis)
17. Two things that are the same in number are _____. (equ)
18. Someone who travels into space is an _____. (astro)
19. Something that makes distant stars look closer is called a _____. (scope)
20. A machine for pulling plows is called a _____. (tract)

Project

Here are some more Latin and Greek roots:

meter	auto	neo	manus
geo	photo	poly	gress
phil	bio	cred	tele

Give the meaning for each root. Then see how many words you can list that contain these roots. Use a dictionary if you need help.

Language Enrichment
Prepositions, Conjunctions, Interjections, Phrases, Clauses

Use what you know about prepositions, conjunctions, interjections, phrases, and clauses to do these activities.

 Amusement Park

Do this activity with three or four classmates. Each of you should write the same 10 interjections on index cards. Interjections should express positive as well as negative feelings. Then take turns describing rides at an amusement park. After a person has spoken, choose the interjection that best expresses your feeling about the ride. See how many members of the group respond with the same interjection.

What Is It?

Look around your classroom and pick several objects. Use prepositional phrases to write four clues describing where each object is. Read the clues to some classmates. See how quickly they can guess what your objects are.

 Handshake

Create your own special handshake and rules for when it should be used. Make a list describing at least four motions that should be made with the hand in greeting a friend, and two rules for using the handshake. Use complex sentences in your description. Teach your handshake to classmates.

CONNECTING
LANGUAGE ↔ WRITING

In this unit you learned about a number of different kinds of words, word groups, and sentence parts. Prepositional phrases, which begin with prepositions, work as adjectives or adverbs in sentences. Conjunctions connect words and groups of words. Interjections express strong or mild feeling. Dependent and independent clauses can be combined to make compound and complex sentences.

◆ **Using Prepositions, Conjunctions, Interjections, Phrases, and Clauses in Your Writing** Learning to use many different kinds of words and groups of words can help you build varied sentences. Pay special attention to how you use prepositional phrases, conjunctions, interjections, and clauses as you do these activities.

Fabulous Trip

Write two paragraphs describing a place you know about. Give information, but also try to make the place sound appealing. Use adjective and adverb phrases, conjunctions, interjections, dependent clauses, and independent clauses to create an interesting variety of sentences.

Living History

You learned about words with Greek and Latin roots on the **Building Vocabulary** pages. Imagine that you can mail a letter to someone from the past. Write a letter to a figure from ancient Rome or ancient Greece. Tell the person about 10 words with Greek or Latin roots that are still used today, and explain how they are used. Use prepositional phrases, compound sentences, and complex sentences in your letter.

Unit Checkup

Think Back	Think Ahead
◆ What did you learn about research reports in this unit? What did you do to write one?	◆ How will what you learned about research reports help you when reading other reports? ◆ How will knowing how to summarize articles be useful?
◆ Look at the writing you did in this unit. How did prepositions, conjunctions, interjections, phrases, and clauses help express your writing?	◆ What is one way you can use prepositional phrases to combine and vary sentences in a report?

Research Reports   *pages 348–349*

Write whether each sentence would come from the *introduction,* the *body,* or the *conclusion* of a research report.

1. Many were amazed by the amount of open land.
2. Scandinavians settled in many Midwest farming towns.
3. These proud Scandinavian farmers have become part of America's success story.
4. Thousands built dairy farms in Wisconsin.
5. They are famous for their delicious cheese.

Connecting Ideas in a Summary   *page 350*

Write a short summary for each of the following topics.

6. a vacation day
7. a favorite television show
8. last Wednesday
9. a topic being studied in social studies
10. a topic being studied in science

Catching the Reader's Interest   *page 351*

Write a striking sentence to begin a research report on each of the following topics.

11. a craft made by a certain group of people
12. Italy
13. your family's history
14. a famous explorer
15. a favorite relative

The Writing Process   *pages 352–362*

Write the letter of the correct response to each question.

16. When you have a general topic for a report, an inverted triangle diagram helps
    a. to narrow your topic.   c. to find another topic.
    b. to cover the topic completely.

17. When writing the introduction to your report,
    a. try to tell as much as you can about your topic.
    b. tell what conclusions you have about your topic.
    c. get the reader's interest, and make the topic clear.

18. In reviewing your report, you find that a sense of completeness is lacking. What should you do?
    a. Add a summary.   c. Vary your sentences.
    b. Add a striking first sentence.

19. Which two editor's marks are used to correct the errors in this bibliography entry?

    Robert Smith, *Green Decade.* **New York: Sunburst Press, 1988.**
    a. transpose and make a period
    b. add a comma and cut something
    c. make a lowercase letter and move something

Prepositions and Prepositional Phrases   *pages 366–367*

Write each prepositional phrase. Then underline the preposition once. Underline the object of the preposition twice.

20. Here is an old picture of my grandparents.
21. It was taken at Ellis Island.
22. They arrived there in 1910.
23. Grandma and Grandpa came from Kiev.
24. Grandpa was sick on the boat.
25. It took a long time to go through the immigration lines.
26. Grandma said all the troubles were worth it because they were now in America.

Prepositional Phrases Used as Adjectives   *pages 368–369*

Write the adjective phrase in each sentence.

27. We attended the Festival of Scotland.
28. A bagpipe band from Edinburgh played Highland music.
29. Meanwhile, men in plaid kilts danced Scottish folk dances.
30. People ate crusty bread with butter.
31. Jamie recited poetry by the Scottish poet Robert Burns.

Prepositional Phrases Used as Adverbs *pages 370−371*

Write the adverb phrase in each sentence.

32. "Our family came here in 2053," said the old man, reminiscing.
33. "My mother and my father left Earth during the Great Migration," he continued.
34. The old man and the young boy sat together under the skies.
35. "From Earth and the other planets, millions arrived," he said.
36. "They were accompanied by their hopes and dreams," added the grandfather.

Choosing the Correct Preposition *pages 372−373*

Find the error in each sentence. Write the sentence correctly.

37. What is Julio's favorite between all his school subjects?
38. He should of taken history this year.
39. History in high school is very different than social studies in elementary school.
40. Julio could of had Mr. Ramirez, his favorite teacher.
41. Julio put his notebook in his new locker.

Conjunctions *pages 374−375*

Write each pair of sentences as one compound sentence. Use the conjunction in parentheses to join the sentences.

42. These old books are beautiful. They are fragile. (but)
43. You must handle them very carefully. You must leave them alone. (or)
44. The old paper can crumble. It can tear. (and)
45. Some of these books are quite rare. They are very valuable. (and)
46. We can't keep the books forever. We can borrow them. (but)

Interjections *pages 376−377*

Find the punctuation error or errors in each sentence. Write the sentence correctly.

47. Wow what a shock that was.
48. Well I never knew my family was famous.
49. Oops I wasn't supposed to tell anyone yet.
50. Psst here comes Karen.
51. Oh she didn't see us.
52. Hey we're over here, Karen.

Phrases and Clauses   *pages 378–379*

Write *phrase* or *clause* to describe each group of words.

53. although *Maslenitsa* is a Russian festival
54. held in early spring
55. waffles or pancakes for breakfast
56. when snow is on the ground
57. after the snow melts

Independent and Dependent Clauses   *pages 380–381*

Write each sentence. Underline the independent clause once. Underline the dependent clause twice.

58. Because our jewelry is beautiful, it is always in demand.
59. Although silver is expensive, it is much cheaper than gold.
60. Much depends on the silversmith who makes the jewelry.
61. Some styles never change, since they are traditional.
62. Although turquoise is the most popular stone, some artists use other materials, such as petrified wood.

Complex Sentences   *pages 382–383*

Combine each pair of sentences into one complex sentence, using the word in parentheses. If the dependent clause begins the sentence, put a comma after it.

63. The Pilgrims arrived at Plymouth Rock. They had little knowledge of American crops. (when)
64. They were so far from England. They had to depend on growing their own food. (because)
65. Many died. The Pilgrims struggled to make it through that first winter. (although)
66. They learned new farming methods. They used the old methods too. (while)

Roots: Clues to Word History   *pages 384–385*

Complete each sentence with a word containing the root in parentheses.

67. We can watch important events on _____. (vis)
68. Another word for *record player* is _____. (phone, graph)
69. A _____ is someone who is thought to have been involved in a crime. (spect)
70. An imaginary line that divides the earth into two parts of equal size is called the _____. (equ)

UNIT

9

Inventing Stories

◆ **COMPOSITION FOCUS:** Suspense Story
◆ **LANGUAGE FOCUS:** Mechanics Wrap-up

A twig snaps—and you wait. You can hear nothing now but your heartbeat. Something is about to happen—but what? That is the question at the heart of every good suspense story. In real life, suspense can be unpleasant. In a story, it can be delicious fun.

Walter Dean Myers has been entertaining young readers for years with stories of danger and adventure. In this unit you will write a suspense story of your own to entertain readers.

◆ === *WARMING UP* === ◆

IN YOUR JOURNAL

What does the word *suspense* mean to you? Describe the feelings you have had when you were in a suspenseful situation.

WORK IN A GROUP

LIBRARY

Look in your school or classroom library for titles of books that might include suspense, mystery, or detective work. Create a list of these books to share with classmates.

Walter Dean Myers developed a keen interest in books in the fifth grade. He began writing short stories and poems while still in school. Today he writes books primarily *to entertain* young readers.

AWARD **Author** WINNING

Reading with a Writer's Eye
Suspense Story

Walter Dean Myers set out to write something that would make readers excited and tense. Read his story, and decide whether he has succeeded. Notice how the writer uses details about people, places, and events to build a feeling of tension.

The Cub
by Walter Dean Myers

"You have to know what it's like, Grandpa," thirteen-year-old Tim Shorter exclaimed. "Motocross is the best! If you could see me ride the trails, you'd understand."

"Sounds dangerous." Grandpa Shorter stopped walking and looked at his grandson.

"Not if you're careful," Tim said. "Anyway, I'm a good driver."

"I'm sure you are." Grandpa Shorter ran his fingers through a thinning shock of white hair. "I don't know about taking chances just for the sake of doing it, though."

Tim sighed. He'd been spending a few weeks this summer at The Pines, as Grandpa Shorter called his place. It was fifteen miles outside of Helena, Montana, but as far as Tim was concerned, it could have been on the moon. Except for his grandfather's cabin and a small shed they used for supplies, there wasn't a house in any direction for miles. Grandpa Shorter didn't even have a telephone. The only modern thing he had was an old pickup he sometimes drove into town. Tim usually liked visiting his grandfather, but right now he felt that the old man was ready to spend the rest of his life in a rocking chair.

"Let's see what we can catch here at the stream before the sun goes down," Grandpa Shorter said, interrupting Tim's thoughts. "I ever tell you about the time I caught a trout here that was so long we had to send to Sears and Roebuck for a bigger frying pan?"

"Grandpa, where do you get all these stories?" Tim asked.

"We used to do a lot of storytelling when I was a young man," Grandpa Shorter said. "Folks were more sociable than they are now."

Tim imagined his grandfather sitting by a stove in a country store, whittling on a piece of wood and listening to stories. It sounded as exciting as sleeping.

"Anyway, my brother and I were out fishing all that day," Grandpa Shorter continued. "We hadn't caught anything and were just about ready to pack up and leave when I got a tug on my—"

"What's wrong, Grandpa?" Tim asked.

"Look over there." Grandpa Shorter pointed toward a tree downstream. At the base of the tree, Tim could see a small animal. It seemed to move from one side of the tree to the other and back again.

"It looks like a raccoon," Tim said. "Probably trying to dig up something to eat."

"No," said Grandpa Shorter. "That's a grizzly cub caught in a trap. Old Man Jenkins and I have found a few traps around here lately."

"If it's a bear, it's too little to hurt anybody, Grandpa," Tim said. "Even you can take that much excitement. I really don't think we have to worry about it."

"Could be . . ." Grandpa Shorter spoke as if he were talking to himself. "But that cub is no more than a couple of months old, so you can bet there's a she-bear in the vicinity. And that much excitement I can't take. A grizzly can run you down and kill you with a single blow. I think we'd better hightail it out of here."

"Yeah," Tim said, looking around him. "O.K., I'm right behind you, Grandpa."

"Keep your eyes open," Grandpa Shorter said. "I don't think that bear will wander off too far from her cub, but you can't be sure."

It had taken forty-five minutes to walk to the stream, but the trip back to the cabin just took them a little over half an hour.

"I didn't think there were many grizzlies around here," Tim said as they reached the cabin.

"Aren't that many," Grandpa Shorter said. "There aren't that many in the country any more. More important is that they mind their business and don't bother anybody. That cub in a trap changes things, though."

Grandpa Shorter got into the pickup and turned the key. The motor whined, coughed, and died.

"We going into town because of the bear?" Tim asked.

Grandpa Shorter ignored the question and tried to start the engine. Again the old motor whined, coughed, and died. The third time, there was a loud clicking sound and no more.

"The cabin looks pretty sturdy to me," Tim offered.

Grandpa Shorter closed both eyes and rubbed his temples with his hands. Then he looked up, took the keys, and went to the little shed he used for storage. Tim sat on the fender of the pickup and waited while his grandpa banged around in the shed. When Grandpa Shorter came out, he had a rifle in the crook of one arm and an ax handle and a package in the other.

"You going to go out and shoot the cub?" Tim asked.

"Shoot the cub?" Grandpa Shorter had put down the package and the ax handle and was loading the rifle. "No, I'm going to try to free it. Its mother will leave it there for a while, hoping it'll free itself. When it doesn't, she'll either abandon it or gnaw its paw off. Either way, the cub will die. I'm going to try to free it before that happens."

"But I thought you said the mother grizzly could . . . you know."

"Yes, that's right, Timmy." Grandpa Shorter's face was grim. "But you don't leave things to suffer and die if you can help it. Not even grizzly bears."

"I'll go along if you want me to," said Tim.

"I don't really want you to," Grandpa Shorter said. "But since I can't get to town for the sheriff, I guess I'll need your help."

The trek back to the stream took another half hour. Tim carried the ax handle and stayed close behind his grandpa. As they walked, Grandpa Shorter told him what they were going to do. Tim tried to imagine himself warding off the mother bear, and more than once he thought about going back to the cabin. By the time they reached the stream, the back of Tim's shirt was soaked with sweat.

"You sure this is going to work, Grandpa?"

"No," Grandpa Shorter said quietly. "You scared?"

"Yeah, I guess so," Tim said.

"Good. This is the time to be a little scared. Just try not to panic."

They stood together, looking upstream. Tim could imagine the cub's mother coming from behind one of the trees at any moment and attacking them.

"You see any signs of the mother?" Grandpa Shorter asked.

"No," Tim said.

"Then let's go."

Grandpa Shorter went first, moving quickly toward the trapped bear cub.

The cub yelped and jumped when it saw him approach. Up close it wasn't as small as Tim had thought. And he froze, horrified, as he saw the cub's paw swing out and its claws make deep, even scratches on Grandpa's arm.

"Don't look at the cub!" Grandpa Shorter said. "Watch for the mother, Timmy!"

Tim turned away, holding his breath. He heard the scuffling beside him and his grandpa's heavy breathing. Then he saw what looked like a huge shadow in the bushes fifty yards away. It was the mother bear, and she was lumbering through the branches into the opening between them!

"Grandpa!"

"The firecrackers, Timmy—quick!"

Tim held his arms together to steady his hands as he lit the first firecracker. It exploded less than ten feet in front of him. The second went a little farther.

The huge bear stopped, made a small jump, and started toward them again, this time more cautiously. Tim saw another bear, a cub as small as the first, behind her. He lit two more firecrackers and threw them toward the mother bear. She took another step, then stopped again and began to circle to her left. She made a noise that was halfway between a growl and a hiss.

"O.K., keep throwing them." Grandpa Shorter's voice was raspy. Tim threw another firecracker, and the huge bear backed away. Then Tim saw the trapped cub scamper toward its mother. Grandpa Shorter had freed it!

Tim looked at his grandpa. The old man was still kneeling, and he had his rifle trained on the grizzly. There was blood on his sleeve.

Tim threw two more firecrackers, then felt his grandfather pat him on the shoulder.

"You O.K.?" Tim asked.

"Just a scratch," said Grandpa Shorter. "When we get back home, I'll put something on it. You did a good job, Timmy. I don't think the bear wanted any part of you and those firecrackers. Especially with cubs to protect."

Grandpa Shorter stopped and grinned at Tim. "She was probably one of those old-fashioned bears. You know—the kind that can't stand much excitement."

Respond

1. Which part of the story do you find most exciting? Explain your answer.

Discuss

2. At which point in the story are you most eager to find out what happens next? What does the writer do to give you this feeling?

3. What did you think was going to happen when you started the story? What does the writer say to make you think this way? In what ways does the story turn out as you expected? In what ways does the writer surprise you?

Thinking As a Writer
Analyzing a Suspense Story

A suspense story is a story in which the possibility of danger builds a feeling of excitement. A suspense story has **characters**, a **setting**, and a **plot.** The plot begins with a **problem. Complications** lead to a **climax** and then to a **resolution.** Study this story map.

The Cub

The **title** gives an impression about the story.

Characters
Tim
Grandpa Shorter

Setting
The Pines, Grandpa Shorter's ranch outside Helena, Montana

The **setting** is the place where the story occurs and the time when it happens.

Characters are the people about whom the story is written. Usually, a story focuses on one of these people, the main character.

Problem
A grizzly bear cub gets caught in a trap.

The **plot** is what happens in the story. It begins with a **problem** the main character or characters will face and tells what happens as the character or characters struggle to solve the problem.

Complications
1. The cub may die.
2. The mother bear may come around.
3. The truck stops working.

Complications are events and discoveries in the course of the story that make the problem worse.

Climax
The mother bear and another cub approach.

The **climax** is the high point of the story, the part where the plot is the most exciting.

Resolution
Tim frightens the bears with firecrackers, and Grandpa Shorter frees the trapped bear cub.

The **resolution** is the ending of the story. It shows how the character or characters solve the problem, and it leaves the readers with a satisfied feeling.

In a suspense story, we know that the characters are in trouble, and we don't know how they will get out of it. As we wait to find out, we feel a special kind of excitement called **suspense,** from a Latin word that means "left hanging."

To build suspense, writers give hints of upcoming danger or trouble for the main character or characters. These hints raise questions that make readers feel nervous and tense and keep readers interested in the story. Look at the underlined details in this section from "The Cub."

"I didn't think there were many grizzlies around here," Tim said as they reached the cabin.

"Aren't that many," Grandpa Shorter said. "There aren't that many in the country any more. More important is that they mind their business and don't bother anybody. That cub in a trap changes things, though."

Grandpa Shorter got into the pickup and turned the key. The motor whined, coughed, and died.

"We going into town because of the bear?" Tim asked.

Grandpa Shorter ignored the question and tried to start the engine. Again the old motor whined, coughed, and died. The third time, there was a loud clicking sound and no more.

"The cabin looks pretty sturdy to me," Tim offered.

How does the cub change things? Will a grizzly bear now "bother" someone? Whom will it bother— and how?

Is something wrong with the truck? What if the characters need to get away from this place quickly?

Why did Grandpa Shorter ignore the question? Is he tense?

Why does the sturdiness of the cabin matter? Is there a creature nearby that can tear apart flimsy cabins?

Discuss

1. Why is it important to introduce the characters and setting first in a suspense story?
2. As you look at the story map, in which part do you expect to find the most hints of future danger? Why?
3. Should the climax always come near the end of the story? Why or why not?
4. In most suspense stories, do you think the longest part is the one that tells about the characters and setting, the problem and complications, or the resolution? Explain your answer.
5. Why is it important for a writer to include elements of suspense in a story?

Try Your Hand

A. Identify Characters and Setting   Read this story beginning. Then list what you learn about the characters and setting.

1.   Rain battered the windshield, and lights continually glared into Ellen's eyes. Exhausted, she gripped the wheel and stared at the road. She had been driving all afternoon without a break, and now, as evening fell, she felt her eyelids growing heavy. Then, suddenly, a pair of oncoming headlights blinded her as a horn blared.

B. Identify Elements of Suspense   What words and details in the paragraph help to build a mood of suspense?

C. Create Suspense   Write details that would add a hint of danger to each of the following passages.

2. Doug carried his heavy radio to the top of Ferris Rock. Here he could finally play his radio at top volume. No one would yell, "Turn that thing down!"

3. Alma and Tim wandered away from the campground after breakfast. Alma wanted Tim to help her find wild strawberries. They walked deep into the woods.

4. Rosanne sat down on the riverbank to eat her sandwich. Across the swift current she saw some children playing on the hillside.

D. Analyze a Suspense Story   Find a short suspense story that you like. Read it with a classmate, and discuss how the writer reveals the characters, the setting, and the plot. Identify the main problem, the words and details that build suspense, the complications, the climax, and the resolution. Then decide whether you think the story is well written and tell why you think as you do.

Writer's Notebook

Collecting Mood Words   A good story has a certain mood. Notice how words such as *horrified* on page 397 and *lumbering* on page 398 add to the mood of "The Cub." Find other words in the story that help create the mood of suspense. Record in your *Writer's Notebook* the words and the sentences in which they occur. Look for opportunities to use words like these when you write a suspense story.

Developing the Writer's Craft
Storytelling: Dialogue and Characters

Good writers let their characters speak for themselves. They write **dialogue,** the exact words characters use as they talk to one another. Dialogue can show what characters are like, how they feel, and what they think of one another. Also, writers often use dialogue to move the plot forward. Compare these two ways a writer could reveal the same information in the story "The Cub."

1. Grandpa Shorter knew that a bear cub was caught in a trap. He and a friend had found some traps around lately.
2. "No," said Grandpa Shorter. "That's a grizzly cub caught in a trap. Old Man Jenkins and I have found a few traps around here lately."

The first example is dull because it simply *tells* us the information. The second example lets us discover the information by presenting what Grandpa Shorter says. In listening to Grandpa Shorter's voice, we also get a sense of what the man himself is like.

When you write a short story, use dialogue to bring your characters and story to life.

Discuss

1. Look at the dialogue between Grandpa Shorter and Tim on page 394. What impression does it give of the characters?
2. Compare the dialogue on page 394 to the one on page 399. How does the dialogue show how the characters changed?

Try Your Hand

Use Dialogue Suppose that you are writing a story about two boys who become lost in the woods. Write a short dialogue between the boys that reveals their problem and at the same time shows what they are like. Exchange papers with a classmate. Discuss how the dialogue you each wrote helped paint the same situation and characters differently.

1 Prewriting
Suspense Story

Writer's Guide

Prewriting Checklist
☑ Brainstorm story ideas.
☑ Think about your audience and your purpose.
☑ Make a story map.

Darrelle wanted to write a suspense story to entertain her friends. She used the checklist in the **Writer's Guide** to help her plan her story. Look at what she did.

◆ Brainstorming and Selecting a Topic

First, Darrelle brainstormed a list of possible story ideas. She got ideas by thinking about stories she had heard or read and by imagining herself in various suspenseful situations.

Then, Darrelle crossed some ideas off her list because she could not think of good plots based on those ideas. She crossed off other items because she did not think she could create a realistic setting for them.

Finally, Darrelle decided to write a suspense story about hearing scary noises in the basement because she could imagine the situation vividly.

Getting caught in a blizzard
Climbing a mountain
Hunting a criminal
Finding and training
a puppy
Hearing noises in the
basement
Getting locked up overnight
in an old warehouse
Getting lost at sea in a
rowboat

Discuss

1. Where do you think Darrelle got each idea on her list? Which way of getting story ideas might work best for you? Why?
2. Look at the ideas Darrelle crossed off her list. Why do you think she crossed off each one?
3. Why would some settings be hard for Darrelle to imagine?
4. What would be some other reasons not to choose certain story ideas?

◆ Gathering Information

After Darrelle selected a story idea, she planned her story. Since she was writing a suspense story, she began by deciding on the main events in her plot. She numbered these events on a time line.

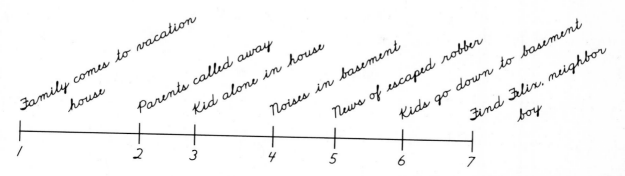

Next, Darrelle thought about the setting of her story. She brainstormed a list of details about the setting. Look at Darrelle's list of details.

Then, Darrelle made some cluster diagrams to get a better sense of the characters in her story. Look at Darrelle's clusters.

lonely gray house
woods all around
gloomy trees
only one neighbor near
peeling paint
thick basement doors
cobwebs

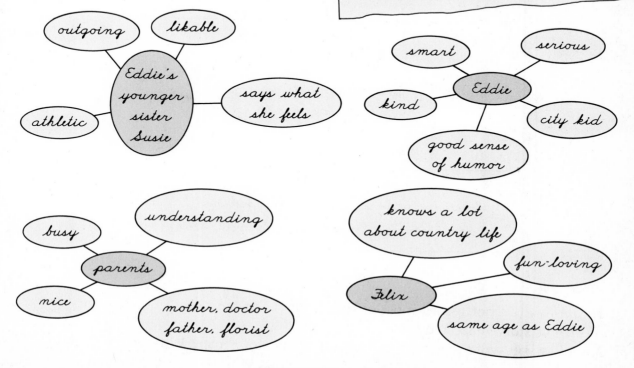

Discuss

1. What makes a time line a useful tool for recording plot ideas?
2. What details might Darrelle have added about her setting?

◆ Organizing the Information

Before she started writing her story, Darrelle decided to organize all her ideas on a story map. Look at Darrelle's story map.

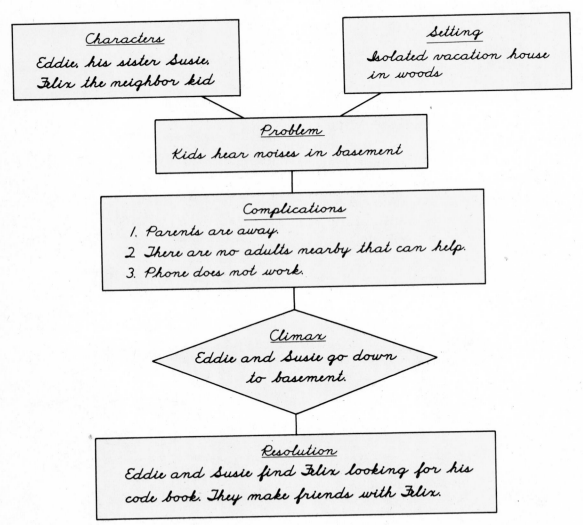

Noises in Basement

Characters
Eddie, his sister Susie, Felix the neighbor kid

Setting
Isolated vacation house in woods

Problem
Kids hear noises in basement

Complications
1. Parents are away.
2. There are no adults nearby that can help.
3. Phone does not work.

Climax
Eddie and Susie go down to basement.

Resolution
Eddie and Susie find Felix looking for his code book. They make friends with Felix.

Discuss

1. Darrelle did not record most of the details from her notes and diagrams on her story map. Why not?
2. Could you write a story based on Darrelle's story map? Why or why not?

WRITING PROCESS

Try Your Hand

Now plan a suspense story of your own.

A. Brainstorm and Select a Story Idea Brainstorm a list of possible story ideas. Use these methods.

◆ Browse for ideas in newspapers, magazines, and other sources.

◆ Think of real events, but change them in interesting ways.

◆ Try putting new twists on plots used by other writers. Think about each idea and your audience.

◆ Cross out ideas that would not be appealing to your audience. If you cannot picture the setting or think of a plot based on that idea, cross it out.

◆ Of the remaining ideas on your list, select the one that you would most enjoy writing about.

B. Gather Information When you have a story idea you like, plan how to gather and organize information for your story. If you lose interest as you go along, brainstorm more story ideas and select a new one.

◆ Work out the main events in your plot. Decide the main problem in your story. List the events that may occur as your characters struggle with the problem. Be sure to include elements of suspense. You may want to make a time line, as Darrelle did.

◆ Picture the setting. Decide when and where your story takes place. Brainstorm a list of details about the setting that can help you describe it vividly.

◆ Develop the characters. Think about the people who will be in your story and what each one is like. You may want to make cluster diagrams as a way of brainstorming details about the characters.

C. Organize the Information Use your notes and your diagrams to make a story map. Include only the most important points about your story in your story map. Be sure your story map includes all the parts of a suspense story.

 Save your notes, diagrams, and story map in your
Writer's Notebook. **You will use them when you draft your suspense story.**

2 Drafting
Suspense Story

Writer's Guide
Drafting Checklist
- ☑ Use your notes, your lists, your diagrams, and your story map for ideas.
- ☑ Introduce the characters and the setting.
- ☑ Reveal the story problem.
- ☑ Write the complications and the climax.
- ☑ Show how the characters solve the problem.
- ☑ Write a title.

Using her notes, lists, diagrams, and story map, Darrelle followed the **Writer's Guide** to draft her story. Look at what she did.

Creak!

Eddie's father stopped the car next to a fallen tree. "Well," he said, "here we are at our new vacation house. What do you think?"

"It's lovely," said Mrs. Hayes.

"But we're in the middle of the woods," gulped six-year-old Susie.

Eddie said nothing. Something about the old gray house made him uneasy.

Discuss

1. What details does Darrelle give about characters and setting?
2. Will readers want to keep reading Darrelle's story? Explain your answer.

Try Your Hand

Now draft a suspense story.

A. Review Your Information Think about the ideas you gathered and organized in the last lesson. Decide whether you need more ideas. If so, develop them.

B. Think About Your TAP Remember that your task is to write a short story. Your purpose is to entertain your audience by creating suspense.

C. Write Your First Draft Follow the steps in the **Drafting Checklist** to write your suspense story.
   When you write your draft, just put all your ideas on paper. Do not worry about making errors. You can correct the draft later.

Task: What?
Audience: Who?
Purpose: Why?

 Save your first draft in your *Writer's Notebook*. You will use it when you revise your suspense story.

3 Responding and Revising
Suspense Story

Darrelle used the checklist in the **Writer's Guide** to revise her suspense story. Look at what she did.

◆ Checking Information

Darrelle cut a sentence that did not help create suspense. She added some dialogue to make her story more exciting. She used this mark ✐ to show what she was cutting. She used this mark ∧ to show where she wanted to add words.

◆ Checking Organization

Darrelle moved one sentence so that her plot would build to a climax. She used this mark ⟳ to show the move.

◆ Checking Language

Darrelle found that she had shifted tenses for no reason. She used this mark ∧ to replace a verb to correct the problem.

> **Writer's Guide**
>
> **Revising Checklist**
> - ☑ Read your story to yourself or to a partner.
> - ☑ Think about your audience and your purpose. Add or cut information.
> - ☑ Be sure that your story is organized in a way that creates suspense. Add more dialogue, if possible.
> - ☑ Check to see that your verb tenses are consistent.

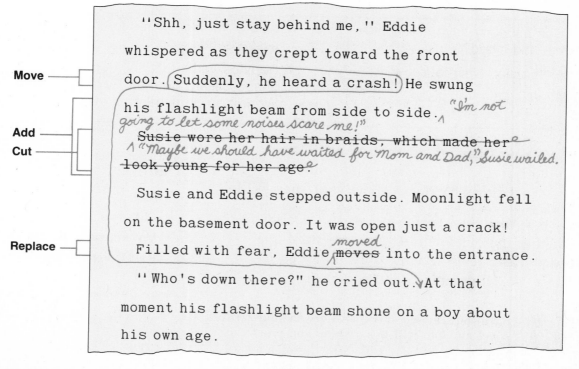

Move

Add

Cut

Replace

''Shh, just stay behind me,'' Eddie whispered as they crept toward the front door. (Suddenly, he heard a crash!) He swung his flashlight beam from side to side. *"I'm not going to let some noises scare me!"*
~~Susie wore her hair in braids, which made her~~ ∧ *"Maybe we should have waited for Mom and Dad," Susie wailed.* ~~look young for her age.~~

Susie and Eddie stepped outside. Moonlight fell on the basement door. It was open just a crack!
Filled with fear, Eddie *moved* ~~moves~~ into the entrance.

''Who's down there?'' he cried out. At that moment his flashlight beam shone on a boy about his own age.

Discuss

1. Look at the sentence Darrelle cut. Could she use this information in another part of her story? Which part?
2. How is Darrelle's revised suspense story better than her draft? Explain your answer.
3. What other changes would you make in Darrelle's story? Why?

Try Your Hand

Now revise your first draft.

A. **Read Your First Draft** As you read your story, think about your audience and your purpose. Read your story silently or to a partner to see whether it is complete and well organized. Ask yourself or your partner the questions in the box.

Responding and Revising Strategies

✔ Respond
Ask yourself or a partner:

✔ Revise
Try these solutions:

Respond	Revise
◆ Is the setting easy to picture?	◆ **Add** vivid details.
◆ Do my characters seem real?	◆ **Add** realistic dialogue.
◆ Does my story plan work to create suspense?	◆ **Add** hints of upcoming danger. **Move** details so that action builds to a climax.
◆ Does my story have an effective tone and mood?	◆ **Add** or **replace** words to create a suspenseful mood.
◆ Is the action easy to follow?	◆ **Replace** verbs that shift tense unnecessarily. See the **Revising Workshop** on page 411.

B. **Make Your Changes** If the answer to any question in the box is *no,* try the solution. Use the **Editor's Marks** to show your changes.

C. **Review Your Suspense Story Again** Decide whether there is anything else you want to revise. Keep revising your story until you feel that it is well organized and complete.

EDITOR'S MARKS

∧ Add something.

⌀ Cut something.

◯ Move something.

∧ Replace something.

 Save your revised suspense story in your *Writer's Notebook.* You will use it when you proofread your story.

WRITING PROCESS

Revising Workshop
Using Consistent Verb Tenses

A good storyteller describes events in a clear and logical order. Beginning writers, however, often confuse their readers because they shift verb tenses unnecessarily. Changing verb tenses without a reason can make events seem to take place out of order. Look at the following example.

> Janis hesitated. She listens for sounds. Was that a creak? She opens the door cautiously.

The passage is confusing because verb tenses change needlessly from one sentence to the next. In the first sentence, an action takes place in the past. In the second sentence, an action occurs in the present. In the third and fourth sentences, the action again shifts to the past and then to the present. Look at the corrected version of this passage.

> Janis hesitated. She listened for sounds. Was that a creak? She opened the door cautiously.

The corrected example is much easier to understand because the writer uses the same tense throughout.

When you write a story, be sure to use verb tenses consistently. Do not shift tenses unless you have a clear reason for doing so.

Practice

Rewrite each passage to make verb tenses consistent. Use the tense indicated in parentheses.

1. Janis has thought about looking for the book in the cupboard. She rummages through the cupboard, but she found nothing. She tried to open the writing desk, but she cannot unlock it. (past tense)

2. Janis had seen the book on Thursday. She comes into the room at ten past noon. She noticed the time because Charley had made some silly remark about her watch. (past perfect)

3. Now it was too late. Janis still comes to visit us on Thursdays, but no one has mentioned the book. (present)

4 Proofreading
Suspense Story

After revising her story, Darrelle used the **Writer's Guide** and the **Editor's Marks** to proofread it. Look at what she did.

Writer's Guide

Proofreading Checklist

☑ Check for errors in capitalization.

☑ Check for errors in punctuation. Be sure you have punctuated dialogue correctly.

☑ Check to see that paragraphs are indented.

☑ Check your grammar.

☑ Circle any words you think are misspelled. Find out how to spell them correctly.

⇨ For proofreading help, use the **Writer's Handbook.**

"So tell me, Felix" Eddie said later, "Did you find your book"?

"Sure, said Felix. Hey maybe we can work on some ~~kodes~~ *codes* together. What do you think"?

I'd like that," Eddie ~~grined~~ *grinned* He had a feeling he was going to like this kid Felix.

EDITOR'S MARKS

☰ Capitalize.

⊙ Add a period.

∧ Add something.

⋏ Add a comma.

ⱽⱽ Add quotation marks.

⤷ Cut something.

⟋＼ Replace something.

∼ Transpose.

◯ Spell correctly.

Ꞧ Indent paragraph.

／ Make a lowercase letter.

Discuss

1. Look at Darrelle's proofread story. What kinds of corrections did she make?
2. Why did Darrelle add the quotation marks? Why did she cut the others?

Try Your Hand

Proofread Your Suspense Story Now use the **Writer's Guide** and the **Editor's Marks** to proofread your own story.

 Save your corrected suspense story in your *Writer's Notebook.* **You will use it when you publish your story.**

WRITING PROCESS

5 Publishing
Suspense Story

Darrelle made a clean copy of her suspense story and checked it to be sure she had not left out anything. Then she and her classmates published their stories in a class story anthology. You can find Darrelle's story on pages 43–44 of the **Writer's Handbook.**

Here is how Darrelle and her classmates published a story anthology.

Writer's Guide

Publishing Checklist

☑ Make a clean copy of your story.

☑ Check to see that nothing has been left out.

☑ Be sure that there are no mistakes.

☑ Share your story in a special way.

1. First, they typed their stories on sturdy bond paper.

2. Then, they illustrated their stories with drawings that expressed the mood of each story.

3. Next, they numbered each page and listed the titles in a table of contents in the order in which they would appear. They also listed the page number where each story began.

4. Finally, they bound the pages and gave the collection of suspense stories a title and a cover design that would attract readers. Then, they invited other students to come in and read some of the stories during their free time.

Discuss

1. Do you think the order in which the stories appear in the anthology could make a difference? Why or why not?
2. How could students find out which of the stories readers find most suspenseful?

Try Your Hand

Publish Your Suspense Story   Follow the checklist in the **Writer's Guide.** If possible, create a class story anthology, or try one of these ideas for sharing your suspense story.

◆ Illustrate, bind, and cover each story separately. Lend your set of stories to the school library for many students to enjoy.
◆ Dramatize some of the stories as Readers Theatre. For tips about how to perform Readers Theatre, see **Tips on How to Dramatize a Short Story** on page 415.

WRITING PROCESS

Listening and Speaking
Tips on How to Dramatize a Short Story

Readers Theatre is the dramatic reading of a story or a play. One person takes the part of the narrator, or storyteller. This person reads the descriptions in the story and the parts that tell what happens. Other people read the dialogue spoken by each of the characters. Phrases such as "he said" and "she said" can be left out of the reading. Follow these guidelines to perform Readers Theatre.

1. Read the story silently.
2. Discuss the following questions with your fellow performers.
   - What is the main mood and tone of the story?
   - What is each character like?
   - What is the purpose of each scene? For example, is the purpose to scare the audience, to surprise them, or to win their sympathy?

3. Assign the parts of all the characters and of the narrator. Then practice reading your part of the story with a partner. Keep practicing until you do not have to look at the words most of the time.

   - Speak as you imagine your character would speak.
   - Experiment with the volume and pace of your voice.
   - Use pauses to get across the feeling of each scene.
   - Ask your partner how your character is coming across. If you are not giving the impression you want to give, decide how to change the way you are reading.
   - Respond to your partner's reading. Listen to his or her expression and tone of voice. Notice what kind of character your partner is creating. Let your partner know if he or she spoke certain parts too quickly or did not speak clearly enough.

4. Practice once or twice with all the other readers.
5. Perform your story for your audience. During the performance, listen to the other performers instead of thinking about what you are going to say. When your turn comes, try to speak as your character would speak, reacting to the other characters.

Writing in the Content Areas

Use what you learned to write about something exciting in a real or an imaginary world. You can write a story or part of a story for students your age anywhere in the country. Use one of these ideas or an idea of your own.

Writer's Guide

When you write, remember the stages of the Writing Process.
◆ Prewriting
◆ Drafting
◆ Responding and Revising
◆ Proofreading
◆ Publishing

Science

Imagine a group of characters threatened by a volcano, a hurricane, or a flood. Write about their adventure. Why do they find themselves in the path of danger? What resources do they use to get away? How do they feel as they find themselves trapped by forces of nature?

Social Studies

Retell the real-life adventure of an explorer such as Roald Amundsen, Vasco Núñez de Balboa, Amelia Earhart, or David Livingstone. Read about the explorer. How did the explorer plan the trip? What hazards and dangers did the explorer face?

Health

Changes in the environment, such as increased air pollution or the warming of the earth's weather, could have serious effects on people's lives. How might one change affect an imaginary group of people? How might a hero begin to reverse the change? What might people do to survive a life-threatening change?

Physical Education

Races and other sports events are full of suspense. How close will the race be? Who will win? Will the winner place first because of skill, luck, or trickery? Make a sports event the central focus of a story, and keep your readers wondering how the event will turn out.

CONNECTING

WRITING ⟷ LANGUAGE

Good suspense and adventure writers keep readers involved with characters and events. How interested are you in what happens to the characters in the rest of this story?

Clark opened the door slowly and entered the hotel room. Juana followed closely behind.

"Montooth must have hidden the microfilm in this room," said Clark, "but we'd better move quickly. He might return at any moment."

Quickly Clark and Juana searched through closets, drawers, and suitcases.

"It's not here," sighed Juana at last. "Do you have any other ideas? We . . ."

The two froze. A key scraped inside the door lock. Montooth was back!

◆ **Mechanics in a Suspense Story** The writer used a period, a question mark, or an exclamation point to show where each sentence ends. The writer also used punctuation marks to show where quotations begin and end. All these punctuation marks make the story about Clark and Juana easier to read. The writer also capitalized the first word in each sentence and people's names. The capital letters help you recognize where a new sentence starts and when the writer is talking about a particular person.

◆ **Language Focus: Mechanics Wrap-up** In the following lessons you will learn more about using punctuation and capitalization and form correctly in your writing.

1 Capitalization and End Punctuation in Sentences

◆ **FOCUS** Every sentence begins with a capital letter and ends with a punctuation mark.

When you speak, you pause to show where one sentence ends and another begins. When you write, you mark the beginning of a sentence by using a capital letter. You mark the end of a sentence with a period, a question mark, or an exclamation point. The punctuation mark you use depends on what type of sentence it is.

1. **Declarative** The plane made an emergency landing .
2. **Imperative** Get that emergency equipment ready .
3. **Interrogative** How could this have happened ?
4. **Exclamatory** What a shock it was when the fuselage cracked !

Guided Practice

A. Identify the word that should be capitalized in each sentence, and name the punctuation mark that belongs at the end of the sentence.

1. the plane took off
2. the passengers relaxed
3. what could go wrong
4. have some lunch
5. suddenly, something banged
6. what was that sound
7. what a frightening experience it was
8. stay calm, everybody
9. could the plane land
10. an ambulance waited nearby
11. the crowd watched nervously
12. the landing was perfect

THINK AND REMEMBER

◆ Begin every written sentence with a capital letter.
◆ End a declarative or an imperative sentence with a period.
◆ End an interrogative sentence with a question mark.
◆ End an exclamatory sentence with an exclamation point.

Independent Practice

B. Using Capitalization and End Punctuation in Sentences
Write each sentence. Add the capital letter and the end
punctuation mark that each sentence needs.

13. jeana Yeager and Dick Rutan are pilots

MODEL> Jeana Yeager and Dick Rutan are pilots.

14. they flew a plane called *Voyager*
15. tell me about their journey
16. where did they fly
17. they flew around the world nonstop
18. was the flight dangerous
19. what a thrilling trip it must have been

**C. Proofreading: Checking for Capitalization and End
Punctuation**   Find the error in each sentence. Write the
sentence correctly.

20. Could the plane cross the Aegean Sea.

MODEL> Could the plane cross the Aegean Sea?

21. the plane traveled 74 miles without fuel.
22. A young Greek pedaled the plane?
23. Why was the plane called *Daedalus*.
24. How close the plane is to the water.
25. the pilot must have been tired.
26. Did the trip take almost four hours.
27. What an incredible feat that was.

D. 28. – 35. Revising: Changing Sentence Types   Rewrite each
sentence in **C** as a different type of sentence. Use correct
capitalization and end punctuation.

28. Could the plane cross the Aegean Sea?

MODEL> Tell me whether the plane could cross the Aegean Sea.

Application — Writing

Story Climax   Imagine that the picture on page 418 shows a scene
from an adventure story. Write the climax of the story, telling how
the pilot brings the damaged airplane down safely. Be sure to
begin sentences with capital letters and to end them with the
correct punctuation. If you need help writing the climax of an
adventure story, see page 42 of the **Writer's Handbook.**

2 Commas and Semicolons Within Sentences

FOCUS

◆ A **comma** is used to separate one part of a sentence from another to make the meaning clear.

◆ A **semicolon** can be used to separate independent clauses in a compound sentence.

Punctuation is used within a sentence to help keep the ideas organized. The most common punctuation mark used within a sentence is the comma. A comma shows readers where to pause. A semicolon may be used to indicate a slightly more definite pause. Use a comma to separate three or more similar words in a series.

1. The detective was used to fear , danger , and excitement.

Notice that a comma goes before the conjunction and the final item in the series. Commas are also used to separate three or more similar phrases in a series.

2. He was alert—at home , on the street , or in the office.
3. The tall man , the slender boy , and the tired girl listened to the footsteps.

Use commas to set off appositives, unless the appositive is needed to complete the meaning of a noun or a pronoun.

4. Raul , a detective , was on a case.
5. This fellow Raul was an expert.

Use commas to set off nouns or pronouns of direct address. A noun or a pronoun of direct address names the person or people spoken to.

6. Listen closely , May , because this is the exciting part.

Use commas to set off mild interjections and other words that introduce or interrupt a sentence.

7. Ssh, the suspect is coming.
8. I'm not sure , however, that he's the one.

Use a comma to separate the clauses of a compound sentence. Be sure that the comma comes before the conjunction. A semicolon may replace the comma and the conjunction in a compound sentence.

9. The suspect came closer and closer , but Raul stayed hidden.
10. The suspect stopped ; Raul froze and stared straight ahead.

Use a comma to separate the clauses of a complex sentence when the dependent clause comes first.

11. As Raul turned, a man stepped out of the shadows.

Guided Practice

A. Read the following sentences. Tell where commas belong in each one.
1. The night was dark and Olmos was worried.
2. He had received some unusual notes letters and telephone calls.
3. His client a famous magician had vanished.
4. Olmos had tried hard but he could not solve the baffling case.
5. Well Olmos would just have to be patient and look for clues.
6. Olmos tried to gather more evidence but he had very few leads.
7. When he returned to the missing magician's home he found several clues.

B. 8.–14. Tell where semicolons can be used and cannot be used in A.

THINK AND REMEMBER

◆ Use commas to separate words and phrases in a series.
◆ Use commas to set off appositives, nouns of direct address, and mild interjections.
◆ Use commas and conjunctions or use semicolons to separate the clauses in compound sentences.
◆ Use a comma after a dependent clause that begins a complex sentence.

Independent Practice

C. Using Commas and Semicolons in Sentences   Write each sentence. Add commas and semicolons where they are needed.

15. Miles McGoo a man in his thirties sat in his office.

MODEL ▷ Miles McGoo, a man in his thirties, sat in his office.

16. McGoo's job was to find lost dogs cats and other pets.
17. Traffic growled a fly buzzed and then the phone rang.
18. McGoo sighed stood up and picked up the telephone.
19. "Oh please help me," said a voice.
20. "My Clyde the sweetest cat in the world has been stolen."
21. "Aha I think I know the culprit," said McGoo.
22. "He's a bad character I'll track him down."
23. McGoo raced to his car but the car would not start.
24. The Clyde case McGoo's toughest case had begun.
25. All of his detective skills would be needed to solve this case he was ready for the challenge.

D. Completing Sentences   Write each sentence correctly. Complete the sentence with the kind of word or words called for in parentheses. Use commas correctly.

26. Clara Jones _____ works at the circus. (appositive)

MODEL ▷ Clara Jones, an animal trainer, works at the circus.

27. The circus animals are _____. (words in a series)
28. One day, Ella Elephant _____ was missing from her cage. (appositive)
29. _____ it was a big mystery. (mild interjection)
30. Clara _____ thought she knew the answer. (appositive)
31. Clara suspected the jugglers _____. (phrases in a series)
32. She also suspected _____. (phrases in a series)
33. _____ Clara was confused. (interrupting word)
34. She told her monkey, "_____ I don't know whom to suspect." (direct address)

Application   Writing, Speaking, Listening

Mystery Story Beginning   Write the beginning of a mystery story to share with your class. Write a mystery that needs to be solved. Provide information about the situation and the suspects. Use commas correctly in your opener. Read the story opener to a group of classmates, and have the group suggest solutions to your mystery. If you need help writing a story beginning, see page 42 of the **Writer's Handbook.**

3 Capitalization of Proper Nouns, Proper Adjectives, and *I*

◆ **FOCUS** A proper noun, a proper adjective, and the pronoun *I* are always capitalized.

The first word and every important word in a proper noun begins with a capital letter. This includes abbreviations of proper nouns, initials, and titles used with names. Capitalize words such as *doctor, senator, boulevard,* and *street* only when they are used with a proper noun as part of the name of a person or a place.

Nouns to Capitalize	
Names of people and pets	Sally Rosenberg Manuel Estrada Aiko Murata Mr. T. R. Brown Ms. Beth Nakamura Mrs. Juana Flores Fluffy Fido Old Floppy Ears
Names of places	Fort Worth Montana El Salvador Missouri River Mount Hamilton Arguello Street Cape of Good Hope
Names of things and events	Empire State Building Erie Railroad *The Gazette* Boy Scouts of America A to Z Hardware Store U.S.S. *Triton* World War I the Renaissance the Civil War

Remember that the pronoun *I* is always capitalized. Proper adjectives are also capitalized.

From Texas plains to African cities, I have roamed the world.

Guided Practice

A. Tell where capital letters are needed.

1. canadian bacon
2. mrs. alfreda cepeda
3. queen elizabeth
4. statue of liberty
5. san angelo
6. dr. e. m. chin
7. miss ann irwin
8. irish sweater

Independent Practice

B. Using Capital Letters Correctly   Write each name correctly.

9. sir elliot pane
MODEL▷ Sir Elliot Pane

10. julio's restaurant
11. acme sea and surf company
12. world trade center
13. president john f. kennedy

14. kelso's department store
15. judge turner
16. salt lake city
17. rio grande

C. Proofreading: Checking for Errors in Capitalization   Find the error in each sentence. Write the sentence correctly.

18. Did you ever meet Captain James r. Mills?
MODEL▷ Did you ever meet Captain James R. Mills?

19. During the war i traveled with the captain.
20. Our ship carried supplies across the atlantic Ocean.
21. I went along as the ship's Doctor.
22. I learned of the position from mister Calco.
23. Many of our supplies came from the calco Company.
24. We traveled from New london, Connecticut, to Africa.
25. One day we were on the Mediterranean sea.
26. Young Lt. Ernie Mays received the british message.
27. A german submarine near the Italian coast had spotted us.
28. Ensign e. Flint prepared us to move quickly.
29. That is a day i will never forget.
30. Later, Captain Mills received the Medal of honor.

Application — Writing

Adventure Story Scene   Imagine that you took a trip on a submarine or another kind of ship. Write a description for your classmates about one exciting event that took place during your travels. Tell who was involved, what happened, and where it happened. Be sure to capitalize proper nouns and proper adjectives.

4 Abbreviations

◆ **FOCUS**   Most abbreviations begin with a capital letter and are followed by a period.

You can save space when you write by using abbreviations or shortened forms of certain words. Most abbreviations begin with a capital letter and end with a period.

Sun. (Sunday)   Mr. (Mister)   Ave. (Avenue)

Use abbreviations of titles and words that mean "street" only with proper nouns.

captain— Capt. Morris.

street—Henry St.

One kind of abbreviation is called an **initial.** It is the first letter of a name used in place of the complete name. Write an initial with a capital letter followed by a period.

John F. Kennedy (John Fitzgerald Kennedy)

Common Abbreviations	
Titles	Mr. Mrs. Ms. Dr. Rev. Jr. Sr.
Days	Sun. Mon. Tues. Wed. Thurs. Fri. Sat.
Months	Jan. Feb. Mar. Apr. Aug. Sept. Oct. Nov. Dec. (May, June, and July are never abbreviated.)
Kinds of streets	Street: St. Lane: Ln. Route: Rt./Rte. Road: Rd. Boulevard: Blvd. Drive: Dr. Avenue: Ave.
Kinds of businesses	Company: Co. Incorporated: Inc. Department: Dept. Corporation: Corp.
Times	"before noon": A.M. "after noon": P.M.

Guided Practice

A. Give the abbreviations or initials for these words.

1. Bluebell Boulevard
2. Hiking Department
3. Reverend Rex Miller
4. Acme Airplane Company
5. Doctor Helen Baylor
6. 7:30 in the evening

Independent Practice

B. Writing Abbreviations and Initials   Write each group of words, using abbreviations. Use initials for middle names.

   7. Arc Metal Company, Incorporated

   MODEL ▷ Arc Metal Co., Inc.

   8. Department of Transportation
   9. Mister Jerry Krant, Junior
   10. 134 Route 12, Willard
   11. Tuesday, July 11
   12. 1512 Royal Boulevard

C. Filling Out a Form   Make up information to complete the form below. Use initials for middle names. Use other abbreviations wherever you can.

CAMP GRIZZLY
WILDERNESS SURVIVAL CAMP
Application Form

MODEL ▷   Name **13.** Jerry M. Poindexter _____

Address **14.** _____

Date of Birth **15.** _____

School **16.** _____

Address of School **17.** _____

Parent or Guardian **18.** _____

Application — Writing

Guidebook Entry   Write a brief paragraph of information about Camp Grizzly for a guidebook that lists summer camps for children. Include information about teachers, counselors, and other workers at the camp. Also, mention where the camp is, how to get there, dates when the camp is open, and what activities are offered. Use initials and abbreviations wherever possible.

5 Letters

◆FOCUS   The parts of a friendly letter and a business letter follow rules of capitalization and punctuation.

The five parts of a friendly letter are the heading, the greeting, the body, the closing, and the signature.

The heading gives the writer's address and the date of the letter. Proper nouns are capitalized. A comma comes between the names of the city and the state and between the date and the year. The postal abbreviation is usually used for the state. This abbreviation contains two capital letters and no period. The postal abbreviations for all the states appear on page 56 of the **Writer's Handbook.**

The first word of the greeting is capitalized.

Each paragraph in the body is indented.

Only the first word of the closing is capitalized. A comma follows the closing.

The signature comes just below the closing.

Friendly Letter

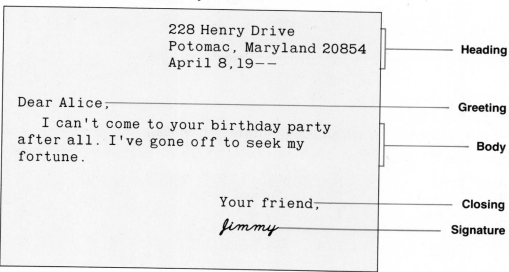

```
                    228 Henry Drive
                    Potomac, Maryland 20854        ———— Heading
                    April 8,19--

Dear Alice,                                        ———— Greeting
    I can't come to your birthday party
after all. I've gone off to seek my               ———— Body
fortune.

                    Your friend,                   ———— Closing
                    Jimmy                          ———— Signature
```

A business letter has six parts: the heading, the inside address, the greeting, the body, the closing, and the signature. The inside address appears above the greeting. It gives the name and address of the person or the company to whom the letter is written. The greeting in a business letter is followed by a colon. A business letter is usually typed. A handwritten signature, however, usually appears between the closing and the typed signature. Study the business letter on the next page.

Business Letter

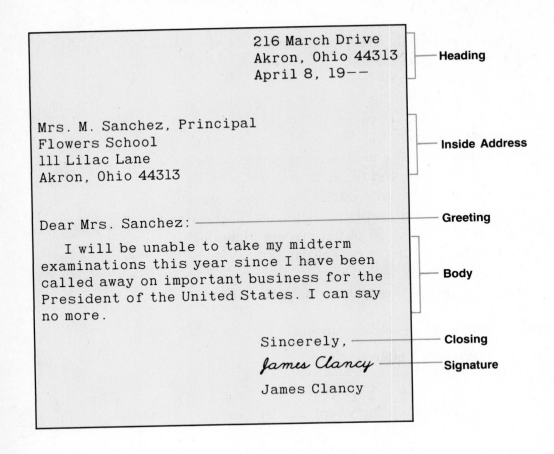

216 March Drive
Akron, Ohio 44313 — **Heading**
April 8, 19--

Mrs. M. Sanchez, Principal
Flowers School — **Inside Address**
111 Lilac Lane
Akron, Ohio 44313

Dear Mrs. Sanchez: ——————— **Greeting**

   I will be unable to take my midterm
examinations this year since I have been
called away on important business for the — **Body**
President of the United States. I can say
no more.

Sincerely, —————— **Closing**

James Clancy —————— **Signature**

James Clancy

Guided Practice

A. Name the part of a letter in which each item might appear.
Some items have two possible answers.

1. 23 Vasona Road
2. Dear Sir:
3. February 8, 1993
4. Mr. Roy Smith, President
5. Bella Dress Design
6. Yours truly,

B. **7.—12.** Tell whether each item in **A** comes from a *friendly letter,*
a *business letter,* or *either kind.*

> **THINK AND REMEMBER**
> ◆ Include a heading, greeting, body, closing, and signature in a
> friendly letter or a business letter.
> ◆ In a business letter also include an **inside address,** the
> name and address of the person or the company to whom
> the letter will be sent.

Independent Practice

C. Identifying Letter Parts   Read each item. Decide which part of a letter it comes from. Then write *heading, inside address, greeting, body, closing,* or *signature.* Some items have two possible answers.

13. Sincerely,

MODEL > closing

14. Dear Pat,
15. 11 Echo Avenue
16. Your pal,

17. Bayport, NY 11705
18. Dear Dr. Mason:
19. Dec. 10, 1993
20. Mrs. Pat Hoskins, Director
21. Youth Science Institute

D. Proofreading: Correcting Capitalization and Punctuation in Letter Parts   Write each item correctly. The information in parentheses tells the kind of letter from which it comes.

22. 456, Carson Avenue (friendly or business)

MODEL > 456 Carson Avenue

23. Dear Dad: (friendly)
24. Your aunt. (friendly)
25. October 9 1993 (friendly or business)
26. Dear Mayor Sonenfield, (business)
27. 10 fellows road (friendly or business)
28. Orlando florida 32821 (friendly or business)
29. with best regards, (friendly or business)

E. Writing Letters Correctly   Write this business letter in correct form.

30.

```
10 montgomery street seattle
Washington 98109
september 10 1993
```

MODEL >

```
              10 Montgomery Street
              Seattle, Washington 98109
              September 10, 1993
```

31.

```
ms meg malone president pirate paradise 10
swamp way winchester ma 01890 dear ms malone
I am currently seeking buried treasure and
am greatly in need of a shovel and a pirate
hat. Please send me your price list. sincerely
robert snow
```

Application — Writing

Letters   Imagine that you are planning an adventure. Write a letter to a friend describing your plans. Then write to a company to order the supplies you will need. Use correct form, capitalization, and punctuation in both letters.

6 Envelopes

◆ **FOCUS** The return address and the receiver's address on an envelope follow rules of capitalization and punctuation.

When you mail a letter, write your own name and address in the upper left-hand corner of the envelope. Write the receiver's name and address in the middle of the envelope, just below the center. If it is a business letter, include the name of the company or the agency under the receiver's name.

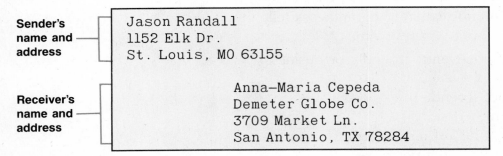

Sender's name and address

Jason Randall
1152 Elk Dr.
St. Louis, MO 63155

Receiver's name and address

Anna–Maria Cepeda
Demeter Globe Co.
3709 Market Ln.
San Antonio, TX 78284

Notice the five-number ZIP Code after the state in each address. Also notice that the postal abbreviation is used for each state. These abbreviations are made up of two capital letters and have no periods. The chart on page 431 shows all the state abbreviations.

Guided Practice

A. Tell where to use capital letters, commas, periods, and abbreviations in each address below.

1. milly brown
   135 oxnard avenue
   red butte north dakota 58201

2. axel penrod
   5014 buchanan boulevard
   dover ohio 44622

3. michele thomas
   745 theoni lane
   fordyce arkansas 71742

4. oscar hudson
   9806 penn street
   graham north carolina 27253

THINK AND REMEMBER
◆ Write your own name and address in the upper left-hand corner of an envelope.
◆ Write the receiver's name and address in the center of the envelope.

Independent Practice

B. Writing Addresses Correctly Write each address correctly, as it would be written on an envelope.

5. maria sanchez   3501 wells drive   roswell new mexico 88201

MODEL> Maria Sanchez
3501 Wells Dr.
Roswell, NM 88201

6. lewis barrymore   6583 palmyra avenue brewer maine 04412

7. gretta darwell   8734 moorhead street fort scott kansas 66701

8. bernard woodward   36072 benedict boulevard   alamo texas 78516

9. pauline wellington   ottaway drive middle valley tennessee 37343

10. jack chang   630 fairbanks road   brighton colorado 80601

11. eleanor porter   36541 ranch avenue   elk city oklahoma 73644

C. Proofreading Envelopes Find one error in each line of each address below. Draw a rectangle to stand for the envelopes, and write the addresses correctly.

12. George m. Hugo

MODEL> George M. Hugo

13. 8765 joyce Dr.
14. Culpeper VA 22701
15. Dean H Jefferson
16. Brinker skate Co.
17. 4502 Reaper ave.
18. Orland Park, ILL 60462

Application — Writing

Envelopes Draw three rectangles to stand for envelopes. Address the envelopes to three of your heroes from real life or from fiction. Make up information you do not know, but be sure to use correct capitalization and punctuation in your addresses.

Postal Abbreviations for States

AL (Alabama)
AK (Alaska)
AZ (Arizona)
AR (Arkansas)
CA (California)
CO (Colorado)
CT (Connecticut)
DE (Delaware)
FL (Florida)
GA (Georgia)
HI (Hawaii)
ID (Idaho)
IL (Illinois)
IN (Indiana)
IA (Iowa)
KS (Kansas)
KY (Kentucky)
LA (Louisiana)
ME (Maine)
MD (Maryland)
MA (Massachusetts)
MI (Michigan)
MN (Minnesota)
MS (Mississippi)
MO (Missouri)
MT (Montana)
NE (Nebraska)
NV (Nevada)
NH (New Hampshire)
NJ (New Jersey)
NM (New Mexico)
NY (New York)
NC (North Carolina)
ND (North Dakota)
OH (Ohio)
OK (Oklahoma)
OR (Oregon)
PA (Pennsylvania)
RI (Rhode Island)
SC (South Carolina)
SD (South Dakota)
TN (Tennessee)
TX (Texas)
UT (Utah)
VT (Vermont)
VA (Virginia)
WA (Washington)
WV (West Virginia)
WI (Wisconsin)
WY (Wyoming)

7 Outlines

◆ **FOCUS** An outline follows rules of capitalization and punctuation.

Before writing a long report, you may want to organize your ideas in an outline. An **outline** is a summary of information broken down into main topics, subtopics, and details. The title appears centered at the top. Each main topic is labeled with a Roman numeral followed by a period. Each subtopic is labeled with a capital letter and a period. Each detail is labeled with a number and a period. There must be at least two items in each category. If you have an item marked *A.*, you must have an item marked *B.* The first word in each line is capitalized. Notice how the parts of this outline are arranged and indented.

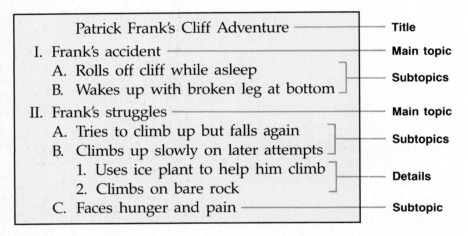

In an outline, each related line should be **parallel,** or worded in a similar way. In the outline above, notice that each main topic is made up of nouns. Each subtopic and detail begins with a verb.

Guided Practice

A. Tell the order in which these additional items from Patrick Frank's adventure should appear in an outline.

1. C. Lifted into helicopter
2. 1. Checks to see if Patrick is alive
3. A. Spotted by a boy jogging
4. 2. Races to tell parents
5. III. Frank's rescue
6. B. Call police
7. IV. The homecoming

B. **8.—14.** Tell whether each item in **A** requires *no indent* or should be indented *one space* or *two spaces*.

Independent Practice

C. Proofreading: Checking for Errors in an Outline Correct the following outline. Use correct capitalization, punctuation, and indentation. The lines of the outline are in the proper order.

Kathryn Yoder and the 1936 johnstown flood

I.   Information about Johnstown
A.   located in western Pennsylvania
b.   Positioned near two rivers
C.   Often has Floods
 1   Earliest recorded flood in 1808
     "Pumpkin flood" in 1871
     Most famous flood in 1889
II. Yoder's Experience
a.   Evacuated home after heavy rains began
B   Waited in hills
C.   worried about dam breaking
d.   Returned home next day after dam didn't break
III. flood damage
A.   forty-one million dollars in losses
1.   Businesses Closed by flooding
2   farmers lost crops and cattle
B.   Hundreds left homeless
C.   Twenty Lives Lost

Application — Writing and Speaking

Outline Read a short article about a famous accident or natural disaster. Then tell your classmates about it. Write an outline of the article in proper outline form to help you organize and remember your material as you give your talk.

8 Titles

◆ FOCUS   The title of a written work follows rules of capitalization and punctuation.

When you write the title of a work, such as a book or a movie, you must follow certain rules to show that it is a title. Capitalize nouns, verbs, and other important words in the title. Do not capitalize unimportant words, such as *a, the, on, or, at, up,* and *for,* unless they come at the beginning or the end of the title.

Underline titles of long works, such as books, magazines, movies, newspapers, musical compositions, and plays. In print such titles appear in italics.

1. Have you read *For Better or for Worse*?
2. The book was reviewed in the *San Carlos Gazette.*

The titles of shorter works, such as poems, short stories, book chapters, articles, and songs, are enclosed in quotation marks. If the title comes at the end of a sentence, the closing quotation marks come after the period. If the sentence ends with a question mark or exclamation point, the quotation marks come before the final punctuation mark.

3. The story "Brainbox" appeared in the book *Lion at School.*
4. Another story in the book was called "Manatee."
5. Have you read "Manatee"?

Guided Practice

A. Identify the words in each title that should be capitalized.

1. the house of dies drear (novel)
2. the ballad of sam mcGee (poem)
3. ladybugs and lucky stars (magazine)
4. the incredible shrinking machine (short story)
5. seven people who disappeared (article)

B. 6. – 10. Tell whether each title in **A** should be *underlined* or enclosed in *quotation marks.*

Independent Practice

C. Writing Titles Correctly Write each title correctly. The word in parentheses tells what kind of work it is.

11. grand canyon suite (musical composition)

MODEL Grand Canyon Suite

12. the incredible journey (novel)

13. the wedding of the hawk (folk tale)

14. how they brought the good news from ghent to aix (poem)

15. in the cave of the one-eyed giant (story)

16. stephen wright's mystery notebook (magazine)

17. los angeles herald-examiner (newspaper)

18. abraham lincoln walks at midnight (poem)

19. for whom the bell tolls (novel)

D. Writing Sentences Containing Titles Write each sentence correctly.

20. The song oh, susannah! was written by Stephen Foster.

MODEL The song "Oh, Susannah!" was written by Stephen Foster.

21. I read about Jesse James in a magazine called westerners.

22. My favorite novel about the West is tree wagon.

23. I enjoyed the article five outlaws on the run.

24. The article appeared in the chicago tribune.

25. Arthur Guiterman wrote a poem titled the pioneer.

26. Our class sang home on the range.

27. Have you seen the movie shadows on the stones?

Application — Writing

List Write several paragraphs, each naming and briefly describing one of the following: your favorite novel, story, movie, poem, song, and television show. Remember to write each title correctly.

9 Bibliographies

◆ **FOCUS** A bibliography follows rules of capitalization and punctuation.

A **bibliography** gives information about sources used in a research report. The sources are listed alphabetically by the authors' last names. Study this bibliography entry for a book. Notice what information is included, how it is ordered, and how commas, colons, and periods are used.

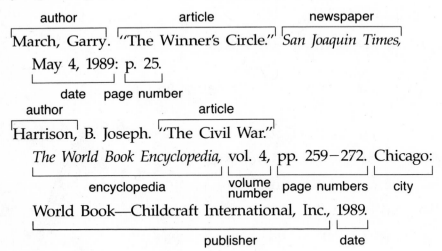

If your information comes from an article, story, or poem, list the magazine, newspaper, book, or encyclopedia in which it appeared. Also, give the pages of the article, story, or poem. If the source is a magazine or newspaper, you do not need to list the publisher or the city of publication. If the source is an encyclopedia, give the volume number as well.

Guided Practice

A. Tell how this information would appear in a bibliography entry.

1. Book: Go Up the Road
Publisher: Atheneum
Place: New York
Date: 1972
Author: Evelyn S. Lampman

2. Article: "Winning"
Newspaper: Clancy Times
Page: 14
Date: March 1, 1980
Author: Paula Williams

Independent Practice

B. Writing Bibliography Entries   Write a bibliography entry for each item.

3. Book: The Hobbit
  Publisher: Houghton
               Mifflin
  Place: Boston
  Date: 1984
  Author: J.R.R. Tolkien

4. Article: "Dreams"
  Magazine: Vistas
  Pages: 19–23
  Date: Nov. 1982
  Author: Emily J. O'Marin

5. Book: Calico Bush
  Publisher: Macmillan
  Place: New York
  Date: 1931
  Author: Rachel Field

6. Story: "Wondering Aloud"
  Book: Happy Choices
  Publisher: Strawberry Publishing
  Pages: 20–24
  Place: London
  Date: 1968
  Author: Glen Adelman

C. Proofreading Bibliographies   Find the errors in each bibliography entry. Write the entry correctly.

7. Tilly, Harriet. Boston: Little, Brown & Co., 1984. Across Western Skies.

MODEL Tilly, Harriet. Across Western Skies. Boston: Little, Brown & Co., 1984.

8. Urson, Yorick. Capturing Wild Animals with a Camera. *The American Photographer* September 16, 1988, pp. 14–18.

9. Willard, Alfred. "Song of My Soul." January 24, 1989 p. 20. *The Phoenix Examiner*

10. Figueroa, Inez. America Before Columbus. Houston Rainmaker Publications, Inc., 1989.

Application — Writing

Bibliography   Make a bibliography of five of your favorite books to share with classmates. Be sure to use the correct form for the bibliography. Remember to put the entries in alphabetical order.

10 Direct Quotations and Dialogue

◆ **FOCUS** A direct quotation follows rules of capitalization and punctuation.

When you write somebody's exact words, you are using a **direct quotation.** Use quotation marks to show where a direct quotation begins and ends. Put end punctuation inside the quotation marks. Begin the first word of the quotation with a capital letter.

1. " That avalanche was so sudden ," whispered Helen.

2. Amy said , "W e're lucky to be alive ."

Notice that a comma separates the quotation from the rest of the sentence. It comes before the quotation marks. A comma replaces a period just before a quotation mark, but it does not replace a question mark or an exclamation point.

3. "I'm so scared !" cried Helen.

4. "Do you hear anything ?" asked Amy.

When other words interrupt a quotation, end the first section with quotation marks. Begin the next section with more quotation marks. If the first section is a complete sentence, use a period after the speaker's name. If the second section begins a new sentence, capitalize the first word.

5. "I thought ," said Amy , "that I heard footsteps."

6. "Let's get closer ," said Helen . "We need to stay warm."

When using direct quotations to write conversation or dialogue, start a new paragraph each time the speaker changes.

Guided Practice

A. Identify the punctuation and the capitalization needed in these sentences, and tell where they are needed.

1. Did you hear that sound asked the first ranger.
2. Let's try digging right here responded the second ranger.
3. Oh, Helen, I hear voices cried Amy. we're being rescued.
4. I never thought mumbled Helen that we'd live through this.
5. The rangers shouted we've found them

Independent Practice

B. Writing Quotations Correctly   Write each sentence. Use punctuation and capitalization where they are needed.

6. The announcer shouted the skaters are off!

MODEL▷ The announcer shouted, "The skaters are off!"

7. There goes our daughter said Mrs. Farr.

8. She's making good time said Mr. Farr. she just might win.

9. Nina Farr cried the announcer has just fallen!

10. Will she get up asked the sportscaster. yes fans she is getting up!

11. Farr is skating hard said the announcer but will she be able to catch up?

12. She's incredible said Mrs. Farr. look at her go!

13. It's over said the announcer and Farr has come in third.

C. Writing Dialogue Correctly   Write the dialogue. Use punctuation and capitalization where they are needed. Remember to start a new paragraph each time the speaker changes.

14. That sudden roar must have been a rock slide cried Mai.

MODEL▷ "That sudden roar must have been a rock slide!" cried Mai.

15. We're done for whispered George unless we can find another way out of this cave. Do you think asked Mai that a search party will come looking for us? I don't know answered George. Let's start looking for light said Mai. I don't want to end my days in here.

Application — Writing, Speaking, Listening

Dialogue   Imagine that you and a partner are story characters facing a dangerous situation. Discuss the situation and how you will get out of it. Then write down your conversation as if it were part of a short story. Use correct punctuation, capitalization, and paragraphing.

Building Vocabulary
Idioms: Lend an Ear

In the best stories, the characters sound like real people when they talk. To get this effect, writers must first listen carefully to everyday speech. They notice phrases not found in formal writing but used commonly in conversations. Many of these phrases are idioms.

An **idiom** is a group of words whose meaning cannot be understood from the meanings of the individual words in the phrase. From long-time use, the group of words has taken on an accepted meaning. The highlighted phrase is an idiom.

It was raining cats and dogs that day.

The phrase *raining cats and dogs* has nothing to do with cats or dogs. It means that rain is coming down very hard.

Many idioms have a colorful history. Today, when you give away a secret, you "let the cat out of the bag."

Long ago, farmers would auction off baby pigs at county fairs. The pigs would come already wrapped in bags for easy carrying. Sometimes, a dishonest farmer would put a cat instead of a valuable young pig in the bag. If anyone gave away that secret, he or she "let the cat out of the bag."

Years ago, hunters would beat around bushes to scare foxes out of hiding. Catching foxes in this way took a long time. The idiom *beat around the bush* has come to mean taking a long time to come to the point.

Idioms give writing the tone and rhythm of real-life speech. You cannot invent idioms, because if you did, no one would know what they meant. Instead, you gather idioms by listening to people talk. In many kinds of writing, you want to set a formal tone, so you should avoid idioms. When you write a story, however, idioms can help give your dialogue a lively, realistic flavor.

Reading Practice

Read each sentence. Study the underlined idiom. Then write a word or words that could replace the idiom in the sentence.

1. I thought I could solve the case quickly, but I soon found I was in for some rough sledding.
2. Every week the robber held up another store.
3. I chased the robber down an alley once, but he gave me the slip.
4. He just disappeared into thin air.
5. Well, I stuck with the case.
6. After a while the case began to get on my nerves.
7. I would be in hot water if I didn't solve the case soon.
8. On Thursday, I got a tip that I should keep an eye on the Lomax Shoe Store.
9. Tips should be taken with a grain of salt.
10. You never know whether or not a tip is on the level.
11. This time, though, I made a beeline for that store.
12. I got there in the nick of time.
13. I caught the robber red-handed.
14. I tell you, I felt like a million back at the station.
15. You see, I could hold my head high once again.

Writing Practice

Write the meaning of each idiom, and then use the idiom in a sentence. Look in a dictionary if you need help. Idioms are listed in bold print at the end of individual entries in some dictionaries. To locate them, look under the most important word in the idiom.

16. horse around
17. meet someone halfway
18. go to the dogs
19. drink in something
20. brush up on something
21. talk turkey
22. on pins and needles
23. run across a friend
24. fall through
25. on your toes

Project

Browse through a dictionary, and find ten idioms you have never heard. On individual sheets of paper, list each idiom and its definition and write a sentence using the idiom. Then make a class book of idioms. Put the idioms together in alphabetical order by the key word in the idiom, and make a cover for the book.

Language Enrichment
Mechanics

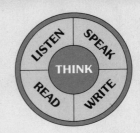

Use what you know about mechanics to do these activities.

 Talk-Show Host

Imagine you are the host of a nationally televised talk show. Decide who today's guest is. Then write the conversation you have with him or her, using correct capitalization, punctuation, and paragraph indentation. Include jokes, humorous remarks, and comments to the audience if you wish. When you are finished writing, act out the conversation with a classmate. Use your dialogue as the script.

 Now Read This

With classmates, keep a classroom bibliography of books you enjoy. Begin the bibliography by writing entries for five of your favorite books. Write each entry on a separate index card, following the form for a bibliography. On each card, write two or three sentences about the book. Use correct capitalization and end punctuation. Add entries as you read books you enjoy. Store the cards in a box in alphabetical order by the last names of the authors. Refer to the bibliography when you are looking for something interesting to read.

 Make a Long Story Short

Think of a hero who had great adventures. He or she could be a real person from history, a character from a book of fiction, or a character from a movie. Write an outline of the person's greatest adventure, using correct outline form. If you choose to write about a real person, look up information in a history book or an encyclopedia. Share your outline with your classmates.

CONNECTING
LANGUAGE ⬌ WRITING

In this unit you focused on punctuation, capitalization, and form in sentences, letters, outlines, and bibliographies.

◆ **Using Mechanics in Your Writing** Periods, commas, and other punctuation marks help keep written ideas organized. Capital letters help highlight ideas and show where new ideas begin. Writers usually use particular forms for material such as letters, outlines, and bibliographies. When writers use these forms, readers can find information quickly and easily. Use capitalization, punctuation, and form carefully as you do these activities.

Boy: *This is the last straw!*

Woman: *Our goose is cooked!*

What's That You Say?

You learned about idioms on the **Building Vocabulary** pages. Use idioms to make an unusual situation seem real. Think of two characters like people you might meet in real life. Now think of them in a suspenseful and dangerous situation. Write the conversation they might have. Use idioms to give the conversation a realistic flavor. Remember to use commas, quotation marks, and end punctuation correctly in this conversation.

Fan Letter

Write a letter to a music or sports figure whom you especially like. Tell the person what you admire about him or her. You might even ask for an autographed photo. Ask the librarian to help you find out how to address the letter. Mail it, and wait for an answer. Use the correct form for a business letter.

Unit Checkup

Think Back	Think Ahead
◆ What did you learn about suspense stories in this unit? What did you do to write one?	◆ How will knowing how a suspense story is written help you enjoy reading one in the future?
◆ Look at the writing you did in this unit. How did mechanics help express your ideas?	◆ What is one way you can use mechanics to improve your writing?

Suspense Stories   *pages 400–402*

Read the suspense story. Then follow the directions.

Unexpected Treasures

The old house stood like a tombstone on the deserted hill. It was the only house on the street.

Tim and Janet crept up to the old house, but they made sure to make some noise.

"We don't want to catch those ghosts unaware. Makes them angry!" Tim said, but his laugh wasn't playful.

"Aw, come on," Janet said. "You know there's nothing in this house."

---

1. Write the title.
2. Name the characters.
3. What does Tim's speech tell you about him?
4. What does Janet say that gives you a hint of danger to come?
5. What is the setting?

Storytelling: Dialogue and Characters   *page 403*

Rewrite each sentence, using dialogue.

6. Tim asked Janet if she said something to him.
7. Janet asked if he heard a dog.
8. Tim said that he heard footsteps.
9. Janet replied that he was imagining things.
10. Both admitted they were more scared than ever before.

The Writing Process   *pages 404–414*

Write the letter of the correct response to each question.

11. Once a topic is chosen, making a time line can help you

    a. develop the plot.

    b. develop characters.

    c. create a setting.

12. In revising your story, you decide that the mood is not suspenseful enough. What should you do?

    a. Add words to create a suspenseful mood.

    b. Put the climax near the beginning of the story.

    c. Change the plot.

13. Which editor's mark would you use to correct the error in this sentence?

    Janet said, Let's get out now!

    a. add a comma ⌃

    b. add a period ⊙

    c. add quotation marks ⌄ ⌄

Capitalization and End Punctuation in Sentences

pages 418–419

Find the error in each sentence. Write the sentence correctly.

14. Did you ever hear of Dian Fossey.

15. she lived for many years in Rwanda, a country in Africa.

16. She lived with and studied the mountain gorilla, a species that is gradually becoming extinct!

17. Fossey devoted her life to preserving these animals?

18. read about this amazing woman.

Commas Within Sentences

pages 420–422

Write each sentence. Add commas where they are needed.

19. The Wright brothers Wilbur and Orville flew the first powered airplane in 1903.

20. Oh what a feeling the first flight must have given them!

21. Orville flew the plane first and then Wilbur piloted it.

22. Other significant dates in the history of flight were 1905 1919 and 1927.

23. Bobby do you know what happened in any of those years?

Capitalization of Proper Nouns, Proper Adjectives, and *I* *pages 423–424*

Find the error in each sentence. Write the sentence correctly.

24. President theodore Roosevelt loved the outdoors.

25. In fact, i believe the teddy bear was named after him.

26. Roosevelt was a New yorker by birth.

27. He took office after president McKinley was assassinated.

28. Roosevelt was a member of the republican Party.

Abbreviations *pages 425–426*

Write each group of words, using abbreviations. Use initials for middle names.

29. 82 Kensington Lane

30. 6:00 in the morning

31. August 7, 1993

32. Taos, New Mexico

33. Charleston, South Carolina

34. Doctor Maeve Ann Collins

Letters *pages 427–429*

Read each item. Decide which part of a letter it comes from. Then write *heading, inside address, greeting, body, closing,* or *signature.* Some items have two possible answers. Next, label each item *friendly, business,* or *either* to show the kind of letter from which it comes.

36. Dear Aunt Julie,

37. October 14, 1993

38. Sincerely,

39. Dear Mr. Greenberg:

Envelopes *pages 430–431*

Write each address correctly, as it would be written on an envelope.

40. patrick pilosi 775 croton avenue ozona florida 33560

41. josé sanchez 828 rio boulevard san diego california 92123

42. greg raynor 1373 wilson drive pittsburgh pennsylvania 15213

43. susan carter 48 university drive knoxville tennessee 37923

44. ruth reynolds 5872 bayshore boulevard galveston texas 77552

Outlines *pages 432–433*

The lines of this outline are in the correct order. Find the error in each line. Write the outline correctly. Remember to indent.

45. A. The Case of the Land Thieves

46. I   Suspects

47. a. Chris Williams

48. 1 Has motive

49. 2. has opportunity

50. B Matt Sooner

51. II. clues

52. A. stamp

53. B Coins

Titles   *pages 434−435*

Write each title correctly. The word in parentheses tells what kind of work it is.

54. Misty of chincoteague (book)
55. We Shall Overcome (song)
56. Star Wars (movie)
57. Life (magazine)

Bibliographies   *pages 436−437*

Write a bibliography entry for each item.

58. a book called In the Shadow of a Rainbow published by W.W. Norton & Company in New York in 1974 by Robert Franklin Leslie
59. a novel by Dashiell Hammett called The Maltese Falcon and published by Alfred A. Knopf in New York in 1921
60. a selection called Bernstein on pages 184−189 in a book about mystery movies called Suspects published in 1985 by Alfred A. Knopf in New York and written by David Thompson
61. a book called Secrets of the Shopping Mall by Richard Peck published in 1979 by Delacorte Press in New York

Direct Quotations and Dialogue   *pages 438−439*

Write each sentence. Use punctuation and capitalization where needed.

62. We're off to the Rockies shouted Mr. Cardozo.
63. I hope we see some bears Ilana said.
64. That added Jeremy is something I want to see, too.
65. Mrs. Cardozo suggested let's unpack the tents.
66. Was I supposed to pack them grinned Jeremy sheepishly.

Idioms: Lend an Ear   *pages 440−441*

Read each sentence. Study the underlined idiom. Then write a word or words that could replace the idiom in the sentence.

67. Mr. Trainor blew his top when his hat was stolen.
68. "You'll have to get up pretty early in the morning to fool me," he said.
69. "I gave Fran Hickox the boot last week, and she would do anything to get back at me," he added.
70. "Mr. Trainor was mean to me," Fran said, "but now the shoe is on the other foot. I admit I hid his hat."

Cumulative Review

Four Kinds of Sentences   *pages 30–31*

For each group of words, write *sentence* or *not a sentence*. For each sentence, write *declarative, interrogative, imperative,* or *exclamatory.*

1. What a wonderful smile Johanna has!
2. A light behind a person's eyes.
3. Do you think people can communicate without using words?
4. Smile when I take your picture.
5. Don't move.
6. When you develop the film.

Subjects and Predicates   *pages 32–33*

Underline the simple subject once and the simple predicate twice. Write *you* if the subject is understood. Write *natural word order* or *inverted word order* for each sentence.

7. Into her room tiptoed Danielle.
8. Write in your journal every day.
9. Is little Tommy following Danielle?
10. This young girl enjoys some privacy.
11. Can you entertain Tommy for a while?
12. Read him a book.
13. The child was very pleased.

Compound Subjects and Predicates   *pages 42–45*

Write the compound subject or the compound predicate from each sentence. Underline the connecting word. Write *compound subject* or *compound predicate.*

14. Marc loves any books about history and reads them often.
15. In fact, Marc and his brother Todd have a large library of history books.
16. Their friends and relatives always know what to give them for gifts.
17. Chinese history and Latin American history are two of their favorite subjects.
18. Todd sometimes writes stories or draws pictures on historical themes.

Common and Proper Nouns   *pages 82–83*
Write the sentence in each pair that has the proper noun. Use capital letters where they are needed.

19. That tall, thin man is mr. baker.
    Tell the baker that we want a loaf of rye bread and six bran muffins.
20. Is that the new jersey you bought to go with your blue pants?
    Where in new jersey do you live?
21. We grow the herb oregano in our garden.
    Can you help us pull some weeds, herb?
22. The mississippi river flows through several midwestern and southern states.
    Let's sit by the river and cool off.
23. My dad works as a truck dispatcher at a shipping company.
    It's noon, dad, so let's leave for the office.

Possessive Nouns   *pages 92–93*
Write the possessive noun from each sentence. Label it *singular* or *plural.*

24. The farmer's days are long and tiring ones.
25. This morning, Mr. Baxter is repairing his oxen's harness.
26. After he finishes that, he will fix his horse's saddle.
27. Horses seem to be able to recognize their owners' footsteps.
28. Rusty, Mr. Baxter's horse, is always excited when he hears Mr. Baxter approach.
29. Rusty doesn't act the same way when he hears Mrs. Harris's footsteps.

Action and Linking Verbs   *pages 128–131*
Write the underlined verbs. Label them *action* or *linking.*

30. Sydelle hoped her birthday present <u>would be</u> a horse.
31. Unfortunately, Sydelle's parents <u>said</u> no.
32. A horse <u>was</u> much too expensive!
33. Besides, where would they <u>keep</u> a horse?
34. They <u>lived</u> in a city apartment building.
35. Instead, her parents <u>gave</u> Sydelle riding lessons for her birthday.
36. That way, Sydelle rode many horses and <u>became</u> an excellent rider.
37. Now Sydelle <u>seems</u> a natural in the saddle.

Subject-Verb Agreement   *pages 140–143*

Rewrite each sentence to correct the error in subject-verb agreement.

38. Becky and her sister Melissa is members of the swim team.
39. Both swims every day after school and on Saturday mornings.
40. They participates in swim meets several times a year.
41. Their mother and father drives them to the competition.
42. Melissa perform superbly at the swim meets.
43. She win a few trophies every year.
44. Everyone think they have a great future in the sport.

Irregular Verbs   *pages 176–181*

Write the past or the past participle form of the verb in parentheses that correctly completes each sentence.

45. People have _____ each other jokes for centuries. (tell)
46. Ancient cave dwellers probably _____ one another laugh by doing funny things. (make)
47. Have you ever _____ to a comedy club? (go)
48. I _____ once. (do)
49. I laughed so hard that I _____ my sides were going to burst. (think)
50. My friend was afraid that his mouth had _____ frozen in a smile. (become)
51. By the end of the evening, I was sure that I had _____ out of laughs! (run)

Agreement of Pronouns with Antecedents   *pages 230–231*

Write each sentence. Draw an arrow from each underlined pronoun to its antecedent.

52. Louise was very grateful to <u>her</u> grandparents.

53. Grandma and Grandpa Stutz had taken Louise with <u>them</u> to Europe on vacation.

54. Grandpa Stutz had been in Europe during World War II, and he said <u>it</u> had changed a great deal.

55. The family said that Rome had been <u>their</u> favorite city in Europe.

56. Louise said, "Grandma and Grandpa, thank <u>you</u>."

Possessive Pronouns *pages 234–235*

Write and underline each possessive pronoun that is used in front of a noun. Write and draw two lines under each possessive pronoun that stands alone.

57. What is your idea for solving the problem?
58. I can't claim that the idea is really mine, but I think it is a good one.
59. We should involve the children in creating their own playground.
60. They will think of it as theirs.
61. Each committee chooses its own task and assigns people to work.
62. Please let me know when you find out what ours will involve.

Reflexive and Indefinite Pronouns *pages 236–239*

Write each sentence. Underline the reflexive pronouns once. Underline the indefinite pronouns twice.

63. Everyone makes mistakes sometimes.
64. You must give yourself a second chance.
65. Libby caused a terrible problem for herself.
66. Nobody would believe her any more because she had lied so many times.
67. Libby realized that the situation wouldn't get better by itself.
68. She apologized to each of her friends.
69. Now, all trust Libby once again.

Adjectives *pages 274–275*

Write each adjective. Label it *article* or *adjective that describes*.

70. Spanish explorers first visited Texas in the sixteenth and seventeenth centuries.
71. Texas became the twenty-eighth state in 1845.
72. The enormous state produces more oil than any other state.
73. Huge cattle ranches are numerous in Texas.
74. Many breeds of cattle were developed by Texas ranchers.
75. Tourists spend over two billion dollars a year visiting the state's exciting cities and beautiful resorts.
76. A wide array of fruits and vegetables is grown in this agricultural giant of a state.

Comparison with Adjectives *pages 282–285*

Write the form of the adjective in parentheses that correctly completes the sentence.

77. Maria is (happy) when she is working than when she is relaxing.
78. Of course, Maria's job is one of the (interesting) jobs you can imagine.
79. She interviews people who are visiting America as exchange students in one of the (good) exchange programs in the country.
80. Some of the real-life stories Maria hears are (funny) than movies.
81. Fortunately, she is the (practical) person I have ever met.
82. Maria always seems to help the foreign students with their problems, no matter how (difficult).
83. Her old job as a museum tour guide was great, but Maria finds this job even (enjoyable).

Adverbs *pages 318–319*

Write the adverb or adverbs from each sentence.

84. The hot, dry wind blew sand everywhere.
85. Lazily, Michelle rose to make dinner.
86. She shut the window completely in order to keep out the sand.
87. Doing this made the room quite stuffy.
88. Michelle looked hungrily at the chicken she had been planning to roast.
89. Thinking about the heat from the oven, Michelle immediately changed her plans.
90. As the yogurt slipped coolly down her throat, Michelle tried to imagine that she had taken a trip to Alaska.

Adverb or Adjective? *pages 326–327*

Choose the form of the adverb in parentheses that correctly completes each sentence.

91. A (bright, brightly) lighted movie scene creates a certain feeling.
92. The same scene, (dim, dimly) lit, changes that feeling.
93. Light can (complete, completely) change the way some objects look.
94. It is (real, really) important for a movie to have good lighting.
95. (Colorful, Colorfully) scenes are enjoyable to watch.

Conjunctions *pages 374–375*
Write the conjunction or conjunctions in each sentence.

96. Your background and mine are very similar.
97. I speak both German and Spanish.
98. You speak German fairly well, but you speak Spanish better.
99. At home, my grandmother and grandfather speak Spanish and English.
100. My parents and my grandparents are bilingual.
101. You could easily get a job translating English or Spanish at a tourist attraction.

Phrases and Clauses *pages 378–379*
Write *phrase* or *clause* to describe each underlined group of words.

102. <u>When I go to a city</u>, I like to see its art and science museums.
103. These museums always tell me something special <u>about the people</u>.
104. <u>Like most of the tourists in this town</u>, I enjoy spending time <u>in gift shops</u>.
105. I plan my souvenir shopping <u>while I'm relaxing over a delicious dinner</u>.
106. The most expensive place to shop is <u>at the international airport</u>.
107. <u>After I've returned from vacation</u>, I enjoy passing out the gifts.

Complex Sentences *pages 382–383*
Combine each pair of sentences into one complex sentence, using the word in parentheses. If the dependent clause begins the sentence, put a comma after it.

108. People enter New York Harbor. They can see a huge, welcoming sight. (whenever)
109. The Statue of Liberty has greeted millions of people. It stands near one of the largest U.S. ports. (because)
110. The statue was a gift to the United States from France. It stands as a symbol of international friendship. (since)
111. People come to this country through New York Harbor. Their first sight is the Statue of Liberty. (when)
112. The statue was in increasingly poor condition. The American people were able to repair it in 1987. (although)

STUDY SKILLS

Contents

1 Finding Words in a Dictionary

A **dictionary** is a reference book that lists words as well as their spellings, meanings, and pronunciations. Each word listed in the dictionary is an **entry word.** You can find entry words quickly by thinking of the dictionary as being divided into three sections.

front: abcde   **middle:** fghijklmnop   **back:** qrstuvwxyz

Decide whether the word you want is in the front, the middle, or the back of the dictionary, and open to the right section. Then turn forward or backward in the book until you find the word.

Entry words are arranged in **alphabetical order.** All the words that begin with the same letter appear together and are alphabetized by their second letters. If the first two letters are the same, the third letter is used, and if the first three are the same, the fourth is used, and so on.

march	melted	mistake	more	murky
quaint	question	quick	quorum	Quran
track	tragedy	tranquil	trap	travel

Guide words appear at the top of every page. The guide word on the left gives the first entry word on a page. The guide word on the right gives the last entry word on that page. All other entry words on the page fall alphabetically between the guide words. In searching for an entry word, check the guide words to find the page with your word on it.

---

appease   appraise

ap·pease [ə·pēz'] *v.* **ap·peased, ap·peas·ing   1** To satisfy: to *appease* hunger.   **2** To calm or soothe, especially by giving in to demands.

ap·pli·ca·tor [ap'lə·kā'tər] *n.* An instrument or device for applying a substance, as a medicine, shoe polish, or glue.

Practice

A. List the words in each group in alphabetical order.

1. plain, plane, placid, plaid
   MODEL⟩ placid, plaid, plain, plane
2. crew, crisp, crisis, crib

3. ransom, right, rabbit, row
4. art, author, arbor, ardent
5. rim, rhyme, really, rhythm

B. Write the words in each group that would be found on a page with the guide words *drill* and *duster.*

6. drop, duty, draw, duck
   MODEL⟩ drop, duck
7. drift, drink, do, dip
8. dye, dream, drip, dune

9. dream, dust, dance, droll
10. dunce, drier, drought, dull
11. droop, draft, dunk, drab

2 Using a Dictionary Entry

Every entry word in the dictionary is followed by one or more **definitions,** or meanings.

> **haz·y** [hā′zē] *adj.* **haz·i·er, haz·i·est** 1 Full of or blurred by haze; misty: a *hazy* sky; a *hazy* view. 2 Unclear; confused: *hazy* thoughts.—**haz′i·ly** *adv*.

Some words have only one meaning. Other words, such as *hazy*, have **multiple meanings,** or more than one meaning. To make it easy to find the meaning you need, each definition is numbered.

Sometimes, two identical words are listed as separate entries. These words are **homographs,** words that are spelled alike but that have different meanings or different pronunciations.

> **tear¹** [târ] *v.* To pull apart or rip by force.
> **tear²** [tir] *n.* A drop of salty liquid from the eye.

Many definitions include an **example sentence** that shows how to use the entry word.

> **pique** [pēk] *v.* To arouse a hurt and angry or resentful feeling in: The rude remarks *piqued* the guests.

Practice

A. Use these entries to answer the following questions.

> **en·trance¹** [en′trəns] *n.* 1 A passageway, as a doorway, used for entering something. 2 The act of entering: No one noticed our late *entrance*. 3 The right, privilege, or ability to enter. 4 The first appearance of an actor in a scene.
> **en·trance²** [in·trans′] *v.* **en·tranced, en·tranc·ing** 1 To fill with wonder or delight; charm; fascinate. 2 To put in a trance.

To which definition of *entrance* does each of the following refer? Write the entry word number and the definition number.

1. put under a spell

MODEL▷ entry 2, 2

2. a door
3. the act of going in

4. to fill with wonder
5. first onstage appearance
6. being able to enter
7. fascinate

B. Write example sentences for those definitions of *entrance* in the box that do not already have them. Follow the order of the definitions given.

MODEL▷ 8. Use this entrance when you come in early.

3 Using a Dictionary for Parts of Speech and Etymologies

Just after the entry word and its pronunciation in a dictionary comes an abbreviation for its part of speech. **Part of speech** refers to the way in which a word is used. A list of abbreviations like this is given at the front of most dictionaries.

n.	noun	*adj.*	adjective	*conj.*	conjunction
pron.	pronoun	*adv.*	adverb	*interj.*	interjection
v.	verb	*prep.*	preposition		

If a word has an **alternate spelling,** it may be listed as part of the entry or at the end of the entry. Study these two entries.

> **pin·ey** [pī′nē] *adj.* **pin·i·er, pin·i·est** Another spelling of PINY.
> **pix·ie** or **pixy** [pik′sē] *n., pl.* **pix·ies** A fairy or elf.

Another interesting item in a dictionary entry is the **etymology,** or history of a word. In some dictionaries the etymology appears after the part of speech. In others it occurs at the end of the entry, as below.

> **as·tro·naut** [as′trə·nôt′] *n.* One who travels in space. ◆*Astronaut* is parallel to *aeronaut,* a balloon pilot, and is formed from the Greek roots *nautes,* meaning *sailor,* and *astro-,* meaning (*between* or *among*) *stars.*

Practice

A. Find the following entry words in a dictionary. List the part of speech of each word. If a word is used as more than one part of speech, list each one.

1. dwarf
MODEL> n., v., adj.
2. empty
3. flat
4. goggle
5. ouch
6. although
7. sink

B. List each spelling variant of the following words. Look up the words in a dictionary if necessary.

8. theater
MODEL> theatre
9. traveler
10. briar
11. favor
12. metre
13. centre
14. adviser

C. Look up the etymology of each word. Use more than one dictionary if needed. Take notes on your findings.

15. coconut
MODEL> Spanish and Portuguese, means "grinning face"
16. dahlia
17. delicatessen
18. five-and-ten
19. czar
20. pretty

4 Using a Dictionary for Pronunciation

Most entry words in the dictionary are followed by a **phonetic respelling,** which shows how the word is pronounced. In a phonetic respelling, each sound is represented by a letter or letters or a symbol. A **pronunciation key,** like that shown below, is used to interpret the symbols in the phonetic respelling. A key usually appears on alternate pages of the dictionary for reference.

a	add	i	it	o͞o	took	oi	oil
ā	ace	ī	ice	o͞o	pool	ou	pout
â	care	o	odd	u	up	ng	ring
ä	palm	ō	open	û	burn	th	thin
e	end	ô	order	yo͞o	fuse	th	this
ē	equal					zh	vision

ə = { a in *above* e in *sicken* i in *possible*
       o in *melon* u in *circus* }

The phonetic respelling also shows the **syllabication,** or how a word is divided into parts. A **syllable** is a word part that includes only one vowel sound. The separation between syllables is usually shown by a dot or a space. Study this example.

rec·re·a·tion [rek′rē·ā′shən]

The phonetic respelling can also tell you where the accents, or stresses, occur in a word. In *recreation,* the primary accent, or main stress, is on the third syllable, and the secondary accent is on the first syllable. A syllable with a primary accent is pronounced with more force than a syllable with a secondary accent.

Practice

Look up these words in the dictionary. Write answers to the questions that follow.

consideration   recommend   descendant   thorough   satellite

1. Which word has five syllables?
   MODEL consideration
2. In which word is the primary accent on the second syllable?
3. Which word's phonetic respelling contains the symbol /û/?
4. Which two words' phonetic respellings contain the symbol /i/?
5. In which words is the first syllable pronounced with greater force than the others?
6. Which words have both primary and secondary accents?
7. Which word has only two syllables?

5 Using a Title Page, a Copyright Page, and a Table of Contents

STUDY SKILLS

When you open a book, the **title page** is usually the first page you see. It lists the title, the author, and the publisher of the book. On the back of the title page is the **copyright page.** This page shows the year in which the book was published and sometimes lists other books from which material was used with permission. Noting the copyright date is important because it tells you how recent the information in the book is.

The **table of contents** in a nonfiction book usually faces the copyright page. It lists the titles of all the chapters in the book and their page numbers. Material is listed in the order in which it occurs. A good table of contents can provide you with an accurate overview of all the information in the book.

THE SOUTHWEST
A Guide to the
Wide Open Spaces
by
Natt N. Arnold
and
Herbert S. Lee
 	
Illustrations by
Wilhelmina Grimm
 	
A Student's
Regional Guide
 	
Lantern Press
New York
	Copyright 1955 by
	Lantern Press, Inc. All
	rights reserved,
	including the Right
	of Reproduction in
	Whole or in
	Part in Any Form.
	Designed and
	Produced by
	The Offset Specialty
	Press, Inc.
	Printed in the
	U.S.A. by Indiana
	Printing and
	Lithography Company.
		CONTENTS
		Meet the Southwest 4
		Touring the Southwest 8
		Indians 17
		Explorers of the West. 40
		The Modern Southwest . . .44
		The Land and
		   Its Life Zones 50
		Birds 53
		Lizards and Snakes 60
		Geological Story
		   of the Southwest 105
		Places to See
		   and Things to Do 120
		Index 157

Title Page	**Copyright Page**	**Table of Contents**

Practice

Answer these questions based on the sample pages above.

1. Which chapters tell about wildlife?

   MODEL ➤ "Birds" and "Lizards and Snakes"

2. Which chapter describes climate?
3. Which chapter of those shown has the most pages?
4. How up-to-date is the information on places to see?
5. Does the book have illustrations? How do you know?
6. Who is the book's publisher?
7. Where is the publisher located?
8. Who are the co-authors of the book?

6 Using an Index

At the back of most nonfiction books is an **index.** The index lists the important **topics,** or sections, in the book in alphabetical order. It may also break down a large topic into **subtopics** or give **cross-references** to other places in the book where related topics are discussed. For each topic and subtopic, the index lists the page numbers on which the topic is discussed.

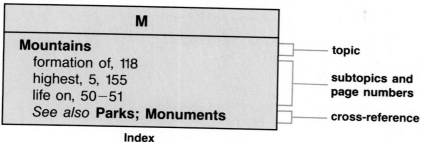

Index

In addition to the index, an **appendix** sometimes appears at the back of a nonfiction book. It contains maps, charts, diagrams, and tables that could not be placed in the body of the book. Statistics from the appendix could be valuable to someone writing a detailed paper or a research report.

Practice

Use the partial index below to answer the following questions.

North Africa, 173–177, 180–181; agriculture, 180; climate, 178; history of, 176–177; oil industry, 180, 181; resources, 180; rivers, 178–179.
North Atlantic Ocean, *See* **Atlantic Ocean**
North Carolina, 429, 456, 458

North Dakota, 448, 449
Northeasters, 435
Northern Hemisphere, 5, 6
Northern Ireland, 61, 66
Northern Rhodesia, *See* **Zambia**
North Korea, 275, 279, 316–318; *See also* **Korea**
North Pole, xiv, xv, 4–7
North Sea, 55, 57, 58, 63, 65, 70, 80, 82, 86, 94, 165

1. Which index topic contains subtopics?
   MODEL ▷ North Africa
2. Where would you find information on North Korea?
3. Which index topic has the most page references?
4. Which index topic refers the reader to *Zambia?*
5. Which topic is found in the pages appearing at the front of the book before the main sections begin?
6. On which pages would you find information about the rivers of North Africa?
7. Where would you find an explanation of northeasters?

7 Using the Dewey Decimal System

Because there are so many books in the library, organizing them logically is very important. The **Dewey Decimal System** provides a way to arrange nonfiction books in the library by subject area. Each of the ten main categories of knowledge is given a range of numbers. The ten categories, their numbers, and examples of books from each category are summarized in the following chart.

000–099	General Works (encyclopedias, atlases, newspapers)
100–199	Philosophy (ideas about the meaning of life, psychology)
200–299	Religion (world religions, mythology)
300–399	Social Science (government, law, business, education)
400–499	Language (dictionaries, grammar books)
500–599	Pure Science (mathematics, chemistry, plants, animals)
600–699	Applied Science (how-to books, engineering, radio)
700–799	Arts and Recreation (music, art, sports, hobbies)
800–899	Literature (poems, plays, essays)
900–999	History (travel, geography, biographies)

Practice

Write the range of Dewey Decimal System numbers and the subject category under which each of these books appears.

1. *Sign Language*
   MODEL ▷ 400–499—Language
2. *A Song in Stone: City Poems*
3. *Great Painters*
4. *The Rights of Candidates and Voters*
5. *Hammond's Historical Atlas*
6. *Twentieth-Century Psychology*
7. *Computer Programming Basics*
8. *Discovering the Guitar*
9. *Machines and How They Work*
10. *Webster's New World Dictionary*
11. *Nine Black Inventors*
12. *World Book Encyclopedia*
13. *Can I Help How I Feel?*
14. *The Illustrated Children's Bible*
15. *A Guide to Literature*
16. *Understanding Poetry*
17. *Flight: A Panorama of Aviation*
18. *Viruses: Life's Smallest Enemies*
19. *Poem Stew*
20. *Folk Tale Plays for Puppets*
21. *Women with a Cause*
22. *What Makes It Rain?*
23. *They Showed the Way: Forty American Negro Leaders*
24. *Fishing for Fun*
25. *In Search of Meaning: Living Religions of the World*
26. *What's a Frank Frank? Tasty Homograph Riddles*
27. *The Mystery of Eastern Religions*
28. *Learning the Violin*
29. *The Animals of Kenya*
30. *The Essays of Ruskin*

8 Using the Card Catalogue

A **card catalogue** is a set of 3″ × 5″ cards that lists every book in the library. The cards are in alphabetical order, usually in drawers. There are three kinds of cards. The **author card** shows the author's last name first. The **title card** shows the book title first. This card is alphabetized according to the first important word in the title. The **subject card** shows the subject of the book first. Subject cards are used when you want a book on a particular topic but do not know the title or the author. The **call number,** in the upper left corner of each card, tells where the book is on the library shelves.

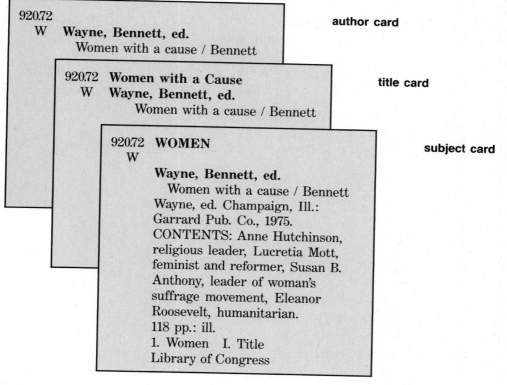

920.72
W   Wayne, Bennett, ed.
        Women with a cause / Bennett   **author card**

920.72   **Women with a Cause**
W   Wayne, Bennett, ed.
          Women with a cause / Bennett   **title card**

920.72   **WOMEN**
W
        Wayne, Bennett, ed.
          Women with a cause / Bennett
        Wayne, ed. Champaign, Ill.:
        Garrard Pub. Co., 1975.
        CONTENTS: Anne Hutchinson,
        religious leader, Lucretia Mott,
        feminist and reformer, Susan B.
        Anthony, leader of woman's
        suffrage movement, Eleanor
        Roosevelt, humanitarian.
        118 pp.: ill.
        1. Women   I. Title
        Library of Congress   **subject card**

Practice

Use the subject card above to answer the following questions.

1. What is the complete title of this book?
   MODEL▷ Women with a Cause
2. Who is the editor of the book?
3. What company published the book? When and where was it published?
4. How many pages are in the book? Is it illustrated?
5. Why might this book have an editor, not an author?
6. Who are the four women whose lives are covered?
7. What do all these women have in common?
8. Where could you look for more books edited by Bennett Wayne?

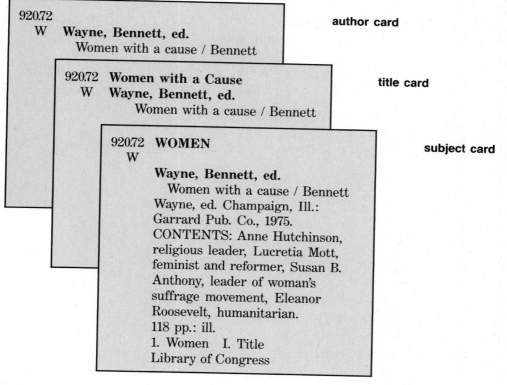

STUDY SKILLS

9 Identifying Kinds of Books

A complete library has at least four, and sometimes five, main sections, each in a separate part of the library. The first large section contains all the books of **fiction**. Fictional works, such as novels and short stories, are based on imaginary characters and events. The books are arranged on the shelves in alphabetical order according to the authors' last names.

In another area are nonfiction books. **Nonfiction** includes books about real people, things, and events. The nonfiction books represent all the categories in the Dewey Decimal System except general works and literature.

A **biography** is a type of nonfiction book that tells about the life of a real person. Biographies are arranged in alphabetical order according to the last name of the subject. Sometimes biographies, especially those about more than one person, are shelved with the call numbers *920* and *921.*

Libraries also have a reference section for books of nonfiction that cannot be checked out. **Reference** books include encyclopedias, dictionaries, and atlases.

Periodicals are works such as magazines and newspapers that are published daily or monthly. They are often located in the reference section. In some libraries, however, they are put in a section of their own where people can browse through them.

Practice

Name the section or sections of the library in which you would find each of the following.

1. an article in *Scientific American* magazine explaining curve balls
   MODEL ⟩ reference *or* periodicals
2. a book about the life of Lou Gehrig
3. a dictionary of baseball vocabulary
4. a book of true sports stories
5. an article in *Black Enterprise* magazine on black baseball officials
6. an encyclopedia of baseball statistics
7. a book called *Unsung Heroes of the Major Leagues*
8. a book of short stories about baseball
9. a newspaper feature on Pete Rose
10. a novel based on the movie *Eight Men Out*
11. a book called *The Business of Baseball*
12. a book called *Baseball's All-Time All-Stars*
13. a novel called *Matt Gargan's Boys*
14. an article about one of the first girls in Little League
15. a history of the Brooklyn Dodgers
16. a book about the history of the Baseball Hall of Fame in Cooperstown, New York
17. a book about the life of Willie Mays
18. an article in *Sports Illustrated* on Tommy Lasorda

10 Using Reference Books

Different kinds of reference books provide different types of information. A dictionary, for example, is a list of words arranged alphabetically. The entry for each word contains one or more definitions, its part or parts of speech, and its pronunciation. Often included are example sentences showing the word's uses and an etymology giving its history.

An **encyclopedia** is a set of books containing detailed information on many subjects. Each book is called a **volume,** and the volumes in the set are arranged in alphabetical order. Printed on the spine, or side, of each book is the first letter or letters of the subjects in that volume. An index in the last volume of the set helps the reader find a topic. Cross-references note where further information on related topics may be found.

An **atlas** is a book of maps. The maps show the climate, the size, the population, and the natural features of various countries of the world. The atlas also contains facts on agriculture, industry, and natural resources.

An **almanac** gives information on general topics of interest, including business, sports, personalities and entertainers, transportation, agriculture, climate, education, and government. Almanacs are usually updated yearly to keep facts current.

Practice

Write the reference you would use to find these things.
1. the pronunciation of the word *Kenya*
   MODEL ▷ dictionary
2. a map showing Kenya and its neighbors
3. a summary of recent events in Kenya
4. the pronunciation of the word *Swahili*
5. an article on the history of Kenya
6. a list of current ambassadors to Kenya and other countries
7. an in-depth discussion of Kenya as a British colony
8. the names of the two highest mountains in Kenya
9. a chart showing how much Kenya trades with the United States
10. detailed information on the various tribes in Kenya
11. a map showing Kenya's agricultural wealth
12. the name of Kenya's present leader
13. a discussion of Kenya's political development
14. information about the annual amount of rainfall in Kenya
15. a map showing Kenya's major cities
16. a history of Kenya's culture
17. a map showing the major roads in Kenya
18. a list or chart showing the easiest crops to raise in Kenya

STUDY SKILLS

11 Using Newspapers

For a written record of the latest news, your best source is a daily or weekly newspaper. A good local or national newspaper has access to news sources all over the world. Most newspapers include the following kinds of information, presented in **articles.**

A **news story** is an article that gives information about a specific event. It reports what happened, who was involved, when and where the event took place, and how it happened. News stories present facts, not opinions.

A **feature** article also presents facts. It differs from a news story mainly in that it concentrates on only one or two angles, or aspects, of the story. These aspects, however, are covered in more depth than they would be covered in a news story. **Regular features** are newspaper columns that appear on certain days every week or every month. Examples of these are movie reviews, advice columns, and shopping features. Well-known reporters who have articles published in many newspapers usually have **by-lines,** which means that their names are printed with every article they write.

An **editorial** is an article expressing an opinion, usually that of one of the newspaper editors, about an issue in the news.

A **display advertisement,** which is not an article at all, contains an appeal to the reader to buy something. Display ads usually contain both writing and pictures to attract the reader's attention.

Practice

Read each description of newspaper information. Write whether it is a *news story,* a *feature,* an *editorial,* or a *display advertisement.*

1. an article giving the facts about a recent fire
   MODEL > news story
2. a review of a recent play
3. a column stating an opinion on a proposed highway
4. an account of the latest traffic accident in town
5. a paragraph appealing to the reader to buy Lox socks
6. a humorous story about a successful local comedian
7. the newspaper's advice for a particular candidate
8. an attempt to convince readers that "Yogurt is Yummy"
9. a behind-the-scenes account of a recent softball game
10. an opinion on conflicting facts in a murder case
11. a short description of a recent hiking-club outing
12. an explanation of the city's lack of low-income housing
13. a report on last week's town council meeting
14. a review of a new restaurant
15. a report on the launch of a space shuttle
16. an article on how to manage money
17. a paragraph and picture promoting a car dealership
18. an article about a new bill passed in the Senate

12 Using the *Readers' Guide to Periodical Literature*

Suppose you want information on a historic house that was first opened to the public about three months ago. You suspect that an article about the house appeared in a magazine or a newspaper, but you aren't sure exactly when. How do you find the article?

Your best bet is the *Readers' Guide to Periodical Literature,* found in any large library. Published every few months, the *Readers' Guide* indexes by subject the articles that appear in every major periodical. Checking one issue under "Historic Houses," you might find the following.

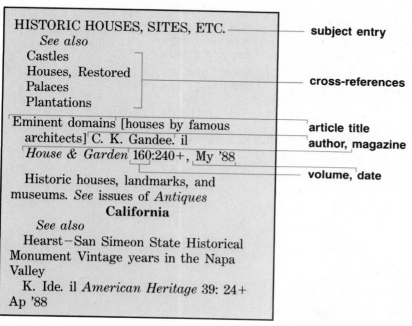

HISTORIC HOUSES, SITES, ETC. ——————— **subject entry**
   See also
  Castles
  Houses, Restored ——————— **cross-references**
  Palaces
  Plantations
Eminent domains [houses by famous ——————— **article title**
  architects] C. K. Gandee. il ——————— **author, magazine**
  House & Garden 160:240+, My '88 ——————— **volume, date**

Historic houses, landmarks, and museums. *See* issues of *Antiques*
        California
   See also
Hearst—San Simeon State Historical Monument Vintage years in the Napa Valley
  K. Ide. il *American Heritage* 39: 24+ Ap '88

Under the subject entry are listed cross-references to other kinds of historic places. Under these come references to specific articles on historic places, giving the title, the author, notations on illustrations, the name of the periodical, the volume number followed by a colon, the page or pages on which the article appears, and, finally, the issue of the periodical.

Practice

Using the subject entry above, write the information requested below.

1. location of the Hearst—San Simeon State Historical Monument
> MODEL   California

2. other subject entries for articles on historic houses
3. author of an article on houses by famous architects
4. date of the article about the Napa Valley
5. name of the magazine that features the Napa Valley article
6. cross-reference for an article about Buckingham Palace
7. magazine referred to for other articles about landmarks

13 Using Records and Cassette Tapes

In recent years, record and tape players have become much more sophisticated. As a result, more and more educational and entertaining material is found on records and tapes. Most libraries own huge collections of recordings.

Finding a record or a cassette tape in the library is just like finding a book. Information on a library's tape and record collection is usually found in a card catalogue that is separate from the book card catalogue. Study this sample card.

The recording form information tells us that the item consists of two long-playing 12-inch records. The description of contents notes that the record has spoken words on Mozart's life as well as recordings of his music.

Practice

Use the sample catalogue card below to answer the questions.

> J
> C
> M681m Music to Have Fun By [sound
>   recording] RCA DEK 1–004–0042
>   [1973] 2 cassettes. National Symphony
>   Orchestra; Howard Mitchell,
>   conductor. Contents. v. 1, Tchaikovsky,
>   Vaughan Williams, Herbert, Bizet,
>   Grieg, MacDowell. v. 2, Copland,
>   Bizet, Cailliet, Gottschalk,
>   Menotti, Copland.

1. What is the call number of the item above?
   MODEL ▷ J-C-M681m
2. In what format was the material recorded?
3. What is the recording number?
4. When was the recording released?
5. Which orchestra is recorded, and who is its conductor?
6. Which composers appear more than once on the program?
7. In what two ways are the recordings *Music to Have Fun By* and *Wolfgang Amadeus Mozart: His Story and Music* different?

14 Using the Encyclopedia

An **encyclopedia** is a set of books, or volumes, containing articles, or entries, on many subjects. The articles are arranged in **alphabetical order.** Letters on the **spine,** or side, of each volume show that articles beginning with those letters can be found in that volume.

On each two-page spread of a volume are **guide words** indicating the first and last articles occurring on those pages. **Key words** that explain important ideas on a page are emphasized in many encyclopedias. An encyclopedia **index** usually includes **cross-references** to related entries.

Stamp Act	guide word
STAMP COLLECTING is one of the most popular hobbies in the world. Young and old, rich and not-so-rich in every country collect stamps.	main entry
How Stamps Differ Stamps may be printed by one of three methods: *relief,* *intaglio,* and *planographic.* They are highly colored.	subhead key words
See also POST OFFICE; STAMP	article cross-references

When you check the index under *Stamp collecting,* you will find the title, the volume, and the page number of the entry often followed by the volumes and the page numbers of related entries. Under *Stamp collecting,* for example, you may find a cross-reference to *Hobby (Collections).*

Practice

Answer the following questions. Refer to the example above.

1. Name one letter that would be found on the spine of the volume containing the article on stamp collecting.

MODEL ▷ *S*

2. Name two other entries that might appear on the same page as the article on stamp collecting.
3. Which key words describe the three types of printing?
4. Name a cross-reference that appears in the article.
5. Name a cross-reference that may appear in the index.
6. How are the articles in an encyclopedia arranged?
7. What is one book of a set of encyclopedias called?
8. What does the guide word on a left-hand page indicate?
9. What does the guide word on a right-hand page indicate?

15 Taking Notes

Taking notes is a helpful way of remembering what you read or hear. You should take notes when preparing to write a report or when studying for a test. When you take notes, you should **paraphrase** information, or put it into your own words. By doing this you show that you understand the material. Study this sample note card.

STUDY SKILLS

FLIGHT
How did the Wright brothers learn theory of flight?

read *Experiments in Soaring* by Otto Lilienthal
read magazine article by Octave Chanute
referred to these sources by Professor Langley at Smithsonian Institution
Both became excited by this reading.

The Wright Brothers by Quentin Reynolds, pages 97–99

The notes above were taken on a note card. Note cards are useful for organizing your notes. When all your information is recorded on cards, you can arrange them in the most logical order. Study these tips for taking good notes.

Tips for Taking Notes

1. Write the topic at the top of the card.
2. Sum up the main idea of each card in a heading.
   The heading can take the form of a question.
3. Record the most important facts and details.
4. Paraphrase the writer's ideas. Write in phrases rather than in sentences.
5. Record the source of your information.

Practice

Read the following story of another group of pioneers of flight—the group that developed *Daedalus,* a plane that set a new record for long-distance human-powered flight. Then make a note card with the most important information about the *Daedalus* itself.

The plane that broke the record for human-powered flight was designed by a team from MIT. The plane has a wingspan of 112 feet, an 11-foot propeller that makes 105 rpm, a body of polystyrene foam, and a weight of only 68 pounds. The "skin" of the plane is Mylar, a thin plastic film. Its propeller is turned by a pilot, a championship bicyclist, pushing bicycle pedals. Every turn of the pedals is translated into one and a half turns of the propeller. A small control stick helps the pilot move other parts of the plane.

---

16 Writing an Outline

Writers use outlines to plan reports and organize their ideas. An outline gives the main ideas and the important details about a topic in the order in which the writer wishes to discuss them. Study this outline. Notice that main ideas are introduced by Roman numerals and important details by capital letters. Notice that the entries are short and that they are similar in style.

A History of Jazz

  I. Sources
     A. West African music
     B. The West Indies
 II. New Orleans influences
     A. The cradle of jazz
     B. The French influence
     C. The Dixieland style
III. American influences
     A. The blues
     B. The spiritual
     C. Ragtime
     D. The work song
 IV. The Jazz Age and after
     A. Radio and the phonograph
     B. Chicago and New York
     C. The big band era
  V. Jazz styles
     A. Afro-Cuban
     B. Bop
     C. Cool jazz
     D. Recent styles

Tips for Writing Outlines

1. Use Roman numerals in front of main ideas. Use capital letters in front of important details. Place a period after each.
2. Indent each subdivision of a main idea.
3. Capitalize the first letter of each entry.
4. Keep outline entries short and parallel in structure. For example, do not use both sentence entries and phrase entries.
5. Make sure there are two or more entries per category. For example, do not write a *I* if there will be no *II* or an *A* if no *B* follows.

Practice

Use the sample outline to write answers to these questions.
1. Name the second main idea in the outline.
   MODEL > New Orleans influences
2. How many important details are given under *IV?*
3. In what order is the outline written?
4. How are the details under *III* parallel, or similar?
5. How does the outline follow tip 5?
6. If you were going to add a section on jazz in outer space, what Roman numeral would you use?
7. Suggest an entry to follow the new Roman numeral. Make it parallel with the others.
8. Suggest at least two important details for the entry.

17 Skimming and Scanning

Report writers have found skimming and scanning useful research skills. To **skim** is to look at material in order to note its general subject, its divisions, and its major headings. To **scan,** on the other hand, is to look quickly at a particular passage, searching for key words.

If you were skimming, you would check the title, the subheads, the illustrations and captions, the introduction, and the summary. Then, if you needed more information, you would look for the main ideas of individual paragraphs.

If you were scanning in an article about farming in China, you would glance down the pages, looking for such words as *farm, farming,* and *agriculture.*

Try skimming for the general subject of this article. Then scan it for details about cave formation.

How Natural Caves Are Formed

Most natural caves are made by water eating holes in underground rock. First, the water finds cracks in the rock and fills them up. As the acid in the water gradually dissolves the limestone over thousands of years, the cracks become larger and larger until they are huge holes filled with water. Then, as the earth changes, the water drains out of the hole, creating a cave.

The general subject can be seen in the title, "How Natural Caves Are Formed." Did you scan for the word *cave?*

Practice

Read the questions. Then scan this paragraph to answer them.

Many mountains in Hawaii have very thin coverings of topsoil. Because the islands are volcanic, there are vast areas of barren lava rock. There are some areas, however, especially in the valleys between mountains, where soil is dense. Because rainfall is heavy, these areas produce a great deal of vegetation. Bougainvillea, hibiscus, and oleanders bloom year-round, while poincianas and plumeria bloom in the spring and summer. The poinsettia, a favorite holiday flower, blooms during the fall and winter.

---

1. What is the general subject of the paragraph?
   MODEL▷ vegetation in Hawaii
2. Scan the paragraph for references to plants. How many different plants are mentioned?
3. Scan the paragraph for a reference to the summer season. In what context is it mentioned?
4. Scan the paragraph for a reference to barren areas. Why is some of Hawaii barren?
5. Scan the paragraph for the word *poincianas.* What is a poinciana?

18 Summarizing Information

A **summary** of a paragraph or a selection is a brief statement of its main idea and important details. Summarizing material often helps you to understand and remember it. When you write a summary, you have an excellent study aid to use as a review for a test.

Read the following paragraph to determine the main idea. Then think about what details you would include in a summary of the paragraph.

> During the early part of the Middle Ages, Western society reached great cultural heights under the rule of Charlemagne. Although Charlemagne never learned to write, he was deeply interested in education. Not satisfied with building schools throughout his empire, he even set up a school in his own palace at Aachen. To the school came learned teachers from all over Europe. For the first time, many ancient manuscripts from classical Greece and Rome were copied and then kept in libraries. Libraries sprang up throughout Europe. This new interest in learning has since been called the *Carolingian Renaissance.*

The main idea is that Charlemagne renewed interest in learning in Europe. Read the following summary of the paragraph.

> Charlemagne advanced education in Europe to such a degree that his times are now called the Carolingian Renaissance.

Notice that only the main idea and one important detail are given in the summary. Someone who has already read the paragraph might easily recall the other details upon reading the summary.

Practice

Write a sentence to summarize this paragraph.

> At the beginning of the Korean War, North Korea was a heavily industrialized country. It had many mineral resources, much of the developed water power on the peninsula, and roughly 90 percent of all the factories. North Korea had a government headed (as it still is today) by dictator Kim Il Sung. South Korea, on the other hand, had a democratically elected government headed by Syngman Rhee. Its economy was heavily agricultural, mainly because of its warmer climate and longer growing season. Its population was also more than twice that of North Korea.

19 Writing a Friendly Letter

Here is a letter written by Ben to his older sister Maggie, away at her freshman year in college.

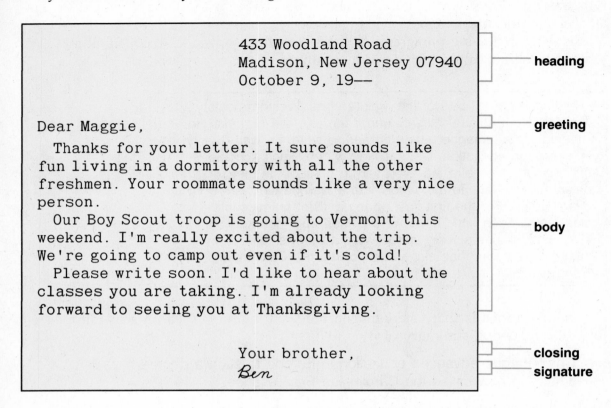

433 Woodland Road
Madison, New Jersey 07940
October 9, 19—— — heading

Dear Maggie, — greeting

  Thanks for your letter. It sure sounds like fun living in a dormitory with all the other freshmen. Your roommate sounds like a very nice person.
  Our Boy Scout troop is going to Vermont this weekend. I'm really excited about the trip. We're going to camp out even if it's cold!
  Please write soon. I'd like to hear about the classes you are taking. I'm already looking forward to seeing you at Thanksgiving. — body

Your brother,
Ben — closing / signature

A **friendly letter** is a letter written to someone you know well. You might write a friendly letter to exchange greetings and to share news. Friendly letters have five parts. The **heading** gives your address and the date on which the letter was written. The **greeting** addresses the person to whom the letter is being sent. The **body** of the letter contains the questions, the news, and the other information that you want the receiver to know. The **closing** is your "sign-off," or your way of saying that the letter has come to an end. The **signature,** as a rule, consists only of your first name.

Tips for Writing Friendly Letters

1. Write your address and the date in the upper right corner of the page.
2. Write the greeting under it and to the left.
3. Write the body in paragraph form.
4. Write your closing and signature in line with the heading.
5. Prepare an envelope with your address in the upper left corner and the receiver's address in the lower middle.

Practice

> 24 Primrose Lane
> Brevard, North Carolina 28712
> December 14, 19—
>
> Dear Emily,
>
>   I hope you are settled in your new home. I sure miss seeing you every day at school. Have you made any friends at your new school yet?
>
>   The picture you sent me of the Gulf of Mexico is beautiful. Do all the Florida sunsets look like that? It sure looks warm there. We had three inches of snow yesterday. It's cold, but the snow has given everyone the holiday spirit. I'll send you some pictures of the Smokey Mountains covered with snow.
>
>   I can't wait for your visit in January. We'll have a great time sled riding!
>
>   See you then.
>
>   Your friend,
>   Vanessa

A. Use this sample letter to answer the following questions.

  1. To whom is the letter addressed?

  MODEL▷ Emily, the writer's friend

  2. Where does the letter writer live? How do you know?

  3. What previous event gave the writer a reason to send the letter?

  4. What news is included in the body of the letter?

  5. What greeting is used in the letter?

  6. What closing is used in the letter?

B. Write a friendly letter to a relative or a close friend who lives in another city. Send some news and ask for news of the person to whom you are writing.

20 Writing a Business Letter

Read this sample business letter. Note how it differs from the friendly letter you have already studied.

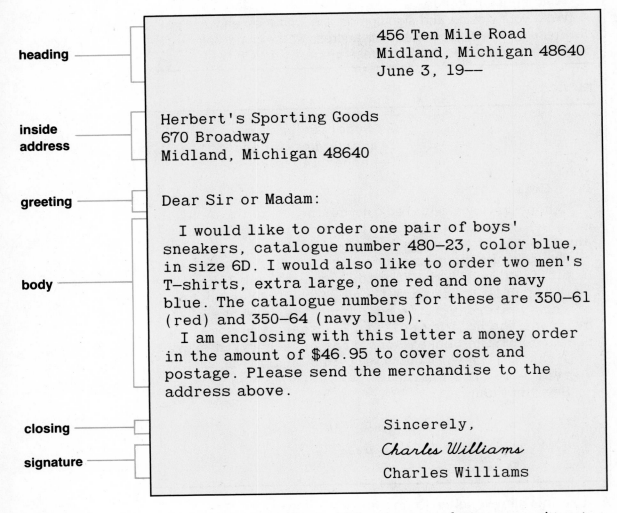

heading

456 Ten Mile Road
Midland, Michigan 48640
June 3, 19——

inside address

Herbert's Sporting Goods
670 Broadway
Midland, Michigan 48640

greeting

Dear Sir or Madam:

body

   I would like to order one pair of boys'
sneakers, catalogue number 480–23, color blue,
in size 6D. I would also like to order two men's
T–shirts, extra large, one red and one navy
blue. The catalogue numbers for these are 350–61
(red) and 350–64 (navy blue).
   I am enclosing with this letter a money order
in the amount of $46.95 to cover cost and
postage. Please send the merchandise to the
address above.

closing

Sincerely,

signature

Charles Williams
Charles Williams

There are many kinds of business letters. Most business letters are written to companies to order merchandise, to ask for information, to complain about faulty products or late delivery, or to request a refund of money sent. Although many companies send catalogues complete with order forms for listing what you want, you can also order by writing a simple business letter.

Notice that the writer uses the parts of the business letter correctly: **heading, inside address, greeting, body, closing,** and **signature.** Notice, too, that he is very careful about the way he orders the merchandise. He lists exact sizes and colors and gives the company's own catalogue number for each item. Then he calculates the exact cost of all three items and adds the shipping charges. Finally, since he may be too young to have his own checking account, he sends the money to the company by money order, which is both safe and convenient.

These tips will help you write business letters correctly.

Tips for Writing Business Letters
1. Write your address and the date in the upper right corner of the page.
2. Write the inside address below and to the left of the heading.
3. Write the greeting under the inside address.
4. Write the body in paragraph form.
5. Write your closing and your signature in line with the heading.
6. Prepare an envelope with your address in the upper left corner and the receiver's address in the lower middle.

Practice

A. Use the sample business letter to answer the following questions.

　1. To whom is the letter addressed?

MODEL Herbert's Sporting Goods

　2. What is the purpose of the letter?

　3. What is the writer ordering?

　4. Where should Herbert's Sporting Goods send the merchandise? How do you know?

　5. What greeting is used in the letter?

　6. What closing is used in the letter?

　7. How is the format of a business letter different from the format of a friendly letter?

B. Write a business letter ordering a boys' Windbreaker, catalogue number 670-18, color tan, size 12, cost $20.49 plus $2.50 for postage and handling. Use your name and address for the heading and signature. Use the address of any local sporting goods store for the inside address. Address the letter to the order department.

C. Write a business letter to John Hanes at the National Forestry Service, U.S. Department of the Interior, Washington, D.C. 20025. Request brochures or other printed material.

　　Explain that you are doing a project about our country's national forests. Ask for information about how the national forests are maintained and how they are protected from forest fires.

One kind of social note is the thank-you note. A thank-you note should thank the giver and express the writer's appreciation for a gift or a special favor.

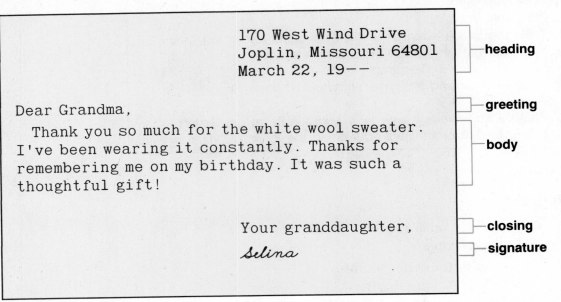

170 West Wind Drive
Joplin, Missouri 64801
March 22, 19—— — **heading**

Dear Grandma, — **greeting**
   Thank you so much for the white wool sweater. I've been wearing it constantly. Thanks for remembering me on my birthday. It was such a thoughtful gift! — **body**

                    Your granddaughter, — **closing**
                    Selina — **signature**

Thank-you notes, like other friendly letters, have five parts. Study these tips for writing social notes with correct content and format.

Tips for Writing Social Notes

1. Place the heading in the upper right corner. The heading contains the writer's address, including city, state, and ZIP code, and the date. Place commas correctly in the heading.
2. Place the greeting to the left of the heading. It begins with a capital letter and is followed by a comma.
3. Organize the body of the letter in paragraphs. Indent each paragraph. If you received a gift, be sure to mention the specific gift you received.
4. Write the closing in line with the heading. Capitalize the first word of the closing. Put a comma after the last word in the closing.
5. Begin the signature in line with the closing.

Practice

Write a thank-you note to a friend or a relative. Use the format shown in the model. Don't forget to show appreciation as well as thank the giver.

22 Writing a Book Report

A book report offers a partial summary of a book and gives the report writer's opinion on it. Study this sample book report. Then read the tips for writing book reports in the box that follows. Notice how the writer followed the tips.

> *In the Year of the Boar and Jackie Robinson* by Bette Bao Lord is the story of the writer's first year in the United States after leaving China in the 1940's. The setting is Brooklyn, New York, where Shirley (the narrator) and her family settle. The main characters, besides the narrator and her father and mother, are her piano teacher, Señora, and her classmates, Emily and Mabel. — introduction
>
> At first Shirley finds life in the United States difficult. Things improve, though, after Emily befriends her and after Mabel teaches her to play baseball. — plot summary
>
> I enjoyed this story because of its realistic characters, its humorous incidents (such as Shirley's early attempts at baseball), and its inspiring theme—that almost all problems can be overcome. — opinion and reasons

---

Tips for Writing Book Reports

1. Write an introduction that includes the title, the author, the setting, and the main characters in the book.
2. Write a plot summary of the main events in the book.
3. Write your opinion of the book, and give several reasons to support your point of view.

Practice

A. Use the sample book report and the **Tips for Writing Book Reports** to answer the following questions.

1. What information should a writer include in the introduction of a book report?

   MODEL ⟩ the title, the author, the setting, and the main characters

2. Does the writer of the sample book report include this information? List the information.
3. Who is the main character in the book? How do you know?
4. Should a writer include in the plot summary a discussion of the minor events in the book? Why or why not?
5. What information does the writer of the sample book report provide in the last paragraph?

B. Write a book report on a novel you enjoyed. Use the same format as in the sample above.

23 Studying for a Test

The thought of studying for tests need not make you nervous. You can be well prepared for any test by following a few simple rules.

Tips for Studying for Tests

1. Pay attention to lectures and class discussions. Take notes on the main ideas presented in class.
2. Ask questions when you do not understand something.
3. Organize your schedule so that you have enough time to prepare each subject well. Spend extra time on your most difficult subjects.
4. Work in a quiet, comfortable place with good lighting and no distractions.
5. Keep any needed books and supplies at hand to avoid unnecessary interruptions, but occasionally take a break to relax and refresh yourself. Be sure to get a good night's sleep.
6. Review all material by going over your study notes and the unit or chapter summaries in the book.
7. Try to predict what questions will be asked on the test.

If you are writing study notes for a test on the American Revolution, for example, try to write notes that answer the questions *who* (Britain, America); *what* (American Revolution); *when* (1776–1783); *where* (the American Colonies); and *why* (some possible reasons: no representation in British Parliament, restrictions on overseas trade of the colonies, and the inability of Britain to rule the colonies from such a great distance). The five *W* questions are excellent for a quick review later.

Practice

Read this description of how Dana studies for a test. Then rewrite the paragraph, correcting poor study habits.

Dana spends most of her time studying her two best subjects. She plays the radio in the background because it relaxes her. Frequently she gets up to get a snack or change stations on the radio. Dana reads the textbook over and over until she has whole passages memorized. If she doesn't understand something, she skips over it. When she has finished her review, she closes the book and writes out as much of the material as she can remember. Dana stays up past midnight studying for tests.

24 Taking a Test

The most important factor in taking a test happens well before the test itself. It is the daily preparation and study of the material to be tested that is critical. When the time comes to take the test, however, don't spoil that test preparation by making careless errors. Read and follow these tips for taking a test.

Tips for Taking Tests

1. Budget your time. Do not spend too much time on any one question.
2. Make sure you understand all directions and questions. If you are not sure, ask your teacher.
3. If you are answering questions on a separate sheet of paper, check to see that every answer is numbered correctly.
4. Skim the entire test before you start. If there are essay questions, read them all before you begin writing to make sure your answers do not repeat information needlessly.
5. Answer easy questions first, then hard ones, unless you are required to answer all questions in order.
6. If you are not sure of an answer, make an intelligent guess, especially if it is a multiple-choice question for which you can eliminate some of the choices.
7. Save a few minutes at the end of the test to proofread your answers.

Practice

For the statements that describe good test-taking methods, write *correct*. Rewrite statements that do not so that they are correct.

1. If you don't understand the directions, make a guess.

MODEL ▷ If you don't understand the directions, ask the teacher.

2. Make sure you have numbered each answer correctly.
3. Always answer questions in order.
4. If there are essay questions, read over each one before answering any.
5. Answer only those questions you are sure of.
6. If you finish the test early, do your homework for the next class.
7. Try to make intelligent guesses on multiple-choice questions you are not sure of.
8. Don't worry about reading all the questions first. Concentrate on one at a time.
9. Answer all the hard questions first and get them out of the way.

25 Taking an Essay Test

To respond well to an essay question, a student is expected to write a thorough answer that may involve more than a single paragraph. Before you accidentally write a wonderful response *to the wrong question,* make sure of what you are being asked to do. Study these tips.

STUDY SKILLS

Tips for Taking Essay Tests

1. Read each question carefully.
2. Watch for these clues to help you understand the question.
   Give an opinion. (Tell how you feel about something and give reasons to support your opinion.)
   Compare or **Contrast** (Show how two things are alike or different.)
   Explain (Give reasons to show why or how something happened; give causes and effects.)
   Describe (Tell how something looks or how it works.)
3. Recall what you know about the topic.
4. Organize ideas for your answer. Then write your response.
5. Read the question again, and look over your answer.
6. Make sure you have answered the question completely.

Read what this student wrote to answer an essay question about Eskimos. The question was *Explain how some Eskimos live close to the land.*

Some Eskimos still use the things of the land to live. These Eskimos use wood or sod to build their homes. They use coal or driftwood for fuel. They hunt and fish for food. The animal skins are used for coats, boots, and rugs. The ivory tusks of some animals are carved into needles or tools.

Practice

Use the tips and the student response in the box to answer these questions.

1. What key words in the question give the student a clue to the topic of the essay?
   MODEL > *Eskimos, close to the land*
2. What key word gives the student a clue about what he or she should write?
3. What is good about the first sentence of the answer?
4. What examples does the writer give to support the topic?
5. Write a sentence that might sum up the response and let the teacher know that the answer is finished.

26 Using Bar Graphs and Line Graphs

Bar graphs are often used to show differences in size or number among several items. The vertical axis, or the line going up the page, measures the size or amount of the item. The horizontal axis, or the line going across the page, describes the item being measured. Study this bar graph. Notice the title that shows what the graph represents.

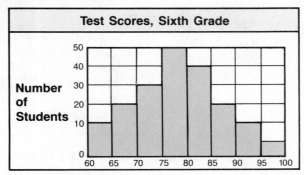

Line graphs like the one below are often used to show changes over time. The vertical axis names the thing that is changing. The horizontal axis describes the time period during which the thing changes. Study the graph. Again, notice the title that shows what the graph represents.

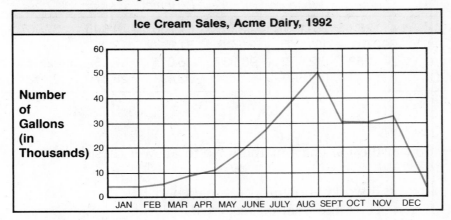

Practice

Use the graphs to answer these questions.

1. How many gallons of ice cream were sold by the end of August 1992?

MODEL ▷ 50 thousand

2. What happened to ice cream sales in September?

3. What happened to ice cream sales in December?

4. What was the most common test score range in the sixth grade?

5. Were there more scores in the 70−75 range or in the 85−90 range?

6. How many students earned scores in the lowest range?

7. How many students earned scores in the highest range?

27 Using Pie Charts and Tables

A **pie chart** shows how a whole is divided into parts. It uses a circle to represent the whole and wedges of the "pie" to show the parts. It is easy to see what part of the total each wedge represents. Pie charts are useful for comparing the relative sizes of different places or things, or for seeing how each relates to the whole.

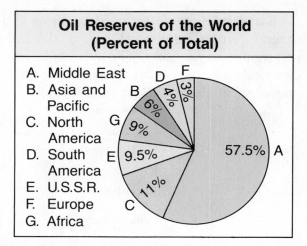

**Oil Reserves of the World
(Percent of Total)**

A. Middle East
B. Asia and Pacific
C. North America
D. South America
E. U.S.S.R.
F. Europe
G. Africa

A **table** is used to show numerical information on one topic. The advantage of a table is that it enables you to compare many different items at a glance.

City Populations by Race and Ethnic Origin						
City	Total	White	Black	Hispanic	Indian & Asian	Other
Austin, TX	410,262	261,166	42,118	64,766	4,645	37,567
Newark, NJ	390,512	101,417	191,743	61,254	2,927	33,171
Norfolk, VA	273,053	162,300	93,987	6,074	8,034	2,658
Oakland, CA	371,779	129,690	159,234	32,491	28,540	21,824

Practice

Use information in the pie chart or the table to answer these questions.

1. Which part of the world shown on the pie chart has the greatest percentage of the total oil reserves?
   MODEL> Middle East
2. Which part of the world shown on the pie chart has the smallest percentage of the total oil reserves?
3. Are the oil reserves of the Middle East greater or smaller than those of the rest of the world combined?
4. Which three areas combined have only about half as much oil as the area with the greatest percent?
5. Which city has the largest combined minority population?
6. Which city has the largest number of whites?
7. Which city has the largest number of Indians and Asians?
8. Which city has a Hispanic population larger than its black population?

28 Using a Map

A **map** is a scale drawing of an area, such as a country or a city. The **distance scale** on the map indicates how many miles or kilometers are represented by a certain measure on the map, such as an inch. Notice that on the map below, the distance scale measures one-fourth of an inch for each fifty miles. The **compass rose** shows which direction is north (and usually east, south, and west as well). Sometimes special marks, or **symbols,** are used, especially on geographical maps, to show areas devoted to certain crops or industries. The meaning of each symbol on a map is shown in a **legend,** or key, found in one of the corners of the map.

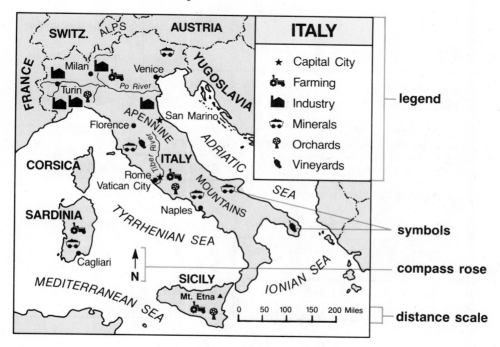

Practice

Using the map of Italy, answer these questions.

1. In which part of Italy is the most industry located?
MODEL ▷ in the North
2. About how long and how wide is the island of Sicily?
3. About how far is Sardinia from the mainland?
4. How is Sardinia different from Sicily with respect to resources?
5. In which river valley is most of Italy's business and industry located?
6. Which major bodies of water surround Italy?
7. Name the four countries that border Italy.
8. Give the name and location of one Italian mountain range.
9. Which river runs through Rome?
10. Which country is closest to Italy on the east?

29 Taking Messages and Using a Telephone Directory

Has this ever happened to you? You receive a telephone message. You believe the message is important, but you can't return the call because the person taking the message forgot to give you some information. When you take a message, remember to include the information shown in this model.

STUDY SKILLS

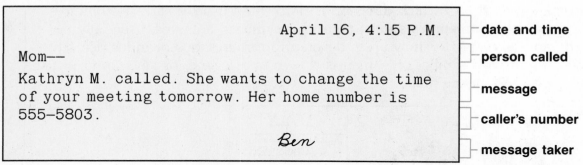

April 16, 4:15 P.M. — date and time

Mom—— — person called

Kathryn M. called. She wants to change the time of your meeting tomorrow. Her home number is 555-5803. — message / caller's number

Ben — message taker

Have you ever been unable to find a person or a business in the telephone directory because you weren't sure how to find the name? These tips may help.

Tips for Using a Telephone Directory	
1. Initials come before first names.	*Ashe, S.* is before *Ashe, Sam*
2. Abbreviations are listed as if they were spelled out.	*St. John's Hospital* is listed as though spelled *Saint John's Hospital*
3. Names that begin with initials are listed first in their alphabetical sections.	*RR Travel Agency* is listed before *Rand Travel Agency*
4. Numbers used as names are alphabetized as if they were spelled out.	*400 Club* is alphabetized as *Four Hundred Club*

Practice

A. Use the tips in the box to answer the following questions.
1. Where would you look for *L & Z Bookstore?*
   MODEL ▷ at the beginning of the *L* section
2. Would *St. Michael's Cemetery* be listed after *Squibb, Jeremy,* or after *Sain, J.?*
3. Would *Low, B.* or *Low, Benton* be listed first? Why?
4. Put the names of these businesses in the order in which you would find them in the telephone directory.
   Walker Shipping, Wallace's Lawn and Garden Shop, Wallsley's Bedding, W. and S. Bookstore

B. Rewrite this telephone message so that it contains more helpful information. (Make up the missing facts.)

Joe called. You can reach him at his cousin's.

30 Completing Forms

To complete a form, directions must be followed carefully. First, make sure you understand what the form is asking for. Read the form carefully before filling in any of the blanks. Next, neatly fill in the appropriate blank spaces. Make sure you have written each piece of information in the right place. Last, read over what you have written to be sure it is correct.

Jake is ordering some back issues of a magazine. Here is the form he filled out.

CIRCLE YEAR DESIRED 1989 1990 ⟨1991⟩ 1992 1993

SHIP TO:

NAME _____ Jake Iselin _____

ADDRESS _____ 2124 Adrian St. _____

CITY/STATE _____ Baton Rouge, LA _____ ZIP CODE _____ 70807 _____

Please send the following items:

_ 1 _ Annual Set(s) @ $34.95 each $ _34.95_

_____ Slipcase(s) @ $4.95 each $ _____

_ 1 _ Cumulative Index(es) @ $2.95 each $ _2.95_

Total Enclosed $ _37.90_

Practice

Copy and fill out this origami (paper-folding) contest application. Make up any information that is necessary.

NAME _____ AGE _____

ADDRESS _____ CITY _____

STATE _____ ZIP _____ TELEPHONE (___) _____

SCHOOL _____ GRADE _____

CITY _____ STATE _____

LOCAL NEWSPAPER _____

TITLE OF MODEL _____

IS IT ORIGINAL? ___ IF NOT, WHO DESIGNED IT? _____

_____

DID YOU LEARN THIS FROM A BOOK? _____ IF YES,
WHAT IS THE TITLE? _____

DID YOU LEARN THIS FROM A PERSON? _____ IF YES,
WHOM? _____

EXTRA PRACTICE

Contents

UNIT 1

1 Sentences *pages 28–29*

A. Identifying Complete Sentences For each group of words, write *sentence* or *not a sentence*.

1. Davis has always enjoyed reading.

MODEL ▷ sentence

2. The universe in the future.
3. Strange languages and customs of other worlds.
4. He had read several books by Robert Heinlein.
5. His favorite is *Red Planet,* a book about Mars.
6. I enjoy books about ancient civilizations.
7. Some books in old, dusty corners of libraries.
8. I especially liked *A Day in Old Rome.*
9. The homes, jobs, and customs of the people.
10. Books about the pharaohs and people of Egypt.
11. I always find interesting books in the library.

B. Making Complete Thoughts Choose the correct word group in parentheses to make a complete thought. Then write the sentence.

12. Our class (with many students, has a book club, of sixth grade).

MODEL ▷ has a book club

13. The members (very intelligent members, discuss their favorite books, meetings once a week).
14. Dan (read a mystery, our best student, reading).
15. He (with many great descriptions, an amateur detective, did not tell us the ending).
16. Darrell and Ivy (together a book of true adventures, spoke next, the story of Amelia Earhart's flight).
17. The meeting (lasted an hour, good, a success).
18. At the next meeting I (about a week from today, first on the program, will discuss a novel).

C. Writing Sentences Add words to complete each sentence. Write each sentence.

19. Bob

MODEL ▷ Bob joined our school's book club.

20. read books about snakes
21. like stories of adventure
22. Pam
23. like stories of magic and monsters
24. In the library I
25. reads about the stars of popular music
26. Many picture story books

2 Four Kinds of Sentences *pages 30–31*

A. Identifying Kinds of Sentences For each sentence, write *declarative, interrogative, imperative,* or *exclamatory.*

   1. Do animals understand us?
   MODEL > interrogative
   2. Animals don't actually understand the words we use.
   3. Do they understand our tone of voice?
   4. Call one of my cats.
   5. Here she comes!
   6. What is her name?
   7. Her name is Fleur de Lis.
   8. What should I do next?
   9. Talk to her softly and gently.
  10. What a loud purr she has!

B. Completing Sentences Choose the correct word group to form the kind of sentence stated in parentheses. Then write the sentence.

  11. many sea animals (declarative)
      do you know, please show me, can be trained
   MODEL > Many sea animals can be trained.
  12. animals at Sea World (declarative)
      obey their trainers, where are the, have you seen
  13. the dolphins and the killer whales (declarative)
      look at, in which pool are, respond to signals
  14. teach them (interrogative)
      what signals mean, trainers can, how do trainers
  15. this picture of a killer whale (imperative)
      where did you get, look at, I really like
  16. an exciting show that is (exclamatory)
      what, have you seen, is this

C. Writing Sentences Unscramble these word groups and add words to form the kind of sentence in parentheses.

  17. other whales each talk (interrogative)
   MODEL > How do whales talk to each other?
  18. songs called noises whales (declarative)
  19. TV whales programs I (declarative)
  20. list programs please TV (imperative)
  21. scientists whales boats studying (declarative)
  22. voices record microphone (interrogative)
  23. sound listen (imperative)
  24. strange sounds beautiful (exclamatory)

3 Subjects and Predicates *pages 32–33*

A. Identifying the Parts of Sentences Write each sentence. Draw a vertical line between the subject and the predicate.

    1. Tim talks on the phone every day.

    MODEL ⟩ Tim|talks on the phone every day.

    2. My friend Alison calls me up every afternoon.

    3. We talk about the day's happenings at school.

    4. Mom allows me to talk on the phone for 15 minutes.

    5. My mom's parents didn't have a phone until 1945.

    6. That must have been terrible!

    7. Dad has a cellular phone in his car.

    8. He communicates with his office every day.

    9. He calls the office on the way to sales meetings.

    10. The office gives him the latest information.

    11. His statistics are always up-to-date.

B. Completing Sentences Add a subject or a predicate to complete each sentence. Write the sentence. Then write *subject* or *predicate* to show what you added.

    12. _____ is a useful communication tool.

    MODEL ⟩ A telephone is a useful communication tool.   subject

    13. Other methods of communication _____.

    14. Television signals _____.

    15. _____ can watch TV shows from the United States.

    16. Satellites in space _____.

    17. _____ was not as fast or easy in earlier times.

    18. Pony express riders _____.

    19. _____ later carried mail in their freight cars.

    20. The telegraph, an even later invention, _____.

    21. Phonograph records _____.

C. Writing Sentences with Subjects and Predicates Use the word groups to write complete sentences. Draw a vertical line between the subject and the predicate of each sentence.

    22. photographs/blurry

    MODEL ⟩ Some of my first photographs|were blurry.

    23. airplanes/mail

    24. large packages/sea

    25. cargoes of grain/by barge

    26. mom/our computer

    27. Language Arts assignments/home computer

    28. family members/computer

    29. family/every evening

    30. watched/tennis tournament

4 Complete and Simple Subjects *pages 34–35*

A. Identifying Complete and Simple Subjects Write each sentence. Underline the complete subject once and the simple subject twice.

1. My mother can speak four languages.

MODEL ▷ <u><u>My mother</u> can speak four languages.</u>

2. Some people can speak nine or ten languages.
3. My favorite aunt can speak several languages.
4. Aunt Jenny works for the government.
5. A friend of hers works for the same department.
6. Between them, they speak eight languages.
7. A neighbor works for a large shipping company.
8. He started in the company as a delivery person.
9. The ambitious youth went to night school.
10. Soon he was promoted to assistant manager.

B. Completing Sentences with Simple Subjects Write a simple subject for each sentence.

11. _____ should understand each other.

MODEL ▷ People

12. Many _____ of the world speak French at home.
13. _____ may live in North America, Europe, or Asia.
14. Their _____ is a rhythmic, flowing one.
15. _____ is one of the Romance languages.
16. Of all the languages, _____ is my favorite.
17. _____ seems to me the most difficult language.
18. Perhaps someday the _____ will be a better place.
19. _____ from all countries will talk to each other.
20. A new _____ of friendship will bring peace.

C. Writing Sentences with Complete Subjects Complete each sentence by adding a complete subject. Write each sentence. Underline each simple subject.

21. _____ speak different languages.

MODEL ▷ My <u>parents</u> speak different languages.

22. _____ learned to speak both Spanish and French.
23. _____ taught me English.
24. _____ have taught me the value of my abilities.
25. _____ were having an argument one day.
26. _____ speaks Spanish and just a little English.
27. _____ learned only French in his school in Haiti.
28. _____ could completely understand the other.
29. _____ listened to them one at a time.
30. _____ straightened out their misunderstanding.

5 Complete and Simple Predicates *pages 36–37*

A. **Identifying Complete and Simple Predicates** Write each sentence. Underline the complete predicate once and the simple predicate twice.

1. Ron wrote a letter to his cousin Ed.

MODEL⟩ Ron <u>wrote a letter to his cousin Ed</u>.

2. Ron Moeller lives in St. Louis, Missouri.

3. Ed Simpson lives in Houston, Texas.

4. Both boys love the game of baseball.

5. In his letter, Ron teased Ed about the Houston team.

6. The St. Louis Cardinals beat the Houston Astros.

7. Later, the Cardinals played the Astros again.

8. Ed had just received Ron's letter.

9. Ed wanted the Astros to win the second game.

10. Then he could write a letter about it to Ron.

B. **Writing Simple Predicates for Sentences** Write a simple predicate for each of these sentences.

11. Mr. Moeller _____ an executive.

MODEL⟩ is

12. He _____ many business letters.

13. At home Mr. Moeller _____ a computer.

14. He _____ letters to people all over the world.

15. The letters _____ always polite but direct.

16. He _____ many deals for his company by mail.

17. His company _____ his excellent work.

18. Sometimes Ron and Amy _____ their dad's computer.

19. They _____ letters to friends.

C. **Writing Sentences with Complete Predicates** Imagine that you are Ron's cousin Ed. Write a complete predicate for each word group. Write each sentence. Underline each simple predicate.

20. I _____ Cousin Ron's letters promptly.

MODEL⟩ I <u>answer</u> Cousin Ron's letters promptly.

21. He _____.

22. Good old Ron _____.

23. In response to his last letter, I _____.

24. Maybe I _____.

25. Actually, he _____.

26. Our family _____.

27. Cousin Ron _____.

28. We _____.

6 Word Order in Sentences *pages 38–39*

A. Identifying Word Order in Sentences Read each sentence. Write *natural* if it is in natural word order and *inverted* if it is in inverted word order.

1. A contented purr came from deep within the kitten.
   MODEL ▷ natural
2. I showed a film to my sister's club.
3. The animal movie made them happy.
4. On the blanket lie nine kittens.
5. Last month they were born.
6. Nearby hovers the mother cat.
7. All over each other tumble the clumsy kittens.
8. "Meow, meow," mew the kittens.
9. At the first sound, the mother awakens.
10. Into the box leaps the graceful gray cat.
11. She grooms the tiny babies with her pink tongue.

B. Changing Word Order in Sentences Change sentences in natural word order to inverted word order. Change those in inverted word order to natural word order. Write each new sentence.

12. Near her sleeping kittens sits the mother.
    MODEL ▷ The mother sits near her sleeping kittens.
13. Into a furry ball curls each little kitten.
14. In groups of two or three lie the kittens.
15. Off the blanket rolls a black kitten.
16. The little kitten scrambles to his feet.
17. His mother rushes to his rescue.

C. Completing Sentences in Natural and Inverted Order Write a sentence using each word group. Write the sentence using the kind of word order in parentheses.

18. with bright, shining eyes (inverted)
    MODEL ▷ With bright, shining eyes gaze the kittens.
19. with their eyes now open (natural)
20. after the misbehaving ones (inverted)
21. from under the bed (inverted)
22. in her mouth (natural)
23. on top of her brothers and sisters (inverted)
24. in the kitchen (natural)
25. using her rough tongue (natural)
26. a few weeks from now (natural)
27. searches the mother (inverted)
28. scamper the kittens (inverted)
29. up the stairs (inverted)
30. before they reached the top (natural)

7 Finding Subjects of Sentences pages 40–41

A. Identifying Simple Subjects Write the simple subject in each sentence. If the subject is *you* (understood), write (*you*).

1. Here is Lisa now.

MODEL ▷ Lisa

2. How gracefully Olympic champions compete!
3. Was it Lisa who surprised her community?
4. How hard the gymnasts have worked!
5. For six years Mrs. Cohen has coached her.
6. "Good luck," yells her best friend.
7. Watch her carefully now.
8. How have her competitors scored?
9. Into the air from the high bar soars Bob.
10. From the television viewer comes a gasp.
11. How does he make those leaps?

B. Writing Subjects of Interrogative and Imperative Sentences Complete each sentence by adding a complete subject. Underline each simple subject. If the subject is *you* (understood), write (*you*).

12. Has _____ been chosen for the team yet?

MODEL ▷ little <u>Lisa</u>

13. _____ all from this state?
14. How old _____?
15. _____ what the coach taught you.
16. _____ do well on the floor exercises?
17. _____ until the end of the special television program.

C. Writing Special Kinds of Sentences Follow the directions for each sentence. Underline each simple subject.

18. Write an interrogative sentence beginning with *Where*.

MODEL ▷ Where will the new <u>gym</u> be built?

19. Write a declarative sentence beginning with *There is*.
20. Write an interrogative sentence ending with *the championship last year?*
21. Write an interrogative sentence beginning with *What*.
22. Write an imperative sentence ending with *when the meet begins*.
23. Write an interrogative sentence beginning with *How*.
24. Write a declarative sentence beginning with *Here are*.
25. Write an imperative sentence ending with *your program*.
26. Write an interrogative sentence beginning with *Who*.
27. Write an interrogative sentence beginning with *Why*.

8 Compound Subjects *pages 42–43*

A. Identifying Compound Subjects   Write *compound subject* if a sentence has a compound subject. Write *no compound subject* if it does not.

1. Rita, Ann, and Kerry are in the drama club.
MODEL▷ compound subject
2. Many students enjoy performing on stage.
3. Kerry and Rita like to do musical comedies.
4. Ann and Toshio prefer Shakespeare's plays.
5. Most plays have three acts.
6. *Fiddler on the Roof* and *Cats* were done last year.
7. Parents and friends came to the shows.
8. Members of the drama club sold tickets.
9. Sets and costumes were made by club members.
10. The actors and actresses attended many rehearsals.
11. Both plays were very successful.

B. Writing Compound Subjects Correctly   Write a compound subject to complete each sentence.

12. _____ and _____ are in our next show.
MODEL▷ Toshio and Ann
13. _____ and _____ are the characters they play.
14. Tomorrow _____ and _____ are going to try out.
15. _____ and _____ are designing the costumes.
16. _____, _____, and _____ are their colors.
17. A _____ and a _____ will be props on the stage.

C. Expanding Sentences with Compound Subjects   Expand each sentence by adding the number of subjects noted in parentheses to give the sentence a compound subject. Write the new sentence. Punctuate each sentence correctly.

18. Al sang in a past show. (Add two subjects.)
MODEL▷ Al, Rose, and Toshio sang in a past show.
19. Rose starred in *The Music Man*. (Add one subject.)
20. *The Music Man* required actors with good voices. (Add one subject.)
21. Some boys do sing on stage. (Add one subject.)
22. *Cats* had music everyone liked. (Add two subjects.)
23. The audience cheered after Act 1. (Add one subject.)
24. Ann danced well in *Cats*. (Add two subjects.)
25. She has danced for ten years. (Add one subject.)
26. Many students' little sisters came to see *Cats*. (Add one subject.)
27. The teachers were proud of us. (Add two subjects.)

9 Compound Predicates *pages 44–45*

A. Identifying Compound Predicates   Write *compound predicate* if a sentence has a compound predicate. Write *no compound predicate* if it does not.

1. Fortunata joined the creative writing group and wrote her first persuasive essay.
MODEL▷ compound predicate
2. Group members meet each week and discuss writing.
3. Both fiction and nonfiction are submitted.
4. David wrote a short story and read it to the group.
5. The members enjoyed it and especially liked the ending.
6. The hero saves his brother and frees a prisoner.
7. Mrs. Hart often attends the meetings.
8. She listens to the readings and makes suggestions.
9. Sometimes members agree and edit their work.
10. The club will publish a literary magazine.
11. The best work will be chosen and published.

B. Writing Compound Predicates   Complete each sentence by adding another predicate.

12. Roosevelt joined the math club and _____ the science club as well.
MODEL▷ may join
13. The science club performs experiments and _____ on field trips.
14. They visited a power plant and _____ how electricity is generated.
15. In the fall they work hard and _____ a science fair.
16. Members plan and _____ science projects.
17. These are displayed and _____ by the school.

C. Expanding Sentences   Expand each sentence by adding the number of predicates noted in parentheses. Write the new sentence. Punctuate each sentence correctly.

18. Alison sings in the school chorus. (Add two predicates.)
MODEL▷ Alison sings in the school chorus, solos in a choir, and sometimes accompanies both groups on the piano.
19. Some students join clubs. (Add one predicate.)
20. Justin takes karate lessons. (Add two predicates.)
21. He gave a karate show. (Add one predicate.)
22. Jan baby-sits for her cousin. (Add two predicates.)
23. She likes small children. (Add one predicate.)
24. The twins play tennis. (Add one predicate.)

10 Compound Sentences pages 46–47

A. **Identifying Compound Sentences**   Write *compound sentence* if a sentence is compound. Write *not a compound sentence* if a sentence is not compound.

1. Sandy is planning a career in broadcasting, but Dan prefers construction.
MODEL⟩ compound sentence
2. Chris is interested in television or psychology.
3. His mother agrees, but his father wants him to join the army.
4. Michele likes books and wants to be a librarian.
5. She could also work in a store, or she could teach.
6. Al and Sam live in the city and dream of reporting on it.
7. Sam writes well, while Al is skilled with a video camera.
8. Sometimes they help with the school's media club.

B. **Combining Sentences to Make Compound Sentences**
Combine each sentence pair into one compound sentence. Write the compound sentence. Underline each simple sentence.

9. Alan and Betsy may take public speaking next year. They may change their minds.
MODEL⟩ Alan and Betsy may take public speaking next year, but they may change their minds.
10. Public speaking is useful. It is difficult to do well.
11. Sarah wrote a speech. She delivered it to the Chamber of Commerce.
12. The school will offer a parent-child communication course. Mr. and Mrs. Lopez will be teaching the class.
13. They will use real-life situations. The class is excited.
14. Jake is taking the course. Hope does not have time.

C. **Writing and Punctuating Compound Sentences**   Add a simple sentence to each existing sentence to make a compound sentence. Write the compound sentence. Punctuate the compound sentences correctly.

15. Pablo once liked art classes best.
MODEL⟩ Pablo once liked art classes best, and now he has become a famous artist.
16. Classes with field trips are always popular.
17. Ms. Anders takes her students to city hall.
18. Students must be polite on trips.
19. The journalism class went to a television studio.
20. Seeing the equipment delighted most students.

11 Avoiding Sentence Fragments and Run-on Sentences *pages 48–49*

A. Identifying Sentences and Sentence Errors Write *sentence, sentence fragment,* or *run-on sentence* for each group of words.

1. Could play a vital role.
   > MODEL   sentence fragment
2. Computers are important have you ever used one?
3. Computers are used by all kinds of businesses.
4. Over one million computers are in use in the United States they store data.
5. Businesses of every kind.
6. Many supermarkets have computerized their checkout systems.
7. The products containing bar codes.
8. The clerk passed the box over the scanner it made a beep sound.
9. Computers are vital to civil engineers.
10. They assist engineers in making calculations they analyze many factors.
11. Computers storing scientific research data.

B. Correcting Sentence Fragments Rewrite each sentence fragment as a complete sentence.

12. the paintings on the walls of the caves
    > MODEL   The paintings on the walls of the caves told many tales.
13. were crude but expressive
14. primitive weapons and tools
15. at a time of prosperity
16. a period of floods
17. storms, lightning, and earthquakes

C. Correcting Run-on Sentences Correct each run-on sentence according to the directions in parentheses. Remember to punctuate your new sentences correctly.

18. Early people probably used sounds words came later. (Write a compound sentence with a connecting word.)
    > MODEL   Early people probably used sounds, and words came later.
19. A caveman may have heard an animal howl he imitated the sound. (Write a sentence with a compound predicate.)
20. The invention of language was important it allowed people to communicate on a higher level. (Write a compound sentence with a connecting word.)
21. Pictures stood for ideas eventually symbols stood for ideas. (Write a sentence with a compound subject.)
22. Sounds could be written as symbols people could communicate with the symbols. (Write a compound sentence with a connecting word.)

1 Nouns *pages 80–81*

A. Identifying Nouns List the nouns in each sentence.

1. The United States has rugged mountains and vast deserts.

  MODEL ⟩ United States, mountains, deserts

2. Parks are for people who like the outdoors.
3. These scenic spots are protected by the government.
4. There are sanctuaries for wildlife at the seashore.
5. Some locations have caves for exploration.
6. Campsites often have tents or cabins for visitors.
7. My brother took a raft down the river through some rapids.
8. He had food, water, a compass, and a first-aid kit.
9. The paddling gave him blisters and a sore back.
10. The wilderness offers fresh air and clear streams.

B. Classifying Nouns List the nouns in each sentence. Then write *person, place, thing,* or *idea* to tell what each noun names.

11. Columbus held the belief that ships could reach India by sailing westward.

  MODEL ⟩ Columbus—person; belief—idea; ships—things; India—place

12. Queen Isabella of Spain had money for his voyage.
13. The ideas of the explorer were odd to his sailors.
14. Their fear grew as the ships sailed far from home.
15. The sighting of land brought joy to the crew.
16. Columbus showed bravery and perseverance during the journey.

C. Writing Nouns in Sentences Write each sentence. Identify each noun. Then rewrite each sentence by substituting a different noun of the same kind for each noun you have identified.

17. Carla visited the Trevi Fountain in Rome.

  MODEL ⟩ Iola visited the Lincoln Memorial in Washington.

18. Tourists come to Florida each winter.
19. People arrive by train in December.
20. The beach is crowded with swimmers and sunbathers.
21. The lifeguard blows his whistle.
22. St. Augustine is an old city with a Spanish fort.
23. Cape Canaveral is the home of the space program.
24. Rick likes Key West in southern Florida.
25. On a fishing trip, his mom caught a swordfish.
26. His dad showed surprise at the size of the catch.

2 Common and Proper Nouns *pages 82–83*

A. Identifying Common and Proper Nouns List the nouns in each sentence. Then label each *C* for *common noun* or *P* for *proper noun*.

1. Old Faithful is a geyser, or spout of water.

MODEL▷ Old Faithful—P; geyser—C; spout—C; water—C

2. Many tourists visit this site in Yellowstone National Park.

3. Grand Teton is another national park in Wyoming.

4. Mr. Nye is a guide in Zion National Park in Utah.

5. Bryce Canyon is another great sight in that state.

6. Rangers protect both campers and animals.

7. My uncle took me to Salt Lake City on the train.

8. We carried water in the Great Salt Lake Desert.

B. Writing Nouns Correctly Choose a word from those listed below that will complete each sentence. Write the word. Then label it *common* or *proper*.

"Old Muddy"	plain	rivers
Colorado	Gulf of Mexico	Rockies

9. Old mountains, like the Appalachians, are rounded, but new mountains, such as the _____ , are jagged.

MODEL▷ Rockies—proper

10. Like mountains, _____ also have a life cycle.

11. The _____ is the river that carves the Grand Canyon.

12. The Mississippi River wanders over a flat _____.

13. This river has the nickname _____.

14. It flows into the _____.

C. Writing Common and Proper Nouns in Sentences Form sentences by adding endings that include common and/or proper nouns. Write the sentences. Underline the common nouns once, and underline the proper nouns twice.

15. The rivers of the world _____.

MODEL▷ The <u>rivers</u> of the <u>world</u>, such as the <u>Ohio</u>, provide <u>transportation</u> for <u>people</u>.

16. The Nile River _____.

17. Each year it floods _____.

18. Near the river _____.

19. Riverboats carry sightseers _____.

20. The Amazon River is _____.

21. It flows _____.

22. In times past _____.

23. Explorers often _____.

3 Capitalization of Proper Nouns *pages 84–85*

A. Identifying Correct Capitalization of Proper Nouns Choose and write the correct form of the noun in parentheses.

1. The (Bay Of Campeche, bay of Campeche, Bay of Campeche) forms Mexico's eastern border.

MODEL> Bay of Campeche

2. The (Sea of Marmara, sea of Marmara, Sea Of Marmara) separates the European and the Asian sections of Turkey.

3. The Philippines lie between the (south China sea, South China Sea) and the Pacific Ocean.

4. The Ruwenzori Mountains of East Africa are also called the (Mountains of the moon, Mountains Of The Moon, Mountains of the Moon).

5. (Truth Or Consequences, Truth or Consequences) is a town in (new Mexico, New Mexico, new mexico).

6. The (Mason-dixon line, Mason-Dixon line, mason-Dixon Line) once divided the North and the South.

B. Capitalizing Proper Nouns Write each sentence. Add capital letters to make it correct.

7. The u.s. department of the interior oversees the well-being of our national resources.

MODEL> The U.S. Department of the Interior oversees the well-being of our natural resources.

8. For years Smokey the bear has fought forest fires.

9. The environmental protection agency works to end pollution.

10. Crowds are a problem in yosemite national park.

11. The lowest point in the united states is death valley.

12. The rio grande separates texas from mexico.

C. Writing Proper Nouns in Sentences Write each sentence. Add an ending that includes a proper noun to each sentence.

13. The redwood trees _____.

MODEL> The redwood trees in Sequoia National Park live for hundreds of years.

14. The peaks of _____.

15. At the mouth of _____.

16. The largest of the _____.

17. A string of islands _____.

18. A well-known bridge _____.

19. Alligators live in _____.

20. If you like to explore caves, _____.

21. From an airplane _____.

22. The giant cactus survives _____.

23. Earthquakes often occur _____.

24. History buffs should try _____.

25. Those who love sailing might want to visit _____.

EXTRA PRACTICE

UNIT 2

4 Abbreviations *pages 86–87*

A. Identifying Abbreviations   Write the abbreviation(s) in each sentence.

1. Mr. Marwick took the class to the Mt. Palomar Observatory on Mar. 2.

MODEL> Mr., Mt., Mar.

2. The distance from Earth to the moon is 238,900 mi.
3. In 1609 A.D. Galileo saw the moon with a telescope.
4. The U.S.S.R. launched Sputnik on Oct. 4, 1957.
5. The first U.S. satellite went up on Jan. 31, 1958.
6. Col. John Glenn was a famous astronaut.
7. Neil A. Armstrong was the first man on the moon.
8. Each of the space shuttle engines weighs 7,000 lbs.
9. The new space shuttle was launched from Cape Canaveral, FL.
10. Edwin Aldrin, Jr., piloted the lunar module.
11. Astronauts train in Huntsville, AL.

B. Using the Correct Forms of Common Abbreviations   Write the correct form of each abbreviation from the choices in parentheses.

12. At 11:03 (AM, A.m., A.M.) today, there will be a total eclipse of the sun.

MODEL> A.M.

13. Scientists at the observatory on Elm Street (S.W., s.w., SW) will monitor it through their telescopes.
14. A lunar eclipse began at 10:00 (PM, P.M., P.m.).
15. We watched it with (Mist., mr., Mr.) Williams.
16. He teaches science at West (Jr., jr, Jun.) High.
17. His class visited Washington, (d.c., Dc, D.C.).

C. Using Abbreviations in Sentences   Read each sentence. Write the correct abbreviation or initial for each underlined word or words.

18. The United States of America maintains two major space centers.

MODEL> U.S.A.

19. The Union of Soviet Socialist Republics also has a space program.
20. The Harris Corporation supplies several components for the space shuttle.
21. Shuttles are launched from the John Fitzgerald Kennedy Space Center.
22. Neptune was discovered on September 23, 1846.
23. The sun set at 7:35 in the evening.
24. In 1682 Mister Halley observed the path of a comet.
25. Senator John Glenn was once an astronaut.
26. Doctor Carl Sagan writes popular books about space.
27. The moon can still be seen at 8:00 in the morning.

5 Singular and Plural Nouns *pages 88–89*

A. Identifying Nouns as Singular or Plural   List each noun. Label the singular nouns *S* and the plural nouns *P*.

1. The leaders of some African tribes are females.
   MODEL⟩ leaders—P; tribes—P; females—P
2. Shepherds of the Issa tribe of Somalia are nomads.
3. A dry climate and poor soil yield little vegetation.
4. Tribe members always move their herds to new land.
5. The Yorubas set up a powerful kingdom in Africa.
6. Yoruba works of art are prized by collectors.
7. Their lands in Nigeria contain forests and farms.
8. Fisheries on the coast are a source of income.
9. The Watusis are often more than 78 inches tall.
10. Pygmies of the Ituri Forest are less than 60 inches tall.
11. Each tribe has its language, history, and customs.

B. Classifying Nouns in Sentences   List the nouns in each sentence. Label the singular nouns *S* and the plural nouns *P*.

12. Some North Americans live near the Arctic Circle.
    MODEL⟩ North Americans—P; Arctic Circle—S
13. The groups live primarily in Alaska, Canada, and Greenland.
14. Alaskan Yupiks are also Arctic peoples.
15. The Lapps live in northern Scandinavia.
16. Other groups live in the Arctic regions of Russia.
17. These humans have mastered life in one of the most inhospitable areas on Earth.

C. Writing Plural Nouns in Sentences   Write each sentence. Complete each one with the correct plural form of each singular noun in parentheses.

18. (Child) _____ who stop at (oasis) _____ eat
    (date) _____ for their (lunch) _____.
    MODEL⟩ Children who stop at oases eat dates for their lunches.
19. The Bedouin are the desert (tribesman) _____ of
    North African and Arabian (country) _____.
20. Some live in (city) _____ or (village) _____.
21. Traditional (man) _____ and (woman) _____ prefer life
    in the desert.
22. (Child) _____ and (sheep) _____ reach the well.
23. Camels eat the (leaf) _____ of (bush) _____.

UNIT 2

6 More Plural Nouns pages 90–91

A. Forming Plural Nouns Write the plural form of each singular noun.

1. chef

MODEL> chefs

2. pinto   4. sheep   6. taco   8. alto   10. man
3. cliff   5. bronco   7. self   9. half   11. sombrero

B. Spelling Plural Nouns Correctly Choose and write the correct form of each plural noun shown in parentheses.

12. Explorers in Kansas found (deers, deer, deeres) and (moose, mooses, meese) plentiful.

MODEL> deer, moose

13. Early settlers in the Midwest found streams teeming with (salmons, salmon, salmones).
14. Barbed-wire fences angered the (cattlemans, cattlemen, cattlesman).
15. They fought with (sheeps, sheepes, sheep) owners.
16. (Burroes, Burro, Burros) were used as pack animals.
17. (Childs, Childrens, Children) of pioneers often worked as hard as adults.

C. Writing Plural Nouns in Sentences Write sentences as directed.

18. Write a sentence using the plural of *half.*

MODEL> Rough wooden fences divide the two halves of the old homestead.

19. Write a sentence about plowing in the days before modern plows were invented. Use the plural of *ox.*
20. Write a sentence about a dense, green forest. Use the plural of *elk.*
21. Write a sentence using the plural of *fish.*
22. Write a sentence about grain stored in a silo. Use the plural of *mouse.*
23. Write a sentence about country food. Use the plural of *half.*
24. Write a sentence about flocks of birds. Use the plural of *goose.*
25. Write a sentence using the plural of *fox.*
26. Write a sentence about wild birds that live in the woods. Use the plural of *turkey.*
27. Write a sentence using the plural of *donkey.*
28. Write a sentence using the plural of *calf.*

UNIT 2

7 Possessive Nouns *pages 92–93*

A. Identifying Possessive Nouns   Write the possessive noun or nouns in each sentence.

1. Saturn's rings contain gases and ice crystals.

MODEL ▷ Saturn's

2. The rings' widths vary, as do their colors.
3. Some of Jupiter's moons are quite small.
4. The moon's surface is pitted with craters.
5. Mercury's temperature is the hottest.
6. It is the sun's closest neighbor.
7. Uranus's density is less than our planet's.
8. Copernicus's theory that the planets orbit the sun is correct.
9. Venus's distance from Earth is 25 million miles.
10. Microwave beams' reflections help to study space.
11. Astronomers' discoveries take years to confirm.

B. Forming Possessive Nouns   Write the possessive form in parentheses that is correct for each sentence.

12. The (Smith's, Smiths's, Smiths') youngest son is an astronaut.

MODEL ▷ Smiths'

13. Mr. (Ryan's, Ryans', Ryans) class saw Sally Ride.
14. The (shuttle's, shuttles, shuttles') orbit is good.
15. These (womens', women's, woman's) designs will be used in the sleeping bay.
16. We have all seen (NASAs, NASAs', NASA's) films.
17. We are curious about the different (astronauts', astronaut's, astronauts) experiences.

C. Using Possessive Nouns in Sentences   Rewrite each sentence so that one word is a possessive. Use both singular and plural possessives.

18. One of the dreams that Thomas has is to travel to Mars.

MODEL ▷ One of Thomas's dreams is to travel to Mars.

19. The surface of Mars was thought to contain canals.
20. The gravity of the moon is less than that of Earth.
21. On the moon, the walk of the astronauts is comical.
22. The schedule of each space mission is complex.
23. The activities of the crew members are planned.
24. The exhibits of the Air and Space Museum include several space vehicles.
25. The smallness of the cabins seems unbearable.
26. The training of the crew prepares them for this.

UNIT 2

8 Appositives *pages 94–95*

A. Identifying Appositives Write each sentence. Underline the appositive in each sentence once. Underline twice the word or words to which it refers.

1. The Gulf Stream, a strong, warm current, brings mild weather to the British Isles.

   MODEL ▷ The Gulf Stream, a strong, warm current, brings mild weather to the British Isles.

2. Earth has great oceans, huge bodies of water.
3. All the oceans, Pacific, Atlantic, Indian, Arctic, and Antarctic, are actually one huge sea.
4. Its surface, 140 million square miles, is immense.
5. Until recently the ocean floor, a mysterious region, was unexplored.
6. Matthew Maury, a United States naval officer, founded modern oceanography.

B. Using Commas with Appositives Write each sentence. Add commas where they are needed.

7. Jupiter the fifth planet from the Sun takes 11.86 years to orbit the Sun.

   MODEL ▷ Jupiter, the fifth planet from the Sun, takes 11.86 years to orbit the Sun.

8. Mars the red planet was named for a Roman war god.
9. In the sixteenth century Tycho Brahe a Danish astronomer studied Mars.
10. Four small moons the moons of Jupiter were discovered by Galileo.
11. Ganymede the largest of Jupiter's moons is 3,260 miles in diameter.
12. Moons also orbit Saturn a ringed planet.

C. Writing Appositives in Sentences Add an appositive to each sentence. Write the new sentence. Be sure to punctuate the sentence correctly.

13. Alison has always wanted to take part in a manned space flight.

    MODEL ▷ Alison, my next-door neighbor, has always wanted to take part in a manned space flight.

14. Her father has encouraged her.
15. She belongs to the Young Astronauts' Club.
16. News stories about space missions interest her.
17. Her family took a trip to Cape Canaveral.
18. Ann Blount invited her to the Air and Space Museum.

EXTRA PRACTICE

EXTRA PRACTICE   **21**

UNIT 3

1 Action Verbs *pages 128–129*

A. Identifying Verbs   List the action verbs in each sentence.

1. This year I decided to be a better person.
MODEL> decided
2. I will spend more time on homework.
3. Perhaps I will watch less television.
4. I will listen carefully in all of my classes.
5. Over the summer I will read about the government.
6. At home I can help my parents more.
7. My mother will assign me some chores.
8. I can iron clothes and wash dishes.
9. My sisters and I often argue and cause trouble.
10. Now I will count to 20 before I lose my temper.
11. If I can do this, no one will recognize me.

B. Completing Sentences with Action Verbs   To each sentence, add an action verb that makes sense. Write the sentence.

12. Ray's father, an engineer, _____ to our class on our recent career day.
MODEL> Ray's father, an engineer, spoke to our class on our recent career day.
13. He _____ us about his work experience.
14. We also _____ what education an engineer _____.
15. Career day _____ us decide on a profession.
16. Lita's mother _____ as a lawyer.
17. She _____ us with her to a trial in a courtroom.

C. Writing Sentences with Action Verbs   To each sentence, add a word group containing an action verb. Write each sentence. Underline the action verb.

18. I _____ a great deal about my career recently.
MODEL> I have been thinking a great deal about my career recently.
19. _____ a job that involves travel.
20. Airline employees _____.
21. My brother joined the Navy, and he _____.
22. My aunt, an antique dealer, _____.
23. Her parents, who were missionaries, _____.
24. Oil companies in Europe frequently _____.
25. _____ work in developing countries.
26. A career in a health field _____.
27. Actors and film crews _____.
28. A good job _____.

UNIT 3

2 Linking Verbs *pages 130–131*

A. Identifying Linking Verbs Write the linking verb in each sentence.

1. Tanya is our class president this year.

MODEL ⟩ is

2. Competition for the presidency was fierce.
3. Tanya feels happy about her victory.
4. She is eager for changes in several school rules.
5. The principal thinks the students are too rash.
6. She and Marcus were on the student council.
7. He became the leader of the dress code committee.
8. Marcus is in favor of a more casual dress code.
9. The present code seems too formal for school.
10. Tanya will be part of his campaign for a new code.
11. They are usually on the same side of an issue.

B. Using Linking Verbs Correctly Write the correct form of each linking verb in parentheses.

12. You (am, is, are) a good student.

MODEL ⟩ are

13. Ms. Brown (were, are, is) our principal again.
14. School (be, is, are) more challenging this year.
15. Our athletes (am, are, be) in excellent condition.
16. Everyone (looks, look, looked) in top form now.
17. Many students (are, is, am) in honors classes.

C. Writing Sentences with Linking Verbs Complete each sentence by adding words that include a linking verb. Write each sentence.

18. _____ on the honor roll last semester.

MODEL ⟩ There were 28 students on the honor roll last semester.

19. _____ the most popular course.
20. Mr. Beck, the history teacher, _____.
21. In college he _____.
22. He still _____.
23. Coaching the school team _____.
24. _____ working with teenagers.
25. _____ more interesting in his class.
26. His students _____.
27. Everyone in his section _____.
28. The end of the year _____.
29. Studying for final exams _____.
30. What to do over the summer _____.
31. Interesting summer jobs _____.

3 Main Verbs and Helping Verbs *pages 132–133*

A. Identifying Main Verbs and Helping Verbs   Write each sentence. Underline the main verb once and the helping verb twice.

1. Did Estrella join the march for peace?

MODEL Did Estrella join the march for peace?

2. She has made a colorful banner.
3. We can watch the march from the corner.
4. The marchers have headed toward the park.
5. At the bandstand our congressman may give a speech.
6. He has supported the peace movement in our area.
7. News about the march may be on TV tonight.
8. Perhaps we could see Estrella and her friends.
9. Should we go to the park too?
10. You and I must hurry.
11. We might not arrive in time.

B. Using Main Verbs and Helping Verbs   Write a main verb or a helping verb to complete each sentence. Write each sentence.

12. _____ Jorge _____ his membership card?

MODEL Does Jorge have his membership card?

13. _____ you ready? We _____ leave immediately.
14. The car _____ waiting. Mother _____ drive us.
15. Tena _____ the keys. She _____ found them.
16. I _____ my book, and I _____ not lost my purse.
17. Here I _____. I _____ lock the door.

C. Writing Sentences with Main Verbs and Helping Verbs   Write each sentence according to the directions. Underline the main verb once and the helping verb twice.

18. Write a sentence about Jorge's future in politics. Use *has* as a helping verb.

MODEL Has Jorge considered a future in politics?

19. Write a sentence about Jorge's plans. Use *has* as a helping verb.
20. Write a sentence about voting. Use *do* as a helping verb.
21. Write a sentence about polls. Use *not* between the helping verb *did* and the main verb.
22. Write a sentence about voter registration. Use *were* as a helping verb.
23. Write a sentence about Jorge's campaign workers. Use the helping verb *will.*

4 Principal Parts of Verbs *pages 134–135*

A. Identifying the Principal Parts of Verbs   Write the main verb from each sentence. Label it *present, present participle, past,* or *past participle.*

1. Megan has planned a career in medicine.
   MODEL > planned—past participle
2. She studied biology in college.
3. Medical schools require a background in science.
4. Zoology had also interested her.
5. She has not picked any particular type of medicine.
6. Megan's mother works as a pediatrician.
7. Many young patients visited her clinic today.
8. Most have only minor injuries or illnesses.
9. Sometimes Megan has helped her mother.
10. Today she has been weighing the children.
11. Nervous children relax around Megan.

B. Using Principal Parts of Verbs Correctly   Write the verb from the box that will complete each sentence. Then write the name of the principal part for each verb.

12. _____ Mario and Joan _____ their careers yet?
    MODEL > Have chosen—past participle
13. They _____ career day at school.
14. Mario, an artist, _____ of being an architect.
15. He _____ this building a great deal.
16. Joan _____ always _____ horses.
17. As a child she _____ to be a veterinarian.

have chosen
dreams
has loved
longed
admires
attended

C. Writing Sentences with Principal Parts of Verbs   Write each sentence as directed.

18. Write a sentence about one of Sarah's goals. Use the present form of *want.*
    MODEL > Sarah wants a job in mathematics someday.
19. Write a sentence about Kay's summer job. Use the past form of *work.*
20. Write a sentence about Charles's hobby. Use the present form of *collect.*
21. Write a sentence about Simon's father. Use the past participle form of *mine.*
22. Write a sentence about Maxine's career choice. Use the present form of *dream.*
23. Write a sentence about Karl's part-time job. Use the past participle form of *assemble.*
24. Write a sentence about employment agencies. Use the present form of *find.*

5 Present, Past, and Future Tenses *pages 136–137*

EXTRA PRACTICE

A. Identifying Verb Tense Write the verb from each sentence. Label it *past, present,* or *future.*

1. Saburo and Greta belong to the Future Farmers of America.
   MODEL > belong—present
2. They joined the club a year ago.
3. Saburo's family owns an organic vegetable farm.
4. They will supply restaurants with vegetables.
5. Greta lives on a large potato farm.
6. Her family also raises animals.
7. Next year she will care for her own pig.
8. She wants a pig for the show at the state fair.
9. Saburo's snow peas won a blue ribbon at the fair.
10. Future Farmers of America sponsors the projects.
11. The members share up-to-date agricultural tips.

B. Choosing the Correct Verb Tense Write the correct form of the verb in parentheses in each sentence. Write the verb tense.

12. Alvin (did attend, attends, will attend) a meeting of the
    Junior Better Business Bureau tomorrow.
    MODEL > will attend—future
13. He (gives, give, gave) a speech at a past meeting.
14. The topic for discussion tomorrow (was, is, will be)
    consumer awareness.
15. The guest speaker (will address, addresses, address) the
    problem of defective appliances.
16. Most businesspeople (will be, was, are) honest.
17. Alvin (owns, is owning, own) a small business.

C. Using Verb Tenses in Sentences Complete each sentence, using the verb and the tense in parentheses. Write each sentence.

18. Tammy Jo _____ as a candy striper at the hospital. (*work*—past tense)
    MODEL > Tammy Jo worked as a candy striper at the hospital.
19. She _____ on the third floor. (*be*—past tense)
20. She _____ nursing school. (*begin*—future tense)
21. Ms. Teng _____ there. (*teach*—present tense)
22. Candy stripers _____ aides. (*be*—present tense)
23. Tammy Jo _____ to patients and _____ them up.
    (*read, cheer*—past tense)
24. Now she _____ new candy stripers learn their tasks at
    the hospital. (*help*—present tense)
25. They _____ that she is a helpful instructor. (*find*—future tense)

UNIT 3

6 Perfect Tenses pages 138–139

A. Identifying Verbs in the Perfect Tenses Write the verb in each sentence. Then write the tense of each verb.

1. Will Robbie have returned home by Tuesday?
   MODEL > will have returned—future perfect
2. He will have been at tennis camp for six weeks.
3. The coaches at camp have improved Robbie's game.
4. He had simply hoped for a fun-filled vacation.
5. Instead, he has become a ranked junior player.
6. By fall, the coach will have trained 10 players.
7. Before camp, Robbie had found serving difficult.
8. He had never eliminated his weak points.
9. Now he has learned concentration.
10. Has he won all his recent matches?
11. Several friends have called with congratulations.

B. Using the Perfect Tenses Add verbs to each sentence so that the sentence makes sense. Write the sentence. Then write the tense of each verb.

12. Rosa and Pat _____ always _____ interested in astronomy.
    MODEL > Rosa and Pat have always been interested in astronomy.—present perfect
13. They _____ a telescope before the comet passed.
14. By May they _____ many nights watching the skies.
15. Shooting stars _____ plentiful this month.
16. Pat _____ Rosa five books by her next birthday.
17. Rosa _____ now _____ becoming an astronomer.

C. Using the Perfect Tenses in Sentences Add words to each word group as directed in parentheses. Write each sentence.

18. Alice _____ about a career in the performing arts.
    (Use the past perfect tense of *think*.)
    MODEL > Alice had thought about a career in the performing arts.
19. Her father _____ an actor before Alice was born.
    (Use the past perfect tense of *be*.)
20. She hoped that his talent _____ off on her.
    (Use the past perfect tense of *rub*.)
21. Lately she _____ second thoughts. (Use the present perfect tense of *have*.)
22. By graduation she _____ what to do.
    (Use the future perfect tense of *decide*.)
23. Alice's friend Enzo _____ always _____ to be a doctor.
    (Use the past perfect tense of *want*.)
24. Recently, however, he _____ about a career in education.
    (Use the present perfect tense of *think*.)

EXTRA PRACTICE

UNIT 3

7 Subject-Verb Agreement *pages 140–141*

A. Identifying Correct Subject-Verb Agreement Write the subject and the verb in each sentence. Then explain why the subject and the verb agree.

  1. Patwin likes forestry.

MODEL ▷ *Patwin*, likes—*Patwin* is singular, so a singular form of *like* is used.

  2. He spends the summer in the woods.

  3. There Patwin visits the forest ranger, Carl Spence.

  4. Carl cares for the trees and the wildlife in his area.

  5. The two men climb up into the tall watchtower.

  6. From above, Carl checks the forest with binoculars.

  7. Rangers send out alarms at the first wisp of smoke.

  8. Forest fires destroy millions of trees each year.

  9. Both men enjoy the silence of the forest.

  10. Together they check the trees for signs of disease.

  11. Carl also knows a lot about the woodland animals.

B. Making the Subject and the Verb Agree Complete each sentence with a verb that makes sense. Write each sentence. Be sure that the subject and the verb agree.

  12. _____ you _____ a career as a nurse?

MODEL ▷ Do you plan a career as a nurse?

  13. June, my camp counselor, _____ to nursing school.

  14. She _____ not _____ a career in a hospital.

  15. Visiting nurses _____ for people in their homes.

  16. Most of their patients _____ elderly.

  17. Close friendships often _____ between nurses and their patients.

C. Writing Sentences with Subject-Verb Agreement Add words to each word group to make a sentence. Write the sentence. Be sure that the subject and the verb agree.

  18. _____ anything to Angelo about his future?

MODEL ▷ Did you say anything to Angelo about his future?

  19. _____ pleased with his work.

  20. The job on the newspaper _____.

  21. _____ as well as anyone in school.

  22. If his column _____, the job _____.

  23. _____ articles about teenagers.

  24. His column _____.

  25. What a great idea _____!

  26. _____ put Angelo's picture in the paper.

EXTRA PRACTICE

8 Agreement of Verbs with Compound Subjects
pages 142–143

A. Identifying Correct Subject-Verb Agreement   Write the subject and the verb in each sentence. Then explain why the subject and the verb agree.

1. Elena and Jim think about a travel agency of their own.

MODEL▷ Elena, Jim think—A compound subject made of two singular subjects equals a plural subject. Therefore, a plural form of *think* is used.

2. They enjoy travel themselves.
3. Unusual destinations and routes appeal to them.
4. Marta and Tarik visit a different place each year.
5. They go by ship whenever they can.
6. A cruise to the Antarctic is one of their dreams.
7. Elena and Jim visit South America each winter.
8. Both students like the variety of climates.
9. Elena's mother lives in Santiago, Chile.

B. Making the Subject and the Verb Agree   Complete each sentence with a subject or a verb. Write the sentence. Be sure that the subject and the verb agree.

10. _____ have always loved animals.

MODEL▷ Tyrone and Felipe have always loved animals.

11. They _____ animals for TV and movies.
12. Tyrone _____ with chimpanzees.
13. His _____ do almost anything people do.
14. _____ specializes in wild animals like tigers.
15. His job _____ obviously the more dangerous one.
16. Their animals _____ with them on a distant ranch.
17. Here _____ pose no threat to neighbors.

C. Writing Sentences with Subjects and Verbs That Agree   Add words to each word group to make a sentence. Write the sentence. Be sure that the subject and the verb agree.

18. Either Ahanu or the twins _____ .

MODEL▷ Either Ahanu or the twins have joined the animal rights movement.

19. All three _____.
20. Members _____.
21. _____ writes congressmen about his concerns.
22. Many laboratory animals _____.

UNIT 4

1 Irregular Verbs *pages 176–178*

A. Identifying Irregular Verbs Write the form of *be, have,* or *do* in each sentence. Identify the tense of each form.

1. Alan lost his appetite; who has it?
   MODEL> has—present tense of *have*
2. Sy had an aquarium with electric eels for light.
3. Al did his flea act at a dog show but lost a flea.
4. Since Ann's pet is an anteater, she has only uncles.
5. The ice had been solid until it lost its cool.
6. Leona has had a chip on her shoulder, so termites keep following her everywhere.

B. Using Irregular Verbs in Sentences Complete each sentence with the correct form of the irregular verb in parentheses. Write the verb.

7. Does Louis _____ a funny hobby? (have)
   MODEL> have
8. Yes, he certainly _____! (have)
9. He _____ collect photos of animals in clothes. (do)
10. In many, dogs _____ sunglasses. (have)
11. Rarer _____ photos of cats in dresses. (be)
12. In one, chimps _____ a tango in capes. (do)
13. Another _____ of a kangaroo with boxing gloves. (be)
14. I _____ amazed by Louis's collection. (be)
15. Louis _____ a favorite picture. (have)
16. In it, two elephants _____ bathing suits on. (have)

C. Writing Irregular Verbs in Sentences Write each sentence as directed. Be sure to use the correct forms of the irregular verbs.

17. Write an amusing sentence, using the past perfect tense of *do.*
    MODEL> Alan had done his homework assignment from his sister's third-grade book by mistake.
18. Write a sentence about Alan's parents' reaction. Use the past perfect tense of *be.*
19. Write a sentence about Alan's teacher's feelings. Use the past tense of *be.*
20. Write a sentence about the homework. Use the past perfect tense of *have* with the word *not.*
21. Write a sentence telling what Alan's teacher said to him. Use the present tense of *do.*
22. Write a sentence explaining what Alan resolved. Use the future tense of *do.*
23. Write a sentence telling what Alan's friends said. Use the present tense of *think.*

UNIT 4

2 More Irregular Verbs *pages 179–181*

A. Identifying Irregular Verbs   Write the irregular verbs in the following sentences.

1. Once upon a time there was a boy named Zack who could read everyone's thoughts.

`MODEL` was, could

2. He knew what his mom thought when she woke him up.
3. "This is the messiest room I have ever seen!"
4. He could tell how his father felt about breakfast.
5. "Eggs again! Why can't Zack make anything but bacon and eggs?"
6. When the mail carrier came, Zack saw through his friendly laugh.
7. "That is the silliest-looking kid on my route!"
8. No one could keep any secrets from poor Zack.
9. One night he came home tired from mind-reading.
10. His mom thought, "How nice that Zack is home."
11. His father gave him a hug and thought, "What did I do to deserve such a great son?"
12. Zack smiled and said, "Things could be worse!"

B. Using Irregular Verbs Correctly   Write the correct form of the irregular verb in parentheses that will complete each sentence.

13. Once there _____ (be) a fish that _____ (fly).

`MODEL` was, flew

14. It _____ (burst) from a lake and _____ (take) off.
15. Its yellow scales _____ (shine) in the sun.
16. The fish _____ (think) it _____ (be) a bird.
17. It had completely _____ (forget) it _____ (have) gills, not lungs, and couldn't breathe air.

C. Writing Irregular Verbs in Sentences   Write five funny sentences about Jerry as directed. Be sure to use the correct form of the irregular verb.

18. Write a sentence using the past tense of *go.*

`MODEL` Jerry went to school wearing one sneaker and one brown oxford.

19. Write a sentence using the past tense of *see.*
20. Write a sentence using the past tense of *sit.*
21. Write a sentence using the present tense of *go.*
22. Write a sentence using the present tense of *take.*
23. Write a sentence using the future tense of *put.*

3 Direct Objects *pages 182–183*

A. Identifying Direct Objects Write the direct object in each sentence.

1. José went fishing and caught a boot.
   MODEL⟩ boot
2. His father gave a shout.
3. "Don't lose that beauty!"
4. José's father took a picture of him with the boot.
5. José is wearing a big grin.
6. He is holding the boot next to a yardstick.
7. It matches the length of his arm.
8. Shall we throw it back or not?
9. Maybe it will fit your brother.
10. "Put your line back in the water, José."
11. "Perhaps you can catch its mate."

B. Completing Sentences with Direct Objects Write each sentence. Add a direct object to each.

12. I need a _____ by tomorrow morning.
    MODEL⟩ I need a costume by tomorrow morning.
13. I have to finish _____ .
14. We rehearse _____ at noon.
15. Iggie can't find _____ .
16. Lettie made _____ out of old tires.
17. I am using my father's _____ as a hat.
18. I wove _____ through the strings of the racquet.
19. The strings won't hold the _____ in place.
20. The racquet uses my _____ as a slide.
21. At any time I may wear the _____ across my face.
22. Next year I will rent a _____ instead of making my own.

C. Writing Sentences with Direct Objects Complete each sentence by adding one or more direct objects to each word group. Write the sentence.

23. The wind whisked _____ off the clothesline.
    MODEL⟩ The wind whisked the laundry off the clothesline.
24. A bear in the neighborhood approached _____ .
25. It grabbed _____ and lumbered off.
26. Mrs. Jenkins collected _____ from the line.
27. She didn't notice _____ .
28. Meanwhile, the bear began eating _____ .
29. Mrs. Jenkins was riding _____ to town.
30. She saw _____ ; it had _____ dangling from its mouth.
31. "Beast, you have eaten _____ !" she shrieked.

UNIT 4

4 Indirect Objects *pages 184–185*

A. Identifying Indirect Objects   Write the letter that precedes the indirect object in each sentence.

1. Dad read my (a) little (b) sister a long (c) story about a timid tiger.

MODEL> b

2. The tiger's (a) mom taught her (b) cub how to (c) stalk.
3. The tiger's father gave the (a) little (b) fellow pouncing (c) lessons.
4. He taught all his (a) cubs a (b) ferocious (c) growl.
5. But (a) none of the (b) lessons gave the timid (c) tiger courage.
6. His (a) family brought the (b) timid (c) tiger food.
7. Father tiger wrote the (a) wisest, (b) oldest (c) tiger a note.
8. "Please (a) give our (b) cub (c) bravery," he begged.
9. The old (a) tiger sent the (b) family a (c) message.
10. "Don't give the (a) meek a (b) hard (c) time," he advised.
11. "They give (a) us a (b) chance at (c) heroism."

B. Adding Indirect Objects to Sentences   Add an indirect object to each sentence. Write each sentence.

12. My brother baked an orange cake with blue icing.

MODEL> My brother baked me an orange cake with blue icing.

13. He also made chocolate ice cream.
14. We threw a Halloween party.
15. My father hired a magician.
16. My mother made silly costumes.

C. Writing Original Sentences with Indirect Objects   Write each sentence as directed.

17. Write a funny sentence about a clown. Use the word *clown* as an indirect object.

MODEL> The circus ringmaster handed the clown a five-foot purple daisy with pink leaves.

18. Write a silly sentence about a cow. Use *cow* as an indirect object.
19. Write a sentence about a mistake. Use *myself* as an indirect object.
20. Write a funny sentence about mud. Use *mother* as an indirect object.
21. Write a sentence about a surprise. Use *teacher* as an indirect object.
22. Write a funny sentence about a harmless practical joke. Use *uncle* as an indirect object.

5 Predicate Nominatives *pages 186–187*

A. Identifying Predicate Nominatives Write the predicate nominatives in the following sentences.

1. Helen's father is president of the Roxwell Book Company.

MODEL> president

2. Her mother is a director of the company.
3. It was she who answered the telephone.
4. The company's books are mostly humorous novels and joke books.
5. Helen's father is also a writer.
6. It was he who wrote that interesting history book.
7. His book was the best one I've read on the history of clowns.
8. He was a clown for several years.

B. Choosing Predicate Nominatives Write each sentence. Choose a word from the box that completes each sentence with an appropriate predicate nominative.

9. The members of the drama club include Trenell and Ann, but the only officer is

_____ .

MODEL> The members of the drama club include Trenell and Ann, but the only officer is she.

she
representative
he
curtain
Damien
item
he
one
she
adviser
I
vice-president

10. Damien received the most votes in the election, so the president is _____ .
11. It was _____ who founded the club two years ago.
12. The drama club, the most respected club in school, is also the hardest _____ to join.
13. It was _____ who wrote about it for the paper.
14. Ann is the _____; that is _____ on the left.
15. Alcot, Inc., is helping us; Mr. Cole is its _____ .
16. What we want to purchase with the funds from our project is a new _____ for the stage.
17. It is a necessary _____ for our upcoming play.
18. Mr. Cole is our _____ on the project.
19. It is _____ who will aid us in our current comedy production.

C. 20.–30. Writing Sentences with Predicate Nominatives Write ten sentences about a funny incident that happened to you. Use five predicate nominatives that are pronouns.

MODEL> 20. The lead skater in our roller derby is I.

6 Transitive and Intransitive Verbs *pages 188–189*

A. Identifying Transitive and Intransitive Verbs Write each main verb. Write *T* after a transitive verb and *I* after an intransitive verb.

1. The trout surprised the fishermen because he talked to them in Latin.

> MODEL > surprised—T; talked—I

2. The fishermen caught the strange fish in a net.
3. They were hauling it in when its mouth opened.
4. One of the fishermen knew a little Latin.
5. Only he could understand the fish when it spoke.
6. The others crowded around him excitedly.
7. "What did it say?"
8. The fisherman scratched his head.
9. He had not used Latin since he went to school.
10. He thought for a while before he found an answer.
11. "Put me back; I'll send you a fish who speaks English."

B. Completing Sentences with Intransitive Verbs Complete each sentence with an intransitive verb and any other words that are needed. Write the sentence.

12. The old convertible _____ .

> MODEL > The old convertible flew into the sky.

13. The passengers _____ .
14. The world below _____ .
15. Feeling brave, Timothy _____ .
16. In the air nearby, birds _____ .
17. Alban and Mary _____ .

C. Writing Sentences with Transitive Verbs Write each sentence as directed. Underline each direct object.

18. Write a sentence with the word *twisted* as a transitive verb.

> MODEL > The circus strong man twisted the iron bar into the shape of a pretzel.

19. Write a sentence with *took* as a transitive verb.
20. Write a sentence with *had* as a transitive verb.
21. Write a sentence with *tried* as a transitive verb.
22. Write a sentence with *crossed* as a transitive verb.
23. Write a sentence with *rode* as a transitive verb.
24. Write a sentence with *applauded* as a transitive verb.
25. Write a sentence with *shouted* as a transitive verb.
26. Write a sentence with *left* as a transitive verb.

EXTRA PRACTICE

UNIT 4

7 Easily Confused Verb Pairs pages 190–191

A. Using Verbs Correctly Write the form of the verb in parentheses that correctly completes each sentence.

   1. May I (lend, borrow) your old Halloween costume?
MODEL▷ borrow
   2. If no one is at home, just (set, sit) the package by our front door.
   3. Will you (teach, learn) me how to make a Halloween costume?
   4. Mother has (set, sat) aside some treats.
   5. I am going to (lie, lay) down for a nap first.
   6. (Leave, Let) me alone until six o'clock.
   7. I want to (lie, lay) in bed for another hour.
   8. Where did you (lie, lay) my costume?
   9. June (lent, borrowed) me a witch's hat.
  10. Did you (learn, teach) to sing that scary song?
  11. The moon (raised, rose) in the sky.

B. Completing Sentences with Correct Verbs To complete each sentence, write a verb from the lesson.

  12. _____ me use a red crayon for my cartoon.
MODEL▷ Let
  13. _____ down and I'll _____ you to draw.
  14. _____ the crayon flat against the paper.
  15. The alligator in my drawing is _____ to play golf.
  16. He _____ his tail, swings, and hits the ball.
  17. He _____ extra golf balls in his mouth.

C. Using Verbs Correctly in Original Sentences Write sentences as directed.

  18. Write two funny sentences using *lie/lay*.
MODEL▷ Lay the elephant on the postage stamp.
        Don't you know you're lying in poison ivy?
  19. Write two funny sentences using *raise/rise*.
  20. Write two silly sentences using *sat/set*.
  21. Write two foolish questions using *borrow/lend*.
  22. Write two ridiculous newspaper headlines using *teach/learn*.
  23. Write two funny sentences using *lie/lay*.
  24. Write two funny sentences using *let/leave*.
  25. Write two funny lines of dialogue using *lend/borrow*.
  26. Write two funny lines of dialogue using *teach/learn*.
  27. Write two lines of instruction from a funny cookbook. Use the words *rise/raise* and *let/leave*.

8 Contractions *pages 192–193*

A. Identifying Contractions   Write the contraction in each sentence. Then write the words from which each contraction was formed.

1. She's wearing a clown suit.
   `MODEL` She's—She is
2. The other clown suit didn't fit John.
3. Now he's going to be a spaceman.
4. The diving suit wasn't his.
5. He couldn't find a helmet.
6. Don't you like to dress up?
7. I've never been to a costume party.
8. Aren't you wearing a mask?
9. My sisters won't ever be ready.
10. They're still sewing sequins on their costumes.
11. I wouldn't miss this for anything.

B. Writing Contractions Correctly   Rewrite each sentence, substituting a contraction wherever possible.

12. I am wearing a chicken suit in our next show.
    `MODEL` I'm wearing a chicken suit in our next show.
13. We will have other barnyard animals on stage.
14. Melissa did not want to play a pig in the skit.
15. She is too vain and will not do it because she would have to pad her body with pillows.
16. Gordon is not so picky about his role.
17. A donkey's big ears and bray do not bother him.

C. Writing Sentences with Contractions   Follow the directions to write sentences about a clown. Remember to punctuate the contractions correctly.

18. Write a sentence using the contractions for *that is* and *is not.*
    `MODEL` That's a flower that squirts water, isn't it?
19. Write a sentence using the contraction for *it is.*
20. Write a sentence using the contraction for *I have.*
21. Write a sentence using the contractions for *there will* and *we will.*
22. Write a sentence using the contractions for *you will* and *will not.*
23. Write a sentence using the contractions for *we have* and *are not.*
24. Write a sentence using the contraction for *cannot.*
25. Write a sentence using the contractions for *do not* and *there is.*

1 Pronouns *pages 228–229*

A. Identifying Pronouns   Write the pronoun(s) in each sentence.

   1. I believe that animals have rights because they have
      feelings just as I do.

MODEL ⟩ I, they, I

   2. I always treat animals as I want to be treated.
   3. Animals trust us, and we must try to keep that trust.
   4. I had a dog named Lumberjack. I loved him a lot.
   5. When I was sad or hurt, he made me feel better.
   6. I found Lumberjack abandoned, and I took him home.
   7. We never understood why the owners deserted him.
   8. They may have been cruel or thoughtless people.
   9. Don couldn't keep this cat, so he found it a home.
  10. Aretha was happy to take it.
  11. We should do whatever we can for the animals.

B. Completing Sentences with Appropriate Pronouns   Write a pronoun or pronouns to complete each sentence.

  12. Alex and _____ want to help all animals when _____
      grow up.

MODEL ⟩ I, we

  13. _____ want to be veterinarians so _____ can treat
      _____ .

  14. Our parents love animals, too, and _____ agree with
      _____ .

  15. As for Kay, _____ wants to run a horse farm.
  16. How do _____ feel about animal rights?
  17. _____ wish that cruelty to animals would stop.

C. Using Pronouns to Avoid Repetition   Rewrite each sentence, using pronouns for the underlined words.

  18. Ann and Leo may run a shelter for homeless animals;
      <u>Ann and Leo</u> will do a good job.

MODEL ⟩ Ann and Leo may run a shelter for homeless animals;
they will do a good job.

  19. If Ann can find a farm or kennel, <u>Ann</u> will buy it.
  20. Ann has received many donations for <u>Ann's</u> work.
  21. When people abandon a pet, do <u>people</u> think about
      what will happen to <u>the pet</u>?
  22. At <u>Ann's and Leo's</u> kennel, Ann and Leo will care for
      the animals and try to find <u>the animals</u> homes.
  23. Animals give much love to those who love <u>animals</u>.

2 Agreement of Pronouns with Antecedents

pages 230–231

A. Recognizing Pronoun Antecedents Write each sentence. Underline each pronoun. Draw an arrow from each pronoun to its antecedent.

   1. Sheila believes firmly in world peace; she volunteers for Young Americans for Peace.

   MODEL▷ Sheila believes firmly in world peace; <u>she</u> volunteers for Young Americans for Peace.

   2. The group has many members; students often join it.

   3. Members work for peace; they talk to world leaders.

   4. The group's president wrote to Sheila and told her that her ideas were helpful.

   5. Several lawmakers have also answered Sheila; they always claim to be in agreement with her.

   6. Sheila has saved many of the letters she has received.

   7. Otto Morosoff arrived from the Soviet Union last week, and he joined the group immediately.

B. Choosing Pronouns That Agree with Antecedents Write the pronoun in parentheses that agrees with each antecedent.

   8. John is working to have (his, her, its) city declared the cleanest city in the state.

   MODEL▷ his

   9. The mayor has said that (she, her, it) agrees with John and will help (he, him, it).

   10. The project is worthy, but (it, they, he) is demanding.

   11. John's sister has promised to help (him, it, he).

   12. Rachel and her friends are hard workers, so (they, she, them) will be a big help.

   13. If enough people are willing to support (them, he, him), the two may carry out their plan.

C. 14.–24. Writing Sentences Correctly with Pronouns Write 10 sentences about feelings or ideas you may have. Use pronouns in your sentences. Remember to make the pronouns agree with their antecedents in number and in gender.

   MODEL▷ **14.** We students should try to protect our environment.

3 Subject and Object Pronouns *pages 232–233*

A. Identifying Subject and Object Pronouns Write the pronoun or pronouns from each sentence. Identify each as a *subject pronoun* or an *object pronoun*.

1. I want to volunteer at the local hospital; it will help me get some experience.

MODEL⟩ I—subject pronoun; it—subject pronoun; me—object pronoun

2. I have a friend there, Dr. Birch.
3. She will help me find a spot where I can be useful.
4. We like her very much, and she is a good doctor.
5. The patients find her sympathetic.
6. My cousin met her when he broke a leg.
7. He spent a week in a ward with four other boys.
8. They became friends, and two of the boys still see him often.

B. Completing Sentences with Subject and Object Pronouns Complete each sentence with appropriate pronouns. Write the sentence.

9. Ron, once shy himself, urged _____ to be more friendly; now _____ am no longer shy.

MODEL⟩ Ron, once shy himself, urged me to be more friendly; now I am no longer shy.

10. _____ meet people and greet _____ pleasantly.
11. _____ used to frighten _____ , but now _____ can't even remember why.
12. Ron and _____ often go places together, and _____ have met many new friends.
13. _____ would never guess that _____ were shy.
14. _____ might say that _____ are now popular.

C. Using Pronouns in Sentences Add words that include pronouns to each word group. Write the sentence. Underline subject pronouns once and object pronouns twice.

15. Eliza chose _____ .

MODEL⟩ Eliza chose me for a good friend.

16. _____ had always liked _____ .
17. People see _____ .
18. Between classes _____ .
19. If _____ were separated, _____ .
20. Next vacation _____ .
21. Being best friends gives _____ .
22. _____ sometimes knows _____ .
23. _____ have told _____ .

UNIT 5

4 Possessive Pronouns *pages 234–235*

A. Identifying Possessive Pronouns Write the possessive pronouns from the sentences. Do not write other kinds of pronouns.

  1. Juana likes her schoolwork, but sometimes its pressures give her a headache.

  MODEL ▷ *her, its*

  2. Math is her most difficult subject.

  3. Its equations and decimals give her problems.

  4. Her brother does his homework with their computer.

  5. Our favorite assignment is writing in our journals.

  6. Juana likes to write about her grandmother, who tells many interesting tales about their family.

  7. Her most recent entry tells about her family tree.

  8. If my grandmother lived nearby, I'd love to hear her stories.

  9. Homework is fun when your family is part of it.

  10. Our parents have forgotten how to do math problems.

  11. If your task is in history, their ideas are useful.

B. Choosing Correct Possessives for Sentences For each sentence, write the correct pronoun in parentheses ( ).

  12. "That idea was (my, your, mine)," said Kathy. "I was using it for (her, my, his) research report."

  MODEL ▷ *mine, my*

  13. Is (your, yours, mine) idea too general?

  14. I narrowed (their, her, mine) to make it more specific.

  15. Josie has already finished (my, her, hers) report.

  16. (Its, Hers, It's) topic is rather unusual.

  17. (Ours, Our, Its) deadline for research is Monday.

  18. Ms. La Croix said that (her, his, our) reports may be written with partners.

  19. There is so much information on (her, yours, my) topic that I may need a partner.

  20. Both partners will get the same grade, however, no matter (whom, who, whose) work is better.

C. 21.–31. Writing Sentences with Possessive Pronouns Write 10 sentences about your feelings and your ideas, using possessive pronouns. Use at least five possessives that stand alone. Underline the possessive pronouns in each sentence.

  MODEL ▷ **21.** I set my goals and standards very high; how high are yours?

5 Reflexive Pronouns *pages 236–237*

A. Identifying Kinds of Pronouns Write the pronoun or pronouns from each sentence. Label each pronoun *personal* or *reflexive*.

1. Roger bought himself a beautiful stamp.

   MODEL ▷ himself—reflexive

2. Roger told himself that it was worth the price.
3. He gave it a page to itself in the stamp album.
4. Roger's mother calls herself a "stampaholic."
5. She and Roger treated themselves to a trip to a stamp collectors' convention.
6. Roger went to some of the exhibits by himself.
7. They introduced themselves to some stamp dealers.
8. Mrs. Fu encouraged herself to buy a rare stamp.
9. She enjoyed herself immensely.
10. "We found ourselves at a booth with especially large stamps," Mrs. Fu said later.
11. "Often the smallest countries make the biggest stamps for themselves," she commented.

B. Completing Sentences with Reflexive Pronouns For each sentence, write a reflexive pronoun that agrees with its subject.

12. Rafael collects baseball cards and has saved all but 20 of a set by _____ .

    MODEL ▷ himself

13. The players had _____ photographed for the cards.
14. Rafael keeps his collection in a drawer by _____ .
15. Do you pay for the cards by _____ ?
16. I told _____ that cards are a good investment.
17. My sister bought _____ football cards instead.

C. Using Reflexive Pronouns in Sentences For each word group, form a sentence by adding words that include a reflexive pronoun. Tell whether the reflexive pronoun is used as a *direct object*, an *indirect object*, or a *pronoun* that follows words such as *by, to,* or *for.*

18. Ed and Bob/trivia games

    MODEL ▷ Ed and Bob like trivia games, and they challenge themselves in every one.—direct object

19. Ed/paces
20. you/a point/for that answer
21. Write/note
22. I/remind
23. Bob's team/the tournament

6 Indefinite Pronouns pages 238–239

A. Identifying Indefinite Pronouns Write the indefinite pronoun or pronouns in each sentence.

1. Anyone can put together all of these jigsaw puzzles.
MODEL > Anyone, all
2. If no one wants to do a puzzle, I will try some.
3. Several are ones I have worked on before.
4. A few of the pieces in each are lost.
5. In none of them have I done all of the sky.
6. The solid red puzzle is another that is impossible.
7. I don't think anyone has ever finished it.
8. Many of these puzzles are easy; others are not.
9. Someone has finished the outside edge of both.
10. Does anybody want help with either of the puzzles?
11. All of the blue pieces are in this box.

B. Completing Sentences with Indefinite Pronouns Write appropriate indefinite pronouns for each sentence.

12. _____ of us wants privileges, but _____ wants responsibilities.
MODEL > Each, no one
13. Carol must clean up before _____ can visit her.
14. If my brother wants to use the car, he will do _____ of the yard work.
15. _____ of us has chores, but _____ do them better than others.
16. _____ of the work is done at the last minute.
17. A _____ of us try to do _____ at all.
18. Almost _____ can keep a house clean.
19. _____ it takes is a little effort.
20. If _____ does the dusting and the vacuuming, _____ should do the cooking and the laundry.
21. _____ should have more than his or her share.
22. To have a clean house, _____ should be overlooked for long.
23. _____ should keep track of the bills.
24. If we are running out of _____ , that item should be put on a shopping list.

C. 25.–35. Writing Sentences with Indefinite Pronouns Write 10 sentences about playing a game. In each sentence, use one indefinite pronoun. Be sure it agrees in number with the verb. Underline the indefinite pronoun.

MODEL > 25. Few of the puzzle-solvers receive a perfect score the first time.

EXTRA PRACTICE

7 Subject or Object Pronoun? *pages 240–241*

A. **Identifying Subject and Object Pronouns**   Write whether each of the underlined words in each sentence is a *subject pronoun* or an *object pronoun*.

  1. I saw him out on the tennis court.
  MODEL > I—subject pronoun; him—object pronoun
  2. He was going to give me a lesson.
  3. We played them until she arrived.
  4. She brought us some lemonade, and we drank it all.
  5. How long have you been playing tennis?
  6. I have only played as long as she has.
  7. They began giving us lessons two years ago.
  8. She is a better player than I am.
  9. If they work hard, you will see them in the finals.
  10. It will be an exciting tournament for her.
  11. We will be playing them in the first doubles match.

B. **Choosing Appropriate Pronouns for Sentences**   For each sentence, write the correct pronoun in parentheses. Identify each pronoun as a *subject pronoun* or an *object pronoun*.

  12. What do (he, you, she) think of the new uniforms?
  MODEL > you—subject pronoun
  13. Did (him, them, he) select the colors?
  14. The shoes are just what (I, her, me) wanted.
  15. (Them, Me, She) likes the blue-and-white ones more than (me, I, us) do.
  16. (Us, We, Him) gave the old uniforms to (they, them, we) to use during practice.
  17. (I, He, She) like (them, they, we) better than the old ones, anyway.

C. **Writing Subject and Object Pronouns in Sentences**   Form sentences by adding words that include subject pronouns or object pronouns to each word group. Underline subject pronouns once and object pronouns twice.

  18. snow skiing or water-skiing
  MODEL > Do you prefer snow skiing or water-skiing?
  19. snow ski better
  20. go to the mountains
  21. to keep trying higher, steeper slopes
  22. the fresh air
  23. new tricks
  24. on the tricky runs
  25. when the weather is hot
  26. borrow a motorboat
  27. Lizzie lives on the lake
  28. a few pointers

8 Who, Whom, Whose pages 242–243

A. Identifying Pronouns in Questions Write the pronoun in parentheses that correctly completes each sentence.

1. (Who, Whom, Whose) shoes are these?
> MODEL Whose

2. (Who, Whom, Whose) is going to do this laundry?
3. (Who, Whom, Whose) did you call about the meet?
4. (Who, Whom, Whose) needs these clean white shorts?
5. (Who, Whom, Whose) racquet needs to be restrung?
6. (Who, Whom, Whose) did you beat in the first match?
7. (Who, Whom, Whose) serve is it?
8. (Who, Whom, Whose) won the last set?
9. (Who, Whom, Whose) will we be watching next?
10. (Who, Whom, Whose) is arguing with the line judge?
11. (Who, Whom, Whose) point is that?

B. Using Correct Pronouns Decide whether *who, whom, who's,* or *whose* correctly completes each sentence. Write the correct word.

12. _____ has Bob invited to the tournament?
> MODEL Whom

13. _____ did Sophie play this morning?
14. _____ trophy is this?
15. _____ playing against last year's champion?
16. _____ in the first match tomorrow?
17. _____ family is here from Argentina?
18. I think we know _____ the best now.
19. For _____ did you bring those drinks?
20. _____ would like a ride home?

C. Writing *Who, Whom,* and *Whose* in Sentences Follow the directions to write each sentence.

21. Write a sentence about a team sport. Use *whom* as the direct object of the verb *choose.*
> MODEL Whom did Ms. Wood choose for the tennis team?
22. Write a sentence about a sport. Use *Who* as the subject and *elected* as the verb.
23. Write a sentence about a sport, using *whose.*
24. Write a sentence about a sport. Use *whom* as the indirect object of the verb *tell.*
25. Write a sentence about a sport. Use *who* as the subject and *lost* as the verb.
26. Write a sentence about a sport. Use *whom* as the direct object of *suspend.*

UNIT 6

1 Adjectives *pages 274–275*

A. Identifying Adjectives Write the sentences. Underline the adjectives that describe once and the articles twice.

1. Ross wrote a scary tale about a haunted farm.
   - MODEL▷ Ross wrote <u>a</u> <u>scary</u> tale about <u>a</u> <u>haunted</u> farm.
2. Two foolish boys go to an old, deserted mansion.
3. They have brought a new camera to record unusual or frightening events.
4. The nervous boys cross the dusty, creaky threshold.
5. Odd noises and cold gusts of air greet them.
6. They begin to tape the creepy sights and sounds.
7. A transparent, expressionless girl floats down the dilapidated staircase and then disappears.
8. Eerie music comes from the rooms and ends abruptly.
9. Terrified but persistent, the boys continue taping until a scary man with a rusty sabre charges them.
10. Escaping the house, the boys play their tape.

B. Choosing Adjectives That Describe Write a word from the box to complete each sentence.

odd-looking
ancient
forbidden
hidden
folded
rusty
gnarled
pitiful
heavy
frightened
ugly

11. The _____ vines twisted around the _____ building on the _____ planet.
    - MODEL▷ The odd-looking vines twisted around the ancient building on the forbidden planet.
12. A _____ hand reached into the _____ mailbox.
13. Inside lay a _____ sheet of _____ paper.
14. The _____ creature gave a _____ gasp.
15. How did the monster find me in this _____ place?
16. Where in the universe can a _____ fugitive hide?

C. Writing Adjectives in Sentences Add adjectives and other words to each word pair to make a complete sentence. Underline the adjectives that describe once and the articles twice.

17. dreams/island
    - MODEL▷ I often have <u>vivid</u> dreams in which I have been shipwrecked on <u>a</u> <u>tropical</u> island.
18. waves/shore
19. trees/shade
20. flowers/smell
21. parrots/silence
22. sails/sink
23. sky/clouds

EXTRA PRACTICE

UNIT 6

2 Proper Adjectives pages 276–277

A. Identifying Proper Adjectives Write the proper adjective(s) in each sentence.

1. The heroine hacked through thick Amazon jungles and broiled under a hot South American sun.

MODEL> Amazon, South American

2. Writing for a London magazine gave the American woman a chance to travel far and wide.
3. She covered the Biafra famine for the May issue.
4. Latin American politics is still her main interest.
5. She has moved to the Chilean or Argentinian capital.
6. For a holiday story she chose Mexican churches.
7. A Panamanian general granted her a long interview.
8. Her Canal Zone article won her a promotion.
9. On a Nicaraguan trip she was delayed by bad roads.
10. Covering the Brazilian Mardi Gras, she spent two weeks in a Rio hotel.

B. Writing Proper Adjectives Correctly Rewrite each sentence so that the proper adjective or adjectives are written correctly.

11. Hilda is researching her swedish ancestors, and Maya is writing to her maltese relatives.

MODEL> Hilda is researching her Swedish ancestors, and Maya is writing to her Maltese relatives.

12. Henry's polish grandfather and ukrainian grandmother tell tales about their trip to America.
13. Maria's puerto rican aunt invited her for a visit.
14. She has a friday flight from the miami airport.
15. Gwynneth has never met her welsh relatives.
16. Helene's french parents promised her a trip to Paris.

C. Writing Proper Adjectives in Sentences Complete each sentence with a proper adjective.

17. I dreamed I helped the _____ hockey team beat the _____ team in the Olympics.

MODEL> I dreamed I helped the American hockey team beat the Soviet team in the Olympics.

18. The _____ and _____ teams were in third and fourth place, respectively.
19. The _____ and _____ teams had the most medals.
20. I wanted to join the _____ bobsledders.
21. The _____ weather was quite cold.
22. Our _____ hosts organized a great parade.

EXTRA PRACTICE

UNIT 6

3 *This, That, These, Those* pages 278–279

A. **Identifying Demonstrative Adjectives** Write the demonstrative adjective or adjectives in each sentence. Indicate whether each word is singular or plural.

   1. Who brought these swim fins to the beach?

   MODEL> these—plural

   2. That ball belongs to the Hall family; use this one.
   3. I can't make this umbrella stick in the sand.
   4. Those ants are on the sandwiches again.
   5. Have you tried this new sunscreen on that baby?
   6. Those messy people are leaving that litter behind.
   7. Perhaps that lifeguard will tell them to clean up.
   8. We came to this beach 30 years ago; in those days there was no lifeguard.
   9. That lighthouse hadn't been built on those rocks.
   10. These children should have some of those oranges.
   11. Don't go back into the water too soon after eating that food.

B. **Choosing the Correct Adjective** Write the correct adjective in parentheses. Then write whether the adjective indicates something near or something distant.

   12. (These, Those, That) scuba gear is Joni's.

   MODEL> That—distant

   13. She left (that, these, those) mask and (this, that, those) fins on her towel.
   14. Please hand me (those, that, this) hat; I can't reach it from here.
   15. (That, This, Those) bathing suit I have on is new.
   16. (This, These, Those) sandals you wore yesterday looked comfortable.
   17. (This, These, Those) cream will protect your nose.

C. **Writing Demonstrative Adjectives in Sentences** Add words, including demonstrative adjectives, to each word group to make a sentence.

   18. love swimming in the ocean

   MODEL> These friends love swimming in the ocean.

   19. girl just dove
   20. dolphins come by
   21. like to watch
   22. boy wants to become
   23. strengthens his muscles

48   EXTRA PRACTICE

UNIT 6

4 Predicate Adjectives *pages 280–281*

A. Identifying Predicate Adjectives Write the predicate adjective or adjectives in each sentence. Indicate which word or words each predicate adjective modifies.

1. Geraldo and Samuru feel good about their chances of winning the bowling tournament.

MODEL ▷ good—Geraldo and Samuru

2. They are ready to face any competition.
3. Samuru seems well again after spraining his wrist.
4. His bowling ball, a gift from his parents, is new.
5. Geraldo's shoes felt tight.
6. He was nervous about them and loosened his laces.
7. The bowling center appears crowded.
8. Friends who came to see them bowl were excited.
9. Their opponents look big and strong.
10. How can they be so confident?
11. The audience is quiet as the tournament begins.

B. Selecting Predicate Adjectives for Sentences Write each sentence, selecting a word from the box to use as a predicate adjective. Underline the word or words each predicate adjective modifies.

12. Rocco and Alma are both _____ at bocce, a game somewhat like bowling.

MODEL ▷ Rocco and Alma are both good at bocce, a game somewhat like bowling.

13. They became _____ at the game in Italy, their native land.
14. The sport is very _____ in that country.
15. How _____ they look when they play!
16. Both seem _____ about being outdoors.
17. The fresh air and sunshine feel _____ today!
18. Lila and Jean seem _____ when they are swimming.
19. They feel _____ in the cool, sparkling water.
20. Swimming laps, they are unusually _____ .

good
wonderful
happy
relaxed
exhilarated
happiest
fast
skilled
popular

C. 21.–31. Writing Predicate Adjectives in Sentences Write 10 sentences about sports or hobbies, using linking verbs and predicate adjectives. Underline the predicate adjectives.

MODEL ▷ 21. Shika feels wonderful after a karate workout.

UNIT 6

5 Comparison with Adjectives: *er, est* pages 282–283

A. Identifying Comparative and Superlative Adjectives Write the adjectives that are in comparative or superlative form.

1. Joanna made the longest jump of all.
MODEL> longest
2. She is the smallest member of the track team.
3. Ellen is faster, but Joanna can do other things.
4. Her jumps are longer and higher.
5. At the hurdles, everyone is slower than she.
6. Ellen is the fastest sprinter on the team.
7. She wins because she has the quickest start.
8. Jan is stronger than Ellen in long-distance races.
9. In the five-mile race, she is the toughest to beat.
10. This meet is the biggest we have ever entered.
11. I hope we are not weaker than our competition.

B. Writing Adjectives of the Correct Form Write the correct form of each adjective in parentheses ( ) to complete each sentence.

12. Sy is a _____ runner than Alonso. (fast)
MODEL> faster
13. Len is the _____ member of the team. (tall)
14. His pole vault is _____ than Sy's. (high)
15. Sy is _____ than Len, but _____ . (small, fast)
16. His _____ event is the high jump. (weak)
17. The fifty-yard dash is our _____ race. (short)
18. Art and Todd are our _____ hurdlers. (swift)
19. Phil is the _____ member of our team. (strong)
20. He is a _____ worker than anyone else. (hard)
21. Phil may become the _____ member of the shot put and discus-throwing squad. (new)
22. He wanted to win a medal at the _____ Junior Olympic meet. (late)

C. 23.–33. Using Forms of Comparison in Sentences Write 10 sentences about skating, using a form of each adjective in the box. Use the positive form in two sentences. Write four sentences using the comparative form and four sentences using the superlative form. Identify the form of each adjective you write.

slow	fast
bold	fine
tiny	clumsy
straight	gentle
safe	healthy

23. Regina's skating is the slowest of all the members of the team.
MODEL> slowest—superlative form

6 Other Comparisons *pages 284–285*

A. **Identifying the Forms of Adjectives** Write any adjective that is used to compare in each sentence. Then identify which form is used.

1. The gym is more crowded today than Monday.
   MODEL> more crowded—comparative
2. Friday is the worst day to reserve a tennis court.
3. It is the least crowded on Monday.
4. Is Sunday less hectic than Saturday for you?
5. Hoyt is a better player than I am.
6. He could be more competitive playing against Bess.
7. I would feel best playing against Tony.
8. Our team had fewer players this year than last.
9. The most hopeless ones gave up playing tennis.
10. We were the most disorganized team.

B. **Choosing Adjectives of the Correct Form** Write the word or words in parentheses that correctly complete each sentence.

11. Of all the swimmers, Toshio is the (able, more able, most able).
    MODEL> most able
12. He is (confident, more confident, most confident) that we will win the meet.
13. We seem (far, farther, farthest) away than ever.
14. Al is (rested, less rested, least rested) than Sam.
15. We've had (little, less, least) practice than most.
16. We will be even (good, better, best) next year.

C. **Using Forms of Comparison in Sentences** Write sentences about track and field events, according to the directions.

17. Write a sentence about the long jump, using the superlative form of *bad*.
    MODEL> Pedro is the worst long jumper in our class.
18. Write a sentence about the hurdles, using the comparative form of *good*.
19. Write a sentence about the pole vault, using the superlative form of *experienced*.
20. Write a sentence about an athlete, using the superlative form of *late*.
21. Write a sentence about weight lifting, using the superlative form of *heavy*.
22. Write a sentence about the fifty-yard dash, using the positive form of *bad*.

1 Adverbs *pages 318–319*

A. Identifying Adverbs Write the adverb or adverbs in each sentence.

1. A very old king once lived in England.
   `MODEL` very, once
2. The king definitely had to choose a successor, but he loved his three sons equally.
3. Finally, he decided to give them a test.
4. The prince who successfully found the tiniest dog would automatically be king.
5. The youngest prince set out gaily and eventually found himself in the court of a lovely white cat.
6. They quickly became friends, and she generously gave him a nut that cleverly concealed a tiny dog.
7. He hopefully asked her aid with another task, to bring back a beautiful princess.
8. Surprisingly, she begged him to kiss her good night.
9. Suddenly she changed into a beautiful princess.

B. Completing Sentences with Adverbs Choose an adverb from the box to complete each sentence. Write each adverb and the word it modifies.

boldly
generously
stealthily
mercifully
cruelly
forever
foolishly

10. Prometheus _____ stole fire from the gods and gave it _____ to people.
    `MODEL` boldly—stole; generously—gave
11. He _____ defied Zeus, who took fire from humans.
12. Climbing into the heavens, Prometheus _____ stole it back.
13. Angered, Zeus _____ chained Prometheus to a rock.
14. A vulture was meant to feed on his liver _____ .
15. Killing the vulture, Hercules _____ saved Prometheus.

C. Writing Adverbs in Sentences Write three sentences as directed. Underline the adverbs.

16. Write a sentence about a Greek myth using an adverb that modifies the verb *flew.*
    `MODEL` Pegasus was a winged horse who flew grandly through the sky.
17. Write a sentence about Pegasus. Use an adverb to describe the adverb *beautifully.*
18. Write a sentence about how the hero Bellerophon must have treated Pegasus. Use an adverb to describe the verb *treated.*
19. Write a sentence about adventures that Bellerophon and Pegasus might have had. Use an adverb to describe the adjective *exciting.*

2 Placement of Adverbs in Sentences pages 320–321

A. Identifying Adverb Placement in Sentences Write the adverb or adverbs in each sentence. Write *before* or *after* to tell where each one is placed in relation to the word or words it modifies.

1. Narcissus fell helplessly in love with his own image.
   MODEL> helplessly—after
2. Narcissus was totally unable to fall in love.
3. The nymph Echo unfortunately fell in love with him.
4. Her love was not returned, so she sadly pined away.
5. After a while, only her voice remained.
6. As a punishment, Narcissus was led secretly to see his own reflection in a fountain.
7. Finally, he fell in love—but with himself.
8. Hopelessly infatuated, he died slowly from grief.

B. Changing the Placement of Adverbs in Sentences Read each sentence, and locate the adverb. Then follow the directions in parentheses.

9. Boldly, King Midas asked for the gift of the golden touch. (Rewrite the sentence so that the adverb comes just before the verb.)
   MODEL> King Midas boldly asked for the gift of the golden touch.
10. Dionysus reluctantly granted his wish. (Rewrite the sentence so that the adverb ends the sentence.)
11. Everything King Midas touched instantly turned into gold. (Rewrite the sentence so that the adverb comes after the verb it modifies.)
12. When his child turned into gold, Midas begged Dionysus pitifully to break the spell. (Rewrite the sentence so that the adverb comes before the verb.)

C. Rewriting Sentences to Vary Adverb Placement Rewrite each sentence in two different ways by changing the placement of the adverb.

13. King Odysseus left his home in Greece regretfully to fight in the Trojan War.
    MODEL> Regretfully, King Odysseus left his home in Greece to fight in the Trojan War.
    King Odysseus regretfully left his home in Greece to fight in the Trojan War.
14. His wife, Penelope, waited loyally for his return.
15. Odysseus fought the Trojans heroically.
16. He cleverly outwitted the horrible giant Cyclops.
17. Skillfully, he dodged the monsters Scylla and Charybdis.
18. Telemachus eventually went to look for his father.

UNIT 7

3 Comparison with Adverbs *pages 322–323*

A. Identifying the Three Forms of Adverbs   Write the adverb or adverbs in each sentence. Identify the comparing form of each adverb. If an adverb cannot be compared, write *cannot be compared.*

1. Early one morning Odysseus bravely sailed from Ithaca to fight in the Trojan War.

   MODEL ▷ early—positive; bravely—positive

2. He was blissfully unaware of the problems ahead.
3. Penelope waited more patiently than most wives.
4. Men wooed her, each more ardently than the last.
5. She slyly promised to accept one after finishing a robe for her father-in-law.
6. Each night she secretly pulled out the threads she had woven during the day.
7. The Norse god Thor most resembles the Roman god Jupiter.
8. Thor treated mortals better than Jupiter and was well known for his kindness.

B. Choosing Adverbs That Compare   Write the form of the adverb in parentheses that correctly completes each sentence.

9. During his travels Odysseus escaped from the Cyclops, a (horribly, more horribly, most horribly) ugly, one-eyed monster.

   MODEL ▷ horribly

10. The Cyclops, (hungrily, more hungrily, most hungrily) than is polite, ate six of Odysseus' men.
11. By planning (slyly, more slyly, most slyly) than ever, Odysseus made the Cyclops sick.
12. Then he (boldly, more boldly, most boldly) blinded the monster.
13. Hiding underneath some sheep, he and his soldiers (quietly, more quietly, most quietly) escaped.

C. Writing the Forms of Adverbs in Sentences   Write the correct comparing form of the adverb in parentheses.

14. Of all the leaders, Odysseus returned to Greece the _____ . (gloriously)

    MODEL ▷ least gloriously

15. Penelope did not _____ recognize him. (easily)
16. Telemachus traveled _____ and _____ than when he began his search. (confidently, wisely)
17. Among the Greeks, Penelope and Telemachus celebrated Odysseus' arrival _____ . (heartily)

4 Negatives *pages 324–325*

A. Identifying Negative Words   Write the word or part of a word that is negative in each sentence.

1. Who hasn't heard the story of the shoemaker and the elves?

MODEL > n't (not)

2. The shoemaker and his wife worked hard, but they never seemed to make any money.

3. At last they had nothing left but enough leather for one pair of shoes.

4. When they went to bed that night, it was not with any optimism.

5. In the morning they couldn't believe their eyes.

6. A beautiful pair of shoes had appeared, but there was no sign of anyone in the workshop.

7. The first customer couldn't resist the shoes.

8. Every morning afterwards the cobbler found new shoes, but no one knew where they came from.

9. As the shoes sold, the cobbler was no longer poor.

B. Avoiding Double Negatives   Write the word in parentheses that best completes each sentence.

10. The queen in the tale "Rumpelstiltskin" hasn't (no, any) idea of the elf's name.

MODEL > any

11. Her father claimed she spun straw into gold when she hadn't (ever, never) done it.

12. The king didn't know (nothing, anything) about their lie when he married her.

13. If she couldn't spin (any, no) gold, she would die.

14. Rumpelstiltskin saved her, but she didn't (ever, never) want to give him what he demanded in return.

15. He thought no one (could, couldn't) guess his name.

C. Rewriting Sentences That Have Double Negatives   Rewrite each sentence to include a correctly stated negative idea.

16. In "The Three Bears," Goldilocks hadn't not ever expected the bears to return so soon.

MODEL > In "The Three Bears," Goldilocks had never expected the bears to return so soon.

17. Goldilocks shouldn't have gone into nobody's house.

18. She hadn't never known the house belonged to bears.

19. She didn't put nothing back after she used it.

20. The bears didn't expect to find no one there.

21. She won't never do it again.

EXTRA PRACTICE

5 Adverb or Adjective? *pages 326–327*

A. Identifying Adjectives and Adverbs Write the underlined words from each sentence. After each word, tell whether it is an *adjective* or an *adverb*.

1. True heroes rarely plan their courageous feats.
   MODEL ▷ True—adjective; rarely—adverb; courageous—adjective
2. Unlikely people may suddenly be heroes in a crisis.
3. Would you dash heedlessly into a burning building to save a helpless baby?
4. Most people probably would.
5. When there is no time to think rationally, we act instinctively.
6. Scientists now say our instinct to save our own kind is as powerful as that for self-preservation.
7. Have you ever been tested in an unexpected way?

B. Using Adjectives and Adverbs Correctly Write the word in parentheses that completes each sentence correctly.

8. During wartime, members of the armed forces (clear, clearly) have chances for heroism.
   MODEL ▷ clearly
9. They learn to respond (quickly, quick) in training.
10. Victory depends on acting (heroic, heroically) during the heat of battle.
11. No one knows beforehand whether he or she will be (brave, bravely).
12. Can one be a hero and not be (fearful, fearfully)?
13. Fear (real, really) produces adrenaline, which helps people to act in emergencies.
14. They become (ready, readily) for "fight or flight."
15. The (true, truly) hero who stays and fights receives the strength and courage to do so.
16. The person who is (interested, interestingly) in self-preservation has the stamina to save himself or herself from a threatening situation.

C. 17.–27. Writing Adjectives and Adverbs in Sentences Write 10 sentences about heroes. Use at least one adverb and one adjective in each sentence. Draw an arrow from each adverb or adjective to the word or words it modifies.

MODEL ▷ 17. Heroes of today are quite different from the heroes of past generations.

UNIT 8

1 Prepositions and Prepositional Phrases pages 366–367

A. Identifying Prepositions, Prepositional Phrases, and Objects of Prepositions Write each prepositional phrase. Underline each preposition once and its object twice.

1. Lewis and Clark sailed up the Missouri River exploring the land of the Louisiana Purchase.

   MODEL > <u>up</u> the <u><u>Missouri River</u></u>, <u>of</u> the <u><u>Louisiana Purchase</u></u>

2. Before the Lewis and Clark Expedition, the land west of the Mississippi River was unknown territory.
3. President Thomas Jefferson had the group follow the Missouri River to its source in the West.
4. Lewis and Clark also traveled over the Rocky Mountains to the Pacific Ocean.
5. With 26 soldiers in their party, Lewis and Clark left St. Louis in 1804.
6. They befriended Indian tribes along the way.
7. The Indians were interested in them; most had never seen white men before.

B. Completing Sentences with Prepositional Phrases Write a prepositional phrase to complete each sentence. Underline each preposition once and its object twice.

8. Many explorers sailed _____ but returned _____ empty-handed.

   MODEL > <u>to</u> the <u><u>New World</u></u>, <u>to</u> their <u><u>homelands</u></u>

9. Two _____ were Coronado and de Soto.
10. They were lured by stories _____ .
11. The Seven Cities of Gold was a legend _____ .
12. De Soto found the Mississippi River _____ .
13. Coronado traveled through the Southwest but went home _____ .

C. Combining Sentences Use a prepositional phrase to combine each pair of sentences. Write each sentence.

14. Henry Hudson left the Netherlands. He departed in a ship.

    MODEL > Henry Hudson left the Netherlands in a ship.

15. Hudson looked for a northwest passage. He wanted to find a northwest passage to Asia.
16. He sailed across the Atlantic Ocean. His ship set sail in 1609.
17. His crew mutinied. They mutinied on the return voyage.

2 Prepositional Phrases Used as Adjectives *pages 368–369*

A. Identifying Adjective Phrases Write the sentences. Underline once the phrases used as adjectives and underline twice the words they modify.

1. The explorers of today travel to distant planets and find objects of great interest.

   MODEL ▷ The explorers of today travel to distant planets and find objects of great interest.

2. Scientists on Earth were eager to study rocks from the moon's surface.

3. Moon rocks taught us something about the Earth.

4. At the museum we saw an exhibit of moon rocks.

5. Several explorers of today are robots.

6. Spacecraft from the United States and other countries send back reports about other planets.

7. We have discovered new facts about the universe.

8. Cameras on the craft gather information.

9. This information about our solar system is then transmitted to tracking stations on Earth.

10. Beautiful photos of Jupiter and Saturn have been sent.

11. Voyages to Jupiter and Saturn last many years.

B. Completing Sentences with Adjective Phrases Write an appropriate prepositional phrase used as an adjective to complete each sentence.

12. Space pioneers _____ may discover new planets _____ .

    MODEL ▷ Space pioneers of the twenty-first century may discover new planets of fantastic beauty.

13. Will other kinds _____ exist on planets _____ ?

14. Stars _____ may have planets _____ .

15. Our solar system is only a small part _____ .

16. Do you believe colonies _____ will ever leave Earth to live on other planets _____ ?

C. Writing Sentences with Adjective Phrases Write each sentence as directed. Underline once the adjective phrases and underline twice the word or words they modify.

17. Write a sentence about a starship, using the preposition *under.*

    MODEL ▷ The tanks under the starship's tail contain fuel.

18. Write a sentence about a space crew, using the preposition *among.*

19. Write a sentence about people landing on another planet, using the preposition *with.*

3 Prepositional Phrases Used as Adverbs pages 370–371

A. Identifying Adverb Phrases   Read each sentence. Write each prepositional phrase that is used as an adverb. Write the word that each phrase modifies.

1. A woman in a long Elizabethan dress walked confidently into the room.

MODEL> into the room—walked

2. Beneath red curls pearls dangled from her ears.
3. She strode with purpose straight to the royal wigmaker.
4. He rose to his feet and greeted her.
5. She acknowledged him with a brief nod.
6. She spoke with authority and gave him an order.
7. The old man replied without hesitation.
8. The queen removed the red curls from her head.
9. The wigmaker replaced them with a new style.
10. The queen looked into the mirror.
11. She smiled at her reflection.

B. Enriching Sentences with Adverb Phrases   To complete each sentence, write the phrase in parentheses that acts as an adverb.

12. The Viking leader strode (with the golden hair, of immense size, toward his longboat).

MODEL> toward his longboat

13. Eric wore a long cape (of animal skins, over his brawny shoulders, with a hood).
14. He spoke to the waiting men (from his clan, in their battle gear, in ringing tones).
15. The expert craftsman carved the prow (of the boat, with the warlike crew, with great skill).
16. The brave men prepared the ship (for its journey, in the harbor, with the tall mast).
17. Storms raged, but Eric calmed his crew (of brave men, with fierce words, of fighters).
18. Eric, the leader of the Vikings, shouted to his crewmen (with broad shoulders, with strong conviction, from the north).

C. 19.–29. Writing Adverb Phrases in Original Sentences   Write 10 sentences about people or nations of the past. Begin each sentence with an adverb phrase. Underline the phrase once and the word that it modifies twice.

MODEL> 19. In ancient Britain lived a king named Arthur.

UNIT 8

4 Choosing the Correct Preposition *pages 372–373*

A. Using Prepositions Correctly   Write the word in parentheses that correctly completes each sentence.

  1. Rachel searched (between, among) the classroom seats to find her contact lens.

MODEL > among

  2. She looked around (in, into) the school cafeteria but found nothing.
  3. She might (have, of) lost it on the playground.
  4. Perhaps it fell (among, between) two floorboards.
  5. Is your vision any different (from, than) mine?
  6. Let's go (in, into) the office and look there.
  7. I've found it (among, between) these paper clips.
  8. You should (have, of) noticed it sooner.
  9. How are contact lenses different (from, than) glasses?
  10. (Between, Among) the two, I prefer contacts.
  11. I can see (in, into) the next room without glasses.

B. Correcting Errors with Prepositional Phrases   Write each sentence correctly. Note: Some prepositional phrases are already correct. If the sentence has no errors, write *correct*.

  12. Narciso walked back in the science room to pick up his forgotten book.

MODEL > Narciso walked back into the science room to pick up his forgotten book.

  13. He strode quickly among the two rows of desks.
  14. He could of jumped for joy when he saw the book.
  15. This class was a little different than his others.
  16. He enjoyed working among all the test tubes.
  17. Botany gave him a view in a totally new world.
  18. "I must of left my book behind when I spoke to Margaret," Narciso thought.
  19. Between all the girls in his science class, Narciso liked Margaret best.
  20. She received excellent grades into science and was a lot of fun, too.

C. 21.–31. Writing Prepositional Phrases in Original Sentences   Write 10 sentences about an ordinary event. Use one of the following prepositions correctly in each sentence.

in   between   from   into   among   than

MODEL > 21. Jan's secret is safe as long as it remains among us three girls.

5 Conjunctions *pages 374–375*

A. Identifying Conjunctions   Write the conjunction(s) in each sentence.

   1. Ancient Roman triremes and Norse longboats were similar in some ways.

   `MODEL` > and

   2. They were galley-style boats and were used for war.
   3. The boats were propelled by oars, but they were also equipped with masts and sails.
   4. For some time, only the Vikings knew how to navigate using the stars or the sun to guide them.
   5. Columbus is credited with discovering America, but Viking ships actually crossed the Atlantic first.
   6. Viking boats had beautifully carved prows, and along the sides were hung the shields of warriors.
   7. At his funeral, a Viking chieftain's body was placed on his boat, and the boat was sunk.

B. Choosing Appropriate Conjunctions   For each sentence, write the most suitable conjunction in parentheses.

   8. Dying in battle was accepted among barbarian warriors, (and, but, or) not surrender.

   `MODEL` > but

   9. In Norse mythology the place for dead heroes is named *Valhalla,* (and, or, but) "the hall of the slain."
   10. Maidens called *valkyries* were either the daughters (and, or, but) the attendants of Odin.
   11. They rode into a battle, chose the warriors to be killed, (and, or, but) carried them to Valhalla.
   12. No one knows how they chose the victims, (and, or, but) certainly no one consulted the warriors.

C. Combining Sentences with Conjunctions   Combine these sentence pairs with conjunctions that fit the context. Write each sentence.

   13. The Carthaginians won one Punic War. The Romans conquered them by winning two.

   `MODEL` > The Carthaginians won one Punic War, but the Romans conquered them by winning two.

   14. In the First Punic War, the Carthaginians were led by Hamilcar Barca. The Romans won and took Sicily.
   15. In the Second Punic War, Hamilcar's son Hannibal crossed the Alps with his army. He invaded Rome.
   16. At the end of the Third Punic War, Rome defeated Carthage. Roman soldiers sowed salt in Carthage's fields.

6 Interjections *pages 376–377*

A. Identifying Interjections Write the interjection in each sentence. Label each interjection *strong* or *mild*.

1. Oh, Mikela lost her ticket for the Trans-Pluto rocket, but she'll buy another.

MODEL > Oh—mild

2. Phooey! I wish I were going too.
3. Alas, is there no way to get a half-fare ticket?
4. Wow! Pluto is my favorite planet as well as my favorite cartoon character!
5. Well, I guess Mikela won't mind leaving us behind.
6. Oh, who else could possibly be going?
7. Oops! Mikela forgot to have her passport renewed!
8. Oh, no! She is so forgetful!
9. Good grief! The rocket will take off without her!
10. Dear me, do you think she'll make it?
11. Hurrah! Here she comes, without a second to spare!

B. Choosing Interjections to Fit Sentence Context Write the interjection in parentheses that fits the context of each sentence.

12. (Ouch! Oops! Whee!) Zero gravity is fun!

MODEL > Whee!

13. (Oops! Whoopee! Well!) My hat just floated away!
14. (Wow! Ouch! Hurrah!) I hit my toe on the landing!
15. (Hmmm, Wow! Oops,) I wonder why the ride has stopped.
16. (Ouch! Well, Oh!) It's Senator Greenly, I'm sure!
17. (Whew! Look! Whee!) He's getting onto the ride!
18. (Oops! Whee! Well,) I hope he watches his toes.

C. Writing Sentences with Interjections Add an appropriate interjection to each sentence. Write each sentence, adding the correct punctuation.

19. The spaceship from Venus is arriving again—for the seven-hundredth time.

MODEL > Well, the spaceship from Venus is arriving again—for the seven-hundredth time.

20. Those Venusians have six tentacles!
21. I forgot; you're married to a Venusian.
22. I'm sure they have other fine qualities.
23. Do you know any other people on the ship?
24. I have a friend who's coming from Rigel II.
25. Most Rigelians need special equipment to live on Earth.
26. Here comes my friend now!

UNIT 8

7 Phrases and Clauses *pages 378–379*

A. Identifying Phrases and Clauses Write each sentence. Underline each clause once and each phrase twice.

1. On St. Lucia's day, Swedish girls wear a crown of candles and serve their families breakfast in bed.

> MODEL> On St. Lucia's day, Swedish girls wear a crown of candles and serve their families breakfast in bed.

2. For weeks Ingrid and Anna anticipate the holiday.
3. For the first time Anna will wear the candles.
4. Both girls are excited about the white dresses that their grandmother is making for them.
5. On the morning of St. Lucia's day they will wake up early so that they can make pancakes.

B. Completing Sentences with Phrases and Clauses Write the sentence part in parentheses that makes the most sense. Identify the sentence part as a *phrase* or as a *clause*.

6. Scandinavians (who live near the Arctic Circle, from the south, in the cities) lay sod on their roofs to keep out the cold.

> MODEL> who live near the Arctic Circle—clause

7. In a Norse story a man brags that he can do his wife's work better (than she can, in winter, without shoes).
8. He puts the cow on the roof to graze (in pajamas, after a bath, on the sod) and drops the rope down the chimney.
9. In the house he ties the rope around his waist (as a belt, so that the cow won't wander off, with a knot).
10. His wife later finds the cow off the roof and her husband (singing loudly, asleep, up the chimney).

C. Writing Phrases and Clauses in Original Sentences Write each sentence as directed. Sentences should be about sports in northern countries.

11. Write a sentence about skiing. Write one or two phrases that are part of a clause.

> MODEL> The Norwegians, whose country is covered with snow for many months, are great skiers.

12. Write a sentence about cross-country skiing. Use an adverb phrase and a clause.
13. Write a sentence about bobsledding. Use one or more adjective phrases in a clause.
14. Write a sentence about skating. Begin with a clause.
15. Write a sentence about building something out of snow. Write a phrase that is part of a clause.

8 Independent and Dependent Clauses *pages 380–381*

A. Identifying Independent and Dependent Clauses Write each sentence. Underline the independent clause once and the dependent clause twice.

1. The Italians are among the best cooks in the world because they love good food.

   MODEL > The Italians are among the best cooks in the world because they love good food.

2. Although the ingredients are simple, they are fresh and flavorful.

3. Though many toppings may be added, pizza is basically bread, tomato sauce, and cheese.

4. When it was introduced in America, pizza was an instant success.

5. Pizza parlors, which sprang up by the thousands, are probably more numerous here than in Italy.

6. Everyone who loves pizza has a favorite version.

B. Completing Sentences with Clauses Write words to complete each sentence. Write whether you added words to a dependent clause or to an independent clause.

7. Spaghetti, which is a dish _____ , seems to be a world-wide favorite.

   MODEL > made of noodles and tomato sauce—dependent clause

8. Pasta, which is another name for macaroni, comes in _____ .

9. Although pasta was thought to have come from China, the story does not _____ .

10. Although noodles are equally popular in China, pasta _____ before Marco Polo's expedition.

11. Because the seasonings _____ , Chinese noodles and Italian spaghetti taste very different.

C. Adding Clauses to Sentences Add a clause to each sentence part. Write each sentence. Then write what kind of clause you added.

12. which grow on vines in the Italian hills

    MODEL > Purple grapes, which grow on vines in the Italian hills, are sweet and juicy.—independent clause

13. not only do most rural Italians make their own wine

14. while elegant restaurants may please tourists

15. Italians often use wine to flavor their cooking

16. they use red wine in many sauces

17. many northern Italians, however, add cheese to sauces

EXTRA PRACTICE

9 Complex Sentences *pages 382–383*

A. Identifying Compound and Complex Sentences Write *complex* for each complex sentence. Write *compound* for each compound sentence.

1. Since Holland is so flat, people can see tulip beds stretching for miles.

MODEL ▷ complex

2. Because most of their country is below sea level, the Dutch have built dikes to keep back the water.
3. When the canals between cities freeze in winter, iceboats use them as highways.
4. In the past the Dutch skated from town to town, as Hans and his friends did in the book *Hans Brinker.*
5. Canals also run through Amsterdam, and they add to the beauty of the city.

B. Completing Complex Sentences Add a clause to make each item a complex sentence. Write the sentences. Be sure to use commas correctly.

6. The Dutch harness the winds to run windmills.

MODEL ▷ The Dutch, who save money on electricity, harness the winds to run windmills.

7. The windmills dot the landscape.
8. The sails make a curious sound.
9. Some people live in windmills.
10. Lighthouse keepers must be like windmill dwellers.
11. Would you rather live in a windmill or a lighthouse?

C. Writing Original Complex Sentences Write each complex sentence about a European city as directed.

12. Write a complex sentence about Paris. Write a dependent clause beginning with *which.*

MODEL ▷ Paris, which is one of the most beautiful cities in Europe, is a center for tourism.

13. Write a complex sentence about a city in England. Include a dependent clause beginning with *who.*
14. Write a complex sentence about Rome. Include an independent clause beginning with *the Coliseum.*
15. Write a complex sentence about a city in Denmark. Include a dependent clause beginning with *where.*
16. Write a complex sentence about a city in Ireland. Include a dependent clause beginning with *which.*
17. Write a complex sentence about a city in Sweden. Include an independent clause beginning *the city.*

EXTRA PRACTICE

1 Capitalization and End Punctuation in Sentences

pages 418–419

A. Identifying Correct Capitalization and Punctuation If each sentence is capitalized and punctuated correctly, write *correct*. If not, write the sentence correctly.

1. Boating on the Colorado River is fun

MODEL ▷ Boating on the Colorado River is fun.

2. Have you ever boated on white water
3. we went on a large rubber raft.
4. There were four of us on the trip
5. How exciting it was
6. we had to work hard to get through the rapids.
7. Did your boat ever capsize
8. It did once, but we were wearing life jackets.
9. the scenery we passed was breathtaking.
10. Sheer cliffs rose up on each side of the river
11. Were we ever exhausted that night

B. Correcting Errors in Capitalization and Punctuation Write the letter in front of each sentence part that is incorrect. Then write that sentence part correctly.

12. (a) Have you ever skied down a (b) mountain.

MODEL ▷ b—mountain?

13. (a) we went skiing in Vermont last (b) winter.
14. (a) How tall the mountain looked to (b) me.
15. (a) I was afraid to go down the (b) slope
16. (a) What made me change my (b) mind.
17. (a) once I began, I never wanted (b) to stop.
18. (a) What a vacation that (b) was?

C. Capitalizing and Punctuating Sentences Correctly Write each sentence, using the correct capitalization and end punctuation.

19. never go camping without a waterproof tent

MODEL ▷ Never go camping without a waterproof tent.

20. we started out on a beautiful sunny day
21. there wasn't a cloud in the sky
22. what a perfect spot we found for camping
23. under the stars, we climbed into our sleeping bags
24. when the rain began, can you imagine how we felt
25. in an instant our sleeping bags were soaked
26. have you ever carried a waterlogged sleeping bag

2 Commas and Semicolons Within Sentences
pages 420–422

A. Identifying Correct Punctuation   If the punctuation within each sentence is correct, write *correct*. If something is wrong, write the sentence correctly.

  1. Since my dad is a pilot he flew me to Nepal.

  MODEL > Since my dad is a pilot, he flew me to Nepal.

  2. On the way we landed in Hawaii Guam and Sri Lanka.
  3. We wanted to see India we also wanted to see Pakistan.
  4. Flying low, you may see deer elephants and tigers.
  5. We tried to spot a leopard alas we failed.
  6. As we neared Nepal, the land became mountainous.
  7. When we passed over villages, we could see people in brightly colored clothes.
  8. The Himalayas were wonderful I enjoyed looking down at them from the plane.

B. Choosing the Correct Punctuation for Sentences   For each sentence, write the item in parentheses that is correctly punctuated.

  9. (Alicia my sister) (Alicia, my sister) (Alicia, my sister,) has been to Africa.

  MODEL > Alicia, my sister,

  10. She lived in (Namibia Chad, and Kenya) (Namibia Chad and Kenya) (Namibia, Chad, and Kenya).
  11. (Brian,) (Brian) (Brian;) you met her in Nairobi.
  12. (When she was there,) (When, she was there) (When she was there) she worked on an archaeological dig.
  13. (My, goodness,) (My goodness,) (My goodness) that must have been an exciting job!
  14. (Yes she liked it a lot,) (Yes, she liked it a lot;) (Yes, she liked it a lot,) and she hopes to return soon.

C. Punctuating Sentences Correctly   Write each sentence, using the correct internal punctuation.

  15. My dog chased the intruder out of the house down the road and into a squad car.

  MODEL > My dog chased the intruder out of the house, down the road, and into a squad car.

  16. Lieutenant Becker the officer in charge was amazed.
  17. Awakened by the noise all the neighbors had come outside.
  18. Mr. Duffy Joanne and Kelly congratulated him.
  19. When things quieted down we gave my dog a treat.
  20. Well that is after all what makes him happiest.

UNIT 9

3 Capitalization of Proper Nouns, Proper Adjectives, and *I* pages 423–424

A. Using Capital Letters Correctly Write each sentence. Correct any errors in capitalization.

1. "The Tell-Tale Heart" is a suspenseful story by the american writer Edgar allan Poe.

MODEL> "The Tell-Tale Heart" is a suspenseful story by the American writer Edgar Allan Poe.

2. The most famous fictional detective is the englishman Sherlock holmes.

3. Holmes and his sidekick dr. Watson were the creations of sir Arthur conan Doyle.

4. They lived on Baker street in london, England.

5. Two of mr. Holmes's cases were recounted in "The Hound of the Baskervilles" and "The Sign of the Four."

B. Choosing Correct Capitalization Write the word or words in parentheses that are correctly capitalized.

6. Robert Louis Stevenson wrote an adventurous story about pirates called (*Treasure Island*) (*Treasure island*) (*treasure island*).

MODEL> *Treasure Island*

7. Jim Hawkins, a young boy, goes to sea on the HMS (*Hispaniola*) (*hispaniola*).

8. The ship is under the command of (captain smollett) (captain Smollett) (Captain Smollett).

9. The search for treasure begins on (Skeleton island) (skeleton island) (Skeleton Island).

10. This book is one of the most exciting (I) (i) have ever read.

C. Capitalizing Sentences Correctly Write each sentence, capitalizing proper nouns, proper adjectives, and the pronoun *I* correctly.

11. Today i contacted the department of tourism for information on trips to the grand canyon.

MODEL> Today I contacted the Department of Tourism for information on trips to the Grand Canyon.

12. The arizona department of highways sent a map of indian pueblo sites.

13. i will be in new mexico in july and august.

14. Shall i visit taos and the rest of the southwest?

15. Perhaps i'll travel northwest to the columbia river valley.

UNIT 9

4 Abbreviations pages 425–426

A. Identifying Abbreviations Write the word for which each of the following abbreviations stands.

1. Tues.
MODEL▷ Tuesday
2. Inc.
3. Rt.
4. Capt.
5. St.
6. Blvd.
7. Fri.
8. Mr.
9. A.M.

10. Ln.
11. Co.
12. Ave.
13. Thurs.
14. Oct.
15. Mon.
16. Sept.
17. Wed.
18. Rd.
19. Dept.

B. Writing Abbreviations Write the abbreviations for the following words.

20. February
MODEL▷ Feb.
21. Mister
22. Senior
23. Reverend
24. Drive
25. Route
26. Saturday
27. August
28. Avenue
29. November
30. September

31. Road
32. "before noon"
33. Incorporated
34. Friday
35. "after noon"
36. Corporation
37. Junior
38. March
39. Company
40. Doctor
41. Sunday
42. January

C. Using Abbreviations Write the following addresses as they would appear on an envelope, substituting abbreviations when appropriate. See page 56 of the **Writer's Handbook** for postal abbreviations.

43. Reverend James Thomas Hill
17839 Holly Lane
San Antonio, Texas 78284
MODEL▷ Rev. James T. Hill
17839 Holly Ln.
San Antonio, TX 78284

44. Captain Mary Tate Ogden
Sheriff's Department
506 Third Avenue
Milwaukee, Wisconsin 53233

45. Doctor Carl Patrick Worthington
1894 Park Place
Newport News, Virginia 23630

46. Mister Paul Stanley Brown, Junior
9000 Pennsylvania Boulevard
Birmingham, Alabama 35203

5 Letters *pages 427--429*

A. **Correcting Capitalization and Punctuation in Letter Parts**   Each letter part is correct except for one error. Explain what is not correct.

1. 10230 Douglas Road
St. Louis Missouri 63123
December 10, 1993

   MODEL ▷ A comma should be placed between St. Louis
   and Missouri.

2. 1821 Gorman Avenue.
Hillsborough, Texas 73906
August 12, 1993

3. Dr. Herbert Krystal
Mercy Hospital
165 Liberty street
Orlando, Florida 32807

4. Sincerely Yours,
Elizabeth Scott

5. Dear Miss Brown

B. **Choosing Correct Capitalization and Punctuation**   Write the correct form of the letter part in parentheses.

6. (Yours Very Truly,) (Yours very truly,) (Yours very Truly,)

   MODEL ▷ Yours very truly,

7. (May 21 1993) (May 21, 1993) (may 21, 1993)
8. (Dear Ms. Diaz) (Dear Ms. Diaz:) (dear Ms. Diaz,)
9. (38 Concord street) (38 Concord st.) (38 Concord Street)
10. (Your Friend,) (your friend,) (Your friend,)
11. (Nashville, Tennessee 37205) (Nashville, Tennessee, 37205)
(Nashville Tennessee 37205)

C. **Writing Letter Parts Correctly**   Write each letter part correctly.

12. (heading) 211 temple street/new haven connecticut 06510/
june 5 1993

    MODEL ▷ 211 Temple Street
    New Haven, Connecticut 06510
    June 5, 1993

13. (closing) sincerely yours/dr louise m adjigian
14. (greeting) dear general Szepansky
15. (inside address) mrs iris lopez/the children's store/945 e
grand avenue/new castle pennsylvania 16101

EXTRA PRACTICE

UNIT 9

6 Envelopes *pages 430–431*

A. Identifying Parts of Addresses Identify the errors in each address. Then write each address correctly. Underline the part of each address that you corrected. See page 431 for state abbreviations.

1. Ms. stacia Gibbs
   8506 Tasmayne dr.
   Elk City, Okl. 73644

   MODEL ▷ Ms. Stacia Gibbs
   8506 Tasmayne Dr.
   Elk City, OK 73644

2. Mister Jack porter
   3234 cuyahoga St.
   brewer, ME 04412

3. dr. Melanie brinkley
   8743 Buckle road
   Alamo, TX 78516

4. Mr. Antonio gomez
   930 Wayne St.
   Flushing, n.y. 11358

5. Mr. martin lynds
   1616 new York Ave.
   Fort scott, KS 66701

6. Ms. caroline Murphy
   87576 bull Rd.
   chicago, Illin. 60614

7. Mr. marshall huggins
   88 Champs Dr.
   Yardley, penn. 19067

8. Ms. wanda Jackson
   894 bradley Avenue
   Weston, ct 06833

9. Doctor david Armstrong
   1845 kennedy St.
   Boston, Mass. 02210

B. Correcting Parts of Addresses Write each item correctly.

10. Vershire vermont 05079

    MODEL ▷ Vershire, VT 05079

11. Mister steve Thomason
12. 89483 silver avenue
13. doctor Sam forrest
14. plymouth michigan 48170
15. San antonio TX 78284
16. ms. Bettie jo Hollister
17. Mr. walter wiznesky
18. Cortez Col. 81321
19. Miz Elise lafontise
20. rockport maine 04856

C. Building Addresses Write the lines of each address in the proper order, correcting any errors.

21. 8783 wallford Blvd.
    Mr. Chris valerio
    chaska MN 55318

    MODEL ▷ Mr. Chris Valerio
    8783 Wallford Blvd.
    Chaska, MN 55318

22. casselberry FL 32707
    Ms. anne Phillips
    7120 Bonaparte Dr.

23. Mz carol Helander
    Newport news, Vg 23630
    666 venus blvd.

24. Doctor Ashford simpson
    19468 Poplar Pl.
    milwaukee, wi 53233

25. Midlothian, Vir.
    Ms. Anita Guggenheim
    1902 Balken Ct.

7 Outlines *pages 432–433*

A. Identifying Correct Outline Form Each outline part is correct except for one error. Explain what is not correct.

1. 1. Tales of adventure and suspense
        A. American authors
            1. Edgar Allan Poe
            2. Shirley Jackson

> MODEL The first number should be a Roman numeral.

2. A. Famous pirates
        1. Captain Kidd
        2. Long John Silver
        3. Bluebeard

3. I. American heroes
        a. Armed forces
            1. General Patton
            2. General Eisenhower

4. I. Fictional detectives
        A. Young detectives
            1. Nancy Drew
            2. Encyclopedia Brown

B. Correcting Outlines Write each outline part correctly.

5. B. british authors
        1. Jonathan swift
        2. Sir Arthur Conan Doyle

> MODEL B. British authors
>   1. Jonathan Swift
>   2. Sir Arthur Conan Doyle

6. A. horror movies
        1. the Phantom of the opera
        2. The Mummy

7. 1. Movie Monsters
        a. King kong
        b. godzilla

C. Writing Outlines Correctly Write each outline part correctly.

8. i. poe's detective stories a. "murders in the rue morgue"
        b. "the purloined letter"

> MODEL I. Poe's detective stories
>   A. "Murders in the Rue Morgue"
>   B. "The Purloined Letter"

9. a. books in the "Oz" series 1 dorothy and the Wizard of oz 2 The land of oz

10. I. characters in The Lion the witch and the wardrobe
        a. aslan b. susan c. Edmund

UNIT 9

8 Titles *pages 434–435*

A. **Identifying Important Words** Write the words in each title that should be capitalized.

1. "the yesterdays and the tomorrows"
   MODEL > The, Yesterdays, Tomorrows
2. island of the blue dolphins
3. trail boss in pigtails
4. my side of the mountain
5. "let's take a trip into space"

6. the war with mr. wizzle
7. the mouse that roared
8. where the wild things are
9. sports illustrated
10. national geographic

B. **Writing Titles** Write the titles as they should be written.

11. the kansas city times (newspaper)
    MODEL > The Kansas City Times
12. saying yes (poem)
13. the secret of the andes (novel)
14. the fountains of rome (musical work)
15. boy's life (magazine)
16. home on the range (song)
17. the fallen spaceman (novel)
18. understanding time zones (article)
19. the pittsburgh press (newspaper)
20. the mystery of sally lee (story)
21. life (magazine)

22. there's no business like show business (song)
23. riders of the purple sage (novel)
24. do not go gentle into that good night (poem)
25. alaska: vacation wonderland (article)
26. the adventures of huckleberry finn (novel)
27. america the beautiful (song)
28. sports illustrated (magazine)
29. a comedy of errors (play)
30. up in the sky (poem)

C. **Writing Titles in Sentences** Write these sentences containing titles. Use correct capitalization and punctuation.

31. Tim's favorite novel is treasure island.
    MODEL > Tim's favorite novel is Treasure Island.
32. Rita sang yankee doodle dandy with the band.
33. Kate always enjoyed the sports section of the batesville bugle.

34. Roger memorized the poem the first signs of spring.
35. For her assignment Sally read an article entitled kite building in france.

9 Bibliographies *pages 436–437*

A. Writing Bibliographic Entries Write a bibliographic entry for each item.

1. Collected Poems of Edgar Allan Poe, Edgar Allan Poe, "Annabel Lee," 1943, New World Publishers, Chicago.

   MODEL> Poe, Edgar Allan. "Annabel Lee." Collected Poems of Edgar Allan Poe. Chicago: New World Publishers, 1943.

2. New York, Charles Scribner's Sons, The Wind in the Willows, 1908, Kenneth Grahame.

3. The Wishing Tree, New York, Random House, William Faulkner, 1964.

4. Oxford University Press, London, Philippa Pearce, Tom's Midnight Garden, 1958.

5. The Young Unicorns, Madeleine L'Engle, New York, 1968, Farrar, Straus & Giroux, Inc.

6. Cynthia Voigt, New York, 1982, Random House, Dicey's Song.

B. Correcting Bibliographic Entries Write each bibliographic entry correctly.

7. edgar allan poe, tales of edgar allan poe, 1945, the purloined letter, new world publishers

   MODEL> Poe, Edgar Allan. "The Purloined Letter." Tales of Edgar Allan Poe. Chicago: New World Publishers, 1945.

8. t. fisher unwin publishers, 1904, new york, the phoenix and the carpet, e. nesbit.

9. pygmalion, george bernard shaw, new york, 1951, seven plays, dodd, mead & company.

10. kate seredy, the good master, 1935, viking penguin books, new york.

11. dell publishing company, the education of little tree, 1976, forrest carter, new york.

12. ranger rick magazine, pages 40–44, national wildlife federation, project peregrine, volume 19, number 6, june 1985.

13. macmillan publishing company, inger mccabe, new york, week in amy's world: new england, 1970.

C. 14.–19. Writing Original Bibliographies Write the bibliographic information on five books you have read.

   MODEL> 14. Welty, Eudora. A Curtain of Green and Other Stories. New York: Harcourt Brace Jovanovich, 1969.

10 Direct Quotations and Dialogue

pages 438–439

A. Identifying Correctly Written Dialogue If the dialogue is correct, write *correct*. If it is incorrect, explain why.

1. "No! cried the detective." "He is guilty!"

MODEL> Quotation marks should be added after <u>No!</u> and deleted after <u>detective</u>.

2. "You've got the wrong man" replied the suspect.

3. I suppose you have an airtight alibi," countered the detective sarcastically.

4. "You bet I have!" shouted the accused man. I was with my sick mother."

5. "Well." said the detective. "we'll have to check up on this sick mother of yours."

6. "I'm afraid that may be rather difficult, the suspect replied sadly. She died this morning."

B. Correcting Dialogue Write each passage of dialogue. Correct the errors.

7. "What are you trying to tell me"? Asked the suspect, "Won't I get a fair trial"?

MODEL> "What are you trying to tell me?" asked the suspect. "Won't I get a fair trial?"

8. The judge responded "of course, you will." "Everybody gets a fair trial in my court."

9. "oops"! exclaimed the court stenographer. Could you repeat that, please"?

10. "Does the accused wish to take the witness stand, asked the judge, to give his side of the story?"

11. I'd rather not talk about it replied the suspect. The subject is too painful for me.

12. If you want the court to consider you innocent "responded the judge" you'd better speak up now.

13. "Well, drawled the suspect, all I know is that I didn't commit any crime." But you might want to talk to my neighbor, Mr. Dewey.

C. 14.–19. Writing Original Dialogue Write at least five lines of dialogue between a burglary victim and the police officers who have come to his assistance. Use all four kinds of sentences. Vary the placement of the dialogue parts of each sentence.

MODEL> **14.** "What is missing from your house?" asked the police officer.

WRITER'S HANDBOOK

Contents

Sentences

- A **sentence** is a group of words that expresses a complete thought. Each sentence is made up of two parts, the subject and the predicate. A sentence begins with a capital letter and ends with a punctuation mark.

  sentence

  T he sun is the center of the solar system .

- There are four kinds of sentences: *declarative, interrogative, imperative,* and *exclamatory.*

- A **declarative sentence** makes a statement. It ends with a period.

  declarative sentence

  The new zoo will open tomorrow .

- An **interrogative sentence** asks a question. It ends with a question mark.

  interrogative sentence

  Did you see the squirrel climb the tree ?

- The subject of an interrogative sentence usually comes after the predicate or between two parts of the simple predicate.

  Did Rosa lend you her bicycle?

- An **imperative sentence** gives an order or makes a request. It ends with a period.

  imperative sentence

  Close the door quietly .

  Please meet me at the main entrance .

- *You* (understood) is the subject of an imperative sentence.

  (you) Feed the cats in the morning.

- An **exclamatory sentence** expresses strong feeling. It ends with an exclamation point.

  exclamatory sentence

  How huge the moon looks tonight !

- A **simple sentence** is a sentence that expresses only one complete thought.

  simple sentence

  Carla drove me to the station.
  I waited for the train.

compound sentence
- A **compound sentence** contains two or more simple sentences joined by *and, or, but,* or a semicolon.

  Carla drove me to the station **, and** I waited for the train.

  Carla drove me to the station **;** I waited for the train.

complex sentence
- A **complex sentence** contains an independent clause and one or more dependent clauses.

  ┌──────────────independent clause──────────────┐
  The California gold rush helped settle the West,
  ┌────────────dependent clause────────────┐
  although many mining towns disappeared
  ┌────────────dependent clause────────────┐
  after all the gold was mined.

subject
- The **subject** of a sentence names someone or something. The subject of a sentence is the part about which something is being said.

  Timmy is playing in the snow.

complete subject
- The **complete subject** is all the words that make up the subject of a sentence.

  The shallow lake froze in the winter.

simple subject
- The **simple subject** is the main word or words in the complete subject.

  complete
  ┌──subject──┐
  A large **fish** swam right near me.

compound subject
- A **compound subject** is two or more subjects that have the same predicate. The connecting word *and* or *or* joins the parts of a compound subject.

  Singers and **dancers** performed in the park.

  Michael or **Marsha** will collect the empty bottles.

predicate
- The **predicate** of a sentence tells what the subject is or does.

  Harold **practices basketball every afternoon** .

  His brother **is the coach of the basketball team** .

complete predicate
- The **complete predicate** is all the words that make up the predicate of the sentence.

  Ann **waved to her friends on the shore** .

- The **simple predicate** is the key word or words in the complete predicate.

┌────complete predicate────┐
Marjorie repaired the broken vase.

┌────complete predicate────┐
The campers can carry their canoes.

- A **compound predicate** is two or more simple predicates that have the same subject. The connecting word *and, or,* or *but* joins the parts of a compound predicate.

Farmers plant and harvest their crops.

They sell the grain or store it in silos.

New machines save time but cost a great deal.

- A sentence is in **natural word order** if the subject comes before the predicate. Most sentences are in natural word order.

┌─subject─┐ ┌────────predicate────────┐
Mark Twain wrote about the Mississippi River.

- A sentence is in **inverted word order** if the predicate comes before the subject. Inverted word order can give part of a sentence more emphasis.

┌──────predicate──────┐ ┌──────subject──────┐
Faster and faster ran the frightened horse.

- Most interrogative sentences are in inverted word order. The verb is usually a verb phrase, and the subject usually comes between the parts of the verb phrase.

May I borrow a pencil?

- To find the subject of a sentence that has inverted word order, change the order to natural word order. Write the interrogative sentence as a declarative sentence.

Can I help you with that problem?   inverted

I can help you with that problem.   natural

- Sentences that begin with *here* or *there* often have inverted word order. *Here* and *there* are never the subject of a sentence. When *here* or *there* begins a sentence, the subject almost always follows the verb.

There is the sketch of my sister.
Here is my other sketch.

- In a declarative sentence beginning with *here* or *there*, the simple subject follows the simple predicate.

Here is my science project.
There will be awards for the best projects.

direct object
- A **direct object** receives the action of the verb. To find the direct object, ask *who* or *what* receives the action.

Lenny baked the cake . baked what?

He chose Clara and me to taste it. chose whom?

indirect object
- An **indirect object** tells to or for whom or what the action of the verb is done. A sentence must have a direct object to have an indirect object. The indirect object is a noun or a pronoun. It is always placed after the verb and before the direct object in a sentence.

      indirect object   direct object
I bought my brother a model airplane.

predicate nominative
- A **predicate nominative** is a noun or a pronoun that follows a linking verb. A predicate nominative renames the subject.

Allan is a boy with a bright future.

Trudy is the captain and the leading scorer on our team.

The secretary of our club is he .

predicate adjective
- A **predicate adjective** is an adjective that follows a linking verb. A predicate adjective describes the subject of a sentence.

The cottage near the lake appeared empty .

She is kind and considerate .

Nouns

noun
- A **noun** names a person, a place, a thing, or an idea. Some nouns are more than one word.

Persons: explorer, Daniel Boone
Places: park, Panama Canal
Things: book, table
Ideas: justice, truth

singular noun
- A **singular noun** names one person, place, thing, or idea.

- A **plural noun** names more than one person, place, thing, or idea. For help with the spelling of plural nouns, see pages 66–67 of the *Spelling* section in this **Writer's Handbook.**

plural noun

Singular	Plural
pioneer	pioneers
planet	planets
branch	branches
comedy	comedies

- A **common noun** names any person, place, thing, or idea.

common noun

The traveler found peace and solitude in the quiet village .

- A **proper noun** names a particular person, place, or thing. Each important word begins with a capital letter. For help with the capitalization of proper nouns, see pages 20–21 of the *Mechanics* section in this **Writer's Handbook.**

proper noun

The Pilgrims of Plymouth Colony celebrated a festival

that we now call Thanksgiving .

- A **possessive noun** shows ownership or possession.

possessive noun

Angela's job   Paul's golf clubs

- A **singular possessive noun** shows ownership by one person or thing. To form the possessive of a singular noun, add an apostrophe and *s.*

singular possessive noun

A stone wall surrounded the king's castle.
King Charles's knights were loyal subjects.

- A **plural possessive noun** shows ownership by more than one person or thing. To form the possessive of a plural noun that ends in *s,* add only an apostrophe.

plural possessive noun

The knights' horses were well trained.

- To form the possessive of a plural noun that does not end in *s,* add an apostrophe and *s.*

Many children's books are about brave knights.

- An **appositive** is a noun or phrase that identifies or renames the word or words that precede it.

appositive

The world's largest desert, the Sahara , is in Africa.

Tina, the manager of the store , hired two more people.

- An appositive is set off from the rest of a sentence by commas. If the appositive comes at the end of a sentence, replace the second comma with the proper end punctuation.

We visited Terlingua , a ghost town in Texas .

Pronouns

pronoun
- A **pronoun** takes the place of a noun or nouns. Pronouns can be singular or plural. The pronouns that are used most frequently are **personal pronouns.**

Personal Pronouns	
Singular	I me my mine you your yours he she it him her his hers its
Plural	we us our ours you your yours they them their theirs

antecedent
- An **antecedent** is the noun to which a pronoun refers. A pronoun should agree with its antecedent in number and gender.

Jane Addams won a Nobel Prize for her work in poor urban neighborhoods.

Ed asked Belinda for a pencil , but she did not have one .

subject pronoun
- A pronoun that is the subject of a sentence is called a **subject pronoun.** *I, you, he, she, it, we,* and *they* are subject pronouns.

We took a ferry across the Hudson River.

I had never been on a ferry.

pronoun-verb agreement
- A pronoun used as a subject should agree with the verb in number.

He likes to play baseball.

They like to play soccer.

predicate nominative
- Use subject pronouns as predicate nominatives.

The winners are they .

WRITER'S HANDBOOK • Grammar

- A pronoun that is a direct object or an indirect object is called an **object pronoun.** Object pronouns are also used after prepositions, such as *to, from, at, by,* and *with. Me, you, him, her, it, us,* and *them* are object pronouns.

object pronoun

> The forest ranger showed us the waterfall.
>
> Lorraine had seen it before.
>
> Two friends had gone with her last summer.

- A **possessive pronoun** shows ownership or possession. It takes the place of a possessive noun.

possessive pronoun

> The team followed the coach's suggestions.
> The team followed his suggestions.

- Possessive pronouns that are used before nouns are *my, your, his, her, its, our,* and *their.*

> The candidates prepared their victory speeches.

- Possessive pronouns that can stand alone are *mine, yours, his, hers, ours,* and *theirs.*

> The blue paintbrush is mine .

- A **reflexive pronoun** refers to the subject of a sentence. Reflexive pronouns are formed by adding *self* or *selves* to some pronouns. The words *myself, yourself, himself, herself, itself, ourselves, yourselves,* and *themselves* are reflexive pronouns.

reflexive pronoun

> Chameleons disguise themselves by changing color.
>
> Alice taught herself Spanish and French.

- An **indefinite pronoun** does not refer to a particular person, place, thing, or idea.

indefinite pronoun

> Everyone anxiously waited for the news.
>
> Someone arrived with a telegram.

- *Who, whom,* and *whose* are pronouns used in questions. *Who* is a subject pronoun. *Whom* is an object pronoun. *Whose* is a possessive pronoun.

who, whom, and whose

> Who found my jacket?
>
> To whom did you return it?
>
> Whose jacket is this?

Verbs

verb
● A **verb** expresses action or being.

I painted those pictures.

This one is my favorite.

action verb
● An **action verb** tells what the subject does or did.

Ray studies astronomy.

He has a new telescope.

linking verb
● A **linking verb** connects the subject to a word or words in the predicate. The most common linking verb is *be*. Some forms of *be* are *am, is, are, was, were,* and *been*. Other linking verbs are *taste, look, smell, feel, appear, seem,* and *become*.

This neighborhood looks familiar.

verb phrase, main verb, and helping verb
● A **verb phrase** is a main verb and one or more helping verbs that work together in a sentence. The **main verb** is the most important verb in a verb phrase. A **helping verb** works with the main verb to express action or being. Most helping verbs are forms of *be, have,* or *do*. Other helping verbs include *could, can, must, would, will, shall, should, may,* and *might*.

The plane is flying at a low altitude.

A heavy fog has covered the city.

The fog will delay your flight.

subject-verb agreement
● A subject and its verb should agree in number. A singular subject requires a singular verb. A plural subject requires a plural verb.

The shipwrecked sailor swims to an island.

The shipwrecked sailors swim to an island.

For more help with subject-verb agreement, see pages 29–30 of the *Usage* section of this **Writer's Handbook**.

principal parts of a verb
● The four basic forms of a verb are its **principal parts.** The principal parts are the *present,* the *present participle,* the *past,* and the *past participle*. Participles are forms used with helping verbs.

WRITER'S HANDBOOK ● Grammar

Principal Parts of the Verb *Open*			
Present	**Present Participle**	**Past**	**Past Participle**
open	(is, are) opening	opened	(have, has, had) opened

- The **tense** of a verb shows time. Verb tenses change to indicate that events happen at different times.

- The **simple tenses** are the *present,* the *past,* and the *future.*

- A verb in the **present tense** tells about what is happening now. Most present-tense verbs that follow singular subjects end in *s* or *es.*

tense

simple tenses

present tense

Marcia hears a strange noise.

She rushes to the door.

- Present-tense verbs that follow plural subjects do not take an *s* or *es* ending.

The artists draw sketches of the city.

- A verb in the **past tense** tells about what has already happened. The past tense is usually formed by adding *ed* to the present tense.

past tense

The magnet attracted the metal clips.

- A verb in the **future tense** tells about what will happen later. To form the future tense of a verb, use the helping verb *will* with the present form of a verb.

future tense

Next year, the city will elect a new mayor.

- The **perfect tenses** are the *present perfect,* the *past perfect,* and the *future perfect.*

perfect tenses

- A verb in the **present perfect tense** tells about an action that took place before the present and that may still be going on. Use *has* or *have* with the past participle to form the present perfect tense.

present perfect tense

Our team has won every game of the season.

- A verb in the **past perfect tense** tells about an action that was completed before some moment or action in the past. Use *had* with the past participle to express the past perfect tense.

past perfect tense

The Vikings had reached North America long before Columbus's arrival.

WRITER'S HANDBOOK • Grammar

future perfect tense

- A verb in the **future perfect tense** tells about an action that will be completed before some moment or action in the future. Use *will have* and the past participle to express the future perfect tense.

By the end of this year, Amy will have saved enough money for a new bicycle.

irregular verbs

- The past and the past participle of regular verbs are formed by adding *ed* to the present tense. The past and the past participle of **irregular verbs** are formed in other ways.

Present: Randy grows tomatoes in his garden.

Past: Randy grew tomatoes in his garden.

Past Participle: Randy has grown tomatoes in his garden.

be, have, and do

- *Be, have,* and *do* are three of the most important irregular verbs. The present-tense form of all of these verbs varies to agree with different subjects. The past-tense form of *be* also varies with different subjects.

Be				
	Present	**Present Participle**	**Past**	**Past Participle**
I	am	being	was	been
he, she, it, and singular nouns	is	being	was	been
we, you, they, and plural nouns	are	being	were	been

Have				
	Present	**Present Participle**	**Past**	**Past Participle**
I, we, you, they, and plural nouns	have	having	had	had
he, she, it, and singular nouns	has	having	had	had

Do	Present	Present Participle	Past	Past Participle
I, we, you, they, and plural nouns	do	doing	did	done
he, she, it, and singular nouns	does	doing	did	done

- Some irregular verbs follow a pattern to change form.

irregular verb patterns

- In one group of irregular verbs, the past participle is formed by adding *n* or *en* to the present form.

Present	Past	Past Participle
take	took	taken
grow	grew	grown
know	knew	known
eat	ate	eaten
see	saw	seen
draw	drew	drawn
give	gave	given

- In another group of irregular verbs, the past participle is formed by adding *n* or *en* to the past form.

Present	Past	Past Participle
speak	spoke	spoken
break	broke	broken
freeze	froze	frozen
choose	chose	chosen

- In a third group of irregular verbs, the past participle and the past form are the same.

Present	Past	Past Participle
make	made	made
sell	sold	sold
tell	told	told
meet	met	met
spend	spent	spent
mean	meant	meant
fight	fought	fought
think	thought	thought
buy	bought	bought

WRITER'S HANDBOOK • Grammar

- In a fourth group of irregular verbs, the past participle and the present form are the same.

Present	Past	Past Participle
become	became	become
come	came	come
run	ran	run

verb contraction
- A **contraction** is a shortened form of two words. Use an apostrophe in place of the letters that are left out when you write a contraction.

he will—he'll	they have—they've	you would—you'd
is not—isn't	were not—weren't	would not—wouldn't

transitive verb
- A **transitive verb** has a direct object.

subject · verb · direct object
The pitcher threw the baseball.

intransitive verb
- An **intransitive verb** does not have a direct object.

The crowd cheered .

Adjectives

adjective
- An **adjective** modifies a noun or a pronoun. Many adjectives answer the question *what kind, how many,* or *how much.*

We climbed the tower of the old building. **what kind?**

Two islands form the country of New Zealand. **how many?**

The children took much pleasure in watching the dolphins. **how much?**

proper adjective
- A **proper adjective** is formed from a proper noun. Proper adjectives are always capitalized.

Australian football is different from American football.

articles
- The words *a, an,* and *the* are special adjectives called **articles.** Use *a* when the article is followed by a word beginning with a consonant sound. Use *an* when the article is followed by a word beginning with a vowel sound.

Robert Peary was a famous explorer.

He led an expedition to the North Pole.

- A **demonstrative adjective** answers the question *which one*. The words *this, that, these,* and *those* are demonstrative adjectives. *This* (singular) and *these* (plural) point out nearby objects. *That* (singular) and *those* (plural) point out distant objects.

> This house has a fireplace.

> Those houses have wood-burning stoves.

- A **predicate adjective** is an adjective that follows a linking verb. A predicate adjective describes the subject of the sentence.

> The old house looks strange .

> Donna is helpful and patient .

- Adjectives can be used to compare nouns. Many adjectives have forms to show comparison. These forms are the *comparative* and the *superlative*. For help with the spelling of comparative and superlative adjectives, see page 69 of the *Spelling* section of this **Writer's Handbook.**

- The **comparative form** of an adjective is used to compare two items. The comparative form of most adjectives is formed by adding *er* to the adjective or by adding the word *more* before the adjective.

> The Nile River is longer than the Amazon River.

> Gold is more valuable than silver.

- The **superlative form** of an adjective is used to compare three or more items. The superlative form of most adjectives is formed by adding *est* to the adjective or by adding the word *most* before the adjective.

> Mount Fuji is the highest mountain in Japan.

> Soccer is the most popular sport in many countries.

- Some adjectives that compare have special forms.

Adjective	Comparative	Superlative
much/many	more	most
good	better	best
bad	worse	worst

Adverbs

adverb

- An **adverb** modifies a verb, an adjective, or another adverb. It answers the question *how, when, where,* or *to what extent.* Many adverbs end in *ly.*

The stream trickled slowly . **how?**

Giraffes have very long necks. **to what extent?**

The walls of the canyon were almost completely vertical.
to what extent?

adverbs that compare

- Adverbs can be used to make comparisons. Some adverbs have forms to show comparison. These forms are the *comparative* and the *superlative.*

comparative form

- The **comparative form** of an adverb is used when two things are compared. The comparative form of most adverbs is formed by adding *er* to the adverb or by adding the word *more* before the adverb.

The sun sets later in summer than in winter.

Large stars shine more brightly than small stars.

superlative form

- The **superlative form** of an adverb is used when three or more things are compared. The superlative form of most adverbs is formed by adding *est* to the adverb or by adding the word *most* before the adverb.

In New Orleans, the rain falls hardest during early summer.

Of all the artists, Paula paints the most beautifully .

special forms

- Some adverbs that compare have special forms.

Adverb	Comparative	Superlative
well	better	best
badly	worse	worst
little	less	least
much	more	most
far	farther	farthest

negative

- A **negative** is a word that means "no" or "not." Common negative words are *no, neither, nothing, hardly, none, nobody, nowhere, barely, not (n't), no one, never,* and *scarcely.*

I ca n't wait to go to the county fair.

I've never been to the fair before.

- Two negative words should not be used together.

> **Incorrect:** Do not never stand near a tree during a lightning storm.

> **Correct:** Never stand near a tree during a lightning storm.

Prepositions

- A **preposition** relates a noun or a pronoun to another word in the sentence.

> Galileo discovered the rings around Saturn.

Common Prepositions						
by	to	from	upon	below	beyond	across
in	at	with	near	above	during	behind
of	off	onto	down	among	between	beside
up	for	over	about	under	through	against
on	into	past	along	after	within	without

- The noun or pronoun that follows the preposition is called the **object of the preposition**.

> How far is Saturn from Earth ?

- A **prepositional phrase** is made up of a preposition, the object of the preposition, and all the words in between.

> The spray from the salty water burned my eyes.

- A prepositional phrase that modifies a noun or a pronoun is an **adjective phrase**.

> The fierce storm threatened the houses along the coast .

- A prepositional phrase that modifies a verb, an adjective, or an adverb is an **adverb phrase**.

> Lewis and Clark journeyed across the Rocky Mountains .
>   modifies verb

> The river is dry during the summer . modifies adjective

> We fell asleep soon after dinner . modifies adverb

Conjunctions

conjunction
- A **conjunction** is a word that connects words or groups of words in a sentence. The conjunction *and* is used to add items. *But* is used to show contrast. *Or* is used to show a choice.

    Pioneer families loaded their wagons and traveled west.

    The train pulled out slowly but was soon speeding through the countryside.

    You can use a pen or a pencil to write your answers.

Interjections

interjection
- An **interjection** is a word or a group of words that expresses feeling or emotion.

    Wow ! You never know what you'll find in a cave.

    Ouch ! This kitten really scratches!

Common Interjections			
whew	well	aha	bravo
wow	ugh	oh	ouch
hey	ah	alas	eek
ssh	hurray	oops	psst

Phrases and Clauses

phrase
- A **phrase** is a group of words that does not contain both a subject and a verb. A phrase is used as a single part of speech.

    Barry lives on the next block .

clause
- A **clause** is a group of words that has a subject and a verb.

- An **independent clause** expresses a complete thought and can stand alone.

    The drought has damaged our crops ,

    but we will still have a harvest .

    Because of the drought, our harvest will be smaller this year .

- A **dependent clause** does not express a complete thought and cannot stand alone. A dependent clause can be joined to an independent clause to form a complex sentence. Dependent clauses often begin with subordinating words such as *while, before, after, when, where, who, that, if, which, until, though, because,* and *since.*

Because the soil is dry , farmers must irrigate the land.

Rita is the one who is winning the race .

Capitalization

- Begin every sentence with a capital letter.

    P umpkins grow on vines.

- The pronoun *I* is always capitalized.

    Tomorrow I am going to the circus.

- Begin each important word in a proper noun with a capital letter.

- Capitalize the names and the initials of people.

    F ranklin D . R oosevelt   E . M . F orster   E llen H ite

- Capitalize the titles of people and the abbreviations of their titles. *Mr., Mrs., Ms., Miss,* and *Dr.* are commonly used titles.

    M rs. Garwood   M r. Shawn   D r. Brennan

- Capitalize the names of the days of the week, the months of the year, and their abbreviations.

    T hursday— T hurs.   D ecember— D ec.

- Capitalize the names of the holidays.

    T hanksgiving D ay   M emorial D ay   F ourth of J uly

- Capitalize the names of historical periods and events. Also capitalize the names of special events.

    M iddle A ges   B oston T ea P arty   W orld S eries

    H omecoming P arade

- Capitalize the names of continents, countries, states, cities, bodies of water, and mountains.

    S outh A merica   F rance   U tah

    C hicago   B ay of B engal   M ount H ood

- Capitalize the names of particular places and things, such as bridges, parks, and buildings.

    T ate B ridge   Y ellowstone N ational P ark

    T ower of L ondon

- Capitalize the names of streets and their abbreviations.

    Maple **S**treet   **B**road **S**t.   **V**enice **B**lvd.

- Capitalize postal abbreviations of state names.

    Delaware— **DE**   Vermont— **VT**   Texas— **TX**

- Capitalize the names of teams, clubs, businesses, and organizations.

    Volunteer **F**irefighters of **A**merica   **M**ilo's **M**agic **S**hop

    Red **C**ross   **F**uture **F**armers of **A**merica

- Capitalize proper adjectives.

    British flag   **C**hinese leader   **A**merican eagle

- Capitalize the first word, the last word, and all other important words in the titles of books, stories, newspapers, movies, and songs.

    *J**ames and the **G**iant **P**each*

    " **V**isit to **M**ars"

    " **A**merica the **B**eautiful"

    *S**pringfield **G**azette*

- Capitalize the first word of the greeting and the first word of the closing in a letter. parts of a letter

    Dear Alice,   **V**ery truly yours,

- Capitalize the first word of a direct quotation. direct quotations

    Carol said, " **L**et's follow the path to the pond."

- Capitalize the first word of the main topics and the subtopics in an outline. outlines

    I. **P**opular sports

    A. **F**ootball

    B. **B**asketball

Punctuation

end marks
- End every sentence with a period, a question mark, or an exclamation point.

> Most people enjoy eating desserts .
>
> When will we visit the zoo ?
>
> That plum is delicious !

period
- Use a period at the end of a declarative or an imperative sentence.

> Edgar Allan Poe wrote mystery tales .
>
> Please leave the door open .

- Use a period after an initial.

> Lyndon B . Johnson   G . B . Shaw

- Use a period after most abbreviations.

> Mr . Mitchell   Oct .   State Blvd .   Mon .

- Use a period within the quotation marks after a direct quotation that is a statement or a command.

> Toni said, "The team members are all here ."

- Place a period after the speaker's name in the middle of a direct quotation if the first part of the quotation is a complete sentence.

> "Bring the basket here," said Mark . "I'll fill it with apples."

- In an outline, use a period after a Roman numeral for a main topic and after a capital letter for a subtopic.

> II . The Grand Canyon
>
> A . How it was formed
>
> B . Scenic attractions

question mark
- Use a question mark at the end of an interrogative sentence.

> What is the largest country in the world ?

exclamation point
- Use an exclamation point at the end of an exclamatory sentence.

> What a beautiful view of the city we had !

- Use an exclamation point after a strong interjection.

  Whew **!** I almost missed the bus.

- Use commas to separate three or more similar words or phrases in a series. Notice that a comma goes before the conjunction that precedes the final item in the series.

  Some important sources of energy are coal **,** oil **,** and natural gas.

  Immigrants faced the challenge of finding jobs **,** learning a new language **,** and adapting to a new culture.

- Use commas to set off most appositives.

  Mount Etna **,** one of the most famous volcanoes in the world **,** is in Sicily.

- Use a comma to set off a noun or a pronoun of direct address.

  Walk carefully **,** Jim **,** or you will step in the poison ivy.

- Use a comma after a word such as *yes, no, oh,* or *well* that introduces a sentence.

  Well **,** you told me the park would be crowded.

- Use a comma to set off a word or a phrase that interrupts a sentence, such as *however, in fact,* or *for example.*

  The penguin **,** for example **,** is a bird that cannot fly.

- Use a comma before the conjunction *and, or,* or *but* in a compound sentence.

  Gene tried to catch the string **,** but the balloon rose too quickly.

- Use a comma to separate the clauses of a complex sentence if the dependent clause comes first.

  Although Grover Cleveland won a majority of the popular vote **,** he lost the presidential election of 1888.

- Use a comma after the greeting in a friendly letter and the closing of any letter.

  Dear Louise **,**

  Sincerely yours **,**

- Use a comma between the day and the year in a date.

  May 9 **,** 1988

- Use a comma between the names of a city and a state.

  Fairmont **,** West Virginia

- Use a comma to separate a direct quotation from the rest of the sentence unless a question mark or an exclamation point is needed.

  "I can show you a map **,** " Rosetta said.

  "How far away are the mountains **?** " asked Ron.

semicolon
- Use a semicolon to separate independent clauses in a compound sentence.

  Some people enjoy winter **;** others like hot weather.

colon
- Use a colon after the greeting in a business letter.

  Dear Ms. Gomez **:**

apostrophe
- Use an apostrophe in possessive nouns.

- Add an apostrophe and *s* to form the possessive of a singular noun.

  The patient followed the **doctor's** advice.

- Add only an apostrophe to form the possessive of a plural noun that ends in *s*.

  Wildlife parks preserve the **animals'** natural surroundings.

- Add an apostrophe and *s* to form the possessive of a plural noun that does not end in *s*.

  The **women's** team easily won the game.

- Use an apostrophe in forming contractions of verbs and the word *not*.

  Some colonists **didn't** favor independence from England.

- Use an apostrophe in forming contractions of pronouns and helping verbs.

  If we arrive late, **they'll** save seats for us.

quotation marks
- Use quotation marks before and after a direct quotation. If a quotation is interrupted by other words, place quotation marks around the quoted words only.

  " Most of the coins are copper, **"** said Pat.

  " I wonder, **"** said Liz, **"** how old they are. **"**

- When a comma or a period is needed with a closing quotation mark, place it within the quotation marks.

"These shells are beautiful," said Mark. "Let's collect some."

- Place a question mark or an exclamation point inside a closing quotation mark if the quotation itself is a question or an exclamation.

"Give me liberty or give me death!" Patrick Henry exclaimed at the end of his famous speech.

"Have you read the entire speech?" the teacher asked.

- Place quotation marks around the titles of short works, such as as poems, short stories, chapters, articles, and songs.

"Stopping by Woods on a Snowy Evening"

"The High Jumper"

"Row, Row, Row Your Boat"

- Underline the titles of books, plays, magazines, newspapers, and movies.

underline

The Wind in the Willows
National Geographic
Boston Globe
E.T.

Troublesome Words

there, their, they're
- Use *there* to introduce a sentence or to indicate where to place something. Use *their* when you mean "belonging to them." Use *they're* when you mean "they are."

    There are six runners in the race.

    Pierre and Marie Curie received a Nobel prize for **their** work.

    They're the youngest swimmers on the team.

two, to, too
- Use *two* as a number word. Use *to* as a preposition. Use *too* when you mean "also" or "overly."

    The **two** largest countries are the Soviet Union and Canada.

    We took a train **to** San Diego.

    The coast is **too** rocky for farming.

between, among
- Use the preposition *between* to refer to two persons or things. Use the preposition *among* to refer to three or more.

    Differences **between** the North and the South led to war.

    There was little agreement **among** the members of the jury.

in, into
- Use the preposition *in* when you mean "already inside." Use the preposition *into* to show movement from the outside to the inside.

    Many people **in** Europe speak several languages.

    Dan stepped **into** the car and drove away.

this, that
- Use *this* to point out a nearby object. Use *that* to point out a distant object.

    This suitcase is heavy.

    That suitcase in the hall is much lighter.

these, those
- Use *these* to point out nearby objects. Use *those* to point out more distant objects.

    These books are about desert animals.

    Those books on the top shelf are about ocean life.

Easily Confused Verb Pairs

- Use *teach* when you mean "give knowledge." Use *learn* when you mean "receive knowledge."

teach, learn

> Mrs. Bradley teaches us a new song every week.
>
> I learned how to play the harmonica.

- Use *lend* when you mean "give something that must be given back." Use *borrow* when you mean "take something that must be given back."

lend, borrow

> Banks lend money to new businesses.
>
> Frank borrowed my umbrella.

- Use *let* when you mean "permit" or "allow." Use *leave* when you mean "go away from."

let, leave

> My friend lets me ride her bicycle.
>
> Dorrie leaves her house at the same time each morning.

- Use *rise* when you mean "get up" or "move higher." Use *raise* when you mean "lift something up."

rise, raise

> Steam rises from the boiling water.
>
> Raise the window a few inches.

- Use *set* when you mean "place something somewhere." Use *sit* when you mean "rest, as in a chair."

set, sit

> Set the packages on the table.
>
> I like to sit in the front row.

- Use *lie* when you mean "rest" or "recline." Use *lay* when you mean "put or place something in a specified position."

lie, lay

> The kittens usually lie on the rug near the door.
>
> Lay the coins in a straight line.

- Use *bring* when you mean "to carry from there to here." Use *take* when you mean "to carry from here to there" or "to remove from a place."

bring, take

> My mother reminded me to bring my lunch.
>
> Please take your coats from the closet.

WRITER'S HANDBOOK • Usage

Pronouns

its, it's   ● Use *its* when you mean "belonging to." Use *it's* when you mean "it is."

Each state has its own form of government.

It's the only playground in the neighborhood.

your, you're   ● Use *your* when you mean "belonging to you." Use *you're* when you mean "you are."

I heard about your trip to Arizona.

You're going to see a film about whales.

subject and object pronouns   ● Use subject pronouns as subjects and as predicate nominatives. Use object pronouns as direct objects, indirect objects, or objects of prepositions.

Subject Pronouns	I	you	he	she	it	we	you	they
Object Pronouns	me	you	him	her	it	us	you	them

He repairs damaged paintings.

It is she who won the prize.

I saw him at the museum.

They gave her a cake.

The teacher handed books to them .

who, whom, whose   ● Use *who* as a subject pronoun. Use *whom* as an object pronoun. Use *whose* as a possessive pronoun.

Who discovered the missing jewels?

To whom did you return the photograph?

Whose bicycle is in front of the gate?

Adverbs and Adjectives

good, well   ● Use *good* as an adjective. Use *well* as an adjective when you mean "healthy" and as an adverb when you tell how something is done.

All of the songs in the musical are good . **adjective**

One of the singers did not feel well . **adjective**

The orchestra played well . **adverb**

- Use *bad* as a predicate adjective after a linking verb. Use *badly* with action verbs to tell how something is done.

bad, badly

> The director of the play felt bad .

> The inexperienced actor had performed badly .

- Never use *more* and the ending *er* or *most* and the ending *est* to form comparatives and superlatives.

comparatives and superlatives

> incorrect: Spain has a more warmer climate than England.

> correct: Spain has a warmer climate than England.

- The adjectives *much/many, good,* and *bad* have special comparative and superlative forms.

Adjective	Comparative	Superlative
much/many	more	most
good	better	best
bad	worse	worst

> Rico says mathematics is more interesting than history.

> He says science is his most interesting subject.

- The adverbs *well, badly, little, much,* and *far* have special comparative and superlative forms.

Adverb	Comparative	Superlative
well	better	best
badly	worse	worst
little	less	least
much	more	most
far	farther	farthest

> Ellen swims better than her brother.

> She swims best in races.

Agreement

- A subject and its verb should agree in number.
- Use the singular form of a verb with a singular subject.

subject-verb agreement

> The detective looks for clues.

- Use the plural form of a verb with a plural subject.

> Scientists find new ways to grow food.

compound subject
- When the parts of a compound subject are joined by *and,* use a plural verb.

    The lion and the tiger belong to the same animal group.

- In some compound subjects the parts are joined by *or, either/or,* or *neither/nor.* Use a plural verb if both parts are plural.

    The teachers or the students plan the schedule.

- Use a singular verb if both parts are singular.

    The glass or the cup breaks easily.

- Make the verb agree with the subject closest to it if one part is plural and the other is singular.

    My sister, my brother, or my parents drive me to school.

    My parents, my brother, or my sister drives me to school.

subject pronouns
- Use the singular form of verbs with the subject pronouns *he, she,* and *it.* Use the plural form of verbs with *I, you, we,* and *they.*

    She collects stamps from foreign countries.

    I collect baseball cards.

- Use the singular form of verbs with singular indefinite pronoun subjects. Use the plural form of verbs with plural indefinite pronoun subjects.

Singular	each	everybody	nothing	anybody
	everyone	somebody	anyone	everything
	someone	anything	nobody	something
Plural	all most both others few several many some			

Each is a famous writer.

Most are from South America.

pronoun antecedent
- A pronoun should agree with its antecedent in number and in gender.

    Louis and Mary Leakey made many of their discoveries in eastern Africa.

    The beautiful beaches and warm climate of Hawaii make it a popular vacation area.

    Lynne asked her friends if they wanted to play volleyball.

Paragraph

- A **paragraph** is a group of sentences that tells about one main idea. A paragraph often begins with a topic sentence. The **topic sentence** expresses the main idea of the paragraph. It tells what all the other sentences in the paragraph are about. The other sentences in a paragraph are called detail sentences. **Detail sentences** add information about the topic. They help the audience understand the main idea.

paragraph

Writer's Guide: Paragraph
1. Write a topic sentence that clearly expresses the main idea of your paragraph.   2. Indent the first line of the paragraph.   3. Write detail sentences that support the main idea in your topic sentence.

South Korea, a small Asian country the size of Indiana, is rapidly becoming one of the important nations of the world. Recovering almost miraculously from the ruins of the Korean War, South Korea has become a major economic power. The country's export of cars and electronics has grown to rival that of Japan. In the last decade, South Korea has become one of America's biggest trading partners. In 1988, South Korea successfully hosted the Summer Games of the XXIV Olympiad in its capital, Seoul.

topic sentence

detail sentences

How-to Paragraph

● In a **how-to paragraph** a writer gives directions or explains how to do something.

Writer's Guide: How-to Paragraph
1. Write a topic sentence that identifies the process you are explaining.
2. Write a detail sentence that lists the materials needed to complete the process.
3. Write detail sentences that explain the steps of the process in the order in which they need to be done.
4. Use time-order words, such as *first, next, then, last,* or *finally.*

topic sentence —

materials —

    Kite making is easy and lots of fun. You need two long, thin sticks, lots of string, some newsprint paper, and glue. Also collect some scissors, a knife, a ruler, a file, and a marker. First of all, cut the sticks to size. Make one stick 24 inches long and the other one 30 inches long. File a notch in the end of each stick. Then, tie the sticks together in the shape of a ''t,'' and set them with glue. Next, run string tightly from notch to notch to make the frame. Tie the string to the last notch, and trace the outline of the frame on the paper. Leave a 1-inch flap along each edge. Finally, fold the parts of the flaps over the string and glue them down. Once your kite is done,

steps —

make a tail and attach it to the kite. Then, make a loop by tying a foot-long string to the short stick in the frame. Tie it about six inches from each end of the stick. Attach the kite string to this loop. Now, you are ready to fly your kite.
    Flying a kite is easy. Here is what you do. First, find a big open space, face away from the wind, and hold the string. Next, have a friend hold the kite and wait for a strong gust. When a strong wind comes, tell your friend to let go, and the wind carries your kite up into the air.

Paragraph of Comparison

- In a **paragraph of comparison,** a writer shows ways in which two subjects are alike. The subjects may be people, places, things, or ideas.

Writer's Guide: Paragraph of Comparison

1. Think of three ways your subjects are alike.
2. Write a topic sentence that identifies the two subjects you will compare.
3. In the detail sentences, give examples that clearly explain the qualities your subjects have in common.
4. Use words such as *neither* and *both* to make your comparisons clear.

    Who will be our "Dog Days Dog" this year--Couch
Potato Pete or Moxie Maxie? Before you decide,
consider the facts. Both dogs are setters, so
either one could set the mood for "Dog Days."
People who know them say that both dogs love people
and neither one barks much.

topic sentence

similarities

Paragraph of Contrast

paragraph of
contrast

- In a **paragraph of contrast,** a writer explains the key differences between two subjects. The subjects may be people, places, things, or ideas.

<table>
<tr><td>Writer's Guide: Paragraph of Contrast</td></tr>
<tr><td>

1. Think of three ways your subjects are different.
2. Write a topic sentence that identifies the two subjects you will contrast.
3. In the detail sentences, give examples that clearly explain the differences between your subjects.
4. Contrast the same categories of information about both subjects.
5. Use words such as *however, in contrast,* and *on the other hand* to signal contrasts.

</td></tr>
</table>

topic sentence

differences

The dogs look different, however. Couch Potato Pete is a black-and-white dog, but Maxie has a red coat. The dogs behave differently, too. Couch Potato Pete's favorite activity is sitting around watching TV. Maxie, in contrast, loves to run and play. "She wears us all out, but she's such fun that we don't care," Betty Hernandez says.

Cause-and-Effect Paragraph

cause-and-effect
paragraph

● In a **cause-and-effect paragraph** a writer focuses on a cause that results in certain effects or an effect that can be traced back to its causes. This type of paragraph can begin with either the cause or the effect.

Writer's Guide: Cause-and-Effect Paragraph

1. Begin paragraphs of effect with a *cause*. Write a topic sentence that tells what happened. The detail sentences should all discuss *effects*.
2. Begin paragraphs of cause with an *effect*. Write a topic sentence that identifies the effect. The detail sentences should all discuss *causes*.
3. Write detail sentences in the order in which the effects or the causes happened.

A hurricane whipped across our state last week. Because of the high winds, many beautiful old trees were knocked down. As the trees fell, they hit power lines. A number of homes were without electricity for over two days. Near the shore, huge waves destroyed many elegant homes that were over a century old. As a result of last week's damage, many towns in the area are taking new precautions against hurricanes.

— cause

— effects

Persuasive Paragraph

● In a **persuasive paragraph** a writer tries to convince the audience to agree with his or her opinion on an issue.

Writer's Guide: Persuasive Paragraph
1. Write a topic sentence that states the issue and your opinion about it.
2. In the detail sentences, include at least three reasons that support your opinion. Explain your reasons with clear examples. Save your strongest reason for last.
3. Be sure to choose reasons that you think will persuade your particular audience.
4. Write a clincher, a concluding sentence that restates your opinion and asks the audience to accept it or to take action on the issue.

topic sentence

detail sentences

clincher

I think someone should start a program to get children and older adults together. The program would be good for kids. They could learn a lot from spending time with adopted grandparents. Adults in the program would benefit, too. Many elderly people could use help with tasks like shopping and getting library books. Starting such a program would be easy for the city or a community group. It would not cost much money. All someone has to do is match up people. Whoever starts this program is sure to feel good about it. An idea like this was tried in Fresh Springs, Nebraska. It worked well there. Let's start a program that gets together the young and the elderly in our community, too.

WRITER'S HANDBOOK • Composition

Persuasive Essay

- In a **persuasive essay** a writer tries to convince the audience to agree with his or her opinion on an issue. A persuasive essay is several paragraphs in length.

Writer's Guide: Persuasive Essay

1. Write an introductory paragraph that states the issue and your opinion about it.
2. Write two or three paragraphs that include reasons that support your opinion. Explain your reasons with clear examples.
3. Be sure to choose reasons that will persuade your particular audience.
4. Write a conclusion that restates your opinion and asks the audience to accept it and to take action on the issue.
5. Write a title for your persuasive essay.

Time to Clean Up!

Recently, a student grumbled, ''The schoolyard is a mess. Why don't they do something about it?'' I think that is the wrong question. Instead, when we see a problem, we should ask, "What can I do?" We students, for example, can clean our own schoolyard--and we should.

For one thing, if we do it ourselves, we can decide when the yard gets cleaned. Who knows how long we will have to wait if the school hires some company to do it?

Furthermore, by working side by side, cleaning up the yard, students can build school spirit. School spirit can help us make every event and program in the school a success.

Finally, cleaning up the yard ourselves will give us students pride and build up our self-respect. That is the most important reason I say we students should all join together for a massive one day schoolyard ''Clean-a-thon.''

Our principal, Mr. Drew, said we can have the Clean-a-thon on Saturday, November 5. The town's Department of Sanitation will send a dumpster for us to use. Everyone should meet at the Whitman Road entrance to the school at 9 o'clock. Please join us. You'll be glad you did.

title

introduction

supporting paragraphs

conclusion

Descriptive Paragraph

descriptive paragraph

- In a **descriptive paragraph** a writer describes a person, a place, a thing, or an event by using specific details. The details should allow the audience to see, feel, hear, and sometimes taste and smell what is being described.

Writer's Guide: Descriptive Paragraph

1. Write a topic sentence that tells what you will describe.
2. Write detail sentences that give specific information about your topic.
3. Choose details that contribute to the tone, or mood, you want to create.
4. Use vivid and colorful descriptive words that appeal to the audience's senses.

A View Worth Seeing

topic sentence —

    The highest natural point in the city is at the top of a rock in Bennett Park. It is a lovely, quiet place in late fall. The rock looks like a wet, gray whale. You can smell damp soil when you stand on it, and you can feel mist on your face. Right in front of you is an empty playground. On the other side of the playground is a path lined with poplars where hundreds of birds twitter among the leaves. From the street just outside the park comes the sound of wet wheels. Beyond, you can see 100 steps leading down to another street far below. In the playground, tire swings hang from beams. You can climb up inside a small red rocket and slide out of it. You can quench your thirst at the silver drinking fountain. This is a good place for children and adults.

detail sentences —

Dialogue

- In a **dialogue** a writer tells the exact words that one person or character says to another.

dialogue

Writer's Guide: Dialogue
1. Place quotation marks before and after the exact words of a speaker.
2. Use a comma to separate a quotation from the rest of the sentence, unless a question mark or an exclamation point is needed.
3. Begin a new paragraph each time the speaker changes.
4. Be sure that the dialogue "sounds" like real people talking.
5. Use words such as *said, called, answered,* and *shouted* to show how the speaker says the words.

"Hello?" said Jimmy as he picked up the phone.   ——exact word

"Hi, Jimmy, it's Robert. Would you like to go camping with me and my family this weekend?"   ——new speaker

"That sounds great!" replied Jimmy. "Let me go ask my parents. Hold on."   ——new speaker

After a few minutes, Jimmy returned to the phone and said, "It's okay with them."

"Super!" said Robert. "We'll pick you up at one o'clock on Saturday. See you then."

Journal

journal • In a **journal** a writer keeps a record of daily events and thoughts. A journal **entry** tells what the writer did and how he or she felt on the day of the entry. A journal can be a good source of writing ideas.

Writer's Guide: Journal
1. Begin each entry with the date.
2. Describe events and feelings that are important to you.
3. Tell *who*, *what*, *when*, *where*, and *why* about each event or idea.
4. Tell your feelings about what you write.

date of entry

July 4, 19—

event or idea

    Today was a special day. My family and I had a picnic at the beach. Mom brought along my favorite food—fried chicken. After we ate, we took turns burying each other in the sand.

    Later, when it got dark, we walked to the park to watch the fireworks. They made an awful noise when they exploded. Little Sammy got scared and hid under the blanket. The colors and shapes in the sky were beautiful. My favorite fireworks were the green ones that fell in long lines of sparkles.

feelings

    The Fourth of July is my favorite holiday. My family always does something fun. Sometimes I wish every day were July 4th. But boy, am I tired!

Personal Narrative

- In a **personal narrative** a writer tells a story about an experience in his or her life.

personal narrative

Writer's Guide: Personal Narrative

1. Write a beginning that gets your audience ready for the story. Tell when and where the experience took place and who was involved.
2. In the middle, write about your experience and how you feel about it.
3. Write what effects the experience had on you.
4. Write an ending that gives the reader a sense that the story is "over."
5. Give your personal narrative a title that captures your audience's attention.

What a Day! — title

I love my little brother Joey, but he sure does drive me crazy sometimes. His weird taste in food, for example, caused me a real headache last week. Looking back, I have to laugh, but at the time it was not very funny. — beginning

It wasn't really Joey's fault, I suppose. It started when I slept through the alarm and woke up late. As a result, I had to rush around frantically getting ready for school. Joey did not help, though. I became all the more discombobulated because he was chasing the cat around and yelling ''Zot! Yodilla!'' (Mom says he's going through a phase.) Anyway, I grabbed my things and rushed off to catch the bus. Imagine how I felt at noon when I opened my lunch bag and found Joey's peanut butter and papaya sandwich and his green milk! — middle

Luckily, a student named Ron must be going through the same phase as Joey. He traded me an apple and a roll for the sandwich. I could not get anybody interested in the milk, though——and I'm not surprised! — ending

Story

● In a **story** a writer tells about one main idea. A story has an **introduction,** a **complication,** and a **resolution.** The turning point in the story is called the **climax.**

Writer's Guide: Story
1. Write the introduction. Identify the main characters and describe the setting. Explain the problem that the main characters must face.
2. Write the complication and the climax. Tell how the problem gets worse and how the characters solve it.
3. Write the resolution. Explain what effects the climax has on the characters.
4. Give your story an interesting title.

title

A Truck, a Tunnel, and One Smart Girl

introduction

Meg Rico and her father were driving across town in Mr. Rico's big semi truck. They were chatting as they approached the low, dark tunnel. Suddenly, with a loud grinding noise, the truck came to a stop. The tunnel was too low. The truck was stuck!

complication

Meg and her father sat silently for a long time before Meg spoke.

"Dad," she whispered. "I——"

"Not now," said Mr. Rico. "I have to think. We need to get out of here before any other vehicles come through the tunnel."

climax

"We——we could let some air out of the tires," said Meg.

Mr. Rico turned and beamed. "What a good idea!" he said.

Mr. Rico climbed down from the truck and let some air out of all eighteen tires. Now the truck was just low enough to get through the tunnel.

resolution

Slowly Mr. Rico drove the truck out. Later he could fill the tires up again, but for now he was happy and proud to have such a smart daughter.

Suspense Story

- In a **suspense story** a writer tells about a series of events that involve suspicious or mysterious actions. A suspense story has an **introduction,** a **complication,** and a **resolution.** The turning point in the story is called the **climax.**

suspense story

Writer's Guide: Suspense Story

1. Write the introduction. Identify the characters and describe the setting. Explain the mysterious event and tell what problem the main character or characters must face.
2. Write the complication and the climax. Tell how the problem gets worse and how the characters solve it. Include elements of suspense.
3. Write the resolution. Explain what effects the climax has on the characters.
4. Give your suspense story an interesting title.

                         Creak!

Eddie's father stopped the car next to a fallen tree. "Well," he said, "here we are at our new vacation house. What do you think?"

"It's lovely," said Mrs. Hayes.

"But we're in the middle of the woods," gulped six-year-old Susie.

Eddie said nothing. Something about the old gray house made him uneasy. It was painted dark gray and seemed to lean to one side. He saw the basement door around the corner from the entrance. It was thick and rough, like the dungeon door in a scary movie.

The family planned to live in the house all summer, while Mr. Hayes wrote a book. In a few days, they had all settled into their new life. Eddie and Susie had fun exploring the woods around the house. At night, they liked to huddle by the fireplace and tell stories or read books.

Then one day, bad luck struck. A neighbor down the road had an accident and broke her leg. Mrs. Hayes had to drive her to the hospital. Mr. Hayes had driven to town for supplies and was supposed to get back before dark. His car broke down on the road, however, and he could not get a tow truck. He called Eddie from a roadside phone to explain the situation.

"It's going to take me a couple of hours to get home," he said. "Why don't you and Susie wait for me over at the Oglebys? It's only a 15-minute walk. Just call first and tell them who you are. They're nice people."

"We'll be okay at home, Dad." Eddie had a shy streak. His parents knew the Oglebys, but Eddie had never met them.

Susie did not take the news calmly. "A couple of hours?" she exclaimed. "But Eddie, we'll be here alone—in the dark."

"Not in the dark, silly. We'll turn on the lights," said Eddie. "We'll build a fire and play a few games of checkers."

By nightfall, they were sick of checkers. Eddie began to wish he had called the Oglebys. The windows were as black as paint. Then the moon came up, and Eddie saw millions of shadows surrounding the house. Every one of them looked like it was moving.

"Eddie, was that you?" Susie squeaked in a tense voice.

"What?"

"Was it you that made that noise?"

"What noise?" said Eddie. "It must have been the wind."

Just then, however, Eddie heard the noise. He knew at once it was not the wind. It came from below his feet, a creak followed by a rustle. Someone—or some *thing*—was in the basement!

"Eddie, I'm scared," Susie faltered.

"Relax, it's probably just a cat or something." Eddie picked up a flashlight.

"Where are you going?"

"To look in the basement." Eddie sounded braver than he felt.

"You're not leaving me alone in the house!" Susie yelped. "I'm coming with you!"

"Suit yourself," Eddie shrugged.

"What if it's not a cat?"

"Shh, just stay behind me," Eddie whispered as they crept toward the front door. He swung his flashlight beam from side to side. "I'm not going to let some noises scare me!"

"Maybe we should have waited for Mom and Dad," Susie wailed.

Susie and Eddie stepped outside. Moonlight fell on the basement door. It was open just a crack!

Filled with fear, Eddie moved into the entrance.

"Who's down there?" he cried out.

Suddenly, he heard a crash. At that moment his flashlight beam shone on a boy about his own age.

"I'm Felix Ogleby," the boy said. "I live down the road."

"But what are you doing here?" Eddie gasped.

"My club used to meet in the basement of this house. I've lost my book of secret codes, and I thought I might have left it here. I'm sorry if I scared you or anything."

"It takes more than a noise to scare us," said Eddie. He invited the boy to come upstairs for a snack.

"So tell me, Felix," Eddie said later, "did you find your book?"

"Sure," said Felix. "Hey, maybe we can work on some codes together. What do you think?"

"I'd like that," Eddie grinned. He had a feeling he was going to like this kid Felix.

Play

- In a **play** a writer tells a story that is meant to be acted out by performers. A play has characters, one or more settings, and a plot. The conversation between characters in a play is called **dialogue.** The writer includes **stage directions,** which tell the characters how to move, act, and speak.

play

Writer's Guide: Play

1. Use dialogue to tell the story. Let the characters' conversations show how the plot develops. When writing a play, do not use quotation marks to show what the characters say.
2. Write clear stage directions, which tell the characters exactly how to move, act, or speak. Put these in parentheses, and underline them.
3. Be sure your play has interesting characters, realistic dialogue, and a well-developed plot.
4. Give your play a title.

Pirate's Treasure — title

(Pirate songs are heard in the background. DESMOND and ALICE are digging in the sand. Suddenly, they find a treasure chest and lift it out of the hole.) — stage directions

ALICE (to herself): I can't believe we found it. It was just where the map said it would be. — dialogue

DESMOND (shouting): We're rich! We're rich!

ALICE (thoughtfully): Wait a minute. There may not be anything in it.

DESMOND (impatiently): Well, let's open it and find out.

ALICE (worried): Wait! Are you forgetting what old Captain Sayles said? Don't you remember his warning about the old pirates taking their revenge?

Lyric Poem

lyric poem

- In a **lyric poem** a writer expresses feelings, usually in a songlike manner. The writer describes people, places, things, or ideas instead of telling stories about them. A lyric poem often has a definite rhyme and rhythm. To help the audience see and feel as the writer does, a poem often contains **figures of speech.** Similes and metaphors are figures of speech. In a **simile** a writer makes a comparison between two things, using the word *like* or *as*. In a **metaphor** a writer also makes a comparison but does not use *like* or *as*.

Writer's Guide: Lyric Poem

1. Use strong and colorful descriptive words to describe your subject.
2. To make your feelings more vivid and clear to the audience, use similes and metaphors.
3. Use rhyme and rhythm to develop feelings in your lyric poem.
4. Give your lyric poem a title.

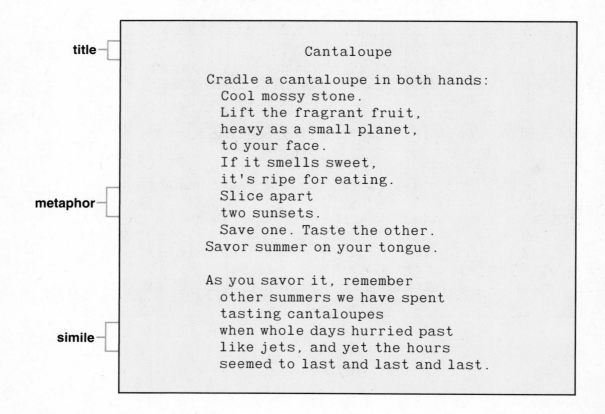

title

```
                    Cantaloupe

        Cradle a cantaloupe in both hands:
            Cool mossy stone.
            Lift the fragrant fruit,
            heavy as a small planet,
            to your face.
            If it smells sweet,
            it's ripe for eating.
            Slice apart
            two sunsets.
            Save one. Taste the other.
        Savor summer on your tongue.

        As you savor it, remember
            other summers we have spent
            tasting cantaloupes
            when whole days hurried past
            like jets, and yet the hours
            seemed to last and last and last.
```

metaphor

simile

WRITER'S HANDBOOK • Composition

Character Sketch

- In a **character sketch** a writer describes a real or an imaginary person.

character sketch

Writer's Guide: Character Sketch

1. Tell the name of the person you are describing in your topic sentence.
2. Describe how the person looks, moves, and thinks.
3. Tell what the person does that makes him or her special. Give clear examples.
4. Explain a situation in which the person shows his or her special qualities.

Emily, my neighbor, is a little smaller than other girls her age. She has sparkling green eyes that stand out on her angelic face. Her pointed nose and small mouth give her a mouse—like look. She eats neatly and moves without wasted motion. Because she is such a neat, well—organized, and responsible girl, she is in great demand as a baby sitter.

topic sentence

description

example of what makes the character special

What most impresses people about Emily, however, is her memory. At home, other members of her family are always asking her to find lost objects. Emily pictures the item, and then she knows where she last saw it. Yesterday, for example, Emily's father had lost his keys. Emily just closed her eyes, pursed her lips, thought for a moment, and then said, ''Ah, yes. I remember.'' She led her father to the kitchen, and there were the keys, just where he had absent—mindedly put them——in the refrigerator.

example of a special quality

WRITER'S HANDBOOK • Composition

News Story

news story

● In a **news story** a writer provides information about a person, a group, an event, an object, or an issue. A news story has three parts: the headline, the lead, and the body. The title of a news story is called the **headline.** The **lead** is the first paragraph of a news story. It tells *who, what, when, where, why,* and sometimes *how* something happened. The rest of the news story is called the **body.** It gives more details about the lead.

Writer's Guide: News Story

1. Write a lead that answers the six news-gathering questions.
2. In the body of the news story, give more details about the lead. Write the most important details first.
3. Write a short, interesting headline. Use a strong verb to attract the attention of the audience.

---

headline ——

lead paragraph —

body ——

```
          Cat Survives 20-Mile Drive in Wheel Well
     Jim Long's father was driving near Springfield,
Illinois, last Monday when he and Jim heard the car
purring--with the engine turned off. Mr. Long had
to jack up the car before discovering a cat wedged
inside the left front wheel well.
     ''My dad thought something was wrong with the
car,'' said Jim. ''Every time we stopped the car, we
heard a high, whining sound.''
     Mr. Long had been driving at between 50 and 55
mph on the freeway. He drove about 20 miles before
discovering the cat. The cat survived the ride
without injury.
```

WRITER'S HANDBOOK ● Composition

Book Report

- In a **book report** a writer summarizes the important events in a book. The writer also gives his or her opinion of the book.

book report

Writer's Guide: Book Report
1. In the first sentence, give the title of the book and the name of the author. Remember to underline the title of the book.
2. Write a summary of the important events. Include the main idea, the names of the main characters, and some interesting details. Do not tell the ending.
3. Tell why a person might or might not like the book, or give your opinion of the book. Support your opinion with reasons.

Zeely, by Virginia Hamilton, is about a girl — **title, author**
named Geeder. Geeder is spending the summer at her
uncle's farm in the country. She keeps seeing a
beautiful woman named Zeely, who is her uncle's
neighbor. Geeder becomes convinced that Zeely is a — **summary**
Watutsi queen. As Geeder thinks more and more about
Zeely, she decides she wants to be just like her.
Zeely is able to show Geeder that it is important
to have dreams, but it is also important just to be
yourself.

I liked this book. The book has very beautiful — **opinion**
pictures, and I think it has an important message. — **reasons**
Also, Geeder seemed like a real person.

Research Report

● To write a **research report,** a writer gathers information from several sources, takes notes from the sources, and organizes the notes into an outline. Then he or she writes the report from these notes and the outline.

Writer's Guide: Research Report
1. Use your notes and your outline to write your research report.
2. Write an introduction that identifies your topic. Make your sentences interesting, to capture the attention of the audience.
3. Write one paragraph for each subtopic in your outline.
4. Follow your outline to write details about your topic.
5. Write a conclusion that sums up the information given or draws a conclusion about the subject.
6. Give your research report a title.

title —

A Land of Many Flavors

introduction —

When you think of Mexican food, do you always picture tacos? Actually, Mexican food includes a great variety of dishes from many different regions. In Jalisco, for example, you can enjoy pozole, a stew made with chunks of pork, corn, and chilies. In the Yucatán, you can dine on sac—kol de jambali——wild boar with peppermint sauce.

subtopic —

Mexican cooking is mainly a combination of Indian and Spanish influences. Hundreds of years ago, the Aztec Indians were already eating the flat corn pancakes known as tortillas. Indians also contributed such ingredients as squash, sweet potatoes, vanilla, chile, chocolate, and tomatoes. The Spaniards, who conquered Mexico in the 16th century, added beef, lard, cheese, and onions to Mexican cooking.

WRITER'S HANDBOOK ● Composition

Turkey with mole sauce is one of the most interesting dishes from Mexico. Mole sauce has 40 ingredients, including chocolate! Turkey mole combines two of the foods Mexico gave to the world--turkey and chocolate. My grandmother says, "It's practically the national dish of Mexico."

— subtopic

Other popular main dishes in Mexico include tacos, enchiladas, chile rellenos, and tamales. Desserts include a baked caramel custard called flan. In the summer, Mexicans may drink liquadas, which are made from fruit juice. On a cold day, they may enjoy hot Mexican chocolate, or cafe con leche, which is hot milk flavored with strong coffee.

— subtopic

From Ensenada to the Yucatán, from Veracruz to Mazatlán, Mexico is a land of many flavors. The best way to learn about this really delicious cuisine is to visit Mexico. Bring your appetite!

— conclusion

Friendly Letter

friendly letter
- In a **friendly letter** a writer sends greetings or news to someone he or she knows. Thank-you notes and invitations are also friendly letters. A friendly letter has five parts.

Writer's Guide: Friendly Letter
1. Write the heading in the upper right corner.
2. Write the greeting at the left margin.
3. In the body, write your message in paragraph form. Tell your friend some news about yourself. Ask your friend some questions about his or her life.
4. Use words that suit your purpose and your audience. Be sure your tone reflects the way you feel about your news.
5. Write the closing and your signature in line with the heading.

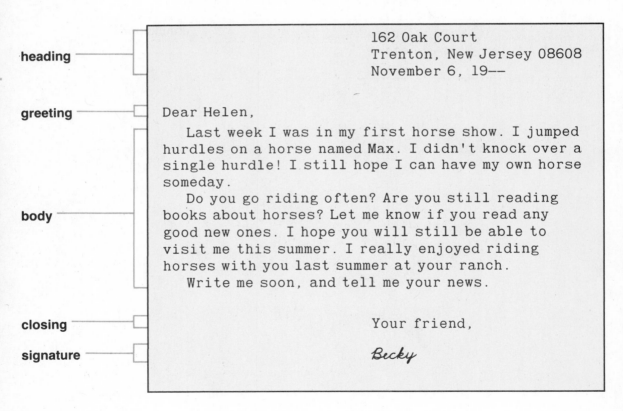

heading

162 Oak Court
Trenton, New Jersey 08608
November 6, 19--

greeting

Dear Helen,

body

   Last week I was in my first horse show. I jumped hurdles on a horse named Max. I didn't knock over a single hurdle! I still hope I can have my own horse someday.
   Do you go riding often? Are you still reading books about horses? Let me know if you read any good new ones. I hope you will still be able to visit me this summer. I really enjoyed riding horses with you last summer at your ranch.
   Write me soon, and tell me your news.

closing

Your friend,

signature

Becky

Business Letter

- In a **business letter** a writer usually writes to someone he or she does not know. The purpose of a business letter may be to ask for information or to order something. In addition to the five parts of a friendly letter, a business letter has an **inside address.** It is the receiver's address.

Writer's Guide: Business Letter

1. Write the heading in the upper right corner.
2. Write the inside address at the left margin.
3. Write the greeting under the inside address. Put a colon after the greeting.
4. Write the body in paragraph form. Tell why you are writing to the person or business. Use a polite tone.
5. Write the closing in line with the heading. In a business letter the closing is usually *Yours truly* or *Sincerely.*
6. Write your signature below the closing. Sign your full name. Then type your name below your signature.

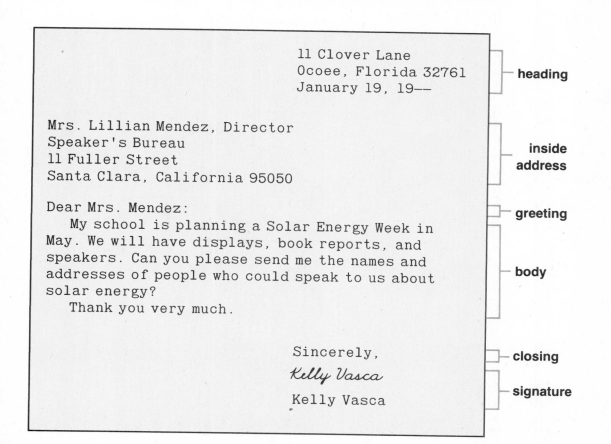

11 Clover Lane
Ocoee, Florida 32761
January 19, 19—— — **heading**

Mrs. Lillian Mendez, Director
Speaker's Bureau
11 Fuller Street
Santa Clara, California 95050 — **inside address**

Dear Mrs. Mendez: — **greeting**

   My school is planning a Solar Energy Week in May. We will have displays, book reports, and speakers. Can you please send me the names and addresses of people who could speak to us about solar energy?
   Thank you very much. — **body**

        Sincerely, — **closing**
        Kelly Vasca
        Kelly Vasca — **signature**

Invitation

invitation

- In an **invitation** a writer invites someone to come to a party or other event or to do something. An invitation has the same five parts as a friendly letter.

Writer's Guide: Invitation

1. Be sure to include a heading, a greeting, a body, a closing, and a signature in your invitation.
2. In the body, tell *who* is invited and *what* the invitation is for.
3. Tell *when* and *where* the event or activity will take place and any other special information your guest must know.

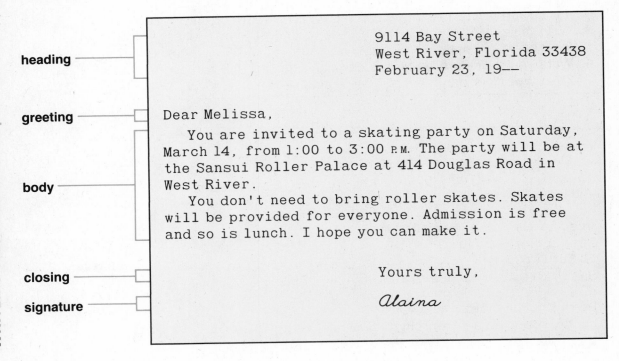

heading

9114 Bay Street
West River, Florida 33438
February 23, 19—

greeting

Dear Melissa,

body

    You are invited to a skating party on Saturday, March 14, from 1:00 to 3:00 P.M. The party will be at the Sansui Roller Palace at 414 Douglas Road in West River.
    You don't need to bring roller skates. Skates will be provided for everyone. Admission is free and so is lunch. I hope you can make it.

closing

       Yours truly,

signature

       Alaina

Thank-You Note

- In a **thank-you note** a writer thanks someone for doing something. A thank-you note has the same five parts as a friendly letter.

thank-you note

Writer's Guide: Thank-You Note
1. Be sure to include a heading, a greeting, a body, a closing, and a signature in your thank-you note.
2. In the body, tell why you are thanking the person.
3. If you have been a visitor somewhere, tell why you enjoyed yourself.
4. If you have received a gift, tell how you are using it.

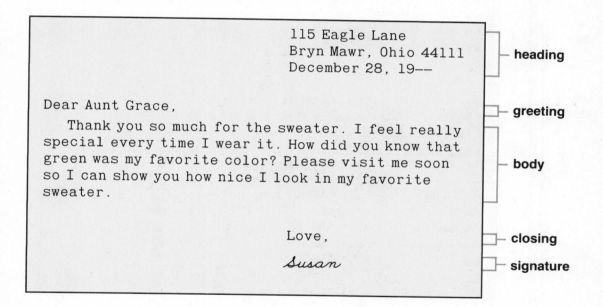

115 Eagle Lane
Bryn Mawr, Ohio 44111
December 28, 19—— — **heading**

Dear Aunt Grace, — **greeting**

    Thank you so much for the sweater. I feel really special every time I wear it. How did you know that green was my favorite color? Please visit me soon so I can show you how nice I look in my favorite sweater. — **body**

Love, — **closing**

Susan — **signature**

Envelope

<dl>
<dt>envelope</dt>
</dl>

- An **envelope** is used to send a letter or a note.

mailing address

- The **mailing address** is the address of the person who will receive the letter. It is written just below the center of the envelope.

return address

- The **return address** is the address of the person who writes the letter. It is written in the upper left corner.

postal abbreviations

- **Postal abbreviations** are used for state names.

ZIP code

- The **ZIP code** is written after the state abbreviation.

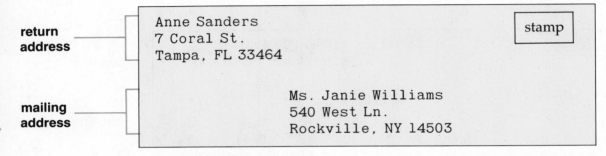

return address

Anne Sanders
7 Coral St.
Tampa, FL 33464

stamp

mailing address

Ms. Janie Williams
540 West Ln.
Rockville, NY 14503

Postal Abbreviations

Alabama	AL	Kentucky	KY	Ohio	OH
Alaska	AK	Louisiana	LA	Oklahoma	OK
Arizona	AZ	Maine	ME	Oregon	OR
Arkansas	AR	Maryland	MD	Pennsylvania	PA
California	CA	Massachusetts	MA	Puerto Rico	PR
Colorado	CO	Michigan	MI	Rhode Island	RI
Connecticut	CT	Minnesota	MN	South Carolina	SC
Delaware	DE	Mississippi	MS	South Dakota	SD
District of		Missouri	MO	Tennessee	TN
Columbia	DC	Montana	MT	Texas	TX
Florida	FL	Nebraska	NE	Utah	UT
Georgia	GA	Nevada	NV	Vermont	VT
Hawaii	HI	New Hampshire	NH	Virginia	VA
Idaho	ID	New Jersey	NJ	Washington	WA
Illinois	IL	New Mexico	NM	West Virginia	WV
Indiana	IN	New York	NY	Wisconsin	WI
Iowa	IA	North Carolina	NC	Wyoming	WY
Kansas	KS	North Dakota	ND		

WRITER'S HANDBOOK • Composition

Vocabulary

- A **base word** is a word to which other word parts may be added to form new words.

base word

- A **root** is a word part that can be combined with prefixes, suffixes, base words, and other roots to form words.

root

Root	Meaning	Example
ped	foot	pedal
mot	move	motion
uni	one, single	universe
ject	throw	reject
port	carry	porter
sect	divide, cut	intersect
tele	far away	telephone
vac	empty	vacation
creat	make	create
cent	hundred	percent

We used a tele scope to study the stars.

Some port able computers weigh less than five pounds.

A ped estal is the lower part of a column.

- A **prefix** is a word part added to the beginning of a word. It changes the meaning or part of speech of the word.

prefix

Prefix	Meaning	Examples
un, in	not, opposite of	unfair, incomplete
re	back, again	retrace, retell
dis	away, off, not	dislike, displace
mis	badly, wrong, not	misjudge, misunderstand
pre	before	preheat, preteen
post	later	postgame, postpaid
over	too much	overcook, overshoot

I agree with the umpire's decision.

Tony disagrees with his brother.

Margaret celebrated her good fortune .

Vincent had the misfortune to injure his leg.

The war left many people without homes.

The country prospered during the postwar years.

● A **suffix** is a word part added to the end of a word. It usually changes the meaning or part of speech of the word.

Suffix	Meaning	Example
er, ist, or	one who	builder, artist, sailor
ness	act of, state of	kindness
ment	as a result of being	enjoyment
ance	act of	assistance
ful	full of, worthy of	powerful
less	without	careless
y	having	dirty
ous	full of	dangerous
able	having qualities of	comfortable
ish	being like	childish
en, n	make, add	thicken, widen

The witness swore to tell the truth .

The people in court believed the witness was truthful .

Harriet admired the smooth wood.

Not a single ripple disturbed the smoothness of the lake.

The ocean appeared green .

Dan used a greenish color to paint the water.

synonym ● A **synonym** is a word that has almost the same meaning as another word. Often, a word has more than one synonym.

The rich man gave money to his poorer neighbors.

The wealthy man gave money to his poorer neighbors.

antonym ● An **antonym** is a word that has the opposite meaning from another word. Sometimes a word has more than one antonym.

I wasn't strong enough to lift the heavy table.

I lifted the lightweight table easily.

homographs ● **Homographs** are words that are spelled alike but have different meanings and, sometimes, different pronunciations.

The library charges a fine for overdue books.

The fine weather lasted all summer.

- **Homophones** are words that sound alike but have different meanings and spellings.

homophones

> Elise bought a new pair of running shoes.

> Would you like a peach or a pear for dessert?

- A **compound word** is a word formed by joining two or more words.

compound word

- A **closed compound** is written as a single word.

> sunlight   fingerprint   latchkey

- An **open compound** is written as two words.

> high school   sign language   fire hydrant

- A **hyphenated compound** is written by connecting the parts of a compound word with hyphens.

> jack-of-all-trades   life-size

WRITER'S HANDBOOK • Vocabulary

Study Steps to Learn a Word

 **Say** the word. Recall when you have heard the word used. Think about what it means.

 **Look** at the word. Find any prefixes, suffixes, or other word parts you know. Think about other words that are related in meaning and spelling. Try to picture the word in your mind.

 **Spell** the word to yourself. Think about the way each sound is spelled. Notice any unusual spelling.

 **Write** the word while looking at it. Check the way you have formed your letters. If you have not written the word clearly or correctly, write it again.

 **Check** your learning. Cover the word and write it. If you did not spell the word correctly, practice these steps until the word becomes your own.

Guidelines for Creating a Spelling Word List

You may want to keep your own spelling word list in a notebook. You can organize your spelling word list alphabetically, by subject areas, by parts of speech, or by other categories. Follow these guidelines.

1 Check your writing for words you have misspelled. Circle each misspelled word.

> *a (poplar) sport*

2 Find out how to spell the word correctly.
- Look up the word in a dictionary or a thesaurus.
- Ask a teacher or a classmate.

> *popular*
> *a (poplar) sport*

3 Write the word in your notebook.
- Spell the word correctly.
- Write a definition, a synonym, or an antonym to help you understand the meaning of the word.
- Use the word in a sentence.

> *popular—liked by many people*
> *The group sang a popular song.*

4 When you write, look at your spelling word list to check your spelling.

> *Soccer is a popular sport in England.*

Frequently Misspelled Words

accept	cushion	manager	shiny
accepted	determined	meant	shoved
afterwards	downstairs	medal	slammed
allowed	drawer	mischievous	sneak
announced	elementary	museum	somewhere
announcer	embarrassed	mystery	straight
annoyed	equipment	nearby	straighten
anxiously	erasers	neighbor	studying
anymore	especially	neighbors	substitute
apologize	everyday	nonsense	surprise
applause	everywhere	nowhere	surprised
assignment	excellent	opposite	themselves
background	excitement	outdoors	throat
backyard	expensive	package	throughout
beginning	experiment	paid	tomorrow
believe	extremely	potato	tournament
believed	grateful	principal	typical
breathe	halfway	probably	unfortunately
business	ignored	professional	unusual
cafeteria	immediately	purpose	upstairs
captain	incident	realized	valuable
ceiling	innocent	receive	video
chalkboard	instance	received	weird
challenge	intelligent	relieved	whatever
college	interest	remembered	whenever
commotion	interrupted	rescued	whose
competition	jewelry	restaurant	wrapped
completely	lightning	ribbon	yourself
concentrate	lose	ridiculous	
concentrating	losing	separate	
congratulated	luckily	shining	

Vowel Sounds

- The short vowel sounds are usually spelled with one letter.

short vowel sounds

  /a/ is spelled **a,** as in *grasp.*
  /e/ is spelled **e,** as in *web.*
  /i/ is spelled **i,** as in *list.*
  /o/ is spelled **o,** as in *sock.*
  /u/ is spelled **u,** as in *run.*

  Note: /e/ is sometimes spelled **ea** as in *ready.*

- Here are eight ways to spell /ā/.

long vowel sounds

  a, as in *navy*
  a-consonant-e, as in *brake*
  ai, as in *complain*
  ay, as in *tray*
  ey, as in *they*
  eigh, as in *sleigh*
  ei, as in *vein*
  ea, as in *steak*

- Here are eight ways to spell /ē/.

  e, as in *equal*
  e-consonant-e, as in *concede*
  ee, as in *sheet*
  ea, as in *eager*
  y, as in *lazy*
  ey, as in *key*
  ei, as in *deceive*
  ie, as in *piece*

- Here are six ways to spell /ī/.

  i, as in *idea*
  igh, as in *high*
  i-consonant-e, as in *rice*
  y, as in *deny*
  ie, as in *pie*
  ei, as in *height*

- Here are seven ways to spell /ō/.

  o, as in *over*
  oa, as in *goat*
  o-consonant-e, as in *rope*
  ow, as in *below*
  ou, as in *shoulder*
  oe, as in *toe*
  ough, as in *although*

- Here are nine ways to spell /o͞o/.

  oo, as in *shoot*
  ew, as in *threw*
  o, as in *to*
  oe, as in *shoe*
  u-consonant-e, as in *rude*
  ui, as in *suit*
  ou, as in *soup*
  ough, as in *through*
  o-consonant-e, as in *move*

ie, ei
- The two vowels *e* and *i* combine in different ways to spell long vowel sounds. Most of the time the spelling for /ē/ is *i* before *e,* as in *piece.* If the word has the /ā/ sound, *e* comes before *i,* as in *reindeer.* If the word has the /ē/ sound after the /s/ sound, the spelling is also *ei,* as in *receive.*

the /ər/ sound
- Here are three ways to spell the /ər/ sound at the end of a word.

  er, as in *teacher, pitcher, dancer*
  or, as in *actor, governor, conductor*
  ar, as in *liar, beggar, scholar*

the /əl/ sound
- Here are five ways to spell the /əl/ sound at the end of a word.

  al, as in *final*
  le, as in *trouble*
  el, as in *tunnel*
  il, as in *pencil*
  ile, as in *fragile*

Syllable Division

- A **syllable** is a word or a part of a word. Each syllable in a word has one vowel sound. Knowing how to divide a word into syllables can help you pronounce the word correctly. Knowing correct pronunciation, in turn, can help you spell a word correctly. Follow these guidelines for dividing words into syllables.

syllable

- When a word has two vowels between two consonants, divide the word between the two vowels.

     truest—tru·est   prior—pri·or

- When a word has two consonants between two vowels, divide the word between the two consonants.

     temper—tem·per   forget—for·get
     puppet—pup·pet   rabbit—rab·bit

- In a word with two syllables, the middle consonant is part of the accented syllable. *Forest,* for example, has two syllables. The first syllable in *forest* is accented, so the *r* sound is part of the first syllable. Here are some other examples.

     travel—trav·el   repeat—re·peat

Verbs

- Add *ed* to form the past tense of most verbs.

past tense

   stamp—stamped   spell—spelled   answer—answered

- If a verb ends in *e,* drop the *e* and add *ed.*

   save—saved   compare—compared   decide—decided

- If a one-syllable verb ends in a single consonant and has a short vowel sound, double the final consonant and add *ed.*

     grip—gripped   pat—patted   beg—begged

- If a verb ends in a consonant plus *y,* change the *y* to *i* and add *ed.*

     try—tried   hurry—hurried   rally—rallied

- For a list of verbs that do not form the past tense with *ed,* see pages 12−14 of the *Grammar* section in this **Writer's Handbook.**

- Add *ing* to form the present participle of most verbs.

    catch—catching   see—seeing   build—building

- If a verb ends in *e,* drop the *e* and add *ing.*

    give—giving   trade—trading   freeze—freezing

- If a one-syllable verb ends in a single consonant and has a short vowel sound, double the final consonant and add *ing.*

    tap—tapping   stop—stopping   get—getting

Nouns

plurals
- Add *s* to form the plural of most nouns.

    train—trains   chair—chairs

- Add *es* to form the plural of nouns that end in *s, ss, ch, sh, x,* or *z.*

    class—classes   sash—sashes
    porch—porches   box—boxes

- To form the plural of nouns that end in a consonant plus *y,* change the *y* to *i* and add *es.*

    city—cities   party—parties

- Add *s* to form the plural of nouns that end in a vowel followed by *y.*

    toy—toys   monkey—monkeys

- To form the plural of most nouns that end in *f* or *fe,* change the *f* or *fe* to *v* and add *es.*

    shelf—shelves   wife—wives

- Add *s* to form the plural of nouns ending in a vowel followed by *o.*

    radio—radios   cameo—cameos

- Add *s* to form the plural of most nouns ending in a consonant followed by *o.*

    solo—solos   piano—pianos

- Some nouns have irregular plural forms.

tooth—teeth	woman—women
child—children	mouse—mice
man—men	goose—geese

- Some nouns are spelled the same in the singular and the plural forms.

moose—moose	deer—deer
fish—fish	sheep—sheep

Compound Words

- A **compound word** is made up of two or more words. Usually, the spelling of the separate words remains the same when the words are combined.

compound word

- A **closed compound** is written as one word.

  airplane   bedspread   newspaper

- An **open compound** is written as two words.

  traffic light   hearing aid   sea lion

- A **hyphenated compound** is connected by hyphens.

  man-of-war   father-in-law   one-fourth

Contractions

- A **contraction** is a short way of writing two words together by leaving out one or more letters. An apostrophe is used to replace the missing letter or letters. Many contractions are formed from a verb and the word *not*.

verb contraction

are + not = aren't	should + not = shouldn't
does + not = doesn't	had + not = hadn't

  Exception: will + not = won't

- A pronoun can be combined with a verb to form a contraction.

pronoun contraction

I + will = I'll	we + have = we've
she + is = she's	they + are = they're

Possessive Nouns

singular   ● To form the possessive of a singular noun, add an apostrophe and *s*.

> I took a hammer from the carpenter's toolbox.

plural   ● To form the possessive of a plural noun that ends in *s*, add an apostrophe.

> The soldiers' uniforms were blue.

● To form the possessive of a plural noun that does not end in *s*, add an apostrophe and *s*.

> The women's meeting begins at noon.

Abbreviations

● An **abbreviation** is a shortened form of a word. An abbreviation usually begins with a capital letter and ends with a period.

titles   ● Most titles for people have abbreviations.

> Mister—Mr.   Doctor—Dr.   Senator—Sen.
> *Mrs.* and *Ms.* are always written as abbreviations.

days, months   ● Here are the abbreviations of the days of the week and the months of the year.

Sunday—Sun.	Monday—Mon.	Tuesday—Tues.
Wednesday—Wed.	Thursday—Thurs.	Friday—Fri.
Saturday—Sat.		

January—Jan.	February—Feb.	March—Mar.
April—Apr.	August—Aug.	September—Sept.
October—Oct.	November—Nov.	December—Dec.

May, June, and *July* are never abbreviated.

kinds of streets   ● Here are some common street abbreviations used in addresses.

Street—St.	Avenue—Ave.	Road—Rd.
Boulevard—Blvd.	Drive—Dr.	Lane—Ln.

Adjectives That Compare

- Add *er* to form the comparative degree of many adjectives. Add *est* to form the superlative degree.   *er, est*

bright—brighter—brightest

- To form the comparative or superlative degree of an adjective that ends in one vowel and one consonant, double the consonant before adding *er* or *est*.

hot—hotter—hottest

- When an adjective ends in *e,* drop the *e* before adding *er* or *est*.

strange—stranger—strangest

- When an adjective ends in *y,* change the *y* to *i* before adding *er* or *est*.

shabby—shabbier—shabbiest

Adverbs That Compare

- Add *er* and *est* to one-syllable adverbs and some two-syllable adverbs to form comparative and superlative adverbs.   *er, est*

slow—slower—slowest

- When an adverb ends in a consonant plus *y,* change the final *y* to *i* before adding *er* or *est*.

hasty—hastier—hastiest

- When an adverb ends in *e,* drop the *e* before adding *er* or *est*.

late—later—latest

Sentence Diagramming

sentence diagram
- A **sentence diagram** shows how the parts of a sentence work together.

simple subject and simple predicate
- The **simple subject** is the main, or key, word in the complete subject. The **simple predicate** is the verb in the complete predicate.

subject	verb

Sam tripped.

Sam	tripped

inverted word order
- A sentence has **inverted word order** when the verb comes before the subject. When you diagram a sentence having inverted word order, place the subject before the verb as usual, and capitalize any words that are capitalized in the sentence.

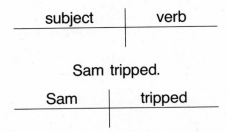

subject	verb

Is Rosa going?

Rosa	Is going

four kinds of sentences
- These diagrams show the simple subject and the simple predicate of each kind of sentence.

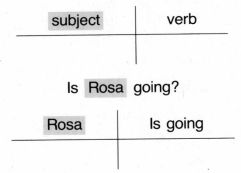

Declarative: Carl ran quickly.

Carl	ran

Imperative: Run quickly.

you (understood)	Run

Interrogative: Did Carl run?

Carl	Did run

Exclamatory: How quickly Carl ran!

Carl	ran

- A **direct object** receives the action of the verb and answers the question *What?* or *Whom?*

direct object

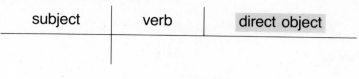

Artists make sketches .

| Artists | make | sketches |

- An **indirect object** tells to or for whom or what the action of the verb is done.

indirect object

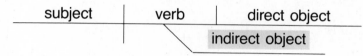

Richard gave him directions.

| Richard | gave | directions |
| | | him |

- A **predicate nominative** is a noun or pronoun that follows a linking verb and renames the subject of the sentence.

predicate nominative

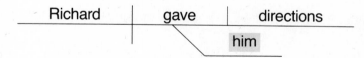

Lincoln was President .

| Lincoln | was | President |

• An **appositive** is a noun or a phrase, often with modifiers, that identifies or renames the word or words that precede it.

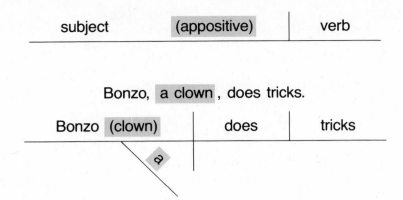

Bonzo, a clown , does tricks.

adjective • An **adjective** modifies a noun or a pronoun.

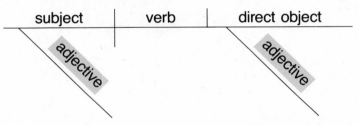

Noisy people filled the large stadium.

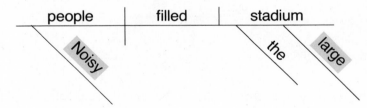

- **Possessive nouns** and **possessive pronouns** precede nouns to show ownership or possession. The **articles** *a, an,* and *the* are special adjectives that always signal a noun.

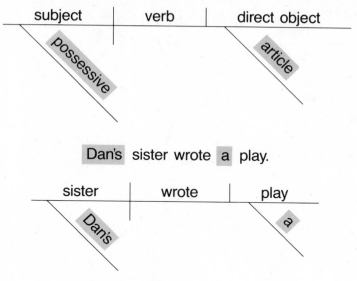

Dan's sister wrote a play.

- A **predicate adjective** follows a linking verb and describes the subject of the sentence.

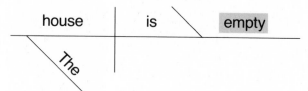

The house is empty.

adverb ● An **adverb** modifies a verb, an adjective, or another adverb.

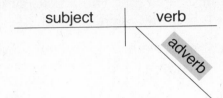

Amy quietly closed the door.

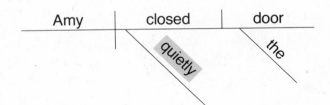

prepositional phrase ● A **prepositional phrase** is made up of a preposition (prep.), the object of the preposition, and all the words in between. The object of the preposition is the noun or pronoun at the end of the prepositional phrase.

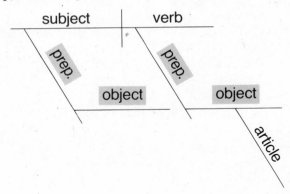

A flock of birds is flying over the lake.

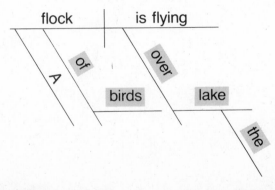

- A **compound subject** is two or more subjects that have the same verb. The subjects are joined by a conjunction (conj.).

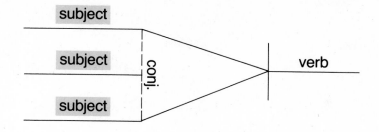

A lion , a tiger , and a leopard escaped.

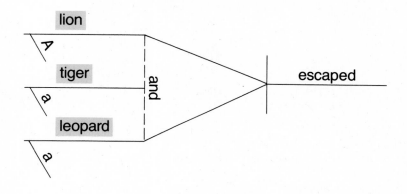

- A **compound predicate** is two or more verbs that have the same subject. The verbs are joined by a conjunction.

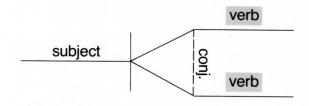

We mowed the grass and watered the flowers.

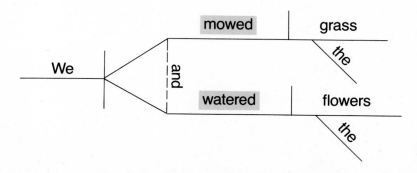

WRITER'S HANDBOOK • Sentence Diagramming

WRITER'S HANDBOOK • Sentence Diagramming

conjunction and a compound sentence

- A **compound sentence** contains two or more related simple sentences joined by a comma and a conjunction or by a semicolon.

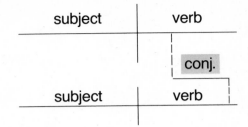

Beth likes vegetables, but she hates meat.

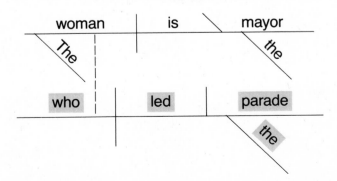

complex sentence with an adjective clause

- A **complex sentence** consists of an independent clause and at least one dependent clause. If the dependent clause functions as an adjective, diagram the sentence like this.

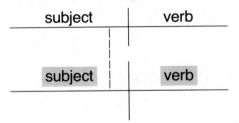

The woman who led the parade is the mayor.

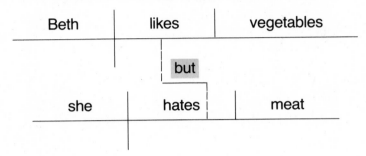

- If the dependent clause in a complex sentence functions as an adverb, diagram the sentence like this.

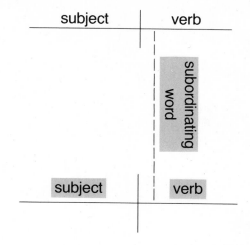

The bell rings when the door opens .

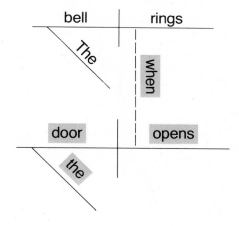

GLOSSARY

Contents

Composition Terms

AUDIENCE *the reader or readers for whom a composition is written* In this business letter the audience is Dr. Patel.

```
Dr. Guta Patel
Mercy Hospital
Aiken, Ohio 44113


Dear Dr. Patel:
```

CLARITY *the preciseness with which the ideas and the intent of a composition are expressed* See how precise the words in these directions are.

Get off at Exit 8A. At the bottom of the exit ramp turn right and go one mile to the first stoplight.

COHERENCE *the orderly arrangement of ideas in a composition* Notice how the changes in these sentences make the passage more logical.

Within days,
~~Soon new growth begins.~~ Despite their damage, forest fires do some good. Scientists can study the rebirth of an environment.

DRAFTING *the actual writing of a composition, beginning with a first draft* This girl is drafting a descriptive paragraph about the painting.

EDITOR'S MARKS *standard symbols for making changes when revising or proofreading* Notice that each mark in these examples indicates a specific type of change.

Use these marks when you revise.

⌒ Move something.	⌃ Add something.
⌐ Replace something.	✂ Cut something.

Use these marks when you proofread.

≡ Capitalize.	⌃ Add something.	⊙ Add a period.
⩔⩔ Add quotation marks.	⌐ Replace something.	✂ Cut something.
∼ Transpose	◯ Spell correctly.	⅄ Add a comma.
/ Make a lowercase letter.		¶ Indent paragraph.

FINAL DRAFT *the finished version of a composition that is ready to be published* This is the final draft of the first draft example below.

Gorillas are an endangered species. Their natural habitat is the mountain areas of Africa.

FIRST DRAFT *the rough version of a composition, in which a writer's thoughts are first put on paper* Notice the unfinished quality of this writing.

Gorilla is endangered species. Mountain areas in Africa are natural habitat.

PREWRITING *the first stage of the writing process, in which the writer gathers ideas and information and begins to organize them* This example shows a cluster as one way of organizing ideas on a topic.

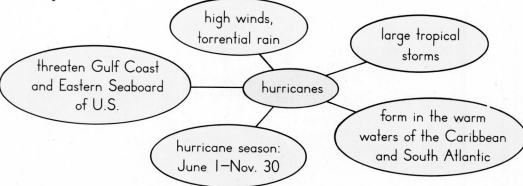

GLOSSARY

PREWRITING STRATEGIES *the activities that help a writer choose and organize ideas and information* The following are examples of prewriting strategies.

- **brainstorming** *an activity that encourages the contribution of ideas from an individual or a group* Making a list is one way of brainstorming. This list shows possible topics for a descriptive paragraph.

> view from the top of the Ferris wheel
> beach at sunset
> Main Street during rush hour
> nature trail at the park
> old oak tree in backyard

- **charting** *a way of classifying and organizing ideas and information*

Setting	Characters	Conflicts
Ohio, 1862	Toby	Toby vs. father
	John	John vs. Confederates

- **clustering** *a brainstorming technique that helps a writer generate and organize facts or ideas around a main idea or topic*

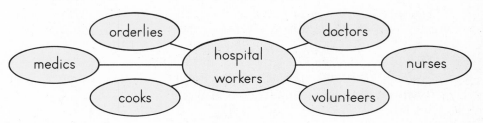

- **diagramming** *a way of showing how ideas are related in time or space*

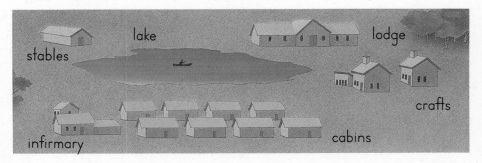

- **using an inverted triangle** *a way of organizing ideas to narrow a topic*

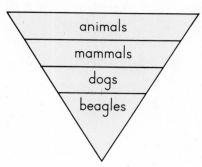

- **listing** *writing, on paper or on the chalkboard, ideas brainstormed by a group or an individual*

Ways to Fly		
airplane	*blimp*	*rocket*
helicopter	*balloon*	*glider*

- **mapping** *a way of organizing ideas to show relationships between them*

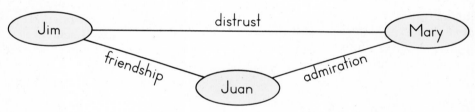

- **slotting** *a brainstorming technique used by an individual or a group to find words or word groups to complete a sentence*

> *Harry was ____ after the marathon.*
> *exhausted   relieved*
> *elated   limping*

PROOFREADING *reviewing a draft to correct errors in capitalization, punctuation, usage, grammar, and spelling*   Editor's marks in this example indicate corrections made by the writer while proofreading.

> *Mia beated ray in Chess*

PUBLISHING *making public a final draft of a composition—for example, by reading it aloud, putting it in a class journal, or displaying it on the bulletin board* This picture shows a bulletin board that displays several students' published work.

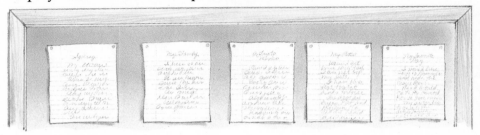

PURPOSE *the reason a composition is written—for example, to describe, to inform, or to persuade* The purpose of this editorial is to persuade.

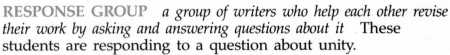

Anita Jones has been a great mayor. A vote for her is a vote for the future.

RESPONDING *a revising activity in which the writer, a partner, or a group asks and answers questions about a composition* Here, a writer questions herself as she reviews her work.

Have I left out any necessary information? Do the detail sentences support the topic sentence?

RESPONSE GROUP *a group of writers who help each other revise their work by asking and answering questions about it* These students are responding to a question about unity.

Boy: *This detail doesn't belong here.* **Girl:** *Maybe you could make the conclusion clearer.*

REVISING *the process of rethinking ideas and correcting errors in organization and language* Notice these changes in a revised draft.

> ~~form~~ ~~warm waters of the~~
> Hurricanes show up in the Caribbean Sea and Atlantic Ocean. They bring high winds and ~~torrential~~ heavy rains to the Gulf Coast and Eastern Seaboard. Hurricanes are large tropical storms.

STYLE *a writer's use of language and sentence structure to create a particular tone* Notice the poetic quality of these lines.

> The mist rose sweet and shimmering from the river, softening the edges of the moonlight as it spread.

TASK *a writing assignment or job* It was Gloria's task to write a thank-you note to her aunt.

> Dear Aunt Nellie,
>   Thank you for the wonderful basketball. It was just what I wanted.

TONE *the feeling or attitude a writer expresses toward the subject of a composition through his or her particular style of writing—for example, a writer's tone may be formal, informal, humorous, or critical* The tone of this example is formal and solemn.

> We are saddened by the death of Mr. Berg. His cheerfulness and love of teaching will be long remembered by all.

UNITY *the presentation of details that support the main idea of a paragraph or a composition, producing an effect of completeness* Here the writer has deleted a sentence that detracts from the unity of a paragraph.

> *Tomás worries about his sister. Will she make nice friends? ~~She is five years old.~~ Will she like school?*

WRITING PROCESS *the ongoing process of prewriting, drafting, responding and revising, proofreading, and publishing a composition* Before writing the final draft, a writer can go back and forth from one stage to another.

GLOSSARY

Literary Terms

ALLITERATION *the repetition of a beginning consonant sound in two or more nearby words* Alliteration is used in this line from the poem "How We Dance" by Lillian Morrison.

> **Bonnie like a beach ball**
> **floating on the sea**

CHARACTERIZATION *a writer's creation and development of realistic characters by describing them physically; by recording their actions, speech, and thoughts; or by commenting on them directly or through other characters* In these lines from a story, the author uses four of these techniques to develop a character.

> **A short, fat man wearing a black suit hopped out, waddled over, and got in line behind us.**

> • • •

> **"I hear you're nearly done with your new book," he boomed. "What's this one going to be about?"**

> • • •

> **"I have reason to believe that he is dishonest."**

CHARACTERS *the people (or animals) in a story, novel, play, or poem* For some authors, creating believable characters by describing their feelings, thoughts, and behavior is more important than writing a complex story; for others, plot comes first and character development second.

FICTION *a story invented by a writer* Works of fiction range in length from one-page fables, tales, and short stories to long novels that have more complex plots and characters.

Historical fiction is based on true events but includes made-up characters and incidents. **Fantasy** may be set in the real or a make-believe world, but its characters do impossible things and the plots are highly imaginative. In **science fiction,** the action is usually set in a future world, which characters often reach through time travel or space travel.

FIGURATIVE LANGUAGE *words used in unusual, rather than in exact or expected, ways* Similes and metaphors are the most common forms of figurative language. In a **simile,** the word *like* or *as* is used to compare two very different things—for example, *Charles dances like an itchy sea serpent.* A **metaphor** suggests a comparison by saying that one thing *is* another—for example, *Charles is an itchy sea serpent.*

FORESHADOWING *a technique used by an author to drop hints about future developments in a story* In *The Mystery of the Missing Coin,* author Ashley Simons uses foreshadowing in the opening paragraph.

> **As Jenny pulled into the driveway, she wondered why the wealthy widower Mr. Van der Horne had called her. When he greeted her at the door and escorted her into the elegant living room, Jenny knew at once that something was wrong.**

IMAGERY *the use of images in writing* Authors often create word pictures by using descriptive language to convey experiences of the senses or the emotions. In the passage at the top of page 10, William Least Heat Moon uses imagery to recount a journey.

Indiana 66, a road so crooked it could run for the legislature, took me into the hilly fields of CHEW MAIL POUCH barns, past Christ-of-the-Ohio Catholic Church, through the Swiss town of Tell City with its statue of William and his crossbow and nervous son.

NONFICTION *any writing that accurately describes something that actually happened, that presents information, or that gives an opinion* Among the forms of nonfiction are **biography,** the story of someone's life, and **autobiography,** the story of the author's own life. **Exposition** is writing that presents or explains information. In a **synopsis,** a writer gives a summary of a longer work.

ONOMATOPOEIA *the formation of words in imitation of actual sounds* Onomatopoeia is used in these lines from a poem.

> The percussionist taps
>   On the cymbals of brass,
> And clashes them together
>   With a big resounding
>   crash!
> Ting   Ting   Ting-Ting-
>   CLANG!

PERSONIFICATION *giving human qualities to nonhuman things or using a character to symbolize a particular quality* The devil, for example, is the personification of evil.

PLOT *the action in a story* **Conflict,** or a character's struggle against opposing forces, is the most important part of a plot. A writer plans a sequence of events around the conflict to hold the reader's attention. In the **introduction,** the setting, characters, and conflict are presented. In the next stage, the **complication,** or **rising action,** the conflict intensifies and the story progresses to a **climax,** in which

the conflict must be faced and worked out. The ending of the story is told in the **falling action** and the **resolution.**

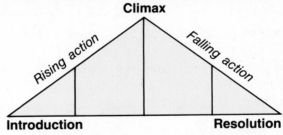

POINT OF VIEW *the choice of narrator through whom an author tells a story* If the story is narrated by a character using the pronoun *I* and seeing events only from his or her perspective, the author has chosen the **first-person** point of view. If the **third-person objective** point of view is used, the narrator is not part of the story, and all characters are referred to as *he, she, it,* or *they.* This narrator only records events and does not offer opinions or reveal the private thoughts of characters. When the narrator is an outsider but is able to tell the reader what the characters are thinking or feeling, the writer is using the **third-person omniscient,** or all-knowing, point of view.

REPETITION *the use of the same sound, word, phrase, or line of poetry two or more times* Repetition can help a writer emphasize an idea or achieve a particular rhythm. Notice how the poet Langston Hughes uses repetition in these lines.

> And the tom-toms beat,
> And the tom-toms beat,
> And the low beating of the
>   tom-toms
> Stirs your blood.

RHYME *the repetition of syllable sounds, especially at the ends of lines of poetry* The rhyming sounds at the ends of lines of poetry may be labeled with letters to describe a poem's rhyme scheme. Notice that Lillian Morrison used an *abab* rhyme scheme in these lines from her poem "Two to Nothing."

Catcher, the ball caller	*a*
knees bent, squatting;	*b*
Pitcher, a slider guider	*a*
peering, plotting	*b*

RHYTHM *the pattern of stressed and unstressed syllables, especially in poetry* A poem may have a regular rhythm, or meter, from beginning to end, or the rhythm may change within the poem. In this verse, the regular meter of the first four lines is changed to emphasize the last line.

> The percussionist plays
>   On the copper timpani.
> Being extra careful
>   When he tunes the key.
> Boom Bim Boom-Bim

SETTING *when and where a story takes place* A writer can choose any time or place in which to set a story. Sometimes the setting is necessary to the plot, as in most science fiction tales, but in stories having plots and characters that could develop anywhere, the setting is less important.

STANZA *a group of lines in a poem that are read as a unit and are comparable to a paragraph in a work of prose* In poems of more than one stanza, the rhyme scheme and meter are usually, but not always, the same in each stanza. Stanzas within a poem may have the same number of lines, or they may be of different lengths. In "African Dance" by Langston Hughes, notice how they differ.

> The low beating of the
>   tom-toms,
>   The slow beating of the tom-toms,
> Low . . . slow

> Slow . . . low—
> Stirs your blood.
>   Dance!
> A night-veiled girl
>   Whirls softly into a
>   Circle of light.
> Whirls softly . . . slowly,
> Like a wisp of smoke around
>   the fire—
>   And the tom-toms beat,
>   And the tom-toms beat,
> And the low beating of the
>   tom-toms
>   Stirs your blood.

THEME *the main idea or meaning of a story* While plot tells what happens in a story, the theme should answer the question "What does it all mean?" The narrator or a character in a work of fiction may actually state the theme at some point, or the author may leave it up to the reader to guess the theme's meaning. Not all authors write with a theme in mind; some stories are written just to entertain.

TONE *the language and sentence structure chosen by a writer to express a particular attitude toward the subject* The tone of a story or poem may be formal or informal, humorous or solemn, critical or enthusiastic. The author must employ a tone that is appropriate to what he or she is writing. In his poem "The Latest Latin Dance Craze," Victor Hernandez Cruz has achieved a joyous, comic tone, as demonstrated in these lines.

> Walking in a double cha cha
>   cha
> Open the door and glide down
> The stairs like a swan
> Hit the street
> Run at least ten blocks
> Come back in through the
>   same
> Door.

WRITER'S THESAURUS

Contents

What Is a Thesaurus?

A **thesaurus** lists words and their synonyms. Like a dictionary, a thesaurus lists words in alphabetical order. Each of these words is called an **entry word.** A list of synonyms follows the entry word. Sometimes a thesaurus lists antonyms.

Look at the parts of this thesaurus entry for the word *beautiful.*

The entry word is in color. It is followed by the part of speech and a definition. An **example sentence** shows how the word can be used.

▶ | **beautiful** *adj.* Lovely; very pretty. Every baby is beautiful to its parents.

Synonyms for the entry word are in italics. Each synonym is followed by a definition and an example sentence.

▶ | *attractive* Pleasing. Your room looks *attractive* with new curtains and new pictures on the wall.
graceful Having or showing beauty or delicacy of form or movement. The ballerina's *graceful* movements were a joy to behold.
lovely Beautiful. Alice has always had *lovely* curls.
pretty Attractive; pleasant. The stationery with the flowered border is very *pretty.*

If an **antonym** is given, it is printed in dark letters.

▶ | **ANTONYMS:** hideous, homely, plain, ugly, unattractive

How to Use Your Writer's Thesaurus

Suppose you are writing a thank-you note to a friend to express your appreciation for a gift. When you read your first draft, you realize that you have overused the word *beautiful*. You open your **Writer's Thesaurus** to find some synonyms. Here are the steps you should follow.

1. Look for the word in the **Index to the Thesaurus.** The Index lists every word in the **Writer's Thesaurus** in alphabetical order.

2. Find the word in the Index.

beautiful adj.

You know that *beautiful* is an entry word because it is printed in color.

3. Turn to the page in your **Writer's Thesaurus** on which *beautiful* is printed in color. Read the entry carefully. Not every synonym may express exactly what you want to say. Choose the synonym that makes the most sense in your note.

Remember: Not every synonym will have the exact meaning you want. Look at the entry for *beautiful* on page 8. Which synonyms fit your writing best?

◆ Sometimes a word is listed in the Index like this:

lovely beautiful adj.

This means you will find *lovely* listed as a synonym under the entry word *beautiful*. Since *lovely* is not printed in color, it is not an entry word.

◆ You will also see some lines in the Index that look like this:

hideous beautiful adj.

This means that *hideous* is listed as an antonym under the entry word *beautiful*.

Index to Thesaurus

F

failure defeat *n.*
fall *v.*
fashionable stylish *adj.*
fat *adj.*
fearful timid *adj.*
fearless timid *adj.*
feeble frail *adj.*
fill stuff *v.*
fluid liquid *adj.*
focused hazy *adj.*
forget remember *v.*
foul fragrant *adj.*
fragile frail *adj.*
fragrant *adj.*
frail *adj.*
free hold *v.*
frightened timid *adj.*
frigid cold *adj.*
frosty cold *adj.*
full empty *adj.*
funny strange *adj.*
fuzzy hazy *adj.*

G

gape look *v.*
gear equipment *n.*
glance look *v.*
gleaming glittering *adj.*
glistening glittering *adj.*
glittering *adj.*
globular round *adj.*
glowing glittering *adj.*
go *v.*
go come *v.*
graceful beautiful *adj.*
grasp hold *v.*
gray *adj.*
greatest most *adj.*
grit powder *n.*
grow *v.*

hard liquid *adj.*
hate love *v.*

hazy *adj.*
hide show *v.*
hideous beautiful *adj.*
highest most *adj.*
hoist lift *v.*
hold *v.*
holder container *n.*
homely beautiful *adj.*
hot cold *adj.*
hot warm *adj.*
humid damp *adj.*
hurry dash *v.*
hushed quiet *adj.*

idolize love *v.*
increase grow *v.*
inexpensive cheap *adj.*
inhabited empty *adj.*
inquire *v.*

jagged rough *adj.*
joyless sad *adj.*

lackluster glittering *adj.*
lad boy *n.*
lake water *n.*
least most *adj.*
leave come *v.*
lengthy long *adj.*
lifeless glittering *adj.*
lift *v.*
liquid *adj.*
locate place *v.*
long *adj.*
look *v.*
loud quiet *adj.*
love *v.*
lovely beautiful *adj.*
loveseat couch *n.*
lower lift *v.*

lowest most *adj.*
luminous bright *adj.*

make *v.*
mature grow *v.*
maximum most *adj.*
melancholy sad *adj.*
memoir memory *n.*
memory *n.*
minimum most *adj.*
miss *v.*
moist damp *adj.*
most *adj.*
move *v.*
muddled hazy *adj.*
muggy damp *adj.*

name *n.*
neglect miss *v.*
nickname name *n.*
nobody everybody
  pron.
noiseless quiet *adj.*
noisy quiet *adj.*
no one everybody *pron.*
normal strange *adj.*
note miss *v.*
notice miss *v.*

observe miss *v.*
ocean water *n.*
odorous fragrant *adj.*
old-fashioned stylish
  adj.
open *v.*
ordinary strange *adj.*
outdated stylish *adj.*
outrageous strange *adj.*
overcome succeed *v.*
overload stuff *v.*
overlook miss *v.*
overweight fat *adj.*

P

paddle swim *v.*
particle powder *n.*
peculiar different *adj.*
peer look *v.*
perfumed fragrant *adj.*
place *v.*
plain beautiful *adj.*
plump fat *adj.*
plunge fall *v.*
populated empty *adj.*
possess hold *v.*
powder *n.*
precipitation water *n.*
prepare make *v.*
pretty beautiful *adj.*
pride *n.*
proceed move *v.*
produce make *v.*
provisions equipment *n.*
puddle water *n.*
puncture open *v.*
push forward move *v.*
put place *v.*

Q

quiet *adj.*
quivering trembling *adj.*
quiz inquire *v.*

R

radiant warm *adj.*
rain water *n.*
raise lift *v.*
recall remember *v.*
receptacle container *n.*
recollect remember *v.*
recollection memory *n.*
reedy fat *adj.*
release hold *v.*
remember *v.*
reply inquire *v.*
respond inquire *v.*
retreat go *v.*
return go *v.*

reveal show *v.*
rise fall *v.*
river water *n.*
robust frail *adj.*
rough *adj.*
round *adj.*
rugged rough *adj.*

S

sad *adj.*
sample taste *v.*
sand powder *n.*
saturated wet *adj.*
saunter walk *v.*
savor taste *v.*
scamper dash *v.*
seat chair *n.*
self-respect pride *n.*
separate different *adj.*
shaking trembling *adj.*
shatter crash *v.*
shimmering glittering
   adj.
shiny bright *adj.*
show *v.*
shrink grow *v.*
shuddering trembling
   adj.
shut open *v.*
shy timid *adj.*
signature name *n.*
silent quiet *adj.*
silky rough *adj.*
similar different *adj.*
skinny fat *adj.*
slice *v.*
slight fat *adj.*
slim fat *adj.*
smart stylish *adj.*
smash crash *v.*
smelly fragrant *adj.*
smooth rough *adj.*
sofa couch *n.*
solid liquid *adj.*
sparkling glittering *adj.*
speechless quiet *adj.*

spherical round *adj.*
springy stretchy *adj.*
squash squish *v.*
squish *v.*
stool chair *n.*
stout fat *adj.*
strange *adj.*
stretchy *adj.*
stride walk *v.*
strut walk *v.*
stuff *v.*
sturdy frail *adj.*
stylish *adj.*
succeed *v.*
success defeat *n.*
supplies equipment *n.*
sweet fragrant *adj.*
swim *v.*

T

take advantage of use *v.*
taste *v.*
thick fat *adj.*
thin fat *adj.*
timid *adj.*
title name *n.*
torrid cold *adj.*
trembling *adj.*
trendy stylish *adj.*
trip fall *v.*
triumph succeed *n.*
trudge walk *v.*
tumble fall *v.*
typical strange *adj.*

U

ugly beautiful *adj.*
unattractive beautiful
   adj.
unclear hazy *adj.*
unlike different *adj.*
unlock open *v.*
unseal open *v.*
unusual strange *adj.*
upset defeat *n.*
use *v.*
usual different *adj.*

V

vacant **empty** *adj.*
vague **hazy** *adj.*
vessel **container** *n.*
vibrating **trembling** *adj.*
victory defeat *n.*
vigorous frail *adj.*
visit **come** *v.*

W

wade **swim** *v.*
walk *v.*
want *v.*
warm *adj.*
warm cold *adj.*
water *n.*
watery **liquid** *adj.*
weak **frail** *adj.*
wet *adj.*
wintry **cold** *adj.*
wispy **frail** *adj.*
worship **love** *v.*

Y

yearn **want** *v.*
youth **boy** *n.*

WRITER'S THESAURUS

animal *n.* A living creature, different from a plant because it can make itself move and has a nervous system. The giraffe is an **animal** that doesn't have a voice.

beast An animal, particularly one that is big and has four legs. The elephant is an intelligent *beast.*

creature Any human being or animal. Every living *creature* deserves to be treated with understanding.

beautiful *adj.* Lovely; very pretty. Every baby is **beautiful** to its parents.

attractive Pleasing. Your room looks *attractive* with new curtains and new pictures on the wall.

graceful Having or showing beauty or delicacy of form or movement. The ballerina's *graceful* movements were a joy to behold.

lovely Beautiful. Alice has always had *lovely* curls.

pretty Attractive; pleasant. The stationery with the flowers on it is very *pretty.*

ANTONYMS: hideous, homely, plain, ugly, unattractive

boy *n.* A young male person. My father was very thin when he was a **boy.**

lad A boy or a young man. My grandfather calls me a *lad* instead of a boy or a teenager.

youth A person in the years before adulthood; an adolescent. The *youth* worked at his parents' farm in the summer.

bright *adj.* Gleaming; shining. I wear my sunglasses when the sun is **bright.**

brilliant Shining brightly; glowing; sparkling. The surface of the lake was *brilliant* in the sunlight.

luminous Full of light; glowing. The face of my watch is *luminous* in the dark.

shiny Bright; gleaming. I polished my bike until it was *shiny.*

ANTONYM: dull

chair *n.* A seat, usually with a back and four legs, meant for one person. Pull up a **chair** and sit down.

bench A long seat, usually without a back. I sat on the wooden *bench* along the wall.

seat Something on which one sits. There is only one *seat* left in this subway car.

stool A seat, usually without a back or arms, meant for one person. Harold sat on a *stool* at the kitchen counter.

cheap *adj.* Not requiring much money, or not worth much money. His **cheap** shoes wore out within a month.

discounted Costing less than the normal price; reduced. I save money by buying *discounted* books.

inexpensive Not expensive; cheap. You can buy an *inexpensive* watch in that discount store.

ANTONYMS: costly, dear, expensive

cold *adj.* Lacking heat; having a low temperature. The room was **cold** because the heater was turned off.

chilly Feeling or causing to be cold; cool. The breeze makes it feel a bit *chilly* today.

frigid Extremely cold; without warmth. Temperatures in the Antarctic are *frigid.*

frosty Cold enough to make frost. You must wear a scarf, a hat, and gloves on such a *frosty* day.

wintry Winterlike. December brings *wintry* weather.

ANTONYMS: hot, torrid, warm

come *v.* To move toward the person who is speaking. Please **come** here at once.

arrive To reach a destination; to come to. Several airplanes *arrive* at Kennedy Airport every hour.

visit To come or go to see. I hope you will be able to *visit* us when you are in Chicago.

ANTONYMS: depart, go, leave

container *n.* Something used to hold something else; a jar, cup, box, or can. Is that **container** for honey or for ketchup?

holder Something that is used to keep things in. Return the unused napkin to the napkin *holder.*

receptacle An object designed to hold something. That *receptacle* is used to catch rain-water.

vessel A hollow container, such as a bowl or a pitcher. We'll fill the big glass *vessel* with eggnog.

couch *n.* An upholstered piece of furniture for seating more than one person. Everyone crowded onto the **couch** to watch the tennis match on television.

divan A long, low couch, often without arms or a back. I like to stretch out on the *divan,* close my eyes, and listen to music.

loveseat An upholstered seat or couch seating two. With the new *loveseat,* we can seat two more people in our living room.

sofa a long, upholstered couch with arms and a back. The arms and back of a velvet *sofa* may wear out quickly.

crash *v.* To fall or to bang into something. If you race through the house, you may **crash** into something.

clatter To make a harsh, metallic sound; to clash. You can hear Gina *clatter* up and down the sidewalk on her rickety bicycle.

shatter To destroy by breaking into pieces. The approaching hurricane may *shatter* our windows.

smash To break into pieces; to crush. Did you *smash* that vase by playing catch in the living room?

D

damp *adj.* A little wet; moist. I removed the towels from the dryer and discovered they were still **damp**.

dank Unpleasantly chilly and damp. The basement is so dark and *dank* that you could almost grow mushrooms in it!

humid Containing moist, damp air, heavy with water vapor. *Humid* weather makes my hair frizzy.

moist Damp. Place a cool, *moist* cloth on the sick child's forehead.

muggy Containing heavy, moisture-laden air. It is so *muggy* that I can hardly breathe.

ANTONYMS: arid, dry

dash *v.* To run fast; to rush. I will **dash** home and be back in a second.

dart To move quickly and unexpectedly. See the lizard's tongue *dart* out.

hurry To act quickly. *Hurry,* before the store closes.

WRITER'S THESAURUS

rush To go or to send in a hurry. Please *rush* that package to the post office.

scamper To run fast. That squirrel may *scamper* down the tree if you offer it some nuts.

defeat *n.* The result of losing; a loss. A **defeat** in one game does not mean that a team will lose the World Series.

conquest An act of defeating or being defeated through force. The *conquest* of Poland by Nazi troops took place in September 1939.

failure Someone or something that has not succeeded. His efforts at finding gold were a *failure*.

upset A defeat of an opponent who is expected to win. The inexperienced team beat last year's champions in an *upset*.

ANTONYMS: accomplishment, achievement, success, victory

different *adj.* Not the same. My sister and I wear **different** sizes of clothing.

peculiar Odd; unusual; unfamiliar. When Hannah laughed at losing the game, her friends thought her reaction was *peculiar*.

separate Not joined; distinct; individual. Every member of a family is a *separate* person.

unlike Different from others. The egg with the double yolk was *unlike* the others in the carton.

ANTONYMS: alike, similar, usual

E

empty *adj.* Containing nothing; having nothing or no one around. The plastic pitcher was **empty** because the juice had leaked out.

deserted Empty because whoever or whatever was there has gone. After the sudden thunderstorm, the beach was *deserted*.

desolate Barren; lifeless. The ghost town was a *desolate* place.

vacant Uninhabited; unoccupied; open for use. In a heavily populated city, it can be hard to find a *vacant* apartment.

ANTONYMS: full, inhabited, populated

equipment *n.* The materials needed for a particular activity. Kneepads are standard **equipment** for football players.

gear Tools and other equipment needed to perform some activity. The mountain climbers carried picks and other *gear*.

provisions Food and other supplies needed for future use. The hikers took enough *provisions* to last them one week.

supplies Goods, such as food and equipment, that can be distributed and used when needed. If you go camping in the wilderness, you should bring food and other *supplies*.

everybody *pron.* Every person. Is **everybody** here now?

everyone Everybody. *Everyone* will get a chance to speak.

ANTONYMS: nobody, no one

fall *v.* To go down suddenly to a lower level. Hold onto the railing so that you won't **fall**.

drop To go down at once; to decrease quickly; to release. When the teacher banged on the drum, the children would *drop* to the floor and pretend to be sleeping bears.

plunge To fall, jump, or dive; to thrust suddenly; to move quickly. When the roller coaster would *plunge* suddenly, everyone would scream.

trip To lose one's footing and stumble. You can *trip* over an untied shoelace.

tumble To fall; to roll or toss about. In judo class Marie learned how to *tumble* without getting hurt.

ANTONYMS: ascend, rise

fat *adj.* Having too much weight on the body; overweight. We will all get **fat** if you keep serving us those huge portions.

chubby Plump; rounded. I was *chubby* before I started walking to school every day.

overweight Weighing too much. Doctors warn that being *overweight* is unhealthy.

plump Slightly fat or rounded. That *plump* chicken has plenty of meat on it.

stout Fat or thickset in body. This store sells clothes made especially for *stout* men.

thick Heavily built; dense. His neck is so *thick* that his top shirt button won't fasten.

ANTONYMS: reedy, skinny, slight, slim, thin

fragrant *adj.* Sweet-smelling. The lilacs are **fragrant** as well as colorful.

aromatic Having an appealing smell. Nothing is more *aromatic* than freshly baked bread.

odorous Having an odor, or smell. If detergent has to be *odorous,* I prefer a lemon scent.

perfumed Having a sweet, pleasant odor, as from perfume. I sometimes carry a *perfumed* handkerchief.

sweet Fresh, pleasant. Smell the *sweet* summer air.

ANTONYMS: bitter, foul, smelly

frail *adj.* Easily hurt; without strength. The newborn calf wobbled on its **frail** legs.

delicate Weak; not sturdy; fragile. One twin had always been big and healthy, while the other had always been small and *delicate.*

feeble Not strong; not convincing. When she didn't want to go to the party, Meg offered the *feeble* excuse that she had to clean her room.

fragile Easily damaged or hurt; delicate. Handle that *fragile* vase with care.

weak Without strength. She felt *weak* after fasting all day.

wispy Thin and delicate. There are only *wispy* clouds in the sky today.

ANTONYMS: energetic, robust, sturdy, vigorous

G

glittering *adj.* Having a bright sparkle. **Glittering** stars dotted the night sky.

gleaming Sending out rays of light; shiny. The *gleaming* car had just come out of the car wash.

glistening Shiny or sparkling, as with reflected light. This detergent will leave your glassware *glistening.*

glowing Shining because of intense heat, especially without flame. To remove a splinter, she sterilized a needle by holding it near a flame until the needle was *glowing.*

shimmering Having an unsteady, glimmering shine. The heat is creating a *shimmering* effect on the highway.

sparkling Giving off sparks or flashes. *Sparkling* dots of sunlight were seen on the water.

ANTONYMS: dull, lackluster, lifeless

go *v.* To move along; to proceed; to move from one place to another. It took courage for pioneers to leave their homes and their friends to **go** West.

depart To go away; to leave. The train will *depart* in 10 minutes.

retreat To withdraw; to fall back. Because of the flood warning, those who lived near the river decided to *retreat* to higher ground.

ANTONYMS: arrive, come, return

gray *adj.* A mixture of white and black; a color or tone that is dark or drab. That **gray** sky tells me that a storm is approaching.

dingy Dull, dirty. Bleach can help make *dingy* clothes brighter.

dismal Gloomy; drab. Bonnie was in a *dismal* mood, so she decided to buy a new outfit to cheer herself up.

grow *v.* To increase in size, amount, age, or maturity. As you **grow**, your appearance changes.

become To turn into; to grow; to undergo change. To *become* good at anything requires effort.

expand To grow or cause to grow larger. Phil wanted to *expand* his knowledge of world geography.

increase To become or cause to become bigger or greater. If you *increase* the volume of that radio, I will be forced to leave the room.

mature To become fully grown or developed. That kitten will *mature* in two years.

ANTONYMS: decrease, diminish, shrink

H

hazy *adj.* Blurred; unclear. Fog makes everything look **hazy**.

confused Mixed-up. The students were *confused* because the explanation wasn't clear.

fuzzy Blurred. If you move the camera when you take a picture, the resulting photo will be *fuzzy*.

muddled Being or acting confused. After missing two nights' sleep, he was so *muddled* that he walked right past his house.

unclear Not understandable; fuzzy. These directions for building an engine are *unclear* to me.

vague Not sharp and exact; unfocused. Joe had only a *vague* idea of what to do with a group of three-year-olds.

ANTONYMS: certain, clear, focused

hold *v.* To carry or to grasp, as in one's hands or arms; to possess. Use both hands to **hold** that large glass bowl.

clutch To hold tightly. *Clutch* your valuables when you are in a crowd.

grasp To hold tightly, as with the hand. *Grasp* the railing if you start to fall.

possess To own or to have. A person cannot possibly *possess* everything he or she desires.

ANTONYMS: free, release

inquire *v.* To ask a question in order to get information. I will **inquire** about my glasses at the Lost and Found office.

challenge To question or dispute the truth or correctness of. The catcher would often *challenge* the umpire's decision.

WRITER'S THESAURUS

contest To question or to challenge. When Mr. Phelps left everything to his cat, his daughter decided to *contest* his will.

examine To ask questions of in order to get information or to test a person's knowledge or skill; to look at closely. The instructor will *examine* the student to see if he knows the driver safety rules.

quiz To examine; to test. I will *quiz* you on the spelling words tomorrow.

ANTONYMS: answer, reply, respond

lift *v.* To pick up or to raise. If you **lift** the sofa cushion, you will find your pen.

elevate To make higher. *Elevate* your foot on that pillow until the swelling goes down.

hoist To lift, particularly with the aid of a machine. The workers needed to *hoist* heavy beams to the roof.

raise To make higher; to increase. *Raise* your racket above your head to serve the ball.

ANTONYMS: drop, lower

liquid *adj.* Capable of flowing; watery. Pour that **liquid** detergent into another bottle.

fluid Flowing; smooth. The dancer moves with *fluid* grace.

watery Full of water; thin and runny, as if water has been added. Whipped cream becomes *watery* if it is kept in a warm place too long.

ANTONYMS: dense, hard, solid

long *adj.* Great in time or in distance. Columbus sailed a **long** way to get from Europe to the New World.

extended Stretched out; made longer; lengthy. We took an *extended* tour of the building.

lengthy Extremely long. If you keep reading that *lengthy* novel and don't give up, you won't be sorry.

look *v.* To use the eyes to see or attempt to see. It is tempting, but unwise, to **look** directly at the sun during an eclipse.

gape To stare with an open mouth, as if surprised. People would *gape* at the odd-looking exhibits in the circus sideshow.

glance To take a hurried look. Try to *glance* at the house as we drive by.

peer To take a close, careful look. The astronomer would *peer* through her telescope for hours.

love *v.* To be strongly attached to; to greatly enjoy. Parents and children **love** each other in a special way.

adore To be devoted to; to feel great love for. Nothing pleased the movie star more than to have audiences *adore* her.

cherish To value deeply. Patriots *cherish* their countries.

idolize To adore; to hold in awe. Some people *idolize* a hero or a celebrity, putting that person on a pedestal.

worship To love someone or something intensely; to treat as godly. The man loves his wife so much that he seems to *worship* her.

ANTONYMS: abhor, despise, detest, hate

make *v.* To bring into being; to cause something to happen. Ann's father will **make** a spaghetti dinner in honor of Ann's graduation.

assemble To put together. The instructions tell how to *assemble* the fan.

construct To build; to make by putting parts together. He decided to *construct* a model of the Sears Tower.

create To conceive and make; to make something new. The artist used her imagination and talent to *create* wonderful works of art.

prepare To get something ready. A sculptor must *prepare* clay before beginning to shape it.

produce To bring into being through physical or mental effort. If you have skill and patience, you will *produce* the result you hope for.

ANTONYMS: break, destroy

memory *n.* Something that a person remembers. The memory of that day will always make her smile.

memoir A story of someone's life and experiences, written either by that person or by someone who knew that person. My father wrote a *memoir* of his war experiences.

recollection A memory. After the accident, Bob had no *recollection* of what had happened.

miss *v.* To fail to hit or reach; to fail to understand. I'm afraid I miss the point of that joke.

neglect To fail to take care of or do. *Neglect* to water the plants and they will not thrive.

overlook To fail to see or observe. An experienced investigator will rarely *overlook* a clue.

ANTONYMS: attend, note, notice, observe

most *adj.* Greatest in number, degree, or power. Our school has the most National Merit Scholars in the state.

greatest Largest; most important; best. Receiving the Most Improved Award was Tom's *greatest* moment.

highest Having the greatest height or degree; top. They climbed to the *highest* peak of the mountain.

maximum Having the highest number, quantity, or degree possible. Fifteen is the *maximum* number of persons this elevator will hold.

ANTONYMS: least, lowest, minimum

move *v.* To advance or to progress; to change position. An artist's model must not move while he or she is posing.

advance To move or cause to move forward or ahead from one point to another; to make progress. Remember to *advance* the film in the camera.

proceed To go forward or onward. *Proceed* to the stop sign, and then turn left.

push forward To make an effort to advance; to go on with difficulty. Although you are discouraged, you must *push forward.*

N

name *n.* A word or words by which some person, place, thing, or idea is known. George Washington is a name people will never forget.

nickname A short or informal name. My friends call me by my *nickname,* Mikey.

signature A person's name written by that person. When you write a check, you must sign your *signature* on the bottom line.

title A name of a book, a play, or a poem, or other written work; a word giving a person's status, profession, or rank. *Macbeth* is the *title* of one of Shakespeare's greatest plays.

O

open *v.* To uncover; to make a space between parts. The windows in many new skyscrapers do not **open**.

expose To uncover and reveal. If you remove the paint, you will *expose* the natural wood.

puncture To make a hole by sticking with a pointed object. A nail can *puncture* a tire.

unlock To open a lock; to reveal. Archaeologists try to *unlock* the secrets of the past.

unseal To open something that has been tightly closed. Jana had to *unseal* the envelope to add another sentence to her letter.

ANTONYMS: close, shut

P

place *v.* To put something somewhere. **Place** your homework on my desk.

deposit To place or to set down; to put. Just *deposit* that heavy package in the front hall.

locate To put; to situate; to find. The architect plans to *locate* the kitchen in the back of the house.

put To place or lay in a particular spot or position. Ted was sure he had *put* his keys on his bureau.

powder *n.* Very fine pieces of something that has been ground down or crushed. The doctor gave the woman a **powder** to apply to her rash.

dust Something fine, dry, light, and powdery, such as dried earth. A thin coat of *dust* covered all the furniture.

grit Little, coarse pieces, as of sand. Rinsing clams and mussels removes the *grit* from inside the shells.

particle A tiny piece or amount. The wind blew a *particle* of dust into Aaron's eye.

sand Tiny particles of broken rocks found on beaches and in deserts. You need to mix *sand* with water to build a sand castle on the beach.

pride *n.* A good feeling about one's accomplishments. Take **pride** in the things you do well.

arrogance Too much self-importance. The fact that he plays baseball very well does not excuse his *arrogance*.

dignity Pride in one's worth; proud bearing. With *dignity* each graduate walked up to the principal and received a diploma.

egotism The state of being habitually boastful about oneself. His *egotism* drove everyone away.

self-respect Adequate pride in oneself. Luisa had too much *self-respect* to allow herself to be insulted.

Q

quiet *adj.* Having or making little or no noise. Students need a **quiet** place where they can do their homework without distractions.

hushed Quiet; still; silent. They spoke in *hushed* voices so that they wouldn't wake the baby.

noiseless Causing little or no noise; quiet; silent. When I use my *noiseless* typewriter, my co-workers nearby don't complain.

WRITER'S THESAURUS

silent Not having or making any sound; noiseless. The teacher asked for volunteers to clean out the closets after school, but everyone was *silent.*

speechless Temporarily unable to speak, especially because of strong emotion. The surprise party in her honor left Diane *speechless.*

ANTONYMS: earsplitting, loud, noisy

R

remember *v.* To recall; to bring back to mind. My mother says she will always **remember** two of her teachers.

recall To remember; to call back to mind. I can't *recall* whether I sent that letter.

recollect To remember. He knew the face was familiar, but he couldn't *recollect* how he knew the elderly woman.

ANTONYM: forget

rough *adj.* Bumpy; not smooth. If a man doesn't shave every day, his cheeks and chin become **rough.**

choppy Short and rough; jerky. The speeding motorboat cuts through the calm water, making it *choppy.*

coarse Not fine; rough. *Coarse* thread is better than fine thread for stitching heavy fabric.

jagged Having sharp, pointy edges. The end of the broken bottle was *jagged.*

rugged Having a rough surface. Only advanced bikers should ride over the *rugged* mountain trails.

ANTONYMS: even, silky, smooth

round *adj.* Shaped like a ball, a circle, or a cylinder. The earth is not perfectly **round**

circular Formed like or having to do with a circle. Horses on a merry-go-round always take a *circular* route.

globular Having the shape of a globe. In models of the solar system, the planets are always *globular.*

spherical Shaped like a sphere; globular. Most pearls are *spherical.*

S

sad *adj.* Unhappy or depressed; sorrowful. The little boy was **sad** when his pet rabbit escaped from its cage.

joyless Lacking in joy; dreary. Cleaning my bedroom is a *joyless* task.

melancholy Having low spirits; gloomy or dejected. He was *melancholy* after being cut from the basketball team.

show *v.* To cause to see or be seen. May I **show** you the painting I made in art class?

demonstrate To show clearly, as when showing someone how to do something. The salesperson began to *demonstrate* the use of the vacuum cleaner.

display To show openly; to exhibit. We will *display* our stories on the bulletin board.

reveal To show something that was hidden. The actor took off his mask to *reveal* his face.

ANTONYMS: conceal, cover, hide

slice *v.* To cut a thin piece from a larger piece. Please **slice** the bread while I pour the milk.

carve To cut up. If Father will *carve* the turkey, we can eat.

chop To cut into pieces. Please *chop* the onion on the cutting board, not on the counter.

squish *v.* To squash or to crush. To make a gallon of grape juice, we had to **squish** a bushel of grapes.

crush To break, force out of shape, or flatten by squeezing. Powerful machines *crush* and stack old automobiles.

squash To crush into a pulpy form; to completely flatten. Put the tomatoes on top where nothing will *squash* them.

strange *adj.* Unusual; out of the ordinary. A **strange**, eerie light seemed to rise from the swamp.

funny Strange; curious; comical. Three o'clock in the morning is a *funny* time to be making a phone call.

outrageous Shocking; out of the bounds of what is expected and proper. *Outrageous* behavior is usually discouraged.

unusual Out of the ordinary; uncommon. It is not *unusual* for children to grow several inches in one year.

ANTONYMS: common, normal, ordinary, typical

stretchy *adj.* Capable of being stretched or pulled. I bought some **stretchy** fabric to cover my bicycle seat.

elastic Stretchy; capable of being pulled or of changing shape. The *elastic* waistband in these pants makes a belt unnecessary.

springy Bouncy; capable of snapping back. This sofa has *springy* cushions.

stuff *v.* To fill. Don't **stuff** yourself, or you will be uncomfortable.

cram To pack; to force in as much as possible. He couldn't *cram* one more thing into his book bag.

fill To load a container to the top. *Fill* the thermos with a refreshing beverage.

overload To fill with too heavy a load. If you *overload* the car, the passengers will be cramped.

stylish *adj.* Modern; in style. Jenny looked very **stylish** in her new outfit.

fashionable Dressing in or otherwise following the latest styles. It isn't always easy to be *fashionable* and comfortable at the same time.

smart Stylishly dressed, in a tailored way. That suit looks *smart* with those matching shoes and that purse.

trendy In step with the latest styles; fashionable to the point of slavishness. Being *trendy* requires frequent shopping expeditions.

ANTONYMS: classic, old-fashioned, outdated

succeed *v.* To win; to reach one's goals. A determined person can **succeed** where others fail.

accomplish To gain an intended end or goal. What did you expect to *accomplish* by writing that letter?

conquer To overcome by effort. Some experts believe that you can *conquer* illness through laughter.

overcome To triumph over; to conquer. Someone who has *overcome* great difficulties feels great satisfaction.

triumph To achieve a victory. In the long run, fair play will *triumph* over cheating.

swim *v.* To propel or tread through water by using your arms and legs. Can you **swim** to the dock and back?

WRITER'S THESAURUS

bathe To immerse; to go swimming. It was my turn to *bathe* the baby.

paddle To use hands, oars, or paddles to push through the water. My little sister can only *paddle* around at the shallow end of the pool.

wade To walk or go through water or anything else that slows one down. I had to *wade* through the stream to retrieve the lost baseball.

T

taste *v.* To learn the flavor of by bringing into contact with the mouth or the tongue. **Taste** the food before you add any more pepper.

sample To test a small part of; to taste. You may *sample* my spaghetti sauce if you like.

savor To taste and enjoy. You can't *savor* food if you gobble it down.

timid *adj.* Fearful; shy. Our puppy is so **timid** that it hides when visitors come.

afraid Scared. Babies are often *afraid* of loud noises.

alarmed Filled with sudden or strong fear; frightened. Kevin was *alarmed* to find the door of the bird cage open and the cage empty.

fearful Frightened; full of fear. To see Connie on the diving board, it's hard to believe how *fearful* of the water she once was.

frightened Filled with sudden fear; scared. The children were *frightened* by the snarling dog.

shy Uncomfortable or nervous around people; bashful. The *shy* young man did not look forward to making a speech.

ANTONYMS: bold, brave, courageous, fearless

trembling *adj.* Shaking, usually with fear, cold, or weakness. He grabbed hold of her **trembling** hand.

quivering Trembling slightly. Although she was frightened, she managed a *quivering* smile.

shaking Moving from side to side or up and down with short, quick movements. The *shaking* vase looked as if it were about to fall.

shuddering Trembling; shivering. Her body, *shuddering* from the cold, needed warmth.

vibrating Moving back and forth quickly; quivering. The *vibrating* platform signaled that a train was coming.

U

use *v.* To put into operation. How long will it be before you can **use** your left arm again?

employ To use for a particular purpose. Exterminators *employ* various chemicals in their work.

exercise To use; to put into action. A leader is in a position to *exercise* power.

take advantage of To make full use of, as an opportunity. George will *take advantage of* his cousin's offer of financial aid.

W

walk *v.* To go forward, one step at a time, without running. Dad can't drive us to school today, so we'll have to **walk**.

amble To walk in a slow, easygoing way. On our vacation we would *amble* along the bay or just sit on the dock and watch the boats.

saunter To stroll. In the spring, people *saunter* through the park, glad that winter is finally over.

stride To walk with long steps. Paul could *stride* across the room in a few steps.

strut To walk in a self-important way, as if wanting to be noticed. You *strut* around as if you owned the world.

trudge To plod; to walk in a slow, tired way. The weary miners would *trudge* home after spending 12 hours in the mine.

want *v.* To desire; to wish for. Do you **want** a slice of this apple?

crave To want strongly or urgently. Sometimes I *crave* a baked potato.

desire To want. Open the window, if you so *desire.*

yearn To want or to wish for deeply. I *yearn* to see you again.

warm *adj.* Comfortably hot; not cold. The **warm** rays of the sun felt good on our backs.

hot Having a high temperature, very warm. Do not touch the *hot* stove.

radiant Glowing with heat, joy, or love. He gave the children a *radiant* smile.

ANTONYMS: chilly, cold, cool

water *n.* A liquid compound made of hydrogen and oxygen. About three-quarters of the human body is composed of **water.**

lake A body of fresh or salt water surrounded by land. Mountains bordered the *lake.*

ocean An enormous body of water that covers much of the Earth. You must cross an *ocean* to reach Hawaii from California.

precipitation Rain or snow that falls on the Earth from the atmosphere. London and Seattle both receive considerable *precipitation.*

puddle A little pool of liquid, especially water. Eddie wore his boots so that he could splash in the *puddle.*

rain Condensed water vapor that falls in drops from the atmosphere. An umbrella is the best protection against *rain.*

river A large natural stream of water. The *river* flows through miles of tropical jungle.

wet *adj.* Covered with liquid. Be careful not to slip on the **wet** floor.

dewy Damp, as with dew. *Dewy* grass feels nice on bare feet.

drenched Soaking wet. Sherry got *drenched* in the sudden storm.

saturated Completely soaked through. That sponge won't absorb more water because it is *saturated.*

INDEX

EP = Extra Practice
G = Glossary
WH = Writer's Handbook
WT = Writer's Thesaurus

◄ A ►

Abbreviations, 86–87, 102, 425–426, 430–431, EP17, EP69, WH68
Addresses. *See* Proper nouns; Nouns.
Adjectives, 273, 274–275, 288, 289, 291, 326–327, 335, 339, 341, 387, 389, 451, 452, EP46–51, EP56, WH14–15, WH28–29, WH69
  adjective phrases, 368–369, EP58
  articles, 274–275, 451, WH14
  that compare, 282–283, 284–285, 293, 340, 452, EP50, EP51, WH15, WH69
  demonstrative, 278–279, 292, EP48, WH15
  predicate, 280–281, 292, 340, EP49, WH6, WH15
  proper, 276–277, 292, 339, EP47, WH14
Adverbs, 295, 317, 318–319, 324–325, 326–327, 330, 331, 333, 335, 340, 341, 387, 452, EP52–56, WH16–17, WH28–29, WH69
  adverb phrases, 370–371, EP59
  that compare, 322–323, 334, 341, EP54, WH16
  placement within sentences, 320–321, 334, EP53
Agreement of subject and verb. *See* Sentences; Subject; Usage; Verbs.
Alliteration, 265, G9
Analogy, 256–257, 258
Analyzing. *See also* Thinking processes and skills.
  business letter (persuasive paragraph), 210–212
  descriptive paragraph, 62–64
  how-to paragraph, 112–113
  lyric poem, 256–257
  paragraphs of comparison and contrast, 158–159
  personal narrative, 12–13
  persuasive essay, 300–302
  persuasive writing, 210–212
  research report, 348–349
  story, 400–402

Antecedents, 230–231, 250, 338, 450, WH8
Antonyms, 286–287, 289, 293, WH58
Apostrophe, 92–93, 103, 107, 192–193, 203, 449, WH24, WH67
Appositives, 94–95, 103, 107, EP21, WH7–8
Articles, 274–275, 451, WH14
Assonance, 265
Audience for writing, 19, 21, 70, 72, 115, 119–121, 125, 165, 167, 214, 217, 218, 220, 263, 266, 268, 308, 310, 312, 327, 356, 358, 407, 408, 410, G2

◄ B ►

Base words, 328, WH57
Bibliographies, 436–437, 442, EP74
Brainstorming. *See* Thinking processes and skills.
Business letters, 207–209, 215–225, 427–429, 476–477
  analyzing, 210–212

◄ C ►

Capitalization, 443, EP66, EP68, WH20–21
  of abbreviations and initials, 86–87, 102, 425–426, 446, EP17, EP69
  in addresses, 430–431, 446, EP70
  in bibliographies, 436–437, 447, EP74
  with direct quotations, 438–439, 447, EP75
  of first word in sentence, 28–29, 32–33, 418–419, 445, EP66, WH20
  in friendly and business letters, 427–429, 446, EP70, WH21
  of *I*, 232–233, 423–424, 446, EP68
  in outlines, 432–433, 446, EP72
  of proper adjectives, 276–277, 423–424, 446, EP68
  of proper nouns, 82–83, 84–85, 102, 106, 423–424, 446, 449, EP16, EP68, WH20–21
  of titles of written works, 434–435, 447, EP73
Castañeda, Omar S., 153–157
Cause and effect, WH35
  connecting, 14, 54
Character sketch, 181, 279, WH47
Characterization, G9
Characters, 403, G9

◀ J ▶

◀ L ▶

◀ M ▶

◄ **Q** ►

◄ **R** ►

◄ **S** ►

continued from page IV

Art Acknowledgments

Shelley Austin: 98, 99, 146, 147, 288, 386, 440, 442, 443; Jane Barton: 84, 97, 175, 238, 317; Suzanne Clee: 44, 146, 208, 297; John Dyess: 34, 96, 374; Michele Fridkin: 38, 127, 134, 135, 176, 370, 378, 382; Randy Galloway: 138; Brenda Johnson: 36, 86; Mark Langeneckert: 30; Marlies Merk Najaka: 46, 92, 276, 420; Judy Nostrandt: 14, 79, 110, 111,130, 186, 273, 284, 322, 365, 372; Sue Parnell: 282; Ralph Perieda: 232, 244; Stephanie Pershing: 42, 77, 82, 154, 155, 156, 188, 230, 242, 264, 278, 280, 286, 320, 326, 368, 417; Walter Porter: 94, 112, 144, 145, 166, 418, 423; David Rickman: 50; Lyn Seward: 136, 236; Joel Snyder: 52, 53, 179, 196, 197, 227, 246, 247, 289, 299, 304, 324, 330, 331, 384, 387; Frank Steiner: 15, 66, 125, 128, 245, 254, 255; James Wattling: 132; Arden Von Haeger: 282.

Production and Layout: Intergraphics

Photo Acknowledgments

PHOTOGRAPHS: Pages 3, HBJ Photo/Rob Downey; 6(t), HBJ Photo/Rob Downey; (b), HBJ Photo/Rob Downey; 7(t), HBJ Photo/Rob Downey; (b), HBJ Photo/Rob Downey.

UNIT 1: 8, HBJ Photo/Charlie Burton; 17, HBJ Photo; 23, HBJ Photo; 25, HBJ Photo; 28, HBJ Photo/Peter Burg; 32, HBJ Photo/Julie Fletcher.

UNIT 2: 58, HBJ Photo/Rodney Jones; 59, Gail Newman; 67, HBJ Photo; 75(l), HBJ Photo; (t), HBJ Photo; (b) HBJ Photo; 76, HBJ Photo; 77, HBJ Photo; 80, Stacy Pick/Stock, Boston; 88, HBJ Photo/Rodney Jones; 90, Herb Lange/West Light.

UNIT 3: 108, HBJ Photo/Rodney Jones; 116, HBJ Photo/Mark Cunningham; 124(l), HBJ Photo/Mark Cunningham; (r), HBJ Photo/Mark Cunningham; 125, HBJ Photo/Mark Cunningham; 142, HBJ Photo/Peter Burg.

UNIT 4: 152, HBJ Photo/Rodney Jones; 162, HBJ Photo; 172(t), HBJ Photo; (l), HBJ Photo; (r), HBJ Photo; 173(t), HBJ Photo; (b), HBJ Photo; 182, HBJ Photo/Wiley & Flynn; 184, HBJ Photo/Bob Daemmrich.

UNIT 5: 206, HBJ Photo/Richard Haynes; 215, HBJ Photo/Mark Cunningham; 223(t), HBJ Photo; (l) HBJ Photo/Mark Cunningham; (r), HBJ Photo/Mark Cunningham; 224, HBJ Photo/Mark Cunningham; 234, HBJ Photo/Jeff Blanton; 238, HBJ Photo/Bob Daemmrich; 240, HBJ Photo/Terry Sinclair.

UNIT 6: 252, Dave Davidson/The Stock Market; 260, HBJ Photo; 271, HBJ Photo.

UNIT 7: 294, HBJ Photo/Richard Haynes; 305, HBJ Photo; 315, HBJ Photo; 318, HBJ Photo/Terry Sinclair.

UNIT 8: 344, Culver Pictures; 345, The Bettmann Archive; 346, Public Health Services/National Archives/Photo Researchers; 347, The Bettmann Archive; 352, HBJ Photo; 361(t), HBJ Photo; (l), HBJ Photo; (r), HBJ Photo; 362, HBJ Photo; 376, HBJ Photo/Julie Fletcher; 380, Cary Wolinshy/Stock, Boston; 382, AP/Wide World Photos.

UNIT 9: 392, HBJ Photo/Rodney Jones; 404, HBJ Photo; 413(t), HBJ Photo; (b), HBJ Photo; 414(l), HBJ Photo; (r), HBJ Photo; 425(t), HBJ Photo/Peter Burg; (b), HBJ Photo/Peter Burg; 434, HBJ Photo/Peter Burg.